CHURCHILL'S WAR

Other Avon Books by
David Irving

GÖRING
HITLER'S WAR
THE TRAIL OF THE FOX

CHURCHILL'S WAR

DAVID IRVING

AVON BOOKS ◢◣ NEW YORK

Originally published in Australia in 1987 under the title *Churchill's War, (Volume One): The Struggle for Power.*

AVON BOOKS
A division of
The Hearst Corporation
105 Madison Avenue
New York, New York 10016

First Avon Books Trade Printing: April 1991

AVON TRADEMARK REG. U.S. PAT. OFF. AND IN OTHER COUNTRIES, MARCA REGISTRADA, HECHO EN U.S.A.

Printed in the U.S.A.

OPM   10   9   8   7   6   5   4   3   2   1

Contents

Introduction

WINSTON CHURCHILL trod carefully into the middle of the second floor clubroom and paused, deliberately surveying the dozen faces that had turned towards him.

As he stood there, short and squat, in a tuxedo that had seen long and honourable service, it occurred to him that he was probably a quarter century older than any of them.

Hosting this dinner at the Union Club in New York City was Henry R. Luce, publisher of the magazines *Time*, *Life* and *Fortune*. It was March 14, 1946: the uneasy interlude after the end of World War II had ended, and everybody could sense it. Luce's fellow editors and executives scrutinized the famous Englishman as if taken aback to find him so small, in the way that movie fans are startled to find that their idols are less than the twenty-foot giants of the silver screen. In the words of a lucid and penetrating memorandum* that Charles Murphy wrote for Luce's private files, there was just a dress-shirted cave where the chest should have been, and a swelling paunch that bore testimony to years of rich fare.

Henry Luce, who had brought him in, turned to greet his other guests. As Churchill swayed alone and splendidly in mid-room, the image struck Murphy of the Cunard Line's *Queen Mary* at the moment when she cast off her tugs in Southampton Water — heavy and loggy, drifting as the Solent's current pressed her hull until her screws bit water and she forged ahead again.

WITH SOFT ROLLS of flesh linking his head and body he looked to Murphy like a congenial, well adjusted bullfrog. The frog's arms and legs were short and stubby, the hands small-boned and white. The complexion was pasty. Then Churchill's expressionless and

---

*The memorandum, sixty-three pages long, is now archived in *Life* executive C.D. Jackson's files in the Eisenhower library at Abilene, Kansas. Among those present were John Billings, John Davenport, Allen Grover, Jackson, Henry R. Luce, Charles Murphy and Charles Wertenbaker.

bloodshot eyes fastened on a portrait on the far wall. The liner's screws began to thump and churn, he swayed across the clubroom and challenged: "Who's that blighter?"

Luce guessed from the portrait's dress that it was an eighteenth-century Englishman; with the smug certainty of Charles Lamb's "wary connoisseur", he confirmed it by a glance at the brass nameplate and pronounced: "William the Fourth."

That it was that blundering and inept monarch took Churchill by surprise. He harrumphed, and said: "Looks more like Lord Rosebery to me. Same heavy jowls."

Behind them was a brooding sculpture of a bald eagle, carved in clear ice some hours earlier by the Union Club's chefs. The wings of this symbol of American might were outstretched; its eyes glittered, and every crevice was heaped with black caviar. The club's heating had been turned up, and rivers of iced water dribbled down its chest. Churchill leered. "The eagle," he announced, "seems to have caught a cold."

He was hypnotized less by the sculptor's art than by the caviar. He waved aside the genteel slices of dry toast an editor handed him, exclaimed: "This stuff needs no reinforcement," and put words into action by shovelling a whopping helping onto a plate, and from there, with scarcely a perceptible interruption, straight and undiluted to his mouth — seemingly unabashed at the appreciative belches that shortly emerged from that orifice. "I hope, gentlemen," he apologized with little evidence of true contrition, "I hope you don't find me too explosive an animal."

Luce misinterpreted the remark. "On the contrary, Sir," he said, "you were only putting into words what was gravely in the minds of many Americans."

* * *

Just over a week earlier, on March 5, 1946, Churchill had delivered an astonishing speech at Fulton in Missouri, accusing the Soviet Union of having imposed an "Iron Curtain" across Europe. On March 10 the entire Soviet press had fired a mighty broadside back, and even Joseph Stalin had joined in the assault, stating in the official Soviet newspaper *Pravda* that Churchill "has now adopted the position of warmonger."

Another mighty belch was Churchill's response to Luce's compliment. Dismissing it with a slice of one hand, he said: "The explosions I had in mind were those given off by my internal pleasure."

He gazed mistily at the spoonful of caviar poised in his hand. Times were when Stalin used to send him a lot of this delicacy. "I don't suppose I'll ever be getting any more," he said.

DINNER WAS NOT YET served. For a few minutes he quietly contemplated the others. Then he began to speak, with a purposeful tone that in Murphy's description cut like a buzzsaw across the grain of idle conversation. Luce signalled with his arm that the others should stop.

They led the Elder Statesman into dinner after that, and Luce seated him at the place of honour on his right.

Clear turtle soup was served, and he gobbled it down. It was followed by terrapin: lowering his head so as to be nearer to this delicacy, he skillfully forked the rare fish from plate to mouth with swift grabbing movements which reminded one onlooker of a steamshovel's grab-bucket at work.

Words and oratory cascaded from him, his tongue now loosened by rare champagne; true, he appeared to be taking only delicate sips, but from the number of refills it was clear that he had imbibed a considerable volume — editor Allen Grover assayed his intake on this evening as one martini, two sherries, four or five glasses of champagne and a formidable balloon of brandy.

Once, he recalled, Stalin had debated with him the real meaning of democracy. Britain, said Stalin, was really a dictatorship because one Party — the party that happened to be in power — controlled everything. Churchill remained a skeptic, committed to Parliamentarianism. He told Luce's dinner guests how, at Potsdam in 1945, he had warned Stalin that he might well find himself replaced as prime minister at the General Election whose results were even then being awaited; Stalin had solemnly commented, "My kind of election is better."

Several remarks showed Churchill's warm regard for Stalin. "Stalin is the one human being in Russia," he said, "I'm sure he doesn't believe any of those awful things he said about me." Later he said, "Stalin always kept his word" — and gave as an example how the Kremlin had adhered to the Soviet-German agreement of August 1939 right up to Hitler's attack two years later. Who actually controlled Russia? Churchill pondered the question, then said: "While Stalin appears to make policy in a sort of vacuum, I doubt very much that he is really free to do what he wants to do."

There was no gainsaying his admiration of the Soviet Communist Party's role in the war. "The Party members are highly disciplined, very brave men," he reflected with unashamed reverence. "They died in very large numbers in the first great battles." But shortly he qualified this attitude. "I have always been for the Russian people; it is Communism that I oppose."

Just as in Europe's feudal past so in the Soviet system the Party officials got the best wages, food, shopping discounts, and accommodation in trains and hotels. As a system of power, the caste structure was hard to defeat, he admitted. "Take your own United States," he said casting a mischievous hand around the tuxedo'd table. "Suppose by some mischance that in this marvellous country three of four millions of people emerged as a self-appointed, highly disciplined elite with all the political and economic controls in their possession. Suppose they had all the privileges — the first-class railroad carriages, the best food, the best food for their children. You would have quite a time, I dare say, trying to shake them loose."

Churchill raised laughter with Vyacheslav Molotov's description of his November 1940 meeting with Hitler in Berlin. Molotov had once asked Churchill if he recalled sending Royal Air Force bombers to Berlin one night in November 1940. Churchill replied that he had a vague recollection of something of the kind.* "Well — Molotov went on — while I was talking to Hitler and other German officials an alert sounded and we all hurried down into an air-raid shelter, a most comfortable place, and I found myself alone with von Ribbentrop. As soon as the door behind us closed, von Ribbentrop turned to me and said, *Let's start dividing up the world*. I replied, But what will England say to that? Von Ribbentrop said, *England is finished, we can forget England*. But I said, if England is finished, why are we here in this shelter. And wherefrom come those bombs which fall?''

From the depths of his fathomless memories he retrieved glittering episodes — his direction of the White Armies of Kolchak and Denikin against the Bolsheviks in 1919; the great community of purpose that had grown up between Britain and the United States. To Murphy his rhetoric seemed like the display put on by a blast-furnace — the incandescent phrases were flung out like pieces of molten metal. ''The impression of them lingers dimly and tantalisingly in memory,'' wrote Murphy, frustrated afterwards, "but somehow the words are gone, like sparks that burned out on the blast-furnace floor.''

Churchill's language captivated his listeners. Several of them urged him to drive home a point that he had made about nuclear power policy

---

*In fact, knowing from British codebreaking operations that Molotov was visiting Hitler that night, Churchill ordered the air raid in an attempt to inconvenience them both.

in the farewell speech he was due to deliver on the next evening at the Waldorf Astoria.

Churchill feigned surprise and asked: "Exactly what did I say? I have already forgotten."

ONLY THIS MORNING, March 14, 1946, he had propped himself up in bed in the Waldorf Astoria and read an editorial in the *New York Times* which catalogued the territories in Europe that had now come under Soviet control. There was Finland, in Russia's sway right up to the tip. There were the Balkans, where Josef Tito was supposedly independent but itching to grab Trieste at Stalin's bidding. In the Far East the Russians had also been given the Kuriles, at Japan's expense. "In short," admitted Churchill, "they have regained in one war everything they ever lost." At every summit conference, he had allowed Stalin to jolly him along with alcohol and frivolity, while the Red Army methodically rolled up the map of Europe.

The United States had done nothing to prevent it. The fruitful association that had joined Britain and the United States in a common cause had withered since the war's end, and Churchill regretted it. As his remarks roamed into this sensitive arena, his bantering tone dropped away. He talked bitterly of the American public's seeming hostility towards Britain's policy in the Far East — what he called "the whole awkward problem of the Colonial peoples who inhabit these vast oceanic regions."

He groped also toward the rawest topic of all, first saying with a half-smile something about British "tyranny in India," and then adding with his customary courtliness, "it is natural that you should wish to hear my views on India" — only to have this topic snatched away from him by Henry Luce, who deftly shut off that debate and lured Churchill back onto more congenial avenues.

There was emotion in his voice when he touched on the adventures that Franklin Roosevelt and he had shared. He had loved "Franklin", as he called the president, like no other. "It's too bad that things were not left to Franklin and myself to handle," he ruminated. "I don't mean the Roosevelt at Yalta. Then he was ethereal. His face was transparent. He was obviously a man preparing to depart."

True, the United States were still powerful, but surely they still needed the British, with their knowledge of the seas, of world trade, and strategy. He talked of the possibility of war with Russia — pointing out that Britain was demobilizing more slowly in Europe than the United States, and adding that the RAF was capable of carrying out any task assigned to it. The Americans must assert their leadership, using the tremendous temporary leverage granted by the atomic bomb. "If Russia had the Bomb," he pointed out, "and you didn't I don't think we'd be feeling so comfortable here tonight."

He lit a long cigar and puffed at it.

John Davenport, an editor, asked Churchill pointblank about Yalta. "How did it happen, Mr Churchill," Davenport challenged, as he applied a match to the end of his own cigar, "that you and Mr Roosevelt were so misled at Yalta as to offer such a high price to the Russians in order to lure them into the Pacific war — a war which was already won?"

There was a pained hush. Many people had nursed the same unspoken question: why had the west, though armed with the atomic bomb, and comforted by the secret knowledge that Japan was already attempting to surrender, fawned on Moscow to such an extent? Henry Luce flushed, and sternly announced: "Mr Churchill, it is hardly necessary to answer that question. Foremost among the subjects on which Mr Davenport certainly is not an expert are the Far East and the Japanese War."

Churchill scowled, ungrateful for Luce's defence. He offered the standard excuse: at Yalta the main thought was to end the fighting. The Rundstedt offensive had destroyed their hopes of an early victory over Germany. And then the fighting at Iwo Jima and Okinawa showed that the losses the Americans might expect if they had to invade the Japanese home islands — probably half a million American casualties or more, and eighteen months more fighting after VE day. "The shadows of the dead," he argued, "were already lengthening at an alarming rate over American homes. Who could wish this to go on an instant longer than was absolutely necessary?"

Of course Iwo Jima and Okinawa were after Yalta, so his argument was artificial. But when this was pointed out, Churchill still refused to abandon his line that the price offered to Russia was reasonable. He just shook his head and mumbled "Oh, no, no, no, there was never any question as to what was the right course."

AT ONE POINT that evening, Churchill just settled back and let his thoughts ramble — over Eisenhower, whom he always called "Ike"; over that vanishing breed, horses; over Drew Pearson and American journalism. Then he eagerly described a new American gadget, the Dictaphone: "Think of being able to talk for twenty minutes into a little green disk that only costs a dime," he said. "But that is not the end of the marvellous accomplishments of this machine. If you wish to ponder what you have said, it is only necessary to flick a switch and it will play your words right back.'' This invention would spell the end of that dreary business of putting down "one miserable little letter after the other." The Dictaphone company had given him two such machines, complete with a lapel microphone which would enable him to dictate as he paced up and down. He had instantly plugged one in and dictated a less than grammatical message of thanks to the company's workers in Connecticut. "This is me, Winston Churchill—" he began, sending a small seismic shock-wave into that corner of the English-speaking world.

Would he ever write a history of this last war? somebody asked. "Quite positively no," he answered. "I am old and, I suppose, in retirement. It would be too much for me to attempt."

The jounalists present that evening would probably never forget their encounter with Winston Churchill. With fire in his eyes, he talked wistfully of the panoply of battle, and he said challengingly: "War is the greatest of all stimulants."

"At moments," wrote one, "the light seemed to pour out of him. One could sense the power in him to summon men, at an hour of universal sinking, to live beyond themselves.

Henry Luce proposed a toast in words which everybody felt exactly right: "We are accustomed," announced Luce, "to drink toasts to people. I propose a toast to Civilisation. But Civilisation is embodied in people. So, to Winston Churchill, the First Citizen of Western Civilization, Defender of the Faith."

* * *

They were sorry to see him leave. Churchill pulled himself to his feet, politely repeated the name of each person as he shook hands with him, and peered intently into that man's face as though fixing it hard upon his memory. He was no longer Prime Minister, but in opposition. A spent force? "The fire has unmistakeably burned low," wrote one observer.

If there was one passage that had fixed itself on their minds, it was when Churchill warmed to the theme of Fulton and the furore that his "Iron Curtain" speech had caused. He dismissed the Soviet reaction as ill-tempered, crude and a typically Communist trick. In fact — and his cheeks positively glowed as he said it — Stalin had used almost the same terms to attack him as had Hitler in his time. "Warmonger, inciter of wars, imperialist, reactionary has-been — why, it is beginning to sound like old times," scoffed Churchill.

Stalin's attack was clumsy and heavy handed, but he was flattered all the same. A sudden idea struck him, and a broad grin creased his pink, baby-soft complexion.

"*You know,*" he said, "*If I had been turned loose on Winston Churchill, I would have done a much better job of denunciation.*"

WHAT SORT OF BOOK would Winston Churchill, the author of *My Early Life* have written if he had set out to denounce Winston Churchill, the statesman?

It is hard for other mortals to write about him but the millions of casualties of World War II demand that his leadership be soberly researched and told. Few families were left untouched by Churchill's wars. They robbed families of fathers, husbands — and wives, mothers and children too. I had spent twelve years researching the life of Hitler. How often Hitler had berated and scorned Churchill! What more natural than that I turn to Hitler's adversary, the free world's hero, over roughly the same period of time?

This is not a hostile biography. How could it be: any writer immersing himself in a subject as lively and human as Winston Churchill is bound to find himself charmed by what he finds within the first few weeks. It is revealing to see from the diaries of the staff at No.10 Downing Street like John Colville and John Martin the transition which they underwent in May 1940, from distraught horror on learning that this "adventurer" was to succeed Neville Chamberlain to grudging acceptance of Churchill for his buccaneering verve and drive, and then outright admiration of his steadfastness. In part this was due to his leadership qualities, in part to his fluent and rapid wit.

Often he told jokes at his own expense. Once he exclaimed, "The world is seething with lies about me — and the damnable thing is that most of them are true!"

His energy was prodigious, indeed startling in a man of his age. He inspected troops, flew in converted bombers, tramped around dockyards, toured bomb blitzed towns, clambered over coastal defences. He wanted to hit the Normandy beaches together with General Dwight D. Eisenhower's armies on D-Day, 1944.

* * *

What scheme have I followed in writing this biography?

Firstly, I have been mindful of Sir Winston's own advice to writers, to heed the dictates of chronology. To his dear friend Mrs Consuelo

Balsan, who had drafted rather untidy memoirs, he once wrote:

> If you get someone to put the dates in the margin opposite each event, you could then see where the pack might be shuffled with advantage. Chronology is not a rigid rule and there are many occasions when a departure from it is a good thing. Nevertheless, I think it true to say that chronology is the secret of narrative.*

Secondly, I attach proper importance to the role of Britain's codebreaking in Churchill's War. He was not allowed to mention it in his own memoirs, nor would it have enhanced his fame if he had. Remarkably, the Official Historians prior to Professor F. Hinsley were not privy to the existence of this Special Intelligence, let alone allowed to refer to it; this surely renders their expensive volumes of questionable value. The background of their ignorance was a July 1945 decision by the Joint Intelligence Committee. Worried by the avalanche of captured German documents reaching Britain, the JIC recognized one danger: that the sheer alacrity of Britain's counter measures to some operations signalled in cipher by the Germans must betray the secret to any alert researcher or Official Historian. "Obvious instances," the JIC figured, "are the rerouting of our convoys to avoid submarine attacks by orders issued immediately after the issue of German orders to their U-boats; the counter measures to meet the GAF [German airforce] attacks on this country, and the routing of our deep penetration raids into Germany; the employment of our forces in the field in face of German dispositions."

Thus the British chiefs of staff circularized all government agencies forbidding their Historians to mention or inquire into Special Intelligence.† National security was placed before historical truth. Those who learned of it — as I did by chance in 1963, by precisely the kind of analysis feared by the JIC, of British and German documents on V-weapons — were forbidden to divulge the Ultra Secret.

The present volume squarely addresses the question why Winston Churchill was so widely mistrusted before his illustrious appointment in May 1940. It is an area about which we have hitherto had little information.

---

*The letter, dated June 27, 1952, is in the Danial Longwell collection at Columbia university library, New York.

† JIC(45)223(O) dated July 20; and COS 187th meeting, July 31, 1945; in CAB79/37. See David Stafford's paper in *Military Affairs*, New York, vol. 42, Feb 1978, 29ff.
The result was a General Directive for Safeguarding Intelligence Sources in Compiling Official Histories. "It is imperative," this laid down, "that the fact that such intelligence was available should *NEVER* be disclosed." Official Historians were forbidden to probe into "apparently unaccountable operational orders." The Pentagon endorsed the decision.

The Churchill family cannot help us, because by the stipulations of the family trust the Churchill Papers are to remain closed until ten years after Dr Martin Gilbert has hewn the final volume of his monumental official biography to which we all owe a genuine debt. What is perhaps more remarkable is that important collections of official documents outside Churchill's archives have been effectively sealed: for example, the letters that passed between Churchill as Prime Minister and His Majesty King George VI, surely the most official of records, are being held at Windsor Castle at the exclusive disposition of Dr Gilbert. In consequence, researchers acting without the warrant of the Churchill family are obliged to carry their inquiries into the four corners of the world.

But this has been a rewarding search. We can screen collections of papers held at the Hoover Library in California, the National Archives in Washington, the Public Archives of Canada in Ottawa, the presidential libraries of Roosevelt, Truman and Eisenhower and Kennedy, the tomes of the Archives Nationales in Paris, the records of the National Library of Australia in Canberra, the French, Czech and Germany foreign ministries. We can trawl through private collections of important individuals in Churchill's life, like those of Henry Stimson and Tyler Kent at Yale University, of Winthrop Aldrich at Harvard, and the *non*-Churchill papers housed at Churchill College, Cambridge (to whose archivist, Dr Correlli Barnett, I am of course indebted.)

A full list of Archival sources will be published in volume two of this biography, but I should like to mention here Madame Reynaud, widow of France's wartime premier, who kindly gave me access to her husband's files in Paris which throw new light on the Dunkirk disaster (particularly useful since Lord Gort "lost all his papers" in the retreat.) Among them are some exchanges evidently missing from Churchill's files, e.g. a telegram on May 24, 1940 which is also among the files captured by the Nazis along with the French accounts of conversations with Mr Churchill.*

I am also indebted to the Soviet authorities for supplying to me copies of all the Russian embassy telegrams from London relating to Churchill, and of his conferences with Stalin, and to Mrs Neham Chalom of the Weizmann Institute of Science at Rehovot, Israel, for allowing me access to the entire file of confidential correspondence between Churchill and Professor Chaim Weizmann, the Zionist eminence grise.

What we find in rare sources such as these both offsets and enhances

---

*Microfilmed by the U.S. National Archives: T120, rolls 115 and 127.

the picture presented by Churchill's own narrower archives, as reflected in Gilbert's writings. Perhaps this is small wonder: we should *expect* to find for example, in the private files of the exiled Polish prime ministers Wladislaw Sikorski in London and Stanislas Mikolajczyk at Stanford, California, and of their foreign minister Tadeusz Romer in Ottawa, rich documents on Churchill's dealings with the Poles. But what European historian could have hoped to uncover in the confidential papers of the Canadian premier and mysticist, William Mackenzie-King, the kind of astonishing tableaux that will be found in this biography?

Readers may be alarmed at some elements in these pages. Few of the visiting statesmen failed to comment in their private papers on Churchill's consumption of alcohol, occasionally coupling their remarks with the puzzled observation that even the hardest liquor appeared to leave him unimpaired. In official American publications, documents have been doctored to omit such passages. There is evidence that on occasions Churchill's temporary incapacitation resulted in political or military decisions that damaged British prestige, and even caused casualties among the soldiers and sailors concerned.

He was at his happiest in war, and said so.

He was rarely a creator, always a destroyer — of cities, of monuments and works of art, of populations, of frontiers, of monarchies, and finally his own country's empire.

His bombing policy led to the slaying of a million civilians in Holland, France, Belgium, Czechoslovakia, Germany and Scandinavia; it seems not to have dismayed him. On the contrary, when I toured his underground war headquarters near Parliament Square twenty-five years ago, I found on permanent proud display, as they had been for his wartime visitors, the sterioscopic photographs of the destruction of Dresden. It is as though Hitler had pinned up colour photographs of Auschwitz or Buchenwald for visiting celebrities.

His indifference to public suffering was documented again and again. In 1944 crowds jeered him when he appeared in dazzling RAF uniform in a newly blitzed suburb of London and declared "This is the thing! It is just like being back in the best days of the Blitz again." While postwar Britain starved he sheltered the flow of tens of thousands of dollars from New York publishers against the depredations of the Inland Revenue while he vacationed with his retinue in North Africa and on the French Riviera. It would be unfeeling to criticize him for an excessive mercenary zeal. What writers are not at times beholden to financial problems? But this book's early chapters are overhung by the enormity of his financial deficit during his years in the political wilderness, a cash crisis illuminated by the papers of his literary agent now on deposit in the University of Oregon at Eugene.

This financial quandary might seem of only vestigial importance, but in following chapters comes the suggestion that he proceeded to sell his soul to a syndicate of politicians and financiers called The Focus, a group which continued to fete and finance him until the outbreak of war.

THE MATERIALS ON this episode are perhaps typical of the sources which I have developed for this biography.

One was a diary of a member of The Focus made available to me by Dr Howard Gottlieb, director of the Mugar Memorial Library at Boston university. This shows that at the time of Munich the Czechs were paying Focus members £2,000 per annum. The papers of the former Czech Minister in Paris, Stefan Osusky, at the Hoover Library, Czech documents now in Prague F.O. archives and captured Nazi intercepts of Benes's secret telephone conversations with Osusky and Jan Masaryk confirm that senior British politicians were being paid by the Czechs in return for a promise to topple Neville Chamberlain's government.

The rarest items come from the most distant sources. From Finnish archives, a telegram from Paris to Helsinki dated March 30, 1940, reporting Churchill's discussions with French premier Paul Reynaud: intercepted by the Nazis, it triggered Hitler's invasion of Norway a week later. From Stockholm archives come the telegrams revealing the extraordinary efforts by Churchill's opponents in the War Cabinet to make peace behind his back in June 1940.

Some material I obtained as gifts — one lady entrusted to me the diary kept by her late husband, Churchill's personal bodyguard, from 1942 to 1945. Churchill's private secretary allowed me to copy his wartime diaries. A stranger telephoned with the text of the Cabinet's message empowering Lord Gort to accept whatever surrender terms at Dunkirk the Germans would offer (the stolen document was in his possession).

Other documents I have had to purchase or even rent — like the daily appointments record kept by Churchill and his staff throughout the war.

Several years ago I was able to photocopy large tracts of the files of the late Lord Cherwell which have since been sealed: these relate to Churchill's role in the allied dealings on the atomic bomb, the Morgenthau Plan, and postwar policy in Germany.

Not all my researches were successful.

In Nazi files I found evidence that the German post office had listened into Churchill's telephone conversations with Roosevelt and recorded them on disks. I found Nazi transcripts of only two of them, however; the rest were evidently destroyed at the war's end.

My search for the corresponding U.S. Navy recordings and transcripts made for the American Bureau of Censorship lasted ten years and has narrowed their probable location to the National Security Agency, but the NSA rarely opens its files. Future historians *must* continue the search; the telegrams that FDR and Churchill exchanged were often drafted by committees, and obviously of less importance than their private conversations, as my chapter "A Telephone Job" in this volume shows.

WHEN SIR WINSTON Churchill died in 1965, modern Britain lost her most fabled son. His place in the world's immediate history was assured. Subsequent decades have already seen the accents change, but it remains true that he towered over his own times.

His spirit was magnificent, his energy prodigious.

What forces of locomotion impelled him in those dark years of the war? Was it the unswerving faith in the rightness of his cause?

He remained unerringly convinced that he was protecting his country and its Empire from its greatest enemy. Yet in reality he had allied himself with that Empire's profoundest enemies, and presided over its dissolution.

Churchill came to be remembered as a champion of peace and freedom and human dignity. In the closing days of his life he murmured to his old friend Sir Robert Boothby, "The journey has been well worth making — once."

Boothby asked, "And then?"

"A long sleep, I expect: I deserve it."

* * *

CHAPTER 1

Faithless But Fortunate

THE ANCIENT GREEKS prescribed that a man of virtue must possess twelve qualities—ambition, gentleness, truthfulness, magnificence, generosity, magnanimity, reverence, justice, prudence, wit, courage and a degree of charm.

Stealing a march into the world on November 30, 1874 after only seven months in the womb of a noted American beauty, Winston Leonard Spencer Churchill proved as years passed to be deficient in prudence, but possessed of other qualities not listed by the Greeks, and that is what this book shall be about.

He learned that he was the first son of the Right Honourable Lord Randolph Churchill, perhaps not the most desirable of fathers.

He learned too that he had English and American blood in equal measure, like many others we shall be meeting in these pages, his mother Jeanette being daughter of one Leonard Jerome, editor and occasional majority stockholder of the *New York Times*. He had no doubt inherited some of the recklessness and most of the enterprise of this grandfather, if little of his material fortune.[1]

He learned that Leonard Jerome had made and squandered four fortunes during his lifetime. "It would have been a fine thing," Winston's younger brother Jack used to commiserate with him, "if Grandfather Jerome had held on to at least one of his fortunes."

His learning continued until Lord Randolph entered him at age thirteen into Harrow, one of England's more fashionable schools. Here it virtually stopped. Years later, when Winston's friend Lord Melchett boasted over luncheon that his son was stroke of the Oxford boat, Churchill crushed him with the retort that athletic or academic achievers were to be distrusted. "I did nothing at Harrow," he reminisced, "but I regard my time there as very well spent." He had whiled away his hours eating ice-cream and candies, he said, and that was the important thing when growing up—to "learn to be an omnivore." His theory was that the energy squandered on academic or athletic pursuits was not available for more vital purposes in adult life.

Upon joining the army he made it a rule not to work after lunch; in fact out in India, he would do no work after breakfast, but whiled away the daylight hours playing endless polo or reading in Gibbon, Plato, Aristotle and Schopenhauer.[2]

Latin and Mathematics had eluded him at Harrow, but Providence had set him before a brilliant English teacher: Winston now found he had a prodigious memory for poetry and prose. He won a prize for reciting Macaulay's Lays of Ancient Rome and began to glow dimly under the radiated power of the Great Masters of the English tongue: his great brain thus fuelled and ignited, he would repay the debt many times over with prose treasures of his own.

Admitted at the third attempt to Sandhurst military academy, he passed out eighth of 150 cadets and was gazetted in March 1895 to the Fourth (Queen's Own) Hussars. A year later his father, a son of the seventh Duke of Marlborough, died alcoholic and incoherent, aged only forty-six.

For a time Winston drifted in the army. Later that year, still aged only twenty-two, he went on furlough to Cuba to observe the Spanish-American conflict. The British ambassador in Madrid, a friend of Lord Randolph's, had obtained the travel documents. He sent back war letters to the London *Daily Graphic*, which had many years before published travel letters sent in by his father.

His regiment left for India. Unenthusiastic about the posting, he took special leave seven months after its arrival at Bangalore, in October 1896, and returned home. Restless and ambitious, he used the influence of his mother and her friends to serve in punitive expeditions and other military adventures on India's Northwest Frontier, in Lord Kitchener's Army of the Nile (1898), and at Khartoum. By the time that the *Daily Telegraph* published his despatches from these battlefields, he had decided on the same public career that five generations of his immediate ancestors had chosen.

He resigned his commission and entered politics.

THE BRITISH PARLIAMENTARY SYSTEM, though still not perfect, had by the end of the century become more democratic than in Lord Randolph's day.

Winston had a hard fight at the hustings, and developed a profound respect for the Parliamentary institutions which he did not abandon even forty years later when at the summit. Once his chief of staff, finding him agonizing over a Parliamentary speech, would suggest offhandedly: "Why don't you tell them all to go to Hell?"

Churchill was shocked. "You should not say those things," he rebuked the general in private. "I am a servant of the House."[3]

This humility before Parliament remained the most surprising of his virtues: while lesser Members merely nodded to the division clerk as they herded through the Division Lobbies, adequately recognized on sight, one member would hear him, by then Sir Winston Churchill—and prime minister—tell him distinctly, "Churchill, W.S."[4]

Defeated at this first election attempt at grimy industrial Oldham in 1899, he returned to the battlefields, reporting the Boer War lucratively for the *Morning Post*. By November he was a prisoner of the Boers in Pretoria; miraculously, he escaped.

"Wanted," read the broadsheet: "Englishman, 25 years old; about 5 feet 8 inches tall, of indifferent build; walks with a little bend forward." The Perils of Winston, of which he circulated his own thrilling version, made him a hero. Funded by his lifelong friend and cousin Sunny, ninth Duke of Marlborough, he was elected as Oldham's representative in Parliament in 1900; he was then aged twenty-six. Vowing to vindicate his father's memory, he took the same seat below the gangway. He aped his father's dress—long frock coat, wide-winged collar and tie—and his debating stance too, leaning forward, jaw jutting, and hands propped on his hips beneath the falls of his frock coat.

He found that he was no mean orator, not that he was a man of ordinary conversation anyway: his talk flowered with verbal finery. A Canadian would observe, years later, that he drew similes from family life and the relationships of tame and wild animals—talking of cat-and-mouse, growling, and getting ones back up.[5] He often used military metaphors, though seldom naval ones. He had a lisp, though it grew less as the years passed, and would punctuate his remarks by elevating his sandy-coloured eyebrows. "His speeches are brilliant," fellow Tory Neville Chamberlain would write after Winston had been a quarter-century in the House, "and men flock in to hear him as they would to a first class entertainment at the theatre. The best show in London, they say."[6]

Enjoying public speaking, he profited from it too—launching himself onto the well-paid lecture circuits in England and then North America under what he called "a vulgar Yankee impressario."

Doubly enriched therefore by the Boer War—both in experience and in wealth to the amount of £10,000—he ceased importuning publishers and family contacts for sustenance. He had his political independence, and that was what mattered. "I care not for your political ideas," remarked one of his mother's friends to Winston, who was experimenting with a moustache, "but my distaste for them is nothing compared to what I feel about that dreadful moustache."

"Madam," he ungallantly replied, "I see no earthly reason why you should come in contact with either."

He soon tired of Arthur Balfour's sluggish Conservative party and its hostility to Free Trade. "I am an English Liberal," he wrote. "I hate the Tory party, their men, their words and their methods."[7] Impatient for high office, in May 1904 he crossed the floor to the Liberals.

It was a timely defection. Sir Henry Campbell-Bannerman's Liberals won office by a landslide in early 1906. He appointed the renegade Churchill as Under-Secretary for the Colonies. Two years later H.H. Asquith, constructing a new Liberal Cabinet, took Winston in as President of the Board of Trade (minister of trade.) He was then thirty-three, an ebullient figure with reddish hair, a hesitant smile and a courtly demeanour that was perhaps a vestige of his birth at the ducal Blenheim Palace.

High office came none too soon for him. Dogged by the specter of Lord Randolph's early cerebral decline, he had become a man in a hurry.

"Surely," somebody once pointed out to him, "you have *years* before you."

Those faint eyebrows rose, "Oh," he replied, "but I *do* need to hurry. I have compelling need of time. You see—we Churchills all damp off after the age of forty."

This was an exaggeration. His illustrious ancestor John Churchill, the first Duke of Marlborough, had not been given an army until age fifty-two. He was Winston's idol. He had commanded Queen Anne's armies from 1702 to 1711 without losing a battle or siege. His victory at Blenheim brought to his dynasty the great estate named after it in Oxfordshire by way of reward. And this in turn had laid the foundation of the Marlborough wealth and political influence.

WOMEN HAD LONG guided the fortunes of the Marlborough dynasty. It was they who had accomplished his transfer of allegiance to the Liberals. Winston's aunt Fanny had married a later Liberal Chief Whip and Cabinet minister, Baron Tweedmouth, and it was he who had arranged his adoption as a Liberal candidate for North-West Manchester. Fanny's sister, Winston's Aunt Cornelia, had married into ironworks money and it was her in-laws the Guest family who, enraged by Joseph Chamberlain's tariff reform in 1903, had put their money behind Winston.

Most remarkable of the female influences on his political fortunes now was the Honorable Clementine Hozier. In September 1908 he had married this forceful girl from Dundee. In the agreeable words of *My Early Life*, published twenty-five years later, he "lived happily ever after." In many ways she had a better understanding of the common people whose destinies her husband was later to rule. She governed and cherished Winston, remonstrating, pleading, guiding and supporting him in the home and at the electoral front.

Marriage mellowed him. He and the Welsh firebrand Liberal, David Lloyd George, had been regarded as pacifists and radicals ("except," as one critic scoffed, "possibly by pacifists and radicals.") Something of that holy fire now went. In February 1910 Asquith moved him up to the Home Office—an important pivot on his way to the Admiralty which was his ambition.

As public unease grew at the navy's unreadiness for war, and professional disquiet about the admiralty's reluctance to appoint a naval staff mounted, Asquith placed the navy under Churchill's control.

Appointed First Lord—navy minister—in October 1911, Churchill rapidly expanded his knowledge of naval affairs, visiting naval establishments and talking endlessly with officers. He could learn fast when he wanted: and having learned he began, to the irritation of the First Sea Lord, to send peremptory orders to the other Sea Lords and even made signals to the fleet without Board of Admiralty approval. The First Sea Lord Sir Francis Bridgeman objected, and became the first to realise the folly of crossing Winston's path: dismissing him, Churchill demonstrated in the words of official navy historian Captain Stephen Roskill his "ruthlessness" by reading extracts of Bridgeman's private letters to the House to foster the notion that the outgoing admiral was in declining health.[8]

As his insight grew, so did his interference. Late in 1913, he took to listening to junior officers gripe against their seniors, and intervened in the fleet's disciplinary affairs in one extraordinary episode that involved ordering the Post Office to intercept a certain letter; the First Sea Lord (whose biographer called Winston's high-handed conduct that of "a thwarted spoilt schoolboy") threatened to resign, as did the Second, Third and Fourth Sea Lords. These episodes did the first damage to Churchill's reputation in naval wardrooms and in the Smoking Room of the House alike.

He became increasingly surefooted as he perceived that the Board was possessed of brains inferior to his own, and that its admirals were less well versed in dialectic. Churchill enforced innovations which partially restored his fame, particularly in the lower deck. He introduced sweeping reforms of the harsh conditions, he abolished some of the humiliating summary punishments that captains could inflict on their men, he updated pay scales unchanged for sixty years, and he made it possible for bluejackets to achieve officer's rank. It was typical of his nature that to discover more about naval aviation, he learned to fly himself.

He hurried the fast and powerful *Queen Elizabeth* battleships through the shipyards, and initiated the conversion from coal to oil firing. But if his fleet was ready in the broadest sense when war broke out in August 1914, it was still imperfect in important details. The magazines of the battle cruisers were vulnerable, naval gunnery was poor, and the heavier shells, mines, torpedoes and other equipment would prove badly deficient when the time came.

* * *

In the World War his personal intervention extended to naval operations, often to awesome effect: he took to drafting signals to the fleet in his own hand and despatched them without consulting the First Sea Lord. It was lawful, but the often ambiguous wording resulted in mishaps like the escape of the German warships *Goeben* and *Breslau* to Constantinople, which in turn encouraged Turkey to come in against Britain.[9]

He was right to want to exploit the Antwerp bridgehead in October 1914 to strike into the German right flank, but he did so in such meagre strength that the result was a fiasco even after he, erstwhile lieutenant in the Hussars, had crossed to Antwerp in person and flamboyantly offered to take charge in the rank of lieutenant-general which Lord Kitchener no less rashly offered him.

In November his navy lost its first action at Coronel, largely because of faulty dispositions ordered from his desk thousands of miles away. His reputation was salvaged by the victory off the Falklands six weeks later, but nothing could expunge the memory of the ill-fated expedition to the Dardanelles in 1915.

Insisted upon with his customary forcefulness, he devised it as a purely naval operation to force the Dardanelles straits and capture Constantinople. Already questionable in concept, it was ill prepared in practice and a bloody failure in execution. Hoping vaguely that his battleships could outrange the Turkish guns and pulverize their forts, he talked the Dardanelles project past his tongue-tied naval and Cabinet colleagues. Too late, at the end of February, he realized that substantial military forces should also be despatched, but he still went ahead with his purely naval assault first, forfeiting the element of surprise.

This naval assault was made on March 18, and was repelled. Writing in his diary the next day Sir Maurice Hankey noted that he had "urged Churchill to have troops to co-operate, but he wouldn't listen, insisting that [the] Navy could do it alone"—hoping, as Hankey suspected, to rehabilitate his name after Antwerp. By the time infantry had been trained and equipped for a frontal assault on the Gallipoli peninsula in April they ran into the machine guns and bayonets of well prepared Turkish positions. Carnage and stalemate resulted.

The First Lord and First Sea Lord, two eccentric, hot-tempered, ambitious characters, had been at loggerheads throughout. The admiral, Sir John Arbuthnot Fisher, kept navy hours, rising at dawn; while his minister was wont to lie a-bed until mid-day and to take afternoon siestas, achieving a bustling crescendo of alertness and activity towards nine P.M.—just as "Jacky" Fisher was normally steering for his cot. By mid-May 1915 Fisher could take it no longer. Undaunted by the sickening bloodshed and mounting warship losses off the Gallipoli peninsula, Churchill demanded that even more ships be sent out. The First Sea Lord suffered a nervous breakdown and quit.

The public was horrified by the debacle and Asquith dismissed his wayward First Lord. Clementine thought Winston would die of grief. In vain he pleaded with his prime minister—first for reprieve, then at least for office, even the most humble; the latter plea suggested to historian Roskill that love of power was a "very strong feature" in Winston's character.

Resigned eventually to paying the political price for failure, Churchill did it in style. He reported for officer training, crossed the Channel as a lieutenant colonel at the beginning of 1916, and served in France as a battalion commander in the Royal Scots Fusiliers for the next five months. He was a popular and efficient officer, but he was careful too to remain in correspondence, both directly and through the assiduous Clementine, with his influential friends in Westminster.

Although a world crisis of Stygian darkness was perhaps not the most appropriate time for such self-indulgence he campaigned for a public inquiry into the Dardanelles, hoping to clear his name by sheer weight of eloquence; in March 1916 he returned briefly to England and stated this demand to the House. Ignoring Clementine's advice, he struck a fitful and ill-advised alliance with his old foe Jacky Fisher and attempted from the Opposition front bench to vindicate them both. But when he ended by urging that Fisher be recalled as First Sea Lord it knocked the bottom from the barrel: his words were received in hostile silence.

Eventually a Select Committee did inquire into the Dardanelles, but its conclusions were anything but satisfying for Winston.

It might have been the end of his career, but Lloyd George—prime minister since December 1916—preferred to have Winston where he could see him and in July 1917 he gave him the ministry of munitions. It was the first of several offices during the six years of Lloyd George's premiership, offices which allowed Winston to complete his knowledge of the workings of modern government.

The next stage was in January 1919 when he became Secretary of State for both War and Air. If it fell short of defence minister, which was the role to which Churchill aspired, it was because Lloyd George was shy of placing that much power in this one man's hands. He must have felt justified in this restraint in February, when Churchill demonstrated a certain instability by fluttering over to Paris on his own initiative and demanding at a summit conference of foreign ministers, that all the Allies intervene against the Bolsheviks in Russia now. "Churchill at his worst," was how Sir Maurice Hankey described it.

Churchill at his worst: that was how the taxpayers might have regarded his campaign, still in this office, for four battleships to be built every year for the next four or five years: in 1920 the only putative enemy was the United States, and war against her was traditionally unthinkable.

Two years later he was back at the desk of Under-Secretary for the Colonies — the same desk he had vacated fifteen earlier. Across that desk now flowed State papers on Ireland, where the "troubles" were at their height. It underlines the garish side of his character that he urged a strongly repressive line against the republicans, supporting what he coyly termed "legalized reprisals" for the murder of British security forces; but his was the statesmanlike hand behind the treaty ultimately signed with the new Irish Free State on December 6, 1922.

Instability continued to be his problem. In September, by his premature release of a communique on the Turkish-Greek conflict in Asia Minor, he nearly precipitated Britain into war with Turkey without first obtaining Dominion guarantees. The Dominions suspected that he was railroading them and Canada and Australia declined their support. The Canadian prime minister was shocked to learn years later from a Privy Councillor that Churchill had been under the influence of drink at the Cabinet meeting concerned.[10] This "Chanak crisis" brought down Lloyd George's coalition. The Dundee electorate expressed their personal displeasure with Mr Churchill at the subsequent general election: they turfed him out of the House for the first time since 1900; to add to his misery, he was ousted by a Mr Scrimgeour — a Socialist and Prohibitionist whom he had defeated at the five previous elections.

He travelled to the Riviera and began to sketch a multi-volume history of the war, *The World Crisis*. The five volumes of what Balfour wittily termed "Winston's brilliant autobiography disguised as a history of the universe" would make him a wealthy man: he expected to earn £5,000 and £8,000 from the first two volumes alone — very large sums of money in those days; he bought Chartwell, worked on further volumes, toyed briefly with the idea of a Centre Party with Lloyd George, and stood unsuccessfully as independent Anti-Socialist at Westminster constituency in March 1924.

Failing there, he went back to the Conservatives. He was returned to the House as a Tory MP after a decisive victory at Epping that

October. Stanley Baldwin rewarded Winston's fickleness with high Cabinet office, as Chancellor of the Exchequer: it was the office his father Lord Randolph had held in 1886.

TWICE A TURNCOAT. If it left him with an uneasy conscience he made light of it. "People often mock at me for having changed parties and labels," he wrote when he was sixty. "They say with truth that I have been a Tory, Liberal, Coalitionist, Constitutionalist, and finally Tory again. . . .

> My own feeling is that I have been more truly consistent than almost any other well known public man. I have seen political parties change their positions on the greatest questions with bewildering rapidity, on Protection, on Irish Home Rule, and on many important secondary issues. But I have always been a Tory democrat and Free Trader, as I was when I first stood for Oldham more than thirty years ago.[11]

To Kay Halle, girlfriend of his only son Randolph, he remarked one weekend at Chartwell upon how his fortunes had improved each time that he betrayed his party. "I've ratted twice," he said, "and on the second rat Baldwin made me Chancellor."

He added, "The family motto of the House of Marlborough is Faithful but Unfortunate. I, by my daring and enterprise, have changed the motto to Faithless but Fortunate."[12]

His five years at the Treasury cannot be glossed over. They were a grim epoch. He came under the influence of powerful City figures who persuaded him to restore Britain to the Gold Standard of 1914. The decision unleashed an economic avalanche. He found the zeros and "damned little dots" beyond his grasp. He resorted to patter and showmanship on the floor of the House to mask his own ignorance.

His naval colleagues watched with particular bitterness as he slashed defence spending to finance eye-catching schemes for social insurance, de-rating industrial property, and sixpence or even a shilling off income tax. This poacher turned gamekeeper attacked every vestige of new naval construction with unremitting zeal.

It shocked his old friends in Cabinet and at the admiralty. "That damned fellow Winston," snorted Hankey, referring to Britain's unreadiness for the new war that slowly loomed, "was largely responsible."[13] Admiral Lord Beatty wrote to his wife on January 26, 1925: "That extraordinary fellow Winston has gone mad. Economically mad, and no sacrifice is too great to achieve what in his shortsightedness is the panacea for evils—to take a shilling off the Income Tax."

Where just one year earlier he had enthusiastically endorsed plans for a new naval base at Singapore, now he mercilessly struck it from the list; he opposed the admiralty's cruiser building programme, and vetoed the increase in submarine strength at Hong Kong.

In particular he scorned the very idea of a Japanese danger to Britain's immense interests in the Far East. "A war with Japan!" he scoffed to Baldwin, "But why should there be a war with Japan? I do not believe there is the slightest chance of it in our lifetime."[14]

The Naval Staff disagreed, arguing in March 1925 that Japan's growing population and need for markets and sources of self-supply would compel her to "push a policy of penetration, expansion and aggression."[15] Churchill as chancellor demurred: "I do not believe Japan has any idea of attacking the British Empire," he wrote, "or that there is any danger of her doing so for at least a generation to come." If she did attack, he believed that Britain's naval power was sufficient to force Japan's surrender after three or four years.[16] At his suggestion the Ten Year Rule—the policy-making assumption that no major war was likely within ten years—was extended in 1926 and again in 1928.[17]

* * *

He was becoming aware that Britain's world position was slipping, and despite his American blood he was inclined to identify the United States as the culprit. At Chartwell he talked of their "arrogance" and "fundamental hostility" to Britain. They wished, he believed, to dominate world politics. In a Cabinet memorandum he urged a similar view: Britain alone should decide how large a navy she required, independently of American desiderata; as for President Calvin Coolidge, he was just a crude amateur with the "viewpoint of a New England backwoodsman."[18] Coolidge delivered an anti-British electioneering speech, which raised Churchill's hackles further: "They have exacted every penny from Europe. . . Surely they might leave us to manage our own affairs."[19] He warned his colleagues against cutting the navy down to "the limits which the United States considers suitable for herself." When Coolidge was now defeated by Herbert Hoover, Churchill described even this as being not good for England. "She is being slowly but surely forced into the shade," he wrote somberly to Clemmie.

By the spring of 1929 this wise woman was writing to warn him that his "known hostility to America" might stand in the way of his becoming foreign secretary: "You would have to try and understand and master America and make her like you. It's no use grovelling or being civil to her."[20]

But the change of feeling which now overtook him was wrought less by Clementine's wise advice than by his growing infatuation with the huge North American continent, as he revisited it on a lecture tour in

September 1929—borne luxuriously from coast to coast by special railroad coaches provided by steel magnate Charles Schwab or his financier friend Barney Baruch, or driven by limousine through the giant Redwood and Sequoia forests of northern California to splash about in a starlet's heated marble pool in Hollywood. He liked almost everything about the country, and even Prohibition held no terrors for him since Randolph the Rabbit—as he affectionately spoke of his son—had filled every flask and medicine bottle in their cases with brandy or whisky: "Up to the present I have never been without what was necessary," twinkled Churchill in a letter home.[21]

By the end of that September his affection for this great new nation was complete. "I explained to them all about England and her affairs," he wrote Clemmie from Los Angeles, still suffused with the thrill of America, "showing how splendid and tolerant she was and how we ought to work together."[22] This visit began a love affair that never ended.

After Labour leader Ramsay MacDonald, the "boneless wonder," captured power in May 1929, all the fun had gone out of politics for Churchill. He had lost interest even in naval affairs. He began to write more, drafted *My Early Life* (published in 1930) and embarked on the four volumes of *Marlborough, His Life and Times* (1933-1938). His style was good, but his desire to find the unblemished truth about the victor of Blenheim was less than absolute. "Give me the facts," he would tell his research assistant, "and I will twist them the way I want to suit my argument."[23]

He would remain out of office for nearly a decade. His enemies mocked him as a Cassandra and warmonger. He was not idle in the House, as we shall see, but he had lost the confidence of the public.

"Here I am," he remarked bitterly to Harold Nicolson, strolling across Horse Guards Parade, "after almost thirty years in the House of Commons, after holding many of the highest offices of State; here I am—discarded. Cast away. Marooned. Rejected. And disliked."

A gardener sweeping up dead leaves noticed him and raised his hat.

"Good ole Winnie!" he called out quite unexpectedly.

Churchill grinned. "The British public," he observed, "is a curious animal. It relishes the familiar. When it has consistently disliked a man for thirty years he becomes a familiar object of abuse. And as such: Good old Winnie."

Perhaps it was providential that he now set out across the lonely wilderness—encumbered with impotent insight and wasted ability. More than once Baldwin seemed on the verge of re-instating him in office, only to hesitate; but more than once in later years Churchill would reflect upon his good fortune in having thus avoided responsibility for the events that tarnished those who remained in power.

Ten years later the Canadian prime minister would suggest to him "There is a destiny about your life. You were meant for these times," and Winston could only agree. The same Canadian would suggest that he had been singled out to be war leader and again Churchill would agree.

"It was fortunate," he added, "that I was out of office for ten years. It gave me time to study the situation."[24]

Why did prime ministers Baldwin and Neville Chamberlain spurn him? It was not just that his name had become a political liability. There was a powerful mistrust of him, and jealousy of his oratory too. The Socialists had no reason to like the politician who had sent in troops to break the miners' strikes, and now he had doublecrossed both Tories and Liberals. In 1917 Lord Esher wrote in one savage indictment that Churchill became too easily intoxicated with his own verbosity:

> He handles great subjects in rhythmical language and becomes quickly enslaved by his own phrases. He deceives himself into the belief that he takes broad views, when his mind is fixed upon one comparatively small aspect of the question.

We have noted that Chamberlain conceded that MPs regarded Winston's oratory as the "best show in London;" but he went on to remark that this was precisely the weak point. "So far as I can judge they think of it as a show and they are not prepared at present to trust his character and still less his judgement."[25] Conservatives like the proprietor of the *Daily Telegraph* suspected he was out for office and even secretly double-dealing with rivals like Lloyd George.[26]

Thus the British followed Baldwin and Chamberlain. They might be dull, but they offered what Britain cherished: tranquillity, safety, and Business As Usual; while Winston thrived on stimulation, danger and risk. Philip Snowden would call him an adventurer and soldier of fortune. To which novelist H.G. Wells added his own telling commentary: "Before all things," he wrote, "he desires a dramatic world with villains and one hero."

Winston Churchill had one enduring ambititon—to become prime minister of Britain. That was natural enough. What was less natural, as a mutual friend remarked at this time to Harold Nicolson, was that he wanted above all to hold that office in a very dangerous war.

The lure of absolute power was always with him.

Entertaining visitors years later at Chartwell, he suggested a party game—"I will ask each of you in turn what is your secret ambition."

The game soon ran out of steam. It was evident that he was more eager to reveal his own than to hear of their ambitions.

"I have two ambitions," he obliged them. The first was, "To become prime minister." He paused, but the other ambition his houseguests would never have divined if they had tried every permutation all weekend.

"The second is," Winston revealed, "to enter into daily telegraphic and written communication with the President of the United States."[27]

Some may have chuckled at that. It seemed unlikely that fortune would smile on him again. He was out of office, and had retired to Lord Randolph's old seat below the gangway.

Here in the wilderness he met another man—it does not matter whom—who asked him which was the more dangerous, War or Politics.

He retorted: "Politics—in war you can only be killed once."

CHAPTER 2

Keeping It Under His Hat

H E HAD NEVER been wealthy, but his outgoings in no way diminished with lessening responsibilities of office. His finances roused curiosity over the years.

Rumours of corruption dogged him. Oscar Wilde's friend and consort Lord Alfred Douglas published one scurrilous pamphlet in 1923 alleging that on behalf of a "Jewish syndicate" including a friend, Sir Ernest Cassel, Churchill had issued a false communique on the Battle of Jutland in return for a £40,000 cut of their Stock Market killing.[1] Churchill had his Lordship jailed for criminal libel.

While in office he had been cushioned by his emoluments as MP and Minister, and he had profited from the traditional perquisites of the high-born—a currency flutter; £500 won at the tables from the Duke of Westminster; a £5,000 fee to handle oil companies' dealings with the government. Even after Baldwin's defeat his contacts in Whitehall were of pecuniary value, and he attracted lucrative directorships in coal storage and transport companies.

Hoping to found a personal fortune, he plunged into the U.S. stock market, and liked the easy money that he made. He began to commune by transatlantic telephone with the financier Bernard Baruch, the head of the U.S. War Industries Board with whom he had dealt when munitions minister. But in vain will the inquisitive search the Baruch papers in New Jersey, for any trace of financial succour – apart from one item, a note in the multi-millionaire's hand acknowledging repayment of five dollars which he had advanced to the Englishman. It was that kind of detail that makes rich men what they are: rich.

Baruch's advice was worth every dollar. In 1929 Winston earned £2,000 from his U.S. electrical stocks; in one three-week period these jumped £5,200 in value, prompting a jubilant letter to Clementine that he had recovered a fortune: "And this, with the information I can get and now am free to use, may earn further profits in the future".

He continued to speculate. But now funds flowed also from his writing. He was commanding substantial fees. He had contracted for twenty-two articles for American weeklies which would earn him no less than £40,000 — so he telegraphed to Clemmie in October 1929.

But his dreams of great fortune dissolved on the twenty-fourth of that month, as he was eye-witness to the New York stockmarket crash. "O Lord," he gasped, stepping out into Wall Street as the Stock Exchange ejected visitors at noon-thirty: "What a day!"

HE HAD SPENT that summer lecturing in North America.

When he arrived back in England on November 5, it was to find that Baldwin, in informal alliance with the Socialists, had agreed to a Royal Commission on the grant of self-government to India.

From that moment, he was overwhelmed by a new obsession — India, "that most truly bright and precious jewel in the crown," as his father had termed the subcontinent forty years before.

Many shared his bitterness at the Viceroy's appeasement of the disruptive, extremist and unrepresentative Indian Congress party led by that "malevolent fanatic" Mahatma Ghandi. Churchill seized the chance to try for the Conservative leadership.

India was part of Churchill's youth: India was an adventure that still lingered in his blood. He could not heed the logic of his critics. Once, the Viceroy Lord Irwin — later Lord Halifax — reproached him for having the ideas of a subaltern a generation ago. "There is a number of interesting Indians coming to the Round Table Conference," Irwin murmured diffidently to Winston, having the usual trouble with his r's, "and I weally think that it would be valuable to you to talk to some of them and bwing your views up to date."

"I am quite shatisfied with my views of India," lisped Churchill in reply. "I don't want them dishturbed by any bloody Indian."[2]

The India Bill was debated on November 7, 1929. Sam Hoare wrote to Irwin afterwards, "Throughout the debate Winston was almost demented with fury and since the debate has scarcely spoken to anyone."

GERMANY WAS NOT at that time among his dangerous obsessions. His baleful eye still glared at Washington. "They are arrogant," he said of the Americans in 1928, "fundamentally hostile to us, and . . . wish to dominate world politics."

But in 1929 a British journal reported that Germany was planning a new 11-inch gunboat and that France intended to go one better. Churchill warned the Cabinet that the secret German plan rendered the current British cruiser programme, currently orientated on the American navy, obsolete.

Soon after Heinrich Brüning's election victory in Germany in October 1930 Churchill lunched with a high official at the German embassy. He remarked that France was justifiably worried about Germany, and voiced the first concern about Adolf Hitler—then only a minor politician leading an opposition party.

"At present," reported the diplomat, quoting Churchill's words in a telegram to Berlin,

> Hitler has of course declared he has no intention of making a foreign war, but he, Churchill, is convinced that Hitler or his supporters will seize the first opportunity to resort to arms again.

When the diplomat, taken aback, remarked upon Germany's "impossible frontiers," and particularly the Polish corridor imposed upon her, Churchill replied, "Poland must have an outlet to the sea."

They found common ground again on the Soviet Union. Churchill roundly proposed that Germany, Britain, and France take concerted action "under German leadership" against Soviet dumping on the world markets. "He sorely regrets," the German official reported, "that the joint offensive against Soviet Russia which he proposed immediately after the war was not approved by the British Cabinet."

In reflective mood, Churchill revealed that he was now writing *The Eastern Front*, and expressed interest in meeting the German field commanders there.

"At the outbreak of war," he reminisced, "it was totally incomprehensible to me and the entire War Cabinet that Germany didn't throw her entire weight against Russia, restricting herself in the west to defending her frontiers. That would have cast France in the role of aggressor in the eyes of the world."[3]

INDIA STILL CONCERNED him more than Germany. To the German diplomat he spoke of the Round-Table Conference being summoned to decide her future, and excoriated the name of Lord Irwin.

"When I think of the way," he reminded his friend Lord Beaverbrook, "in which we poured out blood and money to take Contalmaison or to hold Ypres, I cannot understand why it is we should now throw away our conquests and our inheritance with both hands, through helplessness and pusillanimity."

"My only interest in politics," he added, "is to see this position retrieved."[4]

It was an emotive, crowd-pulling controversy. His opponents on both sides of the House feared that he might ride this horse all the way to Downing-street, rallying followers with the battle-cry, "The Socialists are giving India away!"

An Indian Empire Society was founded. Addressing its first meeting in December 1930 he argued that the practical way to avoid turmoil in India was to improve the lot of the masses, while continuing to assert Britain's will to rule; many times over the next six months Churchill orated in this vein and, with our hindsight of what occurred when India was ultimately abandoned, it is hard to say that he was wrong.

There were times when he cursed universal suffrage. It might well be, he sorrowed in a letter to Randolph early in 1931, that future historians would record that within a generation of "the poor, silly people all getting the votes they clamour for," they squandered the treasure which "five centuries of wisdom and victory" had accumulated.[5]

Releasing India remained his Party's official policy. Regardless of this, he developed his attack on Baldwin, culminating in a speech to the House on January 26:

> Two centuries of effort and achievement! Lives given on a hundred fields! Far more lives given and consumed in faithful and devoted service to the Indian people themselves! All this has earned us rights of our own in India.

He could sense the backbenchers warming to him as he spoke— some began to cheer. There were many Conservatives who regarded Baldwin now as weak or woolly and even "letting down the party."

With this speech, and the letter he wrote to Baldwin that evening formally breaking ties with the Shadow Cabinet, he deliberately put himself beyond the pale.

THAT HIS SELF-EXILE from the inner councils might last eight years did not occur to him. He devoted the early months of 1931 to the attack on the bipartisan India policy, doubting not, as he wrote to his wife, that he had the whole spirit of the Conservative party behind with him.

He basked in the support of the powerful newspaper lords, Rothermere and Beaverbrook. Launching his India campaign, he had made the fiery boast: "Nothing will turn me from it, and I have cheerfully and gladly put out of my mind all ideas of public office."

But nothing would dislodge Baldwin from his complacency. "Decided only to be undecided," Churchill would rasp about the Tory leader: "resolved to be irresolute, adamant for drift." But time was on Baldwin's side. When the hue and cry over India ebbed that summer of 1931, it left Churchill stranded: high and dry, and still out of office, just as Baldwin had known it would.

Churchill surveyed his position. Many said that he was finished. Boats, once burnt, cannot be rescued from the flames.

He was in political isolation; the New York stock market crash had wiped out the fortune he believed safely invested there; he had the upkeep of Chartwell which he had bought in happier times—in 1923, from the proceeds of *The World Crisis* — and he had a sizeable family to support: the eldest Diana, born 1906; the spendthrift Randolph, 1911; the artistic Sarah, 1914; the quiet and helpful Mary, 1922.

He was a man without a party: one newspaper scoffed that while he might change his party with the facility of partners at a dance, he had always been true to the one party he really believed in—"that which is assembled under the hat of Mr Winston Churchill."

> His life is one long speech. He does not talk. He orates. He will address you at breakfast as though you were an audience at the Free Trade Hall, and at dinner you find the performance still running. If you meet him in the intervals he will give you more fragments of the discourse, walking up and down the room with the absorbed self-enraged Napoleonic portentousness that makes his high seriousness tremble on the verge of the comic.
>
> He does not want to hear your views. He does not want to disturb the beautiful clarity of his thought by the tiresome reminders of the other side. What has he to do with the other side when his side is the right side? He is not arguing with you: he is telling you.

* * *

As on earlier occasions when his luck had run out, he slipped out of England for a while. Late in 1931 he again launched himself onto the American lecture circuit to talk about the destiny of the English-speaking peoples.

He hoped to spend some time with "Barney" Baruch. He wrote to Baruch on November 1 that the forty lectures he had arranged would net him £10,000.[6] He travelled with wife, daughter Diana, valet and Scotland Yard bodyguard. In North America he indulged his sybaritic tastes to the full. He surfaced in Hollywood, was photographed with movie starlets, and did not want for either food or drink. Lecture managers were told, "His tastes are very simple: He is easy to please with the best of everything."

It was a hectic pace for a man of Winston's advancing years, and New York city nearly terminated that weary existence.

Visiting Baruch alone on December 13, he had taken a cab to Fifth Avenue and on getting out instinctively looked right instead of left, being a London man. He stepped under the wheels of an onrushing car driven by an Italian immigrant. He collapsed into a bundle of flesh, blood and clothing, and reflected semi-consciously upon his plight. After satisfying the American medical profession's primary concern, his creditworthiness, he was treated at the Lennox hospital. The repair costs—he had broken fifteen bones—and loss of lecture revenue added to his misfortune.

But he would not be Winston Churchill if he could not turn a disaster to his own good fortune. John Wheeler, president of the North American Newspaper Alliance, suggested he write about it.[7] Churchill hired a new private secretary—Phyllis Moir—dictated a wonderful account of his misfortune, which was still painfully in his memory, and pocketed $1,500 for the syndication rights. He blued the money on a three-week convalescence in the Bahamas with Clemmie.

> Somewhere in the black bundle [he had written in the article] toward which the passers-by are running there is a small chamber or sanctum wherein all is orderly and undisturbed.
> There sits enthroned a mind apparently intact and unshaken. Before it is a keyboard of levers or buttons directing the body. Above, a whole series of loudspeakers reports the sensations and experiences of the empire controlled from this tiny headquarters. This mind is in possession of the following conclusion: "I have been run over by a motorcar in America. Here is a real catastrophe. Perhaps it is the end."

The flippant style concealed a deepening worry about his future. Writing to Randolph from the Bahamas, Clemmie reported: "Last night he was very sad and said that he had now in the last two years had three very heavy blows. First the loss of all that money in the [economic] crash, then the loss of his political position in the Conservative Party, and now this terrible physical injury."[8]

Returning to England, he had time on his hands. He built brick walls and otherwise improved upon Chartwell. He painted in oils the canvases recording his meanderings along the French Riviera, Dutch canals, Norwegian fjords, and the cotton plantations of Hobcaw, Bernard Baruch's place in South Carolina. "His friends agree," wrote a benevolent American observer, "that his finest piece of work in this period was a still life of two glasses alongside a bottle of brandy and a bottle of Scotch."[9]

Back in England he enlarged his new profession, journalism, although because of its demands on his time and energy it was at right-angles to his preferred one of politics: but politics were dominated now by the unappetizing coalition of Baldwin and Macdonald, and he was glad to be out of it.

A year before, Harold Nicolson had found him at Chartwell working on three books simultaneously — polishing *My Early Life*, completing *The Eastern Front*, and embarking on a four volume life of the Duke of Marlborough which would fully occupy him until the awful September of 1938. Shuffling books along a thirty-foot table carpentered to his own design, jousting on every page with the long dead historian Lord Macaulay, he laboured to dispel that great historian's accusations against the duke — charges of treason and taking bribes — and to glorify him instead as the hero who had delivered Europe from a despot, Louis XIV.

The volumes painted a magnificent portrait of the times. The glorification was no easy task for Winston, despite the opening to him of the Marlborough archives at Blenheim palace. He found confirmed therein the details of John Churchill's womanizing with well-endowed female objects of his lust and greed. On the weightier charge of high treason, he could only suggest that the letter in question was a forgery; this did not ride well on the lips of a man who had in his own time made political capital out of the Zinoviev Letter of October 1924.

THE MONEY FLOWED in and out of his bank account like an Atlantic tide. He put his literary income for 1930 alone at £35,000. He made an £8,000 deal with the *Daily Mail*, for example, to publish his articles on the North American tour.

This literary income was now indispensible for him. Inevitably, much of it depended on from political posturing that can only be termed irresponsible. The change in several of his tunes can be traced directly to changes in his personal fortunes. He had to toe the line of a fickle international readership, particularly in the United States. Churchill, who in 1929 and 1930 had reserved some of his baser utterances for America and her predatory intentions towards Europe and the Empire, now spoke in his lucrative 1931/32 lecture tour of the need for Britain and the USA to stand together to protect "the distracted peoples of Europe" from Communist tyranny; and he highlighted the absurdity of each country "gaping at each other in this helpless way," and being ashamed of Anglo-American cooperation "as if it were a crime."[10]

In 1920 Mr Churchill had published in one Sunday newspaper an article about "the schemes of the International Jews," in which he had warned against the "adherents of this sinister confederacy," and called them a "world-wide conspiracy for the overthrow of civilisation and for the reconstitution of society."[11] By the 1930's all such ugly phrases had been tailored out of his writings.

His posture towards the Soviet Union was one of consistent abhorrence. In July 1927 he proclaimed that Soviet diplomats were "treacherous, incorrigible, and unfit for civilized intercourse."

Italian Fascism also held few horrors for him. In 1926 he had lauded Mussolini's "commanding leadership;"[12] In January 1927, after several days as Benito Mussolini's guest, he had praised Italy's corporate state, the "discipline, order, goodwill, smiling faces," and even the ubiquitous

Fascist salute;[13] he had declared himself charmed by Mussolini's simple bearing and dedication to the Italian people; and he had gushed to the Roman journalists, "If I had been an Italian, I would have been entirely with you from the beginning to the end of your victorious struggle against the bestial appetites and passions of Leninism. . . Your movement has rendered a service to the whole world."[14]

"Nearly thirty years ago," he wrote for the North American Newspaper Alliance — many of whose readers were of Italian descent,

> I visited the island of Rhodes, then a part of the Turkish Empire. I have just visited it again, under Mussolini's rule. What a change is presented! The dirt, the squalid and bedraggled appearance, are entirely gone. Everything is clean and tidy. Every man, however poor, looks proud of himself. Not a beggar is to be seen, and even the cabmen are well shaved. Yet they all seem quite happy.[15]

As for Germany, Hitler still seemed a long way from office. But Churchill's literary sales there were non-existent; and since he was writing for the greatest democracy in the world — writing so to speak to "the gallery" — he played on the latent anti-German sentiments in the English-speaking peoples. In one American article he denounced the Customs Union established early in 1931 by Germany and Austria as "a revival of the secret old world diplomacy" beneath which lurked *Anschluss* — the dreaded union of German speaking peoples. In his writings for the American Hearst newspapers, he warned of Germany and Austria, towering "grim and grisly" over France, a "boisterous fierce-lapping ocean of Teutonic manhood and efficiency" surrounding the Bohemian "island" of Czechoslovakia on three sides.[16]

Not speaking German, it was easy for Churchill to be anti. In the summer of 1932, still writing *Marlborough*, he toured the duke's victorious battlefields in Flanders and Germany.

Winston took with him the friend who had largely replaced F.E. Smith — who had died an alcoholic in 1930 — in his affections, the German-born Professor Frederick Lindemann. "The Prof" had studied at Darmstadt and Berlin, was fluent in German and conversant with the customs.

Randolph had been in Germany during July covering the elections for the *Sunday Graphic*. ("The success of the Nazi party," he had written, "sooner or later means war.") When their paths now crossed in September in Munich Randolph tried to bring his father together with Adolf Hitler. Winston loafed around the hotel with Hitler's court jester Ernst "Putzi" Hanfstaengel, hoping to see the Führer; but in vain. Neither man set eyes upon the other, nor ever would.

Why should Hitler have seen Churchill then, in 1932? The one's star was in the ascendant, the other's on the wane.

The former Cabinet Minister, who had been feted across the North American continent in special trains and limousines and whose name was a household word in the Empire cannot have enjoyed being frozen out by a former corporal who had never been in office.

His speeches reflected an injury more lasting than any New York motorist could inflict on his esteem. As the Disarmament Conferences now began in Geneva, and there was talk of allowing Germany equality in arms, Churchill found a holy obsession to replace India.[17]

CHAPTER 3

Wuthering Depths

THROUGHOUT THESE EARLIER years of political exile, he was harrassed by accumulating money problems. To keep his country house and feed his family, and to pay off the debts incurred by an increasingly wayward son, he had to devote more time to authorship and less to public affairs; it was a vicious circle, but there was no alternative unless he found philanthropic backers, with all the dangers to his independence that that implied.

As yet, the moneyed aristocracy saw little cause to back him. His enemies had written him off; worse, he had begun to write himself off too. "I'd give up politics entirely," he confessed to a family friend, "if it weren't for the faint chance that one day I shall be prime minister."[1]

To a keen poker player like Beaverbrook he was a "busted flush". At the time of the break with Baldwin, Winston's "Diehard" act over India did not seem to carry conviction. "He has disclosed too many shifting faces to expect to be regarded as immovable now," Beaverbrook commented to a Canadian friend. "His voice lacks that note of sincerity for which the country looks."[2] He was irritated by Churchill's harping on India. "Winston Churchill," he wrote, "is making it his ladder for the moment." To which he added the barbed comment: "Churchill has the habit of breaking the rungs of any ladder he puts his foot on."[3]

He expected Churchill to make one farewell tour, then retire from politics.[4] It was an irony that Stanley Baldwin, who was at heart a Diehard, was leading the campaign for federal rule in India while the Diehards were led by Churchill, who had given Home Rule to Ireland. "The result is," Beaverbrook summed up, "that Baldwin does not feel happy about his policy, and the Diehards are not happy about their leader."[5]

As the campaign against Indian self-government slithered and withered, Churchill threw himself with greater abandon into his other profession. In August 1931 his friend Brendan Bracken landed for him a £7,800 contract with the London *Daily Mail* to write a weekly article for one year. He had the entrepreneurial and literary skills to produce and market sheafs of readable prose even if his ramshackle methods did raise the eyebrows of the more fastidious among his researchers.

* * *

As an author, he rarely originated material himself. Adam Diston, a balding, middle aged Scotsman who sported a butterfly collar, ghosted the weekly articles that Churchill fired off to *Answers* magazine. They spent a few hours in each other's company, then Diston went home to draft the article and sent it to Churchill to amend.[6]

He hired and fired these literary other ranks at will, often treating them little better than a Victorian admiral would the bluejackets below decks. He fluttered across their draft manuscript pages like a butterfly, depositing literary pollen. One such researcher, Edward Marsh, slaved on the galleys for years; his sacrifice was dismissed by Churchill years later with the curt remark that the man had "never been of any use to him at all."[7]

The Times in 1922 furnished assistants to search out chapter mottos for his money-spinning war history. Lesser mortals burrowed in archives, read secondary literature, prepared outlines: he sifted, perused, analyzed, interpreted — and on occasion distorted too.

Marlborough provided instances of this. So did his narrative of the Dardanelles campaign: *The Times* reviewer in 1923 exposed his free-wheeling adaptation of documents;[8] and modern historians with access to the official inquiry's files agree that his responsibility for the disaster was substantially more than would appear from his own tale. "Indeed," concludes one, "Churchill's later account is little better than a pack of lies."[9]

Churchill stood over his devils and skimmed their drafts for style, testing them occasionally on the touchstones provided by acknowledged masters like Gibbon or Macaulay.

"You are very free with yr commas," he lectured Eddie Marsh in 1922 on Colonial Office notepaper. "I always reduce them to a minimum: & use an 'and' or an 'or' as a substitute, not as an addition. Let us argue it out."

Twelve years later he was still educating Edward:

(1) I am in revolt about your hyphens. One must regard the hyphen as a blemish to be avoided wherever possible. . . . I notice Macaulay would write 'downstream' one word, and 'panicstricken' one word. On the other hand 'richly embroidered' seems to me to be two words. . . In 'salt mines' *you* want a hyphen, but who would ever write 'gold-mining shares are good

today?. . . We had a controversy about this last time and arrived at a compromise the principle of which I have forgotten. Would you mind thinking over this again.
(2) 'Judgement' no 'e'. . .

and so on for the whole page of typescript.

And fourteen historic years after delivering this master-class in syntax, Churchill was still plaguing the aide who had become Sir Edward Marsh: "I am still balancing," the now retired war leader wrote, "between 'Goering' and 'Göring' and 'Fuehrer' and 'Führer', etc." To which he added with airy disregard for publisher's expense:

It will be quite easy to change the text throughout by a general directive to the Printer. Curiously I like some one way and some t'other. Let us talk about this.
(2) On the whole I am *against* commas. . .

and thus he had come full circle again.[10]

Many promising young brains were hired by Churchill to assist his. There was history graduate Maurice Ashley, an authority on Oliver Cromwell and the Seventeenth Century, paid £300 per annum to review and sift the treasures of the muniments room at Blenheim Palace.[11] There was Major Desmond Morton, brought in to work on *The World Crisis*: they had met on the western front, where Morton had been subsequently shot through the heart but survived; and there was diplomat Owen O'Malley, who drafted his outline chapters.

Churchill rarely worked with the pen. He declaimed the texts to shorthand girls, while stomping the available floor space and chewing an unlit cigar. He had developed this habit — of dictating manuscripts — while at the Treasury, and freely commandeered his secretary there, one Lettice Fisher, to accompany him on shoots at Balmoral in order that the Muse might not be interrupted.[12]

Thus his written prose was as eloquent as his oratory, a silver torrent of spoken words, often chosen more for their sound than for any precise shade of meaning. A Churchillian sentence crafted with the pen had all the stilted awkwardness of a freshly bricked row of houses: "Everyone may try to make his own bed so long as he is ready to lie in it afterwards", he wrote in a letter to his wife.[13]

In later years he would dictate his masterpieces to Kathleen Hill. She sat at the foot of his bed, typing them into her silent typewriter while inspiration flowed from him. The cigar was still there, but now he sipped iced water or whisky and soda, grunted as though in labour, twitched his toes beneath the bedsheets. At inspiration's end he would bellow "Gimme," seize the paper that rolled out of the platen, and correct it with a fountain pen gripped half way up the barrel.[14]

His output was prolific, but of an enviable quality, particularly the multi-volume histories. He knew how to organize and construct such major opus. In the Thirties he was generating two or three thousand words a day, an entire volume in three months, a major book every year. He told one visitor that he kept two hours free each night for dictating manuscripts.[15]

It would be churlish to deny that they are well composed. He knew his job. In 1930 he would gently admonish a less accomplished friend that writing was like painting. "My teachers used to tell me that the question you must ask yourself is — 'What do you mean to do? What was it you saw that struck you? What was the message you had to give?' "[16]

If, with Churchill, Style vanquished Content every time, what perfect style it was! He could conjure out of a string of unpromising words spontaneous images of a pertinence and sting that probably only a master cartoonist like Illingworth could otherwise accomplish — and then only after hours of draughtmanship.

The consequence of this obsession with style is that when divested of linguistic flora and dissected in the cold light of the late Twentieth Century, some of his most memorable sentences mean little of anything at all.

He sometimes seemed to re-invent the English language. He agonized over principles. Who else but Mr Winston Churchill would dare to inflict Fowler's *Dictionary of Modern English Usage* as a Christmas gift upon the bemused Royal family:[17] was it not rather like bestowing a deodorant stick or nail file on a particularly scruffy friend?

He split no infinitives, that is true. He would wield words carelessly, even wrongly — selecting the rare verb "compass" instead of "encompass" — to intimidatingly archaic effect. The choice of words was baroque and indiscriminate, but the aim was unerring and the results often delightful. Once returning from Harvard he enlarged upon the hope that after the war alliance might be so perpetuated that the *Missouri* — then America's newest battleship — might steam into Gibraltar and "receive cannon balls for her guns."[18]

His entire vocabulary might have been memorized from some newspaper found lining a 19th century escritoire. From the early Thirties he adopted as effective the injunction "pray" instead of "please" — as in "Pray attune your acute mind into [*sic*] analysing this Constitution." Thus he commanded the Prof (Lindemann) one day in 1931 when still stubbornly campaigning for the Indian princes.[19]

But when Winston Churchill ventured forth across the slippery glaciers of the most tangled language forms he did so with the surefootedness of a mountain goat. In that same famous speech to the American Congress in which he would memorably challenge: "What kind of people do they think we are?" he would unabashedly unfurl this ceremonial banner of a sentence:

Sure I am that this day now we are masters of our fate, that the task which has been set us is not above our strenth, that its pangs and toils are not beyond our endurance.[20]

Sentences like this suggest that there were times when for Winston, the Word had become an end unto itself.

* * *

This Leonardo of the English tongue was well paid for his pains. The sales of *Marlborough* in 1929 showed the price his pen commanded: Empire serial rights went to his friend Lord Camrose, the Tory newspaper owner, for £5,000; Empire volume rights to Geo. Harrap's for £10,000 more; and the American to Scribner's for £5,000.[21]

Even £20,000 would not last long, given his outgoings. Undaunted as he sauntered across the threshold and began to plumb the depths of political unpopularity, he cast his mind ahead in the way that authors do to the post-*Marlborough* period, and in October 1932 he took to Cassell's his new idea — a project for a *History of the English Speaking Peoples*, which would alone be worth, he suggested £20,000.

This immense, farsighted construction project, Winston's one-man TVA, mapped out when he was in the foothills of his fortunes, would carry him to the summit of his literary achievements.

"The professors tell me," he would say years later, "that it is very good up to Richard III. But thereafter I am not satisfied with it. Much remains to be done."[22]

His favourite passage was that devoted to the American Civil War — sixty thousand racy, exciting words, bordering at times on a screen-writer's mastery.

In the United States his books did not at first attract large sales. Reviewers acclaimed the third volume of his war history but only 1,000 were sold compared with 11,000 in Britain. But Charles Scribner was a man of fortitude. "We have not lost courage," he would console Winston in 1932, "and will continue to back them until they come their own."[23]

Even in England sales of the final volume on the Eastern front had disappointed.[24]

As book sales declined, Churchill double-banked his income with newspaper and magazine articles. In England, he was already writing for Nash's *Pall Mall* magazine, *Answers* and *Strand Magazine*. Friends now helped to place articles in the USA.

In February 1926 *Cosmopolitan*, then rather more staid than now, published a typical Churchill offering: "When Life Harrasses Me I Ride My Hobby." Though *Cosmo* paid for many, they published remarkably few of these rare Churchill's — spiking four in 1927, one in 1928, five in 1929, and four in 1930; they published only one each in 1928, 1930 and 1931.

His literary agent Curtis Brown had negotiated in 1930 a ten-year agreement with *Collier's* magazine, to write six articles a year at £2,000 per annum. He became an Art Buchwald in striped pants, dilating upon topics as diverse as iced water and Franklin D. Roosevelt, as the Depression and corn on the cob. He would write two articles for *Collier's* in 1930, three each year from 1931 to 1933, two in 1934, five in 1935, three in 1936, five in 1937, four in 1938 and five in the last months of peace, 1939.

UPON HIS RETURN from Germany in the summer of 1932, where he had failed to meet Hitler, he resumed these literary chores.

He was confined to bed, having contracted paratyphoid while visiting Blenheim. There was a rumour — unlikely on the face of it — that he had been poisoned by the drinking water.[25] While convalescing he still dictated to his secretary or read Ashley's latest findings on Marlborough.

He found this new practice of bedroom dictating congenial and convenient: he was after all nearly fifty-eight.

With Ashley's aid he embarked on new money-spinning literary adventures. The literary energy that radiated from the bedroom at Chartwell had a half life that is a-glowing and a-humming to this day in the files of the Chicago Tribune / New York News syndicate archived at Eugene, Oregon.

Probably the oddest literary project revealed by these files is that commenced in September 1932. Curtis Brown had wired him that the *Chicago Tribune* had accepted his latest brainwave, for "the six great stories of the world as retold by Mr Churchill." He agreed to a $1,000 fee — no mean price in those days — for condensing each of the world's classics into 25 pages of double-spaced typescript for American newspaper readers. There is no denying his paternity of these potboilers — the manuscripts are there with Winston's own corrections at Eugene.

It made a striking contrast. In Germany there was terror and turmoil as Hitler made his final bid for power. At Chartwell, Churchill and his devils bent to this eccentric new task.

He rattled off the digests rapidly, getting "A Tale of Two Cities," and "Uncle Tom's Cabin" through the U.S. Customs by November 3, delivering "Moonstone" and "The Count of Monte Cristo" on November 18 and submitting "Tess of the D'Urbervilles" and "Ben Hur" early in January.

He also sold these articles for £2,000 to that discerning readership, the London *News of the World*.[26]

In January 1933 Hitler seized power. In three weeks he was virtual dictator. In England, Mr Churchill was being something of a dictator too — dictating still more digests, though unsolicited. The Nazi menace was far from his mind.

On the last day of January — as the Nazis were staging torchlight processions outside the Reich Chancery in Berlin — Churchill was proposing in a chatty cable to his New York agents that he now digest "Wuthering Heights."

He had a digest of both that and "Jane Eyre" in his agent's hands by February 13.

In Berlin Hitler ordered the secret expansion of his army and airforce, and the liquidation of all opposition. Churchill still had other fish to fry. From New York came a fresh suggestion from his delighted agents that he now tackle "The House of Seven Gables," "Dombey and Son," "The Way of All Flesh," "Ivanhoe," "Ramona," and Dostoievsky's "Crime and Punishment."

FOR THE NEXT year he continued this exiguous existence. He wrote his memoirs, and sold them as *My Life* to the Americans for $6,000 in 1934. He cabled his agents on November 30, "Greatly obliged," and put the package on the transatlantic steamer to them on the appointed day ("Pray communicate this to the *Tribune*") together with forty snapshots from his scrapbooks. Again the *News of the World* bought it, for £4,200. The entrepreneur in him had artfully worked into the American manuscripts puffs for his other books; the Chicago *Tribune* equally neatly excised them.

Early in 1935 he suggested a monthly column syndicated throughout North America. "I don't need to emphasize to you," wrote agent Curtis Brown to the syndicate, "his ability as a journalist for American consumption."[27] Nothing came of it, and he did not return to the idea.

CHAPTER 4

Wild Man In The Wilderness

"IF I WERE elected dictator of the world," Churchill murmured a few days after his final retirement in 1955, "I should kill all the scientists and burn all the books."

He was cruising the Mediterranean with an American publisher when he made the remark.

"Of course," said Churchill, seeing the hurt look of Lord Cherwell, his chief scientific adviser, "I'd make an exception of The Prof. Just simple favouritism, of course, my prerogative as dictator."

His eyes twinkled. "And I should make it a criminal offence for anyone to go around bothering molecules. The little atom should be left in peace for ever."

Clementine leaned over and shouted into his earpiece. "But why, then, Winston, are you always telling the scientists in Britain to get on with it, get on with it?"

Churchill smiled feebly. "Well, quite obviously I am *not* dictator of the world. No, nor is this a platform on which I should be likely to be elected one. So we have to keep our own end up."[1]

IF IT IS TRUE that a man can be judged by the company he keeps, it was not easy to judge Winston in the Thirties, because his friends were so few.

Lord Birkenhead (F.E. Smith) had died in 1930, and it was the Prof who stepped into the gap in the firmament around Churchill. Lord Cherwell — at that time Frederick Lindemann — was to remain his friend and counsellor for the next thirty-five years, while his close cropped hair receded across the Central European cranium, the neat military moustache turned white, and the sallow skin tautened over hollow cheeks.[2]

They had met in August 1921, when the Prof had pandered to Winston's children in the hope of attracting an invitation to Chartwell. Two lonely men, they understood and complemented each other perfectly.

Lindemann was Winston's walking pocket calculator, and a compendium of useful data. Fastidiously dressed in long topcoat and bowler, he was a lifelong bachelor, fanatically abstemious and a cranky vegetarian. By some stroke of ante-natal destiny he had been born on German soil. His father was a product of Alsace, his mother American like Winston's. He had studied at Berlin — under the famous Nernst — and at Oxford. Not deficient in personal courage, he once demonstrated in practice his theory of rescuing planes from the "uncontrollable" spin.

He was wealthy and unscrupulous, both qualities that Winston admired. He was modest, but arrogant too, and vindictive in pursuing former opponents beyond the grave. He was antisemitic, but sheltered at his Clarendon Laboratory the many Jewish scientists who in 1933 began to trickle out of Germany. It was the Prof who gave the first shoulder-heave to the Allied atomic bomb project, and he was the first advocate of saturation bombing; but his first collaboration with Churchill had been on an article for Pall Mall magazine in April 1924 on the "future possibilities of war and how frightful it could be for the human race."

Prof and Politician clung to each other with an oft unseeing loyalty. Repeatedly Lindemann was wrong — in one famous pre-war dispute with Sir Henry Tizard's air defence committee he scoffed at the practicability of radar and suggested backing infra-red devices and "aerial mines" instead. Later he denied the German radio beam navigation, and later still he called the enemy rocket threat a "mare's nest."

But his usefulness to Churchill in his lonely campaigning outweighed all these blemishes.

* * *

Three major issues obsessed Churchill during the mid-Thirties: India, Germany and Disarmament. He boiled each issue down to personalities, and waged a ruthless personal attack on them — Sir Samuel Hoare, Secretary for India, to whom he referred in private as a "dirty dog"; Adolf Hitler, fast becoming dictator of Germany; and the prime minister Ramsay MacDonald, in whose direction he hosed a torrent of corruscating abuse that brought more enemies than friends. Many who later rose to high office under him including Cripps, Eden and Sinclair joined in the protest against Churchill in 1933, while other Members described his attacks in the House as "mean and contemptible," or as a personal vendetta by "a disappointed office-seeker."

His case on India was sound, and it had the makings of a Churchill comeback: many leading Britons, worried about Britain's future in India, looked to him to stop this surrender of Imperial authority. He had the eloquence: appealing to his fellow-Conservatives to reverse the National Government's policy, he would say on February 17, 1933, "One deep-throated growl from the National Union of Conservative Associations would be enough to stop the rot."

But as so often, he poisoned his case with personal animus. His opponents were able to portray his motives as "ill-disguised" — "rather the break-up of the National Government than the safety and welfare of India," said one.

Samuel Hoare squirmed beneath the sting of Churchill's sarcasm. His correspondence with the Viceroy of India, Viscount Willingdon, and the governors of the provinces reveals his real anxiety about Churchill's "entirely selfish and wrecking" campaign.

"Winston and his crowd," he wrote on March 17, to Willingdon, "have been very active and completely unscrupulous." Churchill was out to smash the government, he said: "He will stick at nothing to achieve his end. India gives him a good fighting ground as he can play upon the ignorance . . . of some of the most trusted members of the Conservative party."

> However effective Winston's attack may be, there is a great body of opinion in the country that will never trust him and even the extreme right of the Conservative party, whilst these will use him for their own ends, would never, I believe, take him as their leader.

The House appointed a Joint Select Committee on India. Churchill tried to oppose the move, and was ridiculed by his opponents. "I will say," mocked one Member, "that with all the experience of my right hon. Friend in manual labour, he cannot shovel enough earth over his past to obliterate it from human view."

Hoare invited him to join the committee, hoping to muzzle him. Churchill hesitated, and declined. Hoare wrote sneeringly to Willingdon that at the back of Winston's mind was the belief that Britain was "going Fascist" and that "he, or someone like him" would eventually rule India as Mussolini was governing North Africa.[3]

CHURCHILL SWITCHED HIS attack to the committee. He described the manner in which members had been picked as "a scandal".[4] Three-quarters were known supporters of the government's India policy.

Two — Hoare himself and Lord Derby, the walrus-like Tory man of influence in Lancashire — shortly adopted shabby methods to deflect evidence addressed to the committee particularly by the Manchester chamber of commerce whose cotton interests were at stake.

When Churchill learned of this from private newspaper sources a year later, in April 1934, he saw in it a means of raising a press outcry:

"What will then happen," he told his allies, meeting at the Savoy, "will be an uproar."

He called upon the Speaker to have the matter investigated by a Committee of Privileges. He was entitled, indeed obliged, to do so as a Member of the House. After all, Hoare and Derby had quite clearly tampered with witnesses before a Joint Select Committee. Whatever his entitlements and obligations, his action was of course a clear attempt at forcing Hoare's resignation, collapsing the India policy and perhaps even bringing down the National Government.

Hoare was stunned by the weight of this attack.

I had no word of warning until late on Sunday night [April 15] when Winston sent me a letter saying that he was going to raise a question of privilege on the following day in the House. . . All this was made a thousand times worse by the fact that I had sat next to Winston at luncheon with Philip Sassoon on the previous Thursday, when he had behaved as the best of old friends and colleagues. The very next night he was dining with Lloyd George and Horne for the purpose of arranging an attack. . . Can you imagine a more treacherous way of treating not only two former colleagues in various Governments, but two prominent people in his own party? I now hear that he is mobilizing a terrific case with solicitors, counsel and dozens of witnesses, and he intends to turn the whole business into something in the nature of an impeachment.[5]

Months of acrimonious investigations followed. The mood is illustrated by lines that Hoare wrote on June 1, 1934 to the acting Viceroy, Lord Derby's brother George Stanley: "I do not know which is the more offensive or more mischievous, Winston or his son [Randolph]. Rumour, however, goes that they fight like cats with each other and chiefly agree in the prodigious amount of champagne that each of them drinks each night."

On June 4, 1934 the Committee of Privileges unanimously threw out Churchill's complaint. This was most unjust. The papers of Hoare, the India Office and Lord Derby make it plain that all three had deliberately withheld from the Committee documents which established that he was right.

"I do not mind confessing to you," Churchill wrote to Cyril Asquith two months later, still smarting from the unjustified defeat, "that I sustained a very evil impression of the treatment I received and some day I hope to nail this bad behaviour up upon a board, as stoats and weasels are nailed up by gamekeepers."[6]

The raw truth was that he had fewer friends in the House than Samuel Hoare. In the resulting Debate, the House hounded him mercilessly. Winston, scoffed Leopold Amery, wished to be true at all costs to his chosen motto — *Fiat justitia ruat caelum.*

"Translate!" shouted Churchill, before he could stop himself.

Amery obliged, to hoots of unkind laughter: "If I can trip up Sam, the Government's bust."

THWARTED OVER INDIA, Churchill redoubled his attack on Hitler. Justifying his actions by the failure of the Allied powers to abide by their covenants to disarm after 1919, Hitler was rearming Germany, contrary to the dictates of Versailles. Churchill uttered the first warnings on March 23, 1933.

> When we read about Germany [he had then told the House], when we watch with surprise and distress the tumultuous insurgence of ferocity and war spirit, the pitiless ill-treatment of minorities, the denial of the normal protections of civilized society to large numbers of individuals solely on the ground of race — when we see that occurring in one of the most gifted, learned, scientific and formidable nations in the world, one cannot help feeling glad that the fierce passions that are raging in Germany have not found, as yet, any other outlet but upon Germans.

Much of this was cant. He had himself enforced Britain's ruthless measures of repression in Ireland. Nor would he express comparable concern about Britain's measures in India, where several thousand Congress supporters had been arrested with their leader Mahatma Ghandi. Nor do his other utterances of this period betray any of his later hostility to fascism. In one February 1933 speech, inspired by Mussolini's stout anti-Communism, he had called him "the Roman genius" and "the greatest lawgiver among living men."

He also spoke public words of sympathy for Japan, although her army had now invaded northern China. Britain must try to understand Japan's high sense of national honour and patriotism: "On the one side," he explained, "they see the dark menace of Soviet Russia. On the other, the chaos of China, four or five provinces of which are now being tortured under Communist rule."[7]

HIS OPPONENTS REGARDED the relentless assault on Ramsay MacDonald and his quest for disarmament as prompted by selfish political motives.[8] But it was easy to contrast MacDonald's tireless efforts with Hitler's stealthy rearmament. It made good copy. Europe, Churchill told his Theydon Bois constituents on August 12, lay under an evil and dangerous storm cloud: "Nobody can watch the events which are taking place in Germany without increasing anxiety about what their outcome will be."

Tiring of the one-sided bargaining in October Hitler pulled the plug out of Geneva. He walked Germany out of the disarmament talks and the League of Nations.

This provoked Churchill to even more garish language about Germany. "We read," he told the House on November 7, "of the military spirit which is rife throughout the country; we see that the philosophy of blood lust is being inculcated into their youth in a manner unparalleled since the days of Barbarism."

The exuberance of his own verbosity intoxicated him like little else. A week later he returned to this charge: "The Nazis inculcate a form of blood lust in their children extraordinary without parallel as an education since Barbarian and Pagan times." "It is they," he continued, without offering any source, "who have laid down the doctrine that every frontier must be made the starting point of an invasion."[9]

He also claimed that the Nazis had declared that "war is glorious." Against this might be held his endless conversation about his own glorious campaigns. (The Boer War was "the last enjoyable war," he later remarked to his private secretary.[10]

HE FELT THE lack of friends keenly. He cultivated relations with his opponents like Chamberlain — their correspondence remained on "My dear Neville" and "My dear Winston" terms throughout — and plied him and Baldwin with copies of each scintillating new Churchill volume.

Resolutely barred from office, Churchill pouted and stowed away his inner feelings for later use. He boned up on the art of human relations, patiently replenished the depleted funds of goodwill, and made contact with both newcomers and old men of faded power alike, who slouched around low tables drinking whisky in the smoking room of the House.[11] He felt at home in this familiar room with its smokefilled air, its raucous laughter and lack of decorum.

Fortified by his grasp of history, he was willing to be patient. Somebody asked him at this time why he had so few allies. He replied, "I have one you don't reckon with — events!"[12] He did not know what event he might be waiting for, but as Adolf Hitler was also wont to say — "You must grab the Goddess of Good Fortune by the hem: she passes only once!"

Early 1934 saw him at Chartwell writing up Marlborough's military campaigns. But he also wrote fifty newspaper articles that year and spoke twenty times in the House. His tone became more shrill. Britain preferred not to listen to his unsettling language. Jan Masaryk, the ebullient Czech Minister in London, suggested in one March 1934 despatch that Winston was crying wolf.

In fact it is well known that Winston is going through an alarmist phase and is for ever pointing to the imminence of war and the need for rearmament.[13]

MONEY REMAINED A problem, thanks to his own profligacy and Randolph's gambling. But Churchill was not short of benefactors. In 1931 Lord Rothermere had paid him £2,400 for a dozen *Sunday Pictorial* articles on British personalities, and the *Daily Mail* had backed him on India; but two of this great newspaperman's sons had been killed in the Great War and he was irritated by Churchill's belligerent tone towards Germany. He had begun corresponding secretly with Hilter and would do so with increasing warmth until the outbreak of war.[14]

Churchill evidently sensed this irritation. In August 1934 he wrote to Clementine that he was disgusted at the *Mail*'s "boosting of Hitler," but accepted that Rothermere was sincerely pacifist: "He wants us to be very strongly armed & frightfully obsequious at the same time." The Socialists, he added, wanted Britain to remain "disarmed & exceedingly abusive."[15]

While Hitler became absolute dictator upon President Hindenburg's death, consolidated his power base and eliminated opponents throughout that summer, Churchill submerged himself in his manuscripts and the pleasures of the Mediterranean. Twice that summer he went down there — living in borrowed Riviera villas and sponging off willing friends.

In the second half of August he took the Prof and Randolph down to Golfe-Juan to work on *Marlborough* at the villa of an American actress. Rothermere, it seems, declined to bail him out after heavy losses on the tables at Monte Carlo. Fortunately a Hungarian film producer rescued him. A cigar smoking millionaire with a Homburg hat and an inch-thick accent, Alexander Korda had just produced the first important British "talkie," "The Private Lives of Henry VIII." Churchill told him that the Silver Jubilee of George V was imminent. "London Films," Korda replied in effect, "will commission you to write a film treatment called 'Jubilee,' the History of the House of Windsor." The £10,000 Korda contract reached Chartwell a few weeks later, the beginning of a mutually rewarding friendship. (In 1936 a bemused Tibor Korda who ran the *News Review* was telephoned by a temporarily confused Churchill asking for more.)[16]

Winston put all other work aside, and returned the next day to the Mediterranean, to the yacht of his old brewer friend Walter Guinness, now Lord Moyne. Behind him he left a burgeoning staff of writers and researchers preparing chapters for both *Marlborough* and a new history of the English-speaking peoples.

Quaffing champagne and venerable Napoleon brandy, Churchill cruised the Holy Land and Middle East, worked on the film script, and lectured Korda by letter on how to make movies. He suggested that they might introduce animated historical photographs, and declared himself willing to intone the commentary.

Korda probably needed no lessons. He had arrived in England from Hollywood in 1930 and established London Films two years later. The Prudential were backing him, but would lose every penny. 'Jubilee' was never filmed. Churchill was paid £4,000 nonetheless, and sold off what he could salvage to the *Daily Mail* for £2,500.

Imprudently dispensing Prudential largesse, Korda hired his new friend at £2,000 per annum "to write such scripts as might be needed" although he had little intention of filming them; he put Churchill's daughter on the payroll too.

The film magnate shifted into Winston's social circle. The young Brendan Bracken later introduced him to financier Bernard Baruch as "one of Winston's great supporters in the days when he was running his lonely battle to get Britain re-armed."[17] When war broke out Korda, who had become a British citizen, would move on to Hollywood and produce films flattering Britain's cause. At Churchill's suggestion he filmed "Lady Hamilton" with Laurence Olivier and Vivien Leigh in the title role; Winston would see this film scores of times — just as in Berlin Hitler became hypnotized by the American acress Jeanette Macdonald and the theme music of "Donkey Serenade". There is a suggestion that Korda's offices provided cover for Intelligence activities; others in the film industry including Noel Coward and the urbane Leslie Howard, alias von Ardenne, certainly had minor starring roles in the S.I.S.

In 1942 Churchill allowed Korda the first knighthood in the film industry. Whether his gratitude was for blessings received, or for "Lady Hamilton," or for his toils for the S.I.S. the records do not tell.

* * *

As 1934 progressed, Churchill developed an important subsidiary theme to Disarmament: the growth of German air power. In March the Government had announced a small but timely expansion of Britain's airforce. Labour criticised even that — "The Government," charged Cripps, "has had its hands forced by the wild men like Mr Churchill." Sinclair too derided this foolish and wasteful accumulation of armaments.

Churchill rightly saw through Hitler's various subterfuges like "Air Sport", detecting in them ruses to provide an airforce denied to Germany under the terms of the Versailles Treaty. "I dread the day," he told the House on March 8, "when the means of threatening the heart of the British Empire should pass into the hands of the present rulers of Germany."

Such melodramatic statements were typical of the debating stance that Churchill would adopt over the next five years. Sir John Simon predicted in Cabinet on March 19 that Hitler would move east or into territories of German affinity like Austria, Danzig and Memel. His colleagues were unconvinced that Hitler harbored evil designs on the Empire, and rightly so. We now know from the German archives that even his most secret plans were laid solely against the East; in August 1936 he would formulate his Four Year Plan to gird Germany for war against Bolshevist Russia; and not until early 1938 did he order that Germany must consider after all the contingency of war with Britain — a contingency which, it must be said, Mr Churchill had himself largely created by his speeches.[18]

To many he was a public nuisance. But in a sense he had become a one man Opposition now that Britain was governed by a National Government. That summer of 1934 he found that Britain's weakness in the air was a popular theme, particularly among leading London businessmen. Their doyen Sir Stanley Machin invited him to address the City Carlton Club on it. He developed his campaign on the floor of the House, in newspaper and magazine articles, and in BBC broadcasts too.

What made his campaign difficult to ignore was that by mid 1934 his old friend Desmond Morton was feeding him with data, allegedly from British Intelligence sources on Hitler's rearmament. Morton, a bluff, pink-gin swilling former army major, was repaying a kindness: it was Churchill, while Secretary for War in 1919, who had appointed him to the Intelligence service. Since then Morton had set up the Industrial Intelligence Centre. He lived near Chartwell and now became a regular visitor there, ostensibly as one of Winston's literary researchers. In reality he brought with him secret files which the Prof illicitly photocopied for Churchill — there is no evidence to support the latter's postwar claim that Morton did so with prime ministerial approval; other papers were just filched by Morton and never returned.

Morton's figures reflected the general confusion of Intelligence information at that time. He calculated that Germany would have five thousand planes by the end of 1935, and suggested by comparison that Britain now had nine hundred, France 1,650, Russia 1,500 and Italy a thousand. His figures omitted any consideration of quality or range, but Churchill relied upon them in an effective speech on July 30 alerting Members to the danger of Nazi air raids.

> With our great metropolis here, the greatest target in the world, a kind of tremendous, fat, valuable cow tied up to attract the beast of prey, we are in a position in which we have never been before, and in which no other country is at the present time.

Churchill followed with this announcement: "I first assert that Germany has already, in violation of the Treaty, created a military airforce which is now nearly two-thirds as strong as our present home defence airforce."

By the end of 1935, he warned, Hitler would match Britain's airforce; by 1936 he would overtake it — such was Churchill's claim.

These prophecies of doom met with more scorn than alarm, best summarized in the words of the Independent Labour Party MP, Jimmy Maxton. He suggested that Mr Churchill remember — "from his position of relative irresponsibility below the Gangway" — that his name still counted heavily abroad. "His cynical, sarcastic words in this House," said Maxton, "are taken much more seriously abroad than he takes them himself."

Churchill now had the bit between his teeth, however. He initiated a major Debate on air defense that November. Again Morton supplied the ammunition. Germany might have, he now claimed, three thousand pilots and a thousand war planes by January 1935 — a substantial increase in his earlier estimate. These would include bombers with a five hundred mile radius.

It is plain from the record of November 25 that the Cabinet was concerned about the effect of Mr Churchill's brash campaign on their delicate relations with Germany. Hoare felt they must make clear to the world that his "charges were exaggerated." Chamberlain expressed puzzlement that they themselves had no information backing Churchill's claims — which makes it unlikely that Morton's access to government Intelligence was as close as he implied — and certainly nothing to justify enlarging Britain's airforce in her present economic situation.

Churchill delivered his new attack three days later. His speech was an unabashed attempt at polarizing the House and winning over the more dissatisfied and querulous Members. Resorting to his most alarmist language yet, he now prophesied that in one seven day Nazi air attack on London over 30,000 people "would be killed or maimed." Warming to his theme, he prophesied "a dreadful act of power and terror" in which even incendiary bombs might be used; and he reminded Birmingham, Sheffield and all other major manufacturing centres that they were all at risk.

"We cannot move London," he pointed out. "We cannot move the vast population which is dependent on the estuary of the Thames."

The only direct defence would be the deterrent — the power to retaliate simultaneously: that was why he insisted that Britain double, perhaps even treble, her expenditure on her airforce. Because if both countries continued to rearm at their present rate, in 1937 Germany would have twice the airforce Britain had.

Stanley Baldwin roundly rejected these estimates (and rightly so, as his figures would, years later, prove more accurate than Churchill's). It was left to former prime minister David Lloyd George to urge that Britain stop treating Germany like a pariah — they might later be glad to rely on her as a bulwark against Communism. "If Germany broke down," he said, "and was seized by the Communists, Europe would follow."

WINSTON CHURCHILL WAS two days short of sixty. Perhaps it was the realisation of his own mortality that spurred him to this wild fling in the House. It was unfortunate that his opponents lacked the eloquence and expert knowledge to counter him. They could have pointed out that the German planes then under construction were incapable of carrying a serious weight of bombs as far as London, whether or not they overflew the neutral Low Countries: they could carry the fuel, or the bombs, but not both.

Churchill was right to call attention to the probability that German civil aviation could be converted to military use. But the captured files of the German air ministry reveal both his statistics and his strategic predictions to have been wild, irresponsible, exaggerated scaremongering, delivered without regard for the possible consequences on international relations.

Six years later, in the late summer of 1940, he would find himself hostage to his own predictions. By then the war had raged for a whole year and London, "heart of the British Empire," had still not been touched. It was not until Adolf Hitler was deliberately provoked — as we shall see — in late August of that year that he allowed his airforce to attack the British capital, and part of Mr Churchill's predictions came true.

CHAPTER 5

Sixty

SIXTY YEARS!" BEGAN Churchill, plucking the cigar from his mouth and pausing in his stride. It was November 1934, and he was dictating the manuscript of his life.

"Not so very long ago I thought this a very advanced age. When I was a child I was told that Methusalah [*sic*] and others lived even longer, but I never imagined for a moment that I should compete in such a class."

He paused to let his secretary catch up.

Death was getting busy among his friends. In June his cousin Sunny, Duke of Marlborough, had died, widening the wound left in Winston by the death of Lord Birkenhead. Was he already an old man, a failure? Friends like Lady Lambton pleaded with him not to think like that — "To me," she wrote, "you are still a promising lad."

"Lately," he continued, brightening, "I have not felt the same impression. Sixty now seems to me to be a very reasonable age, when a man may still have vigour of mind and body with knowledge and experience besides."[1] A few hours later the manuscript was finished. He posted it to literary agent Curtis Brown on the thirtieth, his sixtieth birthday.

Age was crowding in on him — absentmindedness, obsessiveness, a one-track mind. Sometimes the often charming, witty and courteous man would huddle in a chair, boorish and indifferent to visitors.

Said Aircraftman T.E. Shaw (Lawrence of Arabia), now a regular visitor at Chartwell: "If Winston was not concerned in a question he would not be interested."[2]

American magazine executive Daniel Longwell found the same, visiting Chartwell. "If his mind is on other things," he reminisced years later, "you are somehow just not 'there' when you're with him. I wasn't 'there' that night at all during dinner." Churchill, still labouring on Marlborough, left them to work on his book.[3]

Not that a Chartwell weekend was unenjoyable.

Churchill had built a round pool into a slope, and with the Prof's hydraulic expertise had directed the water from a spring — the "well" in the house's name — over a series of cascades into it, and rigged up a furnace to heat the water. At eleven the next morning Longwell located Winston and Randolph cavorting in this pool, quoting Ogden Nash poems to each other. He only had to mention that he had worked with Nash at Doubleday to find that he was suddenly 'there' for Winston after all.

He made up a tennis foursome with Clementine, Randolph and a sister while Winston did some bricklaying. Driving him back to London, Randolph explained why he had been invited. "You've seen my father now," he said. "Why don't you tell the editors of *Time* that he is not 'roly-poly!"

Time humoured the request and Longwell was 'there' for ever after that.

THE RELATIONSHIP BETWEEN father and son was singularly uneasy. Randolph was tall and burly, his eyes were very blue, his complexion the pink and ginger-blond of all the Blenheim tribe. He was a heavy drinker and uncontrollably ill-tempered, but possessed of a residual charm. He would mortally offend, then mollify. "Really," he would say penitently, "I ought not to be allowed out in private."[4]

In 1933 Winston had to pay £1,600 of his profligate son's debts. It was a testing time for him, and he found Randolph's jibes impossible to swallow. Conflagrations ensued which even laboured written apologies could not extinguish. "If, infected by the violence of your own language," Randolph would write after one blazing row, "and in the heat of an argument I used words unbecoming for a Son, I should have thought you might have excused such conduct, particularly when assured that it was accidental."

In January 1935 Randolph was just twenty-three when, abetted by his sisters Sarah and Diana, he stood at the Wavertree by-election, adopting his father's line on India. But there was already an official Conservative candidate: Churchill was mortified, and his critics gleeful. Samuel Hoare expressed to one correspondent the hope that Randolph would fare "really badly." Randolph attracted enough votes, even though defeated, to feel encouraged to field a candidate, again against the official Conservative candidate Mr Duncan Sandys, at a London by-election in February.

It provoked another blazing row. His father refused to speak to him for weeks afterwards.

"He has acted entirely against my wishes," he grumbled in a letter to Clementine, "and left my table three days ago in violent anger."

"Randolph seems," he added in a later letter, "to have got a considerable fund through Lady Houston. . . His programme seems to be to put Socialists in everywhere he can, in order to smash up MacDonald and Baldwin." Randolph's candidate came last; Winston was hard put to disguise his relief.

Momentarily thwarted in his ambitions, his son grew a beard and proclaimed he looked like Christ. To Winston he looked uncannily like Lord Randolph, his own father, in the final phase of his fatal disease.[5] Being father to a Churchill was no easier than being ones son.

HE ABANDONED THE fight on India in July that year. He mended his fences, wrote letters of conciliation to the most rancorous of his adversaries, and generally kept his remaining powder dry.

He also sought new allies.

He invited Lord Londonderry, Secretary for Air, to Chartwell.

He put out feelers to Sir Robert Vansittart, the opinionated and embattled Permanent Under-Secretary at the Foreign Office — first telephoning him, then striding into his Park-street house, and finally turning up at his room at the F.O., bringing their connivance into public view to "Van's" dismay.

On the first day of September he set off again to the Riviera. Here he heard from the editor of the *Observer*, J.L. Garvin. On India, the editor commiserated, Churchill could never have won more than one quarter of his party. "On Defence," he wrote however, "you can have three-quarters of it at least with you, for good. . . Your greatest hour is yours now for the taking."

* * *

Churchill was still an outsider, obliged to rely on illicit Intelligence.

He cultivated disgruntled civil servants seeking an outlet for their own opinions. They would come over to Chartwell, float lazily in the pool and whisper secrets to him. Since they were violating Civil Service ethics, Churchill kept it secret when writing his memoirs ten years later. But he may also have been loath to reveal how tenuous were the grounds upon which he built his dramatic attack on the Government's level of defence spending from 1935 onwards.

Primary among his sources was Desmond Morton. He trusted the major implicitly: "We four," he said emotionally one day, waving his hand around a cluster of these friends, "must never part till death mows us down with his impartial hand." The words were from Queen Anne, the emotion from his heart. Morton, it must be said, took a more detached view of Winston. He would write to a friend a quarter century later, "I do not care if I never see him again and certainly would not wish to attend his funeral."[6]

Morton's figures on Hitler's rearmament were, it is now plain, wild and wilful exaggerations. Churchill's biographers have made no attempt to compare them with the *German* files; the latter are difficult of access, couched in an unfamiliar language and follow different criteria. They have also ignored the shortcomings of German plane types. And they have totally disregarded what is surely the most fundamental issue: whether Hitler ever really threatened Britain and her Empire.

Churchill may have suspected the weakness of his case. Outwardly brash and sure of himself, in private he floundered in fathom-deep uncertainty.

Quite properly invited by the secretary to the Committee of Imperial Defence in January 1936 to reveal in confidence any special sources of Intelligence he might have, Churchill decided on balance to rest on his record and not to claim any "daemonic powers." He drafted a reply at some length, but replaced it by terse and unhelpful obfuscation: "I cannot claim any 'special sources of Intelligence' for the figures," he replied, "They are simply my personal estimate."[7] To have revealed that his sole source was a retired army major on the outer fringe of the Intelligence agencies would surely have exposed him to ridicule.

His retrospective search for cast-iron evidence in support of his pre-war claims about the German airforce strength would continue for ten more years.[8] "There must be Germans," he pointed out to the Prof in 1947, "who know what the G.A.F. strength was in 1935."[9] He wrote to American airforce commander General Carl F. Spaatz, but even Spaatz could only supply figures for 1938-39.[10]

The Air Ministry were quietly confident of their (far lower) figures. As they explained to the Cabinet in November they made assumptions "which may not find ready acceptance by those to whom the mass of Intelligence data is not accessible." By September 1935 the breaking of lowgrade German airforce codes had enabled them to identify firmly from call-sign evidence that the Germans had 578 individual aircraft operational.[11]

Hitler was bluffing throughout the mid-Thirties. His airforce was under par, and he pulled the wool over the eyes of his neighbours. When he re-militarized the Rhineland in 1936, he flew the only available fighter squadron from airfield to airfield, repainting its insignia each time. As late as August 1938, when the French airforce commander General Vuillemin visited Germany, every available fighter plane was shoe-horned onto one airfield in southern Germany at which the Frenchman's plane would make a casual stop.[12]

Thus Hitler and Churchill played into each other's hands. Each had reason to talk loudly of Germany's air strength. Mr Churchill had also spoken of thirty to forty thousand dead in the first days of an air attack, and lurid figures like these were easy to remember. In fact even in 1938 Hitler would have only two bomber types capable of reaching London — the Dornier 17F (range 997 miles, speed only 220mph); and the even slower Heinkel 111E (745 miles, 200mph.) Neither could reach Britain without violating the neutral Low Countries, and even then no escort fighter could accompany them to Britain from German airfields.

Despite this Churchill now claimed in the debate on defence spending on March 19, 1935: "Practically the whole of the German bombing air force can reach London with an effective load," and pointed out that few if any British bombers could reach Berlin.

A Labour Member called this speech "scaremongering" and an attempt "to make our flesh creep." But six days later Hitler mischievously claimed to the visiting foreign secretary Sir John Simon that his airforce had already reached parity with Britain. It was a bulwark against Russia, he added, and it is worth noting that his top airforce general Erhard Milch, after meeting him in February to discuss the forthcoming naval talks with Britain, jotted in his pocket diary: "We're banking on Britain. Against Russia."[13]

Hitler's claim put the fat in the fire. In Churchill's words it was a political sensation. "This," he exulted in a letter to his wife on April 5, "completely stultifies everything that Baldwin has said and incidentally vindicates all the assertions that I made."

Fresh informants flocked to his cause. Two days later an impressionable young aide of Vansittart, Ralph Wigram, visited him and began furnishing secret F.O. files including sets of the British ambassador's despatches from Berlin, reporting among other things Germany's growing militancy and Hitler's complaints about Mr Churchill. It was a fruitful association, and when Wigram committed suicide a year later, aged only forty-six, Churchill would attend his funeral as a mark of gratitude.[14]

Others begged him to abandon his irresponsible campaign. On April 13 Lord Londonderry, uneasy at this mounting clamour, telephoned. "I told him that no confidence could deter me from my public duty," Churchill wrote to Clementine. "Ha ha!" "On the whole," he chortled, "since you have been away the only great thing that has happened has been that Germany is now the greatest armed power in Europe."

The flippant tone contrasted with the voice of sincerity that he reserved for the House. Here, on May 2, he now claimed that Hitler's airforce would be "between three and four times" the size of Britain's.

His critics were cowed to silence. Those who did speak did not rise above personal rebuke. "Although one hates to criticise anyone in the evening of his days," sneered one fellow-Conservative, "nothing can excuse the Right Hon. Member for Epping [Mr Churchill] for having permeated his entire speech with the atmosphere that Germany is arming for war."

Hitler was, of course, arming for war but not, as Churchill kept claiming, war against Britain. Behind closed doors alarm was voiced about the dangerous policies toward which Churchill was steering public opinion. The Chief of Imperial General Staff (C.I.G.S.) Sir Archibald Montgomery Massingbird suggested that by aiming at parity "we were issuing a new challenge to Germany in a form of warfare in which we were most vulnerable." Germany had conscription, was larger and geographically better placed, and her industry was infinitely better prepared. Britain, moreover, had important world-wide commitments.

But Hitler's boast had brought to Mr Churchill powerful newspaper allies. Lord Beaverbrook's *Daily Express* apologized for having failed to heed him. When Churchill wrote to Lord Camrose, the tall, distinguished proprietor of the *Daily Telegraph* expressing anxiety at the way in which the Germans had "turned the tables upon us in the air," Camrose replied: "You can rely on us to do all we can."

Only Lord Rothermere still had doubts. Like Londonderry, he began telephoning Winston, who had now leased a two-floor appartment at No.11 Morpeth Mansions not far from Westminster.

"His anxiety is pitiful," wrote Churchill scornfully to his wife. "He thinks the Germans are all powerful and that the French are corrupt and useless, and the English hopeless and doomed. He proposes to meet this situation by grovelling to Germany. 'Dear Germany, do destroy us last!' I endeavour to inculcate a more robust attitude."[15]

Rothermere resisted Churchill's endeavours. On April 29 he wrote flatteringly to Hitler ("My dear Führer") as "one who may occupy the first place in all European history." He was not, he said, taking to heart the current disruption in Anglo-German relations. "The sentiments and views of Parliamentary demagogues," he assured Hitler, making an obvious reference to Churchill, "are capable of quick and unexpected changes." The people's friendship toward the Germans was steadily growing, he added: seven out of ten people writing to his *Daily Mail* were in favour of Germany's claims being entirely acceded to.

Hitler urged Rothermere in his reply not to heed the "Parliamentary demagogues." Nine-tenths of the blood that had flowed in the last three centuries had flowed in vain, Hitler wrote, at least for the interests of the peoples involved. Britain had been shrewd enough to keep out, and her mighty empire was the reward.

Lord Rothermere [appealed Hitler] if today I urge an Anglo-German entente then this is not just something new since yesterday or the day-before-yesterday; in the last sixteen years I have spoken to four or five thousand audiences in Germany, small, large and immense; but in not one speech or line that I have written have I ever uttered the slightest sentiment against an Anglo-German entente.

Then he reverted to his old dream: "An Anglo-German entente," he reasoned, "would form in Europe and thus in the world a force for peace and reason of 120 million of the most superior people. Britain's sea power and unique colonial talent would be united with one of the world's first soldier-races. Were this entente extended to embrace the American nation, then it would, indeed, be hard to see who in the world could disturb the peace without wilfully and consciously neglecting the interests of the White race. . . The Gods love and favour those who seem to demand the impossible!"[16]

The press lord sent a copy of this eight-page confidential letter to Churchill. But Winston had committed himself too stridently against Hitler to change now.

"If his proposal," he rebuked Rothermere in his reply, "means that we should come to an understanding with Germany to dominate Europe, I think this would be contrary to the whole of our history." He reminded Rothermere of the fable of the jackal who went hunting with the tiger — "and what happened after the hunt was over."

FOR A WHILE he tried to form the kind of backbench Conservative pressure group that he had created to defend India, this time "to arouse the country to the peril in which we stand." But it aroused little enthusiasm, and when Lord Londonderry's successor invited him in July to join the Air Defence Research sub-committee of the Committee of Imperial Defence, he agreed. It was an important confidence: it gave him a renewed toehold in the innermost councils, and legal access to important reports on defence affairs. He immediately circulated a memorandum on the "ugly possibility" that Hitler might be able to force a nation to its knees within weeks "by violent aerial mass attack," and he suggested that Hitler was spending £1,000m on military preparations that year alone.*

Whatever the merits of his case, with the co-opting of this fertile brain a sense of urgency and a wealth of administrative experience were

---

*Here he was closer to the mark. German defence estimates fluctuated constantly, but figures entered in Milch's pocket diary on January 12-15, 1935 show that including the *SA* (Brownshirts) the 1935 estimate was 9,600m Reichsmarks (approximately £800m) of which the army claimed 4,000m, the navy 760m, and the airforce 3,300m.[17]

brought to the Committee. He urged clandestine preparations for an emergency expansion of aircraft production, immediate airfield construction, broader pilot training schemes, and the exploitation of Imperial Airways (the forerunner of B.O.A.C. and British Airways) for aircrew training just like Germany's Lufthansa. He put forward other novel ideas too, like infiltrating fast planes to shadow raiding bomber formations; but at the Committee's first meeting on July 25 he learned that work had started on a new radiolocation device, later known as Radar, instead.

* * *

Escaping to the Riviera villa of rich socialite Maxine Elliot in September 1935, he painted, he bored her house guests with diatribes — according to American air attaché Martin Scanlon, one guest who kept a diary — he basked in the sunshine and enjoyed what he called in a letter to Clementine the "contentment engendered by old brandy after luncheon here alone with Maxine."

Back in London he again spoke to the City Carlton Club about German rearmament, wooing wealthy City backers. Instinctively he also began canvassing influential Americans. Late September found at Chartwell the Boston financier Joseph P. Kennedy and his family. Rose Kennedy would afterwards reflect that Winston, "with his puckish face," looked more like a country squire; he had "talked expansively, narrating [and] explaining," urging an imaginative plan for the two English-speaking countries to construct a common navy to police the world and counter the Nazi foe. But, Winston had said with a sigh, there were too many isolationists in America — "too many Irish haters of England," perhaps a tactless remark in view of the Kennedy origins.[18]

His name was becoming a household word in Germany. The Nazi newspapers crudely suggested that his twenty-year friendship with American financier Bernard Baruch was his real motive for dissipating his remaining strength in attacking Hitler. The London correspondent of the Nazi *Völkischer Beobachter* reported that whenever Churchill opened his mouth it was a safe bet that an attack on Germany would emerge.

Every major speech bore this out. "We cannot afford," he thundered in the House on October 24, "to see Nazidom in its present phase of cruelty and intolerance, with all its hatreds and all its gleaming weapons, paramount in Europe."

The November issue of *Strand* magazine published a sulphurous attack on Hitler's record. In this he claimed to have learned from his reading of Hitler's *Mein Kampf* — which can at best have been cursory — that "the French are not the only foreign nation against whom the anger of rearmed Germany may be turned."

He also described how Hitler had exploited antisemitism:

> The Jews, supposed to have contributed by a disloyal and pacifist influence to the collapse of Germany at the end of the Great War, were also deemed to be the main prop of communism and the authors of defeatist doctrines in every form.
>
> Therefore the Jews of Germany . . . were to be stripped of all power, driven from every position in public and social life, expelled from the professions, silenced in the press and declared a foul and odious race.

Churchill had certainly turned a wide circle since publishing his astonishing newspaper attack on the Jews fifteen years before, in which he had called them "the principle inspiration and driving power" behind Bolshevism and underlined that "the prominent, if not indeed the principle, part in the system of terrorism applied by the Extraordinary Commissions* for Combating Counter-Revolution has been taken by Jews, and in some notable cases by Jewesses."

He would have been ill-advised to repeat these obsessive claims in 1935, and it was little wonder that he now adopted the opposite line. Inspired by his robust line against Hitler, the wealthy and influential flocked to become his friends. The South African gold mining industrialist Sir Henry Strakosch started furnishing to him his own data on German raw material imports; Strakosch estimated that Hitler had spent £1,600m on armaments since July 1933.

Authorities like these were hardly reliable or unbiased, but Churchill's was the voice heard on the hustings. When the Air Staff issued a secret memorandum on November 5, 1935 — based, we now know, on its authentic code-breaking sources — stating firmly that the German front line consisted of only 594 planes Churchill sent an exasperated letter to the Committee of Imperial Defence: "It is to be hoped," he wrote, "that this figure will not be made public, as it would certainly give rise to misunderstanding and challenge."

A GENERAL ELECTION was due in mid November. He hankered after his old office as First Lord of the Admiralty but Stanley Baldwin, who had succeeded MacDonald as prime minister in June, had no time for Winston or his warlike election posture. In his own speeches Baldwin

---

*The notorious *Che-Ka*'s. In his 1920 article Churchill had written of the "evil prominence" obtained by Jews in Bela Kun's recent brief "rule of terror" in Hungary and he disarmed one obvious argument by pointing out, "Although in all these countries there are many non-Jews every whit as bad as the worst of the Jewish revolutionaries, the part played by the latter in proportion to their numbers in the population is astonishing."[19]

denied Labour's claims that the Conservatives would "endanger world peace by a vast and expensive rearmament programme."

The Conservatives swept back to power on November 14. It was a landslide. At a party at his London mansion that evening Lord Beaverbrook said over-candidly to Winston, "Your're finished now. Baldwin can do without you."

This proved to be true. Churchill's telephone did not ring.

Disappointed, he left Westminster in December to winter in the Mediterranean. He was glad to be out of London, because passing through Paris on the tenth, he heard the first details of the malodorous Hoare-Laval pact: It would have appeased Mussolini by obliging Abyssinia to surrender twenty percent of her territory to Italy. Under public protest Baldwin dropped the plan, and Hoare resigned.

He was succeeded at the Foreign Office by Anthony Eden. Following these events from afar, Winston dismissed this young politician as a "light-weight" — "The greatness of his office will find him out," he predicted to Clementine.

Seeking the certainty of sun, he travelled first to Barcelona, and then to Marrakesh. He painted from his hotel balcony, played bezique, dictated newspaper articles to his secretary Violet Pearman, sharpened his claws, and drafted manuscript. Something that Marlborough had written in 1708 attracted him: "As I think most things are settled by destiny," the Duke had reflected, "when one has done ones best the only thing is to await the result with patience."

Occasionally he bumped into acquaintances along these shores. Rothermere mockingly wagered Winston £2,000 that he could not foreswear alcohol in 1936. It was a tempting prospect. He would save £500 on liquor, and pick up £2,000 tax free. But he gallantly fought off mammon's temptation.

Before joining Winston here, on December 6 Rothermere had written a further clandestine letter to Hitler, on *Daily Mail* notepaper, volunteering "to stress again the cause of Germany," and asking certain questions. On December 19 the House would reassemble, he said; he asked Hitler to reply the day before: "As you know, I am an ardent partisan of the cause of Anglo-German friendship." One question was whether oil sanctions would end the Italian-Abyssinian war.

"Believe me, dear Lord Rothermere," Hitler replied, "The problem is not whether this or that sanction will to-day bring Italy to her knees, the real problem is whether one is in a position to remove the causes underlying the tensions from which the world suffers at present."

For a hundred million years this earth has moved around the sun. During that long time it has always been filled with the struggle of human beings for nourishment, and later for dwellings and clothing et cetera. . . Countless influences have wrought constant changes in the distribution of property. . . And now, in a certain year [he continued, sardonically] after millions of years in which the earth has moved around the sun, an American professor proclaims the formation of a League of partly heterogeneous nations with completely opposite interests, with a view to banishing future change from this world.

Rothermere had asked whether Germany ought not now to state her colonial claims, but Hitler frowned on this. "I do not want to give the slightest impression that I want to avail myself of your government's present predicament or that of the British Empire."[20]

Rothermere sent copies of Hitler's reply to the prime minister and King George V. A month later the King was dead, and Churchill hurried back to England. He would have preferred to stay abroad longer, to keep at a finite distance from both Baldwin's difficulties and Randolph's latest venture.

Randolph had accepted an invitation to stand yet again against a Government candidate, this time at a Scottish by-election to split the vote and thwart the return of Malcolm MacDonald to Cabinet office. Winston angrily suggested that he had been invited on his "reputation as a specialist in wrecking." It certainly blighted his own chances of being invited back into the Cabinet.

For a time in February he had hoped that a minister of defence might be appointed and that, since his difference with Baldwin over India was now behind him, he would be the first incumbent. This hope dashed, he reverted to the attack on Hitler. The peripatetic American diplomat William C. Bullitt, visiting London at this time, was baffled at the mounting hysteria he found: the German "menace," he reported to Washington, was being played for all it was worth. At dinner tables he heard people say that unless Britain did not make war on Germany soon, Hitler would have his way in Central Europe and then attack Russia. "Strangely enough," wrote Bullitt to President Franklin D. Roosevelt, "all the old anti-Bolshevik fanatics like Winston Churchill are trumpeting this Bolshevik thesis and are advocating an entente with the Soviet Union!"[21]

Churchill shortly put out quiet feelers to the Soviet embassy. He would meet Ivan Maisky, the Soviet ambassador, early in April 1936 and again during May. Maisky assured him that Russia wanted to play her part in keeping the peace in Europe, and Churchill believed him.

ON MARCH 7, 1936 HITLER'S troops had re-entered the Rhineland from which the Versailles Treaty had banned them. His calculated risk came off. Britain and France were obliged by treaty to pitch his troops out, but did not. Neither's public was ready for war. It looked like the end of the League. Eden and Ralph Wigram hurried to Paris to discuss convening a League meeting (Wigram reported to Churchill on his return on the eleventh), and on the twelfth, the French foreign minister Pierre Flandin also came to Morpeth Mansions.*

Addressing the House's Foreign Affairs Committee that evening, Churchill urged collective military action to fulfil Britain's obligations. He contemplated all Germany's endangered neighbours rallying to this cause, but according to the minutes he said nothing about their military preparedness. Hoare sobered the committee down.

Thwarted in Whitehall, Churchill rampaged across the front pages of the press. Remarkably, it was Lord Beaverbrook's *Evening Standard* that began publishing his fortnightly articles on March 13. Through Curtis Brown Ltd these articles — with titles like "How Germany is Arming," "Our Navy Must be Stronger," and "Organise our Supplies" — were also syndicated around the world. Churchill's slogan now was the resuscitation of collective security and the League of Nations.

To Lord Beaverbrook, this was flogging a dead horse. He had once denounced the League as "a greater danger to peace than the armament makers." When the pro-League *News Chronicle* attacked him in 1931, Beaverbrook replied that such treaty obligations compelled Britain to take sides in any quarrel between France and Germany, no matter how remote its cause. "A single shot fired on the borders of [Poland]," he argued, "may send our young men again to the slaughter, and expose our civilian population to terrors of which the last war was but the faintest shadow." He never wavered from this belief. "The British Empire minding its own business is safe," he apostrophized in July 1934 in his own *Sunday Express*. "The British Empire meddling in the concerns of the Balkans and Central Europe is sure to be embroiled in war, pestilence and famine."

The only upshot of the crisis was the appointment of a Minister for Co-ordination of Defence. Again Churchill was by-passed. Baldwin appointed a colourless lawyer, Sir Thomas Inskip, who would excite no enthusiasm as Chamberlain remarked in his diary on the eleventh but would also "involve us in no fresh perplexities."

Shortly, Churchill began canvassing just such a perplexing involvement — to send part of the Fleet to a Russian port to dominate the German fleet in the Baltic. It overlooked a number of impressive snags. "In view of the danger from Germany," Sir Maurice Hankey

---

*Churchill had occasionally written to Flandin asking for French estimates of German air power, always being careful to prompt Flandin with his own estimates first.[22]

wrote to Inskip on April 19, referring to Churchill, "he has buried his violent anti-Russian complex of former days and is apparently a bosom friend of Maisky." He dismissed the Baltic plan as "fantastic".

Worried about the accelerating slide towards war, a leading Tory wrote to Beaverbrook: "The government seems to have committed themselves more than ever to the cause of collective lunacy, and Winston is all out to endorse it, fearing that otherwise there really might be a war somewhere and we not in it. Worst of all, all this folly is calculated to shake the Empire to pieces."[23]

It was not difficult to guess Hitler's next victims: probably Austria, perhaps Czechoslovakia after that. Churchill was haunted by visions of what he called "the great wheels revolving and the great hammers descending day and night in Germany." To flesh out his figures on German rearmament he introduced the financial element, claiming that Hitler had spent £1,000m on *arms* between March 1933 and June 1935 (figures which even Morton deprecated as exaggerated.) In a quaint reference which suggested that his thinking had advanced little since the Great War, he referred to Germany's autobahns as "great military roads where four columns of troops may march abreast."

Winston's influential friends followed his "obsession" with Germany with alarm. Hitler had now talked to Lord Londonderry for two hours, but only about the Communist menace. On May 4 the former air minister reproached Churchill: "Your success was due to your being able to frighten the people of this country by giving them wholly exaggerated figures." He suggested that Churchill visit Germany himself to see things at first hand: but Churchill's reputation was built upon the alarming quagmire that he had himself created, and he did not want it drained just yet.

Nettled by Londonderry's phrase about his "obsession," he sent back a cool reply. "If I read the future aright," he said, "Hitler's Government will confront Europe with a series of outrageous events and ever-growing military might."[24]

There is no doubt that he believed his own figures, in all sincerity. But in April the Air Ministry had checked his estimates and concluded that he was exaggerating: they wrote to him pointing out that he had included in his German first line of 1,210 planes 360 which were in fact second-line. The Air Ministry now put the German first line at 850, while the British was 785.

Churchill preferred his own figures. On May 12, 1936, Ralph Wigram sent him an extract from *Mein Kampf*, pointing out sentences omitted from the authorized English translation. "If one tells Big Lies," Hitler had written, "people will always believe a part."

CHAPTER 6

The Hired Help

SOON AFTER THE NAZIS seized power shadowy groups had evolved in Britain and America, united by the aim of restoring the status quo in Germany. These now jointly and severally approached Mr Churchill.

Their intervention came not a moment too soon for him. By the end of 1935 he had intimidating debts. No amount of writing dismantled his overdraft. It gnawed at his mind, it distracted him from his work. He needed all the financial aid he could get.

The president of the Anglo-Jewish Association, Leonard Montefiore, had begun sending him literature on the plight of the German Jews. But it was the Anti-Nazi Council, later known as The Focus, that would ensure Churchill's political and financial survival.

He wrily recognized who was behind this body. "The basis of the Anti-Nazi League," he would write later in 1936 to Randolph, misquoting its proper title, "is of course Jewish resentment."[1]

The secret of The Focus was kept almost until his death. The codeword Focus glistens like an unrefined gold nugget in the dull and fusty papers of his followers like General Spears and Captain B.H. Liddell Hart. But it remained a mystery. When one of its lesser financiers — a refugee who had left Germany in 1922 — drafted a manuscript about The Focus, Churchill pleaded with him not to publish it during his lifetime.*

These groups had established contact with Churchill during April 1936. Encouraged by Churchill's reborn faith in the League of Nations and in collective security, and particularly by a speech that he delivered to the House on April 6, Lord Robert Cecil put out the first feelers to him on behalf of the League of Nations Union (LNU). At the same moment Churchill received an approach from the Anti-Nazi Council

---

*This was Eugen Spier. On war's outbreak he would put himself at H.M. Government's service. Like most other enemy aliens he was arrested and interned without trial until 1941.[2]

(ANC). Both wanted him to speak at Albert Hall meetings.

The harmless-sounding ANC had its roots in New York. The driving force was local attorney Samuel Untermyer. Hitting back at the Nazis' mindless anti-Jewish boycott, in 1933 his World Jewish Economic Federation had organized a trade boycott of Germany. Together with mayor Fiorello LaGuardia, Untermyer had established the grand sounding "World Non-Sectarian Anti-Nazi Council" in 1934. Later that year he visited Sir Walter Citrine, leader of the Trades Union Congress. Citrine was angered by Hitler's brutal closure of the trade unions. Together they had founded a British "Non-Sectarian Anti-Nazi Council to Champion Human Rights."[3]

Such were the origins of the ANC. A kaleidoscopic panel of Communist fellow travellers, industrialists, financiers, trade unionists and disgruntled Conservatives was quilted together for ANC's headed notepaper. At the bottom of the paper were two slogans. The first was, "Nazi Germany is the Enemy of Civilization." The second was a vestige of the ANC's boycott origins, like the coccyx that remains in Man to remind him of his descent from the lower vertebrates: "Refuse to Trade with the Enemy!"[4]

The reason for the ANC approach to Churchill in April 1936 was this: in London, authoritative Jewish bodies including the powerful Board of Deputies had come out against the more strident boycott activities, lest these provoke the Nazis to more extreme measures; in New York, the firebrand Zionist leader Rabbi Stephen S. Wise, an associate of Untermyer's, disagreed and founded a militant World Jewish Congress based on Geneva. As the Board of Deputies was the principle source of its British finance, the ANC shifted to a political approach in 1936, and began hiring helpers on the political scene.

There followed months of Zionist intrigue and extraordinary contrasts — of union leaders like Citrine banqueting at the Savoy cheek by jowl with the barons of the munitions industries and big chemical combines. Privately commending Citrine years later to Roosevelt, Churchill would write: "He worked with me three years before the war in our effort to arouse all parties in the country to the need of rearmament against Germany." He added his favorite phrase of approbation: "He has the root of the matter in him."[5]

The ANC decision to recruit Churchill had been taken two weeks after Hitler's Rhineland coup. It seemed clear that Austria or Czechoslovakia would be next, but Labour Party policy still flatly opposed rearmament.

At an emergency joint conference with other anti-Nazi forces in London on March 19 and 20, Citrine and Ernest Bevin, the tough transport union boss, opened their campaign for rearmament. Among the speakers were Norman Angell, a communist fellow-traveller, and Henry Wickham Steed. Steed would bulk large in The Focus. Sixty-five, this bearded broadcaster and former editor of *The Times* had been in Czech pay for thirteen years. One is tempted to ask, reviewing Czech documents captured by the Nazis in 1939, who was not? Prague had paid him £23,000 in 1923-24 alone (about a quarter of a million pounds in present terms.)[6] He had a then-fashionable ambivalence about the Jews: although a Zionist at heart, he singled out the Jews among the Germans, whether bankers or Marxists, for particular hatred, believing them to have conspired to make a German master race.[7]

Describing this March 1936 conference some months later Steed recalled that they decided to widen their circle. They decided to hold a private luncheon at which Citrine would again preside, but they would invite Churchill and other prominent Conservative, Liberal and Labour politicians and businessmen to attend as well.[8]

BEFORE THAT LUNCHEON, Churchill received an approach from a third quarter, a letter dated April 21 from Rex Leeper. Aged forty-eight, Leeper was the Foreign Office specialist on central Europe. He was an Oxford educated Australian who had worked previously for Intelligence; he and his brother at the F.O. were also heavily in Czech pay.* Vansittart, his letter said, had asked him to contact Winston about a matter of national importance "in which he hopes very much to enlist your interest."

Churchill welcomed Leeper to Chartwell three days later. Leeper had long campaigned within the F.O. for a program to re-educate the man in the street in favour of the League of Nations. "Our people," he had urged Vansittart in January, "are being given little or no guidance, and yet time presses."

There is no record of what he discussed with Churchill but he told friends afterwards that Churchill was the man Britain needed: "Rex thinks he will come back," wrote one such listener.[10]

Still calling themselves the Anti-Nazi Council, the new group held a private luncheon in Mr Churchill's honour at a hotel in Northumberland Avenue on May 19.[11] ICI industrialist Sir Robert Mond acted as host.[12] Churchill invited Liberal politician Lady Violet Bonham-Carter to sit next to him. She was the daughter of Herbert

---

*Reginald Wildig Allen Leeper was later ambassador to Greece (1943-5) and Argentina. Captured documents show that Prague was paying him and his brother A.W.A. Leeper to thwart Hungarian interests in the F.O.; when Rex's brother died in January 1935 the Czech minister in London Jan Masaryk had organized a fund to which each state of the Little Entente - Czechoslovakia, Romania, Yugoslavia - contributed £500 per annum; £5,000 was set aside for the upbringing of A.W.A.'s daughter.[9]

Asquith; he had been fond of her ever since they met — he a dynamic redhead of thirty-two, she was a stunning beauty of nineteen.

"At this luncheon," wrote Steed afterwards, "Mr Winston Churchill said that a situation which could bring so many political opponents together round one table, to talk across party and above party, must be a grave situation indeed. Nothing less than the freedom and the peace of democratic Europe were at stake."[13]

Winston suggested they find a title that was less cumbersome and negative than ANC.[14] In a short speech, he called upon them to find common ground against Nazi tyranny. They should prepare for the time when "suddenly the tension may rise and we may feel that we could go all lengths together." "That is why," he said, "we ought to keep a little in touch with one another."[15]

Labour theoretician Dr Hugh Dalton suggested that their manifesto "point the finger" at Hitler. Lady Violet disagreed. "There are only two policies to be adopted towards Hitler," she would write a few hours later to Winston, "to hold out the hand or to clench the fist."

In his reply to her Winston set out, perhaps for the first time, his own strategic concept: they should *encircle* "Nazidom," marshalling every country from the Soviet Union right round the Mediterranean — including Mussolini's Italy — to the Belgian coast and back to the Baltic to this end.

* * *

A fresh informant joined Winston's flock of disciples. A jug-eared air ministry official of forty, Squadron Leader Charles Torr Anderson contacted him at Chartwell on the day after this luncheon and wandered into Morpeth Mansions some days later, laden with verbose memoranda on the RAF's unreadiness for war and its pilot training deficiencies. It was all grist to Winston's mill.

Anderson was a sad figure, as should have become clear to Mr Churchill's biographers by now. A brave and severely injured officer who was by 1936 Director of Training at the Air Ministry, he was clearly in the early throes of a behavioral illness — difficult to detect in its early stages — that would lead to his invaliding out of the RAF six years later.[16]

Churchill welcomed all informants whatever their motivation. It was going to be a long haul back. "If all our fears are groundless and everything passes off smoothly in the next few years," he had written to mineowner Sir Abe Bailey — Diana Churchill had just divorced his son — on June 3, 1936, "as pray God indeed it may, obviously there is no need for me. If on the other hand the very dangerous times arise, I may be forced to take a part."

Until that time came, he proposed to expand his power base: he would exploit the ANC and League of Nations Union; he would accept too the invitation to be president of the New Commonwealth Society. "I feel so strongly," he wrote to his constituency chairman, explaining the latter decision, "one ought to do all one can to get this country rearmed and to relieve people from feeling that rearmament means war. In my belief, it is one of the few chances of peace."

He kept strictly out of any controversy not directly in line with his main attack on Hitler. When Lloyd George stoutly declared that Britain would never go to war for Austria's sake the Austrian envoy Georg Franckenstein called on Churchill, as "one of the most brilliant orators," and begged him to repudiate the remark. The latter declined, offering only a tenuous excuse. He was not, he explained, planning to speak in the Debate (which was on Italy and sanctions.)[17]

THE PROTRACTED INTERNAL wrangling continued about the size of Hitler's "first line" airforce. Wing Commander Peter Warburton, air adviser to the Committee of Imperial Defence, thought the air ministry's figures convincing.

"Mr Churchill," rejoined the CID's secretary, Hankey, "does not want to be convinced!"[18]

Over at the ministry an exasperated Lord Swinton put down all this Churchillian "interference" to Baldwin's foolhardy decision to let him see the CID's secret papers: now Churchill was using its air *research* subcommittee as a platform for policy making; but it was none of their business to discuss Hitler's air strength, let alone advise on the strength of the R.A.F. "That," Swinton lectured Hankey, "is the function of the CID and the Cabinet." He suggested that "in view of recent events" they should refrain from letting him see any more secret papers.[19]

Churchill had perfected a propaganda method that might be called The Circle Line. He would declare that the Germans had spent a staggering £800m on arms during 1935. (Hitler had set aside approximately that amount in 1935 for all three armed *services* including armaments and the SA: after all, their cupboard was bare. His defence budget for 1936 would be smaller.)

The figure would be reported by the *Morning Post*, in this case on June 25. An unexpected bonus would be that Neville Chamberlain, chancellor of the exchequer, publicly agreed. Less unexpected was that Ralph Wigram at the F.O. also minuted agreement: "The information in our possession, which generally coincides with that given by Mr Churchill and the *Morning Post*, shows that in 1935 the Germans spent on armaments . . . about £800 million; and are likely to spend as much, if not more, this year."[20]

On July 20, speaking to the House, Mr Churchill would cynically include both the newspaper and Mr Chamberlain as authorities for his £800m figure. Thus his figure completed its circular trip and nobody spotted the sleight of hand.

The Secretary for Air muttered in private about Winston's "fallacious statements about German strength."[21] But Swinton was like a blind dog in a butcher's shop: he could smell raw meat all around him, but could not put his paw on it.

> We are going away on our holidays [Churchill concluded his speech.] Jaded Ministers, anxious but impotent Members of Parliament, a public whose opinion is more bewildered and more expressionless than anything I can recall in my life — all will seek the illusion of rest and peace. . . And the influence of the Conservative party machine is being used through a thousand channels to spread this soporific upon Parliament and the nation. But, I am bound to ask, has not confidence been shaken by various things that have happened, and are still happening?

He asked Baldwin to receive a Parliamentary deputation, and the prime minister agreed. Churchill tried to manoeuvre Labour and Liberal leaders Attlee and Sinclair into his deputation, but they declined to join.

Playing rough, in a speech at Horsham on July 23 he appealed over Attlee's head to trade unionists and Leftist intellectuals.

"All the left wing intelligentsia," he would triumph four months later to his son Randolph, "are coming to look to me for protection, and I will give it whole-heartedly in return for their aid in the rearmament of Britain."[22]

ON THE DAY after the Horsham speech the ten top members of the ANC trooped into Morpeth Mansions, his London pied a terre, for a second conspiratorial luncheon. In response to Churchill's wishes for a less negative title, they now called themselves The Focus but, cat-like, this was a name known only to themselves. The main decisions this day were to set up a research section under Wickham Steed and to draft a manifesto. (According to Steed it was seen by "one American visitor" who insisted it be shown privately to certain associations, which he did not identify, in the United States.[23]).

There were embarrassed coughs when the organizing secretary of ANC, A.H. Richards inquired where the money for all this was to come from; Mr Churchill appeared angry at the question. Richards was taken aside and asked to announce simply that all their requirements had already been met.[24]

Funds had been arranged two days earlier at a private dinner in North London, hosted by the Board of Deputies of British Jews. Its vice-president Sir Robert Waley-Cohen, chairman of British Shell, was a charismatic Zionist extrovert who would become, in the words of his authorized biographer Robert Henriques, the "veritable dynamic force of Focus." At a dinner on July 22 at his home, Caen Wood Towers, he launched the initial secret £50,000 fund for The Focus. His associates signed immediate cheques for £25,000 and pledged the rest.[25]

It was a colossal sum for such an organization to butter around in 1936 — five times the annual budget of the British Council. Personally administered by Waley-Cohen, the fund was used to procure journalists like *Times* leader-writer Captain Colin Coote — who published for The Focus a series of "Vigilance" pamphlets — and for widespread slushing operations coordinated by H.T. Montague Bell.

It was Waley-Cohen who ruled on what The Focus might say. According to Henriques he read each manuscript and amended them profusely, explaining that they had to refute the growing belief among the British public that Nazism had "its legitimate aspects." Even Churchill's writings were not excepted from this editing. A year later he wrote an article entitled "The Better Way". Waley-Cohen made copious alterations on the draft, and Churchill meekly swallowed them.[26]

On July 28, 1936 Churchill took his Parliamentary deputation to see Mr Baldwin. He based his case on Morton's and Anderson's data, and put forward what he called the latest French government estimate of a German first line of 2,000 planes by the end of 1936. He talked of Germany's power to bomb Britain's major food-importation ports as well as London, and freely claimed that Hitler could already drop 500 tons of bombs on London in one mission.

The fallacies are now obvious. He ignored the deficiencies of German bomber types, while highlighting those in the British. RAF bombers, he claimed, could barely reach the German coast. (A few days later the air ministry would wearily refute this: RAF bombers could already reach the Ruhr, no doubt by overflying neutral Holland, as they subsequently did;* and by July 1937 Berlin would be within their range.)

Already concerned by what the Secretary for Air later called the "waste of time" that Mr Churchill was inflicting on everybody — the transcript of this two-day deputation would run to forty printed pages — both Baldwin and Chamberlain were worried about the side-effects of his raucous campaign for rearmament.[28]

It was already affecting relations with Germany. Moreover, if rearmament were begun without proper reason, the diversion of

---

* As First Lord in 1913 Mr Churchill had advocated seizing and holding a naval base on the "Dutch, Danish or Scandinavian coasts" in the event of war with Germany. All were of course neutrals.[27]

of industrial capacity to arms production would also be a catastrophic setback to Britain's struggling peacetime economy.

Baldwin put this argument forcefully to Churchill's deputation. The politician who in public so often cloaked his meaning in vagueness and complacency did not mince his language in private. He had strong doubts, he said, about "the peril itself" as depicted by Mr. Churchill. Were the public to understand that Germany was arming to fight *Britain*?

"We all know the German desire to move East," he said, adding that Hitler had stated it candidly enough in *Mein Kampf*. "And if he should move East I should not break my heart."

Since he was behind closed doors, he used language of exquisite clarity. "I am not going to get this country into a war with anybody for the League of Nations — or anybody else."

Finally: "If there is any fighting in Europe to be done, I should like to see the Bolshies and the Nazis doing it."[29]

BALDWIN WAS NOT the only Englishman to hold that view. In proclaiming that Germany would lead the defence of Europe against Bolshevism, Hitler had devised a slogan of dangerous magnetism. This image, of Britain, Germany and Italy standing shoulder to shoulder across Europe, defending the continent against Comintern subversion, was too alluring for Churchill to accept, although he could not explain why. "It is too easy to be good," he wrote lamely to the French ambassador on July 31.

Events in Republican Spain illustrated the cleft stick in which he was now held. The Red Terror of the Republican government of Juan Negrin was a matter of public record. The evil *Che-Ka*'s, of which Churchill had written in 1920, had been installed in Spain's ancient cities, and were practising executions, assassinations and torture with accustomed expertise. When Nationalist insurgents now began a civil war to overthrow this cruel regime, Mr Churchill declared his sympathies for them and he would maintain this stubborn stand until their victory in 1939.

Germany and Italy ferried aid to the insurgents. But France's Socialist premier Leon Blum, whose new Popular Front government included Communists, supported the Reds. Fearing a divergence of British and French interests from which only Hitler could benefit, Churchill campaigned for both countries to maintain absolute neutrality. Meanwhile he wielded his pen ceaselessly on the insurgent general Francisco Franco's behalf. "A revivified Fascist Spain in closest sympathy with Italy and Germany is one kind of disaster," he polemicized in Beaverbrook's *Evening Standard*. "A Communist Spain spreading its snaky tentacles through Portugal and France is another and many will think worse."[30]

As usual now, he spent September away from his family, painting at Maxine Elliot's villa on the Riviera. Still beset by financial uncertainties he planned to complete there a dozen articles for the *News of the World* — "They are vy lucrative," he explained to Clementine. "It wd be folly not to work them off in view of many uncertainties."

He arrived in Paris on August 30 and conferred with Georges Mandel — born Jeroboam Rothchild, a leading politician like himself without portfolio. Mandel said they were witnessing a breakdown of British and French influence in Europe. General Joseph Georges, who had been Pétain's chief of staff, invited Winston to visit the army's summer manoeuvres with himself and the French generalissimo, Maurice Gamelin. Winston was fatefully impressed by these grave, elderly French generals and their troops. "One feels the strength of the nation resides in its army," he wrote privately to Clementine.

In Paris he drafted a speech about the need to establish a common Anglo-French "front" against Germany. The deputy editor of the *Times*, to whom he sent it for comment, discouraged this word: they should not abandon the hope — supported by so many authoritative pronouncements by the German leaders — that Germany was willing to reach a general understanding with the British Empire.

Churchill delivered the speech late in September all the same. It conjured up an image of a Britain or France under dictatorship: "How could we bear, nursed as we have been in a free atmosphere, to be gagged and muzzled; to have spies, eavesdroppers and delators at every corner; to have even private conversation caught up and used against us by the Secret Police and all their agents and creatures; to be arrested and interned without trial?"

How, he rhetorically asked, could we bear to be "treated like schoolboys when we are grown-up men?"

HIS CAMPAIGN OF speeches urging collective security against Germany aroused fresh anger in Berlin. The *Deutsche Diplomatisch-Politische Korrespondenz* challenged that he was trying to "camouflage personal dislike of Germany" as "practical reasoning." Churchill was delighted to know he was under attack.

On October 15 The Focus met for its third luncheon. Since men of standing were still shy of formally joining, Spier would later relate, ANC finally decided to have no membership at all. On this day they adopted the style of a Focus for the Defence of Freedom and Peace. The drafting committee had produced a manifesto, duly boiled down by Waley-Cohen, Lady Violet, Steed and Angell to a statement of principles. They were unexceptionable — to unite British citizens in defence of freedom, secured by democratic government and public law; and to join with others in preserving peace and withstanding armed aggression.[31]

Churchill merely approved it, in a speech which was not among his best. He had other things on his mind, as will shortly be seen.

"We have the means," he told this luncheon group, "of being the spear-point of all this vast mass of opinion which guards our rights." A few days later he wrote to the secretary, "I do not contemplate the building up of a new and rival society, but only a wielding together of those organisations and galvanizing them into effective use." On October 26 he confirmed: "In my view we are a focus bringing together all these various forces."[32]

The manifesto won prominent men to The Focus, including Sinclair and Sir Austen Chamberlain. A typical secret recruit was disaffected Conservative MP Vyvyan Adams, an official of the LNU, who wrote to Churchill on October 20 of his growing apprehension that the Government was contemplating a deal which would leave Hitler free to attack Eastwards or Southwards.[33]

On November 5 The Focus held its fourth luncheon.[34] Churchiill sent its manifesto to Randolph, writing: "A Peace with Freedom committee has been formed. I enclose a copy of the formula at length adopted. This committee aims at focussing and concentrating the efforts of all the peace societies like the New Commonwealth and the League of Nations Union in so far as they are prepared to support genuine military action to resist tyranny or aggression." "The basis of the Anti Nazi League," he added, "is of course Jewish resentment at their abominable persecution. But we are now taking broader ground."[35]

* * *

Late that October of 1936 the third volume of *Marlborough* was published. What should have been a moment of "post-natal" triumph was clouded by a domestic crisis that momentarily eclipsed all else. Under the eyes of a gleeful press, his daughter Sarah eloped to New York; to join Victor Samek, an Austrian comedian known to vaudeville audiences as Vic Oliver. Oliver had a still undissolved marriage in Vienna.

It was the penalty for a father too preoccupied with himself to care for his children. Quite without his realizing it, Sarah had become a grown-up woman, but he had continued to treat her like a schoolgirl.

She had been a delicate child. She had chosen an acting career, no easy choice for somebody with a famous name. At seventeen she had pirouetted around the gramaphone in Chartwell's dining room imagining herself in the arms of Fred Astaire.[36] By 1936 she was in C.B. Cochrane's chorus line. When she fell in love Winston purpled with paternal anger, and to judge from her letters he left Vic Oliver in no doubt of this.

In a few days' time she would be twenty-two. "I have given up any hope," Sarah wrote in the frantic letter she left behind for her mother, "that you and Papa can ever understand or have any conception what I have been through these last nine months that I have loved Vic — To be in love and to know the weakness of your love — To have to realise not only the incongruity of the situation — but that the man is despised by those who say they love you — To continually and perpetually have him insulted and treated as a low adventurer — To be made to feel you have committed an error."

Clementine had a better understanding of her daughter's feelings. There was not much romance in Winston. Years later she would tell an American airforce general about their own honeymoon in Venice. Winston had insisted on a motor launch. "It is far more healthy than a gondola," he had insisted, "the fumes kill the germs." Not much romance in Winnie, she would sigh.[37]

No one ever asked if I was sad [her daughter's lament continued] or how the long days and nights at Chartwell, with nothing to occupy my mind, ever passed. Then I had a feeling that Papa was not playing quite straight with us — It seemed an ominous silence — Was he . . . just a playing for time in the hope that lawyers working night and day might unravel something in his [Vic Oliver's] past to prevent us marrying?

Faced with blanket disapproval Sarah had eloped to join Vic in New York while her father was still vacationing in France. She chose the German liner *Bremen* to make the crossing. Sailing on October 1, she had written her mother, "Please make Papa understand that I did not just wait till he was out of the country. It was a last minute decision. I just have to go — I'm sorry."

Churchill was aghast. The newspapers went wild. His enemies wrote letters of heartfelt sympathy, and chortled up their sleeves. The ruthless American press steamed disclaimers of any real marriage intent out of Vic Oliver. From shipboard Sarah wrote pitifully to Clementine, fearful lest "Papa might . . . even have me stopped at the immigration place."[38]

She had judged her father's resoluteness well. Post-haste, he sent Randolph across the Atlantic. He had to grapple with fifty reporters to get off the boat. Winston asked Baruch to help; he described it as a "tiresome" affair.[39] Baruch hired for him a slick New York lawyer, Louis Levy, to investigate Oliver and sabotage the embryo relationship if he could.

Pleased to be attracting family attention at last, Sarah ignored her brother's advice. Winston told Levy to press on.

"Papa has the best lawyer in America working for him," Sarah wept in one letter to her mother. "In an informal moment Levy as good as admitted that if *we* were (Vic and I) paying him to get us married, the legal difficulty could have been straightened out in a few days — but I suppose it is his job to prolong the thing as long as possible, to stall and stall and play for time— in the hopes that it may die—or at best circumstances *will* divide us."

"I don't know if you know what Levy has resorted to now," she added. "Failing to find anything on Vic, he has turned his activities to Vienna and in a delicate and for him safeguarded way he has had men suggest to Vic's wife to contest now — at the ninth hour with the first Decree passed! — to contest the case. All her expenses will be paid for her etc. I refuse to believe that Papa knows of this — and that Levy is just over-zealous. Those are apparently just the usual American tactics. Levy is the smartest lawyer and can delay this marriage for some months, if Papa asks him to — equally if Papa asked him to speed it up, we could be married so soon."*

Resorting to the kind of blackmail that favorite daughters often use on indulgent fathers, she added "Considering the situation — and the publicity — I should have thought it [marriage] preferable to me being out here unmarried and still a subject of mystery, gossip and rumours."

Levy's methods failed. Baruch concluded that Oliver was serious and told Randolph so. Winston reluctantly gave consent. While waiting the requisite six weeks to marry, his actress daughter worked the East Coast stages. The wedding was celebrated on Christmas Eve at New York's City Hall.

The papers on this poignant episode are in her mother's personal files. The watchful Clementine never allowed these details of Winston's feudal paternalism to become public property.

Her husband's instincts turned out to have been right. The marriage to Vic Oliver eventually foundered. But Winston Churchill's love for his daughter Sarah endured, and she would return it, becoming a devoted if still troublesome daughter.

THIS NUPTIAL CRISIS late in 1936 destroyed his usefulness to The Focus for many weeks; almost immediately a second emerged, one of historic significance.

---

*In 1940, Churchill instructed J. Arthur Leve of the same Broadway law firm Leve, Hecht, Hadfield & Clark in a libel action brought against him in New York. The British embassy now confidentially warned him that Leve had a bad reputation "owing to his partnership with Louis Levy who was disbarred from federal courts for his connection with bribing of Judge Manton in New York."[40]

CHAPTER 7

Over-Reaching Himself

HIS MARRIAGE TO Clementine was blissfully happy. True, they took separate vacations — he preferring the Riviera, while she took Mary skiing to Austria. But he was beholden to her. "What can be more glorious," he had written at age sixty, "than to be united in one's walk through life with a being incapable of an ignoble thought?"

"I have shown this passage to my wife," he continued impishly, "who says I am to scratch it out, but I won't."[1] He dutifully red-inked it nonetheless, and it did not figure in the thirty-six episode autobiography which the Chicago *Tribune* published in 1935.

On divorce he was very definite — there shouldn't be any. Clementine agreed with a frankness that startled casual acquaintances. "It is difficult to know what to say,"recorded one embarrassed listener, "when the PM's wife goes off into a long account of . . . her father's infidelities and failure to pay the children's allowances specified under a judicial separation, and his habit of pursuing his women friends for ever after in a vindictive spirit!"[2]

As he watched the boyish King Edward VIII nervously opening his first Parliament on November 3, 1936 Churchill could not guess that a matrimonial scandal was about to break upon the very highest plane.

He had kept up the stale wrangle over Britain's air defences, but that campaign was running out of steam. The Cabinet was reluctant to re-arm despite all the arguments marshalled by Eden, the foreign secretary and by Alfred Duff Cooper, the pink-faced secretary for war. Chamberlain warned that the cost of rearmament would place burdens on future generations.

For want of a better cause, Churchill kept up the pressure. Speaking in the House on the twelfth he claimed that the RAF could field only 960 first-line planes against Hitler's 1,500, most of which were what he called in a fit of exaggeration "long distance bombing aeroplanes." Criticizing the inadequate provision of battlefield equipment, tanks and ammunition, he used these famous, scathing words:

The Government simply cannot make up their minds, or they cannot get the Prime Minister to make up his mind. So they go on in a strange paradox, decided only to be undecided, resolved to be irresolute, adamant for drift, solid for fluidity, all-powerful to be impotent. So we go on preparing more months and years — precious, perhaps vital, to the greatness of Britain —for the locusts to eat.

Baldwin offered the lame response that to have announced rearmament would have been to lose the 1935 election — "a squalid confession," as Churchill called it in a private letter. Encouraged by Bracken he refused, like a bulldog with a well gnawed bone, to drop Rearmament in the belief that the marrow must still be in it, somewhere.

He marched a second deputation round to No. 10: the prime minister wearily protested that the first had already wasted an immense amount of the time "of very busy men." Across fifty-eight pages of printed text Churchill haggled and hectored and harangued, still chewing over the disparities between the various estimates of German air power — the air ministry's, his own, the French.

Still the root issues remained unaddressed — Hitler's actual strategic objectives and his capabilities in the air.[3]

* * *

Hovering on the outer fringes of this central debate, The Focus had begun to peel bills off the Jewish Defence Fund's £50,000 bankroll.

Some of those who moved into its ranks were undoubtedly motivated by deeper emotions than those inspired by the persuasive crackle of banknotes. There were men of moral authority and substance like Sir Robert and Henry Mond (Lord Melchett) and the Dean of Chichester; politicians of every hue from the "Gentile Zionists" like Lloyd George, Lord Cecil, Wickham Steed, Amery and Nicolson, to those who had expressed an early coy admiration for fascism like Duff Cooper and Neville Chamberlain's brother Austen, and yet others in whose breasts stirred similar emotions for the Soviet union, like Angell, Boothby and Dalton.

Now that it had funds, The Focus could be choosy. In a letter gently fobbing off one would-be intriguer, Winston referred to "our Group" as consisting of people who had been associated before the Great War, served in the Cabinet or held office. "If the Group is widened at all," Churchill however promised, "I should certainly press for you."[4]

The editors of the influential weekly journals *Spectator, New Statesman, Economist* and *Time & Tide* were wooed and won: Wilson Harris, Basil Kingsley Martin, Lady Rhonda, Harcourt Johnstone.

The Liberals were wooed as well. Dining confidentially with The Focus on November 23 to discuss their first Albert Hall mass meeting — "Arms and the Covenant" — in ten days' time Churchill found both Sir Walter Layton and A.J. Cummings, chairman and chief commentator of the *News Chronicle*, as well as Lady Violet and two B.B.C. executives. Churchill invited Cummings to speak on the platform with him; the newspaperman baulked at that, but later figured at the group's secret functions.[5] Labour also showed interest. "Attlee," said a note passed to him by an MP, "will support you on any rearmament programme. He admires & likes you. The door is open if you want to talk to him."

With good reason, Churchill believed he was riding the crest of the wave.

True, another personal crisis loomed. He owed his bank £2,600 — perhaps £30,000 at current values; he could toss royalty cheques into an overdraft like that, and never hear them hit bottom. And he expected a £6,000 tax demand in 1937.

But he was undismayed: his ship was coming in, of that he felt quite sure. He expected to earn £15,000 from his writings in 1937. A month's lecturing in America would pay off his taxes, and he would bank the dollars in the United States for safety. So he booked the Cunard Line's best cabins and planned to leave on December 22 to spend Christmas in Florida, at Consuelo Balsan's villa in Palm Beach.

He had another purpose — to inaugurate The Focus in the United States. Confidential approaches had been made to him by the American Jewish Committee, and he had given Randolph instructions to talk about it with Baruch, the wealthy financier.[6]

At this buoyant moment his ship of fortune ran aground. An Event happened which was by no means an ally, and he overreached himself.

* * *

At age forty-one, the Prince of Wales had succeeded to the throne on January 20. Modern in outlook and gay in disposition, Edward VIII was a popular Monarch; but uneasy rumours had long been snaking around the diplomatic circuit — rumours that he was "seeing" a married woman, Mrs Wallis Simpson, and intended to make her his queen.

In starch-collar London, of whose morals Stanley Baldwin considered himself custodian, there was outrage: Mrs Simpson was American: Worse, she had a husband and an ex-husband still living.

At Court functions the Churchills and Bracken found themselves sharing tables with handsome monarch and elegant mistress. The King touted her around quite openly. At St Tropez he had rested his nerves in her company. "In the circumstances," commented the Italian consul there, "she seemed to have become an amorous nurse as well."[7]

In February 1936 Baldwin murmured loyal reproaches, but the King felt popular enough to tell him not to interfere.[8] Shortly the prime minister had greater cause for disquiet. The francophile Foreign Office learned that although a high-ranking freemason Edward VIII was an outspoken admirer of Hitler and National Socialism, and that he had developed indiscreet relations with the German ambassador, Leopold von Hoesch.[9] MI5's wiretaps must have echoed this. On March 10 during the Rhineland crisis Hoesch persuaded him to threaten abdication if Baldwin wanted war, and on the eleventh after an audience with the PM the King telephoned the embassy to report success.*

Winston had been his friend for many years. While recognizing all the happy traits of a young man in love, he urged the King at first to sacrifice any idea of marrying the American, if he was to stay on the throne.

Early in July her divorce petition was entered at Suffolk Assizes. To discuss the several niceties, Walter Monckton, the King's legal adviser, visited Churchill, though it is not clear why: perhaps as a senior Privy Councillor. Churchill urged that Mrs Simpson abandon her divorce petition, because of the inevitable scandal for Edward that would ensue. But she went ahead, and late in October won her decree nisi. Shortly, in a fatal miscalculation of the public temper, he changed his opinion: Edward should fight Baldwin, marry Mrs Simpson, and sit tight.

The decree would become absolute in April 1937, a clear month before the Coronation. The implications were obvious: Fleet Street was agog, but Lord Beaverbrook persuaded his colleagues to hold their tongue. American and French newspapers splashed salacious stories however and lurid letters began to pour into No. 10. Undeterred, on November 16 the King informed the prime minister he proposed to marry Mrs Simpson.

Baldwin summoned the Party leaders and Churchill to discuss the crisis. He intended to confront the Monarch with something of an ultimatum: but first he asked for assurances that the others would not accept an invitation to form a government if he did tender his resignation to the King.

Attlee and Sinclair gave them; Mr Churchill kept quiet. We shall probably never know what train of thoughts triggered his

---

*The conversation was cryptic. "Can you hear me? This is David speaking," King Edward said. "Please don't address me by name." He had seen "that bastard" Baldwin and given him a dressing down. "I told him I'd resign in the event of war. There will be no war. Don't worry." The German press attaché, listening on a second earpiece, made a note.[10]

decision to play *va banque*. No doubt he surmised that championing a popular King against his first minister might prove a crusade with a Gaussian force greater than India and Rearmament. Perhaps this was at last the issue on which he could topple the government?

If this be so, the cynicism of his choice now seems obvious. The King's pro-Nazi inclinations can surely not have been any more palatable to him in 1936 than they were to prove, under very difficult circumstances, four years later. It was a clumsily obvious manoeuvre. As Chamberlain once said, when Lloyd George was out for mischief, one might only see the wake of his periscope; but Churchill's hull would be half above water. Winston, Chamberlain mused in his diary, was "moving mysteriously in the background and, it is suggested, expressing willingness to form a Government if there should be any refusal on our part to agree."[11]

Lunching with Churchill on December 2 to discuss their great Albert Hall meeting on the morrow, T.U.C. leader Citrine made quite plain that organized labour would back Baldwin in any showdown with the King.

"I will defend him," retorted Churchill, ignoring this further warning sign. "I think it is my duty."

"What," gasped Citrine, "irrespective of what he has done?"

"He feels it *here*," said Churchill gravely, placing his hand upon his breast.[12]

On the next day, the newspapers broke their self-imposed silence. There were the first ominous signs that Mrs Simpson was not popular. As she fled that evening to Cannes, people clustered outside her house in Cumberland Terrace booing.

THAT DAY, DECEMBER 3, Churchill packed the Albert Hall. The Focus had styled itself a movement for the Defence of Freedom and Peace for this public manifestation. Out at Chartwell, he had laboured for days upon his speech. It scorned Britain's pacifists, appealed not to discard the League of Nations, and derided former Labour minister Sir Oswald Mosley, now leader of the British Union of Fascists. "Fascinated by the spectacle of brutal power," he charged, "his followers grovel to Nazi dictatorship in order that they can make people in their turn grovel to them."*

The loud applause that his speech earned may well have contributed to Churchill's false assessment of his standing at this juncture.

---

*By this time Mosley's blackshirt organisation was being financed by Mussolini. The author located in the Archivio Centrale dello Stato at Rome reports by Italian ambassador Dino Grandi documenting the secret delivery of cash to B.U.F. officials.

There is no doubt that his anti-Hitler campaign was still developing horsepower. "With Churchill," wrote Lord Beaverbrook a few days later, "the man's whole political faith — as he sees it — is bound up in running the anti-German line coupled with a demand for more arms. He has had some success with this already. Indeed he has emerged as the leader of a big armaments, anti-German movement in politics, hostile to the government."[13]

This hard-headed Canadian press lord played a central role in the palace crisis. Fearing that a discredited monarchy might weaken the Empire, he too had urged King Edward to fight. More than one political observer detected this new Beaverbrook-Churchill axis.[14] On the third they were seen together at Beaverbrook's London mansion, Stornoway House, deep in consultation with the King's solicitor George Allen. They recommended that Edward broadcast immediately to his people — over the heads of his truculent ministers.

The King liked the idea, and Baldwin had to warn him that this would be unconstitutional so long as he remained on the throne. Edward asked if he might talk with Mr Churchill, and invited him to dinner at Fort Belvedere, his Windsor home.

Both on the third and fourth Churchill had loudly insisted at Question Time that Baldwin keep the House informed. Out at the fort on December 4 he found the King "debonair" but perceptibly cracking under the strain. "He twice in my presence completely lost the thread of what he was saying," he wrote to the prime minister, "and appeared to me driven to the last extremity of endurance."

Churchill's new advice was that the King ask for time to decide — whether to marry, abdicate, or drop his questionable bride. The King liked that, and suggested that two weeks in Switzerland would be long enough to decide.

Churchill had enough nous to know that leaving England was no way to win support just now. His language adopted a military flavour, always a dangerous sign. Exclaiming, "Sir, it is time for reflection, you must allow time for the battalions to march," he returned to London, again to confer with Beaverbrook ("A *devoted* tiger!" he said, commending the Canadian in a private note to the King, "very scarce breed.") "News from all fronts!" he wrote breathlessly to Edward on the following evening, continuing the military metaphor. "No pistol to be held at the King's head. No doubt that this request for time will be granted."

He assured the King that the issue could be shelved until February or March. "*On no account must the King leave the country,*" he emphasized, adding quaintly: "Windsor Castle is his battle station (poste de commandment)."[15]

In this lather of Royalism he had overlooked the fickleness of public temper. Edward's popularity was ebbing. At the Palladium cinema that Sunday evening the audience shuffled out even while the National Anthem was played.[16] But Winston neither went to vulgar cinemas nor hobnobbed with the hoi-polloi. That Sunday he was in the seclusion of Chartwell drafting a glittering statement to the press. It pleaded for Time and Patience, and did not mince words about those who issued ultimata to their Kings.

It provoked a uniformly hostile comment; only his toady Desmond Morton appears to have endorsed it.

The storm cones were hoisting, but Winston was blind to them. MPs now suspected that he had been playing this painful crisis for his own ends. Harold Nicolson, a stout, florid member sitting that afternoon just one place away from the hunched and pouting Churchill, heard their neighbour Sir George Lambert, former Admiralty colleague and friend of Winston for thirty years, beg him not to speak. "Can't you *feel* the temper of the House?" pleaded Lambert. "You will do yourself irreparable harm."

"I am not afraid of this House," was Churchill's reply. "When I see my duty I speak out clearly."[17]

Baldwin made a statement, but without even listening Winston bounded to his feet and reiterated his plea to the PM to take no "irrevocable step."

The House erupted. There were screams of "Drop it!" and "Twister!" and howls to sit down.

Churchill now grasped the awfulness of his misjudgment. He swayed, twisting his spectacles.

"If," he lisped above the cacophony, pinking with anger, "the House resists my claim to speak it will only add importance to any words I use."

The Speaker called him to order, then directed him to sit down: He was trying to make a speech: It was Question Time: He was out of order.

He stormed out, thunder on his brow. Bracken loped out at his side, and joined him in his car. As Winston glanced out to his left the photographers popped their flashbulbs; he smiled a wan smile. Nicolson described Winston's defeat that day to his wife: "He almost lost his head, and he certainly lost his command of the House." "In three minutes," wrote another observer, "his hopes of return to power and influence are shattered."[18]

WORSE WAS TO follow. The King had decided to abdicate. "Our cock," Beaverbrook grimly telephoned to Winston in a phrase that said everything, "won't fight." Edward wanted only to marry Mrs Simpson. At ten a.m. on the tenth he signed the deed of abdication.

With no course but to retreat, Churchill did so with customary grace and courtesy.

"What is done is done," he said. "What has been done or left undone belongs to history, and to history, so far as I am concerned, it shall be left."

He lunched at Fort Belvedere on the eleventh and left Edward moist-eyed. Teetering upon the threshhold, and tapping out the tetrameters with his walking stick upon the rhythmic flagstones, he recited Andrew Marvell's lines upon the beheading of Charles I: "He nothing common did or mean / Upon that memorable scene."

Two men, one twenty years younger than the other: Their paths would cross again in history. A few hours later Edward, shortly to become the Duke of Windsor, left for Austria where he would remain until Mrs Simpson's decree was made absolute on May 3, 1937; one month later he married her.*

General opinion was that Churchill was done for. He wrote the Duke that he was "feeling rather battered." A year later the latter, reflecting on the crisis, would inform Hitler's deputy at a private dinner that he had been brought down "partly through murky intrigues but mostly on account of his healthy social instincts and Germanophile sentiments."[19] Be that as it may, the relevant sections of those Cabinet proceedings are still closed.

The fiasco left Churchill deeper in the wilderness and more desperate than ever. It had enhanced his public image of instability. The Focus suffered, Spier would recall, because of the criticism attracted by Churchill's posture.

Worse, the American Jewish Committee, which had toyed with bringing him over to inaugurate The Focus there, dropped the idea at short notice: in 1937, a year when sixty-four percent of all Americans believed they shouldn't even have entered World War I, he was too wild a man. According to their historian, the AJC feared that "any known connection between Churchill and the Jews would bring charges of warmongering from anti-Semites."[20] This was no idle apprehension: soon after Europe's tragedy began even Chamberlain was heard to remark that "America and the world Jews had forced England into the war."[21]

---

*In a file of the Italian military intelligence service the author found a whimsical letter from the ex-Kind dated (mis-dated?) Fort Belvedere December 12, postmarked in Hammersmith on the thirteenth. Writing to an English friend in Italy, "Edward P., ex R.I." referred caustically to his brother as "little Tich" and "Stuttering Bertie," to Queen Elizabeth as "his sweet little Queen of Scots" (*dolce piccola reglia scozzesa,*) to himself as "Edward the Confessor" and to Mrs Simpson as the "Baltimore belle." The same *SIM* file contains intercepted British embassy letters on the crisis.

Churchill optimistically hoped the invitation was merely postponed. "I have every hope," he wrote to Baruch on New Year's Day, "that I shall be able to come over to the States in April and hope to inaugurate the Defence of Peace and Freedom movement about which Randolph consulted you. It would have been a great pity," he conceded, "to hurry it unduly." Later in January however the AJC invited Wickham Steed, co-founder of The Focus, instead.[22]

Churchill tried to gloss over this reverse. "The Abdication," he wrote in the same letter to Baruch, "has been most painful and has left far deeper marks among the people than Parliament or the newspapers show. I cannot convince myself that with time and patience it could not have been avoided."[23]

His financial master plan was now in tatters. Hiring Levy's talents against Vic Oliver had not been cheap. His American trip cancelled, he stayed at Chartwell, painting in the pouring rain, or pounding away at *Marlborough*. He would have to finish it by April 1937 just to meet current expenses. To Clementine, still vacationing in Austria, he remarked on how much his ghost writer Francis Deakin was aiding him: "It is quite an effort," he added, "to keep all the points of this argument in one's mind when so much else is afoot."[24]

When Lord Rothermere — who had spent the first week in January 1937 en famille with Hitler — invited Winston to join him on the Riviera, Churchill took his secretary Mrs Pearman with him as well as Randolph: because now he had to write or founder into the icy waters of insolvency. Without a commission, he risked summarizing Russian blockbuster *War and Peace* into thirty-four pages of double-spaced typescript.

It should not be thought that these potboilers did not contain fine prose. Even at his worst, he was superior to most other writers at their best. Pacing the floor of Rothermere's villa he dictated this description of Tolstoi's heroine Natasha, "the jewel of the book"

> — one of the most enchanting creatures 'that Fable e're hath feigned.' All the loveliest things in English poetry might have been written about her: she is made of spirit, fire and dew: her body talks, 'she dances like a wave' her singing might charm a soul from the ribs of death; and she has a decidedly tempestuous petticoat.

He sent the hasty typescript, captioned with scant modesty "A Digest by Winston Churchill of Tolstoi's Great Novel," to the *Tribune* syndicate. They accepted it on the last day of March, coughed up the usual $1,000 — but did not publish it.* That was ominous.

---

*The New York *News* published it eventually, in September 1937; and again in 1943.

To his terror, the hitherto lucrative North American syndication "pot" began to boil dry. He was already digesting Feodor M. Dostoievski's *Crime and Punishment*, but a chill wind had begun to blow from Chicago. When his agency notified the syndicate that he was familiar with the "long and very fine novel" *Jean Christopher* by Romain Holland he met with a rebuff. Evidently his anti-German line had irked Colonel Robert Rutherford McCormick, the *Tribune*'s isolationist publisher.

In October the *Tribune* syndicate would also turn down Winston's project for a major series on the line of Edward Shephard Creasey's classic, *The Fifteen Decisive Battles of the World*. There were too many war features already from Spain and China: that was the unconvincing explanation.[25]

He had painted himself into a corner, and saw no way to get out. May 1937 would probably be the crossroads for him. Baldwin would probably resign then and Chamberlain replace him. His fortune now might lie equally in the City or Whitehall. "I really do not care very much which," he wrote offhandedly to Clementine on February 2. Frederick Leathers, a steamship company director, had held out the prospect of boardroom office, and Winston admitted that it sounded attractive: he would need time to reflect and read if he was to complete his *History of the English-Speaking Peoples* by 1939, and pick up the £16,000 due thereby.

Until then the signs indicated trouble. He wrote to Cassell's, who were to publish the *History*, pleading for another £1,000 advance although he could offer no more than an earnest to begin that autumn. He even talked of selling Chartwell: "If I could see £25,000," he confessed to Clementine on February 2, "I should close with it." The children were nearly all flown, he mournfully explained: "And my life is probably in its closing decade."

He was in the throes of a financial nightmare. Financially, as well as politically, he had over-reached himself in 1936. His outgoings, including the upkeep of Chartwell and Morpeth Mansions, amounted to over ten thousand pounds a year while his gross income from writing, before taxation, seldom exceeded fifteen thousand.* On April 8 he determined to limit the outgoings for 1937-1938 to £6,000: "This cannot on any account be exceeded," he lectured Clementine.[26]

Of necessity his campaigning, even for The Focus, slackened. Lord Davies had urged him on January 7 to use great public meetings of the League of Nations Union or failing that the New Commonwealth or The

---

*Mr Churchill's annual pre-tax income from literary sources had been: Tax Year ending April 1930, £10,695; April 1931, £12,883; April 1932, £15,240; April 1933, £13,981; April 1934, £6,572; April 1935, £13,505; April 1936, £16,312; April 1937, £12,914.

Focus as his vehicle to attain power as "the first Minister." Churchill, he said, only had to play his cards right: "Honestly," he added, "I prefer to see you in the wilderness than play the part of second, third, or any other kind of Minister." Churchill replied that he was under no illusions how little a private person with no access to the B.B.C. could influence Government policy by addressing public meetings.

For months The Focus stagnated, issuing manifestos and organizing multiple-signature letters to *The Times*, mostly drafted by Angell. The first, a letter "For the Defence of Czechoslovakia," on March 10, was published simultaneously in Paris with French signatories, mostly of Leon Blum's Popular Front.[27]

From disgruntled economists, civil servants, arms factory employees, and serving officers, a stream of well-meaning letters continued to reach him: he would invite their authors to lunch, give them a hearing and ask for more information. Armoured warfare expert Brigadier Percy Hobart, Inspector of the Royal Tank Corps since 1933, was one such furtive informant; he had already visited Morpeth Mansions in October 1936. Often Wing Commander Anderson arrived, sat at Churchill's bedside and dictated to Mrs Pearman memoranda on the RAF's weaknesses in tactics or equipment, adding concrete detail like the lack of underground fuel storage tanks. "You must realise," Churchill calmed him once, "that loyalty to the State must come before loyalty to the Service."

NOT ALL OF his informants shared Churchill's unalloyed loyalty to the Empire. Some were pursuing more distant goals, and he was putty in their hands. In April 1936 he had based his frightening (and inflated) £1,000m estimate of Hitler's annual arms expenditure on men whom he would in his memoirs identify only as "two German refugees of high ability and inflexible purpose."

> They understood all the details of the presentment [*sic*] of German budgets, the value of the mark, and so forth.[28]

His reticence is now understandable. One was Leopold Schwarzschild, editor of the Paris *Neues Tagebuch*; the other the economist Jürgen Kuczynski, the furtive editor of the Berlin *Finanzpolitische Korrespondenz*. Aged thirty-two, Kuczynski was a functionary of the banned German Communist party KPD. Some time after he fled to London in January 1936, MI5 expressed curiosity about his wealth and voiced the suspicion that he had brought out the entire KPD funds.[29]

In fact, as he later bragged, he had been financed by Churchill's group. After publishing an anonymous article in Brendan Bracken's *The*

Banker in February 1937, with tongue-in-cheek "calculations" of Hitler's annual arms budget, he had been contacted by "certain circles" and these he had ruthlessly milked of both funds for the Party coffers and secret information for the Soviet Union; these circles, he said by way of identification, were those that came to power in 1940 "with the overthrow of Chamberlain." Kuczynski published an expanded version of the article some months later as a book which his biography would describe as "the first public initiative of the Churchill group in the City against the Hitler regime."

> We can just imagine [adds the biography] the glee of his KPD comrades to see a German comrade marching against German fascism at the head of a section of the City of London.[30]

Kuczynski also drafted a blimpish brochure on *Hitler and the Empire*, to which an RAF air commodore wrote the foreword. "I chose the pen name James Turner," he wrote. "The whole thing was a rather improbable romp." Turner's line was, he chuckled, to deny any personal dislike of fascism — that was a matter for the Germans alone, "If *only* it were not such a danger for the British Empire." The Party printed ten thousand copies. The brochure's closing sentence warned against Hitler:

> Let Great Britain's statesmen be wide awake to the danger to the Empire and act accordingly! Let her take up her rightful place as the outstanding protector of the world's peace and welfare.*

Meeting Kuczynski later, the Soviet ambassador Ivan Maisky roared out these lines, bellowed with laughter, and winked broadly as he did so.

WHO CAN SAY what Churchill really felt about this abyss into which financial misere had plunged him?

Perhaps he had ceased to feel pain. Clementine would reveal to the Canadian prime minister how Winston kept asking her, during these lonely years, whether she thought he would ever return to government, and she would silently shake her head.

In May 1937 Chamberlain became prime minister. Winston was not invited into the Cabinet, and Clementine now told him she did not think he ever would be.[31]

---

*Of this creature MI5 would warn the FBI in 1941, "Since the outbreak of war [he] has been frequently reported as a Communist spreading defeatist propaganda amongst alien refugees." Kuczynski's career climaxed in persuading fellow refugee Dr Klaus Fuchs to defect with Britain's atomic secrets behind the Iron Curtain; both now live in East Germany.

CHAPTER 8

People Are Buying "Churchills"

SOMETIMES, CHURCHILL TOLD a general in 1937, he could not sleep for thinking of the danger to Britain — of how her Empire might be dissipated "in a minute."

"If mortal catastrophe," he would tell the House on March 24, 1938, "should overtake the British Nation and the British Empire, historians a thousand years hence will still be baffled by the mystery of our affairs. They will never understand how it was that a victorious nation, with everything in hand, suffered themselves to be brought low, and to cast away all that they had gained by measureless sacrifice and absolute victory — gone with the wind!"[1]

For a historian born that very day, when the British Empire was at its greatest influence and extent, it is truly baffling to review the archives and compare the specious estimates of Hitler's aims and capabilities in the British records with what is revealed by the German. The former are strewn with the distortions of Britain's foreign-policy making elite, inspired by hatred of Germany imbibed with their mother's milk decades before the Nazis and their atrocities. These men have created legends of magisterial permanence. The legends pollute the history books and have a charm and existence of their own, devoid of any foundation in the archives.

Further comparisons crowd upon the researcher: the businesslike protocols kept by French and German ministries; the total absence of American Cabinet minutes; and the languid letters of self congratulation, oozing self-esteem and virtuosity, in the files of the British Foreign Office. Incoming despatches were slipped into manilla "jackets" on which officials scrawled ironic comments — accumulating collective wisdom like a pearl gathering successive layers of sheen. This was no way to arrive at basic truths. The outcome was a mother-of-pearl reflection of the Office's own culture and prejudices.

Politically, Churchill was staking everything on his claim that Hitler planned to hurl his growing airforce against London, heart of the

Empire. It was now generally believed. The German records, however, reflect only concern about France and the recent treaty between Prague and Moscow which would permit Russia to operate from Czech airfields in a future war.*

At the end of 1936 General Erhard Milch sent to Göring his "Thoughts on Air War."† Contemplating their "probable adversary," he had contrasted the multiplicity of France's targets — munitions and aircraft factories — with Germany's few bomber units (*Staffeln*) even by mid-1937: 96 "heavy" and twelve dive-bomber units (each with nine planes in the first line and three in reserve.)[2]

Meanwhile Mr Churchill and Wickham Steed of The Focus bombarded Whitehall with their own estimates of Hitler's air power and intentions.[3] Sir Herbert Creedy of the War Office warned that further "rebuffs" of Hitler's overtures would change his tune. In scratchy, disjointed handwriting Ralph Wigram — one of Winston's secret sources — inked indignant denials on the "jacket." His minutes during this last year of his young life burgeon with misapprehensions, misspelt names (Ribbentropp) and phobias. "Our only protection seems to be," was one comment, "that if given enough rope the Germans will usually prove to be even more stupid than we are."[4]

Hitler often protested that he had no quarrel with Britain. In the summer of 1935 he naively authorized Göring to offer authentic data on the airforce to Whitehall on condition it was not revealed to other countries (France or Russia). In December he repeated the offer; the F.O. instructed British ambassador Sir Eric Phipps to reject it.[5] Early in July 1936 Milch came over to see Lord Swinton in person, by-passing F.O. channels, and repeated the offer. "General Milch," Swinton told the Committee of Imperial Defence a few days later, impressed, "had made it perfectly clear that he was was not prepared to give information if it were going to be used in Parliament."[6] Overruling F.O. objections, they decided to accept the offer. The figures now released by Milch tallied with the secret estimates worked out by Air Intelligence — a German target of 1,500 first line aircraft by the spring of 1937.[7]

Encouraged, the air ministry sent over to Germany in January 1937 a British mission led by the deputy chief of air staff, Air Vice-Marshal C.L. Courtney.[8] From secret Reich Air Ministry records it is clear that they were furnished with genuine figures.[9] Milch even invited Courtney

---

*The F.O. had reliable evidence that a "subterranean understanding did exist" to this effect. "The balance of evidence," Wigram conceded, "is in favour of General Milch's assumptions."

†The author has been able to use Milch's private diaries and question him exhaustively. He was effectively air minister from 1933 to 1944.

up into his room and let him leaf through the bound volumes containing air plans until the fall of 1938. Reporting this to the Cabinet on February 3 Swinton put Hitler's first line as 1,107 aircraft on New Year's Day, 1937; the British first line consisted of 1,040 in Metropolitan squadrons, 204 in the Fleet Air Arm, and 272 in squadrons overseas — a total of 1,516. The admiralty was receiving German naval data, and had found them bona fide.*

The Churchill group had one obvious recourse, to dismiss the German figures as lies. "Hitler," Sir Robert Vansittart, permanent head of the F.O., wrote to the Cabinet on the following day, "two years ago assured us most solemnly that the German army would never exceed thirty-six divisions and 500,000 men." The manilla jackets collected more ink: it was obvious that "Milch was lying from the start," said one; in June 1937 it was accepted that he had told the truth.

* * *

The motives of the permanent F.O. officials are obscure. Mr Churchill was driven by a different imperative: self-preservation — certainly political, probably financial. He was at his lowest ebb since Gallipoli.

Chartwell had become a financial millstone. His wife had always disapproved of the sprawling mansion. Its extravagance remained a bone between them for forty years. He employed there nine indoor servants — housemaids, personal maids, valets, handyman — as well as three gardeners, a chauffeur, polo pony groom and farmhand. Watching ruin loom, she had begged Winston to watch his step.

Lectured to turn off every light, their children grew up in dichotomy: outward opulence, behind-the-scenes frugality. Sometimes the furniture was dust-sheeted, the mansion closed and a cottage in the grounds opened for the family to hibernate in. None of this financial crisis was visible except to his benefactors, his publishers — whom he importuned for advances — and the local tradesmen whose bills remained unpaid.[10]

Among the benefactors were a new Hungarian and Beaverbrook. The *Evening Standard* was now paying him £60 per article — typical being that on February 5, 1937 which spotlighted the Czechs — "under fear of violent invasion, with iron conquest in its wake."

Already they see the directions given to the enregimented German Press to write them down, to accuse them of being Communists, and in particular,

---

*Hitler was in fact concealing technical breaches of the 1935 Anglo-German naval agreement: the displacements of his new capital ships were more than permitted.

of preparing their airports for a Russian assault upon Germany. Vain to protest their innocence. . .

The Hungarian was Emery Reves. Born Imre Revesz in 1904, he had set up a Leftwing news agency in Paris in 1930. By agreement, he now began to syndicate Churchill's articles around the world. Soon every major Hitler speech was countered by a well-paid Churchill riposte published in most of Europe's capitals — "The new encirclement of Germany!" he quipped to the *Standard*'s editor.[11] Working in tandem with The Focus, Reves commissioned counterfeit anti-Hitler epics still widely cited by the unsuspecting, like Hermann Rauschning's account of non-existent conversations with Hitler.[12]*

Still stockpiling ammunition, against the Government, Churchill accumulated fresh informants. It was all rather hole-in-corner. A typical F.O. "mole" would write a guarded letter from his club, suggest a clandestine meeting, and ask for "a reply to this address and not to the Foreign Office."[13] For months he lay doggo. "W.S.C.," one observer would write to another, "has been very quiet for eight months, which is rather a long time for him."[14]

At the end of March he left for a week's vacation on the Riviera. "I paint all day," he wrote to the near-by Duke of Windsor, to whom he felt bound by the ties of a shared ordeal, "and, so far as my means go, gamble after dark."

Meanwhile, he learned how to manoeuvre at periscope depth. Occasionally he loosed off torpedoes in the House. In mid-April he urged British non-belligerence towards General Franco. There were bellows of Labour dissent. "Winston Churchill," wrote one Tory, "made a terrific speech, brilliant, convincing, unanswerable, and his 'stock' has soared, and today people are buying 'Churchills' and saying once more that he ought to be in the government." "But," added this shrewd observer, "were he to be given office, what would it mean? An explosion of foolishness after a short time? War with Germany?"[15]

In May the new King was crowned. Watching Elizabeth become Queen consort tears of remorse clouded Winston's eyes. He admitted to Clementine the obvious — "The other one," meaning Mrs Simpson, "would never have done." The abdication had cost him dear. Two years later King George VI still spoke unfavourably of his role, and it would be 1941 before Winston was powerful enough to insist, for example, that Canada receive the Duke and Duchess with a guard of honour.[16]

---

*Other Reves beneficiaries included Attlee, Blum, Eden and Duff Cooper. Naturalized British in February 1940, he was whisked out of France in June and transported to New York a year later, where he concocted the "autobiography" of steel magnate Thyssen, *I Paid Hitler*. He later handled the foreign language rights to Churchill's war memoirs.

* * *

Of the new alliances that he forged the most influential was the alliance with the Zionists. This intrusion by Mr Churchill into the history of the barren, holy territories between the Jordan and the Mediterranean was something of an anti-climax.

Since the Canaanites had first settled Palestine for the Arabs in 3500 BC it had been visited by Kings and prophets, by warriors and pilgrims, by warring tribes of Turks, Greeks and Romans, by Moslems and Christians and Jews. Abraham had brought the Jews from Ur of the Chaldees in 2000 BC. Only 380 years later famine drove them to Egypt, where the Pharoahs delivered them into bondage. When Moses led them back to Palestine in 1250 BC, Joshua the son of Nun had commanded his troops besieging Jericho, "Burn ye all that is in the city and slay with the edge of the sword both man and woman, young and old, and ox and sheep, and burn the city with fire and all that is therein." (Joshua, 7:21.) The Jewish kingdom at Samaria (Nablus) fell in 722 BC to Shalmaneser, King of the Assyrians; that at Judah endured 130 more years until Nebuchadnezzar, King of Babylon, put Jerusalem to the torch and transported the Jews to his own country. Seventy years later Cyrus, King of the Persians, returned them to Palestine; they were again conquered there in 332 BC by Alexander the Macedonian.

The Roman legions conquered Palestine in 63 BC and ruled it for seven hundred years, until Caliph the Arab retook it in 637 AD.[17] For nine hundred years the Arabs ruled. Even after Palestine passed under Turkish hegemony in 1517, Arabs and Turks shared government until the Twentieth Century, when British troops moved in upon the break-up of the Ottoman empire in 1918. The League of Nations mandated the territory to Britain. It had fallen to Mr Churchill as colonial secretary in 1922 to draft the terms.

Two years earlier he had written unfeelingly of the Jews, in an article, but even there he had regarded them as an accursed people who should be given a Home of their own.[18] "Nothing could be more significant," he had argued, "than the fury with which [Leon] Trotsky has attacked the Zionists generally, and Dr Weissmann [*sic*] in particular."* "The struggle," he concluded, "which is now beginning between the Zionist and Bolshevik Jews is little less than a struggle for the soul of the Jewish people."

---

*Dr Chaim Weizmann, 1874–1952, an outstanding chemist, was later Israel's first president. From 1921 to 1931 and from 1935 to 1946 he was president of the World Zionist Organization and Jewish Agency for Palestine. The author is indebted to the Weizmann Archives at Rehovot, Israel, for access to their files.

In view of the substantial Jewish financial contribution to The Focus it would have been surprising if Mr Churchill had not become by 1937 a committed Zionist. He explained — to the Peel Commission — that the foreign secretary Balfour, had been motivated by a desire to curry favour with United States opinion when he sent to Lord Rothschild the famous letter ("Declaration") of November 2, 1917 affirming Britain's readiness to establish for the Jews a "home" in Palestine. In London, Zionism had become fashionable: among the Gentile Zionists were Balfour's niece Mrs Blanche (Baffy) Dugdale, Walter Elliot, Leo Amery, Lord Strabolgi and many who turned up in Churchill's secret group, The Focus.

Weizmann would later scan Churchill's *The Second World War* in vain for any reference to his Zionism. "There is not a single word in it," he would write in 1948, "either about Zionism or about Palestine or about his various negotiations with me through these years. It is no doubt a studied omission." He pondered whether to comment on this in his own memoirs. "It will no doubt produce an outburst on the part of Winston," he remarked, "but I really do not care."

Three years later, Churchill used these words in the last letter he ever wrote to Weizmann:

The wonderful exertions which Israel is making in these times of difficulty are cheering to an old Zionist like me.[20]

But in 1937 no colonial secretary could ignore the millions of Moslems in India, balefully watching Britain's attitude to Palestine. The man in the street, wrote Sir Philip Cunliffe-Lister (later Lord Swinton), in November 1933, had no interest in the Balfour Declaration. "The only element we can rely on," he lectured Weizmann and David Ben-Gurion, "is the Moslems." Labour's Jim Thomas, twice colonial secretary despite his humble origins, had roused Zionist anger with a proposed democratic legislative council for Palestine. The 160,000 Jews there were a minority but demanded the majority voice on any council. "It is not fit," Mrs Dugdale huffed in her private diary, "that the future of the Zion should be in the hands of a drunken ex-engine driver."[19] That plan too was dropped. On March 24, 1936 Sir Josiah Wedgwood claimed the credit for having "slain the Palestine Constitution."

I got Churchill and Chamberlain and Amery and Sinclair all to speak and they did, leaving the Rt Hon J.T. Dress-Shirt [Jimmy Thomas] in tears.

Frustrated at the growing stream of immigrants, the Arabs rose in revolt three weeks later. Their rebellion began with the murder of two Jews, and was still smouldering in 1937, costing British lives and siphoning off British troops and arms. A commission under Lord Peel examined Palestine's future, and Mr Churchill was invited to testify before it.

ABRAHAM THE PROPHET; Joshua, son of Nun; Shalmaneser, King of the Assyrians; Nebuchadnessar, King of Babylon; Cyrus, King of the Persians; Alexander the Macedonian, Caliph the Conqueror — the names of those who had determined the Destiny of Palestine were scriptured in the pages of history.

Now, stepping out of the elevator at Morpeth mansions, a Pickwickian figure in temporary financial embarrassment, Destiny in the shape of Mr Churchill took his own place amongst these august arbiters of Zion.

He testified to the Peel Commission on March 12, 1937. His startling proposal was that *all* Palestine be turned over to the Jews. He spoke of their right to immigrate and Britain's "good faith" toward them.

When Peel's deputy Sir Horace Rumbold spoke of the injustice done to the Arabs by this invasion of a "foreign race," Churchill expressed outrage at that phrase, then offered a novel concept of "'just invasions" of which the incumbents of Berlin's Wilhelmstrasse might have been proud:

> Why is there harsh injustice done if people come in and make a livelihood for more, and make the desert into palm groves and orange groves? Why is it injustice because there is more work and wealth for everybody? There is no injustice. The injustice is when those who live in the country leave it to be desert for thousands of years.

As for the "invasion," it was the Arabs who had come in after the Jews, he maintained, and they had allowed the Jewish hill terraces to decay. "Where the Arab goes," he generalized, "it is often desert."

Rumbold may not have known much about the Canaanites, but he did remind Churchill of the Moorish achievements in Spain. "I am glad they were thrown out," was Churchill's only retort. To him all Arabs were wastrels and inferior. Calling for a marked Jewish preponderance he looked forward to the day when Britain had no further duties to "the Arab minority" in Palestine.

Upon reflection he regretted his words about the Moslems and Arabs and asked the commission a few days later to omit them from any permanent record.[21]

The commission decided to partition Palestine between Jews and Arabs, which was less than Mr Churchill asked. He made this clear as principal guest at a small dinner party organized by Weizmann on June 8 at Sir Archibald Sinclair's West London home.

Weizmann disagreed: they should accept partition, but if it was to succeed Britain must allow many more Jews to immigrate each year. Moreover the Jewish state must have defensible frontiers. He chided Leo Amery and Churchill that both had been colonial secretary — yet neither had been able to influence their Government.

"Yes, we are all guilty men," admitted Churchill to Weizmann. "You know, you are our master. And yours," he added pointing to Attlee and Wedgwood, "and yours," to Victor Cazalet and James de Rothschild, the others round the table. "What you say goes. If you ask us to fight we shall fight like tigers."

For all the flowery language, he dismissed Weizmann's proposal for an increase to 50,000 Jewish immigrants a year as a 'mirage.' The Arab rebellion would then become a bloody war. His advice to the commission had been to allow immigration right up to the current limit of 10,000. "By all means let us have a Jewish majority in Palestine," he cried. "I realize we have let the Jews down in the past and it is shameful for us to wake up only when the Jews come unto us in dire distress."

As for partition, he thought it dangerous and unworkable. "The government is untrustworthy," he explained. "They are a lot of lily-livered rabbits. They will chip off a piece here and there."

The Jews, Mr Churchill advised, could do only three things: "Persevere, persevere, and persevere." Later he repeated: "The Jews must hang on."[22] He said much the same to David Ben-Gurion, chairman of the Jewish Agency Executive in Jerusalem. "Our entire tragedy is that we have a weak government."

The Baldwins are idiots, totally lacking in talent etc. . . They are concerned only with deposing and crowning Kings, while Germany is arming and growing stronger, and we are slipping lower and lower.

"But," he prophesied, "this situation will not last long. England will wake up and defeat Mussolini and Hitler, and then your hour will also come."

NEVILLE CHAMBERLAIN HAD just succeeded Baldwin. Still there was no office for Churchill, and his financial crisis remained unmitigated. His new Jewish friends did not desert him. On the first day of June 1937 his attack on the Budget proposals earned plaudits from Lord Melchett ("You are indeed a *very* great man") and Nathan Laski, Harold Laski's father. Sir Robert Waley-Cohen encouraged Churchill to host another luncheon for The Focus on the fourteenth. "I have chosen to go my own way," Winston confirmed on this occasion.[23]

He was navigating into murkier waters. One furtive visitor from Germany was Carl Goerdeler, later hanged as a traitor: Goerdeler, outgoing Prices Commissioner, was conspiring with the disgruntled chief of general staff, Ludwig Beck to overthrow Hitler. As in England, the motives were disparate: Beck had applauded the bloody purge of Ernst Röhm's *SA*, but now he was piqued at Hitler's growing reliance on rival Wehrmacht officers for advice. Visiting London in mid-June 1937 Goerdeler gave economics experts like Frank Ashton-Gwatkin of the F.O. and Sigismund Waley (Schloss) of the Treasury the less than patriotic advice that France and Britain "stand firm" and seize the opportunity to "inflict a diplomatic defeat" on Germany which would enable the moderates to "act."[24]

Czech influence on Churchill also increased, both clandestinely through Wickham Steed and Leeper, and openly through Shiela Grant Duff, the *Observer*'s young correspondent in Prague. In mid-June she begged him to ensure a "firm and unfaltering" attitude by Britain.[25] Churchill encouraged her letters — they were all grist to his mill.

That summer, cash worries crowded his horizon. He interrupted labours on *Marlborough* and the *History* to paste together an anthology of his articles on world personalities; entitled *Great Contemporaries*. It was published in October. To Clementine, vacationing in Austria, he wrote in July that he was overwhelmed with work — "The new book in its final birth throes: articles, & always Marlborough." In an evocative phrase he added, "The well flows freely: only the time is needed to draw the water from it."[26]

The manuscripts laid siege to his senses. When Anderson visited him on August 1 with another airforce officer, worried about pilot training figures, Churchill — unable to listen to Anderson's devotions for long — seized upon the fattening *Marlborough* and recited episodes to the wing commander. "How like the Tory party of those days our present lot is!" he wrote to a researcher months later. "I wish I had studied history at the beginning of my life, instead of at the end."[27]

Of all these historic figures, Hitler fascinated him. Anxious not to offend Beaverbrook, who knew the Führer personally, he published this famous panegyric in the *Evening Standard* on September 17, 1937:

> If our country were defeated I hope we should find a champion as indomitable to restore our courage and lead us back to our place among the nations.

He had moved in a residential secretary — Kathleen Hill, who was musical and widely travelled although only thirty-seven. The costly mansion hummed, and she was bewildered by it all. She had never seen a house like it before — alive and restless, but as still as a mouse when he was away.

Typical of Chartwell was one September evening when Winston

invited down the Prof — to explain a balloon device — and Frank Owen, the *Standard*'s editor. "I found him extraordinarily stimulating," Owen reported to his proprietor, "high spirited, abounding in vigour and full of confidence, very encouraging and kindly." After dinner Churchill turned on the rhetoric, full flood, in defence of liberal democracy against dictators Hitler and Mussolini — "These men of the microphone and murder." Then he switched to the abdication, argued that the Duke should return home. "Better ostracism here," he cried, "than keep a court of dagos on the Loire."

If the Duke flew back tomorrow and drove to the Ritz — "Would there be any demonstration in His Majesty's streets?"

"Not in the streets," laughed Owen, "but probably in His Majesty's Ritz!"

"The kraal of the kaffir," exploded Winston — "the igloo of the eskimo, the sweaty throng of Wall-street — all are more enlightened than the Ritz! God help the State that the Ritz rules!"

Would Fleet Street incite the people to Mob Violence?

I replied [reported Owen] that I confidently expected *The Times* to incite them to Snob Violence.

At this, Winston launched into a diatribe against *The Times* and "the whole sordid crew" in Government. By two a.m. this tireless gentleman had tugged off his outer garments and was marching up and down his bedchamber in his underwear, holding forth on Napoleon, pausing only to fondle a bust of the warlord. He pulled out books of Napoleon's dispatches and declaimed from them to Owen and the Prof, "in execrable French, vilely translated." Owen silently recalled how at Beaverbrook's home, he had seen Churchill urge some Hungarian producer to film Napoleon — the Corsican returning from Elba with forebodings of calamity.

"I think," he wrote that night, "that Winston has both a sense of returning himself, and of the calamity."*

WHEN THE FOCUS lunched secretly at the Savoy on October 3, Churchill invited Eden. Preparing him for the unexpected, he added that Eden would find both Labour and Liberal men there, and even trades unionists; the latter, he suggested, might even be detached from

---

*Entirely without malice — or tact — Beaverbrook sent Owen's uproarious account to Winston on condition that he "treat it with laughter because it is good fun." Churchill was sick with fury. It gave "a loose and sloppy impression" of his remarks, he replied. It would give "gross offence" if ever published. "It gives a vy much better picture of F.O[wen] than it does of me."[28]

particular political parties in the future.[29] Since the foreign secretary had just secured Anglo-French agreement at Nyon on a patrol against Italian submarine piracy, Churchill congratulated him. It looked like a long step towards a Grand Alliance against the dictators.

Hitler did what he could to undermine these exponents of confrontation. He believed friendship with Britain still possible. Sending Joachim von Ribbentrop, the haughty, opinionated businessman who had successfully handled the naval talks in 1935, as his ambassador to London in 1936 he had said "Ribbentrop, bring me back that alliance with Britain!" In May 1937 Ribbentrop recommended that Hitler try to receive Churchill personally — they might still win him as a friend for Germany "as recent personal contacts with the embassy seemed to indicate," a remark he did not amplify.[30]

Churchill and Ribbentrop met occasionally, at social functions like a dinner given by Lord Kemsley. Their dislike was mutual and profound. "If Germany gets too big for her boots," bragged Churchill at one embassy luncheon, "she'll get another thrashing."

Ribbentrop crowed that this time they had the Italians on their side.

"That's only fair," remarked Churchill, puffing at his cigar. "We had them last time."[31]

His only other contact with the Nazis that autumn was when Bradford-born Gauleiter Ernest Bohle visited Morpeth Mansions for an hour's confidential talk; he was chief of Hitler's *Auslands* (Foreign) Organisation which had been coming in for newspaper criticism by Churchill; learning that Ribbentrop was Bohle's bête noir too, Churchill dropped his own attack.[32]

Churchill never met Hitler, but other Britons accepted invitations to Germany. General Sir John Dill, the Director of Military Operations, went over and returned impressed by Hitler's sincerity.[33] The Bristol Aeroplane Company sent aviation expert Roy Fedden around Göring's imposing factories. But now the new British factories were also taking shape; Hankey wrote to Churchill early in October that he had visited half a dozen, huge and well-equipped, covering acres in the Midlands where twelve months before there had been grassland. These were the Shadow Factories — still engaged on peacetime production but laid out with a thought for war.

To Churchill's irritation the air ministry invited General Milch over again, returning his hospitality in January. "How we have been let in for this visitation at the present moment," wrote Group Captain Lachlan MacLean gloomily to Churchill, "is beyond imagination."

"We have invited the German Mission over," Churchill echoed, in an incautious letter to Sir Maurice Hankey on October 16, "— Why, I cannot tell. Highly competent men are coming. A desperate effort is now being made to present a sham-show. A power-driven turret is to be shown, as if it was the kind of thing we are doing in the regular way. Ought it to be shown at all?"

In peaked caps and leather greatcoats the German airforce generals were photographed outside Adastral House, home of the air ministry. On Swinton's orders they were shown over the shadow factories and selected RAF establishments including Cranwell; prototypes of modern military planes — the Wellesley, Blenheim, Harrow, Battle and Whitley — were flaunted to them.

On October 20, Churchill met Milch, a stocky cigar-smoking James Cagney figure, face to face. "Boom" Trenchard had invited the generals to dinner at his Club.

"What d'you think of gliding as a sport?," ventured Churchill, adopting a bantering tone, "D'you think I could pick it up, if I tried to at my age?"

Milch offered the services of the gliding schools in Germany.

"If you value gliding so highly," said Churchill through the cigar smoke, "could you not with profit dispense with powered flight entirely? That would eminently solve our difficulties!"

There were delighted chuckles from his party — Amery, Lord Camrose and Duff Cooper.

"I am convinced," said Milch thickly, "that our Führer would accept such a proposal." He had one condition. "Oh," said Churchill, "and that is?"

"That the Royal Navy revert to those beautiful old sailing ships."

"One-nil to Milch," boomed Swinton.

Back in Berlin, Milch reported to Hitler for two hours on November 2. Hitler questioned him closely about Churchill, and emphasized again his desire for friendship with Britain.[34]

IN PROTESTING ABOUT the Milch visit in his letter to Sir Maurice Hankey, Churchill had betrayed an over-detailed knowledge of the air defences. Hankey sent a blistering reply, regretting that serving officers in a disciplined force had felt able to communicate "backstairs information" to a politician and critic rather than to their proper military superiors. He reminded Churchill that even when years passed before such distasteful episodes were revealed they could annihilate reputations: had not Field Marshal Sir Henry Wilson's reputation been soiled long after his assassination when his wife published his diary, revealing his "trafficking with the Opposition leaders" before the War?[35]

If this was a hint that Hankey knew of Churchill's own "trafficking" with Eden, Attlee, Sinclair and The Focus, he missed the allusion. Stung in his dignity, he made a haughty reply:

I certainly did not expect to receive from you a lengthy lecture when I went out of my way to give you, in strict confidence, information in the public interest. I thank you for sending me the papers back, and you may be sure I shall not trouble you again in such matters.[36]

Unabashed by the magisterial rebuke, only two days later he invited Lord Derby to the next clandestine luncheon on November 2. "We have a small 'focus'," he wrote, "which aims at gathering support from all Parties, especially those of the 'left', for British rearmament, for the association of the two western democracies (France and Britain), and for the maintenance of peace through British strength."

Again Eden, the foreign secretary, joined this little circle at the Savoy.

Churchill also continued to solicit secrets from his sources. In mid November 1937 Anderson handed him another secret memorandum. The wing commander's mental instability was showing — Mrs Pearman, who took his 'phone calls, suggested that the RAF officer "brooded too much" owing to his lonely and introspective life. After one 'phone call now, she typed this note to Churchill: "He said *himself* that you were *not* to think he was not 'balanced', because he was so pessimistic." But it cannot have been easy to regard him as stable. In January 1938 he sent more papers, writing to Mrs Pearman: "Will you give the attached papers to Papa."

While Churchill plodded away through November and December 1937 at *Marlborough*, Mr Chamberlain searched for an alternative to confrontation and rearmament. Göring had extended an invitation to Lord Halifax to visit Germany, and Chamberlain welcomed it. Seeing Eden, their star acquisition, being bypassed, The Focus tried to sabotage the trip but failed.

The Halifax visit was debated in Parliament on December 21. Churchill attacked Hitler's record on the Jews, and argued that Europe's security was better founded on "the power of the French Army and the power of the British fleet." Halifax's success however, encouraged the Cabinet to review Britain's defence budget, "changing the present assumption as to our potential enemies," as Sir Thomas Inskip, Minister for Co-ordination of Defence, delicately put it. "Germany," he pointed out, "has guaranteed the inviolability and integrity of Belgian territory."[37]

An ineffable weariness was overcoming Churchill. At this crucial moment, he went off to spend January 1938 at Maxine Elliot's villa on the Riviera. On the way, he arranged private meetings in Paris with certain French politicians — among them Alexis Léger, Edouard Daladier, and Leon Blum. "I am anxious to persuade him [Blum] to pay us a visit over here," he notified the British embassy, "and I would give him a luncheon at our 'focus' of which I will tell you more when I come."

He was worn out — "He came away on the 2nd," Pearman wrote to the secretary of The Focus, "not before he needed it, as he looked very tired."[38]

There was little sunshine, apart from a brief visit by Eden, and it rained incessantly. Work on *Marlborough* consumed every hour. He had bought a Discavox machine, which recorded his dictation on thin discs of gelatine, but its recording time was only a few minutes, and he abandoned it.

It was early February before he returned to Chartwell. During his month's absence, Churchill was appalled to learn, Chamberlain had removed Vansittart, head of the anti-German F.O., and given him an empty post (Chief Diplomatic Adviser). In Berlin, Hitler had sacked his foreign minister, appointed Ribbentrop in his place, and used two sordid sex scandals both to replace his army commander and to take over the Wehrmacht himself. "Now," Churchill wrote to Maxine, "the whole place is in the hands of violent men."

Ribbentrop was in no doubt as to Britain's earnest (later wartime propaganda to the contrary notwithstanding). "Today," he had warned Hitler, writing in December 1937, "the British governing class is ready and willing to go all the way, i.e., to the point of war, to protect its vital material interests and its position as a world power, so long as there is the slightest chance of victory."

In January 1938 he had underlined this: "In my view, sooner or later Britain will always fight."[39]

Writing this, perhaps Ribbentrop had his altercations with Mr Churchill in mind.

CHAPTER 9

The Grand Alliance

HE MIGHT BE out of office, but by early 1938, Churchill had his own foreign policy and had established his own direct links with foreign governments. While waiting for The Event, he called upon foreign statesmen, sent out personal envoys like Sheila Grant Duff, Francis Deakin or General Spears — Tory MP for Carlisle — and encouraged the diplomatic corps to look upon Morpeth Mansions as a second Court of St James.

That corps in January 1938 was an eccentric gallery.

Joachim von Ribbentrop had left, but re-appeared like a bad penny. The Austrian envoy was Baron Georg Franckenstein, a guilt-stricken diplomat of sixty who would shortly become a British subject and join the British Secret Service rather than risk returning home.[1] The Romanian minister Viorel Virgil Tilea would be stripped of his nationality three years later for his activities in London.

The Czechs were affably represented by Jan Masaryk, fifty-two —a heavily built, well dressed six-footer. Tainted with madness from his maternal ancestors, Masaryk spoke a rapid mid-Atlantic brogue larded with "eloquent profanity," as an American newspaperman wrote; he admitted to being the kind of man who liked to eat hamburgers with the mustard dribbling through his fingers.[2]

Stalin's man in London was Ivan Maisky, a shrewd, porky, Munich-educated Bolshevik of fifty-four. His slant eyes betrayed proud traces of a distant Mongolian ancestry. His job was not easy. Anglo-Soviet relations were at sub-cryogenic temperatures since the appeasement of the Nazis had begun. "Your Neville is a dolt," Maisky had told Winston; "he thinks you can ride a tiger." Churchill was saddling up a different tiger: In his memoirs he owned to "friendly relations" with Maisky, adding that the Russian also "saw a good deal" of Randolph.[3] But Moscow archives show there was more to their meetings than that.

Europe was awash with secret embassy funds. Sir Charles Mendl had destabilised several French governments since his appointment as press attaché in Paris in 1926.[4] The Italians were making lavish "presents" to Mosley.[5] The German embassy wielded substantial sterling funds but their press attaché would bleat: "Buying influence is all but impossible in Britain; neither press nor MPs are corrupt. The only way to influence them is by the lavish luncheon or dinner customary here" — to which he added the not unfamiliar grouch: "Given London prices, this method comes costly enough."[6]

The Czechs were most prolific, although relevant British investigatory files have been closed for seventy-five years.[7] When Robert Boothby, once Churchill's private secretary and now a member of his Focus, was later obliged to resign ministerial office over irregularities involving Czech funds and a certain Mr Weininger he advised the House, as an MP of sixteen years' standing, not to set impossible standards "in view of what we all know does go on and has gone on for years."[8]

The Czech president Dr Edouard Benes had been buying foreigners since the Twenties and not just H. Wickham Steed — ex-editor of *The Times* — and the Leepers. In his files the Nazis found receipts signed by some of the most famous names in British journalism and politics.* By 1938 Czech payments to Englishmen both direct and indirect, were staggering. Spears alone was getting "£2,000 a year from [the] Czechs."[10]

As the 1938 crisis climaxed Benes increased the secret funds to his legations: emergency credits totalling two million crowns were rushed to Masaryk, and the same amount to Stefan Osusky in Paris. The first instalment went to the Midland bank account (£6,988 on May 26 — a significant week in Czech history — and £2,600 on June 10.) The second instalment, of £7,182, would go direct to Masaryk's personal account at Barclay's on September 20. After Benes fled, his successors sent investigators to London; Masaryk refused to co-operate, citing the "unorthodox manner in which the funds had been applied."[11]

VACATIONING ON THE Riviera in January, 1938 Churchill had several times driven down to Cannes. He joined Anthony Eden moodily playing roulette at the Casino. One evening they stacked their chips on No. 17 repeatedly, confounded the laws of probability, and left well rewarded. Neither forgot how number Seventeen kept turning up to redeem their fortunes.[12]

---

*Several are still alive (1987). Nazi radio in Munich reported early in 1939 that Benes had kept such lists and that according to *Cyrano*—a Paris magazine incidentally being "helped" by Mussolini—the Quai d'Orsay had requested Prague not to publish them. The British Foreign Office, pricking up its ears, asked their envoys in Prague and Paris to establish who had "received Czech money during the [Munich] crisis." The envoys stonewalled—it was a "delicate matter".[9]

During Eden's absence on the Riviera, Chamberlain took charge of foreign affairs. His principal advisors were Sir Horace Wilson and Sir Joseph Ball. Ball, director since 1929 of the Conservative Research Department and connected with MI5, was keeping Churchill and other dissidents under surveillance for Chamberlain; Wilson, former industrial adviser to the government, moved into the Treasury a few steps from No.10, becoming one of Churchill's most implacable enemies.

Through Ball, by-passing the obstructive Foreign Office completely, Chamberlain had made overtures to Italian ambassador Dino Grandi in October 1937; Mussolini dealt direct with the PM's sister-in-law, Lady Chamberlain. These illicit contacts continued even after the foreign secretary returned in mid January 1937. Eden's amour propre, already injured beyond repair, was further violated by an episode involving an approach from Roosevelt which Chamberlain fended off without even consulting him. A ridiculous quarrel began which continued for weeks without the Cabinet learning of it.

Unfortunately, neither Ball nor Wilson left notes or diaries; in Cabinet files is only one narrative by Wilson on the crisis that now followed, written three years later. It refers to Eden's "vacillation" over whether or not to improve relations with Italy.

Chamberlain arranged to see Grandi with Eden on Friday the eighteenth to talk about recognizing Italy's claim to Abyssinia. Late on the seventeenth, at a private meeting of MPs — many of them now in The Focus — Churchill urged that they back Eden to the hilt. "We must call a halt," he said, and roused vehement approval. The record of this stirring meeting was placed in Eden's hands, we do not know by whom, on the following morning. It stiffened his resolve.[13]

When they met Dino Grandi that Friday, he and Chamberlain were at loggerheads. They clawed at each other "like two fighting cocks," the chortling Italian telegraphed to Rome.[14] On Saturday the Cabinet learned of their differences. Unexpectedly for the taut, angry Eden and those in his corner, Chamberlain refused to climb down. Unexpectedly too, he did not refer the matter to the House, but left it to the Cabinet to decide which should resign, prime minister or Eden. Eden put up a highly strung performance, and one senior Cabinet member concluded that he was "both physically and mentally ill."[15]

Late on Sunday word was telephoned to Chartwell that Eden's resignation had been accepted.

Winston was shocked. From the ringside, he had followed the infighting with the same predatory relish as the run-in to the Abdication. Now Eden had jumped right out of the ring and was flat on his face. Many times in later years Churchill chided him over the resignation, even when they were at Yalta. But he also asked himself if he had not egged

Eden on. He would spend ten years re-furnishing and re-decorating his memory for his memoirs.

> I had heard something of [the emerging Cabinet differences] but carefully abstained from any communication with Mr Eden. I hoped that he would not on any account resign without building up his case beforehand, and giving his many friends in Parliament a chance to draw out the issues.[16]

Beaverbrook was not taken in. "I have been told differently," he wrote.[17]

Churchill's memoirs also devoted twenty-five melodramatic lines to the sleepless night after Eden's resignation. ("I watched the daylight slowly creep in through the windows, and saw before me in mental gaze the vision of Death.") But what kept Winston awake was a profound relief to other men: more than one wise counsellor slept more soundly for the knowledge that Anthony Eden had put himself beyond the pale. "Today," wrote Hankey, the Cabinet's veteran secretary, setting out his reaction to the news, "I felt there just a possibility of peace;" while Inskip found he could sleep until eight a.m. instead of lying awake, bathed in anxiety.[18]

Indulging his wanderlust Eden trailed back to the Riviera. He would not bother the House with his presence until mid May, but idled at Cap Ferrat, leafing through local newspapers and listening to Radio Vienna, until it became a blaring subsidiary of the Grossdeutscher Rundfunk.

THE FOCUS — NOW domiciled at No. 54 Fleet Street in London — made what capital it could out of his departure. Labour called a vote of censure, Churchill spoke, and over twenty Tory MPs including all of those now embraced by The Focus abstained; among them were Harold Nicolson, Derrick Gunston, Ronald Cartland, Paul Emrys-Evans and Harold Macmillan, a leftwing Conservative who had been brought into the group by Waley-Cohen; one Focus man, Vyvyan Adams, even voted *against* the Government.

The Focus confidentially circularized other MPs who had abstained. One was General Spears. The letter invited him "at the personal request of Mr. H. Wickham Steed" to "a small meeting of our Focus to discuss questions of policy" on March 1. He was assured that he would be present in his private capacity and that the "Defence of Freedom and Peace" (as The Focus overtly styled itself) was not a new and rival political party, just 'a Focus' of influential people meeting periodically for "discussions across the gulf of politics."[19]

At the Savoy on the appointed day Spears found his friend Churchill presiding over the expensive luncheon. After the platters had been cleared and brandy and cigars passed round, Winston rose and spoke scathingly of his Party leader's policies. He talked of Britain nosing from door to door mooing dolefully like a cow that had lost its calf, now in Berlin, now in Rome — "When all the time the tiger and the alligator wait for its undoing."[20]

The campaign lost him some benefactors. He had written flatteringly of Hitler in September 1937, and of Mussolini as recently as October. Beaverbrook still bristled, and printed a lead article accusing Churchill of "lending himself to the most violent, foolish and dangerous campaign to drive this country into war since he drove us into it himself against Russia in 1919."[21]

DURING THESE MONTHS Churchill had developed his strategic theory of a Grand Alliance — a formal alliance between Britain and France, to replace the present loose, unstipulated arrangements; to this new alliance should be added the Soviet Union and the smaller countries of Central Europe.

Chamberlain was pragmatic. He told Lord Halifax, the languid, easy-going successor to Anthony Eden, that in a crisis the Czechs would appeal not to "collective security" but to France and Britain, neither of whom was ready for war. "Therefore," argued Chamberlain, "this problem must be settled practicably." He repeated these words to the new American ambassador later that day, March 4.[22]

The ambassador was Joseph P. Kennedy, one of the more controversial appointments made to the Court of St James. To Dorothy Schiff, publisher of the *New York Post*, Roosevelt would guffaw that sending a millionaire Boston Irishman to England was "the greatest joke in the world." But he had other reasons than purely jocular. Kennedy had part-financed his campaigns; but when he nonetheless gave the U.S. Treasury to Henry Morgenthau Jr., Kennedy had become a virulent critic. "Kennedy," F.D.R. remarked to Morgenthau, "is too dangerous to have around here."[23] That is why he had shipped him abroad.

Joseph Kennedy lunched with Winston and Randolph at Morpeth Mansions on Wednesday March 9, 1938. He was a man with the kind of tall, loose-limbed charm that unlimited wealth does bring. He was pushing fifty, a Harvard graduate who had grown wealthy by sleazy stock dealings; he had made millions from the merger of Pathé and RKO, many said by defrauding stockholders.

Kennedy waved aside the proffered glass and smiled a toothy grin. He didn't drink, smoke or gamble, so any real intimacy with Churchill seemed unlikely. Powerful men did not intimidate him, he confessed later: peering at them through eyeglasses in circular rims set close together, he slyly visualized them in red frilly underwear and lost all awe of them. He had sparse sandy hair like Churchill's but there the similarity ended. "He has an athlete's figure," *Liberty* wrote a few weeks later, "a clean-cut head, clear straight-shooting eyes, a flashingly infectious smile and faultless taste in dress."[24]

Churchill told the new ambassador of the deal that Ribbentrop was offering: Germany undertook not to proceed westwards, but wanted her colonies back; and Britain must turn a blind eye on what Hitler undertook to the east. It was pure "fallacy," said Churchill, to delay the showdown until Britain had rearmed. He wanted it now, on whatever pretext. Hitler's army would soon be larger than the French, and his airforce was gaining on the RAF with every month.[25]

Kennedy had both family — four sons — and fortune, and didn't propose to lose either in somebody else's showdown, as he put it later. He told Washington that he had found in Britain's prime minister "a strong character and realistic mind;" but, as for Mr Chamberlain's most powerful opponent, it may well be that as Kennedy left Morpeth Mansions he found himself visualizing the paunchy, cigar-smoking Englishman in frilly red underwear.

"EVENTS!" CHURCHILL HAD once proclaimed: they would be his ally.

Later that same Wednesday he learned that — in apparent violation of an agreement that had been extracted from him at Berchtesgaden by Hitler — the Austrian chancellor Dr Kurt Schuschnigg had announced a snap plebiscite for Sunday March 13.

Perhaps The Focus had urged this risky idea on Vienna. (The Anti-Nazi Council, its *alter ego*, maintained offices in Vienna as well as London and Prague.) Writing in the *Standard* as early as March 4, Churchill had certainly touched upon a plebiscite, expressing confidence that if they could vote fairly and without fear, two-thirds of all Austrians would support their country's independence.

In the upshot, there was little to choose between Schuschnigg and Hitler when it came to rigging referenda: only *Yes* ballot forms were printed in anticipation of that Sunday; the text made it treasonable to vote *No*; voters had to insert their addresses; and the voting age was raised to twenty-four, above the average age of Austrian Nazis.[26]

The ballot never took place. Hitler's tanks clattered into Austria early on Saturday March 12 — the sound of music in Churchill's ears: who would deny the truth of his assertions now?

Ten years later he wrote a characteristic memoir: as chance would have it, he claimed, he was that very day attending Chamberlain's farewell luncheon for Ambassador von Ribbentrop at No.10 Downing Street — telegrams interrupted their repast — Hitler was invading Austria — his mechanised forces were advancing upon Vienna. He clearly recalled how the villainous von Ribbentrop had deliberately "tarried for nearly half an hour," engaging Chamberlain "in voluble conversation" to keep him away from work and telephone, ignoring every hint to leave.

> At length Mr Chamberlain said to the Ambassador, "I am sorry I have to go now to attend to urgent business," and without more ado he left the room. . . The Ribbentrops lingered on, so that most of us made our excuses and our way home. Eventually I suppose they left.

"This," his ungenerous narrative would conclude, "was the last time I saw Herr von Ribbentrop before he was hanged."[27]

As so often, the truth was different: Ribbentrop's records, which outlived him, show that Hitler treated him no better than Chamberlain treated Eden; he was completely in the dark.[28] Moreover, the farewell luncheon with Churchill was on Friday March 11, the day *prior to* the invasion; and the Churchills left *before* the day's telegrams, ominous enough in themselves, arrived.[29]

True, a restlessness did pervade the luncheon company toward the end: but it was the impatience of Neville Chamberlain as he waited for Winston and Clementine to leave: he had an urgent personal message for Hitler to discuss with Ribbentrop — alone.

Eventually Winston gathered up his hat. "I hope," he lisped to the Ribbentrops, "England and Germany will preserve their friendship."

"Be careful you don't spoil it," Frau von Ribbentrop rejoined.

The telegrams were from Vienna: The Nazis were insisting that the plebiscite be postponed; Schuschnigg had cancelled it; on instructions from Berlin Dr Arthur Seyss-Inquart, the Nazi lawyer appointed minister of the interior as a result of the Berchtesgaden talks, had issued an ultimatum to appoint him chancellor instead. Schuschnigg resigned.

The finality of it all took Churchill's group by surprise. That same Friday, Bracken was writing to Bernard Baruch: "No one here knows what may happen in Austria on Sunday. There is a rumour — probably a baseless one — that Hitler may march his troops into Austria on the pretext of 'keeping order'." Significantly, Churchill's friend hoped that this would lead to "a showdown with the German bullies."[30]

On Saturday morning Hitler's troops crossed into Austria at the new chancellor's bidding. "There can be no doubt," Churchill grumbled in a letter to Unity Mitford, repeating his *Evening Standard* prediction, "that a fair plebiscite would have shown that a large majority of the people of Austria loathe the idea of coming under Nazi rule."[31] He hurried back to London on Monday March 14, past bands and populace trudging down Park Lane chanting "Chamberlain Must Go!"

> Europe [he told the House that day] is confronted with a programme of aggression, nicely calculated and timed, unfolding stage by stage,

and there is only one choice open, not only to us: . . . Either to submit like Austria, or else to take effective measures while time remains.

He now stated his call for a solemn treaty of mutual defence organized by Britain and France, "what you may call a Grand Alliance."

Later that afternoon he and Chamberlain discussed the idea with Halifax and Cadogan.

The PM was scornful: "You have only to look at the map," he wrote his sister a few days later, "to see that nothing that France or we could do could possibly save Czechoslovakia." The frontier facing Austria was virtually unfortified. He had abandoned any idea of guaranteeing Czechoslovakia.[32]

Chamberlain's attitude was guided by realism, not pessimism. With Churchill's warning of the enemy "knock out blow" against London firmly in their minds, his chiefs of staff agreed with him. Britain, they advised the Cabinet, was totally unprepared for the world war that must result. She could send only two poorly equipped divisions to the Continent. Of twenty-seven fighter squadrons, twenty were obsolete; there were no medium or heavy anti-aircraft guns, and no air-raid shelters. If Italy and Japan joined in, the Empire would be wide open to attack.[33] The Cabinet decided to press Dr Benes to come to terms with his German minority.

Would France go along with appeasement? Chamberlain, whose crony Joseph Ball was privately monitoring certain telephone lines, suspected that Leon Blum's French government was "in closish touch with our Opposition." "There are all sorts of intrigues afoot," wrote Cadogan in his diary, mentioning Winston's name; he added: "God help us all."[34]

Churchill made plans to fly immediately to Paris; but for various reasons he postponed it by a week.[35]

ONE OF THOSE reasons was the personal crisis that now towered over Churchill. He was living from hand to mouth in the shadow of a sheer granite overhang of revenue demands. Late in 1937 he had begun pirating his own works, selling a ten-part variant of "My Life" to the Sunday Chronicle.[36] His foreign markets were shrinking. As Austrian Nazis hounded down their opponents and oppressors, the Vienna newspapers stopped printing his articles syndicated by Emery Reves.

In the second week of March 1938 a slump wiped out Churchill's American stockholdings. Becoming uneasy about them while still at Cannes he had inquired of Baruch whether to sell. Baruch had telegraphed back: "See it through. Bernie."[37] The advice was wrong: the stocks collapsed; suddenly his share account with London stockbrokers

Vickers, da Costa & Co was £18,000 in the red, and they wanted payment.

Stricken by this cruel misfortune, he told Bracken on the eighteenth that he was quitting politics for good. He wanted time to complete his *History*; completion by the due date — the end of 1939 — would enrich him by £15,000. "But how," observed Bracken, this Man Friday, in a memo, "is he to do this while events run at this pitch, still less if he should be required to devote his whole energies to public work?"

Bracken passed word of Churchill's insolvency around City financiers. "I cannot tell you," Winston wrote to him, "what a relief it would be if I could put it out of my mind; and take the large decisions which perhaps may be required of me without this distraction and anxiety."

HE MADE A final throw, although it was a paradox of which he was himself aware. Having for years castigated the government for Britain's military inferiority he now began demanding, as he had urged on Kennedy three days before Hitler invaded Austria, a preventive war. His brassy reasoning was that now Germany and her opponents were equally matched. Later the gap would widen.

Vestiges of this ambivalence still showed when he met mutinous MPs at Pratt's Club on March 16. He talked of their "blind and obstinate" leaders, and threatened to refuse the Whip and take fifty Tory MPs with him unless Britain staged a showdown: "We stand to lose everything by failing to take some strong action," he growled on this occasion. But then he reverted to the "knock-out-blow" theory he had propagated so often before. "If we take strong action," he prophesied, "London will be a shambles in half-an-hour."[38]

Two days later his *Evening Standard* article was less equivocal in justifying an early showdown:

> Many high authorities believe that the German army is not yet in a condition to undertake a major aggressive land war. Neither her stores of raw materials nor the state of her officer-cadres are sufficiently complete to encourage during the present year a hasty challenge to a group of well-armed States, with Great Britain and France at the core.

Churchill had high hopes of the French army. Those who knew her statesmen and generals, he would write a month later, realized her immense latent strength better than the casual observer: "They see the French army always on the watch. Part of it mans the ramparts round the country. The rest constitutes," he maintained. "the most perfectly trained and faithful mobile force in Europe."[39]

The PM and foreign secretary did not share his awe of either French or Russian might. Halifax called Mr Churchill's plan unrealistic: under it, the French army, merely by manning the Maginot Line, was to deatin large German forces while Czechoslovakia engaged the rest; it did not explain how the French defenders could detain forces if the enemy declined to address them — as happened a year later. Churchill's plan for a British-French-Russian alliance, warned the foreign secretary, would look as though Britain was "plotting to encircle Germany."

AWARE THAT CHAMBERLAIN would make a major foreign policy statement to the House on the morrow, Churchill invited the Soviet ambassador to breakfast at Morpeth Mansions that morning, March 23. Gnome-like, Ivan Maisky's feet seemed not to reach the floor as he sat at the table.[40]

Churchill began by expressing concern about Stalin's purge of the Red Army; he needed to know the facts for the next day's debate. "Twenty years ago," he told Maisky, anxious to assuage the Russian's natural suspicions about him, "I fought with all my strength against communism. I considered communism with its doctrine of world revolution the greatest threat to the British Empire. Now," he continued, "Communism does not pose such a threat to the Empire. On the contrary, now the greatest threat to the British Empire is Nazism, with its doctrine of world domination by Berlin."

"As I've several times told you in the past," he explained, "I hate Nazi Germany and am campaigning hard for the formation of a 'Grand Alliance' within the framework of the League of Nations for the struggle against Germany." While this alliance ought to embrace all "peace-loving nations" the main role would devolve upon Britain, France and Russia. "A strong Russia is absolutely essential," he continued, "but people keep telling me that as a result of recent events Russia is finished as a serious factor in international politics. Pray set aside my doubts."

Maisky explained the rationale behind Stalin's ruthlessness. (A decade later he would barely escape the same dictator's anti-Jewish purge.) Churchill listened keenly, puffing at a cigar, occasionally interrupting with intelligent questions or observations. "When I had finished," Maisky reported to Moscow, Churchill exclaimed,

> "Well, thank God you've set my mind at rest! I loathe Trotsky, and I've been following his activities for a long time. I considered him the evil genius of Russia. I am all for Stalin's politics. He is creating a powerful Russia, and that's what we need — more than anything."

Churchill outlined his own plan: Ought not the Soviet army demonstrate that rumours of its demise were an exaggeration? Some kind of action was called for: Maisky asked what he had in mind and Churchill suggested a solemn declaration that Russia would give significant aid to Czechoslovakia if invaded. "This need only be, of course," he added, "on condition France fulfils her obligations. But of that I have no doubt."

Maisky replied dubiously that it was common knowledge that the Soviet Union honoured its obligations.

"I am aware of that," interjected Churchill. "Stalin is a solid and reliable fellow. He keeps his word. All the same, there are times when it is important to emphasize even something that is common knowledge. Now, for instance."

MAISKY CHANGED THE subject: how were things in England?

Churchill replied that a "ministerial crisis" had threatened Chamberlain a few days before, and he had agreed to modify his policies. The PM had given him certain undertakings, and he had accordingly agreed to delay his visit to Paris. He promised Maisky that he was going to trip up Chamberlain wherever he could in the next day's debate: an early Cabinet reshuffle would soon see Churchill and perhaps Eden as well back in office, perhaps in a coalition with the Opposition. Major legislation — on conscription, trades-union reform and the abolition of restrictive practices to step up arms production — would need Opposition support, and they loathed Chamberlain.

He was confident that Hitler was not planning an early strike against Czechoslovakia. He might try meanwhile a backdoor annexation of Hungary, then go on to Romania, isolating Czechoslovakia from the outside world; she could then be destabilized from within using the Sudeten German minority and economic pressure. "She will lose her nerve," he predicted, "and drop into Hitler's hands like ripe fruit."

> Hitler is aiming at creating a "Central European Bloc" from Germany to the Black Sea and the Mediterranean. In four or five years he'll be able to realise his dream if he isn't stopped in time.

This, reasoned Churchill, was why they had a common interest in fighting Hitler. "If," he concluded, "the fascist threat to the Empire were to disappear and re-emerge again in communism, then — let me be completely frank with you — I would resume the fight against you. But I don't foresee such a situation arising in the immediate future. Certainly not before I die."

Maisky calculated: the Englishman at the far end of the breakfast table was sixty-three.

"For the time being," said Churchill, "you and we must travel the same path."

* * *

In the House on March 24, 1938 Chamberlain agreed to step up rearmament. But Britain, he defined, would use force only to defend the Empire's immediate interests, which included France, Belguim and certain other countries with which she had treaty obligations.

This did not satisfy Churchill. He demanded a formal military alliance with France, and a Ministry of Supply to ensure the orderly manufacture of war materials. He blamed the slowness of rearmamanet on the Cabinet system of government.

"Twenty-two gentlemen of blameless party character," he declaimed, "sitting round an overcrowded table, each having a voice — is that a system which can reach decisions from week to week and cope with the problems descending upon us?"

The system had broken down hopelessly in the last war — they needed a new system for this one: because this was not peace in which they were living now. "Is it not war without cannon firing? Is it not war of a decisive character, where victories are gained and territories conquered, and where ascendancy and dominance are established over large populations with extraordinary rapidity?"

He decided to visit France that weekend. As Ivan Maisky had reported, Churchill's "politics and intrigues are without a doubt unique and of the highest order."[41]

THAT DAY LORD Beaverbrook delivered a right hook to this apostle of confrontation. The *Evening Standard* ended his lucrative contract, with the barest minimum of notice. The newspaper proprietor who had boasted so often of his liberalism towards his writers, would tolerate no longer that Winston both ran with the hare and hunted with the hounds. It was an abrupt end to the Beaverbrook-Churchill axis.

It should have come as no surprise. The Canadian newspaperman was by 1938 everything that Winston wasn't: anti-League, a closet admirer of Hitler, and anti-war. Still an isolationist, in recent weeks he had become a believer in rearmament, but only for its deterrent value. When a *News Chronicle* leader writer — now covertly in The Focus — badgered him to campaign for Winston's return to office, Beaverbrook sent this withering reply: "Unhappily he would bring pressure upon the government forthwith to give a guarantee to Czecho-Slovakia that we will fight in defence of that artificial nation, brought into existence by Messrs [Lloyd] George, Clemenceau, and [Woodrow] Wilson." He wanted the soldiers to stay at home, guard Britain, her Empire and its outposts.[42]

Beaverbrook was aware of the rumours as to who was bankrolling the Bring Back Winston campaign. Upon his recent return from Miami, he had used infelicitous words about the people sabotaging rapprochement. "There are twenty thousand German Jews in England," he wrote "in the professions, pursuing research, in chemical operations, etcetera. These all work against such an accommodation."*

"The Jews have got a big position in the press here," this Press lord rasped in another exasperated, ill-considered letter. "One third of the circulation of the *Daily Telegraph* is Jewish. The *Daily Mirror* may be owned by Jews, the *Daily Herald* is owned by Jews. and the *News Chronicle* should really be the *Jews Chronicle*. . . I am not sure about the *Mail*." For years, he continued, he had prophesied there would be no war. "But at last I am shaken. The Jews may drive us into war. I do not mean with any conscious purpose of doing so. They do not mean to do it. But unconsciously . . . their political influence is moving us in that direction."[44]

The ending of the *Standard* contract might have been the coup de grace for Churchill. We can imagine with what bitterness he now asked *The Times* to advertise his beloved Chartwell for sale. The advert would appear on the second day of April, inviting offers of £20,000 (about £1m in today's values.)

A few days before that date, on March 28, 1938, he was saved.

Bracken's South African friend Sir Henry Strakosch, the Gold mining millionaire and chairman of Union Corporation Ltd., agreed to pay off Churchill's debts.[45] Strakosch was a Jew born in Moravia, Czechoslovakia. Chartwell was withdrawn from the market, and Churchill campaigned on.

---

*For what it is worth, the Aga Khan would assure a diplomat in 1940 that Churchill had "for years" been in the pay of the Jews *and* Lord Beaverbrook![43]

CHAPTER 10

"Let's Wait And See," Said Maisky
(April-May 1938)

THE PLEBISCITE HELD under Nazi auspices did not bring the result Churchill had predicted. Forty-nine million Austrians and Germans were jointly asked, "Do you accept Adolf Hitler as our Führer, and do you thus accept the reunification of Austria with the German Reich as effected on March 13, 1938?" Over ninety-nine percent voted "Yes."*

It jolted the British Foreign Office. "I can't help thinking," observed the new permanent head, "we were very badly informed about feeling in that country." Britain, he felt, would have been very wrong to prevent the Anschluss against the wishes of "to put it mildly" such a majority; she had only vetoed the Anschluss, he now recognized, "to spite Germany."[2]

Czechoslovakia was obviously next. This artificial implant in post-war Central Europe had been vigorously rejected by her neighbours: her only friends were in Moscow, Paris and London. Her population consisted of Czechs and Slovaks, but of Poles, Hungarians, and Ruthenes too — and of three million Germans in the Sudeten region.

As part of his eastward strategy Hitler planned to get those Germans back. On March 19, 1938 his propaganda minister circularized Nazi editors to soft-pedal the term *grossdeutsch* — greater German: It might be taken to imply that Germany's appetite was "satisfied" with Austria. Nine days later we find Hitler and Ribbentrop conniving with the Sudeten German leader Konrad Henlein, and the High Command ordering the reinforcement of Austrian road bridges on the way to the Czech frontier. On April 5 the general staff told General Wilhelm Leeb that he would command Seventh Army, operating from Austria into Czechoslovakia.†

---

*Voting was on April 10, 1938. The ballot was secret, but in some districts concealed markings were used to pinpoint spoiled and "No" votes for future reference.[1]
† *The War Path*.

CHURCHILL TINKERED AT his Grand Alliance. He flew to Paris on March 25, arousing the curiosity of London diplomats. What was he up to now? Was he working for or against Chamberlain?³ He spread rumours that he was on a semi official mission — to get France's statesmen to agree on a government of national concentration; Whitehall assured Italian ambassador Dino Grandi that these press stories were untrue: Mr Churchill had gone of his own volition. Reporting to Rome, Grandi sized him up as "the most authoritative representative" of a group of "ambitious, malcontent and power-hungry" opponents of Chamberlain.

True, Churchill was ambitious. But he was no fool: he arranged the Paris meetings through the embassy, and slept under its roof. When he asked to meet known Communists, however, the ambassador drew the line.

It was a mad gourmet weekend. Winston dined tête-à-tête with Edouard Herriot, president of the Chamber; he lunched with Paul Reynaud and supped again with foreign secretary Joseph Paul-Boncour and prime minister Leon Blum. "Why do you French," he asked each one of them in turn, "bother to vote large sums of money to increase your Navy?" British naval superiority over the German and Italian navies was absolute and could cover all France's Mediterranean interests. "You," he urged, "should concentrate on your airforce." The French had only 250 obsolete fighters and 320 bombers.

Like a streetcleaner after a cavalry parade, Sir Eric Phipps followed Churchill round the Paris salons, bucket and shovel in hand, cleaning up. He cautioned the French politicians to take what Winston said with a grain of salt: he spoke for only a tiny minority: he was "not the arbiter of our destinies."⁴ After Blum's tottering government was shortly replaced by one under Edouard Daladier, the ambassador suggested that Halifax now visit Paris with Chamberlain to "put things into somewhat better proportion than they have been left by Winston."

To France's statesmen Churchill was a phenomenon. He spoke an eccentric — some said execrable — French. Declaring to Blum: "We must make good," he translated it literally by, "Nous devons faire bonne!" This might be loosely translated as "We've got to make the house-maid."⁵'' It was an emotional evening. Leon Blum was in distress over his wife's death, and Phipps saw both men's eyes filled with tears.⁶

Churchill spent some hours with Louis Marin, Jules Sauerwein of *Le Soir*, colonial minister Georges Mandel and Camille Chautemps — Blum's immediate predecessor — advocating staff talks and grand alliance. The chief of general staff Maurice Gamelin had doubts about that alliance. "The Red Army," he objected, "has soldiers, officers, arms, planes, tanks — all of these, but does it have *morale*?"⁷

Churchill particularly liked what he saw of Alexis Léger, the dapper, fifty-year old secretary-general of the French Foreign Office. Léger was the Vansittart of the Quai d'Orsay — obsessively anti-German, and at the forefront of the intrigues against Daladier.[8] On Phipp's advice he was not included in Daladier's visit to London in April, and was eventually dismissed: No. 10 awarded him the GBE and a KCVO, and Mr Churchill would in 1940 urge even higher honours.*

Churchill returned to London from Paris on March 29.

Perhaps unwilling to be seen in too frequent communication with the Soviets, he sent his son to report to Ivan Maisky on the trip. Young Randolph told the ambassador that they had found support there for the Grand Alliance, but that feelings towards Moscow were cool. Winston had extolled the French army, and wanted Maisky to know that France would honour her commitments to Czechoslovakia.

> Randolph Churchill also notified me [Maisky told Moscow] that very influential Cabinet members are working on Chamberlain about the need to bring his father into the government immediately.

Winston's plan was, confided his son, to make Lord Swinton the scapegoat for the poor condition of the RAF and to replace him as Secretary for Air.

"I have heard so often before," reflected Maisky in his secret telegram to Moscow, "about Churchill's imminent re-admission into the Cabinet that I am inclined to view such information somewhat skeptically."

> The root of the matter lies in Churchill himself — powerful and headstrong at a time when other Cabinet members are distinguished only by colourless mediocrity. . . Churchill would tower head and shoulders over the lot of them, especially in a crisis.

Still, some Conservatives might feel it expedient to have this voice muted inside the Cabinet, rather than outside.

"Let's wait and see," he said.[10]

CHURCHILL HAD BEGUN clumsy efforts to school Randolph with the wider virtues as he grew older. He was harnessing him at that moment to extracting and editing his major speeches for *Arms and the Covenant*. But Randolph had a drinking problem and was difficult to handle. A typical scene blazed up that spring of 1938 when Randolph taunted his father over what he — probably correctly — perceived as naive

---

*"As M Léger's services have been dispensed with by his Gov't," minuted Sir Alexander Cadogan, "I fear it would not be a good moment at which to confer on him a signal honour."[9] Léger thereupon emigrated to Washington and joined the Library of Congress as a consultant.

attempts to curry favour, and over one dinner he tactlessly reminded his father of one such gift sent to War Minister Leslie Hore-Belisha in February.

Winston found this jibe "singularly unkind," and, as he wrote curtly to his son, "offensive, & untrue." He refused to speak to Randolph. His son wrote a contrite apology, which attracted a further paternal slap: "I was about to write to you," wrote Winston haughtily, "to ask you to excuse me from coming to luncheon with you on Thursday, as I really cannot run the risk of such insults being offered to me, & do not feel I want to see you at the present time."[11]

In a reply of almost feline jealousy, Randolph retorted that he did not see why his father should not show him the same friendship and respect that he showed to "that amiable flibbertigibbet," Brendan Bracken. This extraordinary mutual flagellation of frustrated father and only son continued in letters for several days, illustrating vividly the flaring tensions consuming them both as they saw a famous career seemingly draw fruitlessly to a close without the Event it needed.

A FEW DAYS after the confidential briefing of Maisky, Winston spoke to a lady who had the ear of Prague about his hopes of persuading Russia to help against Germany.[12]

Inevitably, it meant compromising on some of his beliefs. A week before seeing Maisky he had written nobly in the *Evening Standard* of the right of the Sudeten Germans to expect "good treatment and equal citizenship" from Prague. Since then, the Moravian born Strakosch had paid off his £18,000 debts; and Churchill no longer had to humour Beaverbrook. By May 7, in a letter to his stockbroker, he would be calling the Sudeten Germans "the best treated minority in Europe."

Significantly, he also evacuated his shell-cratered position on the Spanish civil war. It had taken sustained bombardment after he published praise of General Franco on August 10 and 21, 1936, even more after the articles of January 8 and April 2, 1937. On April 14 of that year he had defiantly told the House: "I will not pretend that if I had to choose between Communism and Nazism I would choose Communism."

Since then he had shifted his weight to his left foot. "Until recently," he admitted in conversation on November 1, "I was for Franco for this reason: victory for the Reds in Spain would put tyrants and extremists into power and their inevitable atrocities would estrange British public opinion." The Italian ambassador, to whom a mutual friend quoted these remarks, reported him as adding: "If the British find Bolshevism right on their doorstep they'll react against it." Then no British government could establish close links with a Radical Socialist France against Hitler. Contemplating the further danger of Italian bases in a fascist Spain, Churchill now expressed doubts that it would be "expedient to allow Franco to win."[13]

After seeing Maisky he developed this theme in public:

> A thoroughly Nazified Spain [he wrote on April 5, 1938] retaining its German nucleus would be a cause of profound anxiety both to France and Britain.

The more he wooed the Kremlin, the more pronounced became his hostility. "Nothing," he would scoff two days before the end of 1938, "has strengthened the Prime Minister's hold upon well-to-do society more remarkably than the belief that he is friendly to General Franco and the Nationalist cause in Spain." He added, "It would seem that today the British Empire would run far less risk from the victory of the Spanish [Republican] Government than from that of General Franco."

With Franco's victory in April 1939, the transformation was complete: on the twentieth of that month Churchill would claim that Franco was preparing to attack British Gibraltar. Reports, he further claimed, were streaming in of "concentrations of troops and preparations of aerodromes behind the Pyrenees, and of submarine bases on the north coast of Spain."

To those who had followed his career since 1935 it rang familiar. His four-seasons attitude to Franco was, albeit on a larger canvas, a copy of one cameo in October 1937 that he had probably forgotten: in one Friday's *Evening Standard* he had headlined an article: "War is Not Imminent." In the *Sunday Chronicle* two days later he uttered a cry of alarm about the peril of war descending at that very moment upon Europe.[14]

AMONG THOSE TORY MPs who had joined The Focus was Sir Louis Spears. Born Spiers in 1886, this military gentleman had been British liaison officer to the French high command, and had anglicized his name in 1918. Retiring as a brigadier-general, he had married a lady novelist from Chicago; her brother lost every penny of the Spears fortune when Wall Street crashed, but since then Spears had gone into business and was now earning £15,000 per annum.[15]

Like many in the Churchill group, he was financially in the thrall of the Czechs. The Czech president Dr Edouard Benes, a friend for twenty years, had invited the MP onto the board of the steelworks at Vitkovice, sited in Moravia within tempting distance of both Poland and Germany. This gave Spears a hefty interest in Czechoslovakia indeed, quite apart from other "considerations" and in 1938 he shuttled between

Prague, London and Paris in a way that Churchill could not politically afford.[16]*

Two days after Hitler's troops entered Austria Benes told Spears his tactics: he had his 1924 treaty with France; about a million Czechs had been trained, and he was going to "play for time" to complete his defences. On the previous day, he added, the Russians had promised him "an absolute minimum" of one thousand planes; his airfields were ready to receive them.[17]

That was in mid-March 1938. Early in April, Churchill directed his good looking young researcher Francis Deakin, who was also about to visit Prague, to ask Benes what "we can do to help."[18]

Despite these clattering distractions, Winston had to keep writing. The *History* overwhelmed his hours. On the sixth, the *Daily Telegraph* nervously agreed to a six-month trial of his articles; encouraging the newspaper's proprietor, Lord Camrose, he mentioned the Reves syndicate as evidence of worldwide interest in his articles — "Though as the Nazi power advances, as in Vienna," he admitted ruefully, "planks are pulled out of it."

His "interface" with the political power centres was still The Focus. Not surprisingly, the archive material about the links between Churchill and The Focus under its various aliases, and about its fringe activities, is sparse — but the circumstantial evidence is strong: He was its powerhouse. He hosted its luncheons, he was its sole protégé. It shared members, finance, and operational addresses with those who now ventured into less passive fields. And this it now did, after Austria: on April 13 Wickham Steed circuitously explained to Spears that he was now "getting our 'focus' into action" in support of a positive policy.

The first such operation would be an orthodox mass meeting funded by The Focus at Manchester, calling itself here "Peace and Freedom within the League." When first approached for this away fixture by the Focus on April 2, Churchill showed reluctance. Sir Henry Strakosch had paid off his debts five days before; perhaps he felt he could dispense with The Focus? But he himself had once said that he who rides a tiger finds it difficult to dismount. The Focus called a special luncheon in strict privacy at the Savoy four days later: "Winston wobbled a good deal," Wickham Steed described afterwards to Spears, "but has now agreed to kick off at Manchester on May 9, with [Lord] Derby in the Chair."[20]

---

*The Wittkowitz Bergbau-und Eisenhütten-Gewerkschaft manufactured armourplate, partly for British navy contracts. The Austrian Rothschilds held the 53 percent controlling share. In 1938 the well-informed Rothschilds transferred the company to the Alliance Assurance Company, a London Rothschild firm. Blackmailing the family to sell off their controlling interest to Germany, the Nazis imprisoned Louis Rothschild in Vienna. Even after they physically seized Vitkovice in March 1939, the haggling went on until the bargain was struck for £3.5m.[19]

He was slithering to the Left. After this luncheon the *New Statesman*'s editor put out secret feelers to influential Liberal and Labour politicians: would they join a putative Churchill coalition with Eden as foreign secretary, if their minority parties were strongly represented in his Cabinet? It was their first sniff of power for some time: Attlee agreed in principle, but retired into his shell soon after the editor sounded him; Greenwood and Morrison showed more interest, and Bevin was also rumoured to be willing, if offered the ministry of labour. These remarkable soundings, described by Kinglsey Martin to Hugh Dalton a few days later, were an echo of things to come.[21]

Ten days later, Churchill put out cautious feelers to Eden, ex-foreign secretary, still sulking on the Riviera; his letter was critical of the PM's new agreement with Italy. Eden, still reluctant to gang up openly with Churchill, replied in terms of polite endorsement.

Using Waley-Cohen funds, The Focus now set up a publishing company and this brought *Headway*, the official monthly of the League of Nations Union, under its control.[22] It had a circulation of 60,000 copies, but to some it seemed a further leftward lurch. "The policy of the new *Headway*," wrote co-financier Eugen Spier, disagreeing with the purchase, "would be to turn out the Conservative government."

At Waley-Cohen's request Brendan Bracken released German-born Werner Knop who had been foreign news editor of his *Financial News and Banker* since 1935. The Focus set him up in an office in the fountain yard of one of the ancient Inns of Court near Fleet Street. Knop's "front," Union Time Ltd, disguised as a press agency, was funded "by a group of British businessmen and newspaper editors."[23] It agitated for an anti-German foreign policy; it financed the pamphleteering into Nazi Germany by Commander Stephen King-Hall, and, Knop claimed, funded at least one attempt on Hitler's life.[24]

There were other, lesser issues that April to perplex Churchill, of course, like the treaty abandoning British sovereignty over naval bases in southern Ireland. "You are giving away," protested Churchill, "the sentinels of the Western approaches."

But his main target remained Hitler. "The destruction of this thug," he told Sheila Grant Duff, one of his clandestine contacts to Prague, "would justify even great sacrifice by the rest of the world." He reassured her that neither he nor Eden had any intention of joining Chamberlain's "government of cowards."

Unfortunately the British showed little enthusiasm for war with Germany, as he had admitted to a friend some months before. That would involve conscription and utmost exertions; while to defeat Italy would involve only the "gentlemen of our gallant fleet."[25]

In Czechoslovakia he espied the germs of a preventive war in which by one concerted effort Britain, France and Russia could dispose of Hitler before he became too strong. He said so quite frankly on April 8 and 11 to Miss Grant Duff, who was now the *Manchester Guardian* and *Spectator* correspondent in Prague. He would wager fifty to one, he said, that Hitler would not attack yet. "He expressly said," wrote a Prague official, quoting the report she sent him, "that he would prefer Czechoslovakia to provoke war now."

If they waited a year, the country would be destroyed from within. He thinks we would certainly win a war against Germany this year. Next year that would be less likely, while in 1940 all hope would have gone. Today the German army is far weaker than the British, and the British fleet is very good. True, Britain is short of planes, but the war won't be won in the air.

"If the Germans bomb London," Churchill had told this young woman journalist, using words which viewed from the other side of 1940 leave a sediment of suspicion, "they will provoke the profound embitterment of a people that is still proud and, once awakened, will hold out to the end."[26] But it certainly was his real fear then: on the first Sunday in May he warned the four million readers of the *News of the World* about the lack of anti-aircraft guns.

Britain must not withhold one penny to consign to a sure doom the "accursed air murderer," for so the Winston Churchill of 1938 adjudged the "bomber of civilian populations."

The attack on the nests from which the hostile vultures come, as well as the attack on the military depots, railway junctions, mobilization centres of the enemy army, if vigorously and successfully maintained, will very soon compel the aggressor State to withdraw their aeroplanes from merely murdering civilians, women and children, the old, the weak and the poor, and come back to the fighting fronts in order to concentrate upon military targets.

On the ninth he addressed The Focus mass meeting at Manchester called in the "defence of freedom and peace." Here, in public, he spoke with a different tongue. The world must avoid war, he said, by strengthening the League. He called upon other nations to join in grand alliance with the "two great western democracies." To link friendship with Germany with any agreement to return her colonies or give her a free hand in Central Europe would be a "disastrous decision." If they had begun rearmament two years earlier than they had, he said, Britain would have been spared many humiliations.[27]

His warmest references were to Moscow, and the Manchester audience fiercely applauded them. This worried his Essex voters. His constituency agent telephoned at breakfast time on May 12 to warn that while they liked the speech they disapproved his "over familiar tone" about Russia.

EAVESDROPPING ON THIS 'phone call from across Churchill's breakfast table was once again the Soviet ambassador. Again neither Churchill nor his biographer ever made any reference to this clandestine meeting.

Churchill wanted to draw Maisky's attention to the *Manchester Guardian*'s extensive coverage of his "large and highly successful" meeting. It was the first of many, he added; Eden, with whom he had talked the other day upon his return from the Riviera, was adamantly refusing to back Chamberlain and might yet come out in open support of Churchill's campaign. It was being organized, he confided, by men from all three parties.

As Mr Churchill explained, his aim is to create a mass movement of a non-party character to demand the concerted resistance of all peace-loving nations against the aggressors, especially Germany.

He himself had devised its slogan, *Arms and the Covenant*: that had something for both right and left.

His Grand Alliance was, as the ambassador pointed out to Moscow, in essence the old League of Nations without the aggressor nations but with a stronger commitment to mutual armed defence. "In actual fact," reported Maisky, "he considers that without the U.S.S.R. nothing will come of his Grand Alliance. . . Without Moscow's close co-operation there will be no peace in Europe."

Winston admitted that he had had to express reservations at Manchester about aspects of the Soviet internal regime, but only because he had to take account of the feelings of his constituents.

He had particularly praised Stalin's strategy in the Far East, said Maisky — "The way we maintain neutrality and simultaneously help China with arms."

Open Soviet military intervention on China's side would rouse anti-Soviet feeling . . . making it more difficult to form the Grand Alliance which Churchill now sees as the sole salvation of mankind.

Referring tactfully to Stalin's sanguinary liquidation of Army officers, Churchill hoped that any "complications" in the Soviet forces had been purely transitional and had since been "rectified." He unabashedly angled for an invitation to the next Red Army manoeuvres. "So long as I'm pressing for collaboration with the Soviet Union," he said, "It's important I form my own impressions of your army." Randolph also asked to go, as he wanted to write newspaper articles on Russia.[28]

CHURCHILL REFUSED TO consider visiting Germany. Perhaps he preferred to keep Hitler at arm's length, as the Devil he Didn't Know.

He had little gut feeling against Nazis as such — each important Nazi who came to London usually crossed the Welcome mat at Morpeth Mansions.

On the day after he saw Maisky, May 13, he was visited by the leader of the Sudeten Germans, Konrad Henlein, an athletic forty year old — suspected by Heinrich Himmler of homosexual tendencies.[29] Professor Lindemann interpreted; Winston invited two cronies — Colonel Malcolm Christie, a former air attaché in Berlin, and Archie Sinclair — to attend.

Stressing the need for secrecy about his visit, Henlein promised these gullible drawing-room conspirators that he had received no instructions from Berlin.* But affable, charming and persuasive though he was, his mission was to drive a wedge between the Czechs and their allies — to prepare the coming war of nerves. Back in Berlin nine days later Henlein would be assured by Hitler that as soon as the West Wall fortifications were complete, in eight or ten weeks' time, he would finish off Czechoslovakia.[30] He left Churchill with the impression that he would restrain Hitler, work with Benes and persuade his Sudeten Germans to limit their demand to local "autonomy."[31]

Churchill sent copies of Lindemann's notes on Henlein to Chamberlain and Halifax; they thanked him politely.[32] This private fawning upon Chamberlain and Halifax, about which latter he had expressed contempt to Ivan Maisky, suggests that he hoped to stay near the inside track — or, to coin an apter phrase for this kind of ungainly manoeuvring, to run with one leg on each side of the fence.

The Focus was still campaigning for Chamberlain's overthrow, but Winston would have accepted office even under him, as Randolph made plain to Maisky. To create the necessary opening, he had sedulously aroused the House against Lord Swinton over alleged inadequacies in the RAF's repair organisation, its shortage of ammunition and bombs, and its inadequacies inevitably showing up in bomber pilot training and squadron serviceability now that it was expanding.[34]

Swinton was obliged to resign on May 16. Winston wrote him the customary letter of condolences, but Chamberlain gave the air ministry to someone else (Sir Kingsley Wood.) "The Government," Churchill explained in a wistful note to a young Tory MP ten days later, "have a solid majority and Chamberlain will certainly not wish to work with me. If of course the foreign situation darkens, something in the nature of a National Government may be forced upon us, but events, and great events alone will rule."[35]

---

*But preserved among the papers of Hitler's adjutants is a note signed R[ibbentrop]: "I received Konrad Henlein before and after his trip to England and took the opportunity to discuss in detail with him the tactics to be pursued."[33]

He shifted his aim now to the War Office, writing on June 3 to Leslie Hore-Belisha, secretary for war, alleging scandalous deficiencies in flak, in Bren guns, and in anti-tank rifles. Hore-Belisha took it coolly, replying that the allegations were not accurate.

SINCE EVENTS WOULD not oblige, circles in London took a hand in creating them.

Through Spears, Churchill had the assurances of Benes that Czechoslovakia could mobilize seventeen active and seventeen reserve divisions. As he had told Miss Grant Duff, Winston wanted a showdown now. A still unexplained chain of circumstances later in May 1938 nearly brought it about. On Friday May 20 Intelligence officials in London passed on to Czech colleagues[36] information that eleven German divisions were approaching the Czech frontier.[37] German archives make plain that this was not true.[38] Prague mobilized 175,000 reservists. For twenty-four hours, Europe teetered on the brink.

What was the origin of the canard? Did Masaryk talk with Churchill in those crucial days? The ebullient Czech was certainly spotted on the day before the crisis in conclave with Vansittart.[39] Without instructions from Prague, Masaryk requested the British Foreign Office to intervene in Berlin. Chamberlain and Halifax were out of London for the weekend. At the F.O. press conference on Saturday Rex Leeper — whose close association with both Prague and Churchill has earlier been noted — announced that war was imminent. When Britain's ambassador uttered the requisite admonitions in Berlin he was manhandled by an outraged Ribbentrop — innocent once again, as now turns out.

This was precisely what Masaryk had wanted. "You are aware," he gloated to his superiors in Prague, "of how unpleasant Ribbentrop was to Henderson and how much that has aided us."[40]

When no tanks rolled into Czechoslovakia, Leeper poured fuel on the flames, flaunting it as a triumph of "collective security'" over Hitler's ambitions.

LEEPER'S POSTURING BROUGHT about what The Focus had been working for for many months: the inevitability of war with the Nazis.

Months later, Hitler would still betray a smouldering bitterness over the episode: despite every assurance to Henderson, as he told an adjutant, that not one German soldier had been set in motion, Fleet Street had crowed over Germany "bowing to British pressure."[41]

His patience had snapped. At the beginning of May 1938 a joint conference between his admiralty and airforce staffs in Berlin had already begun analysing the changing situation: "Britain," they concluded, "is emerging more and more as Germany's principle opponent."[42] Now, on May 24, Hitler told his naval aide to telex his admiralty that they must assume that Britain and France would be on the enemy side, and prepare the immediate acceleration of battleship construction. He hurried back to Berlin.[43]

Unseen from Mr Churchill's "poste de commandement" at Morpeth Mansions, the May 1938 crisis had thus set torch to fuse. For Hitler, it was a severe blow: on his confident instructions, Raeder had been building the wrong navy and Göring the wrong airforce for war with Britain. He ordered work stepped up on the West Wall.[44] On May 28 he harangued his generals at the Chancery. "It is my inflexible resolve," he pronounced, "that Czechoslovakia shall vanish from the map."[45]

General Milch made a note of the likely airforce figures given a "mobilisation day" on October 1 (the beginning of the new military year.)[46]

The fuse was slowly burning. It was not the immediate showdown that Churchill had hoped for; but it was the next best thing.

CHAPTER 11

Choosing Between War and Shame

THAT SUMMER OF 1938 he took a corner seat and was content with it, as he wrote to one MP hovering on the threshhold of The Focus.[1]

He remained at Chartwell, savouring the Weald of Kent and the country home he had so nearly lost; he even toyed with the idea of revisiting California.

Prague had begun exasperatingly slow negotiations with Henlein; Churchill's writing load allowed little time for the history of any other peoples than the English-speaking. Mademoiselle Curie had sent him a new book about her clever mother; but he found no time to read it. He was "horribly entangled," he wrote to Lord Halifax, with Ancient Britons, Romans, Angles, Saxons, and Jutes — "all of whom I thought I had escaped from for ever when I left school!"[2]

"So much to do, so little time" — Cecil Rhodes' final words might have described this period for him. He turned down General Spears' invitation to speak at a regimental anniversary. "No, No, dear Louis," he mix-metaphored: "Let us keep our powder & shot in hand."[3]

For his oldest friends he made exceptions. Bernard Baruch had announced back in April he was coming over on Roosevelt's behalf on about June 13, to investigate the dictators' airplane production and the democracies' rearmament.[4]

Six foot four, Baruch had the spare, athletic frame of the boxer he had once been. Brendan Bracken once wrote to him, "Nature made you and Winston for each other and it does you both great good to meet."[5] They had done so often, since their first encounter at the 1919 Peace Conference — in New York or at Hobcaw, his plantation in South Carolina. Once the American philanthropist had ordered up three redheads from the local cat-house for the virile English politician: before delivering them that Thursday their Madam had had to concoct one with dye; fortunately her colour lasted until the return to base on Monday.[6] "Faithless," Churchill may well have murmured once more as he contemplated the offerings, "but fortunate."

Thirty-five years later Baruch would write him this fond pen portrait:

> I wish the world could see you for a few moments walking with your dog, Rufus, about your garden, marvelling at the beauty of a rose, or lecturing the fish in your pond as you feed them. The world should be a guest at your dinner table and enjoy the treat of hearing you talk, with a bottle of wine always at hand, of military tactics in the American Civil War, of your early adventures in South Africa, of Gibbon and Macaulay and of the knaves and fools you have known.

Sometimes he would slump into a chair, listening to the others argue and murmuring merely, "No, Bernie dear."[7] He could not conceal from Baruch his disillusionment with life. He talked about going into business. He talked of his farm or horses, and then of the approach of war. Once he pointed to the side of the house and exclaimed, "Look at that beautiful vine with its lovely flowers! That is something man cannot do — he can never equal what nature has done there."

Baruch saw how these bleak years had eroded Winston's spirit, and tried to hearten him. "I know," he wrote, to Churchill fifteen years later, "how keenly you felt the accusation of 'warmonger' that was hurled at you, for that was the epithet pinned upon me in the United States."

"Well," remarked Churchill on the night before Baruch left, "the big show will be on very soon. You'll be running it in America. And I'll be on the sidelines here."[8]

TANTALIZINGLY, BARUCH — WHO had been initiated by Randolph into The Focus at the time of the Abdication crisis — would reminisce to Churchill: "I have been wondering for some time how you were going to treat certain subjects in your book. It will be difficult to ignore them or to gloss them over."[9]

Churchill also made time for The Focus. On June 2, 1938 he spoke on "peace and freedom" on a League of Nations Union platform at Birmingham. He talked scornfully of Franco and his fascist aid, predicted that he would demand unconditional surrender, and confessed that he found it difficult to maintain his previous "impartial neutrality" on Spain. Referring to the recent Czech crisis, he crowed over Hitler's apparent climbdown on May 21 — claiming it as a definite success for collective security — and scoffed at the critics of rearmament:

> Is there then to be only one armed camp, the dictators' armed camp, and a rabble of outlying peoples, wandering around its outskirts, wondering which of them is going to be taken first and whether they are going to be subjugated or merely exploited?[10]

Basil Liddell Hart was now The Focus military adviser, but this tank warfare expert found that during their meetings Churchill did not really take in a point except where it fitted his own theories. Liddell Hart tried unsuccessfully to warn of the coming of fast, fluid armoured warfare; later, Churchill would admit that he had not kept pace with such developments.[11]

AT ONE WEEK'S notice The Focus called a secret meeting at the Savoy for June 22, 1938 ostensibly "in view of the present international situation." Most probably their guest was Dr Hubert Ripka, a high Prague Foreign Intelligence official whom Churchill certainly met at this time.[12]

Somewhere out there in the wilderness of the last two years was the old, anti-Bolshevik skin that Winston had now shed: but in the darkness of such conversations as with Ripka, as Czech archives reveal, the new skin glowed in warmest pink. Years before, strolling with Baruch in a frosty Bois de Boulogne during the 1919 Paris peace conference, he had jabbed his walking stick at the East and growled, "Russia! That's where this cold weather is coming from."

Now he confided to Ripka how distressed he had been by the internal weakness and decay in the Red Army. "This was why," the Czech reported, "he was so pleased that Stalin had liquidated Marshal [M.N.] Tukhachevsky, who had certainly been plotting with Germany.* He spoke frankly of his great admiration for Stalin, and of his hopes that he can bring the convulsions presently disrupting Russia under control."

They talked of the Sudeten Germans. Churchill repeated what he had told Henlein — that Britain would intervene if Hitler attacked. "We used rough and minatory language to Henlein," he said, "because that's the only way to speak to a Boche." But then he talked of the good impression Henlein had made, and of how he seemed to be keeping his engagements. Ripka choked, and pointed to Henlein's less roseate interviews with senior Daily Mail journalist G. Ward Price, and Karl Frank's conversations with British reporters in Prague. At this Churchill lost his composure: Prague must come to terms with Henlein, he said; it would be an error to rely too "carelessly" on British aid.

"Every one of us leading politicians," he lectured Ripka, "has to ask ourselves whether we have the right, whether we can in all conscience force our country into war — whether we can permit London to be destroyed, and our Empire to be shaken once more." He added with rare candour, "I cannot say that I would not act similarly to Mr Chamberlain, if I had the responsibility as head of government."

After this outburst something of the heroic, lachrymose Churchill returned. Ripka stammered that the Czechs would defend themselves,

---

*He had not. Tukhachevsky had been framed by the S.S.

and were no longer vulnerable to a sudden mechanized thrust across the frontiers. Tears shot into Winston's eyes.

"Masaryk was right," he cried, referring to Jan's father Thomas. "Death *is* better than slavery." If war did come, he contined, mopping his eyes, this time they must wage it against the Boche so thoroughly that he wouldn't recover for generations. "We'll smash them to smithereens," he snarled, "so they don't trouble us for a century or more."

After a while he spoke of "Herr Beans," as he pronounced the name of Czechoslovakia's president, Edouard Benes. Churchill

> called him one of the greatest men of our epoch, and praised the resolution of the Czechs to fight for freedom with such vehemence that he began to cry all over again.

IN MID JUNE 1938 he had accepted an admiralty invitation to tour the underwater weapons establishment at Portland. Here he inspected Asdic, the new secret acoustic device for locating submarines; he concluded that the submarine threat had been defeated.

Writing in the *Daily Telegraph* on June 23 he pointed out that an aggressive Hitler would have to contend with France, Russia and eventually Britain too. After a horrendous report from a "Refugee from Vienna" appeared in *The Spectator*, he pleaded with the Foreign Office to give him material about Austria; Cadogan could only suggest some punning phrases about taking people for "Joy (through Strength) rides." "It is easy to ruin and persecute the Jews," Winston wrote in the resulting article, "to steal their private property; to drive them out of every profession and employment; to fling a Rothschild into a prison or a sponging-house."[13] (Louis Rothschild was still imprisoned in Austria, held hostage until the family agreed to sell the Vitkovice steelworks to Germany.)

Churchill nursed his clandestine contacts with the French and Czechs. On June 28, July 19 and September 4 General Spears paid visits of several days to Paris where his close friend Sir Charles Mendl was the embassy's bag-man.[14] The moody, melancholy Jan Masaryk was an equally frequent visitor to Winston — while Neville Chamberlain did not receive him until September. At the end of June Masaryk flew home to report; it was Chamberlain's opponents whom he saw on his return. "Churchill," he advised Prague, "as well as Eden and Sinclair are constantly in touch. I think there'll be a showdown this autumn, if the Gods grant us peace until then."[15]

Another of Hitler's henchmen called at Morpeth Mansions that July — Albert Forster, the thirty-six year old gauleiter in beleaguered Danzig. Again Churchill was oddly impressed, commenting to him favourably on the lack of anti-Jewish laws in the Free City, and admitting according to Lindemann's note that while anti-semitism was a "hindrance and an irritation," it was "probably not a complete obstacle to a working agreement," — meaning between Britain and Germany. When the gauleiter urged him to come and see Germany for himself, Churchill asked with gentle irony whether August and September would not be "unhealthy months" for that. Hitler was not thinking of war, Forster responded with a smile to Churchill: The Führer's immense social and cultural plans would take years to fulfil. As for disarmament, he reminded Churchill of how often Hitler had even offered to prohibit aerial bombardment; Churchill did not know the answer to that, but replied in broad terms that only Hitler could remove the shadow of war from the world.[16]

After Forster had left them, the Prof told Winston of one remark tactfully omitted by the gauleiter's interpreter: Forster had suggested that Britain and Germany "divide the world" between them. Winston invited Halifax to dinner on the strength of it.[17]

He was in an odd, uncomfortable limbo — between impotence and influence, between pariah and persona grata. Later that month he was graciously allowed to accompany their Majesties on their State Visit to Paris and Versailles.

* * *

Hitler now had one and a half million men under arms. He completed his western fortifications, ranted about war, but probably still had not made up his mind — the prerogative of him who takes the initiative.

Downing-street dithered, appalled at the slithering towards war. Two army divisions — forty per cent of Britain's total field force — were tied down in Palestine, keeping Arab and Jew from each other's throats. With only two infantry divisions available to send to France, with only ten capital ships in service, with the new eight-gun monoplanes like the Spitfire still far from operational, Britain was powerless.

Late in July Mr Chamberlain sent a deaf and decrepit liberal peer, Lord Runciman, to arbitrate in Czechoslovakia — a country that he could not with certainty have located on the map until quite recently. "I think," Churchill lamented in a letter to Lloyd George, "we shall have to choose in the next few weeks between war and shame."[18]

Another German came to see him, this time an anti-Nazi army officer — the landowner and gentleman farmer Major Ewald von Kleist-Schmenzin. The young *News Chronicle* journalist Ian Colvin had picked him up at his exclusive Berlin club and introduced him to Englishmen

like Lord Lloyd. Von Kleist, quoting a "top army general" — probably
Hitler's chief of general staff, the lamentable Ludwig Beck — told all and
sundry that Hitler would attack Czechoslovakia on September 28. The
general begged Britain to announce that she would fight, promising:
"Then I'll put an end to this regime." It is not apparent why Beck needed
the London stimulus — why he could not squeeze the trigger of his pistol
the next time he met Hitler, with the same salutary effect.

Von Kleist settled discreetly into London's Park Lane hotel on
August 18, his exit-visa having been furnished by the traitorous
Intelligence chief Vice-Admiral Wilhelm Canaris. That evening he
repeated "September 28" to Vansittart. The next day Randolph brought
him down to Chartwell.

Some of his reactionary proposals were not for tender ears: his client
generals, he promised, could instal a new regime "probably of a
Monarchist character" within forty-eight hours; they wanted the
liquidation of the irksome Polish corridor — a somewhat inopportune
demand, felt Winston, since even Hitler was not yet asking that.[19] He
humoured "Monsieur de K.," as the transcript discreetly called him, and
— after obtaining sanction by telephone from Halifax — drafted a letter
for von Kleist to brandish at his turncoat generals, setting out the horrors
of war but going no further than had Mr Chamberlain in his speech of
March 24.

Kleist was emphatic that Germany couldn't fight longer than three
months, and that Hitler's defeat was certain. "H.," he disclosed,
"regarded the events of May 21 as a personal rebuff."

Winston sent Randolph's transcript to Halifax, and to the PM four
days later: "I do not suppose it can do much good, but every little
counts."[20]

* * *

His romantic meetings with these renegades were not entirely
without profit. By putting to them the alluring notion that he was "anti-
Nazi and anti-war," but *not* anti-German, Churchill lit a slow burning
fuse in their minds: the belief — misguided, as time would show — that
if they rose against their dictator they could count on Winston Churchill.

Chamberlain was too hard-boiled a politician for cloak-and-dagger
fantasies. In July 1938 he had referred dismissively to them as
"unchecked reports from unofficial sources." The files bulged with them.
In April Vyvyan Adams had visited Benes, Hodza and Krofta, like
Spears and Deakin before him.[21] Wickham Steed had sent material later
that month from "a German financial expert on Central and South-
Eastern Europe," a week later from a "competent British observer

visiting Czecho-Slovakia," and in mid-June a further rambling, anonymous summary.[22] Once, he had warned of serious defeatism in Whitehall — secretary for war Leslie Hore-Belisha had told American journalists on April 27 that government policy was to let Hitler "eat his belly full."[23]

As for von Kleist, whose treacherous career would be terminated by the Nazi People's Court in 1944, this officer and gentleman reminded Chamberlain of the loathsome Jacobites at the Court of France in King William's time: "I think," he noted to the foreign secretary, "we must discount a good deal of what he says."[24]

ON AUGUST 19, 1938 The Focus secretary wrote to the group about a national campaign to "rally the people to the support of a resuscitated League of Nations." But ideas had crystallized in Churchill's mind, since seeing Major von Kleist, that some kind of a Joint Note might trip up the mad dictator Hitler in full gallop. He talked it over with the foreign secretary and the Cabinet considered it on the thirtieth. Halifax pointed out that Mr Churchill's other prospective signatories — France and Russia — might ask what *Britain* proposed to do; this would be embarrassing, because the answer was: "Nothing until late 1939"[25]

Ignorant of this discussion, Winston pressed on. On the following day he invited Maisky down to Chartwell — another meeting not mentioned in his memoirs.

"Today," the Soviet ambassador cabled to Moscow afterwards, "I lunched with Churchill. He seemed very much on edge."[26] Churchill said that war might be imminent. The Czechs would fight, France would probably go to their aid, and even Britain might eventually abandon her present reserve.

> According to Churchill, feelings in Britain — both amongst the masses and in government circles — have clearly hardened against Germany and in favour of Czechoslovakia over the last ten days.*

He had a plan that might prevent this catastrophe: If Benes made what Lord Runciman felt was a decent offer and Hitler rejected it, then Britain, France, and the Soviet Union must issue a Joint Note to Hitler, unmistakeably pointing to the consequences of aggression. Simultaneously, their ambassadors in Washington would formally show it to Roosevelt and invite him to associate the United States with the Note. That would lend it greater authority. It was in his opinion the only hope of preventing world war.

---

*As with all Maisky's telegrams from Soviet foreign ministry archives, these have been translated from the Russian.

> Churchill particularly hopes [reported Maisky] to secure Vansittart's approval — a man who in his words is gaining in influence. However, I myself don't share Churchill's optimism.

Churchill obviously wanted to know the Kremlin's attitude to his plan. For the rest of their discussion, said Maisky, he spoke about Germany with unmitigated hatred. As the evening drew on he declared that he had thought up a new slogan: "Proletarians and free-thinkers of the world, unite against the fascist tyrants!"

INSPIRED BY THIS eccentric approach the Russians formally suggested that London and Paris concert their plans with Moscow while there was still time. When French foreign minister George Bonnet inquired through diplomatic channels what Russia planned to do, his Soviet counterpart Maxim Litvinov informed the French chargé d'affaires Jean Payart on September 2 that they would honour their 1935 alliance with Czechoslovakia; but that Moscow felt more entitled to know *France's* position in advance. In particular, since neutral Romania and Poland were refusing to allow Soviet troops through to Czechoslovakia, the League of Nations would have to vote upon the matter.[27]

Notified of these remarks on the same day, Maisky telephoned Chartwell and asked to see Churchill again, urgently. The little Russian diplomat arrived the next day, September 3, related Litvinov's important guarantee to fulfil Soviet obligations and suggested that Churchill obtain government pressure for the summoning of the League of Nations council. Without — rather curiously — revealing that it was Maisky who had informed him ("I have received privately from an absolutely sure source the following information. . .") Churchill passed this on to Halifax immediately. But nothing came of this important project. The foreign secretary said merely he would keep it in mind.[28]

There were other eclectic visitors to Chartwell early that September. Through an indescretion of Clemmie's sister, leaked in the *Daily Express*, we know that under a personal guarantee of secrecy Dr Heinrich Brüning, the last of the Weimar Chancellors, had come down from Oxford, where he was a deeply respected Research Fellow at Queen's College. Anti-Nazis had asked him to get Churchill to influence No. 10 to "speak plainly to Hitler."

We have no note on what they discussed; but perhaps this is the place to mention that ten years later Dr Brüning wrote to Churchill's publishers, enjoining them not to publish a letter he had written to Winston on August 28, 1937 about the tragic error of those guilty of funding Hitler before his rise to power. Industrialist Friedrich Flick and the I.G. Farben company had been forced to contribute only after the

Nazis came to power, he said; but he knew from bitter inside knowledge as Chancellor that others, including the French secret service, had voluntarily financed the Nazis into office:

> I did not [Brüning wrote to the Editors of *Life*, prohibiting the use of his letter, in 1948], and do not even today, for understandable reasons, wish to reveal that from October 1928 the two largest regular contributors to the Nazi Party were the general managers of two of the largest Berlin banks, both of Jewish faith, and one of them the leader of Zionism in Germany.[29]*

It must have been a lively household that September of 1938, but Churchill always made time for wealthy and influential American emissaries. On the ninth he was visited by Alfred Bergman, whose fortune came from the Royal Typewriter company's European concession (which included Czechoslovakia) and influence from his friendship with Roosevelt. Churchill asked him to send regards to Roosevelt — "the outstanding leader of our century," an accolade he had only recently bestowed on Benes — and boasted that he himself did not have the civilian's fear of war.

"How far is America willing to go?" it occurred to him to ask.

Bergman replied that America would back the British provided they did something — "Which up to now they have not."[30]

Churchill told him of his new Joint Note plan: he was going to put it personally to Chamberlain the next day, and F.D.R. would be invited to give moral support.

By this time however Hitler's campaign against Czechoslovakia was approaching its climax. As Churchill walked into No. 10 the Big Four crisis committee (Chamberlain, Halifax, Simon and Hoare) stepped out of the Cabinet Room.

Winston demanded that they issue his Joint Note as an immediate ultimatum to Hitler — "It's our last chance of stopping a landslide."

But Chamberlain had trumped his old opponent again: he had just revealed secretly to the other three a long prepared plan for a dramatic flight to Hitler. They had no interest in his plan now.

Churchill repeated his demand on September 11, now limiting it to Britain alone: she must issue a simple ultimatum — if Hitler set foot in Czechoslovakia, he would have Britain to contend with.[31]

They did not heed him: why should they have? They were in office, and he was not. To one of his benefactors, the Guinness brewery owner, Churchill now repeated his gloomy phrase: "We seem to be very near the bleak choice between War and Shame."[32]

---

*Brüning stated that the French secret service and Schneider-Creusot works had made up one half of Hitler's revenue from 1921 until 1932; and he added that before 1933 the SA (Brownshirts) and SS had been equipped with revolvers and machine guns made in the United States.

CHAPTER 12

Here Today, Gone Tomorrow

NO EVENT YET had seemed to offer Churchill an opportunity like the 1938 Czech crisis. He had lain submerged on the political seabed all summer, filling barely an inch of the Index to *The Times* with his doings. Now Chartwell reverberated to the blast of ballast tanks discharging as he rose towards the surface, manned stations, and prepared to do war. The Event, the showdown of which he had so often talked, seemed to have come.

Not everybody shared his relish. "Public opinion here," the American ambassador reported at the end of August, "is definitely against going to war for the Czechs."[1] In France they liked it even less.

If Roosevelt, Hitler, Benes, Churchill and certain of his friends in Paris were similar in this respect their motives were very different.

"The President," dictated one American official two days after a White House Cabinet meeting on September 16, "thinks that economically the United States will fare well whether Europe goes to war or not. He looks for an improvement in business during the winter months and he says that [Treasury Secretary Henry J.] Morgenthau agrees with him." Europe's Gold, explained F.D.R., was now flooding into the United States to purchase munitions — they might even have to use navy ships to ferry the Gold across. British and French citizens owned U.S. securities of enormous value, and would be forced to sell them if war broke out: the United States, Roosevelt concluded, could only profit from a war.[2]

Hitler, let it be said, was no less cynical. "Clausewitz was right," he liked to remind his more nervous generals: "War *is* the father of all things."* Even the Czech president Edouard Benes looked forward to it after some unseemly wobbling. As he "happily" signed the mobilisation papers later in September he rejoiced that the die had been cast: "We are heading for war."[3]

The War Path.

He had been supported, as this chapter will now show, by Stefan Osusky and Jan Masaryk, his envoys in Paris and London — and by Mr Chamberlain's principal opponent, Winston Churchill, who also regarded war as one of the highest aspirations of mankind.

Neither Chamberlain nor his French counterpart, the short, squat Edouard Daladier, wanted war. Daladier had been an artilleryman in the World War and had seen what war was like. He rasped at Georges Mandel, one of his ministers, that he wasn't going to sacrifice the flower of France's manhood to whitewash the "criminal errors" that he had committed at Versailles with his chief, Clemenceau.[4]

Nor, it must be said, did Göring relish the prospect of war. Late in August his chief of staff had ordered the western Luftflotte 2 to prepare bomber units in case of war against Britain; General Hellmuth Felmy replied on September 22 that unless they could operate from the Low Countries their planes had neither the bombloads nor the range.[5]

If this was a shock for Göring it would have been an even greater shock for Mr Churchill who had widely publicized that Hitler intended to deliver an immediate "knock out blow" when war began. Although Göring's pilots used their radios freely, British air intelligence had no evidence of any such preparations — of units training, stockpiling bombs, or concentrating in the north-western exit corner of Germany.[6]

AT FIRST WINSTON fought alone. Eden was away; Duff Cooper, First Lord of the Admiralty, cruising in the Baltic.[7] Churchill did not share Chamberlain's apprehensions about a showdown. Britain with her fleet, France with her army, seemed invulnerable. The battleship seemed the embodiment of power. Privileged to have seen the Asdic, he assured his readers in the *Telegraph* that the submarine was in "undoubted obsolescence" as a "decisive war weapon."

That summer, he scattered such valuable opinions freely: Airforces decided nothing in land battle; they were "an additional complication rather than a decisive weapon" — so he wrote on the first day of September 1938, exactly twelve months before Hitler proved him wrong. He scoffed at the "air experts" who claimed that British battleships costing millions could be sunk by enemy airplanes costing thousands. "Aircraft will not be a mortal danger to properly equipped modern war fleets, whether at sea or lying in harbour under the protection of their own very powerful anti-aircraft batteries reinforced by those on shore." Come 1942, and he would be wiser in this respect as well.

Chamberlain was not blind to the dangers below. He had a kind of Asdic too. At a nod from Sir Joseph Ball the home secretary Sam Hoare placed wiretaps on Eden, Macmillan, and Churchill — all future prime ministers.[8] MI5 was already tapping embassy telephones.[9] Vansittart, wise to the ways of ministers, eschewed the telephone and contacted Winston and Labour conspirators only in their private homes.[10]

The intercepts raised eyebrows, but the English were gentlemen — Neville Chamberlain betrayed no feelings when Messrs Churchill and Attlee were heard conniving with Maisky and Masaryk, undertaking to overthrow his government; nor when Masaryk telephoned President Roosevelt direct; nor when the Czech used language which could only be termed infelicitous. "I would not let my dog," he once said, "lift his leg in [Sir John] Simon's left eye."[11] Asked by one conspirator whether Chamberlain was getting firmer, Masaryk hooted: "Firm! About as firm as the erection of an old man of seventy!"[12]

MI5 has declined to make available the British transcripts although the requisite thirty years have long elapsed. The German intercepts of London embassy communications indicate that Masaryk was furnishing documents and funds to overthrow the British government.[13] The fight that he put up earned grudging praise from Hitler after reading the German intercepts.[14] "They won't look me in the eye," Masaryk was heard shouting down the line to Prague early on September 14: "They're just a rabble here." "I'm in telephone contact with Roosevelt." "As for France, they're a load of ratbags too." "I must hang up now, Eden's here." After it was all over, and Masaryk had lost fatherland and legation, Sam Hoare recommended he be awarded the Grand Cross of the Victorian Order — despite having "consorted with Winston and his friends."[15]

Chamberlain's ministry would have needed strong stomachs to look Masaryk in the eye that day. Winston learned of the reason for their evasiveness over lunch with the First Lord at the Admiralty.[16] Duff Cooper, his soft complexion looking pinker than usual, sitting with his back to the light so that his disconcerting squint was less noticeable, told him that the prime minister proposed to see Hitler the next morning — making his first airplane flight ever — and would agree to a plebiscite in the Sudeten areas that Hitler was demanding.

Even under Czech supervision, its outcome would be a foregone conclusion. The choice was not between war and a plebiscite, Duff Cooper had objected in that morning's Cabinet, but between "war now, and war later." The idea was, it seemed, to take the wind out of Hitler's sails. "The stupidist thing that has ever been done," exploded Churchill.[17] His sails were now empty too.

Masaryk telephoned the ugly news to Prague at ten p.m.

BENES: Impossible!
MASARYK: That sow Sir Horace Wilson's going too.

Relief swept Paris. This British initiative was opposed, as the U.S.

ambassador William C. Bullitt observed, only by communists, Soviet agents, and certain Jews like Mandel; even Leon Blum approved. Apart from Reynaud and permanent officials at the Quai d'Orsay — meaning Léger — nobody, he added, wanted war just to maintain France's traditional power in Europe.[18]

Foreign minister Georges Bonnet had warned Britain's ambassador, Sir Eric Phipps, that France would not intervene even if Czechoslovakia were attacked.[19] When his clandestine sources at the F.O. leaked this to Churchill there was hell to pay. He and The Focus ran the telephone lines to Paris red-hot. Bonnet complained to Phipps that Churchill and General Spears had pestered him and other ministers by telephone. "Presumably," the boozy ambassador cabled to the F.O., Churchill had "breathed fire and thunder . . . to binge Bonnet up."[20] He urged Halifax to remind the two that the Germans were probably tapping their conversations.*

Masaryk did not give up. That Friday noon, September 16, even before Chamberlain returned to England, the Czech was on the telephone to Prague:

> MASARYK: Yes, before anything happens, if anything's to be done, I'd like money.
> BENES: Yes.
> MASARYK: I need just enough here — you know — and right now.†

Chamberlain's dealings with Hitler produced uproar among Focus members. Writing to its secretary A.H. Richards on the seventeenth Churchill predicted that if the Government was going to let Czechoslovakia be cut to pieces "a period of very hard work lies before us all."[23]

Daladier and Bonnet came over for talks on Sunday, September 18, with "their tongues [hanging] out," as American ambassador Joseph Kennedy heard, eager to avoid war; Vansittart was kept out of the conferences because of his intriguing with Léger and Churchill. They talked emotionally of France's honour and Czechoslovakia's plight. "We must," they repeated, "take a realistic view."[24] Their airforce was negligible, their army qualitatively inferior: of sixty-eight divisions facing Germany only two were "light armoured divisions," equipped with antiquated Hotchkiss H-35 and Somua S-35 tanks. They were strong in artillery but not in anti-tank guns, and that was what mattered.

---

*Mussolini's agents were certainly intercepting high level calls in 1936; Gestapo agents tapped one Reynaud–Chamberlain conversation in May 1940.[21]

†This passage is lined in British files. Czech archives show that four days later the National bank sent one million crowns, £7,182 to Masaryk's *private* account at Barclays bank. He refused to tell later Czech investigators how he disposed of the money "because of the unorthodox manner in which the funds in question had been used."[22]

Churchill learned little of this that Sunday. By circuitous route — Sheila Grant Duff telephoned it to him at Chartwell — he gathered confirmation that Chamberlain had some "miserable plan" to impose on Prague. He assured her he was going to issue a powerful declaration on Wednesday. Until then, everything depended on the Czechs: they must be willing to fight at all costs. She passed this on to Ripka, their agent in Prague.[25]

At the end of that day, the British and French governments sent an ultimatum to Benes, to transfer the primarily German areas to the Reich.[26] On Monday Eden and others advised Masaryk that Prague must play for time — perhaps they should reply that first they must consult their Parliament as it was a matter of such "entirely unexpected" concessions.[27] Later on Monday, at three-twenty p.m. Masaryk spoke with Benes.

> MASARYK: The uncles are still in session here and haven't breathed a word to anybody. . . Yes, you know what? They're even speaking of ceding territories without a plebiscite.
> BENES: Yeah, yeah.
> MASARYK: I'm not going over there [to Whitehall] at all. They haven't sent for me. So what I say is: Shit them, Mr President.

Playing for time, he feigned sickness. When Halifax sent for him, he sent back a note that recent surprises had been "a little too much" and he was suffering gallbladder problems: "My 'vet' thinks that I must stay in bed for a couple of days." He had just telephoned with Benes, he said, who was still waiting for "the verdict."[28]

That evening Churchill bore down on the foreign secretary. Halifax educated him to the weakness of the French, particularly in the air; General Gamelin had warned that war would end in a debacle. Winston emerged muted and chastened.[29]

> BENES: I wanted to ask what people like Churchill —
> MASARYK: They're hopping mad, think it's absolutely shocking.
> BENES: — Couldn't you ask their advice?

Masaryk already had; they had replied they were in no position to offer advice, but "hoped we wouldn't put up with it." Benes became evasive.

> MASARYK: And what line do we take on this?
> BENES: That's obvious!
> MASARYK: *Yes or No?*
> BENES: *No* of course. That's obvious.

NOW THAT EDEN was on the same side of the net, though not yet in the same team, Churchill set to work on Labour Party leader Clement

Attlee. He telephoned congratulations on Labour's declaration in the morning papers: "Your declaration," he lisped, "does honour to the great British nation."

Attlee answered in clipped tones: "I'm glad you think so," and replaced the receiver.[30]

Prague had still not replied to the Anglo-French demand. Chamberlain needed the reply urgently, as he was about to meet Hitler again at Godesberg. The intercepts reveal the reason for Prague's delay.

> BENES: What I'm looking for is a formula which isn't *No* and isn't *Yes*. Briefly one that lets me negotiate honourably.
> MASARYK: Yeah, the Old Man's packing his bags again and he's on hot bricks.

That evening, Prague's formal refusal reached the F.O. "It is not only the fate of Czechoslovakia that is in the balance," this said. Together with Halifax and Cadogan, the PM and Sir Horace Wilson drafted a muscular ultimatum to Dr Benes demanding that he withdraw his refusal and accept the Anglo-French plan — "before producing a situation for which France and Britain could take no responsibility."

Masaryk meanwhile checked with Prague, learned that half "his fortune" was being transferred immediately and the rest later.

> MASARYK: Just as soon as possible. That's what matters to me. . . Any moment now the balloon will go up I've nothing to go on.

Spears contacted Robert Boothby, Churchill's former Parliamentary secretary. Boothby said there was nothing they could do as a group, meaning that night. He also predicted that Eden "would not come round." This, he pointed out a few days later, proved right. Spears relayed to Winston that Boothby was no longer interested in Czecho-Slovakia.[31]

* * *

Disappointed in his friends, Churchill flew over to Paris to "stiffen the French government."[32] His literary agent Emery Reves met him at Le Bourget airport. Winston had an impulse to telegraph to Benes, to stand fast — "*Fire your canon and all will be well.*" [33] But sensing that it might be unwise to put such words in writing, he left the cable unsent.

He had flown into a French hornet's nest. At two-fifteen that Wednesday morning the British and French legations in Prague had delivered the ultimatum to a disheveled Dr. Benes. Prague radio announced it some hours later.

It evoked consternation in Paris. Dr Stefan Osusky, a career diplomat of impeccable credentials, had been Czech minister there for twenty years. Not until 1942 did his papers, filed for an abstruse libel action in London, shed light on the two Anglo-French ultimata to Benes, on his evasiveness, and on his search for honourable ways of saying neither Yes nor No. On the seventeenth, these papers suggest, the French minister in Prague had pressed the president about the crisis; Benes had *volunteered* to cede territories to Germany. He had outlined them on the map — the move would have transferred a million Germans to Hitler — but then suggested that London and Paris confront him with an ultimatum so he could save face. Small wonder that his sudden rejection of that ultimatum had aggrieved his allies. Osusky now learned that Daladier had revealed this background in confidence to his Cabinet. The foreign minister did not reply to Osusky's shocked inquiry; but Daladier confirmed it in an interview with him.[34]

At eight a.m. on September 21 this telephone conversation was found going on between Prague and an anonymous voice in Paris.

> PRAGUE: Benes has accepted the London plan upon the nocturnal demarche of the British and French Ministers, since both countries threatened to ditch us completely if he didn't. There's only one hope: You've got to contact Blum immediately — leader of the biggest Party in France — and try everything you can to make Herriot head of government. And contact Attlee to do the same in England. I'm going to try and get through to Attlee from here too. There's not a moment to lose, you must act immediately.

By ten-thirty Churchill had contacted Osusky. His advice was plain, as the Nazi wiretappers reported.

> OSUSKY: You've got to hold out!
> BENES: Yes, but how long?
> OSUSKY: Well, what deadline did they give you?
> BENES: They want it [the reply] this afternoon.

Osusky asked him to think it over calmly.

> BENES: The choice is simple enough: either we hit out or we don't.
> OSUSKY: I was taken aback because I phoned Masaryk in London and he told me it was all over already—
> BENES: We haven't made our reply yet.
> OSUSKY: — because he asked me to tell Churchill, who's in Paris today. So I told Churchill it's all over and you'd accepted I told him I've heard nothing about it from Prague myself. He didn't know anything and couldn't tell me anything. I told Churchill, "Jan Masaryk asks me to tell you it's all over — they've accepted.

Osusky said he didn't know.

> BENES: They're not going to march now?

OSUSKY: I told you already, what matters is for us to present a united front. Their Government is here today and gone tomorrow.

Osusky did what he could to unseat Daladier. "In this uncertain situation," he would testify, "I approached my political friends for support and help."[35] He told Mandel, Campinchi, Reynaud, and others of the new Anglo-French ultimatum to Benes; three of the ministers said they would resign if Daladier did not withdraw it.

Reynaud had entered Churchill's name in his desk diary at mid-day and that of Spears that evening. (Spears was also in Paris seeing "discontented ministers.") Churchill told Benes, years later, that he found both Reynaud and Mandel depressed and talking of resigning.[36] He told Benes he had argued them out of it. Reynaud's memory was different: Churchill tried to persuade Mandel and himself "to insist on resigning."[37]

Winston certainly intended Benes not to cave in. "After his Paris talks with Mandel and Reynaud," noted the private secretary of Benes, "he wanted to telegraph us to put up a fight, but afterwards he dropped the idea because he didn't feel he could do so on his own responsibility."

While still in Paris, Churchill issued to the British press association the declaration he had foreshadowed to Sheila Grant Duff on Sunday. It described the "partition of Czechoslovakia under Anglo-French pressure" as a surrender to the "Nazi threat of force," and talked of "the prostration of Europe before the Nazi power."

The idea that safety can be purchased by throwing a small state to the wolves is a fatal delusion.

It was a call for an immediate showdown.

German war power, he warned, would grow faster than the Anglo-French preparations for defence. Parliament, in short, must be recalled.

* * *

He had the feeling that Chamberlain's hours in office were now numbered. Back in London on Thursday, September 22, he triumphantly told Jan Masaryk that three French ministers had submitted formal protests to Daladier. Now he needed to know precisely how the Anglo-French ultimatum had been worded. Whitehall and the Quai d'Orsay alike refused to release the details.

MASARYK: Please have the original text of the plan read through to us.
BENES: Original? We already sent it in a telegram!

Masaryk explained, without comment, that it had not reached him.

BENES: Aha!

MASARYK: Things here are snowballing in our favour.

That afternoon, Masaryk's staff telephoned solid chunks of disinformation to Prague. His deputy Karel Lisicky predicted that "that swine" Bonnet and the British Cabinet would resign within hours; his military attaché Josef Kalla confirmed it, and spoke of huge demonstrations sweeping London. At all costs Benes must hold on until Monday the twenty-sixth: then, Churchill hoped, Parliament would reconvene.

It was time to call The Focus. Churchill telephoned its Peers, MPs and journalists to meet him at his apartment at Morpeth Mansions at four-thirty p.m. First he steered his cab driver to No. 10 to learn the latest news from Godesberg, where the PM was conveying Benes' agreement to Hitler; Chamberlain hoped to attach certain terms to it. Then Winston drove on to his apartment where the first arrivals were already waiting for the lift. They rode up together.

"This is hell," said Harold Nicolson.

"It's the end of the British Empire," was how Churchill put it.[38]

Standing behind the fire-screen nursing a whisky and soda, "rather blurry," as Nicolson affectionately described him, and "rather bemused," Churchill outlined the Cabinet's conditions for agreement.

"Hitler will never accept such terms," pointed out Nicolson.

"In that case," replied Churchill, "Chamberlain will return tonight and we shall have war."

That would make it mildly inconvenient, observed someone, for Mr Chamberlain — to be in enemy territory.

"Even the Germans," observed Churchill, "would not be so stupid as to deprive us of our beloved prime minister."

During the evening, Attlee phoned: Labour was now prepared to come in. "Let us form the Focus," said Churchill. From Pratt's to the Beafsteak, the mood was one of despair.

IN PARIS THE rebellion had fizzled out. The three ministers marched in to see Daladier — Reynaud's desk diary shows his appointment, together with Mandel and Champetier de Ribes, at four p.m.; but when the premier told them Benes had accepted the ultimatum, and had suggested the original ultimatum himself, they saw no further cause to resign.

Churchill had left Spears in Paris; he visited their mutual friend Alexis Léger. Léger blamed Britain for ditching Czechoslovakia. Several others of The Focus were in Paris too that day: Stephen King-Hall — the pamphleteer hired by Union Time Ltd — had an appointment with Reynaud at eleven; T.U.C. chief Citrine was seen haggling over his room price at the Lutetia; Dalton cornered Blum, and whispered *"Courage!"* into his ear. Blum mistook the encouragement and kissed the towering Labour intellectual on one cheek.[39] Boothby flew in, then on to Geneva to meet Litvinov at the League of Nations. "The Russians will give us full support," he confirmed after to Spears.[40] But nobody at No. 10 was interested in that.

The talks at Godesberg broke down on the twenty-third. Hitler increased his demands, rendered mistrustful by his knowledge of the Masaryk-Benes conversations; Chamberlain was only willing to forward, but not to recommend, those demands to the Czechs.

Thus the crisis seemed at hand. Recalling Churchill's June 1937 advice to wait until Britain's hour of distraction, Chaim Weizmann, Israel Moses Sieff and the other Zionists bore down on Jan Masaryk late that afternoon, urging war. "Perhaps God is doing all this so that the Jews may go back to Palestine," said the Minister of Health that evening. "I believe that will be the result."[41]

At four-thirty p.m. the Foreign Office telephoned to their Prague legation a telegram to inform the Czechoslovak Government "that the French and British Government cannot continue to take the responsibility of advising them not to mobilize." Benes was told at six. Halifax told Jan Masaryk at six p.m., adding: "For God's sake, do it quick!"[42] Benes signed the mobilisation papers and later recalled having been most happy: he turned to his wife and to Jan's sister Alice, said that the die was cast. "We are heading for war."[43]

* * *

Churchill drove down to Chartwell for the weekend. That Saturday morning, September 24 he knew that if Hitler's Plan was rejected, it would bring Europe to the brink of war.

MASARYK: Mr President, first of all please send me by cipher the text of the telegram with which they advised us to mobilize.
BENES: Yes, right away.
MASARYK: Second, how does the Plan go?
BENES: The one we're to get now?
MASARYK: Yes.
BENES: We haven't yet got it.
MASARYK: I've told people here we've gone as far as we can go.
BENES: It's right out of the question for us to abandon our position.
MASARYK: Our troops must stay right where they are at any price, come what may! . . . And the moment anything comes at us, we open fire.

Evidently the Czechs were not planning to honour any agreement to withdraw. How useful it was, Masaryk commented, that Chamberlain was at Godesberg. "People" hoped the mobilization would not upset the Old Man there. "People here are only afraid we may give way again." "Things here look very different now." "I think all the Parties are with us now, even *The Times* sees we've got the upper hand. The tours de force have all stopped."

At mid-day that Saturday, Masaryk saw the Plan. He telephoned Eden, then hurried round to show it to him, saying his government could never accept it.[44] From there he telephoned the F.O. to arrange to see the Map at about four. From what he told Spears, the foreign secretary was evidently glowing with the Hitler-radiation that Chamberlain had brought back from Godesberg: the Führer, he echoed, would be satisfied with the Sudetenland.[45] France would not fight. ("His Majesty's Government should realize," Phipps had by that time telegraphed from Paris, "extreme danger of even appearing to encourage small, but noisy and corrupt, war group here."[46]) Three hours later, Masaryk handed out to Dalton, Attlee, Greenwood and others the first copies of the "petrifying" pre-dawn ultimatum that the British and French had slapped on Benes three days before.[47] That evening, General Spears and seven others of The Focus including Harold Macmillan sent an urgent letter to Lord Halifax, threatening a Tory revolt if the screw was turned on Benes any tighter as Hitler was demanding.[48]

THAT SUNDAY, SEPTEMBER 25, Randolph Churchill and Desmond Morton lunched down at Chartwell with Winston. One of the Sunday newspapers, *Reynold's News*, had leaked accurate details of the ultimatum to Benes, supplied by a mole at the F.O. L.W. Carruthers, a Finchley journalist for *Time & Tide*, rushed copies down to Churchill and Spears. He urged Churchill to challenge Chamberlain to produce the Note to Parliament. Around mid-day, Lady Spears telephoned. Sir Derrick Gunston, one of the Focus MPs who had signed the last night's letter, had telephoned with rumours that half a dozen ministers were now threatening to resign. Winston said, "There is nothing to be done yet," but drafted a new statement demanding Parliament's recall.

Knowing that Daladier was coming over to see Chamberlain, Churchill and his colleagues winced at the thought that No.10 might yet persuade Benes to accept.[49] But Masaryk came down to Chartwell for lunch, and put his mind at rest. Earlier that morning, at 8:37 a.m. he had 'phoned Benes·

> MASARYK: After lunch I'll be coming together with some of the most important people and I think it'd be a good thing if this afternoon I tell the French and British something. When Daladier gets here I'll say I have a message for him and the British. "*I much regret,*" I'll announce, "*to have to say that this document cannot be accepted.*"

Over lunch Winston hammered that point home. Masaryk must deliver a firm No from Benes. The way that he expressed it breathed new life into the drooping Czech. On his way to No. 10, Masaryk called in on R.W. Seton-Watson — another of his legation's "clients" — for tea; he told him the decision. Masaryk's tail was up for the first time in days.[50]

Now that war seemed inevitable, some people like Lord Cecil felt that evening that Winston should be PM. Others felt sure that Chamberlain would pull back from the brink, but be swept aside in the resulting humiliation. Wise men disagreed: "If we have peace," said Zionist sage Chaim Weizmann, "people will forget their wrath and only remember that they have been somehow saved from war under their present rulers."[51]

At four p.m. the BBC announced that Prague had rejected Hitler's terms. When Spears telephoned Georges Mandel in Paris, the Frenchman reassured him that the mandate that Daladier and Bonnet were on their way to express at No. 10 was to back the Czechs.[52]

At five-thirty Masaryk handed over the formal rejection Note to Halifax and Chamberlain, and explained why, conscious that he was making history. "They called me in," he told Benes immediately afterwards, "and we talked for an hour. Their ignorance is so abysmal you wouldn't believe it." They had asked, however, whether Czechoslovakia would agree to an eleventh hour conference "at which we'd all participate?" That would at least stave off the evil hour set by the latest scandalous proposals. "Well, then," said Benes, still playing for time, "yes. Yes."

Fresh in funds, The Focus began printing millions of leaflets and booked a London hall for a protest meeting on Thursday to throw out the Chamberlain Four and set up a National Government.[53] That evening the Cabinet met — in a "blue funk," as Winston later said — then waited for the Frenchmen.[54] It was nine-thirty p.m. before they arrived, breathing new determination; but under painful cross-examination by Sir John Simon they could offer little account of what France could actually do for Czechoslovakia.

Since there was no word yet of Parliament being called Churchill sent out overnight telegrams from Chartwell to The Focus summoning a council of war at four p.m. the next day at Morpeth Mansions.[55]

WHEN HE RETURNED to London on that Monday morning, September 26, he was conscious that the week ahead might be one of the most crucial in history, and that he might end by playing the central role. On the previous evening, Masaryk had handed out copies of the Hitler map to British and American journalists,[56] and now Fleet-street splashed

Hitler's demands as well as Churchill's insistance that Parliament be recalled. Masaryk telephoned Prague.

> MASARYK: Everthing's going fine here. Every newspaper is 100 percent behind us. There's not one backing the other side.

But a terrible anguish overwhelmed the more vulnerable. Gripped by a clammy fear of the knockout blow, parents evacuated children to the country, fired their less essential below-stairs staff, hid their treasures, packed the family silver and sent it to the bank. "Will I be sent to a concentration camp?" asked one elderly German Jewess, fearing internment in England. "It is probable," was Lady Spears' bleak reply.

That Monday Winston opened a telegram from Baruch: "In case of war," said Baruch, "send the children and expectant mother [Diana Churchill] to me." But Diana would be an air raid warden in London. Winston replied: "Now is the time for your man to speak" — meaning Franklin Roosevelt.[57]

Hitler announced that he would broadcast that night. In the privacy of No. 10, the prime minister read to his Cabinet Churchill's appeal for the recall of Parliament and added that he would wait two more days.

He had one more card up his sleeve, but seems to have feared that it would no longer be enough. Chamberlain had sent Sir Horace Wilson with a letter to Hitler. It offered a conference to decide the means of implementing the Anglo-French plan. When Churchill was shown in at three-thirty he found Chamberlain "an exhausted and broken man," as he told Leo Amery. He urged the PM to issue a warning that Britain, France *and* Russia were united against Hitler: they must mobilize the Fleet: they must call up all reserves. The prime minister promised to do so one hour after Hitler's broadcast if it was not conciliatory.[58]

Churchill hurried back for the four o'clock Focus meeting at his "poste de commandement," Morpeth Mansions. He found them apprehensively awaiting his return.[59]

In Berlin that afternoon, in the marble halls of the Reich Chancery, Hitler issued an ultimatum to Sir Horace Wilson: aware from the wiretaps of Prague's delaying tactics, he gave Benes until two P.M. on Wednesday to agree to his terms. Come what might, he declared, he would have his troops in the Sudeten German territories on Saturday.

In Westminster, at No.11 Morpeth Mansions, Winston Churchill poured himself another weak whisky, and dilated at length upon what he had told Chamberlain: now they must press for a National Government, for immediate war measures, for the . blockade of Germany, for conscription — "We must get in touch with Russia." Unaware of his trafficking with Ivan Maisky, Leo Amery warned that wooing Russia would dismay Conservatives. They decided that Winston should go to Lord Halifax and persuade him to put out a threatening communique *before* Hitler's broadcast. This would force Chamberlain's hand and leave him no room for further manoeuvres.

The original intention of the Focus was to have a forty-second announcement broadcast in German over Nazi wavelengths in the pause just before Hitler spoke. All Germany would then hear of England's resolve to fight.*

Just how the document came to be drafted, and whose voice dictated the words it contained, are not clear even now: it spoke of "Russia" instead of "Soviet Union," but it was headed "official communique" and typed on Foreign Office notepaper. Rex Leeper, one of Masaryk's "clients" at the F.O. who had steered Britain to the brink in May, sent it to Reuter's agency. (Afterwards the F.O. and the French foreign ministry immediately disowned it. Phipps told the Quai d'Orsay it was not genuine; Bonnet told journalists that it was the work of "an obscure underling" of Vansittart.)

> The German claim to the transfer of the Sudeten areas has already been conceded by the French, British and Czechoslovak Governments, but if in spite of all the efforts made by the British Prime Minister a German attack is made upon Czechoslovakia the immediate result must be that France will be bound to come to her assistance, and Great Britain and Russia will certainly stand by France.

WHATEVER THE EXHILARATION these underground schemes produced amongst The Focus and in Whitehall, the ordinary citizens, and not a few of their MPs, viewed coming events with a foreboding whose intensity became apparent only after the shadow was dramatically lifted. Not since the Abdication, in fact, had Churchill so overlooked the darkening chasm that occasionally opens between public and published opinion. Reading Tuesday's *Daily Sketch*, one day before Hitler's ultimatum would expire, Lady Spears nervously wrote in her diary: "Worse than we thought. We feel on the brink. Curious atmosphere." Either the Germans overthrew their Führer — an echo, that, of Goerdeler and von Kleist — or: "We'll be at war by Saturday."

That early autumn Tuesday morning, September 27, Londoners glimpsed scenes whose like they had not seen for twenty years — lines outside libraries where gasmasks were being issued; volunteers digging air raid trenches in the Royal parks; evacuees crowding railroad stations, glancing at the skies; a solitary anti-aircraft gun in Hyde Park. From Wellington Barracks to Eton college ramparts of sandbags were being

---

*In the event no break-in was made into German wavelengths. The BBC, said Lindemann, fumbled or refused to break international wavelength agreements, so it went out over the conventional channels only, an hour after Hitler's speech.[60]

filled and stacked. Spears arranged for all Jewish refugees who wanted to fight to write him saying so. He phoned his wife: "Arrangements have been made" — in fact by The Focus — "to broadcast Chamberlain's speech in German." She unhung their better pictures and drove their valuables to their cottage in the country.[61]

That afternoon the prime minister instructed the First Sea Lord to mobilize the Fleet as Churchill had suggested; Duff Cooper, the navy's minister, was only informed later. Even before learning of this, Hitler partially shifted his ground: he sent a telegram assuring Chamberlain that German troops would not advance further into Czechoslovakia than the territory which Prague had already agreed to cede. "I feel certain," Chamberlain replied in a perhaps unfortunately worded telegram, offering to fly over yet again, "that you can get all essentials without war and without delay."

From Prague, Ripka telephoned Sheila Grant Duff that the Foreign Office was applying "great pressure" on Benes to knuckle under. She telephoned the news to Churchill. He was furious — he had seen Chamberlain and Halifax the day before, he shouted to her, and they had assured him the pressure was at an end; he was so angry that he slammed down the telephone when he finished speaking.[62] Shortly, he received from Masaryk bare details of what the Czech called the "Hitler-Chamberlain auction," with full permission, to use them — "Just please not verbatim so some of my 'friends' will not have a pretext to send me away from London. The map will be ready tonight."

Churchill listened at Morpeth Mansions as Chamberlain broadcast at eight that night, in deepening gloom as the familiar, grating voice talked of the letters that were pouring into No. 10. "How horrible, fantastic, incredible it is," the prime minister said, "that we should be digging trenches and trying on gas masks here because of a quarrel in a faraway country between people of whom we know nothing." These careless words aroused in those closest to the Czech cause, — whatever their motives may have been, bankers, diplomats, journalists, and politicians in The Focus, — "bewilderment," in the words of one, "and grief."

Around nine-thirty Winston telephoned General Spears and commanded him to telephone Reynaud in Paris, to assure him that the speech did not reflect the feeling of the country. But Spears found a strange drumming noise on his telephone and a three hour wait to get even Long Distance: it was the mobilization of the Fleet, they reflected; later a friend telephoned from Brussels and through her they got Reynaud to telephone at midnight.

Over dinner with Duff Cooper at the Admiralty Winston learned that the Fleet had been mobilized. He sent round to the *Evening Standard* an anonymous item for its Londoner's Diary, congratulating the First Lord on this move and reminding readers that Mr. Winston Churchill had taken the same steps on the Tuesday before the declaration of World War I.[63]

BRONZED AND FIT, the MPs streamed into Westminster for the recalled Parliament that Wednesday September 28, 1938. Before going down to the House Lady Spears looked around their Bayswater home, decided the servants' lavatory would be safest in an air raid and sent a servant out to buy black paint for the skylight. Passing the bank she withdrew £10 for emergencies.

If the rank-and-file MPs had opinions, they still kept them to themselves. At eleven o'clock the Focus caucus and a hundred other dissidents met in uproar over Chamberlain's broadcast in a tense Committee room, issuing notes to Party leaders. Into this mood of rising panic, the BBC broadcast two hours later air raid and child evacuation regulations.

Churchill drove down to the House.

Over at the Carlton grill, his friend Chaim Weizmann saw his hour coming too; he lunched in style, and invited several Gentile Zionists to discuss how to exploit the Czech crisis in the context of Palestine. Britain had only two divisions there, and only two more available for France. He thought he had Chamberlain over a barrel now. A year earlier a Foreign Office memorandum had pointed out that the Zionist policies of the Colonial Office were rousing anger throughout the Moslem Middle East, and that there was a powerful argument for revising them if the air situation was as perilous as Mr Churchill claimed.[64] Since then the PM had replaced William Ormsby-Gore by Malcolm MacDonald as Colonial Secretary; and now, in September, MacDonald had made it clear that partition of Palestine was a dead duck. On this famous Wednesday he sent for Weizmann and notified him that should war now break out Palestine would be subject to martial law and further immigration halted. Weizmann wrote to him that same day, warning that the British must choose between friendship of Jewry and of Arabs.

Blanche Dugdale returned from the Carlton to the House in time to hear a roar of applause lift the roof. She entered to find MPs giving Chamberlain a standing ovation. Churchill was sitting, ashen faced, with arms folded; his friends were seated with him, while 600 MPs stood and cheered. Up in the Speaker's gallery, the Queen Mother watched intently as Conservatives waved order-papers. The Party had rallied to their Leader just as Weizmann had predicted days before.

Half an hour before, Chamberlain had spread out his papers before him and embarked on a painfully ordered narrative of the Czech crisis while messengers hurried along the oaken benches handing out the telegrams and pink telephone slips that were descending on the Palace of Westminster. Churchill had stacked his telegrams ostentatiously in front of him, held together with an elastic band: confident that his hour had come.

As the deadpan prime minister's narrative advanced into the recent and unknown, the clock beneath the peers' gallery where Churchill had espied his old enemy Lord Baldwin sitting, moved on to twelve minutes past four. The PM had reached "yesterday morning" in his narrative — when a sheet of F.O. foolscap was rapidly passed along the front bench and handed to him.

"Herr Hitler," he announced, interrupting his own speech, and straightening up from his notes, "has just agreed to postpone his mobilization for twenty-four hours and to meet me in conference with Signor Mussolini and Monsieur Daladier at Munich."

War had been averted: the world was back from the brink. There was that instant of silence that demagogues know so well — a silence, broken by thunderous applause.[65] It sends a thrill into the marrow of the speaker; today it chilled Churchill's to the bone. Unjustly, he suspected that his crafty rival had stage-managed this very scene: he certainly did not forget the lesson when he came to announce the sinking of the enemy's biggest battleship some years later.

The House broke up in joyous cacophony. Were they tears of jealousy that welled into Winston's eyes, or of remorse?

He gripped Chamberlain's hand as the PM swept out of the Chamber.

"By God," he growled at him, *"you're lucky."*[66]

CHAPTER 13

Outcast

ONLY A SLICK of oil remained on the bubbling Parliamentary surface to mark the failure of Churchill's torpedo run. There followed eleven months of bitter personal despair.

If Chamberlain stubbornly refused to give him office in those months he had more than enough reason: He was concerned about Winston's growing recourse to alcohol, as he showed by remarks to Joseph Kennedy. Moreover, Winston's group had fought dirty; they had sold themselves to the Czechs for their own ends.*

The wounds never entirely healed between the vanquished and the victor. Chamberlain did not crow, but kept his lamentations private, telling only his sister what he was learning from the wiretaps: "I had to fight all the time against the defection of weaker brethren and Winston was carrying on a regular campaign against me with the aid of Masaryk the Czech minister. They, of course, are totally unaware of my knowledge of their proceedings; I had continual information of their doings & sayings which for the *n*th time demonstrated how completely Winston can deceive himself when he wants to, & how utterly credulous a foreigner can be when he is told the thing he wants to hear." In this case, added the PM, Churchill's message had been: "Chamberlain's fall is imminent."[2]

Winston's methods had also ruffled Britain's allies. The Cabinet's secretary noted in his diary that his sudden flight with Spears to Paris — and his visit only to Mandel and other government members opposed to Daladier's policy of peace — was most improper: The French foreign minister complained about it, and asked what Britain would say if prominent French statesmen did the same?[3]

---

*The principal Czech agent in London reported on October 20 that Masaryk had told him in July 1938: "I know that neither Sinclair, Seton-Watson, nor Attlee can save us: they're Opposition. What we've got to do is get amongst the members of government and the Conservatives." Now for the first time this agent received substantial funds from Masaryk: "I never had such a guilty conscience," he reported to Prague, "as when I was handing out the money the Minister played at my disposal."[1]

THE WORLD REJOICED as the news broke about the Four Power conference. As Chamberlain packed for Munich a two-word telegram from President Roosevelt lay on his desk: *"Good man!"*[4]* Come Sunday, and the whole of Fleet Street would have performed a complete somersault in Chamberlain's favour..

But the news left Winston more cast down than before. In London's clubs that Wednesday night, September 28, MPs spat out his name like snake venom. Anthony Crossley, a young Tory MP who had teetered on the brink of The Focus, listened to them discussing the recent "disreputable intrigues" and told Winston afterwards that, frankly, his name was mentioned.

"The last word has not been spoken yet," replied Churchill, affecting indifference.[6]

The plans of The Focus had come unstuck. They met that Thursday in private over luncheon at the Savoy — Churchill, Lady Violet, Lord Lloyd, Nicolson, Spears, Wickham Steed and many MPs.[7] Glasses of cognac stood amongst newspapers whose front pages already carried wire photos of Chamberlain being cheered through the streets of the Bavarian capital. That afternoon Lloyd, Cecil, Sinclair and Churchill signed a telegram entreating him not to betray the Czechs but to draw upon Russia's aid.

Eden refused pointblank to sign, seeing it as a "vendetta against Chamberlain."[8] Attlee, when found, also ducked out: first, he said, he must secure the approval of his Party who were meeting, as Lady Violet recalled, "at some watering-place a fortnight hence."

The Focus meeting dragged on until evening, gloomily aware that nothing could be done. Nicolson saw that even Winston had lost his fighting spirit. His eyes were wet as the meeting broke up. On the nine o'clock news Spears heard of the first British proposals at Munich. His eyes brimming with tears, he told his wife he had never been so ashamed, so heartbroken. Together they went round to Morpeth Mansions, but all the fight had gone out of their champion.

"It's too late to do anything," Churchill muttered.

Spears replied, "It's never too late."

In a towering rage at the refusal of Attlee and Eden to sign the telegram, Churchill dined at the Savoy with the Other Club.[9] When he re-emerged hours later, the early editions carried the Munich terms. These directed Benes to pull his troops out of the Sudetenland including the vital fortifications over the next ten days.

---

*Ten years later Chamberlain's widow sought White House permission for its release. President Harry S. Truman deemed it inadvisable in a presidential election year. In 1950 she tried again. Truman scrawled, "I do not think it should be released. HST."[5]

Spears soldiered on. Through an emergency committee set up the next day he issued a million leaflets, "Czechoslovakia's Martyrdom." There were no problems of finance.[10]

Overnight Churchill too recovered his old spirit. At Morpeth Mansions Nicolson glimpsed on Winston's face on Friday morning, September 30, a grim expression he could only describe as utterly blank, and heard him exclaim to Lord Cecil: "I feel twenty years younger."[11] After telephoning Masaryk that Friday evening to implore Dr Benes to dig his heels in and refuse to pull Czech troops out of the vital fortifications for the next forty-eight hours at least — he assured Masaryk that "a tremendous reaction against the betrayal of Czechoslovakia is imminent" — he climbed into his black Humber and drove down to Chartwell. Chamberlain's wiretappers had also picked up this final incitement to war — for such there would have been if Benes were now to disregard the Four Power agreement. The head of the Foreign Office recorded in amusement that Winston, Lloyd and others were still "intriguing with Masaryk and Maisky."[12]

By the time that the prime minister landed at Heston airport at six o'clock that evening, to declare to the enraptured throng that he had gained peace with honour, Mr Churchill, author and broadcaster, had resumed work on his *History of the English-Speaking Peoples*. On the following day, Saturday October 1, he had an appointment with a young producer from the BBC, fresh out of Cambridge and already secretly in the pay of the Soviet Government. We don't know what they discussed, but they seem to have found common ground because after their talk he inscribed a copy of *Arms & The Covenant*: "To Guy Burgess, from Winston S. Churchill, to confirm his admirable sentiments."

It poured with rain that weekend. Lady Diana Cooper phoned Chartwell to report that Duff Cooper had resigned as First Lord. She heard Winston sobbing. Chamberlain gave the admiralty to Lord Stanhope.

Trying to rebuild a united front against the prime minister, Churchill telephoned the economist Roy Harrod. "This is Winston Churchill speaking," he began, and explained what he was attempting. Harrod suggested that he try the more eminent trade union leaders.

"I have done that already," came the icy reply. "They're worse than Chamberlain."[13]

CHAMBERLAIN GAVE ORDERS to buy up Prague's surplus arms to stop them getting into the wrong hands (in Spain or Palestine.)[14]

He viewed the Zionists and Winston with the same loathing as he bestowed on Dr Benes and Jan Masaryk, and it would not have surprised him had he known that as Masaryk walked into Weizmann's home late that Saturday, October 1, the whole company rose in mute acknowledgement and the ladies kissed the diplomat. Mazaryk found there the Marks & Spencer's directors Simon Marks and Israel Moses Sieff, discussing ways of destroying Chamberlain's policies on Palestine;[15] a few hours earlier MacDonald had informed Weizmann that if war broke out Palestine would come under martial law and the *yishuv*, the Jewish community, would be conscripted. "We can only work by every means," wrote one virago attending that evening's conclave on how to end the British mandate, "fair and foul . . . to buy land, bring in men, get arms."

Masaryk revealed that he had tackled Sir Alexander Cadogan about the wiretap records handed over by Hitler, and had denied using such language. "From one friend to another," was Cadogan's reply, "be careful."[16]

The downpour continued throughout Sunday.

After a brief ultimatum, Poland seized Teschen, a Czech mining town. A bedraggled Churchill lunched at Bracken's house with the Polish ambassador — whose name he could never remember. They had last lunched together on the day of Chamberlain's announcement of the Munich conference. Now whatever sympathy he had entertained for Poland had evaporated: if war came, the world would leave her to the Nazis and their Schrecklichkeit.

Count Edward Raczynski inquired, "But do you think there will be war, Mr Churchill?"

"My dear Polish ambassador," said Churchill, sidestepping that elusive name, "There is war *now!*"[17]

It had not yet occurred to the Poles to court the democracies. In Warsaw they introduced vicious nationality laws to prevent Polish Jews returning home from emigration; in Berlin, they coquetted with Hitler over a grand alliance against Russia; in Washington their ambassador complained about the "almost 100 percent Jewish control" of American radio, film and newspapers, and about the Jews' coarse but effective propaganda line: "The American people," this noble diplomat, Count Jerzy Potocki, informed Warsaw, "are told that peace in Europe is hanging only by a thread and that war is inevitable." He identified the men behind this campaign as Baruch, Morgenthau, Judge Felix Frankfurter, and the Governor of New York State — they posed, he said, as defenders of democracy but in the final analysis were "connected by unbreakable ties with international Jewry."[18]* The Poles would remain pariahs until March 1939.

---

*The Nazis captured Count Potocki's telegram in Warsaw and published it in March 1940. Baruch wrote him icily: "I think this requires an explanation."[19] Potocki denied the document's authenticity (it was genuine. The original carbon copies of all his telegrams are in the Louis P. Lockner collection at the Hoover Library.)

For four days beginning that Tuesday, both Houses debated the Four Power agreement. Winston manoeuvred for one final torpedo run: he sent Macmillan to ask Dalton to bring his leader Clement Attlee to a meeting of dissident Tories at Bracken's house. Attlee ducked the meeting again, and it went ahead without him. The MPs agreed tactics in the big debate: Should the Tory dissidents vote against Chamberlain or merely abstain? Anxious to see as many MPs abstaining as possible, both on the Government's motion and on the Labour amendment, Churchill asked Dalton not to make the latter too patently a vote of censure. Dalton said his friends were not frightened of that.

"We must not only be brave," Churchill lectured him. "We must be victorious."

Dalton liked him, preferring Churchill's toughness to the "wishy washiness" of Eden whom Churchill had also persuaded to attend.

Overshadowing all the Tory dissidents was the fear that Chamberlain might call a snap election and withdraw the Whip from them. Few of Churchill's group could afford to lose an election: General Spears would be "faced with the prospect of losing £2,000 a year from Czechs," as his wife wrote disarmingly in her diary, adding almost as an afterthought: "And his seat in Parliament."[20]

Churchill asked if Labour would agree not to contest constituencies where the dissidents were opposed by official Conservative candidates: Dalton refused to commit himself.[21]

* * *

At ten past five on October 5, 1938, Churchill rose to deliver the most important speech in his career.[22]

Years before, he had studied Lord Randolph Churchill's style of oratory, and perfected it as his own. "Never peek slyly at your notes," he would say in 1945, tutoring a colleague on the art.[23] "They should be flagrantly waved in the face of the MPs." He took his time and studied his notes quite openly, grasping the lapels of his coat and standing well back from the Box; with his special glasses he could read his typescript at five feet. "Do not touch the Box lightly with your hand — that only distracts the audience's attention. If you touch the Box at all, then bang it solemnly with the fist at an appropriate moment." And, he added, a menacing scowl glowered at the audience would add theatrical effect.

In this speech he made a fatal error: he set those notes aside. He had begun to praise Duff Cooper as the real hero of Munich, when Lady Astor loudly interrupted: "Nonsense!"

Rattled, he looked up to answer her.

"She could not have heard the Chancellor of the Exchequer admit," he began, "in his illuminating and comprehensive speech just now that Herr Hitler had gained in this particular leap forward in substance all he set out to gain."

It was an obscure, uncharted side-track, but he rattled further down it. "The utmost," he floundered, pausing, "my right Hon Friend the Prime Minister has been able to secure by all his immense exertions, by all the great efforts and mobilisation which took place in this country, uh, the utmost he has been able to gain –"

"– Is *peace!*" shouted several Members in delight.

After that his speech fell off its hinges. At one point he attacked the Munich settlement in a laboured witticism: "One pound was demanded at the pistol's point. When it was given, two pounds were demanded at the pistol's point. Finally the dictator consented to take one pound seventeen shillings and sixpence, and the rest in promises of goodwill for the future."

> There can never be [he went on] friendship between the British democracy and Nazi power, that power which spurns Christian ethics, which cheers its onward course by barbarous paganism, which vaunts the spirit of aggression and conquest, which derives strength and perverted pleasure from persecution, and uses, as we have seen, with pitiless brutality the threat of murderous force.

As Churchill thundered this denunciation, Chamberlain tossed his head in scornful denial.[24] Sir Harry Goschen felt Winston should have held his tongue; the speech had been trumpeted all round the world and had set back Britain's reputation. The *Times* scoffed that he made Jeremiah look an optimist by comparison, the *Express* derided it as "an alarmist oration by a man whose mind is soaked in the conquests of Marlborough." Only the *Telegraph* stated thoughtfully that Mr Churchill's earlier warnings, seemingly verified by events, entitled him to be heard.

When the vote was taken, the mutiny squibbed. Only thirty MPs abstained, with thirteen including Churchill remaining seated.

He found it hard to forgive his valiant friends who now voted for the Government. One he abused "like a Billingsgate fishwife," and cancelled their firstname friendship. Another, Robert Boothby, reprimanded by Bracken for "crumpling," bleated in a note to Churchill that he had in fact – surreptitiously – abstained. "I do not think I have 'crumpled'; but confess I cannot regard the events of the past few days, which I sincerely believe portend the doom of at any rate my generation, without agitation." "I really have not changed my mind at all," Boothby explained to Spears, "But after Munich I was given certain information by two people who knew the facts, which led me to the conclusion that in the event of war we should probably have been defeated within three weeks. In these circumstances I don't think Chamberlain had any alternative but to come to terms."[25]

His position secure, Chamberlain adjourned the House until November 1, pointing out that it was for the Speaker to decide if it should be recalled earlier. "But," Churchill loudly interjected, "only on the advice of His Majesty's Government!" — an offensive remark which Chamberlain haughtily called "unworthy." Churchill pinked with anger and demanded that the PM retract, which attracted this reply on Downing Street notepaper: "You are singularly sensitive for a man who so constantly attacks others."[26]

A month without Parliament would allow tempers to cool. There was no knowing what mischief the bellicose would reap if they continued to sow disharmony from that ancient platform.

By a hair's breadth, peace had been preserved at Munich. So Chamberlain remarked in a letter to his sister. "Unhappily," he continued, "there are a great many people who . . . do all they can to make their own gloomy prophecies come true."[27]

For several days Churchill tried to prepare a fresh torpedo run. It was Cripps who suggested that a small group of men "prepared to take their political lives in their hands" should sign a national appeal.[28] Dalton asked fellow Labour Party leaders Attlee and Morrison to join him in a three-a-side conference in the Conservative Harold Macmillan's flat; this time Eden got cold feet and Duff Cooper would not come without him. "Only Churchill would have met us," wrote Dalton, "and this we judged could be done without so much elaboration."[29]

Winston shrugged and returned to Chartwell. Observing him, Macmillan felt he was relapsing into a complacent Cassandra: "Well," seemed to be Churchill's attitude, "I've done my best. I've made all these speeches. Nobody has paid any attention. All my prophesies have turned out to be true. What more can I do?"[30]

* * *

One reason for the crumbling of support at this stage was the drying up of funds. Masaryk had resigned; on the advice of the Czech agent mentioned earlier the legation was purged of Leftists, Polish and German emigrés, and staff of Jewish origin. Benes also resigned and shortly arrived in England with his wife.[31]

He found he was not popular. Many Czechs disliked him even more than Chamberlain. When Chamberlain announced a £10m credit for Czechoslovakia,[32] a Mr Samson, whom the British authorities identified as "a Jew long resident in Britain" tipped off the Foreign Office that Benes and his former prime minister Milan Hodza had transferred £3m in English banknotes out of Prague and deposited them at his, Samson's, Lloyds Bank safe deposit at Stamford Hill. When Cadogan recommended a Treasury investigation, an F.O. official fobbed him off, suggesting an examination of Samson's mental health instead.[33]

Such intrigues seem germane to this account: Benes was later baffled by Churchill's hesitancy to recognize the exile government he formed.[34] There were more such dubious transactions. On December 20 Masaryk tried to transfer £21,000 out of Prague using the Lord Mayor of London's Czech Refugee Relief Fund as a currency evasion device; part of these funds also belonged to Benes.

Churchill's stocks had sunk to near zero. Replying to a commiserating letter from *Winnipeg Free Press* editor John W. Dafoe, Winston wrote on October 11, 1938: "I am now greatly distressed, and for the time being staggered by the situation. Hitherto the peace-loving Powers have been definitely stronger than the Dictators, but next year we must expect a different balance."

Over the next weeks a new bloc had begun to form including Eden, Duff Cooper, and Cranbourne. Lady Spears thought they were "making a mistake in not wanting to include Winston." On November 6 Eden invited Gunston, Amery, Spears, Cartland, Crossley, Macmillan and others to a meeting, but not Churchill. Nicolson was relieved, finding that the old man had become embittered, "more out for a fight than for reform." Discouraging the notion of inviting Eden to their next luncheon, Churchill explained on the twelfth to The Focus secretary: "I doubt if Mr Eden would come. he is very shy at present." Shy was the wrong word: One cold morning, visiting Stornoway House, Winston asked Lord Beaverbrook to get Eden on the 'phone. A voice said he was just coming, until Max said: "Mr *Churchill* wants to speak to him." After some delay, the voice said: "He's out walking," and put the phone down.[35]

Beaverbrook wrote off Churchill. "This man of brilliant talent, splendid abilities, magnificent power of speech and fine stylist," he wrote on the tenth, "has ceased to influence the British public."[36] A week later, in a debate on the need for a ministry of supply, Winston passionately appealed for fifty members to vote with him: only Macmillan and Bracken did so.

WHAT BROUGHT CHURCHILL back into the limelight was the Nazi propaganda campaign that began nine days after Munich. Speaking in his snarling, guttural Austrian dialect to fortification workers at Saarbrucken, Hitler picked on him by name. "It only needs for Mr Duff Cooper or Mr Eden or Mr Churchill," he declared, rolling the r's in Chu*rrr*chill, "to come to power in Britain in place of Chamberlain, and then we can be quite sure that the aim of these gentlemen would be to start a new world war. They make no bones about it, they speak of it quite openly."

Shortly, Hitler's propaganda officials issued a secret circular: "In future the German press is not to pass up any opportunity of attacking Eden, Churchill and Duff Cooper. These men are for ever picking on Germany and stirring up hatred of her. We must repay them in their own coin. In the eyes of the world Churchill and Duff Cooper are to be branded as warmongers and provocateurs whose schemes have been thwarted by Munich. Newspapers close to the three are putting it about that they are candidates for high Cabinet posts. The German press is to adopt such a censorious attitude to these three that without our uttering one word to this effect the entire world decides of its own volition that for such personalities to be given high office would be the gravest affront to Germany."[37]

The barrage continued when Hitler spoke on November 6 at Weimar. "I recently named three of these globetrotting warmongers by name. What stung them was not the allegation, but my audacity in naming them."

> Mr Churchill [he continued] has openly declared his view that the present regime in Germany must be overthrown by internal forces who are standing gratefully by to make themselves available to him.
> If Mr Churchill would mingle more with Germans and less with emigré circles, with venal traitors in foreign pay, he would see the absurdity and stupidity of such vapourings.

Hitler asked "this gentleman who appears to be living on the Moon" to believe that no force capable of turning its hand against the regime existed in Germany.

If this campaign was the first turning point for Churchill — since British public opinion instinctively rallied to his defence — the second came very shortly. On the seventh a young Polish Jew demented by Warsaw's new nationality laws gunned down a German diplomat in Paris. Dr Goebbels' own newspaper *Der Angriff* claimed "a direct link" between Churchill and the assassin. The diplomat died two days later, and Goebbels touched off a vicious pogrom in revenge: synagogues and businesses flamed; Jews were manhandled, murdered or thrown into concentration camps.

Just when his isolation seemed final and complete, this Nazi Night of Broken Glass saved him. The loathsome pogrom made Germany an international outcast; and it released substantial Jewish funds into the 1939 campaign to draft Churchill into No. 10.

It was a sickening setback for appeasers like the American ambassador. Like Chamberlain, Joseph Kennedy preferred peace at any price. His habitat was the Clivedon set. His views were poison to Churchill, whose men were already canvassing round the backdoors of the White House, demanding the ambassador's recall. "I may say in passing," Bracken wrote privately to Baruch, "that your Ambassador in London exhausted the resources of his rhetoric in praising the Munich pact." Hobnobbing with his German colleague Herbert von Dirksen, Kennedy — like Count Potocki — remarked upon the "baleful influence" of the Jews upon American journalism and government. At the Trafalgar Day dinner three weeks after Munich, he declared that democracies and dictatorships should settle their differences — "After all," he said, in a passage which Bracken drew to Baruch's attention, "We have to live together in the same world whether we like it or not." To London friends he described Roosevelt's Democratic policy as "a Jewish production."[38]*

Churchill made no secret of his adherence to the Zionist cause. When Palestine was debated on November 24 he criticized Chamberlain's policy. "The Court is august," he said finding some of his former eloquence, "the judges are incorruptible, their private virtues are beyond dispute, but the case is urgent and all they have been able to do in three whole years of classic incapacity is to paulter, and maunder, and jibber on the Bench." Regardless of the uproar it would cause in the Moslem world, he recommended allowing up to 25,000 Jews to immigrate into Palestine annually for the next ten years.[40]

Kennedy meanwhile sailed for the United States in December 1938, and would not return until late February.

IN MID NOVEMBER 1938 Clementine Churchill left England for the West Indies. To her long letters Winston replied with only the patchiest of telegrams. He was still swamped with work on the *History* "I have been toiling double shifts," he dictated on December 18, "It is laborious: & I resent it & the pressure." He softened the typed letter with a few lines in "his own paw." Writing a few days later about the death of her oldest friend, he reflected upon mortality — upon the many now dying whom he had known when they were young. "It is quite astonishing to reach the end of life & feel just as you did fifty years before. One must always hope for a sudden end, before faculties decay."[41]

He was the kind of driven man who seldom contemplates suicide, however bottomless the slough. The post-Munich strain might have

---

*Biographer James Landis studied Kennedy's (still inaccessible) 1938 diary and wrote him informally ten years later: "I've been over the October and November stuff. You get busier and busier, not to speak of the Jews starting to mess the thing up." And — justifying a draft chapter on "the Jewish propaganda following Munich," — "You personally were very conscious of it at the time."[39]

pushed other men over that brink. "Winston, Eden, and the rest of us who regarded Munich as a great surrender have been much abused," wrote Bracken, most intimate of his conspirators, to Baruch.[42]

But Churchill never lost his curiosity about what the future still held in store for him. One evening ten years later, in the Smoking Room at the House, he reminisced about films — he had seen some, like Alexander Korda's "Lady Hamilton," twenty times. "You know, one can't help admiring the Almighty," he said, in that voice he used when working up to a point, "He's been telling this Story of Life for thousands of years, he's never repeated himself once, nobody knows what the end is going to be — but only one in ten thousand walks out in the middle!"[43]

FOR A WHILE he tried to unseat Leslie Hore-Belisha at the War Office.

He saw his chance when his MP son-in-law Duncan Sandys, a first lieutenant in the army, was disciplined by the Army after revealing secret data on anti-aircraft deficiencies in the House. Sandys claimed this was a breach of Parliamentary privilege. "For the Churchill clique," smirked a German diplomat in London, "the affair is grist to the mill, and that is why Churchill egged Sandys on to raise the matter." This was also the War Office view, where Sir Henry Pownall wrote that Sandys was a "slippery young gentleman" backed by Winston, and that both hated the secretary of state and longed to catch him out. The Committee of Privileges found in Sandys' favour, but to Churchill's dismay it later turned out that it had been furnished with inaccurate facts. Sir John Simon wrote to the PM, "I have the impression that Winston and Co . . . would not be sorry to see it dropped provided, of course, that they escape the discredit which may come to them."[44]

Months later, on December 5, the house debated the affair. Churchill declared that Hore-Belisha had been too complacent over the Territorial Army. "When?" demanded Hore-Belish, rising to his feet. "And where?"

"I have not come unprepared," replied Churchill.

But he fumbled his notes, and those press clippings he read out mitigated the minister rather than condemning him. Hore-Belisha challenged, "Will the Right Hon. Gentleman go on reading!" Each succeeding sentence demolished Churchill's own argument the more. "He is becoming an old man," remarked one Tory MP; to another it was like watching a tiger miss his spring.[45]

Personal indebtedness still oppressed Churchill as 1939 began. He hoped to earn £22,420 that year including £7,500 on the completion of the *History* — he was now fighting the Wars of the Roses, having put Joan of Arc to the stake — £4,880 from the *Telegraph* and £4,200 from the *News of the World*. Chamberlain had no intention of distracting him from his literary endeavours. "If Winston walks in at the door," he had once said to Baldwin, "*I* walk out of the window." He quoted this in mid-December to one of Roosevelt's intimates who brought him a private message — that in the event of war he "would have the industrial resources of the American nation behind him." People could not expect to walk in and out of governments at will, said Chamberlain, particularly if they had made things difficult at an anxious moment.[46]

Privately, Churchill did not believe that Britain was Germany's next target. He predicted on December 22 to Clementine that when Hitler moved again, probably in February or March, it would be against Poland. In fact he cared little for that country: she had attracted disdain by her "cynical, coldhearted behaviour" in seizing Teschen.

For tactical reasons, however, he wanted the British to believe that they were at risk, and equally that the Soviet Union presented no danger at all. "War is horrible," Churchill told Kingsley Martin for the *New Statesman*, "but slavery is worse, and you may be sure that the British people would rather go down fighting than live in servitude."

At the same time he urged closer co-operation with the Kremlin. "Soviet Russia," he averred, in an interview for *Picture Post*, "has never made the blunder of thinking the welfare of its people could be increased by looting its neighbours. However much one may disagree with its political and economic theories, it has hitherto shown no trace of the aggressive intentions which appear to inform the three partners of the so-called axis."[47] Before many months had passed he would be wiser in this respect.

By January 1939 Whitehall was awash with rumours of Hitler's next strike. Sources spoke of a sudden coup — of a knockout blow against Britain, of an invasion of Holland. Perhaps malignant forces in England were keeping tension high. Lord Halifax hinted at this in a telegram to Washington later that month: some messages had come, he said, from highly placed Germans of undoubted sincerity, others from refugees claiming links with leading German personalities.[48]

Churchill did not take them seriously. On January 7 he left to vacation on the Riviera. Passing through Paris, he lunched with Reynaud, met with Phipps and Mendl, listened to Blum's opinion that those two "ruffians" Hitler and Mussolini would soon be off again, then headed for the Mediterranean by overnight train. Courage had returned to the French generals as the threat of war receded: he learned from Blum — who had it from Daladier who had it from Gamelin who had it direct from General Georges — that the French could have pierced Hitler's West Wall by Day Fifteen of the Czech war at least.[49] Perhaps it was fortunate for their self-esteem that they never knew that Hitler had planned to have his Panzer divisons in Prague by Day Three.

His feelings towards his own Party were of unmitigated bitterness. His local officials at Epping had now suggested that Britain come to terms with Germany, and indicated that they preferred an MP of that view. Winston wrote to Clementine on the ninth not mincing his language about "these dirty Tory hacks who would like to drive me out of the Party".

He lazed at his usual château, lying abed and dictating 1,500 words a day of manuscript. In the evenings he played the tables, preferably with other people's money. "Just as at Chartwell I divided my days between building and dictating," he teased Clementine, "so now it is between dictating and gambling."[50]

He dined frequently with the Windsors who lived near by. An American friend of the Duke's, a colonel from their London embassy, was also there, writing a copious and contemptuous diary about the wealthy foreigners he encountered on the Riviera. "We dined with Maxine Elliot at her villa," he wrote one night, identifying among the other guests Mr Churchill, Lady Drogheda and the flamboyantly lesbian Marchioness of Milford Haven: "The Duke does not like people with her reputation." After dinner they played vingt-et-un, and Churchill began to monologue, disapproving of Charles Lindbergh for visiting Germany and accepting a decoration. The American winced at some of his remarks, "But knowing his gift for oratory and my inarticulateness I remained silent." He thanked God he could leave early.[51] Churchill dominated these evenings. Often he deprecated Franco's coming victory. After dwelling upon the illusions which had made Franco popular among the "well-to-do" a chauffeur drove him down to the Casino. "It amuses me very much to play," he explained to Clementine, "so long as it is with their money."[52]

On the day after he wrote these words, he and the Duke of Windsor sat by the fireplace and argued fiercely about Franco.* Perched on the sofa's edge the slim ex-king tore into Churchill's latest article about Spain, and mocked at his proposed alliance with the Kremlin.

The paunchy politician was the kind of checkers player who sweeps the pieces off the board when the game goes against him.

"When our kings are in conflict with our constitution," he roared, with gravelly voice, "we change our kings."

---

*Five months into the war, Spears was told by a French officer friend that the Duke had told him, "Moi, j'aime les allemands!" While the Duchess asked the French senator De la Granges and others, "After all, does anybody know what we are fighting for?" And, "Will we be any better at the end of it all?"[54]

Britain, he cried was in the gravest danger of her long history. Some of them may have pondered why then he was desporting himself down here; others probably reflected, as had Chamberlain, that the danger of war was lessened with each day that Winston was far from Westminster. Of course nobody dared to provoke the famous temper by uttering such lèse-majesté out loud. "The rest of us sat fixed in silence," wrote one guest.[53]

A FEW DAYS after Winston's return, Chamberlain replaced Inskip by Lord Chatfield as Minister for Co-ordination of Defence.

Winston took it as a fresh snub. "How indescribably bloody," he wrote to his sister-in-law, "everything is!"[55]

He resumed his wooing of Labour. On February 9, 1939 several Labour MPs were invited to the Savoy for a "strictly private" luncheon with The Focus. Lord Halifax was principal guest; he spoke briefly and answered questions. His secretary made a private note that one of the Labour men, Rennie Smith, had become very pro-Halifax "since the Focus lunch." Smith approved the plan that Churchill, who had presided, set out for encircling Germany with a ring of peace-loving states.[56]

That spring of 1939 the heavily financed publicity push for Churchill began. It was to characterize the middle months of 1939. *Picture Post's* Hungarian born editor Stefan Lorant, who had fled Germany in 1933, ran three prominent articles on his background and political views. The first, written by Wickham Steed, promised that Churchill's "greatest moment" was about to come. There were spreads of photographs of Chartwell and his family.[57] Asked in one episode about his policy at home, Winston explained: "I think it will be necessary to form a government upon a broader base and ensure the cooperation of the great mass of the working people if we are to carry through a strong foreign policy."

He was happy to let the publicity machine gather momentum without him. Resolving his personal indebtedness still had first claim to his time. Turning down a request from Spears to speak at Carlisle he explained that it was "absolutely necessary" for him to be down at Chartwell every possible night of 1939 in order to complete his *History*.[58]

CHAPTER 14

Still Hibernating

WHILE FIRST PRAGUE, then Danzig began to smoulder, Churchill barely lifted his head from the desk where the final chapters of his magisterial *History of the English-Speaking Peoples* were taking shape.

He rarely ventured forth from Chartwell. Once General Spears invited him to speak in July. He replied declining: "I am so rarely in London now, and so busy on my *History*. . ." He would still be marshalling source books, directing researchers and dictating manuscript weeks after war broke out.

Munich had made him enemies and he knew it. Determined attempts were made to unseat him and he had to speak at several constituency meetings defending his record. Visitors found him in resigning mood. When he looked to the future, beyond Neville Chamberlain, he saw only the grinning features of Lord Halifax as Britain's next prime minister. Over lunch one day in March he said as much to Ambassador Kennedy — the tide was running so strongly for Chamberlain that it would be better to lie low.[1]

In Central Europe, Czecho-Slovakia began to break up from within, subverted by Hitler's agents. On the third Prague's Intelligence service reported to their British colleagues that Hitler planned to invade in mid-March.[2] On the eleventh Cadogan had like messages from both MI5 and the SIS; he wrote a bland "Maybe" in his diary. On the twelfth the banker Tony Rothschild forwarded to Churchill's informant and benefactor Sir Henry Strakosch a similar "ear witness" report.* The latter's protégé Sir John Simon commented sardonically on the rotten luck of Ribbentrop & Co, unable to communicate their horrible designs

---

*Characteristically, this report's hard factual kernel about Prague was cocooned in hooey: Franco about to be overthrown by Serrano Suñer; Mussolini about to hand an ultimatum to France; Italy about to swoop on Switzerland using paratroops and the Göring Regiment; and Germany about to invade England with flat bottomed boats massing in northern harbours.

to the general staff without "ear witnesses" giving the game away. Equally authoritative warnings had pinpointed March before, he pointed out, and scoffed to Halifax: "Well, the Ides of March have come, but not gone."[3]

Chamberlain cared little for the Czechs. According to German intercept records he sent a secret message to Berlin on the fourteenth expressing disinterest in Czecho-Slovakia.[4] Dr Goebbels notified Nazi editors: "London will show the utmost reserve even if there should be an external attack on Czecho-Slovakia."[5]

Late that day the new Czech president visited Hitler. Under menace, he signed over his strife-torn country to Germany's protection. Even before he arrived at the Reich Chancery an elite SS unit had occupied the Vitkovice steelworks to keep it from the predatory Poles — a serious blow for the Rothschild consortium who owned it and for General Spears, whose membership of the board would probably seem less necessary to the Führer than it had to Dr Benes. By dawn of March 15 Hitler himself was in Prague.

Chamberlain took it calmly. In the House that afternoon he declined to associate himself with those who charged Hitler with a breach of faith. His Intelligence authorities were less sanguine, having lost valuable resources in Prague, and invited the head of the Czech Intelligence service to transfer his staff to Britain; that gentleman accepted, passed through Paris on the eighteenth and directed the Czech legation there to send its war contingency Intelligence funds to him in London through the British embassy.[6]

TO HIS CREDIT, Lord Halifax refused to swallow Hitler's occupation of Prague. Upon his insistence, Chamberlain found belated words of indignation and spoke them at Birmingham on March 17. Churchill was impressed. Back at Chartwell, he received a letter from secretary of The Focus welcoming the PM's apparent recognition that he could not "shoo off dictators with an umbrella."

Prague galvanized several associates of The Focus into action — though for different motives. Wickham Steed asked the Foreign Office to grant immediate asylum to a number of Czechs; he guaranteed the Foreign Office that their maintenance would be assured by himself "acting on behalf of Dr Benes and certain wealthy Czech-Americans."[7] Spears badgered the Treasury to take action over Vitkovice, its account at N.M. Rothschild & Co., and the hapless Nazi hostage Louis Rothschild.[8] And Mr Churchill's former secretary Robert Boothby also hurried to the Treasury on Friday the seventeenth, though on a different mission of humanity.[9]

He had been hired by a wealthy Czech resident emigré, Richard Weininger. Weininger had assets of £242,000 blocked in Prague; promising the Tory MP ten percent of any proceeds, he had advanced to him £1,000 in February and asked him to get any monies available in London — for example Britain's loan to Prague — released to people like himself.[10] On March 17 Boothby was at Downing-street urging the blocking of all Czech assets in Britain. Five days after that he spoke thus in the House: "Every person, and I would apply this to Czech residents in this country as well as to British subjects, who can prove assets held in Prague ought now to be paid out of the [Czech Loan] Fund."[11] His campaign resulted — as he would confide to Weininger in June — in a Treausry decision in favour of holders of Czech cash and bonds.

Churchill, by way of contrast, lay low in the countryside. He was momentarily distracted from his writings by a sudden fear of an all-out Nazi air attack, the spectre that he himself had conjured up, and wrote to the prime minister on the twenty-first suggesting that with such a man as Hitler — under intense strain, fearful of British encirclement plans — anything was possible. He might be tempted to throw a surprise attack at Britain's capital or her aircraft factories. Winston urged Chamberlain to announce that Britain's anti-aircraft defences were manned now.

"It is not so simple as it seems," the PM replied.

ONE BY ONE the props defending the fragile peace in Europe were being knocked aside. At any moment the dreadnaught of war would begin its slide down the slipway. A growing number of politicians in London wanted precisely that: Hitler, it seemed, was getting away with everything, and nobody was willing to call his bluff.

Can we not discern their hand in that month's odd Romanian episode? We can call it the Tilea Untruth. Two days after Prague the Romanian minister in London, Viorel Tilea — intimate friend of The Focus — told Lord Halifax that Germany had issued an "ultimatum" to his government. Bucharest, astonished, denied the ultimatum but Tilea stuck to his story. Robert Boothby would brag a few days later over lunch with Dorothy Macmillan at Quaglino's that he had himself "entirely invented'" the story — he had called on the legation to obtain a visa, Tilea had mentioned that Germany was asking Romania to concentrate more on agriculture and he had persuaded Tilea to tell the F.O. that this was an "ultimatum"; he himself had then sold the story to the newspapers.[12] According to a German intercept, Tilea admitted to another Balkan diplomat that his instructions had only been to talk of an "economic ultimatum"; he had "made the utmost possible use of his instructions."[13] Whatever the background, he shortly retired a wealthy man; he purchased a farm and maintained a monklike silence until his death. The Foreign Office took note that among Tilea's effects in January 1941 was a pound of solid Gold.[14]

The consequences of the Tilea Untruth were serious. Fearing new Hitler schemes, this time against Romania, Chamberlain began drafting a Four Power declaration to be signed by Britain, France, Poland and Russia, to "act together in the event of further signs of German aggressive ambitions."[15] But an important meeting of his Foreign Policy Committee on March 27 accepted that Poland would not join a system that gave Russia the right to pass troops through her territory. Britain quietly decided therefore to include Poland, rather than Russia, in the non-aggression scheme.[16]

While Churchill bent over his *History*, reports about German designs on Poland also quickened: on March 22 an Intelligence (CX) report stated that the German *Aufmarsch* was to be completed by the twenty-eighth; five days later a similar source claimed that the Germans in Danzig were standing by for a coup on April 1. These reports were entirely false, but seemed serious enough when viewed from London.

On the last day of March Sir Horace Wilson, who now had a private office at No. 10, was told that Military Intelligence concluded that Hitler was forcing the pace, hoping to obtain Danzig in the next few days by force or agreement, or to intimidate Warsaw.[17]

CHURCHILL REMAINED IN political hibernation. By March 23 — the day that Germany regained Memel from Lithuania — many associates were asking The Focus why he was not giving a lead. When the League of Nations Association invited him to speak, he lifted his head long enough to make the truculent reply that since his 1938 speaking campaign had made no impact he would reserve his declining energies for the House.

Even here his influence seemed on the wane. When he and Eden set down a resolution late in March demanding conscription and a national government equipped with special powers over industry, it attracted only thirty-six signatures including Duff Cooper and Harold Macmillan, and was flattened by a counter-resolution signed by 180 Conservatives. Churchill returned to his manuscript.

One of his private Intelligence sources was young Ian Colvin, the *News Chronicle*'s correspondent in Berlin; then aged twenty-five, Colvin was used by anti-Nazi elements in Berlin as a vehicle for scare stories. Churchill showed no dismay at the fall-rate of Colvin's prophecies: in January 1938, before the Anschluss, Colvin had alleged that Hitler planned to invade Czechoslovakia that spring; after the November pogrom he had described a "speech" made by Hitler to three foreign ministry officials setting out his aversion to Britian and Chamberlain, and describing how he was going to get rid of the Jews, the Churches and private industry in Germany (there was no such speech).[18]

Now, on March 29, he arrived in London. Cadogan found him a "nice young man, rather precious" — but together with Halifax listened with disquiet to the newspaperman's latest report, that an attack on Poland was imminent. This too was untrue: four days earlier Hitler had secretly assured his commander in chief that he was not going to tackle the Polish problem — yet.[19]

Together the F.O. officials walked Colvin over to No. 10. Given the delayed shock of Hitler's entry into Prague, and the nervousness generated by Tilea, Chamberlain was determined not to be caught napping. After some reflection, because he disliked being stampeded, he decided to guarantee Poland immediately — before it was too late.[20]

He announced the guarantee in the House that Friday, March 31.

Its effect was not what he intended. Within an hour of the news reaching Hitler, he sent for General Wilhelm Keitel — as the diary of his adjutant shows* — and ordered the High Command to draw up a directive for Case White, war against Poland.

This, and the further remarkable British guarantees that shortly followed to three Balkan countries, were welcomed by The Focus. They were like tripwires. As Iverach McDonald, diplomatic correspondent of *The Times*, would later write, they were justified in the eyes of a growing number of Tory MPs and journalists for one simple and overriding reason: "The sooner that war came the better."[21] In this curious, even base desire they were at one with their greatest enemy. On April 3 Keitel signed the Case White directive, outlining a contingency which might make war on Poland necessary on or after September 1.

Roused at last by the rattle of these events, Mr Churchill found himself in broad agreement with the government for once, and declared so in the House on that same day, April 3. Again he commended Stalin to Mr Chamberlain as a partner; later, he strolled down to the lower smoking room to clink glasses with the Soviet ambassador.[22] Poland, he pointed out to Ivan Maisky, would want to know that any Russian troops she allowed in would also eventually get out.

"Can you give us such assurances?"

Maisky gave no reply.

The prime minister did not share Winston's benevolent appreciation of the Kremlin. He feared that Soviet motives were quite remote from western ideas of liberty. Despite "painstaking examination," Sir Horace Wilson would recall, writing in October 1941, Mr Chamberlain could not believe that the Soviet policy was anything but selfish — "mixed with a strong desire to see civilized Europe ruined by a conflict between

---

The War Path.

England an Germany." And, he continued, nothing that the Russians did up to the time of his death suggested to Chamberlain that he was mistaken.[23]

ON GOOD FRIDAY, while England warmed to the Easter bank holiday weekend and Mr Churchill applied himself once more to his *History*, Benito Mussolini occupied Albania.

The next day, April 8, Churchill and Macmillan lunched at Chartwell and pored over maps of the Mediterranean; Winston learned that the British fleet was scattered throughout that sea and that three of its five capital ships were actually "lolling about" Italian ports. He spent much of that Saturday hectoring the PM by telephone and messenger-borne letter, begging him to order the Fleet to seize the island of Corfu that night — to pre-empt further Italian plans in those waters.

Chamberlain found out that Churchill had also contacted his cronies in the French government. The distant whiff of cordite had revived Churchill's flagging spirits, but it appalled the PM; he wrote his sister about how Winston had "badgered" him to recall Parliament, telephoning at all hours of the day.

> I suppose he has prepared a terrific oration which he wants to let off. I know there are a lot of reckless people who would plunge us into war at once, but we must resist them until it becomes really inevitable.

On April 13, intending to announce Britain's guarantee to Romania, Chamberlain invited Winston to call on him before they went into the Chamber. Churchill wrongly grasped that the invitation meant he was about to be offered a new Ministry of Supply. But more than ever since Saturday's Corfu intermezzo the PM mistrusted his judgement; the invitation had been uttered merely in a mood of reconciliation, hoping to keep the House united. Before tossing to his disgruntled rival some morsels of secret background information, he revealed nonchalantly that he was quite aware that Winston passed on such secrets through Randolph to journalists and "others" — no doubt meaning the French and Ivan Maisky.

Winston allowed that he would be making a "not unhelpful speech."[24] He thought he had phrased it carefully, but neither its acid undertone nor the cheers that it attracted from Labour benches escaped the prime minister; when he shortly set up a Ministry of Supply, he gave it to somebody else. Churchill remained in the wilderness.

The polemics in the newspapers increased, hostile to Hitler, favourable to Winston. Typical of Fleet-street's spring campaign was the reader's letter prominently printed by the Odham's Press *News Review* on April 6: "When we fight Germany again," a Mrs E. Heffer wrote, "give her a thorough beating, exterminate the German men and divide Germany between Britain and her Allies!" The publication of such a letter was widely commented upon in Germany.

Largely to spike Mr Churchill's guns, Chamberlain now introduced conscription, having first sent a secret message to reassure Hitler.[25] As Chamberlain put it, in a cutting private remark about Churchill, "The nearer we get to war, the more his chances improve, and vice versa." The *Sunday Pictorial's* young editor Hugh Cudlipp wrote to Winston that he had received 2,400 letters overwhelmingly in his favour, and accepted an invitation to Chartwell in return; pleasingly few of the correspondents had recalled Gallipoli. Winston's stock was rising. Ambassador Kennedy agreed to be principal guest at The Focus luncheon on April 25,[26] and after Churchill addressed the House two days later, still dissatisfied with Chamberlain's Military Training Bill, Lord Camrose's *Daily Telegraph* printed a flattering report of MPs pouring in to hear him.

IT WAS FORTUNATE that he had not committed himself to Chamberlain's Cabinet, because in May 1939 he was called upon to attack it again. Dismaying word had reached Chaim Weizmann in Jerusalem of Britain's probable future policies in Palestine — a White Paper would propose an independent Palestine with a Jewish population limited to one-third of the total, settling only one small "ghetto" area.

Weizmann sent a menacing cable to Chamberlain — with a copy in code to Mr Churchill — warning that the Jews in Palestine would oppose such a policy with all their strength. It would destroy all Jewish hopes and surrender them to what he called "the Arab junta responsible for terrorist campaign." "Jews are determined make supreme sacrifice," he warned, "rather than submit to such regime." Begging Churchill to get the White paper postponed, he spoke of the "grave consequences" if Downing-street announced the new policy or authorized the use of force against the Jews: "It will engender further bitterness between Jews and Arabs and drive Jews who have nothing to lose anywhere to counsels of despair."[27]

A further telegram to Churchill followed on May 4. With Italy and Germany poised to invade Egypt and Libya, Weizmann suggested, Britain could ill afford to alienate the "single group in Middle East whose loyalty absolute and war potential [are] not inconsiderable." The Jews could produce 40,000 disciplined men to reinforce Britain in the Middle East, as well as bringing over reinforcements from Eastern and Central Europe and America.

The government however suspected that different motives underlay the desire to arm the immigrants in Palestine. The potential nuisance value of the Moslems, they reasoned, far outweighed that of the Jews.

Besides, if war did come with Hitler, the Jews would have no option but to support Britain. The White Paper was issued on May 17 heedless of the blandishments from Jerusalem, and debated in the Commons a few days later.

Churchill's group was outspoken against it. He himself delivered a fine oration, which he rehearsed to Weizmann over lunch that day at Morpeth Mansions. It derided the notion of prohibiting Jewish immigration after 1944 unless Palestine's Arab population agreed. "Now there is the breach," he cried. "There is the violation of the pledge. There is the abandonment of the Balfour Declaration. There is the end of the vision, of the hope, of the dream." It was another Munich, he mimicked — *"They're on the run again!"*

There were many abstentions. Chamberlain's majority fell to eighty-nine. The Focus associates — Amery, Bracken, Cartland, Cazalet, Law, Locker-Lampson, Macmillan, Sinclair, Nicolson and many others — all voted with Churchill against the White Paper.

"Words fail to express my thanks," Weizmann wrote that day, and Bob Boothby echoed him: "One of the few things in my life of which I am proud is that . . . I have hitched my waggon to your star."[28] Churchill, his prospects of Cabinet office receding still further, returned to his *History*.

* * *

He had healed the breach with Eden. Eden too emphasized the need for an early alliance with Russia, and was to be heard when speaking to his constituents early in May 1939 quoting the words of Churchill — "whose exceptional talent the nation will wish to see employed in its service at this time." On the fourth he was to be seen in a huddle with Churchill in a corridor of the House. "Fancy having thrown away the Czechs, a gallant and democratic people," Winston exclaimed, loud enough for Hugh Dalton to hear, adding with evident distaste: "And now we have to do the best we can with the Poles."[29]

That day's *Daily Telegraph* carried his article urging the Poles to accept Russia as an ally; a "definite association" between Poland and Russia would soon become indispensible. What Poland feared was precisely the association that Moscow defined three months later — that between the meal and the monster. But Churchill was out of office, and could afford the luxury of over-simplification. In mid June he would refer to "Poland, a new force, and behind it, the Russian pad."[30] These were words, phrases, images — devoid of political reality.

In the *Telegraph* on June 8 he reverted to his call for an immediate Triple Alliance. He guessed that time was running out. Late in May, a former British air attaché in Berlin had furnished to him a report from inside the War Ministry: according to this a German traitor had written to him on May 8 warning that Hitler was seeking a Russo-German alliance and had ordered editors to tone down their articles on Russia.[31]

Time was running out in another sense for Churchill. He was like a gambler, whose pile of chips was steadily declining. Strained by the upkeep of Morpeth Mansions and the Chartwell estate, his funds were nearly exhausted. Thanks to That Man, as he soon took to calling him, ever fewer countries were now willing to syndicate his articles. Poland, Romania, Greece — all found his articles too risky to print. "The net is closing round our activities," he lamented in a letter to international literary agent Emery Reves on May 8, "through fear of Germany."

But he sensed that his hour was nigh. His oldest friends reassured him. Blum came over and met with associates of The Focus at the Berkeley Hotel, and several times that summer Paul Reynaud noted Winston's name in his appointment book in Paris. One old comrade reflected after dining with Winston that he was charming and friendly and looked younger than for years. "He too regards a more or less early war as certain!" noted P.J. Grigg.[32]

Joe Kennedy also accepted the inevitability of war that summer. Over dinner in June the senior American columnist Walter Lippmann related this to Winston, while adding that the ambassador was also convinced that Britain would be defeated. Whisky-and-soda in one hand, cigar stub in the other, Churchill loudly disagreed, delivering a fine oration in rebuttal of this "tragic utterance." His speech vibrated with familiar rhetoric about perils, ordeals and jeopardy, about trials and disasters, and about veritable rains of fire and steel, scattering death and destruction. "I for one," he ended, "would willingly lay down my life in combat, rather than, in fear of defeat, surrender to the menaces of these most sinister men."

Such was Harold Nicolson's recollection of his words, while Lippmann jotted down Churchill's prediction that Hitler's Wehrmacht could never pierce the French carapace. When in form like this, nobody liked to contradict him. Puffing at his cigar, he suggested that only one argument counted and that was the use of force: "At [Germany's] first provocative action, cut German railway communications with Europe and defy them to do anything about it!"[33]

Once he touched upon the alleged threat from Japan. In March he had dismissed it. "Consider," he had written then to Chamberlain, "how vain is the menace that Japan will send a fleet and army to conquer Singapore."[34] Now, in June 1939, he repeated that insouciance. Were he in power, he said, he would cut his losses in the Far East; "no dispersion of the fleet," scribbled Walter Lippmann; and, "settle with Japan after the war."

Two weeks later Churchill spoke to probably the largest lunchtime audience of the City Carlton Club. "I was not deceived last year," he maintained, "and I warn you not to be deceived this year."

His prediction now was that after the crops had been harvested July, August, and September would see tension rising in Europe. Could he but address Germany's Führer direct — speak to him right at the summit, he would declaim: "Pause, consider well before you take a plunge into the terrible unknown. Consider whether your life's work, which might now be famous in the eyes of history, in raising Germany from prostration and defeat to a point where all the world is waiting anxiously upon her actions — consider whether all this may not be irretrievably cast away."[35]

That day, June 27, 1939, he published another potboiler, *Step by Step*. In its proof copy, the book had closed with a chapter entitled, "Will Hitler Make Napoleon's Mistakes?" predicting that Germany would ultimately invade the Soviet Union.

At the last moment Churchill excised this prophetic essay.[36]

CHAPTER 15

Two Fisted

YEARS LATER, INCREASINGLY deaf and a prisoner to his thoughts, he occasionally looked back in contrition upon the holocaust that had ensued. Once a historian would see him pacing his room at the House murmuring, "Europe is a sea of blood and it is all our fault."[1]

Perhaps it could not have been foreseen by the democracies in that summer of 1939. Other matters seemed paramount: the rise of antisemitism, the resurgence of nationalism, the infectious spread of racial intolerance.

At the beginning of that summer Churchill was visited by an eminent American whom some researchers now regard as having been a clandestine emissary from President Roosevelt — Felix Frankfurter.

The meeting was seemingly confidential, for neither man's biography mentions it. Judge Frankfurter had emigrated as a boy of twelve from Vienna, risen through the ranks of the American judiciary, and was now one of the president's most respected advisers; appointed to the Supreme Court in January, he had begun sending handwritten messages to the White House on the Court's small notepads — about Weizmann and Ben-Gurion, refugees, and the repeal of the neutrality law.[2]

Frankfurter was close to the American Jewish Committee (AJC) which stood — at one or two removes — behind The Focus. Perhaps unconsciously he also used its jargon: in one note on May 24 he urged Roosevelt, even when talking on domestic issues, to stress at all times the Nazi threat to "freedom and peace."* Shortly before Frankfurter's visit to Mr Churchill, as his surviving papers show, there had been meetings to discuss the most seemly manner of spending the $3m dollar

---

*Churchill wrote to Clementine on January 8, 1939 that Chamberlain had adopted the very phrase he had been repeating for the last two years, namely "freedom and peace"; and he commented particularly that Chamberlain "put, as I have always done, 'freedom' first."

propaganda fund raised by the AJC. At one meeting, called in New York on December 22 to discuss the rising antisemitism, somebody had suggested using Hitler's Germany as a kind of lightning conductor — to "deflect" the endemic hatreds from Jews wherever they were to Nazi Germany.

It was an ingenious but disturbing suggestion. At a second secret meeting in April 1939, chaired this time by Frankfurter himself in Washington, he expressed alarm at the AJC's "present secret and undercover methods"; such methods, he suggested, implied "a distrust of the very democracy in which, as Jews, we profess to believe."

In his view they must either continue to use respectable front organisations — he instanced the Conference of Jews and Christians — or they must use only methods respectable enough to stand investigation. Suppose a snap Congressional investigation exposed the AJC's current $3m campaign? It would embarrass the entire Jewish community. "And," he warned, "what capital its enemies would make of such an attempt to mould public opinion in this country!"[3]

Invited to Oxford to receive a doctorate in law, Frankfurter told Sir Maurice Bowra, Warden of Wadham College, that Hitler was a threat to freedom and peace everywhere. Bowra ensured that Lindemann took him to Churchill.

We know little about his visit except that Frankfurter thanked the Prof for arranging it. "That talk with Mr. Churchill," he wrote, "was one of the most exhilarating experiences I had in England — it made me feel more secure about the future."[4] He wrote to a fellow judge afterwards that all his friends in Britain expected war. One of them evidently predicted that Hitler's clock would begin to run on August 21.[5]

SIMULTANEOUSLY WITH FRANKFURTER'S departure from London, an extravagant publicity campaign began on Churchill's behalf. In a pleasingly artless paragraph of his memoirs the latter professed surprise and ignorance of its origins:

> Thousands of enormous posters were displayed for weeks on end on Metropolitan hoardings, "Churchill must come back." Scores of young volunteer men and women carried sandwich-board placards with similar slogans up and down before the House of Commons.

"I had nothing to do," he pleaded, "with such methods of agitation."[6]

Mysterious agents rented advertising hoardings — a typical one photographed on July 24 in The Strand bore only three huge words: WHAT PRICE CHURCHILL? By rumours, innuendo and outright statement Fleet-street suggested he was actually about to return; newspaper editorials and readers' letters debated the issue.

It was the *Daily Telegraph* which started this great paper chase on July 3. "No step," argued this, the flagship of Lord Camrose, "would more profoundly impress the Axis Powers with the conviction that this country means business." The *Star, Sunday Graphic, Observer* and *Yorkshire Post* took up the cry, with the *Mirror, Evening News, Daily Mail* and the communist *Daily Worker* hard on their heels.

This virtual editorial unanimity was impressive, not to say unique. Several diplomats suspected that it was orchestrated. In Berlin, the appalled British ambassador told the equally disgusted Lord Kemsley, owner of the *Sunday Times, Sunday Graphic* and *Sunday Chronicle*, just what he thought of "brother Camrose's Churchill campaign."

In London, the American embassy recalled having seen periodic agitation for Churchill earlier, but never on such a scale; over at Carlton Terrace, the German ambassador ascribed it to dissidents trying to subvert the Cabinet and sabotage its constructive policies on Germany — "mainly Anglo-Jewish circles with the Churchill group in their wake."[7]*

Vexed by the *Telegraph* editorial, Chamberlain sent for Lord Camrose and explained in confidence just why he would not hire Winston: The man was bad-tempered and his ideas and memoranda "tended to monopolize" everybody's time in government, an argument of some validity as events had shown. He enlightened Camrose about the strange Corfu Saturday, citing it as an example of Churchill's uneven judgement.[9] He detected in the agitation a conspiracy involving the Soviet ambassador — his sources reported that Maisky was in close touch with Winston's son. On July 8, after a visit from the Australian High Commissioner the prime minister wrote to his sister that the Dominions thought like him — that if Winston was in the Government "it would not be long before we were at war."

Truth called the "blatant press campaign" an intrigue to enable Winston to "muscle into the Cabinet;" it quoted one admiral as making clear that he did not want "the indispensable Mr Churchill" back in the Government, let alone at the admiralty. "Sir Walter Layton wants Mr Churchill in the Cabinet," mocked *Truth* on July 14. "Why not make a job of it and have [his comedian son-in-law] Vic Oliver too?"[10]

ONCE THAT JULY, when the agitation was at its height, Churchill flew to Paris, thrilled to the Bastille Day parade down the Champs Elysee, and returned flushed with military panoply and the cognac of the Ritz, where he had lunched with his principal accomplice Paul Reynaud.

---

*The ex-Queen of Spain told Ambassador von Dirksen on July 6 that a letter from Churchill to the Republican prime minister Negrin had been found listing the art dealers in Holland suitable for disposing of the Spanish treasures.[8]

Friends and rivals were struck by his liquor consumption. Lord Rothermere wagered £600 that he could not foreswear cognac for a year; Chamberlain too mentioned this minus element of the Churchill equation when the American ambassador called on the twentieth. Kennedy commented on the raucous press campaign — which had climaxed, he reported to Washington, three or four days earlier — and inquired why the PM refused to yield. Chamberlain replied that he did not believe that Winston could deliver one-tenth as much as people thought. "He has developed," he murmured "into a fine two-fisted drinker." Reverting to a prevailing theme, he added that Churchill's judgement had repeatedly proven unsound; had he been in the Cabinet he was convinced Britain would have been at war by now.[11]

As suddenly as it had begun, the agitation subsided. Sam Hoare explained, perhaps unjustly, to Lord Astor, "Anything that Winston attempts is overdone" — in this case it had only stirred up reaction against him.[12] By the twenty-second the American embassy could confirm that the campaign had ended. It had, in Kennedy's picturesque phrase, "fallen out of bed."[13]

The "Bring back Churchill" campaign certainly irritated Hitler. When he received Lord Kemsley at Bayreuth on July 27 he "referred particularly," as the press lord confidentially informed the Foreign Office, "to Mr Winston Churchill and his powers of expression." Kemsley advised the Führer not to attach undue importance to the Opposition; Mr Churchill in particular had been unfortunate in his campaigns several times in the past, "starting with the Abdication."[14]

Churchill buried his head in his manuscripts at Chartwell; occasionally august visitors came down to see him. General Sir Edmund Ironside, the army's commander-in-chief, was one, on July 24. In December 1937, Winston had visited him, had listened approvingly as the general poured out laments about the new secretary for war, Leslie Hore-Belisha, and had attempted some clumsy flattery. The general had stiffly replied that he had never influenced his career "by asking or intriguing for things." Churchill had hastily explained that he had not either, but "I've had my ups and downs."[15]

Down here at Chartwell they talked until five a.m. The birds were chorusing the arrival of the dawn as they retired to bed — Ironside overwhelmed by Churchill's conviction that war was inevitable. Standing in front of the six-foot square map of Europe that adorned the wall above his writing desk, the politician had lectured the C-in-C about the likely sequence of events: Poland destroyed; diversions by Mussolini, then an Italian invasion of Egypt; a German advance through Romania to the Black Sea, and finally "an alliance with Russia when the latter sees how the land lies." It must be said that his prophecies were a tour de force.

Winston also outlined a plan he had himself devised to send battleships into the Baltic. Months later, he would elaborate it under the codename Catherine. It was never executed, although it did feed his obsessive interest in Scandinavia.

Churchill had once called Ironside the finest brain in the British army; but this view was not held widely or for long. Kennedy would report to Washington that people said the general could talk twelve languages but doubted he could think straight in any of them; while Cadogan privately thought him "so stupid as to be impervious to anything." General Ironside could not get Winston out of his mind, and days later still pictured him walking up and down his study, chafing at the inaction — "a man who knows that you must act to win."[16]

If during this July 1939 press agitation Mr Churchill himself had avoided the limelight it was for a more pressing reason than diplomacy. His year's gross income was lagging some £10,000 behind expectations; but he was nearing the end of his half-million word *History*, and upon completion would be entitled to collect £7,500. His manuscript had reached the imperial reign of Queen Victoria; but now, in mid 1939, the British Empire with its accretions at Versailles was even more majestic, farflung and prosperous than in her time. If ever in later years he cast a backward glance upon the vanishing empire, perhaps in that brief mood of contrition after the ensuing holocaust, he must have realised that it was his own stewardship of office that marked the passing of its prime.

OCCASIONALLY HE VENTURED up to London that summer, but in strict privacy — usually for one of the mysterious Witches' Sabbaths organized by The Focus. From its office at Southampton Buildings in Chancery-lane, its secretary arranged a luncheon to enable Dr Benes "to meet, quite privately, just a few associates of our Focus" upon his return from America.[17]

Since earlier chapters have made repeated reference to this cabal it will serve a historical purpose to identify some of the forty "associates" of The Focus who lunched in that private room at the Savoy on July 27, 1939. Fortunately Benes retained the guest list, and this reveals among those present Messrs Churchill (who presided) Ronald Cartland, Colin Coote, Cummings, Eden, Emrys Evans, Henderson, Greenwood, Layton, Nicolson, Salter, Seton-Watson, Sinclair and Spears, as well as Mr and Mrs Wickham Steed, Captain B.H. Liddell Hart, Miss Megan Lloyd-George, Lady Violet Bonham-Carter, the Lords Lytton, Lloyd and Davies, and of course Sir Robert Waley-Cohen whose committee was providing the funds.

The Czech record tells us that in his "secret speech" Mr Churchill praised their venerable guest for his moderation during the Sudeten crisis; as long as he, Churchill, lived he would seek to undo the terrible injustice done to Czechoslovakia, and as he said this the tears were seen to trickle down his cheeks.[18]

Writing in February 1943, Sam Hoare would urge Beaverbrook to remember the oppressive mood, that summer of 1939.

> It was an atmosphere of peace at almost any price; the Peace Ballot, the Labour opposition against any service estimates and conscription, the pressure of business and industry against war. Neville was not the man to fight this opposition, for at the bottom of his heart he sympathized with it. Nor, I believe, would Churchill have fought it if he had not been in Opposition.

Parliament dissolved. Outside the Chamber, Churchill buttonholed Chamberlain and protested that he could not trust his judgment during the coming vacant weeks. The PM replied that this was mutual.

This stung Churchill to repeat Archie Sinclair's charge that if Parliament had met earlier last September Britain could have mobilized her fleet, reached agreement with Moscow and saved Czechoslovakia. It seemed to the PM a "fatuous and imbecile proposition." Winston stormed into the Chamber purple with fury.[19] Here he delivered a speech demanding Parliament's recall later that same month. Hitler, he claimed, had a habit of perpetrating his felonies when the Members were on holiday: Chamberlain checked and found that on the contrary the House was in session on every such recent occasion.

In an ironic broadcast on the eighth Churchill invited his American audience to listen to the tramp of armies "going on manoeuvres—"

> Yes, only on manoeuvres! Of course it's only manouevres — just like last year.
> After all, the dictators must train their soldiers. They could scarcely do less in common prudence, when the Danes, the Dutch, the Swiss, the Albanians — and of course the Jews — may leap out upon them at any moment and rob them of their living space, and make them sign another paper to say who began it.

Before leaving on vacation, Churchill wrote a lengthy letter, at Lindemann's suggestion, assuring the secretary of state for air, Sir Kingsley Wood, that the development of an atomic explosive such as recent press scares had suggested would take "several years," and that Mr Chamberlain must not allow himself to be bluffed by any German or "Fifth Column" threats of a secret weapon, "some terrible new secret explosive, capable of wiping out London."[20]

That letter sent, he left to vacation in his own way — with his beloved French. His notorious affair with France still raised indelicate titters in the less francophile sections of society. During the French State

Visit to London over Easter ("Frog Week") one Tory MP remarked upon Churchill, who was no art-lover, and "all the pro-Frog boys" going to Covent Garden.[21]

As with all affairs of the heart, his emotions blinded his common sense. Oblivious of the fetid odour of decay arising from her army and society, he still saw across the Channel the France of 1914. He had assured Ironside in 1937 that the French army was an "incomparable machine." His solid confidence was fortified in mid August when he and Spears toured the Maginot fortifications at Gamelin's invitation. Wearing a natty light-coloured pinstripe and trilby and with only the wispiest gold chain across his waistcoat, he explored the subterranean workings and tunnels without pausing to reflect upon the psychological ill effects of such monumental defensive positions upon the offensive spirit of an army.

Looking grave and slim in his gold-braided kepi the local field commander, his old friend General Georges, drove him down to where the broad, fast-flowing Rhine formed the frontier with Germany. Winston suggested that monitors — ships mounting heavy guns on a protected deck — would help thwart a German offensive here. He returned to Paris pleased to find the platform at the Gare de L'Est crowded with photographers and gawking railway workers.

He checked into the Ritz, collected Clementine and Mary, and went on to vacation at Consuelo Balsan's. The artist Paul Maze joined him; sometimes they fished together off a local humpback bridge, but mostly Winston marshalled canvases, brushes and tubes and set off to paint the old manor house or nearby Chartres cathedral.

He was aware by now that Hitler's clock had already begun to tick. In Moscow, the Anglo-Soviet talks were stalled. Modest British and French military missions had arrived there on the eleventh, but Stalin had responded to Hitler's flirtations and now stated impossible demands to the British and French. In London a week later Vansittart learned from a secret source with access to communications between Berlin and Rome that Hitler was going to attack Poland on the twenty-fifth or soon after.

On August 23 Berlin radio broke the extraordinary, awful news of the pact between Germany and the Soviet Union.* Poland, caught between them, was doomed. Elder statesman Maurice Hankey, summoned urgently by Chamberlain to No.10 Downing Street to advise him on how to set up and run a War Cabinet, wrote in his diary: "He

---

*Washington even learned of the secret protocol dividing Poland between Hitler and Stalin. Hans-Heinrich von Herwarth, a traitor in the German embassy in Moscow, betrayed it a few hours later. He was appointed ambassador to Britain after the war.[22]

then consulted me about personnel: Should Winston Churchill be in? I agreed with him that public opinion would expect it."

Catching the unmistakeable whiff of gunpowder in the air, and frantic lest Chamberlain set up his War Cabinet before he could return, Winston called briefly on Paul Reynaud at the ministry of finances, dashed off an article for the *Daily Mirror* ("At the Eleventh Hour"), then flew home by the first available plane, leaving his wife and daughter to follow. As his plane circled Croydon he was already picking out deficiencies in the airfield's camouflage, shelters and defences.[23].

He was in no doubt that the Event was upon them: Chamberlain was about to be tripped up — by his own tripwire, the Polish Guarantee.

When Archie Sinclair phoned after dinner he found Winston in high fettle; he had just telephoned Reynaud, and the Frenchman had assured him that all was going well — "By which he means war," Harold Nicolson supposed, hearing of this.[24]

Hearing rumours of 20,000 "organized Nazis" lurking inside England, Winston decided to take precautions: he took out and checked his own revolvers; and he called his former Scotland Yard detective Inspector Thompson out of retirement, and told him to bring his pistol with him.

The prime minister was dazed by these events. On August 23 Kennedy had called upon him, shocked by his haggard looks, and asked how things stood. Chamberlain replied, downcast: "It appears as if all my work has been of no avail." The guarantee to Poland had not worked. "The thing that is frightful," he stated, "is the futility of it all. After all, the Poles cannot be saved." Now Britain could only wage a war of revenge; this would leave Europe in ruins and her own position in the Far East progressively weakened.[25]

Parliament, recalled on the twenty-fourth, enacted an Emergency Powers Bill. In the streets, hired women mutely paraded sandwich-boards bearing one word: CHURCHILL.

Chamberlain squirmed at the name. To invite this troublesome man into his Cabinet would be to scuttle every last prospect of an accommodation with the dictators. When Sir Nevile Henderson had called upon Hitler on the previous afternoon he had mentioned this stout refusal to employ Churchill as the ultimate proof of the PM's desire for peace; according to the German record, Henderson explained that the hostility in Britain was being whipped up by "the Jews and the enemies of the Nazis."[26]

Unable to understand why even now Chamberlain was not sending for him, despite his premature return from France, Churchill dined gloomily that evening with Duff Cooper, Eden, Sinclair and Sandys at the Savoy. Afterwards he drove to Chartwell to continue on the *History*.

THROUGHOUT 1939 HE had barely thought about Poland: such feelings as he entertained for her were of contempt.

Now it was Munich all over again — with Masaryk's place taken by that Polish ambassador whose name he could never recall. Day after day he now picked up one of the two 'phones on the wall shelves in his study, and telephoned the ambassador to beg Warsaw not to weaken or give in.[27] Others in The Focus kept up the pressure — Lord Lloyd, Harcourt Johnstone, Hugh Dalton, Brendan Bracken and Duncan Sandys all 'phoned or called upon Count Raczynski.

For the last days of August Churchill invited General Ironside down to Chartwell — the General had just paid an official visit to Poland and was full of what he had seen. Churchill had also continued to correspond with Eden, who had now joined a rifle battalion as an officer, and when Parliament was recalled on August 29 photographers caught them walking together to the House — Eden immaculate in striped tie, Churchill more sombre in spotted cravat, dark three-button suit, black homburg and gold knobbed walking stick.

He believed that Hitler was in a corner. He called up Eddie Marsh and told him so on the phone: the Führer was rattled, he said, but in mortal fear of climbing down. Fearing that Chamberlain might yet force a compromise upon Warsaw, upon Churchill's urging the Polish ambassador now risked doing as Masaryk had done in 1938 — transforming himself from a diplomat into an agent interfering in British internal politics, "and, what is more," he admitted, "in opposition to the Government." His most willing accomplices were "the politicians of various shades grouped around Churchill."[28]

As August 1939 ended, Winston Churchill stood at the long inclined trestle table that he had carpentered and plucked at the reference books stacked up along it. Peering at their pages through circular, metal rimmed spectacles, in a zip-fronted romper suit that he called his "siren suit", clenching a damp, unlit cigar in his mouth, he applied himself again to his *History*.

As the first hours of September 1939 dawned, his head was still bowed over his manuscripts; he had now completed 530,000 words. it was an overrun, he would have to cut it back.

* * *

The rattle of the telephone woke him at eight-thirty: it was Count Raczynski, announcing that Hitler had invaded his country.

As Winston drove back to London that Friday morning he glimpsed the placards: DANZIG PROCLAIMS RETURN TO REICH: GERMANS BOMB POLISH TOWN. Invited to No. 10, he learned from the PM that he had decided to form a small War Cabinet of half a dozen ministers without portfolio, including Mr Churchill — who agreed without comment — and Lord Hankey, who told his wife his job appeared to be to keep an eye on Winston.

Behind black-out shades the crowded House met in subdued lights at six p.m. Since Chamberlain's hands were tied by the French there was little he could report; for once the Soviet ambassador was absent from the gallery. Now that Stalin was Hitler's ally, it would not have been tactful to appear.

"THE DIE IS cast," Chamberlain had told Churchill that morning. Yet nothing came of his offer of War Cabinet office for several days. The new War Cabinet did not even meet.

Churchill worked out that its average age would be sixty-four (his own) and sent a note that night urging the inclusion of younger men like Eden and Sinclair. He told Colin Coote of The Focus that he was stating "very heavy terms" and did not believe Chamberlain would last out the week.[29]

The strain of this final baffling wait for Cabinet office was cruel. When Lord Hankey went to the House on Saturday the second, he found Winston in the smoking room ("The amount of alcohol being consumed was incredible!") holding forth to some of the younger MPs. Embarrassingly, Churchill had allowed the press to announce his appointment to the War Cabinet — an item that was both premature and unhelpful because Chamberlain still dimly hoped to restore the cumbling peace.

With his face as black as thunder, Winston hung around the House waiting for the summons to No. 10. He muttered to Bob Boothby — who confided it over drinks to Blanche Dugdale — that he had refused Cabinet office unless there were other changes. The temper in the bars and smoking rooms of the House was curdled by Chamberlain's inactivity. When, at 7:42 p.m. he read a statement speaking of the chance of further talks, Arthur Greenwood swayed to his feet and said that he spoke for the Labour Party. Somebody shouted, "Speak for Britain!" Startled by the uproar Churchill nearly rose, according to Walter Elliot, to move a vote of No Confidence; but he had learned caution since Munich and the Abdication and bit his tongue,

Meanwhile Hitler's panzer divisions were rampaging eastwards, laying claim to ever greater areas of Poland. That evening Churchill's associates foregathered at Morpeth Mansions — Eden, Boothby, Bracken, Sandys. Duff Cooper also arrived from the Savoy, bringing two junior ministers, Harold Balfour and Euan Wallace. The mood was dismay: it seemed that the Anglo-German talks might even now be resumed. Once Winston telephoned Raczynski, anxious for news: the ambassador told him that London and Paris were still undecided.

Speaking slowly and in a strangled voice, Winston replied: "I hope — I hope that Britain will keep — will keep its —"

The Pole heard the familiar voice tail away, then what sounded like a sob — was it anxiety or humiliation?

Later that Saturday evening, the Morpeth Mansions group sent one of their number — Duncan Sandys — round to tell the ambassador they had resolved to overthrow Chamberlain if he showed further signs of weakness.[30]

His ambitions cruelly slighted, Churchill sent a hurt letter to Downing-street after midnight:

> I have not heard anything from you since our talks on Friday, when I understood that I was to serve as your colleague, and when you told me that this would be announced speedily.
> I really do not know what has happened during the course of this agitated day; though it seems to me that entirely different ideas have ruled from those which you expressed to me when you said "the die was cast".

Again he urged the PM to bring Labour and the Liberals in; and at least to let him know where he stood before the Debate at noon on Sunday.[31]

Chamberlain had more urgent matters on his mind. A British ultimatum had been telegraphed during the night to Berlin. It expired at eleven a.m. on the third and he broadcast the announcement declaring war on Germany.

As his broadcast ended, London's sirens sounded. Many now expected the all-out attack that Churchill had prophesied.

Winston himself recoiled to the street shelter clutching a brandy bottle and other comforts.

Shortly, he ventured the few hundred yards to the House; he received a note to visit the prime minister in his room after the Debate; he himself rose to speak at 12.21 p.m.

> In this solemn hour [declared Churchill] it is a consolation to recall and to dwell upon our repeated efforts for peace. All have been ill-starred, but all have been faithful and sincere. This is of the highest moral value. . . This moral conviction alone affords that ever-fresh resilience which renews the strength and energy of people in long, doubtful and dark days. Outside, the storms of war may blow and the lands may be lashed with the fury of its gales, but in our own hearts this Sunday morning there is peace. Our hands may be active, but our consciences are at rest.

Later, he received a summons to the prime minister's room. Chamberlain offered him the admiralty. It was the office he had coveted more than any other. It would afford him the means of expunging the misfortunes of Gallipoli and the Dardanelles; it would solve his rather more personal problems too. He could sell of his apartment at Morpeth Mansions and move into the First Lord's official residence.

* * *

Their Lordships of the Admiralty now signalled to the fleet these words: "Winston is back."[32]

CHAPTER 16

A Foot In The Door

LIKE A NEW boy at school he spent the first days of the war avoiding antagonizing his prime minister. Members might lash and lambast, but Churchill sat in his new place on the front bench with arms folded; biding his time. The opposition cliques still met, but Winston Churchill, First Lord of the Admiralty once more, was no longer in them. This was perhaps the very reason that Chamberlain had brought him into his War Cabinet. On the third he had also invited Eden to head the Dominions Office; although this lowly position would be outside the War Cabinet, the former foreign secretary reflected that half a loaf was better than no bread and took the job.[1]

Here in the middle ground, Churchill was ill at ease. One Member wrote on September 3 that his first war speech "sounded rather grandiloquent and forced."[2] MPs regarded his appointment to the Cabinet as a ploy to stifle criticism of the government: "They hope Winston will be so busy with his own department," General Spears observed, "that he will not make a nuisance of himself." On the sixth this MP heard from the Tory Chief Whip that underlying Hankey's appointment as Minister without Portfolio was Chamberlain's hope that he would "act as a kind of tame elephant to Winston."

Churchill had in no way abandoned his ambitions. Though he now lived in the admiralty building on the far side of Horse Guards Parade, he wanted to hang his hat permanently on the peg marked prime minister near the Cabinet room of No. 10 — taking precedence over all the other pegs labelled Lord Chancellor, Lord President, Lord Privy Seal, and the rest. Even so, as First Lord he had his foot securely in the door.

"Rhetoric," Stanley Baldwin had once caustically defined, "is the harlot of oratory" — and Winston had made a blowsy, gutsy rhetoric his handmaiden ever since his youth. As a wartime minister now, he spoke a dynamic tongue that both moved and thrilled the uneducated masses as well as swaying even the most erudite of his colleagues into reconsidering their often healthier views and re-tailoring them into accordance with his own.

In a famous index entry to his war memoirs he would revile Baldwin for putting "Party before country;" his own actions while First Lord can be indexed in the same shorthand way: he put war before law; offensive before defensive; initiative before inaction; propaganda before absolute truth; and often, probably without realizing it, the interests of Mr Winston Churchill some way ahead of those of Britain and her Empire.

In his own mind, his interests became inseparable from those of his country. He saw himself as Britain's natural ultimate leader, and trod down the basic rights of other nations in that quest for power. Having achieved it, he would hang on to it regardless of the cost to Europe, to his own people and to their hard-won Dominions. His famous phrase, of "blood, toil, tears, and sweat" could with equal aptness describe the tools with which his British forebears had pieced together that incoherent crimson patchwork across the world's atlas, the British Empire. One monarch's demented follies had finally lost the transatlantic colonies to Mr Churchill's own rebellious American ancestors, but the truncated Empire had continued to grow, reaching its greatest extent in the aftermath of Versailles. The coming war would bring about Britain's financial ruin and the Empire's dissolution.

The Dominions had responded immediately to Britain's clarion in September 1939, but not without muted alarm: we shall see how Mr Churchill, deaf to those voices, heeding only the desiderata of the clever and sophisticated Franklin D. Roosevelt whom the American peoples had had the greater gift to elect their president, reeled down the path of power politics into those tenebrous years.

"We have been outwitted," was the candid admission he would once make in the coming months, after Hitler had checkmated him. It would make an appropriate epitaph for the Empire that crumbled apart at the hands of his great transatlantic friend.

HE DID NOT of course confine himself to naval matters at the admiralty. Eden told their mutual friend Hugh Dalton that Winston was adopting a more active, wider role in Cabinet. "You can't imagine his remaining silent," said Eden, "and thinking only about submarines when a general conversation develops!"[3]

Winston knew what he was after. One colleague likened him to an Indian elephant — there again, that elephant comparison — hauling a load of tree trunks through the jungle, trampling bush and undergrowth underfoot: not really knowing the precise route, but forging on by instinct all the same.

Thus he rampaged across the preserves of generals and ministers. His speeches and memoranda marauded over foreign and military affairs; oblivious of precedent and protocol, he would correspond with presidents and foreign notables as though they were his equal. To Lord Halifax he would write artlessly, "I hope you will not mind my drawing your attention from time to time to points which strike me in the Foreign Office telegrams, as it is so much better than that I should raise them in Cabinet;" a few days later, urging Halifax to bring Bulgaria into the Balkan defence system, he added tongue-in-cheek, "I shall equally welcome any suggestions about the Admiralty which at any time occur to you."[4]

Tireless in his criticism of the dictators' barbarity, he could survey the privileges of neutrals and the rights of non-combattants with equal disdain. Once this century the unredeeming Gods of war had already trailed death and ruination across the poppy fields of Belgium; yet Churchill was unable to grasp that small nations such as these were unwilling to invite those same Gods back in again, this time in the garb of French and British troops, to meet a putative invader. A concept like the indivisibility of right and wrong was foreign to him: it was a crime for Hitler to invade Poland; but Stalin's subsequent invasion roused from Morpeth Mansions not a whimper.

He had waxed indignant in his speeches about Gestapo terrors in Bohemia and Moravia; the liquidation by the Poles of the German ethnic minority, in the days before and after Hitler's invasion, aroused no horror in Mr Churchill. Only occasionally did the sapient man inside the First Lord struggle to the surface: learning in October that a British warship had tricked a U-boat into surfacing and then destroyed it, he commented privately to the First Sea Lord that it was "odious" that that warship's crew had picked up the submarine's survivors and murdered them "one by one during the next twelve hours, the last two found hiding in the screw alley."[5]

He treated the laws of war with abandon. A year later the chief of air staff would refuse to allow assassins to parachute into France in plain clothes. When the Air Staff submitted legal objections to his project for mining enemy rivers, Churchill scored through their heading ("Note on the Use of Mines laid by Aircraft in Inland Waterways") and angrily wrote instead: "Some funkstick in the Air Ministry running for shelter under Malkin's petticoat."[6] He broke international conventions with little more compunction than his enemy. In October he would endorse the Panama agreement for a 300-mile zone free of hostilities, then ordered the German pocket battleship *Graf Spee* attacked inside it. In December he recommended mining neutral Norway's waters.

To his more queasy colleagues he offered the unusual argument that since Britain had declared war in accordance with the Covenant of the League, no infringement of International Law, "so long as it is unaccompanied by inhumanity of any kind," could rob Britain of the "good wishes" of the neutrals.

This stocky, pink faced figure in black jacket and striped pants felt he was somehow above International Law. Much evil flowed from that belief. Had Europe been privy to his views — its cities laid to ruins by 1945, and its lesser nations newly enslaved under the secret agreement he reached with Stalin the previous October — she would have scarcely credited his language of 1939. "We are fighting," he had postulated, "to re-establish the reign of law and to protect the liberties of small countries. Our defeat would mean an age of barbaric violence, and would be fatal not only to ourselves, but to the independent life of every small country in Europe." This, he argued, gave Britain the right and indeed the duty to abrogate the very laws she sought to reaffirm.[7]

He himself would do so without a second thought. In February 1940 he would order the seizure of a German supply vessel in Norway's waters; in June he would browbeat the French to transfer to Britain the Luftwaffe pilots they had taken prisoner, although a Geneva convention specifically forbade such transfers by the detaining power; in July he would bombard a French naval squadron at Mers-el-Kébir — a war crime by any definition, since it was an unprovoked attack on an allied force without declaration of war; in August he would recommend Dum Dum bullets as the best way of "killing Huns;" and reply, when his son pointed out they were illegal, that since the Germans would make "short shrift" of him he had no intention of showing any mercy.[8] He would suggest drenching invasion beaches with poison gas, arguing that he could do as he liked on his own territory — which was certainly not a view held at Geneva; and four years later, demanding that his forces use bacterial warfare and poison gas, he would write: "It is absurd to consider morality . . . It is simply a question of fashion changing, as she does between long and short skirts for women."[9]

Implicit in everything he did in the late Fall of 1939 was a nervous, urgent desire to see action against the enemy. Hitler was making all the running. He was defeating his enemies in detail, sometimes without firing a shot. Churchill was determined to wrest the initiative from him.

This was sound strategic reasoning, although there was also an underlying cause for Hitler's triumphs: a dictatorship is better tailored for seizing initiatives than the committee system enshrined in a democracy. "I see such immense walls of prevention, all built and building," Churchill would write to Halifax in a lament about bureaucracy, "that I wonder whether any plan will have a chance of climbing over them." "Victory," he lectured, "will never be found by taking the line of least resistance."[19]

He sat on some of those committees himself, still as a junior member, and endowed with little authority outside naval affairs.

But inside the admiralty he was absolute lord and master, possessed by the need to take the offensive. Lacking the means yet to inflict direct damage on Hitler's Germany, he found himself planning minor operations on the periphery — mining rivers like the Rhine or the coastal waters of Scandinavia, and even bombing the Russian oilfields at Baku. Developing such subsidiary theatres was, a later C.I.G.S. remarked, a weakness of many statesmen.[11] But it grieved the admirals, who failed to talk him out of them. "His battery of weapons," wrote Admiral John Godfrey, director of naval intelligence, "included persuasion, real or simulated anger, mockery, vituperation, tantrums, ridicule, derision, abuse and tears."[12]

Godfrey recalled drily that when Mr Churchill became their "chief asset" they found that he lived largely on this exotic diet — "the carcases of abortive and wildcat operations." The First Sea Lord was prepared to indulge him, but it involved setting up duplicate planning, operational and intelligence staffs.

It will suffice here to take one such plan, Catherine — named after the Great Russian Empress, because Russia was never far from his thoughts: Three days after his return to the admiralty, Churchill offered his project for a foray by fifteen-inch battleships into the Baltic, across which passed Hitler's only links with Norway, Sweden and Finland. By the twelfth he had drafted the plan in outline.[13] The attack would have to be in March when the ice melted; oil tankers would fuel this fleet for the three months that it rampaged around the Baltic. He did not consider what would happen if the tankers were sunk. Churchill of course believed that battleships were at no risk from air attack — that their guns would be sufficient defence. As Admiral Godfrey pointed out, the fleet would be right under the German fighter umbrella and well outside British air range. "Don't worry," Pound quietly assured him, "it will never take place."[14]

Nor it did. Nonetheless the investment in planning was substantial. Winston appointed a special unit under his old friend Admiral the Earl of Cork & Orrerey to report to him.[15] In his memoirs Mr Churchill claimed that Pound's deputy Rear Admiral Tom Phillips had supported Catherine; having gone down with his battleship in 1941 — sunk by air power in a sea far larger than the Baltic — Phillips was in no position to dispute this. Godfrey, his friend and term-mate, confidentially dismissed Churchill's postwar claim as "nonsense."[16]

AS THE SILENCE of the graveyard descending upon Poland that October, Mr Churchill burrowed in Whitehall.

His primary tool in these undermining operations was S Branch — a private statistical office he set up under Professor Lindemann. To staff it he raided Godfrey's own statistical section, claiming that he wanted to investigate shipping statistics; but he would direct the Prof on October 9 to use these men for "special enquiries" — to doublecheck Cabinet papers submitted by other ministers. Godfrey watched with chagrin as the section became a "private piece of machinery," operated for the furtherance of the First Lord's ambitions.[17]

Typical of the wide net that Winston now flung out, harvesting public anxieties, was a note to Hoare criticizing needless blackouts, gasoline restrictions, and food rationing. He also suggested a volunteer "Home Guard" of half a million over-forties. All this was of little direct concern to a navy minister, but he was unabashed. "I hear continual complaints," he wrote, justifying his intervention, "from every quarter of the lack of organization on the Home Front. Can't we get at it?"[18]

* * *

At six p.m. on September 3, after attending his first War Cabinet, Churchill hastened over to the admiralty, a sprawling Portland-stone office labyrinth under the lofty telescope of Admiral Lord Nelson. From his private entrance he was escorted up to the First Lord's room: not that he needed any escort — he knew it well.

Casting around, he missed an octagonal mahogany table; it was found elsewhere and brought back into the room. Little had changed since the Dardanelles disaster. The map case containing naval charts of 1915 was still behind the sofa where he had last seen it. Pound came in and the two men eyed each other — "amicably if doubtfully," as Churchill recalled. He had publicly criticized the dispositions of Pound's fleet at the time of Albania. But Pound had useful qualities — he was forgetful, quiet and complaisant. Humourless and remote as well, he was never seen to read a book; he was at sea if any conversation steered into non-naval topics. He regularly dozed off in staff meetings (the consequence of an undiagnosed brain tumour.) He was a prey to rare phobias too, believing that ratings ashore conspired to avoid saluting him.[19]

Later that evening, Churchill lowered himself into the familiar leather-backed chair in the Board Room, bade Pound introduce his staff and then adjourned them with the words: "Gentlemen — to your tasks and duties." "From today," he rasped down the telephone to the Polish ambassador at eleven p.m., "I am First Lord of the Admiralty. If you should need me, I am at your disposal any time."

From that first moment he fired off orders and inspirations, catechizing, querying and carping, a volcano of aggressive instinct that for ten years had lain dormant — some had hoped extinct. He called for statistics on Hitler's U-boats and their capabilities; he set up a map room in the library, flagging the onward march of the merchant ships and escorts bringing in supplies; he railed at the neutrality of the "so-called Eire;" he ordered faster construction of escort destroyers — Cheap and Nasties, "cheap to us, nasty to the U-boat." These messages became known as "First Lord's Prayers" because of his style which substituted "Pray" for "please," as in "Pray let me know your views."

In his search for an initiative, his eyes had lit upon Narvik, the ice-free port in northern Norway through which Sweden plied her iron ore trade with Germany during the winter when her own Baltic port of Lulea was icebound. Until Lulea reopened each spring the iron ore ships had to hug the coastal waters of Norway, as they headed south to Germany. At an admiralty staff meeting on September 18 somebody, probably Churchill himself, recommended halting those iron ore shipments even if it meant violating Norway's neutrality. On the following day he put to the War Cabinet a scheme for mining Norwegian waters.

* * *

Throughout the war each month's appointments would be entered on large-format cards — the first was an eleven-thirty a.m. War Cabinet on September 4; it was at first marked as being in the Cabinet War Room bunker, as London still expected Hitler's knockout blow, then amended to No. 10. Across these cards, which were salvaged by his admirable A.D.C.,* parade the notables of Churchill's War — dukes and duchesses and peers and admirals who might go down in ships and history. September 1939 saw Cork & Orerry, Drax ("if train punctual"), Evans, Tyrwhitt, Wake-Walker; press lords (Beaverbrook) and journalists like the American H.R. Knickerbocker; different hands pencilled in appointments with his trusty friends from the wilderness like Vansittart or "Dr Revesz" (Reves, his literary agent) or the Romanian, Tilea; on September 25 a "Mr Spier" was pathetically entered — Eugen Spier, earliest financier of The Focus, was about to be interned.

Once or twice Field Marshal Ironside came. He had few admirers in the soldiery — "It's a mercy his soldiering days are over," one general assessed a year earlier. "There's always been more bluff and brawn than brain." Their minister, Hore-Belisha, told those who would listen that Ironside's appointment was the fault of politicians who did not know the man *au fond*, "notably Winston."[20]

---

*The author purchased them from Tommy Thompson's heirs and has donated a copy to the Public Record Office, London, where they form part of PREM 10.

Of course bare names, like those of Colonel Stuart Menzies, who shortly became head of the SIS, and Sir Vernon Kell, head of MI5, give little clue as to the subjects discussed. The colour has to be filled in from other sources — like when Winston dined at Lord Kemsley's. At the end of the meal the newspaper owner invited him to a chair at the top of the table and asked in a stage whisper what new intrigues he was hatching against Chamberlain; the First Lord purpled, rose, rang for a servant and sent for his car.[21]

Churchill's influence grew throughout that month. He was appointed to the Land Forces committee. It met on September 7 and resolved to raise fifty-five divisions by late 1941 and to build the factories to sustain them.[22] On the next day Churchill told the American ambassador that fourteen merchant ships had already been sunk by "U-boat" warfare; but he spoke encouragingly of France's immense army of four million.[23]

In Cabinet he turned out much as the others expected — in Sam Hoare's words rhetorical and very reminiscent; Churchill struck him as an old man, easily tired and over emotional.[24] The much younger secretary for war Leslie Hore-Belisha expressed frustration at the way his more elderly colleagues wasted time phrasing communiques rather than preparing for a major war.[25] After one flowery Churchill monologue Hoare heard a colleague scoff: "Why didn't he bring his six-volume *World Crisis*?" Churchill, he snidely commented in his diary, was no doubt already writing new memoirs.[26]

Scepticism about Churchill's vitality was probably justified. The real war had yet to begin, and that was the stimulus he needed. Not until the ninth did elements of the Expeditionary Force even cross to France. Their commander, General Lord Gort, followed two evenings later after Churchill and Lord Camrose had dined him at the Other Club — the cliquish dining club which Winston had founded with F.E. Smith in 1911. According to Camrose's notes, Churchill predicted that they would master the present U-boat menace quite rapidly; but he perceptively added that in about a year's time it would revive.[27]

As yet there was little that Britain could do. Dalton expressed shock that Chamberlain had made no realistic plans for aiding Poland after guaranteeing her. Churchill replied that as a Cabinet member he could not voice open criticism. "I have signed on for this voyage," was the way he put it. He was still groping for a strategy, uncertain of himself. In a sense, he was still living the Great War; his mental images were those of Jutland and Gallipoli, of fleet actions and of bayonet charges on Turkish trenches. Pacing the floor, he told Dalton that he had a dream of all the states of southern and south-eastern Europe moving ultimately against Germany, and of the flags of freedom fluttering in Prague and Vienna (curiously, he made no mention of Poland's capital.) A few days later, to the Cabinet, he was more specific: he wanted "all the Balkan countries and Turkey" dragged in:

> We needed as many Allies in the Balkans as we could secure, and it was not at all to our interest that the Balkans should be kept in a state of quiet, whilst France and ourselves were left to bear the full brunt of the German assault on the Western Front.

"But," he told Dalton on the thirteenth, "all this is very far away, and there will be a long, grim interval first."

"If only we had the Czechs as well as the Poles!" he sighed. Britain might have won over the Russians too — "But at the end they played a deadly game!"

"I sit here," he mused out loud to Dalton, "and I only get bad news — of our ships sunk. I don't get the good news, when their submarines go down." He was confident that the U-boats would be defeated. He pictured in vivid words to the Socialist intellectual the effects of depth charges on submarine crews — the sudden concussion, the claustrophobia.[28]

Donning a spurious naval uniform he left to inspect the northern-most naval bases at Scapa Flow and Loch Ewe, which he had last visited a quarter century before: the fleet had been berthed at this hideout on the west coast of Scotland, for the same reason as now, the unreadiness at Scapa. He returned to the admiralty three mornings later to learn that the aircraft carrier *Courageous* had gone down with her captain and five hundred of her crew escorting a convoy in the Bristol Channel.

"Gentlemen," he began his Admiralty report to Mr Chamberlain's Cabinet that morning, "I have a piece of bad news to give you" — and he reminded them that although old, she had been one of their most valuable warships. He was stoical about such casualties; in fact loss of life affected him far less than the loss of personal prestige, particularly when the former was somebody else's and the latter was his own. Some months later the troopship *Lancastria* would be sunk by enemy aircraft off Saint-Nazaire, drowning 3,000 British soldiers; he ordered the news suppressed, and confessed six weeks later when it leaked out in America that it had entirely slipped his mind. Now, as even more sinister news came that the Red Army was invading eastern Poland, he reminded Hankey of how exactly twenty-five years before they had lost the *Aboukir*, *Cressey* and *Hogue* to enemy submarines, and that this was not the first time Russia had defected.[29]

Powered by conflicting emotions — the desires to punish Germans and to act aggressively, while not scandalising neutral opinion — on September 10 he advised Chamberlain against taking any initiative in bombing. "It is to our interest," he wrote, "that . . . we should follow and not precede the Germans in the process, no doubt inevitable, of deepening severity and violence.[30] Count Raczynski came to the Admiralty, followed on the thirteenth by Hugh Dalton, to argue that bombing Germany would bring relief to their reeling Polish allies.

"If we disregard Poland," replied Churchill, disagreeing, "it is unquestionably in our interest not to make the first move in air warfare in the West." British aircraft factories were still gearing up. "If we can," he said with measured cynicism, "let us secure that the first women and children to be hit are British, and not German." For maximum effect on American opinion it was vital that *messieurs les assassins commencent.*[31]

Towards the Italians he still showed a vestigial affection — having met and rather liked the "bluffing gangster" who presided over them. But there was a hard core of rationalism too. Mussolini, he reminded Dalton, had one hundred submarines.[32] So in Cabinet he recommended selling airplanes to Italy and buying motor boats as ways of developing a fruitful Anglo-Italian trade.[33] Detente with Italy would be one way of retrieving British forces from the Mediterranean and the Middle East.[34]

Another would be if British troops in Palestine could be partially replaced by a Jewish contingent. The Jewish Agency had offered a truce over the bitterly contested White Paper for the duration of the war and Jewish support worldwide in the fight against Hitler. But in return they demanded a not inconsiderable concession — the right to raise a Jewish army in Palestine.

Over dinner with Winston and Brendan Bracken at the admiralty on the nineteenth Chaim Weizmann claimed that 75,000 young Jews had volunteered in Palestine and that more could be recruited from Romania and Poland. "What is important," he explained, "is to create cadres and establish a military organization."

Churchill saw no objection. "Once the Jews are armed," he agreed, "the Arabs will come to terms with them.""

He directed Bracken to liaise with Weizmann and to comply with every wish. But the first wish that Weizmann expressed when Bracken visited him at the Dorchester — London's only bombproof hotel, now filling with the rich and influential — was not so simple to fulfil; the Zionists wanted permission to erect a Jewish arms factory in Palestine. Over this, the War Office would dig in its heels.[35]

MANY MEMBERS OF Parliament came to look upon Churchill during those first weeks as a source of spirit and moral uplift. One speech by him could change the temper of the House.

On the last day of September a statement by the prime minister had been greeted with funereal gloom. Beside him sat Churchill, silent, true to the Cabinet solidarity he had explained to Dalton, but visibly unhappy; looking in one observer's words like the Chinese God of Plenty suffering from indigestion.[36]

As he rose he was cheered from all the benches — no longer just by the Labour opposition. He set out Britain's naval prospects, and could not forebear to remark how strange was the experience of finding himself after a quarter century in the same room at the admiralty, poring over the same maps, and fighting the same enemy.

"It is the sort of thing," he added, grinning hugely and with a sidelong glance at Chamberlain who could raise no more than a sickly smile, "that one would harldy expect to happen."

There were MPs who felt that he had hauled himself closer, in those few minutes of oration, to the coveted premiership than ever before. Even the Chamberlain faction was overheard in the lobbies exclaiming, "We have now found our leader."

Over in Grosvenor Square, as this momentous opening month in Europe's bloodiest war came to an end, the American ambassador composed a broad survey for his president. As he viewed it, England was once more fighting for her possessions and her place in the sun: "Regardless of the God-awful behaviour of the Nazis," wrote Kennedy, "surely the fact is that the English people are not fighting Hitler — they are fighting the German people, just as they fought them twenty-five years ago, because 45 million Britons controlling the greatest farflung maritime Empire in the world and 80 million Germans dominating continental Europe haven't learned to live together peacefully."

He saw it as a sign of decadence in London that nobody had told the British the truth about their plight. They had no leaders, and he doubted whether their Parliamentary machine was capable of throwing up one.

Many people, continued the ambassador in this challenging dispatch, doubted whether Chamberlain could survive a serious reverse: "Who is to replace the Prime Minister? Possibly Halifax, possibly Churchill. But for all Halifax's mystical, Christian character, and Churchill's prophecies in respect to Germany, I can't imagine them adequately leading the people out of the Valley of the Shadow of Death."[37]

CHAPTER 17

Naval Person

TOWARDS THE END of that first month of war, September 1939, the prime minister's private secretary admitted to himself that perhaps Mr Chamberlain ought to stand down in favour of somebody more forceful; but he feared that Mr Churchill seemed too old to succeed him.[1]

Churchill's performance in the House soon dispelled such fears. One M.P. who had been in The Focus — and who would be buried eight months later near Dunkirk — was jubilant at the manner in which their champion confounded critics who had been whispering that "the years had been taking their toll."

> I know that the *nation* will never let him go now that, at long last, he is back in the Cabinet.[2]

From time to time Winston's mind strayed across the North Atlantic. He had been born half American but considered this no misdemeanor. A genealogist, that rara avis of historical research, would establish that in the eighth generation he shared three pairs of ancestors with President Roosevelt.[3] The seat of the Jeromes, his maternal ancestors, was Rochester in New York State, and his mother had been born in Brooklyn. Directly descended on her side from a captain in George Washington's armies, Churchill could claim to be a member of the Cincinatti: so in 1776 he would have had loyalties to both sides of that historic quarrel.[4]

Before speaking at the turn of the century at New York's Madison Square Gardens, this gentleman of much-mixed blood had been introduced by Mark Twain with these words: "I give you the son of an American mother and an English father — the perfect man!" Half a century later, when Mr Adlai Stevenson came down to Chartwell to solicit a message for the English Speaking Union in London, Winston would growl: "Tell them I *am* an English speaking union."[5]

Though it might derelict the interests of the old world, he never entirely overcame this maudlin affection for the new. In New York in March 1946, recalling their victorious alliance in two world wars, he would mistily ask of his dinner guests: "Why do you have to wait for a war to bring us together?" A year after that he would emotionally remark to an editor of *Life*, "America needs good men, for America has to save the world." Laying aside his brandy glass, he murmured very slowly: "America — is — the — world."[6]

HE HAD SOON made himself at home at Admiralty House. The desk was cluttered with toothpicks, gold medals used as paperweights, countless apothecaries' pills and powders, and the special cuffs he used to prevent his dark jacket sleeves from becoming soiled; the table beside it carried the bottles of liquor.[7]

The First Lord was probably the one popular figure in the government and he knew it. The public had the feeling that *they* had chosen him, a delayed reaction from the mysterious poster campaign of that summer. The newspapers wrote of him as a future prime minister.[8]

On the first Sunday in October he delivered a wartime broadcast. Churchill sent for his Intelligence chief Rear Admiral John Godfrey to make sure his facts were right; the admiral, a frank, open faced officer, saw an efficient typist with a silent typewriter skimming out the text in triplicate on half sheets of foolscap, while a dishevelled Mr Churchill, fortified by two long drinks and two enormous cigars, paced the room dictating, dropping cigar ash and spilling whisky over his waistcoat. "The sentences," recalled the admiral, "seemed to emerge without any effort."[9]

He spoke briefly of Poland's unquenchable spirit and prophesied: "She will rise again like a rock, which may for a spell be submerged by a tidal wave, but which remains a rock." He lingered on the Russian conundrum; he announced that the Cabinet was preparing a war of at least three years. It was an unaccustomed, archaic language that flowed from the loudspeakers, but the English understood it and were enthralled. There was danger developing in Hitler's submarine offensive — "But the Royal Navy has immediately attacked the U-boats and is hunting them night and day, I will not say without mercy, because God forbid we should ever part company with that, but at any rate with zeal, and not altogether without relish."

Congratulations reached him from all round the listening world. "Your broadcast magnificent," prime minister William Mackenzie-King cabled from Ottawa, "as perfect in its appeal to the new world as to the old."[10] But from across Horse Guard's Parade there glowered the green of envy behind the windows of No. 10. Writing up his diary Chamberlain's secretary now suspected that Winston would be PM before long. "Judging from his record of untrustworthiness and instability," this official mused, echoing his master's oft-stated views, "he may in that case lead us into the most dangerous paths.

AT THE AMERICAN embassy, Joe Kennedy had also listened to the broadcast. He was worried by this war: he had asked Sir John Simon two days before, "Just what are you fighting for now? You can't restore Poland to the Poles, can you?"

"No," replied Simon, "not all of it."

"You can't talk about aggression," he had argued, "and permit Russia to retain half of Poland and have its claw over the Balkan States as well as the Baltic States?"

"Possibly not," the chancellor agreed.

People coming from Germany had assured Kennedy that if Hitler went there would be chaos, and Germany might turn communist. "The cost to England and France," he prophesied, "will be so great that it will reduce them to a mere shell of their present selves."

Simon, Halifax and Chamberlain all shared this bleak view, or so he reported to Roosevelt. "If they were to advocate any type of peace," he continued, "they would be yelled down by their own people who are determined to go on." He urged the president to help Britain end the war while she still could.[11]

"Of all the wars that men have fought in their hard pilgrimage," Winston had declared in this broadcast, "none was more noble than the great Civil War in America nearly eighty years ago." Less felicitously he added,

> All the heroism of the South could not redeem their cause from the stain of slavery, just as all the courage and skill which the Germans always show in a war will not free them from the reproach of Nazism with its intolerance and brutality.[12]

Kennedy choked on these words and rushed word to Winston that this comparison would not commend him to Southern editors. Winston suggested putting out a suitably contrite statement to mitigate the faux pas, but it turned out that the American press had ignored his broadcast; and while there had been some comment "in the Senate cloakroom," Roosevelt himself was said to be quite pleased.[13]

On the morning after the broadcast Kennedy came to lunch at the admiralty. Eyeing the fine silver and mahogany, he asked what would happen if Hitler now offered acceptable peace terms — a possibility troubling many minds that week.* Privately he believed Britain hadn't

---

*The Irish Foreign Office allowed the German embassy in Dublin to learn on October 3 that Mr Chamberlain and people of influence around him wanted peace provided Britain's prestige could be preserved. In the British archives the F.O., Chamberlain, Wilson and Hankey files covering this episode have been closed until the 21st century.[14]

a chance. Two weeks earlier he had told an officer of the Coldstream Guards that Britain and France would both be "thrashed;" and his son Jack had interjected that even the repeal of neutrality legislation would not help, because Britain hadn't got the Gold to buy in America.

Answering the ambassador's question, Churchill confirmed that Britain might agree to an *armistice*, but only to gain respite.

He had clearly written Poland off. Kennedy expressed curiosity as to why Britain had not declared war on Russia, who had also invaded Poland.

"The danger to the world," Churchill gravely responded, "is Germany, and not Russia."

An uneasy discussion followed on the Nazi air raids that everybody expected, but which still had not begun. Churchill was looking forward to them — hoping that the inevitable "air massacres" might draw in the United States. The ambassador's ears picked up at remarks like these. "It appears to me," he telegraphed immediately to Washington, "that there is a feeling that if [British] women and children are killed . . . the United States will tend more towards their side."

One theme that Churchill developed was to be repeated in different variations many times over the next two years. "If the Germans bomb us into subjection," he pointed out, "one of their terms will certainly be that we hand over our Fleet. And then your troubles will begin."[15]

Kennedy knew what was behind Churchill's remarks. "Every hour will be spent by the British," he predicted, "in trying to figure out how we can be gotten in."

Later he prophesied that when he finally succeeded Winston would charge his brandy glass and say, "I have done my duty. Victory is ours! This is my crowning achievement! God save the King!"[16]

* * *

Immediately after this luncheon on October 2 Churchill's remarkable correspondence with Roosevelt began. A letter arrived by diplomatic pouch from Washington for Ambassador Kennedy to deliver *sealed* to the First Lord.

The ambassador was resentful at having been by-passed but before revealing it to the morning Cabinet on the fifth Churchill tactfully invited him to the admiralty and read out to him Roosevelt's bland, almost over-innocent letter.

Dated September 11, it congratulated Winston on his appointment and continued: "It is because you and I occupied similar positions in the World War that I want you to know how glad I am that you are back again in the Admiralty." F.D.R. invited Winston to enter into correspondence. "What I want you and the Prime Minister to know," he said, "is that I shall at all times welcome it, if you will keep me in touch personally with anything you want me to know about. You can always send sealed letters through your pouch or my pouch." After this veiled invitation to by-pass regular channels, F.D.R. concluded, "I am glad you did the Marlboro' volumes before this thing started — and I much enjoyed reading them."[17]

It was an unorthodox communication on any count: a Roosevelt could write to foreign heads of state or government, but hardly to anybody lesser; it violated every convention.

As Churchill launched into a monologue, Kennedy still felt bitter: the more he heard the First Lord's effusions about neutrality and "keeping the war away from the U.S.A.," the more his Irish blood was roused.

"Maybe I do him an injustice," he brooded in his diary,

> but I just don't trust him. He almost impressed me that he was willing to blow up the American embassy and say it was the Germans, if it would get the United States in.[18]

AT THE ELEVEN-THIRTY Cabinet, Mr Churchill persuaded his colleagues to let him develop this secret correspondence.

It is clear from what we now know that he took a delight in clandestine communication — the secret courier, the scrambler telephone, the unofficial telegraph. We have noted his extramural dealings with Maisky, with Masaryk and Mandel. We shall soon see him establish private radio links with his favourite commanders during the Narvik and Dunkirk episodes, enabling him to circumvent both the ground commander and the Board of Admiralty with directives and instructions.

Throughout the coming war he would commune regularly with Roosevelt by channels which prevented the Foreign Office and Britain's ambassador in Washington from automatically reviewing the messages. The two men had evidently communicated informally through third persons like Frankfurter before this correspondence began, and Churchill may even have identified himself as Naval Person in such billets doux. How else can we explain Kennedy's usage of the phrase "Naval Person" in his four p.m. telegram despatched in advance of Winston's reply to the President later that day, October 5? "The Naval Person," he now wrote, will not fail to avail himself of invitation and he is honoured by the message."[19] That person, he added, would write immediately: and it is only in the reply that now went off, drafted in fact by Pound's wiry, irascible deputy Tom Phillips, that we find the first recorded use of the Mr Churchill's famous soubriquet: "The following from Naval Person. . ."[20]

Perhaps transatlantic telephone conversations had preceded this. While dining at Morpeth Mansions that same night, Churchill was telephoned by President Roosevelt from three thousand miles away — again by-passing the prime minister; an admiral who chanced to be his guest witnessed it.

The background of this urgent 'phone call suggests that F.D.R. shared Kennedy's appreciation of Mr Churchill's wily capabilities. Grand Admiral Raeder, whose cryptanalysts had broken the main British naval cypher,[21] had called in the U.S. naval attaché in Berlin at mid-day on the fourth and handed him in confidence a Note warning that an American steamer — the 6,209-ton coaster *Iroquois* — was to be sunk off the East Coast of America "under *Athenia* circumstances,"* possibly by concealed explosives; the vessel had left an Irish port on the second laden with refugees including Americans; German naval Intelligence had learned of Churchill's alleged plan from "a particular source."[22] Roosevelt told his Cabinet, ordered Raeder's claim publicized immediately — and telephoned Churchill.[23]

"Admiral," said Churchill, returning to his dinner guests, "I think you must now excuse me. This is very important and I must go and see the Prime Minister at once."[24]

THE F.D.R.—CHURCHILL TELEGRAMS were extraordinary in several respects. No attempt was made to paraphrase them before transmission — a security lapse which must have delighted British codebreakers, who took as keen an interest as the Germans in reading American telegrams.[25] Since the American diplomatic cypher (Gray) was already an open book to codebreakers — legend has it that at one Washington banquet a diplomat delivered his entire speech in Gray — it was perhaps of only academic interest whether the First Lord showed the F.D.R. messages to his prime minister or not.[26]

Lord Lothian, ambassador in Washington, was as displeased as Kennedy at being sidetracked and the foreign secretary, Lord Halifax, asked Churchill on January 6 to desist from using non-F.O. channels; Churchill replied on the twelfth that it would be a pity to close down "this private line of communication through the American Embassy and the State Department."

> I have availed myself of your permission to send such messages with the most scrupulous care to keep strictly within the lines of your policy.

---

*The *Athenia* had been torpedoed in the Atlantic on September 3 with the loss of 112 lives, including twenty-eight Americans. The Germans righteously denied blame — Hitler had embargoed attacks on passenger liners — but later learned that a U-boat was indeed responsible. Seeking to embarrass Churchill, the Nazis continued to blame him.

Regretting that Lothian had been by-passed, he suggested that future communications might go simultaneously both by F.O. and American embassy channels, thus "giving the President the feeling that he has a special line of information."[27]

At the White House only two officials were allowed to handle these "Naval Friend" messages. "Many a night," one of them, —the White House communications officer Captain Donald Macdonald, —would state in 1970, "I was out on a party and I'd get a call because one of these messages came in and I'd have to come and break them down and then notify the President that the message was in. And the President invariably would send me over to talk with Morgenthau, whom he had ticked off to be his man to work with the British. . . This was kept very, very quiet, what we were doing."[28]

As their intimacy became more profound the two men relied increasingly on the transatlantic radiotelephone link. Roosevelt certainly resorted to it when need arose to by-pass cumbrous diplomatic channels.* So did Churchill, who would call him from a privy-like booth in the underground War Room. On its outer door a circular brass dial marked Vacant or Engaged; the door opened to reveal a short passage and a second green baize door behind which was the special scrambler telephone, a black instrument with a green dial standing on a small table next to a leather-seated chair. Above the door was a ship's clock with an extra red pointer to remind him of Washington time.

Nor were these the only secret channels developed by the two inventive statesmen. The unclassified archives contain some 950 items originated by Churchill and eight hundred by F.D.R., but these files are clearly incomplete: they contain almost no reference to either Ultra or Magic, the solution of German and Japanese codes so important to their wartime decisions.[29] Perhaps these messages can be found in the archives of the S.I.S. and the National Security Agency. By mid 1941 certain of their communications were definitely flowing through a radio link established between S.I.S. headquarters in London and the F.B.I.'s North Beach radio facility on Chesapeake Bay. In the twelve months following June 1940 two or three hundred messages a week used this channel using the F.B.I. one-time pads, a cypher considered invulnerable, or other cyphers exclusive to the British, and J. Edgar Hoover was told that this was in part traffic between Churchill and the president.†

* * *

---

*See page 526
†See page 561

Kennedy had again detected in Churchill at this October 5, 1939 interview what he termed "a soft and appeasing policy toward Russia." The Soviet Union, the First Lord implied, was justified in occupying eastern Poland as that territory was "really Russian soil." Imperceptibly Britain's war aims had shifted from guaranteeing Poland's independence. On the previous day, Kennedy had discussed Churchill with Lord Halifax who had couched his views in terms that showed little respect for Churchill's judgment: at a recent Cabinet, he said, the First Lord had mentioned the torpedoing of a Greek ship — and had then launched into an oration about how the wind had shrieked and the waves grown high and fearsome.

Kennedy urged the foreign secretary to give due consideration to Hitler's peace terms when they came and in an unappealing turn of phrase again commented on the Jewish influence on the British press.

Hitler, victorious now in Poland, announced his proposals to the Reichstag on the sixth. He confirmed the neutrality of his neighbours, and told France he would not even claim Alsace-Lorraine. The speech was devilishly cunning: it attracted favourable comment in American newspapers, but Fleet-street condemned it in such intemperate language that at next day's Cabinet Lord Halifax murmured that the press commentaries were entirely unauthorized.

Of 2,450 letters that poured into Downing-street over the next few days, 1,860 begged Chamberlain to end the war. The Cabinet however was agreed that Hitler's offer was unacceptable; it remained only to discuss how to reject it. Halifax, Churchill, Cadogan and Vansittart all drafted possible replies. Churchill suggested the briefest possible text, mentioning the fate of Roosevelt's final peace attempt in August as an example of the uselessness of negotiating with Hitler.

He was still struggling to finish off the fourth and final volume of his *History*, aided by his trusty scribes. Deakin was reviewing the proofs on the Victorian age and a young ghost called Alan Bullock was completing Canada. While Deakin delegated Ashley to deviling ten thousand words on Cromwell, Bullock began rough-hewing a similar quantity of Churchillian prose on the origins of the Empire in the antipodes. "By December," records Martin Gilbert, in whom this manner of literary endeavour struck no odd chord, "only Waterloo and Trafalgar remained to be done."[30]

WHILE ESTABLISHING CLANDESTINE channels to the west, to Washington, Winston did not neglect his relations with the Russians. The Soviet ambassador had steered clear of him since the Hitler-Stalin pact and Churchill's inclusion in the Cabinet; but with visions of Catherine — the proposed naval foray into the Baltic — dancing before him the First Lord had reiterated his pro-Soviet line in his broadcast on the first, and at ten p.m. on the sixth Maisky groped his way through the thickening London fog to the unfamiliar building.

Churchill reminisced about the history of this room and showed off the relics of earlier wars. "This," he said, opening the map case let into the wall behind his desk, "is the very map I used to follow the German grand fleet's movements on."

He admitted frankly his regret that Britain and Russia were not allies against Germany. Maisky blamed it on Chamberlain.

"I know, I know," commiserated Churchill. "But byegones must be byegones."

Their basic interests were the same, he said, and he was certain that Britain and Russia would eventually come together. Meanwhile he was doing what he could to further Soviet interests in Cabinet: he had persuaded his colleagues not to oppose Soviet naval bases in the Baltic, arguing that anything that hurt Germany must be in the British interest.

Maisky answered cautiously. "I would not like to speculate what will happen in the future."

Churchill smiled indulgently. His reply was gently veined with sarcasm, "Yes, time will tell."[31]

A few days later Günter Prien's U-boat skulked into the fleet anchorage at Scapa Flow and sank the battleship *Royal Oak*; eight hundred sailors perished, from admiral to seaman. It turned out that the admiralty had been warned in April that the defences were inadequate. That was before his time, but Mr Churchill ruled against holding an inquiry.[32] He assured his colleagues that even giving the complete picture and not "slurring over" setbacks he could satisfy the House by "leading up to a happy conclusion;" and sure enough that afternoon saw his rhetorical skill — a fine example of how to appease ones critics by abject acceptance of broad responsibility, while still rejecting it in detail.

Such verbal gymnastics were his forte. Immediately after taking office he had lectured Rear Admiral Godfrey, his Director of Naval Intelligence, that the admiralty bulletin must "maintain its reputation for truthfulness."[33] This was not the same, of course, as telling the truth. Describing his minister's approach to that elusive commodity, the D.N.I. would recall in a confidential history, "He did not hesitate *not* to tell the truth or to paint a rosy picture that had no connection with reality."[34] As the U-boat war went from bad to worse, the next weeks produced samples of this dexterity. Admiral Godfrey would recall that since Winston preferred to compose later broadcasts unaided, "the truth regarding our anti U-boats measures got fogged."

Churchill's memorable juggling and jousting with statistics had started before the war when he claimed that Hitler had secretly built more submarines than allowed under the 1935 Anglo-German naval agreement — a canard that he would even sustain in his memoirs.[35] Years later Godfrey would analyse the U-boat war using captured German records. Hitler, he found had started the war with only the fifty-seven allowed by the agreement; most of them training in the Baltic. But Churchill had claimed that the enemy had sixty-six, explaining to his puzzled staff that many were operating in the South Atlantic (in fact none would be south of Cape Saint-Vincent before June 1940.)

He began an extraordinary multiplication game, to conceal the disappointing results from the British public. Before his Sunday broadcast on November 12, the D.N.I. correctly informed him that six U-boats had been sunk (out of his "sixty-six"); but on the air that evening Winston announced: "The attack of the U-boats has been controlled and they have paid a heavy toll." Reminded three days later that the true figure was six, Churchill forbade its circulation except to Pound, Phillips and himself.

Naval Intelligence consistently estimated right. Admiral Godfrey was shocked at the widening discrepancies. "I assumed," he wrote in a confidential admiralty history, "that his perversion of the truth was part of Mr Churchill's technique of heartening the nation at a time when all news was bad."

In December 1939 Godfrey had reported eight sunk; the actual figure was nine; Churchill claimed *twenty-four*. In January the figures were nine, ten and (Churchill) *thirty-four*; broadcasting on the twentieth, the First Lord claimed: "It seems pretty certain tonight that half the U-boats with which Germany began the war have been sunk, and that their new building has fallen far behind what we expected." (He had taken the nine known sunk, added sixteen "probables" and rounded the total upwards.)

In February 1940 the figures were ten (Godfrey), eleven (actual) and *thirty-five* (Churchill). The First Lord was fully aware that there had been no sinkings at all for several weeks since he minuted on the seventh, "I am sorry that we sunk no U-boats in the two months between December 4th and January 30th," and ordered "this gloomy view" restricted once again to Pound, Phillips and himself.

So it went on: On February 17 he added 17 "probables" to fourteen "known sunk," called the resulting thirty-one "a working hypothesis," and added in green ink on the docket, "I think forty-five will be nearer the truth." The actual figure was sixteen; Churchill announced *forty five*.

When Admiral Pound's wretched Director of Anti-Submarine Warfare, Captain A.G. Talbot, concluded that by March 10 all the attacks had failed except fifteen of which they had actual "remnants" and that as many as forty-three enemy submarines were still fit for service,

Churchill angrily retorted that clearly the Germans could not have more than twelve left: because he himself had publicly said so. He insisted on Talbot's dismissal ("This conclusion leads me to think that it might be a good thing if Captain Talbot went to sea as soon as possible"); Pound had the decency to ensure that Talbot was given command of an aircraft carrier.[36]

Not until mid-April was a document captured from an enemy submarine, U-49, listing Hitler's entire submarine fleet. The canard was exposed, but only to those in the know.[37] When he left the admiralty shortly thereafter Mr Churchill was able to limit the secret to the smallest possible circle of admiralty officers; he deceived the Cabinet about the true figures; and even his successor was kept in the dark — the new First Lord believed as late as July that during Churchill's admiralty stewardship thirty U-boats had been sunk, saving the Atlantic lifelines of the nation.

He embroidered upon the shipping losses in like manner. After he accounted to the House on December 6 ("We are buffeted by the waves but the ocean tides flow steady and strong in our favour") it did not escape one M.P. that in totting up the empire's surviving tonnage Winston had included the ships operating on the Canadian lakes.[38]

Captain Talbot was only the first of a number of staff officers whose head was brought into the First Lord's room on a platter. The next was the Director of Plans, Captain V.H. Danckwerts: he had the temerity to criticise Catherine, and was summarily dismissed. A hush fell upon the admiralty, and captains and admirals wondered who would be the next foolish virgin sent into the wilderness. Godfrey had the impression that during this initial *furore*, Mr Churchill was unconsciously including the admiralty establishment among those he blamed for keeping him in the wilderness for so many years; the procession of Directors, Sea Lords and others evicted by him from the admiralty certainly damaged morale.

One final example will illustrate this aspect of his tenure. "It became his habit to cheer everyone up in his Wednesday broadcasts," Godfrey would write: "Good news was made to seem better; bad news was toned down, delayed or sometimes suppressed." When particularly spicey news came in, its release was routinely held up so that the First Lord might include it in his Wednesday broadcast. "No one," reasoned the admiral, "was more conscious than Mr Churchill of the popularity of the bringer of good tidings." Woe betide any officer who stole his thunder. Vice Admiral Theodore Hallett, who controlled the admiralty's press section did so — thrice; Winston dismissed him too, and posted him to sea.[39]

CHAPTER 18

The Joybells Will Ring

LEO AMERY OBSERVED in September 1939 that with Winston's exception the government was entirely devoid of fighting spirit.[1] This was true, but as First Lord he still had only limited authority to act. In October he reverted to his pre-war habit of dealing with foreign statesmen independently of No.10. He decided to renew his contacts with Mandel and other pre-war associates; General Spears, sent over to Paris to set these meetings up, soon found however that Whitehall had warned official Paris that he was a creature of Winston's and connected with *des affaires louches* — "bent dealings."[2]

When the First Lord arrived at the Ritz on November 2 Mandel asked to see him alone. Cannier now than when he was out of office, Churchill decided it would not do, as he told Spears, to be "caught" in an intrigue and invited Mandel to a larger dinner on the fourth. Meanwhile he drove out to French navy headquarters and — perhaps rashly — offered to the fleet commander Admiral Jean-Louis Darlan the British anti-Submarine device, Asdic.[3]

Later he visited the C-in-C Maurice Gamelin — a Gallic general so diminutive that even with his platform heels he encountered problems in decorating taller Nordic officers like Ironside, since a certain amount of kissing both cheeks was involved. Churchill set out to him a novel scheme just suggested to him by the Prof: The French should float special mines down the Rhine, creating consternation among the Germans and sinking barges and damaging bridges.[4]

He dined his French associates at the Ritz on the fourth. Prime minister Edouard Daladier, invited to attend, had curtly made his regrets having telephoned first to inquire about Winston's other guests. The table plan shows that to his right were two of Daladier's most venemous critics, Paul Reynaud and Alexis Léger; to his left were navy minister César Campinchi; Spears; Phillips; Darlan; Mandel; the British ambassador; Blum; Winston's A.D.C., Tommy Thompson, and son-in-law Duncan Sandys.

AS AUTUMN SHADOWS lengthened, London was depressingly empty except for hundreds of air-raid wardens and extra police now wearing steel helmets in anticipation of Hitler's knockout blow. The streets were dominated by uniforms. Sometimes the sirens sounded and the silvery-white barrage balloons were winched up into the yellow, smoggy air, like slow bubbles rising in champagne.

From his embassy window Joseph Kennedy could see the balloon tethered in Grosvenor Square: it seemed like a big white elephant to him. The war was clouding the entire Anglo-U.S. financial horizon; Hollywood film imports were to be cut from $35m to $5m annually.[5] "Yes," Sir Frederick Leith-Ross, director-general of the ministry of economic warfare, agreed in a tone of flat finality, "If the war goes on our Gold will be gone, our export trade gone and our foreign securities sold."[6]

The British government had acquired $800m of assets in New York by compulsory purchase from its citizens; $500m of these assets would now have to be sold off to finance 1940 alone. The huge sale was overhanging Wall Street like a reservoir about to burst its dam.

Kennedy had not tired of trying to halt this unpopular war. "Make no mistake," he wrote to Roosevelt early in November, "there is a very definite undercurrent in this country for peace." The British didn't want to be finished econimically and politically — "which they are beginning to suspect will be their fate if the war goes on very long."[7] A few days later twenty Labour MPs appealed for a more considered reply to Hitler's October offer; and Mr Attlee openly stated on November 8, "We wish the German people to know that they can now secure if they will an honourable peace."[8]

Only Churchill seemed to desire hostilities to continue. His prime minister deeply mistrusted him — Joseph Kennedy reassured himself of that when he visited No.10 — but preferred to have him inside the Cabinet; it was easier to handle him there. "As for the prime minister-ship," Chamberlain calmed the American ambassador, "I don't think there's one man in the Cabinet who'd vote for him. People are getting on to Churchill. He can't keep up this high pace all the time. I really hate the whole thing, Joe, but I just won't let Churchill get away with it."[9]

This underlying desire for peace was cruelly exploited by Hitler's Gestapo. Two of his generals turned up on the German-Dutch border offering to overthrow him. Lord Halifax was inclined to take them seriously, but his ministerial colleagues hesitated to reply in Winston's absence. "Cabinet did nothing about reply to Generals," noted one senior F.O. official in disgust, "as Winston away till Sunday night! . . No one dares answer without his approval."[10] Halifax undertook to talk him round.

On Sunday the fifth, Winston returned from France. On the following morning his appointment card read: "10:15. Halifax comes over." He evidently persuaded Churchill, because an invitation duly went to the German generals to meet on the Dutch frontier as soon as possible.

The First Lord was by nature an optimist — "I call him the Great Optimist," the C.I.G.S. told Kennedy. He took German army dissidence as a welcome sign of imminent collapse, brought about by his blockade. Chamberlain shared this belief in Germany's internal breakup. "I don't believe it will last beyond next spring," he told Kennedy, while waiting for the outcome of the frontier rendezvous.

The next day, the S.I.S. station chief at The Hague went in person to the historic rendezvous with the dissident enemy generals. The latter turned out to be Gestapo heavyweights in disguise. After a shootout in which a Dutch Intelligence officer was killed, the S.I.S. men were kidnapped, dragged over the border into Germany and tossed into Dachau. In London, a D-notice was issued to editors forbidding mention of the fiasco.

AFTER THAT, CHURCHILL was contemptuous of all feelers from Germany. "Your predecessor was entirely misled in December [sic] 1939," he would admonish the foreign secretary in 1941, not without a triumphant undertone. "Our attitude towards all such inquiries or suggestions should be absolute silence."[11] Though he was loath to do so, Chamberlain now rebuffed appeals for peace submitted by King Leopold of the Belgians and Queen Wilhelmina of Holland. Broadcasting a few days later, Churchill robustly demanded Germany's unconditional withdrawal from Poland. "The Germany which assaults us today," he urged his listeners, "is a far less strongly built and solidly founded organism than that which the Allies and the United States forced to beg for an armistice twenty-one years ago."

In this broadcast he uttered several prophicies about the enemy.

As they look out tonight from their blatant, panoplied, clattering Nazi Germany, they cannot find one single friendly eye in the whole circumference of the globe. Not one! Russia returns them a flinty stare; Italy averts her gaze; Japan is puzzled and thinks herself betrayed; Turkey and the whole of Islam have ranged themselves instinctively but decisively on the side of progress.

By 1941 these prophecies of Nazi isolation would be mercifully forgotten. R.A. Butler, the under-secretary at the Foreign Office, thought the broadcast "vulgar" beyond words, but reassured the protesting Italian ambassador that only a tiny minority in Whitehall was as inflexibly belligerent as Mr Churchill; there was no question, said Butler, of demanding that Hitler pull out of Poland as the price of negotiations. "This is not the only instance where Mr Churchill's language has been out of line with official government policy. He speaks only for himself."[12]

THAT WINTER HE still lacked a sense of direction.

He lunched with Eden at the Savoy, he received American journalists, he talked business with Reves, he conferred with ancient friends like Sir William Wiseman, who had headed the secret service in North America in the World War, and occasionally he conducted more formal business with "C" — the head of the S.I.S. — or his own D.N.I.; he conspired with Oliver Stanley and General Ironside on ways of eliminating Hore-Belisha from the War Office, he listed a Privy Council meeting — noting, in evident disappointment, "ordinary clothes."

On the day after his broadcast Paul Reynaud came over to see him, dapper and bustling, eyebrows arching more like circumflexes than ever; Reynaud was still conspiring against Daladier — their jealous feuding, partly over a woman, would have grave consequences for the Allies before the spring was over. He was a picturebook Frenchman with thin moustache, twinkling eyes and receding hair parted down the middle. He looked younger than his age but his size had saddled him with a lifelong feeling of inferiority. Their papers show them dining with Sinclair and Attlee, but we do not know what they discussed.[13]

While waiting for events, Churchill stimulated his own flow of adrenalin by cobbling at his naval staff. A deputy director in the operations division inked this remark into his illicit diary on November 17: "The Fifth Sea Lord [Vice-Admiral the Hon. Sir Alexander R.M. Ramsay] has been pushed out by Winston with his usual charming way — a chit left on his table. [Captain C.A.A.] Larcome goes too — a pity. I feel Ramsay was about the only S[ea] L[ord] on the staff side who ever spoke his mind — a failing sometimes, but an immense attribute in war."

Overnight, Churchill's first real crisis began. From mid-day on the eighteenth hourly reports came in, of ships sinking off the east coast. A new enemy mine was causing the trouble. Admiral Pound brought him the grave news at Chartwell that Saturday: six ships had sunk in the Thames. Winston hurried back for a special Sunday Cabinet "blaspheming against the Germans," but relishing every moment. "He enjoys this sort of life," wrote the operations officer. "Extraordinary man."

Fortune played into his hands. By Wednesday a naval officer had salvaged one of the new mines at low tide near Shoeburyness; the First Lord hauled the lieutenant-commander, J.G.D. Ouvrey, before eighty admiralty officials on Thursday night to relate the weapon's secrets.

"You have dissected this monster," Mr Churchill summarized his narrative, "divided it into pieces and now you can examine it at leisure!"

The mine's detonator was magnetic — the mine would be triggered by the magnetic shadow of any ship passing within range.[14]

The episode had tangential consequences. The German use of this indiscriminate weapon would justify employing the equally illegal fluvial mines against Rhine shipping. The Cabinet authorized him to proceed.[15] By Thursday Major Millis Jefferis had already demonstrated a five-pound prototype to him; two weeks later they were tested in the Thames. Of course the whole operation (now code-named Royal Marine) would first need France's sanction, and *there* would be the rub; meanwhile Churchill directed that the test report be kept in an "O" box — O for offensive — and ordered several thousand manufactured.

* * *

During the winter Winston Churchill's predatory gaze fell upon Norway, that luckless, lustrous land of trolls and sleepy inlets. Norway was a neutral in this war. But Churchill knew that Hitler's blast furnaces were deriving most of their iron ore from Swedish mines at Gällivare; that during the cold months Sweden's own ore port of Lulea was icebound; and that the ore was then freighted by train to Narvik, in the far north of Norway, and by ship down Norwegian coastal waters to Germany.

In October, Churchill proposed that Britain stop this traffic.

It was a correct strategic decision; it should have been possible to effect it almost immediately. But in the six months that followed the British high command was beset by doubt and dither — between Mr Churchill, the Cabinet, and the French general staff who had begun nourishing strategic ambitions of their own including an invasion of Russia from north and south (Scandinavia and Syria) and the total destruction of Hitler's Soviet ally.

As it will be a tangled story, a broad review will not be out of place. Churchill's strateic objective never varied: to choke off Hitler's ore supplies, either en route, or at source. His first plan (Wilfred) was to mine the Norwegian waters and force the ore ships into the open sea where the gentlemen of the Navy could deal with them; shortly, he favoured a bolder plan to capture Narvik; as the weeks passed, and with them the colder weather that kept Lulea closed, he developed an even more hazardous plan — to advance from Narvik into Sweden and seize the orefield itself. Out of all plans there thus evolved by March 1940 a plan to turn Norway and Sweden into a major theatre of operations against Hitler.

All these plans were unfortunately quite illegal. They would involve British troops invading neutral waters and even going ashore with or without permission; neutral citizens who got in the way would be killed. As will be seen, this aspect disturbed many of Churchill's staff ("I thought we were fighting for Law & Order!" wrote Captain Edwards) and ways were sought around their objections.

Mr Churchill offered various solutions. His own minor violation, Wilfred, might goad Hitler into committing a major infraction, such as invading southern Norway; this in turn would justify Britain executing her own large plans. After Russia attacked Finland on the last day of November, Churchill suggested an expedition to help the Finns; first, of course, Finland must appeal for aid; but Helsinki dithered, and by mid March the appeal had still not formally come.

Churchill's private remarks show that he was interested in Finland *only* as a pretext for getting troops into Norway and Sweden. When Lord Cork, still planning Catherine, suggested on December 5 that the Soviet aggression might be the last chance to mobilize anti-Bolshevik forces of the world, Churchill was horrified. "I still hope," he replied, "war with Russia may be avoided and it is my policy to try to avoid it."

CHURCHILL DECIDED TO sound Roozevelt before initiating Wilfred. To stimulate interest in the war he had sent over to the White House a colourful account of the loss of *Royal Oak*: "We must not let the liaison lapse," he explained to Admiral Pound.[16]

He winked at Washington outrageously and often. "The great English-speaking Republic across the Atlantic Ocean," he postulated in his November broadcast, "makes no secret of its sympathies or of its self-questionings, and translates these sentiments into actions of a character which anyone may judge for himself." Whether blind ardour or wishful thinking, it remained unreciprocated. He even offered Roosevelt the secrets of Asdic in return for the Norden stablized bombsight; the president refused to be drawn.

Churchill knew that Ambassador Kennedy was planning to spend Christmas at Palm Beach reading detective stories and relaxing, and on November 28, the eve of Kennedy's departure, he invited him around, hopefully offered him a whisky-and-soda — the ambassador was teetotal and declined — then disclosed his secret plan to mine Norwegian waters. How, he asked, would the president react? Adopting the conspiratorial tone that he felt was appropriate in dealings with the First Lord, Kennedy told him he would certainly ask the president: if Roosevelt disapproved, he would cable, "Eunice had better not go to the party;" presidential approval would be signified by the message, "My wife cannot express an opinion."[17]

Kennedy left the next day; from Lisbon the *Manhattan* would take him to New York. Before boarding her he pleaded with the State Department to announce that even if this vessel mysteriously blew up in mid Atlantic with an American ambassador on board Washington would not consider it a cause for war.

"I thought," wrote Kennedy in his scurrilous unpublished memoirs, "that would give me some protection against Churchill's placing a bomb on the ship."[18]

* * *

Callous of Britain's larger agony in the fight against Adolf Hitler, the Zionists had begun a private war against her over the White Paper on Palestine. But they had made no headway against War Office and Colonial Office hostility to their scheme for a Jewish army; by November 1939 forty-three members of the Hagana were awaiting trial for illegal possession of arms, a serious offense in Palestine.

Ben-Gurion visited the colonial secretary on the fifteenth and warned of bloodshed; in vain. Frustrated by Churchill's passive attitude, Weizmann tackled their mutual friend Brendan Bracken. "Winston," apologized Bracken, "is terribly worn and is not sleeping." In fact he wondered whether Churchill could hold out much longer.

In mid December, Weizmann wrote to Churchill urging that he arm the Jews and oppose the White Paper. The First Lord invited him round briefly at seven p.m. on the seventeenth and expressed his usual optimism about the war.

"We have them beat," he told the Zionist leader.

Weizmann was more interested in Palestine. "You stood at the cradle of this enterprise," he reminded his friend. "I hope you will see it through."

Churchill asked what he meant by that.

"After the war," was the reply, "the Zionists would wish to have a state of some three or four million Jews in Palestine."

"Yes," said Churchill mechanically, "I quite agree with that."[19]

Weizmann was leaving for New York — Bracken had arranged the passage. He took careful note of those words; and over the weeks that followed Churchill and Bracken kept him informed of the Zionist Office's continuing struggle against Lord Halifax and Malcolm Macdonald — using a code designed to foil British Postal Censorship.

* * *

The *Manhattan* arrived intact in New York, and Kennedy visited the president on December 8.

While Roosevelt sat up in bed and poured out a coffee from a Thermos, the ambassador tackled him about the irksome secret correspondence with the First Lord. Roosevelt's explanation showed little esteem for Churchill. "I have always disliked him," he drawled, "since the time I went to England in 1918. He acted like a stinker at a dinner I attended, lauding it all over us. I am giving him attention now because there is strong possibility that he will become the prime minister and I want to get my hand in now."

We cannot divine his motives for now encouraging Winston's Norwegian adventure. When Kennedy traced out on Roosevelt's bedroom highboy the shipping lanes that the British planned to mine, the president nodded assent. Kennedy sent off the pre-arranged message: "My wife cannot express an opinion."[20] Churchill in turn notified the Cabinet — Roosevelt's secret response had, he claimed, been "more favourable" than he had hoped.[21]

He even suggested an operation much wider in scope: suppose the "trend of events" forced Norway and Sweden into war with Russia — "We would then be able to gain a foothold in Scandinavia with the object of helping them, but without having to go to the extent of ourselves declaring war on Russia." Then Britain could seize the Norwegian ports of Narvik and Bergen. By the sixteenth he had put finishing touches to his plan. Throttling Hitler's iron ore supplies, this suggested, was one way of "preventing the vast slaughters which will attend the grapple of the main armies."[22]

ONE INCIDENT BRIGHTENED Churchill's war that December. A British naval force hunted down and damaged the enemy raider *Graf Spee* which had sunk many ships in the South Atlantic. Unable to effect repairs at Montevideo where Uruguayan officials had been bribed — perhaps on Churchill's instructions — to deny her a long enough stay, her captain took the pocket battleship out to sea, scuttled her and shot himself upon her bridge.

One night during this battle admiralty staff saw Churchill clad in a strange night garment appear in their operations centre, itching to transmit instructions to Commodore Harwood in the South Atlantic; Admiral Pound convinced him that Bobby Harwood probably knew best. In later weeks, the Director of Naval Intelligence later wrote, Churchill resorted to many a subterfuge to get his way: "Not the least tantalizing procedure was his trick of drafting telegrams as if they originated in the Admiralty." The D.N.I. was astonished that Pound allowed it, and attributed it to his failing powers of resistance.[23]

While Churchill broadcast a few days later a homily on the freedom of the seas, his warships continued entering the new 300-mile war-free zone of South America to seize or sink ships trading with Germany. To his dismay even Roosevelt's administration joined in the chorus of neutral protests. On Christmas Eve he apologized in a message to the president and reassured him that he had now given instructions "only to arrest or fire upon [enemy ships] out of sight of United States shore." The *Graf Spee* battle had been well within the 300-mile zone, of course, but the First Lord was unrepentant and dismissed the neutral clamour. "Much of world duty is being thrown on Admiralty," he chided Roosevelt. "Hope burden will not be made too heavy for us to bear."

He was human enough to understand what underlay American official aloofness — the coming presidential election. "Roosevelt is our best friend," he explained to Chamberlain, "but I expect he wants to be re-elected and I fear that isolationism is the winning ticket."[24]

Not until February 1940 did F.D.R. even acknowledge Churchill's narrative on the *Graf Spee*, and when he did write it was to carp at British warships searching American merchant vessels: "There has been much public criticism here."

ON DECEMBER 20 Churchill dined Admiral Darlan at Admiralty House. A proud and honourable sailor, the Frenchman remembered that in this same dining room a British officer had once told him that no Briton could sleep easily so long as there was one French submarine in the Channel. Two years later he would be liquidated with a pistol provided by the S.O.E., one of Mr Churchill's secret agencies.

The French were independently warming towards a Norwegian operation. At the Supreme War Council meeting in Paris on the nineteenth Edouard Daladier announced that Hitler's exiled steel magnate Fritz Thyssen had recommended disrupting the iron ore supplies.[25]

The French also wanted to speed aid to Finland — though for her own sake and not, as Mr Churchill preferred, merely as a pretext to land troops in Scandinavia. General Ironside even talked of sending 4,000 ski troops to seize Gällivare, reassuring the Cabinet's military co-ordination committee on the twentieth that the ore fields were too remote for any accidental entanglement with Russia.[26] When Churchill again talked of his original uncomplicated plan to mine Norwegian waters, Lord Halifax objected that this might endanger the "larger plan" for seizing Gällivare.[27]

Probably it was here that Winston made his mistake. Instead of insisting that they keep their eye on the ball — stopping the ore traffic — he too now became enthusiastic about larger operations.

HIS INTERMEDIATE AMBITION was to become Minister of Defence.

Uprooting the obstacles in his path, he engineered the dismissal of Hore-Belisha from the War Office — whom only a few months earlier he had praised for forcing through conscription. The minister, a Jew, detected Churchill's hand in it, and that of "Tiny" Ironside who often dined with him; he suspected Ironside of scheming to become military dictator. He had certainly become acutely unpopular with the generals at B.E.F. headquarters. "A fine day's work for the army," General Pownall called the dismissal in his diary: Fleet-street was in uproar, but Gort's chief of staff put this down to the alarm of "the Jew-controlled press" like the *Daily Mail* at seeing "one of their champions and nominees" removed.

Offered the Board of Trade, Hore-Belisha refused it, assuring friends that he would make a come-back as prime minister. *Daily Mirror* editor Hugh Cudlipp had to advise him that the increasing antisemitism generated by the war would rule out his chances. So, emulating Churchill, he began to write for the salacious *News of the World*, evoking from another editor the chuckling comment that without Winston's strength he would be unable to serve as "a cloak for dirty stories" and get away with it.[28]

His successor was a pleasingly complaisant man, Oliver Stanley, a personal friend of Mr Churchill. The latter now reverted to the Norway problem. "If they [the Germans] did invade Norway, I would be glad," Churchill told his Cabinet colleagues. "They would become involved in a serious commitment." But still no decisions were taken. On the twelfth he exclaimed that the debate had now dragged on for six weeks — he had heard every argument in favour of doing nothing; they were letting the initiative rest with Germany. But the old fears remained, that Wilfred might prejudice the "larger plan" to seize Gällivare. Meanwhile although Winston had privately secured Roosevelt's endorsement of Wilfred, nobody had bothered to consult the Dominions.[29]

That day Spears brought their old friend Admiral Sir Roger Keyes to lunch at the Admiralty. "When things seem to be going smoothly," Winston philosophized, "you may be perfectly certain Fate is preparing some particularly unpleasant trick for you."

What form would it take? Perhaps the knockout blow against London? He speculated there would be violent action soon, probably the invasion of Holland which would bring the German bombers within range (Lindemann had now explained to him that they could not reach London without overflying the Low Countries.) A German courier aircraft had crash-landed two days earlier in Belgium carrying (genuine) staff plans for an invasion of the Low Countries. Churchill clearly thought them genuine, but the B.E.F. commander dismissed them as obvious fakes in the best Hollywood traditions — "reminiscent," he scoffed, "of the famous railway train plan of the days before the last war."[30]

Still struggling against the Soviet invaders, on January 20 Finland appealed for immediate British help — for about ten Hurricane fighter planes, with British volunteer pilots and ground crews. Whitehall still prevaricated. Churchill supported the idea and Finland's fight attracted broad space in his broadcast that night. "Only Finland — superb, nay sublime — in the jaws of peril — Finland shows what free men can do."

> Let the great cities of Warsaw, of Prague, of Vienna banish despair even in the midst of their agony. Their liberation is sure. The day will come when the joybells will ring again throughout Europe, and when victorious nations, masters not only of their foes but of themselves, will plan and build in justice, in tradition and in freedom a house of many mansions, where there will be room for all.

HOW EPHEMERAL ARE the finest dreams of man! Many a citizen of Central Europe, entering the Russian army's unremitting thrall five years later, might well have pondered on these words in Winston's peroration. But even in January 1940 no neutral was deceived by his hollow verbal architecture, however grandiose and filigree. Oslo and Stockholm huffed at his insinuation that they "yielded humbly" to German threats; Geneva and The Hague suspected that Britain's turbulent First Lord coveted their countries for battlefields.

The Foreign Office saw his broadcast as a setback to every effort to win neutral sympathy. "Would you think it unreasonable of me," Lord Halifax pleaded on January 26 in that over-courteous tone he used to express extreme annoyance, "to ask that in future, if you are going to speak with particular reference to Foreign Policy, you might let me see in advance what you had it in mind to say?"

Besides the clattering events of war, Churchill's January appointment card had been dotted with publishers, ghost writers and literary agents. Once he nipped over to France with Randolph and Spears for another reassuring look at the Maginot line and a talk with General Georges about operation Royal Marine. Towards the end of January the Cabinet sent over General Ironside for staff talks with the French. "As Daladier says," the C.I.G.S. wrote in his diary, "time is slipping on and we are doing nothing but talk."

"Winston," he added, "is mad to start something. . ."

CHAPTER 19

Nobody Questions The Victor

A SAVAGE WINTER locked all Europe in an unwanted embrace. The Rhine traffic was paralyzed in its glacial grip, the lakes and canals congealed, the railroads were halted.

A similar paralysis gripped Allied planning as the British and French argued out their own strategic beliefs — whether to mine the Rhine, invade Narvik, seize other Norwegian ports, or intervene in Finland's far north at Petsamo. At staff talks held at the end of January 1940 the French high command showed that they believed they had time: that Finland would not collapse under Soviet attack, and that Hitler would not attack on the west for many months — perhaps even until 1941.[1]

On February 2 the British Cabinet agreed to ask the French to abandon their Petsamo plan. That day Churchill invited Scandinavian journalists to lunch; Ribbentrop would later claim that he blurted out a number of "incautious remarks" about Norway, and that these shortly reached Berlin.[2]

A Supreme War Council was convened in Paris to resolve the strategic controversy and Chamberlain invited Churchill to join them. Wearing what one notable described as "a strange, spurious naval costume" and clasping a red Lord High Admiral's flag Churchill took the Cabinet party by special train to a destroyer at Dover. Lord Halifax eyed Winston's nautical garb with amusement: "He was in grand form," he dictated later, "and I have never seen anyone so pleased at being in a party." On the train down, Chamberlain showed him telegrams concerning a peace mission being undertaken by the American under-secretary of state Sumner Welles in European capitals; in his telegram of reply Chamberlain had urged caution upon Washington lest Welles be exploited by Nazi propaganda.

> Winston [noted one diarist] after a second sherry, read them through and, with tears in his eyes, said "I'm *proud* to follow you!"

"So *that* was alright," concluded the diarist, Sir Alec Cadogan;

Churchill had evidently chosen the flattery with care, because he referred to the very words ten years later when writing his memoirs, and Lord Halifax also quoted this, "Winston's immediate comment," in his diary, adding, "An interesting specimen of his quick generosity."

They stayed at the British embassy in the Rue Saint-Honoré. The French Cabinet came to dinner, "less [General Maurice] Gamelin," as Halifax remarked, "who has [taken] a vow not to dine anywhere in war." The next morning Churchill woke early, breezed into Halifax's room at 7:30 a.m. in a dressing-gown and staggered the sleepy foreign secretary with a two hour harangue about the war in general. The speech seems to have exhausted him, and neither the British nor the French text shows Winston uttering a word during the ninety minutes Supreme War Council at the war ministry. "I have just seen a miracle," gasped Admiral Sir Dudley Pound, the First Sea Lord, to Oliver Stanley: "I have just attended a meeting for three hours without Winston making a speech."

This silence was not only unChurchillian but regrettable: had he insisted on going straight for Narvik and Gällivare much evil might have been averted. But a determined Soviet offensive had now begun in Finland, and there were fears of an early collapse. Daladier approved all of Chamberlain's proposals except for the total abandonment of the Petsamo plan, which was now to be exploited if Norway and Sweden refused to co-operate with the large plan aimed at seizing Gällivare. Daladier and Chamberlain agreed that a total of three or four divisions should be sent across Norway and Sweden to Finland by mid April, which seems further proof that no German offensive was expected that spring.[3]

There were obvious snags: Lord Gort's expeditionary force had taken a month to move the few miles to France; this new army would have to cover a far greater distance before the Finns collapsed. But the party that trooped back aboard Winston's destroyer behind their prime minister — Halifax, Oliver Stanley, and Kingsley Wood — were satisfied. They looked to one observer like happy-go-lucky schoolchildren following a popular master on a Sunday outing; the First Lord, he noticed, trudged up the gangplank by himself; while General Ironside was clutching a kilogram of French butter. Halifax had slept badly, disturbed by "Winston's snores [from] next door" aboard the train to Boulogne; he went below. A hot soup was carried up to Chamberlain on the bridge.

The First Lord had his unusual red flag run up the halyards, lit a cigar and descended to the wardroom; here he warmed body and soul with a decanter of port and pages of scantily clad ladies in *Blighty* respectively.[4] As their destroyer ran into Dover, his flag attracted a signal from an ignorant — nay, foolhardy — destroyer captain: "Why the Red Ensign?"

THE CROSSING HAD not been without hazard.

When *Sunday Pictorial* editor Cecil King came to lunch on the following day with the Churchills at Admiralty House, Winston told him that they had encountered several mines and had hit one with a shell; instead of exploding, the top flipped into the air and came hurtling down towards them. "Ch[urchill] said it was rather frightening, as it weighed fully fifty pounds and they couldn't tell quite where it would fall."[5]

The newspaperman found Clementine good looking but dry and nervy. Winston himself had come in wearing zip-sided black boots but looking puffy and old. A rather loud American lady who had joined them handed him a bottle of brandy, but he set it aside: "I'm giving it up for a while," he said, and drank port and beer alternately during the meal.

They talked of Hore-Belisha. Recently, Churchill had told this journalist that the man was one of Chamberlain's best ministers. Now he disparaged the ex-minister ruthlessly: the editor correctly divined that the new war minister, Stanley, was a social friend of the Churchills; he suspected that Winston had dislodged Hore-Belisha to make place for him. As for the PM, Churchill went out of his way to praise him — he was tough and belligerent.

King replied that Chamberlain was old and dreary; the country regarded Churchill as their leader, he said.

Churchill refused to be drawn.

No.10, he observed modestly, was not much of a prize these days anyway. "I would take it only if offered by common consent." He was amused to hear that the public opinion polls showed that a clear majority wanted him to succeed Chamberlain, followed by Eden.

When the talk turned to the shipping war King was sceptical: Winston's complacent figure of 140,000-tons sunk ignored neutral shipping completely. "The story Ch[urchill] seemed to believe," the editor wrote in his diary, "is the one he puts over in his radio speeches."

> The only thing he said he was afraid of was the effect of unrestrained aeroplane warfare on our highly complex industrial organisation.
> I said I thought Hitler had done more harm to us by *not* bombing than he could have done by bombing.

Without air raids, Cecil King pointed out, the peace movement would thrive. Churchill feigned ignorance of this movement, but the editor warned that it embraced a third of the Labour party. Churchill replied that when organized labour realized they were earning more than in peacetime it would stabilize public opinion in favour of war. The editor bridled at this "harping on money" but confined his distaste to his diary.

> Ch[urchill] took a poor view of the Labour leaders and said they wanted to win the war and then give away our colonies.

Before the ladies withdrew, the newspaperman suggested bringing the battlescarred cruiser *Exeter* — coming home for repairs after the *Graf Spee* battle — up the Thames into the very heart of London.

"What's the good of that?" asked Churchill dismissively, "it could only come up to the Pool. People couldn't go on board."

King replied that the Pool was the centre of London ("though not," he reflected, contemplating the well-lunched Mr Churchill, "of *his* London"). People could go up one gangway, along the deck and down another. Churchill's youngest daughter Mary, a "real winner" with generous eyes and mouth, excitedly suggested a City dinner for the sailors; Clementine chimed in, "—in the Guildhall!" If *Exeter*'s sailors paraded to the Guildhall, said King, all London would pour into the streets.

Churchill betrayed not a flicker of acceptance. Perhaps he was remote from public feeling; perhaps he disliked the lower deck; perhaps his mind was elsewhere — on the political struggle for absolute power. It was three-fifteen and time for his siesta.

HE WAS CERTAINLY up to something, probably in cahoots with the French field commander General Georges, and probably to the discomfiture of Edouard Daladier. He had loathed Daladier since Munich; nor had the French prime minister cut an impressive figure at the recent War Council — his game leg in plaster, his face blotched with alcohol. Now, on February 10, Winston flew his friend Spears over to Paris on an extended hole-and-corner mission that might last as long as a month. The general wrote secretively in his diary:

> I had a special and very confidential mission given me by Winston which I was able to carry out satisfactorily though it was quite on the tapis that I might have had to go back to London, in which case he offered me a plane or a destroyer as the case might be; this turned out not to be necessary.

Although the entry continues, "I sent him a report which he told me on my return was quite perfect and he so informed the PM and Halifax," this may well have been a smokescreen; why else should he have noted next to this passage, when he marked the diary up years later for publication, "*Not in*"?[6]

* * *

One of those Events for which Churchill was always waiting now occurred. The 15,000-ton supply ship *Altmark*, which had ministered to the late *Graf Spee*, had nearly completed her long trek home from the South Atlantic. Below decks he knew she was carrying three hundred sorrowing prisoners, the seamen taken from victims of the pocket battleship.

After weeks of radio silence on February 14 she signalled (in a cipher which the British could not yet read) that she was about to enter the Leads, the rocky Norwegian coastal waters. She was entitled to use this channel, being an unarmed merchant vessel.[7]

Churchill followed the ship's progress closely. Meanwhile he took the night train to Plymouth for the homecoming of *Exeter* — "A most moving and impressive sight," the Chancellor, Sir John Simon, recorded in his notes. "The Captain conducted us over her and traced the course of various enemy shells. . . One eleven-inch shell landed between the two forward turrets and ricochetted above the bridge where the Captain was standing. . . Everyone there, twelve or fourteen in all, were instantly killed or wounded except the Captain himself."

On the fifteenth the admiralty heard rumours that *Altmark* was off the Norwegian coast. The Germans shortly deciphered a British admiralty signal notifying the cruiser *Glasgow* and three submarines that Tromsö had sighted a German tanker. Since *Altmark* was now in neutral waters the Germans were not as yet unduly perturbed.[8] Later that day a British reconnaissance plane sighted the ship. On the sixteenth Churchill recommended Admiral Pound to send warships to "sweep northwards" up the coast "not hesitating to arrest *Altmark* in territorial waters should she be found."

At 4:30 p.m. the destroyer *Cossack* (Captain Philip Vian) found her. The German ship had fled into the ice-packed Jössing Fiord. There was one nasty complication — two Norwegian torpedo boats were holding off the British destroyers, claiming to have searched the German and seen no prisoners.

"Can we sink 'em if they interfere?" pondered Captain Ralph Edwards, Churchill's Deputy Director of Operations, in his diary.

Churchill himself provided the answer. He tramped down to the War Room — a dingy hole in the old Admiralty Building's basement — accompanied by his secretary and the Vice Chief of Naval Staff, Tom Phillips. At 5:25 p.m. he dictated a signal to Captain Vian: *Cossack* was to board the *Altmark*, which had now run aground, and liberate the prisoners, opening fire if necessary on the Norwegians.

"Get that cyphered up," he barked to the Duty Signal Officer, "and be quick about it. I've told the Secretary of State that those orders are going at a quarter to six unless we hear to the contrary."

For a few minutes he walked up and down, flapping his coat tails and chewing his cigar. Then he turned to the Duty Captain: "I can't wait," he said, "Get me Lord Halifax."

He sat in the green armchair next to the desk and took the telephone.

Halifax suggested adding a sentence to the effect that Vian should notify the Norwegian officers that to submit to force majeure was no derogation of their sovereignty (wording of which, perhaps, Hitler himself would have approved).

"Now get that off at once," Churchill told his staff, and lounged off towards the stairs.

At the door he turned and remarked to the assembled officers, "That was *big* of Halifax."

For the rest of that night, there was silence. *Cossack* did not bother to report. Later, Admiral Pound would invite Captain Vian to picture the scene—"the First Lord and myself sitting in the Upper War Room at three o'clock in the morning, wondering what was happening."

Adrenalin pumping, Winston's imagination ran riot. Had anything gone wrong? Was Vian trying to refloat the *Altmark*? It was an anxious night before the admiralty received Vian's "very full" report.[9]

He had executed the boarding with great dash. What Mr Churchill would term a "hand-to-hand fight" had followed. According to the German captain's Report of Proceedings, the boarding party fired blindly on his unarmed crew and machine-gunned the seamen fleeing across the ice (a point that upset Norwegian opinion.) Six were killed: the survivors looted at gunpoint: the captives—303 all told—liberated. "Winston rang me up at seven o'clock in the morning," dictated Lord Halifax, "to tell me that they had got the *Altmark* prisoners and from his point of view all was well; my fun would, no doubt, begin. . . I have no doubt at all," reflected Halifax, "that the general public will be delighted and won't trouble too much about the niceties of international law."

In fact the *Altmark* incident was such a flagrant violation of international law that it attracted grudging admiration from Herr Hitler, no dullard in this respect. "History," he pointed out at a ceremonial luncheon for new corps commanders the next day, "judges by success or failure, that alone. Nobody questions the victor if he was in the right or wrong."[10]

Churchill's in-laws echoed this attitude. "It's comforting to know we can be ferocious," wrote Pamela after watching *Cossack* disembark the rescued prisoners at Leith in Scotland.

Mr Churchill would write that both this and the *Graf Spee* episode strengthened his hand as well as the prestige of the admiralty. He ordered maximum publicity for the arrival of the rescued seamen, and ordered newspaper photographers up to Scotland to obtain pictures of starving, emaciated seamen; however they had all been well cared for aboard the supply ship and he imposed censorship on the resulting photographs instead.

In little things, it might be added, his honesty was absolute. Learning later of the looting, he rebuked his admirals: "Anything of this kind must be stopped." To which he added his own idiosyncratic interpretation of the Hague Rules for Warfare: "Personal property of enemies may be confiscated by the State" — it can't — "But never by individuals."[11]

Hitler drew far-reaching conclusions from the episode. Evidently the British were equally disposed to thumb their nose at neutrality: but a Norway in Allied hands would be a disaster for Germany. He called one of his most capable generals, Nikolaus von Falkenhorst, to the Reich Chancery and ordered him to draw up a plan of attack.[12] Mr Churchill's spectacular coup would shortly lead to the whole of Norway falling under the Nazi yoke, at a tragic cost in Allied lives.

* * *

As he entered his heavy black limousine to drive to the City — he had put to his staff the bright idea of inviting HMS *Exeter* right up the Thames to the Pool; her sailors would parade through cheering crowds held back by bobbies, and be entertained at the Guildhall — two other problems were on his mind. These shall illustrate the extraneous stresses to which this remarkable First Lord was often subjected during months in which the navy was the only force seriously engaging the enemy.

The first plague upon him was inflicted by those merchants of joy, the legal profession. No stranger to the libel courts himself, he found himself being sued for libel in New York. The anti-British publisher of the Sunday *Enquirer*, one Griffin, was claiming that Churchill had once told him that if America had not made the "horrible mistake" of joining in the world war Britain could have made peace in 1917, saving a million lives: that Winston, then a hard-up writer, had used these words in August 1936 when trying to peddle ten articles for $5,000: and that, when questioned on the eve of Hitler's war by a Philadelphia *Evening Bulletin* reporter, Winston had called Griffin a liar and denied having heard of him: wherein lay the libel. Griffin was claiming £200,000 damages.

Since the courts had allowed Griffin to attach all Winston's earnings from New York publishers he could not let it go by default.[13] He instructed his New York lawyer J. Arthur Leve, whom it will be recalled he had hired to discredit Vic Oliver in 1936; that legal gentleman's advice boiled down to getting the F.B.I. to hound the plaintiff. Winston received it on the eve of the *Altmark* crisis, and asked the F.O. to act accordingly through the State department. "There is no doubt in my mind," he minuted, "that this man Griffin is set on by German agents, which would fully explain his malignity against this country."

The British ambassador in Washington disabused him of this notion; there was no foreign money behind Griffin. But Lord Lothian also warned that Leve had an unsavory reputation as the law partner of one Louis Levy, an attorney disbarred from Federal courts in connection with the bribing of a New York judge. "I am advised," he added further-more, "that Leve is not a very sound lawyer and would be likely to overcharge."[14]

Like all litigation, the case lasted a long time; in justice, let us see it rapidly to its conclusion. The British embassy instructed new lawyers; in September 1940, as aircraft whirled across the skies of England, Leve submitted his account to Mr Churchill (whose new lawyers deemed it indeed "excessive") Two years later, when towns as yet unheard of filled the headlines, like Stalingrad and Alamein, the New York courts awarded him judgment with $20 against Griffin. By that time America would again be in a world war and the *Enquirer* under indictment for lowering the morale of U.S. armed forces.[15]

The second plague upon him was Palestine. The Zionists had used the interval since May 1939 to buy up land to pre-empt the White Paper's provisions while their political agents in London fought a delaying action against it. On February 13, 1940 — the day he received Leve's advice to use the F.B.I. — Winston was defeated in Cabinet by MacDonald over the White Paper.[16] On the day of the *Exeter* parade he received from New York a distressed telegram from Chaim Weizmann bristling with threats about rousing American opinion. "Am informed introduction [of White Paper] land measures likely almost immediately," cabled Weizmann. "Sentiment here in general friendly to Allies, but highly sensitive. Am deeply convinced this measure would have most deplorable reactions not alone in Jewish circles." He hoped "most earnestly" that Winston could persuade the prime minister to delay the Palestine land measures until Weizmann saw him in person.[17]

* * *

The various plans to intervene in Scandinavia were mired in difficulties. Under German pressure Stockholm was now refusing to hear of Allied troops crossing to Finland. The Finns themselves had begun secret armistice talks in Moscow. Both Paris and London urged them to fight on, and Daladier offered 50,000 troops by the end of March, perhaps realizing that the pledge would never have to be honoured.[18] Helsinki stalled for time in Moscow, while asking Chamberlain and Daladier to rush aircraft and troops to Finland immediately.

Churchill was inclined to write off Finland. He voiced relief, telling his colleagues that it would have been an unprofitable diversion. The enemy was Germany, and Britain should not send aircraft or troops to a theatre where Germans could not be engaged.

The direct assault on Narvik however remained his obsession. He told Admiral Pound on March 6 that Britain should not be deflected from that purpose just because Sweden had got cold feet. Once in Narvik, he reminded the First Sea Lord, "we have got our foot in the door."[19]

The Finnish tragedy drew to its close amidst haggling over legal technicalities that seem quite incomprehensible now. London and Paris begged Helsinki to make a formal appeal for aid, since under League of Nations rules they could then apply pressure on Sweden and Norway to allow transit. The Finns played for time.[20] Under the circumstances, Chamberlain delayed sending off the fifty precious Blenheim bombers he had earmarked for Finland until the appeal actually arrived.

Window-dressing now, aware that his own political position was become shaky, Daladier dictated a long telegram on March 9 to the Finnish government: this voiced puzzlement that the appeal was still not forthcoming. "We are ready to come to your assistance immediately. The aeroplanes are ready, the expeditionary force is ready to start." The sting of Daladier's message was in the next sentence, "If Finland will not now make an appeal to the Western powers, it is evident that these cannot take any responsibility at the end of the war for the final arrangement of Finnish territory."[21]

PEACE INITIATIVES HAD borne down on London from several directions. One came through the pacifist Lord Tavistock, who had ascertained Hitler's peace proposals through the German legation in Dublin on January 18; Lord Halifax ridiculed them after they were leaked in the press.[22]

Ambassador Joseph Kennedy loathed the European war and lingered in the United States until the eve of the Sumner Welles mission to London. He searched for ways of ending the madness. In February the British authorities intercepted a telegram from him to Grosvenor-square asking urgently for samples of "pacifist literature."[23] Arriving at London's airport, Kennedy emphasized to waiting reporters that isolationist feeling was growing in America.

Sumner Welles arrived at the same airport on March 10. The second ranking official in the State department, he was touring European capitals in a search for peace. Kennedy briefed him on the attitude of Chamberlain and Halifax to peace, but Welles knew where the obstacle would lie. "What about Churchill," he asked. "When's he going to supplant Chamberlain?"

"Chamberlain," replied the ambassador, "is convinced that he can handle him."

He doesn't think Churchill is conspiring against him. Of course, Churchill is always bringing in a lot of plans that Chamberlain has got to turn down, but Chamberlain thinks he takes all that in good grace. In fact, Chamberlain told me he thinks Churchill feels free to advocate some pretty wild ones because of the certainty that they *will* be turned down.[24]

Invited to tea at Buckingham Palace on Monday the eleventh, Welles mentioned Ivan Maisky. The King misheard the name as Mosley: wrongly assuming that Kennedy was privy to certain transatlantic arrangements he reminded him of "our agreement that the United States could do something — if the Mosleys don't take over."[25] (Sir Oswald Mosley was leader of Britain's Italian-financed fascist party.) Sumner Welles cocked a quizzical eye at Kennedy; the ambassador was as baffled as he was, and never cleared up the mystery.

IN LONDON THE chiefs of staff decided on that Monday March 11 to go ahead with Plan R3, the expedition to seize Stavanger, Bergen and Trondheim, as well as Narvik.[26] "A bit late I'm afraid," Captain Edwards regretted in his diary, "though we are only just ready."

Simultaneously the first awful rumours arrived that Finland was about to stop fighting. This would remove the pretext for Allied intervention altogether. On the request of the Finnish legation Chamberlain announced, in reply to a planted question by Attlee, that the British government was prepared "in response to an appeal" to help Finland "using all available resources."

Winston meanwhile hurried over to Paris. He had originally intended to fly over about another matter; London had now authorized his Rhine mining operation (Royal Marine), but Paris was now unexpectedly withholding approval — General Gamelin was said to be expressing concern about possible enemy reprisals. In Paris he tackled Gamelin in person, but the general would not go beyond agreeing in principle. Over dinner with Daladier and Léger he met the same response. They blamed their air minister Guy la Chambre; he was asking, they said, for three weeks to move the three hundred aircraft assembled on Villacoublay airfield to safety from any reprisals.

While in Paris, scene of many of his old intrigues, Churchill evidently had a rendezvous with his old conspirator Paul Reynaud, Daladier's rival and minister of finances. "I share, as you know," he would write to Reynaud ten days later, "all the anxieties you expressed to me the other night about the general course of the war, and the need for strenuous and drastic measures."[27]

Churchill persuaded Reynaud to turn the screw on Finland. She must not sign any armistice — not just yet. On Tuesday morning after seeing Winston the Frenchman spoke with the Finnish envoy, Harri Holma. Holma telegraphed to Helsinki at three-thirty p.m. that Mr Churchill had assured Reynaud that an Allied expeditionary corps was about to sail for Norway — in fact it would sail, he said, on March the fifteenth — provided that Finland sent an immediate appeal for aid. Britain and France would then "notify" Oslo and break off diplomatic relations with the Soviet Union.[28]

It was a fatal indiscretion. Either Holma's cipher telegram to Helsinki or his confirmatory telephone call at four p.m. to his foreign minister Väinö Tanner in Helsinki was intercepted by Hitler's Intelligence service (the landlines crossed German soil.)[29] Acutely concerned, Hitler accelerated his own invasion preparations still further. As he would later say, "If Churchill and Reynaud had kept a still tongue in their heads, I might well not have tackled Norway."[30]

CONVOYS OF WAR material were now bound for Scapa Flow en route for Norway; warships were about to embark the British invasion troops. But would the Finns collapse first? Uncertainty led to hesitation in London. Upon his return to the admiralty that Tuesday, March 12, Mr Churchill found that the War Cabinet had wavered once again, deciding now to go for Narvik first, to be followed only if successful by a second landing at Trondheim.

Small wonder that Sumner Welles had told Kennedy on the day before that he was not impressed by the leaders he had so far seen.

Attlee, he said, had lectured him about teaching the Germans that force would not prevail ("You mean," Welles had queried, "German force?" and smiled a cherubic smile.) Sinclair had spoken only platitudes.

All the greater was the curiosity with which Sumner Welles presented himself with Ambassador Kennedy at five p.m. on the twelfth at Churchill's famous office at the admiralty. They found the First Lord sitting in a big chair at an open fireplace reading an evening paper; there was a highball at his elbow, and he was smoking what seemed to Welles like a "twenty-four inch" cigar. "He offered us a drink," recalled Kennedy, "but we declined." In fact, as Welles wrote chattily in his secret report to the president, "It was quite obvious that he had consumed a good many whiskeys before I arrived."[31]*

Winston launched easily into a brilliant cascade of oratory and wit which would have impressed Welles more had he not recently boned up

---

*The author's text is from the original report in Roosevelt's files. A doctored version was published in the offical *Foreign Relations of the United States,* 1940, vol. i, omitting offensive remarks about Churchill.

on the First Lord by reading his volume *Step by Step*; it contained the original version of this familiar address — how he had warned against Germany but nobody had heeded him. He gestured as though speaking to an audience of thousands.

"Russia, to him," observed Welles, "offered no real menace and no real problem." The Nazi government was "a monster born of hatred and of fear." There could be no peace without the total destruction of Germany. "All this will cost us dear," Churchill admitted, "but we will of course win the war and that is the only hope for civilization."

Welles said somberly that when the real fighting started it would bring devastation and ruin for everybody.

"I am not so sure of that," replied Churchill. "The last war did not bring about conditions of that type."

His monologue lasted one hour and fifty minutes — "in the course of which he became quite sober," as Welles observed. Then the First Lord unfurled charts showing Britain's purported shipping losses: "What we have lost on balance," he assured the American, "is not significant." Of a total of eighteen million tons the net loss was about 220,000 tons — that is, sinkings over new construction. The magnetic mine had been defeated; forty-three enemy submarines, he claimed, had been sunk.

Afterwards he led the Americans to the War Room to see the Intelligence maps about convoys and shipping movements. Churchill had made his mark on Welles, who asked the F.O. that he be so informed; Sir Alec Cadogan decided not to do so, taking comfort, as he minuted, from the fact that Mr Churchill would already have that conviction — "so nothing is lost."

BY THE TIME Winston ushered the Americans out into Whitehall — as a special parting gift he had pressed upon the distinguished visitor an autographed copy of *Step by Step* — the BBC correspondent in Helsinki had reported the signing in Moscow of a Soviet-Finnish armistice.

Once again, Winston's Narvik project seemed to have been spiked.

> The Government [Captain Edwards recorded the next day] has decided to mark time with Plan R3. Why they don't cancel [it] now I can't imagine. Convoys ordered to Scapa & ships about to sail or embark troops turned over to their own duties again. Much work. . . Late in the evening Plan R3 was cancelled.

The prime minister invited Sumner Welles to dine with his colleagues at No.10 and seated him next to the First Lord.

The mood was fluid. Some were relieved that Britain had avoided the odium of invading a neutral country and opening fire on the Norwegians (even if "in self defence"); others seethed with angry disappointment.

Kennedy's meagre reservoir of tact was now bone dry: "If you can show me one Englishman that's *tougher* than you are Winston," he crowed at the crestfallen First Lord, "I'll eat my hat."[32]

As the evening proceeded, many inhibitions were dissolved. Sam Hoare paraded his hostility to Churchill openly.* "Of course," he scoffed, jerking a thumb at him, "*he* would be willing to fight for a hundred years." Later, Welles urged Churchill to announce that Britain would in future respect the 300-mile Panama Congress zone. "Don't let Winston do the talking," interrupted Hoare. "America is too *afraid* of him!" Encouraged by the laughter, as the pink of Churchill's complexion deepened, Kennedy revealed how he had warned Cordell Hull not to declare war on Germany if *Manhattan* blew up mysteriously, as he would not put it past Winston to put a bomb aboard.

"Not I," retorted Churchill, adding gravely. "I am certain that the United States will come in later anyway."[34]

Afterwards, Chamberlain took Welles aside, into the room where he kept souvenirs of his famous father. "I hope your mission will make it possible for the president to succeed in his desire to avert this calamity," he said now that they were out of earshot, "and to help the world to save itself."

As they passed through rooms hung with portraits of earlier first ministers the American visitor noticed only one photograph, a signed portrait of Benito Mussolini.

Empire hostility to the war went deeper than he had first expected. Stanley Bruce, the Australian high commissioner in London, assured Sumner Welles that the Dominions had no desire to annihilate Germany.

But few men in Whitehall wanted peace in 1940. "The old men who run the government," Joseph Kennedy pondered, after Sumner Welles had left, "are all so near the grave that they run the war as if there were no generations to follow them." The younger looked upon it as a vocation: they loved it: they would not give it up. "There seems no real fire anywhere, no genius, no sense of the shambles that are to come."[35]

---

*This was mutual. Cecil King had asked Churchill whether he ought not to get out of the admiralty while he still could: any naval disaster of sufficient gravity to dislodge Chamberlain would unhorse him too. Churchill replied that he was no coward like Hoare — who "ran away" from the admiralty because it was politically dangerous, and then while at the Home Office refused to implement air raid precautions because that, too, was dynamite.[33]

CHAPTER 20

Tit For Tat

THERE WAS A side-result of the Sumner Welles meeting with Churchill that did great harm: Welles put it about official Washington that the famous Englishman was an alcoholic. He told Ickes that Churchill was a "drunken bum;"[1] he told Berle he had found the First Lord "quite drunk;"[2] he was explicit about it in his report to Roosevelt.

The latter passed it around North America. He regretted to the visiting prime minister of Canada that Winston "seemed to be drinking too much;" he amplified this a few days later to the remark that "Churchill is tight most of the time." "This is shameful," wrote Prime Minister Mackenzie-King, scandalized, in his diary, "that he should have been in this condition when Sumner Welles went to see him. It is that arrogance and the assumed superiority that some Englishmen have that have made so many nations their enemies today."[3]

By any standards Churchill was not a modest drinker. When he was a young subaltern in the South African War the water was unfit to drink, he would say: "We had to put a bit of whisky in it. By diligent effort I learned to like it."[4] "Alcohol," he would aphorize, "can be your master or your slave. For many long and anxious hours it has sustained me and I have used it for my own purpose."[5] According to Lady Cunard's butler Ronald Perkins, Winston would arrive at dinner parties equipped with his own brandy or Black Label, which his driver would hand over to the butler. Alec Bishop, a clerk at the Cabinet offices, noticed that Churchill was regularly served three or four small whiskies when working each evening.[6]

Such being the ambivalence of the times, both family and public liked him the more for it; drinking has always been projected as a sign of bonhomie and sophistication. "There he goes, off to his bloody brandy — and good luck to him!" was a typical wartime by-stander's remark, quoted by a biographer. His colleagues smiled indulgently. "Some discussion of tea ration," recorded one bemused civil servant after a War Cabinet meeting — adding: "And a discussion of this topic between Winston and A[rthur] Greenwood [an inveterate lush] can be *quite* dispassionate!"[7]

Why did he drink? Probably for the usual reasons — to mask stress or suppress inhibitions; or to feel more capable. But there is a rising price to pay for such blessings. Alcohol also anaesthetizes the brain centres affecting judgment, knowledge, and social controls. In extreme cases it can cause the permanent loss of higher mental functions. Under the stress of war, people were readier than usual to accept this price. Sir Robert Bruce Lockhart later remarked upon how many ministers resorted to alcohol.

Drinking was important to Churchill — one of the classic symptoms of the alcoholic. He camouflaged his craving behind good humour, but it remained a craving all the same. Travelling in Prohibition America in the Twenties he had gone to some lengths to camouflage and conceal the liquor in his luggage; in non-Prohibition England, the balloon of vintage Hine or Remy Martin had become as much part of the Winston image as the Havana cigar.

Talking with Bruce Lockhart, Beaverbrook expressed concern about what he frankly called Winston's "alcoholism." There are clues that, clinically speaking, this word was not too strong: Churchill suffered pneumonia and certain infectious diseases to which alcoholics are particularly prone. A more specific list of symptoms would include his drinking alone; his drinking before noon; his drinking to build up self confidence or drown sorrows; his getting angry when people mentioned the drinking; and his turning down invitations if drinks were not to be served.

Although our narrative has paused momentarily at March 1940, we can isolate specific, and in any other circumstances trivial, episodes. For example, when Mrs Eleanor Roosevelt dined with Churchill and their Majesties in October 1942 she commented in her unpublished diary that Churchill had seemingly imbibed "too much champagne," because "he repeated the same thing to me two or three times."[8] Another minor incident occurred at Casablanca in 1943. Officials found Churchill "in the vilest of humours" because there was no liquor at a dinner given by Roosevelt for a local Moorish potentate, the Moors being abstemious.[9] As a second version of the same episode had it, Churchill became "very grumpy because there was nothing to drink."[10] In whatever spirit the president may have kept relating this to his colleagues — and he did — it did not redound to Mr Churchill's credit.

His alcoholism was a family heirloom. His father had died of drink; there was the same problem in Clementine's family and it was an affliction inherited in turn by their offspring. It would lead to Sarah's arrest for disorderly conduct in California and to her remand in a women's prison in London.[11] It plagued Randolph all his life. An F.B.I. agent informed J. Edgar Hoover in July 1942 that "Randolph Churchill was in 'El Morocco' until four a.m. today [and] . . . was tight. A pretty picture."[12] Randolph stormed out of a New York television interview when questioned about his drinking. When Winston's grandson was only three — so Beaverbrook tut-tutted to the little boy's mother — he ran down the hall "to ask me to have a cocktail with him."[13]

Churchill settled his substantial London liquor bills with Hatch Mansfield, his wine merchants, on the morning he became prime minister. "One bill he would never pay, however," recalled Ralph Mansfield to the *Daily Telegraph*, "was his wife's gin bill." Clementine always had to settle that herself.

The family made light of this curse. Writing to her mother about a raging tooth-ache, Sarah would add humorously, "So far, the only relief has been obtained by an old fashioned treatment of which Papa will approve! Holding neat whisky in my mouth. Oh delicious anaesthesia! Local, then total!!"[14]

Winston would quaff '28 and '34 Pol Roger champagne throughout a meal rather than any wine, and made light of that as well.[15] Several times he called upon the Prof to compute his total consumption assuming he had drunk half a bottle a day for the last half century: the Prof made the slide-rule calculation once on the way over for the Atlantic meeting with Roosevelt in 1941 and gave him the result in liquid tons of champagne. Churchill was disgruntled to find that it would not even half fill the dining saloon.[16] Ten years later Churchill was still inquiring the total.

> At dinner [wrote Dean Acheson] he made [Lord] Cherwell get out his slide rule and compute the depth of the inundation which would take place in the dining room if all the champagne Mr Churchill had drunk in his life were poured into it. The results were very disappointing to the Old Man. He had expected that we would all be swimming like goldfish in a bowl whereas it would hardly come up to our knees."[17]

Starchier statesmen were irritated by it all. Mackenzie King had primly foresworn liquor for the duration of the war and was the butt of much Churchillian mockery in consequence; he lectured the Englishman on the virtues of abstaining — he would find himself better in "health and judgment." Churchill chortled that he felt no less well for the stimulants he took, and Mackenzie King replied that much depended on "the habits a man had from youth," adding charitably: "If you were to give up completely it would probably kill you."[18]

At least once, as the Canadian prime minister's papers suggest,

Churchill's little problem had nearly pushed Britain into war. Lord Greenwood revealed to him — under the Privy Councillor's oath of secrecy — his inside knowledge of the Chanak Crisis of 1922; Greenwood had been in the Cabinet during the very heated debate. "As a matter of fact," Mackenzie King dictated afterwards, "Churchill, Lord Birkenhead and Lloyd George had all been out dining pretty well that evening [September 15] and the decision to fight the Turks and to send out the appeal [drafted by Churchill] to the Dominions to aid in preventing the advance of the Turks was made under those conditions." Greenwood remarked that when national leaders were under the influence of alcohol it put entire nations "into the peril of their lives."[19]

The secret reports filed by Ambassador Kennedy and Sumner Welles about Churchill's inebriation — although excised from the published texts — damaged Britain's cause. On the day that Churchill finally comes to power we shall see Roosevelt dismiss him in an aside to his colleagues as a drunken bum.[20] The private diaries of his staff — Alanbrooke, Cunningham, Edwards and others — are peppered with exasperated references to his drunken incapacitation. But so it would go on. In January 1945 Roosevelt was informed by his special emissary, who shared the PM's sense of fun, that despite the unfavourable location of Yalta "Churchill . . . feels that he can survive it by bringing an adequate supply of whisky."[21]

Such supplies were not always easy to come by. Upon arrival at Fulton, Missouri, a year later to deliver his "Iron Curtain" speech, he demanded a whisky. Fulton was a dry town, and it took the president's military aide some time to locate a pint of the golden liquor, an ice bucket and a pitcher of water.

"Well, general," croaked Churchill, when the aide reappeared. "Am I glad to see you. I didn't know whether I was in Fulton, Missouri or Fulton, Sahara."[22]

* * *

This was the position in Mr Churchill's political affairs that we had left in March 1940: In Norway, even the pro-British had been disturbed by the *Altmark* affair — indeed, outraged that the violation of neutrality had been rewarded with Britain's highest medal for gallantry.[23] In Germany, Hitler had been alerted by intercepts and had ordered General von Falkenhorst on March 12 to include an *emergency* invasion of Scandinavia among his more prosaic calculations. But now that Finland had collapsed he eased this pressure, directing that planning continue "without excessive haste and without endangering secrecy."[24]

To Churchill, the Finnish collapse was "a major disaster" for the

Allies. Rightly, he wanted to press on with the seizure of Narvik — the decision would be "unpleasant," he argued, but the subsequent capture of the Swedish orefield would save casualties on the western front in the long run. His argument was unimpeachable. Deeply concerned about the leisurely course the war was taking, he wrote at length to Lord Halifax pleading for Britain to take an initiative now. "The days are full of absorbing work," he admitted: "but they cost six millions each. Never was less result seen for money."

> There never was any chance of giving effective help to Finland; but this hope — or rather illusion — might have been the means of enabling us to get to Gällivare. All that has now fallen to the ground; because so cumbrous are our processes that we were too late. Now the ice will melt; & the Germans are the masters of the North. Can we suppose they have not been thinking about what to do? Surely they have a plan. We have none.

Events, he feared, were taking an increasingly adverse turn: "In spite of all their brutality the Germans are making more headway with the neutrals than we with all our scruples." It was not enough for ministers merely to discharge their duty faithfully: "We have to contrive & compel victory." The Germans were now more at their ease than ever before — "Whether they have some positive plan of their own wh[ich] will open upon us I cannot tell. It wd seem to me astonishing if they have not."[25] He repeated this robust line at that day's War Cabinet: Britain's "real objective" was still Gällivare. True, she had lost Finland as a "lever," but she could always take the line that her national interests were directly threatened by "the possibility of Russia making her way through Scandinavia to the Atlantic."

Since the war began, his restless brain had spawned extraordinary offensive projects, of which Catherine, Royal Marine, Wilfred and Cultivator No.6 were only four: the last-named was an immense armoured machine weighing hundreds of tons but capable of burrowing a man-high trench straight through enemy lines. A prototype was built and tested, but events overtook it before it could be introduced in France. After lunching with him on the twentieth, Eden afterwards told a friend that Churchill was "full of ideas — not all good — but how could they be with a man who had so many?"[26]

Chamberlain just survived the Finland fiasco, although he was given a rough ride by Sinclair, Dalton and Macmillan when he delivered to the House an over-conceited account of Britain's assistance to the Finns. When Ambassador Kennedy visited the First Lord after the debate — to protest at the continued harrassment of American shipping by the British navy — Churchill showed concern at the prospect that Welles might succeed in his mission; he hoped that Roosevelt would not be so misguided as to offer a peace plan. "It would just embarrass us," he told the ambassador. "For we won't accept it. In fact I would fight Chamberlain if he proposed to accept it."[27]

IN PARIS, THE effect of the Finnish debacle was more dramatic than in London. Daladier effectively lost a vote of confidence and resigned as prime minister on March 21. Suddenly Winston's old friend and fellow campaigner Paul Reynaud was prime minister. His tenure of office was fraught with unexpected problems. Daladier remained minister of defence; a former peasant — with all the bad qualities of that class, as the British ambassador shortly warned — he was a dedicated foe of Reynaud. For the next months France's two leading politicians fought like tomcats, distraught by rivalry for a certain lady's favours.

Winston was exhilarated by the appointment of his *confrère*. "I rejoice that you are at the helm," he wrote to Reynaud on March 22, "and that Mandel is with you." Mandel was to remain minister for the colonies, and Winston asked to be remembered to him. "We have thought so much alike during the last three or four years," he added encouragingly, "that I am most hopeful that the closest understanding will prevail."[28]

These two musketeers met a few days later at No.10: Reynaud had come over with Gamelin and airforce commander Joseph Vuillemin for a Supreme War Council being held in Downing-street to decide the next move against Hitler. Daladier did not come: he had ducked out at the last moment, pleading his damaged leg.[29]

From the first moment there were arguments. The British wanted to mine the Rhine and cut off Hitler's iron ore, the French were more interested in attacking his oil, and they contemplated even more desperate measures. Second on the British agenda was, "The case for going to war against Russia" — France had developed a long-range bombing project against Stalin's oilfields at Baku and Batum, to deny Hitler further oil supplies and paralyze the Soviet economy, and during the winter the French had begun preparing a major campaign against the Soviet Union. At French airforce headquarters a secret wall map showed two large arrows plunging into Russia and meeting to the east of Moscow: one arrow began from Finland, the other from Syria and Lebanon via Baku.[30] On March 19 Churchill had hinted to Kennedy that a major event might take place in July, which Kennedy later deduced was a reference to an attack on Baku.[31]

There were some reservations against fighting Russia; a note on Chamberlain's file for this War Council meeting warned that "Socialist opinion" in Britain and France might find it difficult to swallow. For want of anything better he now adopted Churchill's two projects—

Wilfred, for mining Norwegian waters, and Royal Marine, mining the Rhine.[32]

Churchill was again curiously taciturn. Of 15,000 words on the record barely forty were spoken by him — to say that Britain saw Royal Marine "as a reprisal for German attacks on our merchant shipping and other illegal acts of war;" and that mining other rivers by air would have to wait for the full moon in mid-April.

The French were unenthusiastic about these projects. Reynaud wanted to bomb Baku; he did not think the result would be war with Russia — given the peculiar Russian mentality it might even encourage them to brush up their relations with the Allies. He had reason to believe that Turkey would tolerate overflights by Allied bombers operating from Syria or Northern Iraq. He wanted the necessary ammunition dispatched immediately to Syria. Chamberlain however feared that this would drive Stalin further into the arms of Germany.

The upshot was that this highest Allied authority gave conditional approval to Wilfred and Royal Marine, and a timetable was drawn up: formal protest notes would now go to Oslo and Stockholm about the German abuse of their territorial waters; the Allies would mine the Rhine on April 4 and the Norwegian waters on the fifth. The British agreed to study Baku, while a joint committee examined the broader question of whether to declare war on the Soviet Union. The meeting concluded with a formal declaration of Allied solidarity — that Britain and France would "neither negotiate nor conclude an armistice or treaty of peace except by mutual agreement."[33]

The strategic decisions were controversial. At the admiralty, Captain Edwards called the decision to lay mines in Norwegian territorial waters "a vast mistake."[34] Since a German riposte was inevitable against Norway, Admiral Darlan pleaded with Daladier to prepare the necessary means immediately to convey French troops to Norway.[35]

Intelligence was now arriving through Sweden indicating that Hitler was preparing his own move. Admiral Phillips urged that this was a "last opportunity" to execute R3, the plan to seize Gällivare. Churchill gained Cabinet approval to load British troops for an immediate expedition to seize Narvik the moment that Hitler invaded southern Norway in revenge for Wilfred. R3 was resurrected, and by the last day of March battalions of infantry were being loaded aboard cruisers in Scotland, equipped with winter clothing and the kind of light equipment they would need for an unopposed landing in Narvik and other Norwegian ports.

AT THIS JUNCTURE an extraordinary change of mind occurred in Paris and London: a flurry of jealous intrigue between Reynaud, Daladier, Churchill and Chamberlain led to the loss of four vital days.

The Supreme War Council had made its agreement to the launching of Royal Marine conditional on French cabinet approval. On March 30 Daladier blocked it: he talked of the fear of German reprisals, but his real motive may have been to spite Reynaud.

It was a remarkable and unnecessary stalemate. France supported the expedition to Norway, but not the mining of the Rhine. The former, major, venture needed the British fleet; the latter, minor, operation required France's permission. Britain should have swallowed her pride and proceeded immediately with the Norwegian venture. But when the French ambassador came to No.10 to explain that Daladier was the culprit Chamberlain ruled quite simply: "No mines — no Narvik!"[36]

The records throw no light on the reason for Chamberlain's stubborn loyalty to Winston's river-mining scheme. The petulant decision caused division and chaos in the Allied military staffs. Distraught, Admiral Darlan asked Gamelin on April 2 to specify how many transport ships would be necessary for the French to transport men to Narvik.[37]

Churchill remained preoccupied with his now-orphaned Royal Marine. Listening to Oliver Stanley talk at the War Cabinet on April 3 of a "somewhat garbled" report that Hitler was massing troops in a Baltic port, he stated that every preparation had now been made to stage an Allied landing in Norway if necessary. "But," he added dismissively, "I personally doubt whether the Germans will land a force in Scandinavia."

He suggested flying over to Paris to tackle Daladier in person about Royal Marine, and Chamberlain agreed.

AS PART OF a general rearrangement of his Cabinet, Chamberlain had just elevated him to a position of considerable importance, effectively that of a defence minister: he gave to Churchill the Military Co-ordination Committee, of service ministers and chiefs of staff. Lord Chatfield resigned as chairman on the third, and Chamberlain announced Churchill's appointment on the fourth. "We are on the eve of great events," wrote Sir John Simon in a diary note that reflected the eager anticipation at Cabinet level that day, "and the refurbishing of the Cabinet is merely the prologue."

Hitherto Chamberlain had shared the widespread doubts as to Churchill's stability: he had once remarked that Baldwin would never risk making him foreign secretary — he "would dread to find himself waking up at nights with a cold sweat at the thought of Winston's indiscretions."[38]

He had told Churchill of the new appointment on the day before the Supreme War Council. The First Lord told a mutual friend it was "the best talk with the PM he ever had," although Chamberlain turned down both his "pet suggestions," for taking Sinclair and Beaverbrook into the government. While Winston had evidently said nothing in Anthony Eden's behalf, Churchill would assure this junior minister when they met afterwards that he had urged Chamberlain to give him the air ministry. The PM gave it back to Sam Hoare, however, no friend of either of them. There would be more chances, "many more," Churchill encouraged Eden, "on this rough voyage."[39]

Privately he truckled to the prime minister. "It is very good thing that Sam has come up to the scratch in good form," he wrote to Chamberlain, and added: "I value highly the confidence which you are showing in me; and I will try my best to deserve it."[40]

So Churchill seemed to have turned over a new leaf, and it touched Chamberlain deeply. For all his violence and impulsiveness, he commented to his sister, Winston was very responsive to a sympathetic handling. "To me personally he is absolutely loyal and I am continually hearing from others of the admiration he expresses for the PM."

The new appointment as acting chairman of the military committee attracted applause and relief from the press — where Churchill's experience from the Great War was still highly rated — and a pleasing reaction from Bath where his daughter was on the stage: "Darling Papa," wrote Sarah,

> There was such a lovely picture of you on the Newsreel the other day, and the buzz and excitement that swept through the theatre suddenly made me feel so inordinately proud that I was your daughter, and it suddenly occurred to me that I had never really told you, through shyness and inarticulateness — *how much* I love you, and how much I will try to make this career that I have chosen — with some pain to the people I love, and not a little to myself — worthy of your name — one day. . .[41]

AS THE RUMBLINGS from the Baltic increased Churchill yanked his friend Spears away from lunch at the Ritz on April 4, picked up a final plea that Chamberlain had written to Daladier, and made the boneshaking flight over the Channel to Paris in an elderly Government Flamingo.

He was on a ticklish mission. With some experience of Anglo-French diplomacy, Spears advised him to call briefly on Reynaud, then to telephone Daladier at once as his opposite number, saying he had come over to see *him*. Churchill ignored the advice and invited both Reynaud and Daladier to dinner at the embassy. Daladier inevitably made some petty excuse; only now did Churchill realize that there was such bad blood between the two men.

"What will centuries to come say," he burst out, mortified, to Spears, "if we lose this war through lack of understanding?"

He decided to dine alone with Reynaud. The new French PM told him he had tried for three hours to talk Daladier round; but, he pleaded, he could hardly overrule his own minister of defence on strategy. To Daladier, Churchill's fluvial mine was just a "dangerous toy."

To his chagrin, Spears was confined to locating General Georges and arranging luncheon next day with Winston. "To go over with Winston," he grieved in his diary, "and not be included in his dinner with Reynaud was to diminish my own value and importance."

Smarting, he telephoned Churchill the next morning and huffed that he was going back to London. Winston smoothed his ruffled feathers, and went off to see Daladier. Daladier, somehow, talked him round. He emphasized the vulnerability of his aircraft factories to German reprisal; as for operation Royal Marine, he did promise a firm date later — three months later — and Churchill expressed himself satisfied with that.

Before driving off to Laperouse for a gourmet luncheon with Generals Spears and Georges, Churchill passed Daladier's final decision by telephone to Downing-street: it would indeed be an error, he now suggested, to twist French arms any further over Royal Marine.[42] At No.10, Chamberlain greeted Winston's *volte face* with derision — it was like the story of the pious parrot, purchased to teach manners to a parrot which used bad language. "It ended," he scoffed, "by learning to swear itself!"[43]

In the First Lord's absence Chamberlain broke the log jam in Allied strategy. He recommended the Cabinet to forget Winston's Royal Marine and to proceed with Wilfred (the operation to mine Norwegian waters) in four days' time — on April the eighth: Hitler would react in southern Norway: Britain would then spring R4 on him, the seizure of Narvik and capture of Gällivare. . .

The naval staff viewed it with mixed emotions.

"The more I think about [Wilfred]," wrote the acting Director of Operations on the fifth, "the more convinced I am that it's a political blunder of the highest order."

> It's against our principles and it cannot in my opinion achieve the results its protagonists claim. We deliberately infringe neutral waters & therefore the Law — I thought we were fighting for Law & Order. Another blunder to the account of Mr Winston Churchill — curse him.

The leisurely pace continued. As the main minelaying force for Wilfred sailed that evening at 6:45 p.m. it occurred to Reynaud to notify General Gamelin that Narvik was going ahead. The general in turn notified Admiral Darlan, and the fleet commander requisitioned the transport ships he needed.[44] Even so, the preceding four-day "tit-for-tat" delay had serious consequences for the timetable: The first British troops could not now sail before the eighth; this in turn would delay

French embarkation until the sixteenth, as there was a limit to how many ships even the friendliest Norwegian ports could handle.

While Churchill had lingered in France, significant messages had piled up on his admiralty desk. The Danish government had passed to the American minister in Copenhagen a message from a German traitor about Hitler's intentions. The British envoy had telegraphed the details to London soon after midnight: Hitler had issued

> definite orders to send one division in ten ships moving unostentatiously at night to land at Narvik on 8 April occupying Jutland on the same day.

The Foreign Office flatly disbelieved it. That afternoon an even more alarming message had arrived from Britain's Copenhagen envoy — "Troops actually embarked 4 April." Churchill read these reports when he arrived back from Paris an hour before midnight. Alerted by these ominous "mutterings" Captain Edwards had warned that a move against Norway was imminent; he found he was considered an alarmist. Mr Churchill sat down to pen a note to Chamberlain, but concerned himself only with Royal Marine and Daladier's objections.[45]

Daladier had handed to him an unyielding reply to carry back to No.10. While Royal Marine might impede Rhine traffic, the Frenchman's letter conceded, his *comité de guerre* could not ignore the risk, of which they had been warned by air minister Guy la Chambre on March 11 and by his successor on the thirtieth, of enemy reprisals against the aircraft factories. Likening the air industry to a snake changing its skin, Daladier observed, "The snake must not be touched while performing this operation." Daladier's advice was to concentrate on Germany's iron ore and oil supplies. "As I said to Mr Churchill this morning, in any case it is only a postponement and not outright cancellation."[46]

"It is vy long winded," Churchill apologized, forwarding this to the PM, "but they are serious in their alarm about their aviation; and it wd be dangerous to press them against their judgment."[47]

Meanwhile, Captain Edwards had sent out spotter planes, and at 9.00 a.m. on Sunday morning a Coastal Command Hudson sighted a German cruiser and six destroyers north of Heligoland. The First Lord refused to take them seriously, and debased a useful signal to the Home Fleet summarizing the Intelligence evidence on Hitler's intentions with the unhelpful words: "All these reports are of doubtful value and may well be only a further move in the war of nerves."[48]

At 4:45 p.m. that afternoon a belated message reached the admiralty reporting that Bomber Command had sighted a German battle cruiser, two cruisers, and a large number of destroyers steering north or north west at high speed off Jutland Bank. Edwards noted this in his diary, added: "I wanted and tried hard to get Wilfred cancelled." The First Lord would not agree. At 5:27 p.m. he ordered the fleet to raise steam.

Not for one moment did Churchill consider that Hitler was about to invade Norway. To him, it looked as though the enemy battle cruisers were attempting a breakout into the Atlantic. The dispositions he now ordered are explicable only on this assumption, since they left the central North Sea uncovered. He gravitated to the Operational Intelligence Centre in the multi-storey bunker from which naval operations were directed, to take personal command.

Forgetful of the recriminations after the Goeben incident and the Dardanelles he intervened that day and the next: his imprint is unmistakeably upon many of the imperious signals that now issued, even when they bore, as his post-1915 prudence dictated, Admiral Pound's name as originator. He did not bother to consult the First Sea Lord — a senile admiral gnawed by osteo-arthritis and a brain tumour, who drooled and fell asleep during staff meetings. Pound's hair was snow white, his face lined and pallid, a marked distortion in one eye. The admiral would have been no match for this thrustful politician even if he had been in London that Sunday, April 7: but he was not; he had gone salmon-fishing on the Mountbatten estate near Romsey. When he returned, late that evening, Captain Edwards found him "dead beat," his deputy Tom Phillips equally tired, and the First Lord perceptibly well dined.[49]

On this particular evening Churchill had eaten substantially with the outgoing air minister Kingsley Wood, and was inevitably in no shape for taking decisions. Trashing Wilfred, R4 and all his own predictions about Hitler's moves against Norway: ignoring the puny size of Hitler's navy when compared with Britain's: Winston Churchill could only think that the enemy Grand Fleet was emerging, that Hitler was endeavouring to pass his battle cruisers through one of the northern exits to the Atlantic. Visions of Jutland danced in his head.

At 8:30 p.m. Admiral Sir Charles Forbes led the Home Fleet out of Scapa in the battleship *Rodney*, with *Valiant*, *Repulse*, two cruisers and ten destroyers. Poor Forbes! He had earned the soubriquet "Wrong Way Charlie" in previous naval operations when his warships had repeatedly found themselves heading away from the enemy. Now, at the behest of his First Lord, he took Britain's fleet out at high speed to the north-east, followed at ten p.m. by the cruisers *Galatea* and *Arethusa* from the Clyde.

During this day, troops for R4, the seizure of Stavanger and Bergen, had been loaded aboard the cruisers *Devonshire*, *Berwick*, *York*, and *Glasgow* at Rosyth. But now that Admiral Pound returned that night, enfeebled from his fishing outing Churchill prevailed upon him to order the troops ashore and sail the cruiser squadron into battle without them. The decision to dump Plan R4 was taken without reference to Forbes, to the chiefs of staff or to the War Cabinet, let alone to the Supreme War Council; in the early hours it was telephoned to Admiral J.H.D. Cunningham at Rosyth. At one hour's notice the bewildered troops were turfed out onto the dockside, and saw the cruisers proceed to sea with their bags and baggage still aboard them. Years after the blunder became apparent, Churchill nudged the blame onto the Commander-in-Chief: he claimed in his memoirs to have concerted "all these decisive steps" with Admiral Forbes. But his memory was at fault: the admiral was with his fleet on the high seas, maintaining radio silence. It was Churchill's decision alone.

> Plan R4 [penned Captain Edwards in his diary] had to go by the board . . . so as to supply enough destroyers. . . . Winston taking a great personal interest. He wants to interfere & I'm sure he's wrong. An astonishing man.[50]

THAT NIGHT THE opening moves were made in perhaps the most catastrophic week of the naval war, silent as the shifting of chessmen on a board: in the jaws of a filthy gale the destroyers of the Wilfred force, their decks slimy with ice, laid the first mines off West Fiord at 4:32 a.m. on the eighth. An hour later the job was done. A few hours after that a destroyer of the covering force, *Glowworm*, vanished without trace into the darkness off the Norwegian coast. We now know that the luckless craft had been trampled down by the northward march of Hitler's entire battle fleet: her captain had bravely hurled his warship against the cruiser *Hipper*, blowing up a few moments after the ramming.

What had gone wrong? The Nazis had been reading the admiralty signals. They knew of Mr Churchill's plans. Now Hitler had taken the biggest gamble of the war. Within twenty-four hours he was going to bring the entire Norwegian coastline under his control in the biggest naval gamble in history.

CHAPTER 21

Completely Outwitted

GIVEN THE TOTAL lack of discretion as to the plans discussed at the Allied conferences," Admiral Darlan wrote as the awful disaster unfurled, "the German high command could scarcely have failed to know of our decision."[1]

The indiscretions were legion. Churchill's nephew, a Beaverbrook reporter, had been sent ahead to Narvik — a treason, Hitler called it, "typical of his American-Jewish journalistic character."[2] Late in March 1940 German agents had eavesdropped on the French prime minister assuring a foreign diplomat that "in the next few days the Allies would be triggering decisive and momentous events in Northern Europe."[3] On the thirtieth Mr Churchill had broadcast that Britain would no longer tolerate pro-German interpretations of neutrality — the allies would fight the war wherever they had to, however little their desire to extend it to other theatres.[4] Alerted by these and other indiscretions on April 2 Hitler had ordered Norway invaded in the darkness before dawn of the ninth.

Disturbed by the apparent failure of his secret service, Mr Chamberlain set up an immediate inquiry.[5] Lord Hankey grilled Colonel Stuart Menzies, the mild-mannered, aristocratic head of the Secret Intelligence Service, and reported that he had alerted at least the admiralty in good time: as early as May 1939 his predecessor had sent to Naval Intelligence a German book claimed (correctly) to be Hitler's "sea Gospel," Admiral Wegener's *Die Seestrategie des Weltkrieges*; this volume argued that Norway must be seized before any future assault on England.[6]

Subsequently, Hankey found, the S.I.S. had sent over to Mr Churchill's admiralty, since this was a purely naval affair, the accumulating evidence that since December a German expedition to Norway had been prepared, exercised, trained and loaded in north German ports. They had reported alleged predictions by Grand Admiral Raeder that he would "smash the British blockade" by operating from

Norway, and described two OKW and interservice conferences held during March. Hankey exonerated the S.I.S. "But," he reminded Chamberlain, "we did not get any warnings as far as I can recollect from the Admiralty."

Reading this damning report even as the catastrophe began, Chamberlain's adviser Horace Wilson felt that things might look clearer now in retrospect — and in justice to Mr Churchill this should be emphasized — but he suggested a further investigation into whether this Intelligence "ought to have led to a different disposition of our naval forces than was, in fact, ordered?"[7]

THE LACK OF boldness and vision that Mr Churchill displayed in these dispositions throughout April was humanly understandable: until the last moment, the axe of political oblivion hung over him. On April 8 we find the diary of Captain Edwards remarking upon "a lack of firm decision" in the admiralty; he could have made that entry each day of the campaign.

It was a legacy of 1915. Wary of being wrongfooted in this, his home-run to power, the First Lord stumbled and fumbled throughout the Norwegian campaign. His new chairmanship of the military co-ordination committee acted like a Dead Man's Handle on all the other control panels of military authority. Within a very few days, loud cries of protest were raised in the War Office about the "serious strategical mistakes." Winston's committee, the deputy C.I.G.S. protested, was usurping the functions of the War Cabinet, the chiefs of staff, and all the expert planners.[8]

It was a campaign without much point now anyway: not enough that Germany was dependent on neither Narvik nor the Swedish ores (her steelworks were fed to a significant degree on scrap iron);* not enough that by April the snows were melting anyway, and Lulea would soon reopen. By mid April the campaign had become a war for its own sake: a spectacular military diversion: a smashing of china in foreign shops. The Norwegian public showed little enthusiasm to join in on either side.

* * *

On the eve of Hitler's move, Monday, April 8, the admiralty was still labouring under the after-effects of Winston's heavy evening. "All the S.O.'s [senior officers] very tired," observed Edwards, adding: "The Fleet is still steaming madly to the North!"

---

*On April 13, Hitler himself signalled General Dietl that he must defend Narvik at all costs: "If necessary destroy ore railroad through mountains beyond repair."[9]

Convinced that Hitler was slipping his battle-cruisers out into the Atlantic and that all else was a diversion, Churchill had tossed ashore the two infantry battalions loaded for Bergen and Stavanger, and despatched their cruisers post-haste to the north. Still convinced that he was right, he now abandoned the other section of Plan R4, Trondheim and Narvik, and ordered the cruiser *Aurora* to "proceed with all despatch without troops on board, repeat, without troops on board" to join Admiral Sir Charles Forbes with the Fleet.[10]

Conscious of the historic hour, at eleven a.m. he presented himself in the Board Room to the lens of society photographer Cecil Beaton. Half an hour later he announced to the War Cabinet that the Wilfred minefield had been laid off Narvik and that "all our fleets were at sea." Lord Halifax, informed that the minelaying in Norwegian waters had gone smoothly, dictated this comment in his diary:

> So now we shall wait for the wails and protests of the neutrals and the fury of Germany. Winston rang me at breakfast to tell me that it had all gone without a hitch, and my first anxiety that we might find ourselves in Norwegian bloodletting is therefore so far removed.

"Winston," he continued, "reported to the Cabinet that a considerable force of German ships was out in the North Sea, which the Government were taking appropriate steps to deal with. He seemed optimistic. I hope he is right."

Some of his colleagues felt that Hitler might even have ordered his troops to seize Narvik, but Mr Churchill scoffed at the idea. "It might also be the intention," he suggested dismissively, "when the force had been landed, to send the *Gneisenau* out into the oceans as a raider. In any case the whole operation seemed to be a most hazardous venture."

Forbes had sent a Sunderland flying boat ahead of his fleet and at two p.m. it sighted warships 220 miles southwest of West Fiord — but steering unmistakeably west. This provided further support for Mr Churchill's break-out hypothesis, and encouraged him to ignore the gathering signs of a major German invasion operation. In fact it was the *Hipper* group, cruising in random patterns before going in to Trondheim.

Shortly, the secret service telephoned his Intelligence division to warn that a hundred German ships were heading northwards past Denmark. At eight p.m. Forbes reversed his fleet's northwesterly course to meet them.

By this time, Mr Churchill had left to dine with Hoare and Stanley. The incoming telegrams piled up in his absence; among them a Reuter's agency message from Oslo reporting that a German freighter torpedoed off southern Norway had spewed forth troops, and that these were claiming to be bound for Bergen to protect it against the Allies. Several hours passed before the First Lord even forwarded this to Forbes.

The feast with his two ministerial colleagues infused him with fresh spirit. "Winston," wrote Hoare that night, "[was] very optimistic, delighted with mine laying, and sure he had scored off the Germans."[11] Significantly, the First Lord said nothing of any invasion threat.

For a while his optimism fizzed like champagne.

When he teetered back into his Operational Intelligence Centre it was nearly eleven p.m. and the bad news was stacking up. At seven p.m. a submarine had spotted three enemy cruisers and a destroyer heading north past the Skaw.[12] Later that night, his mousey private secretary Eric Seal stammered to a newcomer, "The entire German navy seems to be heading for Norway."

By five a.m. the fizz had gone flat. Hitler had invaded Norway. Trondheim, Bergen and Stavanger were under his warship's guns. At eight-thirty German transport planes were already debouching troops on Oslo's Fornebu airfield. The War Cabinet, meeting at that hour, heard that no German ships had been reported at Narvik but a hung-over Churchill, unable to conceive even now the scale of Hitler's coup, suggested that all this might well be just a prelude to an offensive against France — an assessment which overlooked the inability of Hitler to commit his airforce to two theatres at once.

Churchill reported that destroyers were standing by "to stop enemy transports entering Narvik." But then the teletype brought incredible press reports that the Germans were already there too. Two clear hours earlier the Austrian Major-General Eduard Dietl had hoisted the swastika over Narvik. "Winston," recorded Lord Halifax, charitably reflecting that it was difficult to assess the Navy's problems from only a small-scale map, "again is sanguine that at Narvik anyhow the Germans ought to be what he calls 'cut like flowers'."

These events were nonetheless a cruel shock.

"Germany," Winston suggested to his colleagues, still fiercely optimistic, "has made a major strategic mistake."[13] This was not the view of the naval staff. "What a chance we've missed," wrote Edwards.

ADMIRAL FORBES PLOUGHED a southwards furrow through rising seas during the night, looking for the enemy fleet. Joined early on the ninth by nine cruisers and thirteen destroyers, he had a considerable force with which he could have caught the Germans in mid-disembarkation, in several places. At six-twenty a.m. he found himself closest to Bergen and detached four cruisers and seven destroyers for the assault, willing to run the risk that Bergen's coastal batteries were in enemy hands and working (they weren't). He would have caught *Köln*, *Königsberg*, and

Bremse in harbour there.

But upon his return to the Operational Intelligence Centre after the War Cabinet the First Lord vacillated. On balance, he had already decided against invading Trondheim: two German warships were known to have entered that fiord. Now, under pressure from the First Sea Lord, he also intervened to forbid the attack on Bergen; which done, he went off to lunch.

It was an "ill judged" intervention.[14] "Pure cold feet," was the appreciation of his acting Director of Operations in a diary whose tone towards the admiralty's political master was clearly deteriorating.

> Winston ratted & so did 1st S.L. — never win like this. Blast &damn them. Winston is an infernal menace, and may well lose the war for us. We should go to Trondheim too. It's the key — Bergen isn't.

A vastly more ominous development was the scale of the German air attack that now developed on the Home Fleet in these waters. By noon, Forbes had had to turn away to the north, having lost a destroyer and taken a heavy bomb on his own battle-cruiser. Some of his ships expended 40 percent of their Flak ammunition — a taste of what would have happened to Churchill's Catherine. Air cover was not available: in the hurry to put to sea the carrier *Furious* had not embarked her fighter squadron.

AFTER LUNCH CHURCHILL had retired to bed for two hours, taking Nelson the admiralty cat. Both were in need of consolation, Nelson having just been doctored to put an end to his amorous affairs.

The First Lord propped himself up with pillows and pawed the maps of Scandinavia. He was sure Hitler was only bluffing in Norway. How could the German navy do otherwise under the noses of the mightiest navy in the world? But what was he really up to? An Atlantic breakout, or war in the west? General Pownall, Gort's chief of staff, summoned back from Gort's headquarters to the War Office during the day, learned that the fateful plan to send to Scandinavia three or four of the ten B.E.F. divisions was "definitely *off*," unless "the Crazy Gang" (as Winston's military co-ordination committee was termed in Whitehall) disposed otherwise again. "With Winston as Chairman," reflected Pownall in his diary, "they are likely to be extremely volatile. . . What a struggle and a mess up it has been — a full seven weeks delay in formations alone."

At four p.m. Churchill went over to No.10 for an emergency meeting with the French leaders. Their *comité de guerre* that morning had decided to rush troops to Norway. But now each ally had a rude shock for the other. Reynaud had learned from Gamelin that the French expeditionary division was still in the Jura mountains, to avoid espionage. And Oliver Stanley had to apologize to the French, who included Admiral Darlan, that the five British battalions embarked for Plan R4 had been put back on dry land, since Mr Churchill had sailed their cruisers; moreover, all their equipment was still on board.

As for the press report about Narvik, Mr Chamberlain now suggested it must be a mistake for Larvik in southern Norway, while Mr Churchill still hoped to occupy Narvik before the Germans. "The actual operation of clearing any Germans out of Narvik should not present great difficulty," he said, according to the French record. "At this moment," he however admitted, "the admiralty hasn't the slightest idea what is going on at Narvik. We don't even know if there are any Germans at all there."[15] He was sending destroyers into West Fiord to find out.

Playing his hunch about the West, he suggested they invade neutral Belgium immediately to forestall Hitler there. Once again he ran into Daladier's opposition. It was unwise, said the French minister, to antagonize the Belgians — they could be very sensitive. "Too right they are," snorted Churchill. "They just have no desire to get into a war!"[16]*

Trying to clear up the confusions, that evening he invited his fleet commander to break wireless silence and explain what he was doing and why. "I consider," he added, in blithe reassurance, "Germans have made strategic error in incurring commitments on Norwegian coast which we can probably wipe out in a short time." He repeated his conviction that the western front would soon begin.[17]

There would be two Narvik task force commanders, Major-General "Pat" Mackesy and Churchill's elderly but offensive minded World War naval friend Lord Cork & Orrery. Cork had not been to sea for years: but as an admiral of the fleet he outranked both Pound and Forbes.

Late on the ninth Churchill and Pound briefed the two task force commanders separately, verbally, and wholly inadequately. They would sail in different cruisers: they were not introduced: Mackesy believed that his naval counterpart was still Admiral Sir Edward Evans, whom Churchill had however sent to Stockholm. While Field-Marshal Ironside did give Mackesy explicit written orders,[18] Churchill endowed Cork only with a private cypher and a secret line of communication to him behind the backs of his admiralty colleagues.† At 9:30 p.m. he invited the admiral to attend his military committee; he also invited him to drive

---

*Thus the French record in Reynaud's papers. On April 10 the Belgians moved more forces against the French frontier.

†The naval staff did not find this out for twelve days. It is borne out by a signal on May 9 from Cork to Churchill that he had sent a signal on the seventh "by S.P.02328 [the naval cypher (N) held by Lord Cork] which I believed ensured private communication with yourself."[19]

down Whitehall the next day to the House, to the plaudits of the onlookers. But several days would pass before the reassembled task force sailed.

By the time the "Crazy Gang" met, late on the ninth, Churchill knew the worst: Hitler had packed ten destroyers and several thousand mountain troops into Narvik. Five British destroyers were patrolling off West Fiord and their commander Captain B.A.W. Warburton-Lee bravely signalled London: "Intend attacking at dawn high water." Cruiser reinforcements were readily at hand; but instead of telling him to await these Churchill replied at ten p.m. — by-passing both Forbes and the cruiser squadron commander — giving discretion to attack: "We shall support whatever decision you take."[20] In the resulting gallant but unequal action two destroyers were lost and Warburton-Lee killed. By that time however, Mr Churchill had long been manoeuvred into his cot by Eric Seal.

THE MORNING SIGNALS were brought into his bedroom: Hitler was now unquestioned master of Norway and Denmark. "Although we have been completely outwitted," he dictated to Pound, in a fit of candour, "there is no reason to suppose that prolonged and serious fighting in this area will not impose a greater drain on the enemy than on ourselves."[21]

The naval staff was anxious to attack, and scathing about the absence of decision. "The Germans," wrote Edwards that day, "can't have constituted satisfactory defences yet."

Edwards tried to have the 32,000-ton battle cruiser *Repulse* sent in to "clean up the mess" at Narvik. But an important reputation was at stake: from within his panelled Board Room Churchill sensed the distant crowing not just of Hitler, but of his Whitehall rivals too; to Anthony Eden, visiting that evening, he spewed venom about air minister Sam Hoare, calling him "a snake" and incapable of inspiring the airforce at times like this — as though that were at the root of the affair.[22]

The enforced inaction gnawed at him. As he drove to the House that Thursday morning newspapers headlined rumours that British troops had already liberated Trondheim, that their navy was inside Oslo fiord and had issued an ultimatum to the Germans. The *Star*'s placards proclaimed: BERGEN CAPTURED — OFFICIAL. It would fall to Winston to reveal that their troops were still in Britain.

Pallid and unwell, he took refuge in vague, euphonious language and stumbling gibes. He muddled his notes, clipped the wrong spectacles to his nose, once confused Denmark with Sweden. He tried to persuade the House that Hitler had made a "vast strategic error." Confining his own profound scepticism to his diary, Sir John Simon observed that on the contrary Hitler "has certainly achieved for the moment a vast tactical success." In answer to a question, the prime minister confirmed that Winston had been chairing the military committee since April 4.

He lingered in the bar, then drowned his surviving sorrows in the admiralty. At a staff conference that evening Churchill was visibly the worse for drink; Edwards jotted an angry description in his diary of "a very long meeting with W.C., who was half tight."[23]

They wrangled until midnight, then he staggered across Whitehall to the War Office to arouse Field-Marshal Ironside and tussle with him. "Winston," wrote Edwards, "lost his temper just when everything looked like being settled."[24]

That evening, the British expedition finally sailed for Norway, three days late. The recapture of Narvik might yet restore the First Lord's fame, and for the next seven weeks it would become his guiding star.

* * *

On the twelfth the War Cabinet began glancing at alternatives to this remote northern port. Eyeing Sweden, Lord Halifax murmured that an attack on Trondheim offered greater political effect. But Mr Churchill predicted a "bloody repulse" there, and a memorandum written that day for the joint Planners showed he contemplated only staging a "menace" to Trondheim since a full scale landing could not be undertaken in the present month. Groping for the word "inspired," but finding only "dispirited," he dictated: "The Norwegian resistance will be inspirited by British landings." His secretary dutifully took down the nonsense word as dictated.[25] The Cabinet dissolved in mutual recrimination, with Churchill trying to score off the foreign secretary because the British envoy at Copenhagen, Howard Smith, had fallen into Nazi hands.

"You have no right to talk," retorted Lord Halifax, "as your Communist nephew [Giles Romilly] was captured at Narvik."

"That causes me no concern at all," sniffed the First Lord. "The Nazis are welcome to him."

The naval staff blamed him for their misfortune. "Winston," wrote an indignant Captain Edwards, "is at the bottom of it all."

> He will try & be a strategist and run the Naval Side of the War. Nothing is yet settled on the question of where the other landings are to take place. However at last they ordered C-in-C [Forbes] to send in a force to attack the enemy ships at Narvik with a B.S.

On Saturday the thirteenth Churchill showed a closer interest in Trondheim after all. Writing to the French leaders about events at Narvik ("We are to-day attacking with the Fleet") he predicted that the important British forces arriving "in the neighbourhood" on Monday or

Tuesday would "settle the matter" before the arrival of the French contingent on April 21.

> Therefore we must consider extreme importance and urgency of operations against Trondheim.[26]

He was further swayed in that direction when the 31,000-ton battleship *Warspite* charged into Narvik's fiord with nine destroyer consorts and sank all seven surviving German destroyers; viewed from the battleship the half-drowned seamen struggling up the snow covered slopes were taken for a rout. Admiral Whitworth recommended that Narvik be occupied without delay by "the main landing force." But the cruisers with their battalions were no longer on hand, and reports of a rout were greatly exaggerated. Winston's five p.m. military committee talked of landing small parties of troops *near* Trondheim. He decided to go further and send a note to Stanley urging him to stiffen this improvised force with regular troops.[27]

The renewed shift of emphasis appalled his naval colleagues. "Indecision reigns supreme," sighed Edwards; the muddle was "indescribable." Angered by Churchill's overriding of chiefs of staff, Cabinet and planners, the deputy C.I.G.S. sent a formal complaint to Ironside about the chaotic conduct of deliberations: "Meetings," he complained, "have been held continuously until all hours of the night without adequate time for thought." Everybody was exhausted — "None of the Staff can work under these conditions and give of their best."

With the recent boozy wrangling still in vivid memory, Field-Marshal Ironside fervently agreed. He wrote to Stanley pleading that the chiefs of staff be relied on for military advice; Winston's "military co-ordination committee" could always screen it before it went to the Cabinet. But the M.C.C. must not get bogged down in details.

> That has been fatal. Personally, I think that the M.C.C. should be used for long term projects. It cannot be used as a species of "super-generalissimo" in being.[28]

Overnight Winston's Trondheim plan took shape. By telephone he persuaded his friend Reynaud to allow the French contingent to be switched to Trondheim; by wireless, without consulting higher authority, he diverted two of the five British troopships to Namsos, near Trondheim. "It will be an operation of much difficulty and risk," Winston admitted in a letter to the King, "but we must not fail to profit by success and speed."

The confusion was now complete.

The 146 Infantry brigade was switched to Namsos, while its commander, Brigadier Phillips, was on a ship continuing to Narvik.

Troops were separated from equipment, gunners from guns, guns from ammunition. Norway was mantled in snow deeper than the British troops had ever seen; they had no snow clothing, let alone skis.

Thus they landed at Harstad some sixty miles from Narvik: *Southampton* with General Mackesy and two rifle companies, followed on the fifteenth by *Aurora* with Admiral Lord Cork and the remaining troopships. Mackesy was left with about 1,800 troops all told (Mr Churchill, masking the consequences of the diversion, would write of "four thousand" in his memoirs.) Arrayed against him were two thousand elite, if poorly provisioned, Austrian mountain troops, to which were now joined over two thousand sailors off the sunken destroyers. Well might Mr Churchill call it "this ramshackle campaign."

The newspaper billboards read B.E.F. IN NORWAY – OFFICIAL.

But at three a.m. that Monday, April 15, the admiralty received disquieting word from a small naval party landed at Namsos: the little port was totally unsuited for troopships and exposed to air attack.

This was a serious complication. Worse was to come. As Mr Churchill waited confidently for word that Mackesy and Cork had clubbed their way into the abandoned streets of Narvik he learned that their ships had come under determined machine-gun fire: they had decided not to attack.

The expedition had not been equipped for an opposed landing. Both he and Field-Marshal Ironside had banked heavily on the Norwegians; but the latter showed an almost treasonable unwillingness to assist the Allies or resist the enemy.[29] Churchill postponed Hammer, the assault on Trondheim, until the twenty-second.

Naked revolt now stirred against him. When he chaired his military committee as usual that evening Sir Edward Bridges, the Cabinet secretary, caught the growing "uneasiness" over Winston's conduct of its affairs. The First Lord had continuously called upon the chiefs of staff for advice without letting them confer; he had squeezed out the planning staffs altogether; and now there was to be yet another postponement. "Air marshal afraid of air menace," commented Edwards after that day's meetings – "sea admiral afraid of S/Ms [submarines], field marshal afraid of everything."[30]

At dead of night Churchill sent a pained inquiry by his private link to Admiral Lord Cork: "All our plans for urgent operations to the southward [Trondheim] depend upon our knowing at earliest what you propose and what you do at Narvik. . . Cabinet desire to know by a.m. to-day, Tuesday, what you decided and did, yesterday, Monday."

TEMPERS WERE FRAYING at both ends of the chain of communication. On Tuesday the sixteenth, after reading an "awful" reply by Forbes to a signal made by Churchill, Captain Edwards mused in his diary: "Why they don't relieve him I can't imagine. W.C. asked him to reconsider attack on Trondheim. It is vital to the Allied cause. Forbes simply sticks his toes [in] etc. & won't play."

That day a second expedition sailed, destined for Andalsnes south of Trondheim. It had been delayed by a storm. There was growing impatience at the delays. Simon, Kingsley Wood and Hankey voiced anger at the postponement of Hammer, and there was restlessness that Churchill was dictating war policy without even token reference to the Cabinet. These operations were likely to be hazardous, yet they had seen none of the customary written appreciations from the chiefs of staff.[31]

Partly in an attempt to "clamp together the various & changing plans wh[ich] are now afoot," but also to secure Chamberlain's backing Churchill sent him a memorandum that day promising that Narvik would be disposed of by the twentieth and that he could then use the regular brigade from there to invade Trondheim two or three days later. He described how the batteries would be quelled, the fiord forced, the airfield silenced by naval bombardment, the enemy at Trondheim distracted by subsidiary operations at Namsos and Andalsnes. But in the scribbled covering note he clearly foresaw trouble closer at home: "In the event of difficulties arising w[ith] the Committee I shall have to invite yr assistance."[32]

Those difficulties had already arisen. His disagreement with the chiefs of staff over Hammer was so vocal that General Sir Hastings Ismay, his staff officer, visited Bridges during the morning to warn of "a first class row" if Churchill took the chair at the military co-ordination committee again.[33]

To the relief of its members — the service ministers and chiefs of staff — when the committee met at mid-day Chamberlain himself took the chair; and he convened it at No.10, not the admiralty.

Since Bridges had also adjured Ironside, Newall and Pound to keep their tempers, and since Chamberlain for all his faults was a much better committee chairman than the loquacious First Lord, the committee began to hum.[34]

If Chamberlain was surprised that even Winston expressed his gratification at this there was more to come: the First Lord invited the PM to continue to take the Chair — "At any rate while the present affair was in progress."[35]

That he so willingly abdicated his most coveted office, effectively that of a Defence Minister, deserves comment. Probably he had witnessed too many military disasters from high office in the Great War not to recognize the outlines of one in embryo now. He did not want to be midwife to one yet again. But was there more to it than that? In his entourage there were some who suspected him of wicked disloyalty in these weeks. "I'm quite certain," Edwards would write, as the Norway fiasco finally emerged in all its ugliness from the womb of war, "he's played the whole of the last eight months to become PM, often at the expense of helping to win the war."[36]*

In private, he made no bones of his seminal responsibility for the fiasco. Years later, a mere author once again, grappling with the shifting command structures of these weeks, and picking Ismay's brains, he would write wryly, "I certainly bore an exceptional measure of responsibility for the brief and disastrous Norwegian campaign — if campaign it can be called."[37]

* * *

We now know that on April 17 Hitler had an unseemly breakdown, lost his nerve and ordered Narvik evacuated; but that General Alfred Jodl refused to forward this order.† Victory at Narvik was that close.

But General Mackesy had postponed his advance there until the snows melted. Churchill found the news "unexpected and disagreeable," choked on it far into the night, then wrote to the committee on the seventeenth: "One of the best regular brigades in the Army will be wasting away, losing men by sickness and playing no part."[38] Using his secret cypher link he dropped a broad hint that Lord Cork ask for Mackesy's recall.

> Should you consider that situation is being mishandled it is your duty to report either to me personally or to admiralty on it, and what you would do yourself.

Cork however endorsed Mackesy's view, and added that any naval action to wear down the enemy garrison at Narvik would destroy the town and kill Norwegians; besides which they lacked the proper ammunition for a naval bombardment. "Short of a direct order," he informed the First Lord, "soldiers refuse to entertain idea of assault."

In a further message that began with the conciliatory words, "Very well we will do what we can," Mackesy set out his troops' deficiencies: they had not one field gun or anti-aircraft gun between them, and practically no mortar ammunition.

Confronted with this stalemate at Narvik, and with Admiral Forbes' shortage of Flak ammunition, the chiefs of staff shelved the frontal assault on Trondheim. They would beef up the flank attacks from Andalsnes and Namsos instead. Churchill willingly abandoned Hammer

---

*Quoted in full in next chapter.

†*Hitler's War.*

— it would release the *Warspite* and troop reinforcements for Narvik, the town on which he saw his reputation depending.

"We move," he estimated, relieved, "from a more hazardous to a less hazardous operation."

BY APRIL 19 both Hitler and Churchill, for different reasons, had developed an unbecoming callousness towards the Norwegians. Hitler on that day ordered his airforce to destroy any towns reported by the British as occupied, and particularly Namsos and Andalsnes, "without regard for the civilian population."

Churchill, angered at the supineness of the Norwegian population, ordered Narvik destroyed for much the same reason. "Of course," he notified Lord Cork that day, "the less the town is knocked about the better for our own accommodation, but we must get in to Narvik or its ruins as soon as possible." Later that Friday evening he explained his urgency in a personal message on their private link: "Once this is achieved," he told Cork, "we have the trophy at which all Europe is looking, we have a bridge-head for further landings, and our men sleep under such shelter as may be left, while the enemy sleep in the snow."

Getting his way again, on the twentieth he persuaded the War Office to subordinate the dissident general Mackesy to Lord Cork. ("I gather," wrote Captain Edwards, "that general & admiral are growling.") Churchill warned the admiral not to expect any reinforcements for a fortnight, and emphasized the political reasons why Narvik must be captured without delay. His plan was for a saturation naval bombardment followed by an amphibious assault. That afternoon he received assurances from Cork that he had prepared a plan closely following these suggestions. "Starting harrassing fire to-day Saturday 20th April."

It soon became plain to the naval staff that Mackesy was unimpressed by the plan, considered any seaborne assault impossible and would rather resign than attempt it. "It appears that there's a first class row brewing or in progress between Cork & Mackesy," wrote Edwards. "The 1st Lord has taken a hand in the game." After a personal reconnaissance Mackesy then reported to London that an amphibious assault from open boats would lead to the slaughter of his troops. He doubted that Lord Cork's naval bombardment would dislodge the defenders. "Those of us," he signalled, "who have seen and experienced far heavier and better directed bombardment . . . must know only too well that British and German troops are not so demoralized and that machine gun detachments always come up when bombardment ceases."

In a stinging message, he reminded Lord Cork and Churchill that there were 5,000 Norwegians in Narvik; that killing them would prejudice future operations in Norway; and that such a bombardment would violate the instructions* which he, Mackesy, had received from the Cabinet: "I submit that it should only be undertaken on a direct order from the Cabinet."

This rebuff created a muffled sensation. At the admiralty many already felt that the First Lord's proposal was "very wrong." But Mackesy, seeing his military career at an end, made a renewed protest, couched in terms of even more heroic candour, which he specifically asked Lord Cork to convey to the government. "Before proposed action against Narvik commences," this read, "I have the honour to inform you that . . . there is not one officer or man under my command who will not feel shame for himself and his country, if thousands of Norwegian men, women and children in Narvik are subject to bombardment proposed." Admiral of the Fleet Lord Cork, no fool he, appended to Mackesy's signal, "I have no remarks."[39]

Churchill was under pressure to show results. Encouraged by his utterances, Chamberlain had written in private on the twentieth, "I shall be very disappointed if we haven't practically captured Trondheim before the week is out." But they had reckoned without Hitler's ruthless air attacks on the two positions flanking Trondheim. Those on Namsos were so violent that the French mountain troops could not land, and the British commander Carton de Wiart talked of taking to the ships. Edwards' only comment was the forbidden phrase, "Shades of Gallipoli!"

Under this lowering sky Churchill foamed at Mackesy in a secret message to Lord Cork: "If this officer appears to be spreading a bad spirit through the higher ranks of the land force, do not hesitate to relieve him or place him under arrest." He repeated: he wanted Narvik rendered uninhabitable to the enemy — scorched earth. If Lord Cork concurred, he suggested six hours' notice to the townsfolk to get out, and then the naval bombardment.[40]

That signal sent, he flew with Chamberlain to Paris for a Supreme War Council. The long suffering lord Halifax found that his hotel room, next to Winston's, offered less than the repose he had prayed for:

> We got to bed about eleven and about twelve Winston came up to bed in the next room to me and made as much noise as a moderate earthquake. At seven o'clock next morning I heard a knock on the communicating door which meant that he had had some brainwave which he wished to impart to me. I . . . pretended to be asleep therby postponing his incursion 'till 7:30! 9:30 we began the Supreme War Council at the Quai d'Orsay.

---

*These bear quoting: "It is clearly illegal to bombard a populated area in the hope of hitting a legitimate target which is known to be in the area but which cannot be precisely located and identified."

It conferred for two days, but dwelt only briefly on Norway. In his own short contribution Churchill played down the significance of Trondheim. Looking ahead, Reynaud gloomily remarked that Britain had only ten divisions in France now and anticipated only twenty by the end of 1940, while Hitler might well raise three hundred. Again he suggested marching into Belgium now. When Chamberlain proposed bombing Hitler's refineries, the French showed the now familiar nervousness about their aircraft factories and for their part raised again their plan to bomb Baku.[41]

THE NEWS ON Chamberlain's return to No.10 was that the Namsos force had retreated to a small beachhead. Preparing him for the worst, Churchill drafted a note warning of "a head-on smash" looming in Norway; but he scratched that out and wrote flummery instead: "I am vy grateful to you for having at my request taken over the day to day management of the Military Co-ordination Cte."

On the twenty-fourth Lord Cork's ships bombarded Narvik but as Mackesy had predicted the Germans did not surrender. In London, energetic buck-passing began. The prime minister's secretary heard Bridges call Winston "maddening" — he was making the most unreasonable proposals.[42] He wanted to demand even wider powers; but before he could state them, a letter arrived from Chamberlain — wanting to discuss the "rather unsatisfactory" Norwegian situation with him in private. Over at No.10, Churchill demanded outright control of the chiefs of staff, blaming the "hopeless muddle" on them. Chamberlain humoured him with a half solution — a military secretariat of his own headed by Ismay, who would also join the Chiefs of Staff Committee.[43] It was a major concession, but Winston apparently blackmailed him with the threat that he would go to the House and disown all responsibility. Speaking of him a few hours later to Sir Alec Cadogan, the prime minister remarked: "He's grand — when things are going right!"

The chiefs of staff now faced up to the possibility of abandoning southern Norway altogether. "Position to be put before War Cabinet," wrote Edwards. "If politically essential to hold on, we must attack Trondheim. Otherwise prepare to withdraw." On April 26 the Cabinet formally discarded Trondheim, and the naval staff began to talk seriously of evacuation which would be, Edwards realized, a most difficult operation. "If we scuttle out of Norway the political effect will be incalculable." Chamberlain suggested they describe a successful evacuation of Namsos and Andalsnes as a "strategical triumph." Churchill pointed out that Narvik had always been their real objective.

Among those stung by the decision was Admiral of the Fleet Sir Roger Keyes: he had led the Zeebrugge raid in 1918, and even now offered to command a naval assault on Trondheim; Churchill spiked the idea. The seniority problem alone would have been stupendous. Keyes refused to be fobbed off, and sent him a long critique of Admiral Pound, calling his conduct of the sea war "deplorably pusillanimous and short-sighted." "This opinion," Keyes wrote, "is shared with bitter resentment by many naval officers [and] is pretty prevalent throughout the fleet."[44] For several days Admiral Keyes, lively and brave beyond his years, lobbied ministers and fellow MP's; when they stonewalled him, he told anybody who would listen that if the navy had only moved faster this entire fiasco would never have occurred.[45]

The French government was equally unhappy about the evacuation plan. Reynaud appealed to Chamberlain that quite apart from its effect on domestic prestige such a setback would damage Allied morale with the neutrals, large and small.[46] On April 27 Reynaud came over for a Supreme War Council: his military adviser Lieutenant Colonel Villelume recorded, "The British are inclined to evacuate Central Scandinavia; M le President [Reynaud] asks them to await the outcome of the imminent Narvik operation before putting it into effect." The French believed that the British had agreed, but the British recorded the decisions as the immediate dropping of Trondheim and a realization that the evacuation of Andalsnes might at any time become necessary.[47] Immediately the French visitors had left London in fact the chiefs of staff gave orders for the evacuation of Andalsnes on the last day of April. Two days passed before the French ambassador learned of this breach of faith.[48]

Thus only Narvik was still to be attempted. Chamberlain penned these private lines: "This has been one of the worst, if not *the* worst, week of the war. We hadn't reckoned on the way in which the Germans had poured in reinforcements of men, guns, tanks, and aeroplanes. In particular this brief campaign has taught our people, many of whom were much in need of teaching, the importance of the air factor."

The First Lord returned to his manuscripts, to chew over his *History* with Lord Birkenhead and historian F.W. Deakin. Elsewhere in the building, Edwards was writing his own pocket diary:

> This is too awful, the way we're going to scuttle out of Norway. Winston thinks we can save our face by holding Narvik.

Viewed from the Operations division, this seemed "utter nonsense." Viewed by Churchill, however, it was not just saving face. He saw Narvik as a major base for a mighty Allied army. He began drafting a paper setting out its future defences — half the scale of Scapa's in guns and searchlights; the airfield enlarged, the anti-submarine installations improved. For the time being, however, it was still in an Austrian general's hands.

Among the messages that Captain Edwards saw on the twenty-eighth were "pertinent questions from Paris." Reynaud was baffled by what was going on; the French contingent at Namsos had their tails well up, he said, and on the twenty-ninth he cabled Ambassador Corbin to urge the British not to evacuate.[49]

On the last day of April, as the evacuation nonetheless began, Chamberlain circularized his colleagues about Winston's new military secretariat. The First Lord accepted the new arrangments in a smug note: "I shall try my best to make all go smoothly."[50]

He had decided that the assault on Narvik should continue. "To implement this decision (of the 1st Lord's)," as Captain Edwards now underlined in his diary, "we impose a terrible strain on the fleet."

> An enormous L[ine] of C[ommunications] across the enemy's new front door. I am not clear why we want Narvik unless it's to walk into Sweden & seize the ore mines. We now have no national policy or no naval policy and we just muddle along. It's deplorable.

That night, Intelligence gave fresh warning that Hitler was about to attack Holland. Desperately tired Edwards ran Churchill, Pound and his deputy to earth in the First Lord's room ("They were all talking about Narvik . . . all half asleep") and persuaded them to move minelayers to the south and warn the War Office.

At about the same time Paul Reynaud got on the telephone to Chamberlain about the plan to bomb Stalin's oilfields. He said that General Maxime Weygand, French commander in the Middle East, could be ready by May the fifteenth. Chamberlain remarked on the delay. Reynaud explained that Turkey was raising "steeper demands each day" for overflight permission.

A Gestapo agent in Paris obtained an illicit transcript of their conversation from his mistress, a French telephone operator. He rushed it to Berlin. With minor changes, Hitler would use it in the Reichstag in partial justification for the next outrage he was about to spring upon the world.[51]

CHAPTER 22

Hence Prime Minister

YEARS LATER, WHEN Churchill wrote about Norway, he would tidy up the blunders and distemper over the shortcomings — the rash unloading of the troops, the reloading only for an unopposed landing; the incorrect weapons, the inadequate equipment, the inappropriate ammunition, the insufficient instructions; the bomber pilots equipped only with a 1912 Baedeker; the admiralty charts that showed no contours around Narvik; his own over-confident diversion of half of Mackesy's infantry and all his snow-trained French mountain troops from Narvik to Namsos on April 14.

One thing was beyond dispute. His own role in the disaster had been central. A tide of dismay lapped around the government. Hore-Belisha, the former War Minister, was seen lobbying Members about how Mr Churchill had landed guns in one fiord and gunners in another, and talking of other admiralty oversights. Ominously, he reminded those who would listen that there was a precedent for a Select Committee of Inquiry — after the Dardanelles disaster.[1]

As the Cabinet privately rehearsed excuses for the fiasco, Anthony Eden wondered if Hitler conducted his councils in this manner.[2]* "The Tapers and Tadpoles are putting it around," wrote one Tory, alluding to the two Party fixers in Benjamin Disraeli's novel *Coningsby*, "that the whole Norwegian episode is due to Winston."[4] But his public esteem was too high to dismantle easily. Chamberlain sighed to Sir John Reith that somebody else would have to debunk him.[5]

The month ended with ugly allusions to Gallipoli in the columns of *The Times*, and the First Lord's prestige as low within the admiralty as it was without. Incoming signals of April 28 had seen the Admirals

---

*He did. Referring to Hitler's unforgiveable nervous crisis on April 17, 1940 over Narvik, an O.K.W. officer wrote angrily a week later: "The consequence was a string of orders which delved almost exclusively into details scarcely capable of being judged from Berlin, and which were often changed soon after."[3]

Forbes and Cork having "their usual bicker," as Captain Edwards called it in his extraordinary diary. "Winston entered the fray & decided against the staff's decision — oh, the interference & we aren't strong enough to stand up to him. Scuttle from Norway goes on."

LET US NOW return to his political friends, of whom we heard little during the excitement of the military campaign.

As April 1940 ended, fierce political manoeuvring began. The bitter plight of the troops at Narvik, the perils of the evacuation, the imminence of the western campaign: all were set aside — and it was not only the English politicians who saw their chance to profit from Britain's misfortune. Unsurprisingly, at the Zionist Office there was talk of using the Norway crisis to show "how ill the Allies can do without Jews if war spreads," and to warn of the "risk of bloodshed in [the] Holy Land if present policy continues."[6]

To people like Beaverbrook and Bracken, Churchill's career seemed in danger of eclipse. "Brendan," recorded a witness of one conversation between them, "made defence of Winston, said it was untrue that he lost his nerve."[7]

If Mr Churchill was to mend his fences, he could do so only in the lobbies of the House. "Politics," Lord Roseberry had once said, "is an evil smelling bog," and shortly the First Lord was mired into that bog right up to his chin. Everybody knew what Winston was about. Visiting No.10 on the first evening in May, as an unseasonally cold gust of wind rafted the leaves and litter across Horse Guards Parade, he commented, "If I were the First of May, I should be ashamed of myself," and the PM's secretary reflected: Personally I think *Churchill* ought to be ashamed of himself.[8]

It was close-hauled, the struggle that now began. The older hands recognized that for Chamberlain this was the end-game. By inviting Churchill to chair the Military Co-ordination Committee on April 4, he had fed out a few more inches of hangman's rope to him. But whose head would now be in the noose? And if Chamberlain fell, who could succeed him — Halifax? Eden? Few thought seriously of Churchill. He was the only obvious successor, reflected Ironside in private; only to dismiss that thought from his mind — perhaps recollecting the First Lord's "half tight" visit to his office on the eleventh. "He is too unstable."[9]

Lord Davies urged Beaverbrook to "plump for Winston" and topple Chamberlain as once he had brought down Asquith.[10] The press lord returned an impassive reply. His daily newspaper published an article playing down the Norway fiasco, but in private his views were uncompromising. "Churchill?" he expostulated to an associate at this time, "He's the man who let the Germans into Norway."[11]

In the event other heads would roll, those of Forbes and Mackesy, and finally of the prime minister himself. As the government crashed in flames Mr Churchill survived, and this portly Phoenix would write with one suspects more than a trace of relish: "Failure at Trondheim! Stalemate at Narvik!. . . It was a marvel that I survived and maintained my position in public esteem and Parliamentary confidence."[12]

He survived because he and his friends had tilled the swampy ground of Parliament assiduously, and he could now watch his seedlings grow with seeming detachment. The PM's secretary jotted down one government official's assessment that while Winston himself was remaining loyal to the prime minister, "his satellites" — and here the names of Duff Cooper and Leo Amery were mentioned — "were doing all in their power to create mischief and ill-feeling."[13]

This mischief making had begun earlier in 1940. Duff Cooper told a Zionist assembly in Washington D.C. that in face of rising antisemitism Britain must unambiguously side with the Jews, and that there were large areas elsewhere for the Arabs "should they be reluctant to stay on in Palestine." "I feel that Churchill will take Chamberlain's place," one London newspaper reported him as saying. "He is a great organizer, and has the confidence of the people."[14]

"Winston," observed one diarist MP "is being lauded by both the Socialist and Liberal oppositions, and being tempted to lead a revolt against the PM." That evening, May 1, as the painful evacuation of six thousand troops from Namsos began, Members saw him drinking and roaring with laughter in the Smoking Room with Archie Sinclair the Liberal leader and Socialist A.V. Alexander — "The new Shadow Cabinet," as one witness prophetically recorded.[15]

BRITISH INTELLIGENCE HEARD rumblings like those preceding Norway — indications that Hitler's next move was imminent. They were ignored. No naval steps were taken. On May 1 Captain Edwards found no forces available for the Channel front other than five destroyers at Dover. Everything else was tied down by Churchill's "wildcat adventure up to Narvik," where Lord Cork was still drafting plans for his assault.

> They're "crackers" on the project and I'm quite sure we shan't be able to hold it without expending a disproportionate effect on doing so. Winston again — ye gods, he's a menace.

The First Lord surfaced at the House on the following day, tired out, barely able to recite his speech before having to be literally led away. Commented one Fleet Street veteran, "It is in times like these that age and excessive brandy drinking tell."[16]

Chamberlain was optimistic about the political crisis, writing to his sister on the fourth from Chequers, "I don't think my enemies will get me down this time." But as the post-mortem began on Norway — as the shot and shell began to fall around Chamberlain — Churchill edged away from him, perhaps doubting his own immortality. "I had some very unhappy experiences in the last war," he told A.V. Alexander, "when my Naval advisers, after the event, said they had differed from me all along."[17] Alexander repeating this to Hugh Dalton, added that some people were saying that Winston had lost his nerve, that he could not forget the Dardanelles, that he was acting now "like a singed cat." This saddened Winston's admirers in the Labour Party: they were setting store by him as their last hope of effecting a Socialist revolution in England.

For a while Churchill wilted. The adrenalin had ceased to flow. At one committee on the fourth Ironside found him somnolent and listless. "He took quietly what we said," he wrote, puzzled, "without demur." The trouble was still Narvik — "He wants it taken, and yet doesn't dare give any direct order to Cork."[18]

On the sixth the latter admiral forwarded fresh objections from the generals — they lacked landing craft, information, suitable beaches, smoke shells, and any means of digging into the frozen, rocky ground.[19] Edwards called him "a busted flush." He saw that Cork's proposals would mean a protracted battle of problematical outcome — "Not at all suited to Mr W.C." The Cabinet were doing their utmost to drive the admiral to action. Edwards commented, "Political face saving is so necessary."

IT WAS PARLIAMENT that lit the political powder keg when it met to consider Norway on the seventh. As Chamberlain entered there were ironic cries of "missed the bus!" — his jibe at Hitler of the month before.

At first the debate proceeded smoothly. Both Labour and Liberals were still undecided to make it an issue of confidence. That afternoon the *Evening Standard* hinted at an early general election but Labour had no desire for that: Hugh Dalton adjudged that Chamberlain would wipe the floor with them. Thus they trod a narrow plank between criticism and censure, willing to wound but afraid to destroy. Archie Sinclair spoke early, and did not spare Churchill for all their thirty years of friendship. "Is it not a fact," he challenged, "that the Prime Minister and the First Lord have led the people to believe the impossible about this adventure, which was never thought out and which was never taken to the end?"

In the course of that day the prime minister made one odd mistake, which may have saved Mr Churchill's bacon: asked by Labour's Herbert Morrison when the arrangement had been made for Winston to chair the military co-ordination committee, Chamberlain in his reply gave mistakenly the date on which he had *confirmed* it to the House, April the eleventh. He should have said the Fourth, five days before the Norwegian operation. But even when asked whether the appointment covered the period of the Norwegian operations, he replied: "I appreciate the point. No, it was not before the Norwegian operation; it has only been made recently."[20]

The injury to his administration after that first day's debate was grievous, but not fatal. Still angered about Trondheim, Admiral Keyes had entered in full uniform with six rows of medal ribbons, delivered a powerful attack on the naval staff, and sat down to thunderous applause. Captain Edwards recorded, "Roger Keyes spilled the beans but ruined it all by saying W.S.C. was the genius we should trust. Nothing could be worse!"

Overnight, however, Fleet Street — itself partially to blame for having raised such false hopes early in the campaign — began braying for Chamberlain's blood. On the second day, May 8, Labour decided to risk a vote of confidence. Somehow Churchill rode out the storm in one of the most tortuous performances of his career. Kennedy attributed his salvation to the Party organization handled by Margesson the Chief Whip, "like a cheer leader or like the Tammany bosses used to handle Tammany." The American ambassador, watching from the distinguished persons' gallery, found himself wondering what would happen if Hitler now invaded Holland: Would the opposition temporarily abate?[21] He would shortly have his answer.

Rattled by the clamour, Chamberlain conceded that Britain had suffered a loss of prestige. Under attack by Keyes and Lloyd George, to Kennedy he looked in bad shape. Churchill played his hand magnificently — generous, protective, deprecatory, spirited, charitable, confessive. When Lloyd George flamboyantly insinuated that the First Lord had been let down by his admiralty colleagues, he jumped to his feet to declaim: "I take full responsibility for everything that has been done at the Admiralty." Lloyd George retorted that Mr Churchill "must not allow himself to be converted into an air-raid shelter to keep the splinters from hitting his colleagues." Churchill murmured to Walter Elliott, "Absolutely devastating."

At ten p.m. he rose to conclude for the Government, a masterpiece of debating skill — still insisting that it was Hitler who had blundered, that on balance the result rested with the Allies. This, he declared, was the time to set aside feuds and hatreds and conserve them for their common enemy. His private staff, who crowded the official box, were uneasy about the scintillating performance: his secretary John Peck felt that "somehow it did not ring entirely true." Their master was enjoying himself more than was seemly — relishing, as Chips Channon also observed, the irony of defending a cause in which he did not believe.

The speech was full of fire, but it was the cold flame of artificial pyrotechnics, and lacked warmth. The vote was distasteful for Chamberlain. His majority was disastrously reduced — sixty Tories had abstained, thirty had voted against him; 281 had voted for his government, and two hundred against; the No lobby buzzed with speculation. While the Chamber refilled, there rose a rhythmic stamping of feet on the wooden floor, and the opposition benches rang with the cry of "resign." Josiah Wedgwood started singing Rule Britannia, drowned in turn by a chant of "Go, go, go, go!"

As Chamberlain stalked out of the rowdy Chamber, the Chief Whip signalled to his henchmen to rise and cheer; the prime minister was visibly pale and angry.[22]

In later private conversation Churchill would often hark back to that debate and the tactical mistakes that Chamberlain made. It had presented him with a wonderful opportunity: "The stars in their courses fought at my side," he reminisced. "I was able to defend my Chief to the utmost and win only esteem and support in so doing." No one could say, he would add, that he had been disloyal: "I never have done that sort of thing."[23]

At the admiralty the officers were aghast at the distinct possibility that Churchill would profit from Chamberlain's humiliation.

> The danger to my mind [wrote the acting Director of Operations that night] is that out of it will come . . . a Govn headed by that arch-idiot Winston. I'm quite certain he's played the whole of this last eight months to become P.M., often at the expense of helping to win the war. As witness the way he never backed us against the Air.

To which uncharitable speculation he added, exasperated: "The high ups . . . still insist on going on with the mad Narvik project."

To maintain that operation the admiralty was still committing to those waters one battleship, three aircraft carriers, seven cruisers and twenty-one destroyers.[24]

* * *

On the second day of this great Debate the admiralty had sent a cautiously phrased signal to Lord Cork, saying that according to "our information" the German effort at Narvik was flagging.[25] In January the S.I.S. had made its first major break into the German airforce codes. More significantly, in mid April they had manually solved the special code introduced five days earlier for the German airforce and army in

Norway. These early intercepts have vanished from the files, but it would explain Mr Churchill's frustration with Lord Cork and General Mackesy if he had read echoes of the frantic signals from Berlin when Hitler lost his nerve and seemed about to abandon Narvik.

* * *

So wrapped up was Churchill in the political jockeying that he did not act upon the accumulating evidence that Hitler was on the point of attacking Holland and Belgium. On May 8 the Dutch naval staff notified Gerald Dickens, the British naval attaché at The Hague:

> The same source in Berlin who predicted the attack on Denmark has telegraphed that an attack on Holland and Belgium and the western Front will start to-morrow morning if flying conditions are good: if not, within a few days. . . The Dutch have also had warning of an early attack from a Vatican source.*

The British attaché informed the French government direct. At five p.m. the Dutch cancelled all leave.

Independently of this the headquarters of the British airforces in France (B.A.F.F.) — whose reconnaissance planes that day had sighted 400 tanks massing in woods to the east of the Ardennes — warned units of the B.E.F. that an enemy attack on Belgium was "likely within a few days."[26]

Both in the B.E.F. and in Whitehall the warning was disbelieved. At I Corps some key personnel were still on leave. The War Office announced that there was still no sign of imminent invasion of Belgium or France.[27] Over in the admiralty the politician who had so vehemently warned of Hitler's military ambitions, was now preoccupied with the fulfilment of ambitions of his own.

Chamberlain had still not resigned, but all Whitehall was mooting his successor. Bracken confided to Kennedy that while not objecting to a Halifax Cabinet, Mr Churchill would not join it; which effectively squelched that.

Later that evening Kennedy strolled over to Beaverbrook: his diplomats had learned that Hitler would attack in the morning; the newspaper owner recalled having telephoned Winston. The ambassador himself telephoned around Mr Churchill and the other notables. "Everybody is mad," he noted, after hours on the telephone. "They all

---

*The author found this warning in Reynaud's papers. Colonel Hans Oster, a traitor in the Abwehr, had tipped off the Dutch military attaché in Berlin, Major G.J. Sas; the German wiretap agency *Forschungsamt* heard Sas report it to The Hague. The Vatican's tip-off had come from Dr Joseph Miller, another Abwehr traitor.

want to do something and go places; but nobody has the slightest idea of what should be done. Chamberlain, Halifax and Churchill are unquestionably tired men."[28]

MAY THE NINTH: The day had dawned clear and warm, tulips carpeted the London parks. Flying conditions could hardly be better. From Naval Intelligence came word that Germany had suddenly sailed a minelaying force, had severed communications with Holland, had transmitted a string of radio signals to German merchant vessels such as had preceded Hitler's Norway coup.[29] At Admiralty House Churchill's mind was still elsewhere.

As he took his Valet safety razor he sent for Eden and told him — while shaving — that in his view a National Government would have to be formed. Chamberlain would have to resign, since he would be unable to persuade Labour to come in.[30] They had already refused him in September.

Churchill and Eden met several times that day. Coming over to Admiralty House to explain the German fleet movements and the naval staff's hope of catching them, Captain Edwards found them both in a huddle with the Liberal leader Archie Sinclair too. "Cabinet meeting?", Edwards mused sarcastically in his diary: that was what he suspected.

Labour and the Liberals had an ambivalent attitude toward this war. A year earlier they had opposed National Service. Now Labour seemed to prefer Lord Halifax to Mr Churchill. The latter had sent Bracken to ask Clement Attlee outright a day or two before whether he would serve under Winston; but the prim, schoolmasterly Labour leader had replied that they "had never forgiven Churchill for Tonypandy," when he had ordered soldiers to fire on striking miners.[31]

On the eighth the leading Labour doctrinist Hugh Dalton had told Halifax's under-secretary, R.A. Butler, that there was much to be said for his master. Butler set out in a letter, which is among Halifax's papers, the terms on which Labour would enter a National Government. Halifax was their only choice; "Churchill," quoted Butler, "must stick to the war." Now, on May 9, Attlee's position softened — he agreed it lay between the two contenders.[32] Churchill probably heard of this when Beaverbrook came to see him during the forenoon. "Do you intend," Beaverbrook asked, according to his pencilled notes, "to serve under Halifax?" "I will serve," Churchill replied, obliquely, "under any Minister capable of prosecuting the War."[33]

When Randolph Churchill telephoned him from his Territorial Army unit at Kettering, his father said: "I may be in a big position tonight."[34] By noon Ambassador Kennedy had learned that the 1922 Committee — the powerful body of Conservative backbenchers — had sent for Chamberlain at two-thirty p.m. and demanded a Cabinet reshuffle. By lunchtime, Churchill had learned — because over that meal he passed it on to Eden and Kingsley Wood — that Chamberlain had decided to resign.

How to ensure that the ancient tree, shortly to be felled, toppled in the right direction? Suppose the PM recommended to His Majesty, as was his traditional right, Lord Halifax? Kingsley Wood suggested that Chamberlain would be rooting for Halifax, and would invite Churchill to give his blessing. *"Don't agree,"* — that was Kingsley Wood's urgent advice to his long-time friend — *"and don't say anything."*[35]

AT FOUR-THIRTY P.M. that day, Churchill walked across Horse Guards Parade to see Chamberlain and Halifax together — knowing it was to be the most important hour of his life. Chamberlain talked of national unity and confirmed that he was ready to resign if Labour refused to serve under him.

There followed the discussion which Kingsley Wood had rehearsed with Churchill. Chamberlain said that Lord Halifax was the man mentioned as most acceptable.

All too generously, Halifax replied, "I think Winston would be the better choice."

If he expected a modest shake of the head from Churchill he was disappointed. The First Lord remained Sphinx-like — immobile and silent. ("Winston," Halifax related to Sir Alec Cadogan shortly afterwards, "did *not* demur.")

Halifax courteously continued. It would surely be impossible for him to function as prime minister from the House of Lords. "It would be a hopeless position," he said. "I should be a cypher."

Churchill with equal courtesy agreed. The Chief Whip and others, he ventured, believed that feeling had been veering towards him. (In fact Margesson had advised Chamberlain the House would prefer Halifax.[36])

At 6:15 p.m. he sent for Attlee and his deputy Greenwood and put the questions: would they serve under the present leadership; or under any other? The two Labour leaders laboriously wrote these questions down and explained that they must consult with their brothers down in Bournemouth — their Party, with exquisite sense of national priorities, had convened its annual party conference at this South Coast resort.[37]

Churchill, nothing if not a wily warrior, "at this point made an impassioned plea to them to join under Chamberlain." So Kennedy learned from one participant. Attlee and Greenwood were unmoved and left for Waterloo station.

Churchill returned to the admiralty, to sketch his first Cabinet. Over dinner with Anthony Eden, he explained that Halifax did not wish to succeed to the premiership. He, Churchill, would invite Mr Chamberlain to remain as leader of the House; he would appoint Anthony to the War Office; he would assume for himself the style of "Minister of Defence" as well as prime minister.[38]

From all sides came voices from the past, confirming that the battle was won. Robert Boothby, his former secretary, wrote about the feeling of the House: neither Labour, nor Sinclair, nor "our group" — which had met that afternoon — would "touch Chamberlain" at any price. Boothby was now working to harden opinion against Lord Halifax; the concensus was that Winston was the "inevitable Prime Minister."[39] Lady Violet wrote in the same, if more flowery, vein.

* * *

While these jealous democrats had prowled around each other in London, the dictator in Berlin had acted. A secret train had conveyed Adolf Hitler and his staff overnight to the western front.

Before dawn of the following day, a mild and lovely late spring morning, he suddenly uncoiled his armies westwards. Ghastly messages gate-crashed Churchill's triumphant slumber at Admiralty House. The first, at 5:20 a.m., was that the Wehrmacht had stormed across the frontier into Holland. Still in his silken pyjamas, he telephoned the French ambassador: would both Allied armies nonetheless move forward into Belgium now? Monsieur Corbin called back almost at once — the Panzer divisions were rolling into Belgium too. Hoare and Stanley arrived, still ministers for Air and War, and conferred with him over breakfast. Hoare, a timorous soul, marvelled at the First Lord's composure: tucking into eggs and bacon and chomping on a cigar as though nothing untoward was happening.[40]

Setting aside — briefly — the struggle for power, his mind was on the movements of fleets and armies again. The risks were real, and adrenalin was flowing in the old way.

By seven a.m., when his Military Co-ordination Committee met, both the indignant neutrals had appealed for Allied help. Mr Churchill had ordered the B.E.F. across the frontier into Belgium. No vacillations or last-minute hitches this time: a well-oiled scheme was working. "All our movements," wrote Halifax, relieved, "[have] been for once prepared to the last gaiter-button."

Churchill was exhilarated; but so too was Hitler. Months later, with his armies already hammering on the gates of Moscow, Hitler would still remember the thrill of that instant: "When the news came that the enemy was advancing [into Belgium] . . . I could have wept for joy! They'd fallen right into my trap! It was a crafty move on our part, to strike toward Liege — we had to make them believe we were remaining faithful to the old Schlieffen Plan."[41]

An emergency War Cabinet had been called for eight a.m.

Before Churchill and his two colleagues set out from Admiralty House, his son came on the phone again. "What about what you told me last night?" he asked.

"Oh," replied Winston, affecting a nonchalant air. "I don't know about that. Nothing matters now except beating the enemy."[42]

The mood at No.10 was overcast by a joyless stream of incoming reports: enemy paratroops were already dropping into Holland. Churchill's report was the only bright news — he assured his colleagues that he had set in motion the pre-arranged advance into Belgium.

IN ENGLAND LIFE went its normal way. With doughty defiance of Hitler and his grand strategy, the entire National Executive of the Labour Party had again caught the 11:34 for Bournemouth. Dalton, sharing a black cab with Attlee to Waterloo, asked for the Ministry of Economic Warfare when the National Government was formed.[43]

At No.10 however Chamberlain was having second thoughts. "As I expected," he wrote to Beaverbrook, "Hitler has seized the occasion of our divisions to strike the great blow and we cannot consider changes in the Government while we are in the throes of battle."

The logic was compelling. He persuaded Hoare, he convinced Sinclair, he repeated it to another minister in a personal letter which the American ambassador saw. "Hitler's picking the moment to strike when we are divided has changed the entire situation," this letter read. "I propose to remain. The next three or four days' battle will determine the fate of civilization for the next one hundred years."[44]

But his enemies, having dislodged him this far, were not going to be cheated now. Bracken was heard to snarl, "It's as hard getting rid of him as getting a leech off a corpse."[45] He jangled the alarm to Paul Emrys Evans. Evans phoned Lord Salisbury, and his Lordship told them to insist on Churchill's appointment as prime minister before the day was out.[46] Kingsley Wood, to whom Churchill had promised the Treasury, was no less disconcerted at the change that had come over Chamberlain, and persuaded him of the need for a National Government to confront this crisis and told Churchill of this at ten a.m.

Some of the Labour leaders wanted Parliament recalled immediately. More seasoned hands like Dalton advised against it, arguing that "this would give the cheer leaders and crisis-exploiters a chance to rehabilitate the Old Man."[47]

With so much at stake — his political future — Churchill had little of his mind on the great land battle in Holland and Belguim. The Dutch Ministers had arrived from Amsterdam to see him, with horror written across haggard faces. But what could he offer by way of comfort? That naval demolition teams were even now crossing the Channel in destroyers to blow up the great Dutch refineries and port installations to prevent Hitler getting them?[48]

The War Cabinet met again at eleven-thirty. On his recommendation, it sent his querulous friend Sir Roger Keyes to liaise with the King of the Belgians.[49] Other plans were put in hand. British forces would seize Curaçao in the Dutch West Indies to prevent Nazi sabotage to the oil facilities there. The first fluvial mines would be fed into the Rhine that evening.

As Churchill gathered his thoughts, he lunched alone with Beaverbrook. At the third War Cabinet at four-thirty the news was that Nazi paratroops had seized Rotterdam airport and that troop carrying planes were landing; but in Belgium British troops had already advanced to the line of the River Dyle. The Chief of Air Staff, Sir Cyril Newall, suggested they now bomb the Ruhr, Germany's vital industrial region, but that decision was postponed.

Late that afternoon a note was handed to Chamberlain, and he told his colleagues that it was Labour's answer. Speaking from a coin 'phone in Bournemouth a Labour spokesperson had telephoned their Party's refusal to serve under him.[50] Mr Chamberlain accordingly declared that he proposed to resign that evening, in favour of the First Lord.[51]

The news struck a chill through the admiralty.

> Winston is P.M. [wrote Captain Edwards that day.] He told me so himself when I took him some news about yesterday's operations. . . I distrust the man and think it is a tragedy. God send I'm wrong.

The fleet had also watched the "racket in Parliament" with distaste, bordering on dismay. "They think more of politics than they do of the war," wrote the Commander-in-Chief, Mediterranean, in a private letter. "Winston has got what he has been intriguing for. I don't know if he will stick the course. He lives at a high rate."[52]

THE ROYAL SUMMONS reached Churchill some hours later, and he hurried to the Palace.

The Monarch had doubted his integrity every since the Abdication, but was prepared to see what this new leader could do. "I suppose," he stuttered with forced humour, "you don't know why I have sent for you?"

Truckling to his style, Churchill replied: "Sir, I simply couldn't imagine why."

Back at the admiralty, he wrote fine words to Chamberlain:

The example which you have set of self-forgetting dignity and public spirit will govern the action of many, and be an inspiration to all.

His telephone rang: it was Ambassador Kennedy, profuse with congratulations. In his jaunty manner, the American claimed that he himself had played a vital role in securing for him the keys of office.

"You," he continued to the puzzled First Lord, "conceived the plan to mine the Norwegian territorial waters. But I was the one to obtain Roosevelt's consent."

Churchill still did not understand.

Kennedy chuckled. "Hence Norway," he said, and laughed out loud. "Hence prime minister!"[53]

Let us end this chapter of Mr Churchill's life not with the irreverence of the American ambassador, but with the sombre, historic note that he himself struck in recalling his emotions in his memoirs. "I felt that I was walking with destiny," he would write of this day, "And that all my past life had been but a preparation for this hour and for this trial."

CHAPTER 23

Rogue Elephant

WAR IS A game to be played with a smiling face," Churchill had once declared.[1] The new prime minister smiled as he blamed the defeat in Norway on traitors like Vidkum Quisling and on his compatriots who had failed to destroy tunnels and viaducts to prevent German reinforcements reaching Trondheim.[2] As Hitler opened his western offensive, Winston smiled again, blamed the overrunning of the Low Countries once more on traitors, and relied on his friend General Georges and his indomitable Army of the North-East for victory in France.

For the time being he remained at Admiralty House, as an act of charity to Mr Chamberlain; but also because he knew how fragile were the buildings in Downing-street.

The staff at No.10 feared it was the end of an era all the same. Chamberlain's secretary dourly hoped that his old master would soon be back in office.[3] Overseas reactions to Winston's assumption of power were equally mixed. Canada's Mackenzie-King cabled support, but Roosevelt did not — when the news irrupted into his own Cabinet he remarked that though Churchill was the best man that England had he was drunk half of the time. Winston was, he could not forget, one of the few public men who had ever been rude to him.[4]

For the first three days, Churchill barely applied his mind to the battle. He had old accounts to settle. Lord Hankey had rebuked him in 1938 over his "pumping [of] serving officers" for material to abuse the government with; suspecting that Winston had never forgiven him he wrote a letter of resignation but was awarded a minor ministerial office.[5]

Visiting Churchill on the eleventh to report on the XD teams' swift demolition of oil, power, harbour and coastal installations in the Low Countries, Hankey found the offices in chaos and Chamberlain in despair. "The dictator," he wrote to Sam Hoare, "instead of dictating, was engaged in a sordid wrangle with the politicians of the Left about the secondary offices." He saw some hope of stability in the solid core of Churchill, Chamberlain and Halifax: "But whether the wise old elephants will ever be able to hold the Rogue Elephant, I doubt."[6] (The allusion was to a memorable cartoon by Mark Sykes.)

Labour had been swept out of office in 1931; recently, they had feared that a snap election would bury them for good. Now they were exploiting the military crisis to ram vital elements of the class struggle down Churchill's throat, divining that there were few high Tory principles he would not sacrifice to entrench his government. That afternoon he offered two War Cabinet seats out of five to Labour men — Attlee and Greenwood. Ernest Bevin, the earthy, honest and capable boss of the transport workers' union, agreed to serve as labour minister — but only after extracting promises that union legislation would be revised.

Winston's stalwart friends of The Focus were well rewarded. He brought into No.10 a wagonload of friends described by shuddering permanent officials like Alec Cadogan as "the most awful people." Lindemann, Morton and Bracken headed the list, and joined eagerly in the massacre of the rest. Sir Horace Wilson, head of the civil service and Chamberlain's chief adviser, was physically evicted immediately. "The day Winston took over," Harold Macmillan snickered to a Labour intimate, "Sir H. Quisling came to his room as usual, but found that the 'parachute troops' were already in possession. Bracken and Randolph Churchill, the latter in uniform, were sitting on the sofa. No words were exchanged. These two stared fixedly at Sir H.Q., who silently withdrew, never to return." Churchill gave Wilson until two p.m. to get out. "Tell that man," exploded Winston, when Wilson pleaded for four more hours, "that if that room is not cleared by two I will make him Minister to Iceland."[7]

Pandering to the other Party organizations, he selected the Liberal leader Archie Sinclair as air minister, and A.V. Alexander, a Labour politician, as First Lord. These men would hold those offices throughout the war, in name at least: neither would seriously oppose him. Eden became secretary of war by virtue of the same distinction. As for Winston's own new post of Minister of Defence, he told his chief of staff Pug Ismay, "We must be careful not to define our powers too precisely" — in fact he intended to set the limits at infinity. Alexander, a former grocer, impressed few (though it is fair to mention that Sir Robert Menzies, Australia's most enlightened prime minister, grew to admire the new First Lord). His appointment confirmed Captain Edwards' suspicions as to Churchill's real reason for remaining at Admiralty House: "I suspect him of becoming PM *and* 1st Lord. God help the Empire. It's a disaster."

The reshuffle met with a frosty royal disapproval. The King later confided to Roosevelt's emissary that he had a low opinion of Churchill's ministers. He baulked at having to appoint Winston's carrot-topped retainer Brendan Bracken to the Privy Council. Mr Churchill was adamant. "Mr Bracken," he reminded the King's private secretary, "has sometimes been almost my sole supporter in the years when I have been striving to get this country properly defended, especially from the air. He has suffered as I have done every form of official hostility."

The King frowned even more upon Lord Beaverbrook; he had not forgotten the Abdication crisis, and knew of Canadian hostility to this man.[8] Churchill hired him nonetheless and did not regret it. He had been out of power too long, perhaps, and needed a political insider whose brains he could pick. So we find them eating together on the eleventh, and whiling away a whole afternoon together on the twelfth. Shamelessly fawning on the new PM, a few hours later Beaverbrook wrote him: "I remember a trainload of Blue Jackets at Victoria Station cheering you wildly after you were dismissed from the Admiralty in 1915"[9] Having learned in Norway belated lessons about air power, Churchill created a new ministry, of aircraft production, and gave it to this potent Canadian — one of the more inspired appointments in his Cabinet.

As for the rest, Churchill appointed the Cockney London leader Herbert Morrison to the ministry of supply. Telephoning Hugh Dalton to offer him the ministry of economic warfare that he coveted — at the controls of the subversive war — he apologized, "Well, if you'll excuse ceremony, I'll have that announced tonight. Time is pressing, and it's a life and death struggle." "You'll take the oath tromorrow," he added, "the Privy Council office will tell you when."[10] The Treasury found itself handed to the insipid Sir Kingsley Wood, a politician singularly innocent of qualifications. *The Economist* called it a disaster, but we know from Dalton's diary that Wood, like Macmillan, had judiciously kept in cahoots with Labour. The succession of Winston's other champion Duff Cooper to the ministry of information caused pain throughout Whitehall.

Not everybody was willingly seduced. Offered a lowly post at the ministry of food, Emanuel Shinwell telephoned that it was "a bloody insult."[11] Churchill bestowed it on Boothby instead. Stanley, eased out of the War Office to make way for Eden, also refused a lesser office. "There were a number of times," he confessed to the new PM, "on which I questioned your judgment."[12]

This process of Cabinet-making distracted him until three a.m. on the thirteenth when he grew bored with the process. "My government," he told Macmillan, "is the most broad based that Britain has ever known."[13] He summoned them to the admiralty that afternoon. "I have nothing to offer," he told them, "but blood, toil, tears and sweat." He rather liked the sound of that. Glancing up as though the skies might fill with Hitler's bombers at any moment, he commented to Dalton afterwards, not without pleasurable anticipation, "I expect all these buildings will look a bit different in two or three weeks' time."[14]

* * *

His popularity was still volatile. He stepped into the Chamber that day to near silence, while Chamberlain was cheered — "a terrific reception" as one MP recorded in puzzlement.[15]

When it was Winston's turn to rise, he repeated those ringing words: "I have nothing to offer but blood, toil, tears and sweat." "You ask," he said, "what is our policy? I will say: it is to wage war, by sea, land and air, with all our might and with all the strength that God can give us; to wage war against a monstrous tyranny, never surpassed in the dark, lamentable catalogue of human crime. That is our policy."

As his car left him at the back gate to No.10, he heard voices murmur, "Good luck, Winnie," and, "God bless you."

"Poor people," he reflected, "I can give them nothing but disaster for quite a long time."[16]

THEN HITLER SPRUNG his ugliest surprise, and hurled his panzer divisions against France.

In four days the catastrophe would be so complete that the confusion over Norway was as nothing in comparison. Cabinets would meet several times a day; meetings would overlap; orders would be issued, re-issued, countermanded: frequently no records would be taken.

Churchill was a driven man — propelled by a purpose more profound than any other: military victory alone, whatever the cost to his country, would expunge the blemishes left on his name by a history of defeats from Gallipoli to Norway. Such manic purpose was unlikely to prosper rational decision.

The horrifying, unexpected crisis in France broke on the afternoon of the fourteenth with a telephone call from Paul Reynaud. "The German army," he announced, "has smashed through our fortified lines south of Sedan." He implored Winston to send over ten more fighter squadrons. Without them he could not halt the enemy advance. "Between Sedan and Paris there are no fortifications."[17] There followed a hastily written note from the French ambassador appealing for massive air support: "M Paul Reynaud assesses that Germany has now unmasked her real intentions by throwing in everything she's got."

Now Churchill's affection for the French nearly proved Britain's undoing. Blinded by that emotion, he laboured mightily to give her those extra squadrons, although the air ministry warned earnestly that Britain herself needed sixty and was already down to thirty-nine. Meeting at six p.m. the chiefs of staff warned him not to humour France's panicky request.[18]

An hour later Reynaud telephoned again: monstrous tanks had crossed the Meuse and were trampling through the anti tank defences. Nothing stood between them and Paris. Churchill now agreed — so Reynaud told the American ambassador William C. Bullitt who saw him moments later — to send over every available plane.[19] But a gloomy and unpleasant Cabinet meeting again prevailed upon him to hesitate before further denuding London, heart of the British Empire. Even so, the reply which his secretary dictated by phone to Paris was not wholly discouraging — they were considering the French appeal, this said, but it would take time.[20]

STILL PUTTING THE finishing touches to his government Churchill retired to Admiralty House with his Chief Whip. Shaken by the day's events, he telephoned Beaverbrook to come over. The press lord had been drinking heavily. He listened to the ferocious news of Sedan and fled.[21]

Eden, Sinclair and Ismay dropped by, joined around midnight by the American ambassador with an alarming rumour from Rome — Mussolini seemed about to spring to Hitler's aid. The scene was well depicted by John Colville whom the PM had inherited from Chamberlain as private secretary: "They walked about," he wrote, "talking to each other, while Winston popped in and out, first through one door and then the next, appointing Under-Secretaries . . . talking about the German threat to Sedan with Eden, and listening to the alarmist, and, I think, untrustworthy opinions of Mr Kennedy."[22]

According to Kennedy, Churchill blurted out that the war was lost, and he was going to appeal to Roosevelt.

"What can we do," inquired Kennedy, "that won't leave us holding the bag?"

He cabled Washington immediately he returned to the embassy, at two a.m.: "He [Churchill] considers the chances of the Allies winning is [sic] slight with the entrance of Italy."

"You know our strength," I said. "If we wanted to help all we can, what could we do? You don't need credit or money now; the bulk of our navy is in the Pacific ocean, our army is not up to requirements, and we haven't sufficient airplanes for our own use. So what could we do if this is going to be a quick war all over in a few months?"

Churchill suggested America lend thirty or forty old destroyers (Britain had lost nine off Norway.) He himself would never give up, "even if England were burnt to the ground." "Why," he told Kennedy, "the Government will move, take the fleet with it to Canada and fight on."[23]

Churchill drafted a telegram to Roosevelt, signed "Former Naval Person." It began, "Although I have changed my office, I am sure you would not wish me to discontinue our intimate, private correspondence." He predicted that Hitler would attack Britain soon. "If necessary," he reiterated, "we shall continue the war alone and we are not afraid of that." He warned what would happen if Roosevelt should hesitate too long. "You may have a completely subjugated, Nazified Europe established with astonishing swiftness, and the weight may be more than we can bear." Britain's first need, he amplified, was for the loan of "forty or fifty" destroyers; after that, aircraft; anti-aircraft guns; ammunition, and steel. "We shall go on paying dollars for as long as we can," he promised, "but I should like to feel reasonably sure that when we can pay no more you will give us the stuff all the same."[24]

HE SNATCHED A few hours of sleep. At seven a.m. the telephone rang: it was the French prime minister again, in extreme agitation — "Nous sommes battus! We're beaten!" The enemy was cascading through a fifty mile breach. The road to Paris was wide open. More British squadrons must be thrown in. "Nous avons perdu la bataille!" he kept repeating. "We've lost the battle!"

"*Impossible*!" shouted Churchill — in fact Reynaud told Bullitt that he screamed.[25] "That can't have happened so fast. All experience shows that after a time an offensive comes to a halt of its own accord. Remember March the Twenty-first, 1918!" This was no time to panic — surely the invaders must now be at their most vulnerable.

"Everything's changed," he heard Reynaud say. "There's a torrent of panzers pouring through."

Wide awake, Churchill retorted that whatever France elected to do, Britain would fight on — "if necessary alone."

He promised to urge his colleagues to release more fighter squadrons. Meanwhile he asked to speak to General Georges.[26] Locating the general was not easy: there were no communication links at all between Georges, the British commander Lord Gort, and General Gamelin, the French commander-in-chief. It was ten-thirty before Georges came on the phone. He confirmed the serious breach at Sedan, but was optimistic that it had been plugged.

Photographers, sensing the crisis, snapped Winston as he hurried across Horse Guards Parade to No.10 — scowling, in sombre suit, heavy watch chain and black homburg, carrying leather gloves and cane. Evasively, he assured the chiefs of staff that he had warned Georges that Britain had no squadrons to spare; Georges, he said, had "quite understood."[27] But the note of panic in Reynaud's voice had not escaped him, and he was contemplating crossing immediately to Paris to "sustain" his government.

The chief of air staff had received a direct appeal from Gamelin for ten fighter squadrons.[28] Bluff, broad-shouldered, Sir Cyril Newall was worried that Winston might fritter away their last squadrons in France. He persuaded his colleagues to give Sir Hugh Dowding, chief of R.A.F. Fighter Command, a hearing. Dowding made plain that he was against parting with a "single additional Hurricane." A gaunt moustached air chief marshal, Dowding was widely disliked in Whitehall. He had trodden on many toes; he had become a spiritualist too (though careful to reveal his belief in the occult only to those who shared his mystic persuasions, like Dill and Mackenzie-King.)*

Dowding carried the argument about squadrons into the War Cabinet that morning, May 15. Temporarily convinced, Churchill persuaded his colleagues to approve the strategic bombing of Germany as from that night — "the soundest action which we could take in the present situation," in Dowding's words. Luring the enemy airforce over Britain, Churchill explained, would relieve the pressure on France. The Cabinet decided to send no more squadrons to France "for the present."[30]

Of course, there were fallacies in the strategic argument: the bombers that would be used for an attack on Britain were very different from the units engaged over the battlefield; but Churchill had political reasons for wanting the air attack on Britain to begin, as will become apparent. He candidly repeated the strategic argument in a letter to Reynaud justifying the negative decision on the fighter squadrons.

> We are all agreed that it is better to draw the enemy onto this Island by striking at his vitals, and thus to aid the common cause.

He repeated his earlier observation on the phone: all experience of earlier wars lectured that the enemy's real difficulties were about to begin: they would certainly not be lessened merely by making a "bulge" in the front; they would in fact increase with each kilometre that the enemy advanced. So he reassured the nervous French prime minister.[31]

---

* In 1942 a Sunday newspaper mischievously reported a statement by Dowding: "I am sure that our war dead live on. I have read messages from them." He claimed to have received these through automatic writing. In April 1943 he offered to let Beaverbrook "see a number of messages from men killed on the battlefield in this war." His lordship understood what was meant, and tactfully declined.[29]

The fighter controversy continued on the sixteenth. Sinclair, the air minister, took the same line as Dowding. But the chiefs of staff had news that Hitler's troops had penetrated the vaunted Maginot Line. Stampeding refugees were clogging the roads. Gamelin again demanded ten squadrons, this time in a telegram to Churchill.[32] Churchill felt that he should comply, if only to put heart into the French soldiers. Newall advised sending four squadrons; Churchill suggested they add two more by weakening the Scapa defences, but Sinclair rebelled at this excessive generosity.

SEVERE THOUGH THE blow of the Sedan breakthrough had been to the French, its effect on the B.E.F. was traumatic.

Lord Gort's papers were lost, but the private diaries kept by his chief of staff Sir Henry Pownall reveals him as clutching at straws, unnerved by trivial setbacks and elated by the palest gleams of better news. His corps commanders shared these faults. On the fifteenth Lieutenant General Alan Brooke, commanding II Corps, was already imagining both flanks being turned and the force having to "extricate" itself: "But," he wrote, "I still have a firm conviction that Right must conquer over Wrong." Entries like these in his leatherbound, locked diary betray little confidence. He had lived in this idyllic spring countryside of cuckoos and cowslips for months, sentimental, homesick and under-employed, and Hitler's offensive had caught him, like the B.E.F., literally napping. Lieutenant General Michael Barker, commanding I Corps, suffered a partial nervous breakdown. Small wonder that as Gort saw the B.E.F. being unhinged, encircled and swept towards the sea he proved incapable of developing a consistent offensive strategy to thwart the audacious German plan, although his force did not encounter the full weight of the enemy at any stage during the retreat — Hitler had singled out the Dutch, the Belgians and the French for his main assault.

The B.E.F. had reached its forward defensive line in Belgium on the thirteenth. Two nights later Gort authorized its withdrawal. As it leapfrogged back from one line to the next, it forfeited stores, communications networks, officers' morale, and the confidence of its allies. The alliance would end at Dunkirk with lawless French soldiers murdering Major General Bernard Montgomery's operations officer, with mutual recriminations and with allegations of betrayal.[33]

By the sixteenth at least one of Churchill's colleagues — perhaps Lord Halifax — had written off the French. Quoting him, Kennedy secretly warned Roosevelt to face up to a possible Allied collapse. "This crack-up can come like a stroke of lightning," he added, "It is the view of my friend that nothing can save them from absolute defeat unless by some touch of genius and God's blessing the President can do it. This is absolutely reliable information."³⁴

Churchill refused to concede defeat so easily. "It is ridiculous," he exclaimed, "to think that France can be conquered by 120 tanks!" By five p.m. he was in Paris, being shown into the prime minister's study at the Quai d'Orsay. He found Reynaud and Gamelin a picture of Gallic desolation. Daladier was barely on speaking terms with Reynaud; a certain lady still came between them. Gamelin for that matter was not on speaking terms with Georges. Churchill's own temper can be gauged from his reply when told — wrongly — by Gamelin that railroad strikes in Belgium had hampered troop movements: "Shoot the strikers!" he rasped.³⁵

Warning that enemy tanks might be *in* Paris by midnight the city's military governor had recommended the government to flee. The political archives were already being destroyed. Ancient officials were heaping government files onto bonfires.³⁶ "A mass of charred paper is flying around the garden of this office building," pencilled Daladier in his notes. "The files are being burnt. Smoke-laden atmosphere."

On a wall map Churchill espied the offending Bulge at Sedan.

"Churchill believes," noted Daladier, "that the salient can be tied off just as in 1918. I have to tell him you can't compare the two wars."

Roland de Margerie, Reynaud's secretary, recorded the short discussion that developed on the German tank danger. Churchill still declined to take it seriously. "Unless," he said, "the tanks are supported by considerable infantry forces they are just coloured flags stuck into a map — no more and no less. They can't support themselves or keep themselves supplied." What they were looking at was not, in his view, a real invasion.

He asked General Gamelin when he was going to strike at the flanks of that bulge. The Frenchman shrugged — a gesture of hopelessness that stuck in Churchill's mind long after³⁷ — and spoke of "Inferior numbers. Inferior equipment (armament.) Inferior methods (doctrines.)"

Churchill wheeled his kitchen French into action. "Where is your mass of manoeuvre?" There was that shrug again, and this time Gamelin emphasized it by turning up the palms of both hands. "Aucune! — None," he said. He talked about giving up the Namur-Wavre line in Belgium.

"Now that we have got there," objected Winston, "why should we retire? Let us fight on that line."

The French asked for six fighter squadrons in addition to the four arriving that day. Churchill doubted they would make any difference.

"The French," said Daladier, "believe the contrary."

His record mirrors the blistering exchanges as the British argued that it would delay the Germans if they bombed the Ruhr.

I declare it absurd in my view to believe this [wrote the French war minister.] Damage to the Ruhr will leave them stone cold, they're not going to let their prey slip away like that. No, Britain's fate is being sealed in this salient.

Britain can't send over one more division to France (and there are only eight here now!) because their men are not trained (after eight months!) So let Britain at least send airplanes. London has to be defended right here.

Churchill drove back to his embassy to talk it over with London. At nine p.m. he dictated a recommendation that the Cabinet release the six squadrons. "It would not be good historically," he reasoned, "if their requests were denied and their ruin resulted." (His aides in London sardonically commented: "He's still thinking of his books."[38]) His message ended with purple prose: "I again emphasize the mortal gravity of the hour."

In London this attracted a remark about his "blasted rhetoric," but it did the trick. At midnight he received their telegram of agreement expressed in the Hindustani word for *Yes* — a language Pug Ismay understood.

Half an hour later they drove up to Reynaud's apartment. It was swathed in velvety darkness, and their gaze fell upon a lady's fur coat in the drawing room. Reynaud emerged; they read out the telegram; they prevailed upon him to fetch Daladier.

"I gave Churchill's hand a grateful squeeze," recorded Daladier in his diary, perhaps oblivious of the fur coat.

Since enemy tanks might at any moment roll into Paris, Churchill rose at crack of dawn and was back with his Cabinet at ten a.m. His stamina was truly remarkable.

THIS DAY, MAY 17, 1940 was the beginning of the great betrayal. Churchill had not missed the significance of that Bulge. He confided to young Colville who had met him at Hendon airport that Gort's force might be cut off.

Anxious to know Roosevelt's reply to his appeal, he telephoned Grosvenor-square from Hendon; at eleven Ambassador Kennedy was shown in.

The president's message offered legalisms, verbiage and little else. Lending destroyers would require the sanction of a hostile Congress. In response to Winston's hint that part of the U.S. fleet should move to Singapore — "I am looking to you to keep the Japanese quiet in the Pacific, using Singapore in any way convenient" — Roosevelt replied that the fleet would remain at Pearl Harbour.[39]

The original survives, drafted in his own hand, so there is no denying the authorship: was Roosevelt's unhelpful attitude guided by lethargy, composure, or calculation? He had received an even less cheering telegram from his Paris embassy. Bullitt had cabled into his "most private ear" that France was about to be crushed. "You should have in mind," warned Bullitt, "the hypothesis that . . . the British may install a government of Oswald Mosley. . . That would mean that the British navy would be against us." He urged Roosevelt to ensure — perhaps by "some direct arrangment with the officers of the British fleet" that it moved to Canada in time.[40]

A fresh appeal had arrived from Gamelin for air support, pointing out the obvious: "The thrust threatens the British army's line of communications."[41] After admitting to Kennedy that Hitler's purpose was now clear — to cut off the northern part of the Allied line — Churchill charged Chamberlain to study the evacuation of the B.E.F. through the Channel ports.[42]

For a while he dropped into his bed at the Admiralty to catch up on his sleep. Nobody grudged it ("A grand man!" marvelled Dalton.) Then he hurried over to the Palace, late though it was.

SINCE WASHINGTON WOULD not help, the Anglo-French plan to blast Stalin's oilfields was quietly put on ice. At Lord Halifax's suggestion, the Cabinet decided to send Sir Stafford Cripps, an influential Left-wing Socialist, on an exploratory mission to Moscow.

"If it goes wrong," said Dalton, "don't blame me."

Churchill made the wan reply: "You're on velvet."[43]

In Belgium the retreat went on. Brussels, an open city, was left to the enemy on Friday the seventeenth, after Gort's troops had wrecked its telephone exchange; in Antwerp that Saturday Royal Navy demolition teams torched the oil installations.[44] In London, Churchill gave his Chief of Imperial General Staff, "Tiny" Ironside, the dubious order to "concert plans" with Gort to safeguard the B.E.F. in "various eventualities" — even though the force came under French orders.[45]

That decision taken, Churchill sought sanctuary in the countryside. At five p.m. Colville handed him a cryptic message — evidently about the attempts to seal the enemy breach — dictated over the phone by Brigadier John Swayne from Georges' field headquarters.

Patient is rather lower and depressed. The lower part of the wound continues to heal, but as I expected, the upper part had started to suppurate again, though they tell me that so far they have not seen much pus. The effect of the injection will not be known for some time, but I have asked the Doctors to let me know as soon as possible the general effect, which, as you will realize, must be the combined result of many local injections.[46]

He had wanted to spend Trinity Sunday, May 19, at Chartwell, ministering to the goldfish and the one black swan that had survived a marauding fox.

But at mid-day the telephone rang. A message had come from Lord Gort about basing himself on Dunkirk, a little French port across the Straits of Dover, and fighting it out with his back to the sea.

* * *

Lord Gort was accustomed to fighting offensive actions, unversed in the defence — a Manstein rather than Model. To be instructed to concert plans for "various eventualities" was hardly calculated to inspire. He was faced by difficulties that seemed insuperable: his signals communications were fraught by premature demolitions, by power failures, by dispatch rider shortages, and by the reluctance of truculent Belgian postal and telegraph officials to assist a failing ally against Germany, an ancient and substantial neighbour.

That Sunday morning Lord Gort was already alarmed by wildly inaccurate reports from the French general charged with co-ordinating the Allied armies, G.H.G. Billotte, about enemy formations getting in behind them.

When Lord Gort now called the apprehensive corps commanders to what one of them, Brooke, called "a momentous" conference at Armentières that morning, their eyes were fixed on Blighty. "GHQ had a scheme," Brooke wrote that day in his diary, "for a move . . . toward Dunkirk, establishing a defended area round this place and embarking all we could of the personnel of the B.E.F., abandoning stores and equipment."

Counter-attacking, the alternative, was easily dismissed. "To go south west was impossible," summarized Pownall in his diary. He and Gort favoured Dunkirk; Brooke, fearing that a rush for the French ports would prompt an immediate Belgian defection, imperilling the B.E.F., suggested those in Belgium.

This was why, towards mid-day, Pownall had telephoned the War Office to set out "what might become necessary" — a retreat to Dunkirk, whence it might be possible to ship some troops home.* An hour or two

---

*Thus the bare bones of Pownall's conversation with the Director of Military Operations, Major-General R.H. Dewing. According to *his* record Pownall stressed they would not withdraw unless (unspecified) French operations to the south failed. His note was drafted retrospectively — he evacuated his genuinely contemporary diary that same Sunday to his wife in England — and for an evident purpose, because he invited Gort and the corps commanders Brooke and Barker to sign the handwritten endorsement: "I heard the GHQ end of this conversation and the above is a fair summary."[47]

later he telephoned again to discuss the Belgian ports as an alternative; he revealed that Gort had already authorized Air Vice-Marshal C.H.B. Blount to send some of his airforce component back to England. One way or another, the B.E.F. was quitting.

At the Cabinet to which Winston was summoned in London that afternoon Ironside declared that he had turned down Gort's evacuation plan. Churchill agreed: On the contrary the B.E.F. must strike south to Amiens, cutting off the enemy spearheads. The Cabinet broke up in dejection. Ironside murmured to Eden, "This is the end of the British Empire."[48]

The indomitable prime minister wanted to fly out to Gort himself; he had a suitcase packed before he could be persuaded to leave the mission to Ironside.

Instead, he made an impromptu broadcast, incredulous that three or four million French soldiers could be overwhelmed by a sudden "scoop or raid of mechanized vehicles."

He warned that Hitler might in a few days turn against Britain.

> Behind the armies and fleets of Britain and France — gather[s] a group of shattered States and bludgeoned races: the Czechs, the Poles, the Norwegians, the Danes, the Dutch, the Belgians — upon all of whom the long night of barbarism will descend, unbroken even by a star of hope, unless we conquer, as conquer we must; as conquer we shall.

AFTER HIS BROADCAST he ordered a study of the fighter cover needed for an evacuation; he called for the chiefs of staff, he summoned Eden, he sent for Beaverbrook. Together they listened while Professor Lindemann drafted a bullying message to Washington, trading on the possibility that Britain might surrender her fleet to Hitler.

"Here's a telegram for those bloody Yankees," Churchill barked at Colville. "Send it off tonight." Ninety minutes after midnight it went to the American embassy. The duty officer, Tyler Kent, scribbled a copy for his own purposes.

"I am very sorry about the destroyers," Churchill's message said. "If they were here in six weeks they would play an invaluable part." Britain also urgently needed Curtiss P40 fighters. Then came the threat:

> If members of the present Administration were finished and others came in to parley amid the ruins, you must not be blind to the fact that the sole remaining bargaining counter with Germany would be the Fleet, and if this country was left by the United States to its fate no one would have the right to blame those then responsible if they made the best terms they could for the surviving inhabitants. Excuse me Mr President putting this nightmare bluntly.[49]

It was muscular language. Even Churchill got cold feet, and asked

Group Captain William Elliot, one of Ismay's staff, to have it stopped. Double-checking, the American embassy contacted No.10 but learned that the PM still lived at Admiralty House. "The prime minister," Elliot apologized, rather stating the obvious, "is rather unorthodox in his methods. . . Mr Churchill was asleep and could not be disturbed. . ." Finally he raised the Prof. "As it turned out," Elliot concluded nonchalantly, "it was he who sent the message in the first place."

The next morning, May 20, Churchill decided to let the message stand. "I fetched this back during the night for a final view," he told Ismay, "but decided not to alter anything. Now dispatch."[50]

"THE ADMIRALTY," he directed at his eleven-thirty Cabinet that Monday morning, "should assemble a large number of small vessels in readiness to proceed to ports and inlets on the French coast."

Ironside had flown over to straighten out Lord Gort; but, increasingly disenchanted with Ironside, Churchill had also sent over the Vice C.I.G.S., Sir John Dill, to recommend an energetic south-west offensive personally to the French high command. He now telephoned Dill to warn them that failing this, Britain would take whatever steps she could for the security of her forces; "This might involve withdrawing to cover the Channel ports."[51]

Ironside telephoned to say that Gort was blaming the slowness of the B.E.F. push southwards on refugees choking the roads. In fact Gort had briefed the 5th and 50th divisions only on Sunday evening to make "a small offensive" from Arras on Tuesday.[52]

The age-old problems of military coalition were surfacing in Flanders — the British found the French undisciplined and temperamental; the French found the British pedantic and pigheaded. The intervention from London strained already taught tempers at B.E.F. Pownall described the instructions brought by Ironside, to attack south west towards Amiens, as "scandalous (i.e. Winstonian)" and "quite impossible." Drawing attention to "some enemy mechanized parties" in that area he and Gort convinced their visitor of the folly. The French high command found Gort's obstinacy mystifying. Over at his headquarters, purple-faced from shouting, Billotte persuaded Ironside and Pownall that the full-scale counter-attack must go ahead.

Taking an increasingly hardnosed view of the future, Churchill ordered the navy's XD teams to prepare — of necessity, in secret — to demolish the northern French ports and installations. That afternoon he received confirmation from Dill that he had passed the warning about the consequences of failure — independent action by Britain — to generals Georges and Weygand at mid-day. (Weygand had arrived from the Middle East to replace the discredited Gamelin, whom Reynaud suspected of sabotaging his orders.)

The Dardanelles, Norway, and now Dunkirk: Churchill was facing yet another fiasco. By Tuesday May 21 Hitler's tanks were bearing down on Boulogne. Ironside flew back from Belgium, saw Winston that morning and wrote in his diary: "[He] persists in thinking the position no worse." "It is a shock," admitted one of Winston's staff, "that the Germans should have penetrated so far." Something like fatalism had grasped him. Recalling a happier Riviera evening two years earlier, he remarked grimly to Eden, "About time Number Seventeen turned up!"[53]

But it was Hitler who had rolled high and was winning. That day his spearheads reached the estuary of the Somme at Abbeville. Ecstatic with praise for his generals, he talked of the generous peace he would now offer Britain: he had no claims on her: he had taken pains not to injure the B.E.F. "The British can have their peace," he exclaimed, "as soon as they return our colonies to us."*

Churchill had no intention of giving up. He talked of the perils of invasion, envisaged a paratroop assault on Whitehall itself. At that evening's Defence Committee he learned that thousands of soldiers in the depots had never taken a rifle to their shoulder; there were only 150,000 rifles in the whole kingdom.[54] Undismayed, he ordered sandbagged machine posts set up covering the streets and arches of Whitehall.[55] Over in Belgium, at a 4:15 p.m. conference that afternoon Lord Gort told his corps commanders the B.E.F. would fall back on its original frontier defence line the following evening.

AS THE FRENCH waited for Lord Gort to comply with Billotte's orders to counter-attack, the exchanges between Paris and London sharpened. At six p.m. Reynaud's secretary handed to the embassy Weygand's stiffly worded demand that Churchill "invite" his airforce "to initiate bombing operations on the battlefield as requested by General Billotte who is," the new C-in-C reminded the British, "co-ordinating the operations of the French, British and Belgian armies in Belgium."[56]

But the R.A.F. was away bombing targets in the Ruhr; and Billotte's prestige with the British was in decline — some documents called him supine and useless. Trying in vain to raise Reynaud by telephone Churchill rasped, "In all the history of war I have never known such mismanagement."

That evening, Colville broke news that Billotte had been critically injured in a car crash. The prime minister decided to fly again to Paris, and preach the Gospel of attack.

_____
*Hitler's War.

There is no doubt that a bold counter-attack would have thrown the Germans into disarray, though for how long will always be open to dispute. Battle-fatigue was making itself felt among the German troops; Hitler was nervous about his armour's flank defences, and General Fedor von Bock, commanding the Army Group facing the British, noted growing concern about his own lack of reserves.

On that afternoon, May 21, two British divisions had launched their "small offensive" south of Arras and advanced eight miles. They found the territory thinly defended, inflicted casualties, took four hundred prisoners, suffered few losses, and bestowed a mortal fright on General Erwin Rommel, commanding the 7th Panzer Divison here: for the first time his tank crews found themselves fighting the British, and engaging a tank — the Matilda Mk II — that their 37mm gun could not pierce; justifying his setback here, Rommel would declare he had been attacked by five divisions. But then the British, mystifyingly, pulled back. By Wednesday May 22 even the timorous General Pownall had begun to see the B.E.F. corps commanders as "unduly pessimistic."

LONG BEFORE DAWN on that Wednesday, Churchill had flown to France. He reached Reynaud's office after some aerial detour at mid-day and they drove on out to Weygand's fortress headquarters at Vincennes. The new C-in-C was seventy-three but fighting fit. Billotte having now died of his injuries, his place as army group commander was taken by the French General J.M.G. Blanchard, who visibly did not relish it.

Weygand received the two Allied premiers in his Map Room. He was optimistic. Altogether there were forty divisions — French, Belgian and British — north of the German thrust line. He refused to hear of retreating but demanded a full-blooded offensive southwards, meeting a similar northwards offensive by French forces massing under General Frère on the Somme.[57] Churchill grunted frequent approval, according to Villelume's record, but Weygand wanted more than noises. He asked "in firm and exact, although courteous, terms" for promises of greater British air support. Churchill so promised. He drafted a formal agreement to the Weygand Plan, which both Reynaud and he himself initialled at one-fifteen p.m. Under this Plan, eight of the forty divisions would launch a strategic counter offensive toward Bapaume and Cambrai, beginning on the morrow: they would liberate Amiens: they would meet Frère advancing from the South.[58]

By seven-thirty he was relating the Weygand Plan to the War Cabinet; his buoyancy was washed away by Eden, who had been telephoned at five p.m. by Gort's ADC, Lord Munster. "Boy" Munster had had to come to the Belgian coast to telephone, since the cross-Channel telegraphic cable at Dunkirk had now been interrupted.[59] The

B.E.F., his lordship had said, was running out of food and ammunition: and he believed the French had got cold feet about the projected offensive. Eden reported that Munster would like to be fetched home by a destroyer "if we wished to see him."[60] (They didn't.) Between them, Eden and Gort killed the counter-offensive.

The War Office had set up a direct radio circuit to Gort, enabling Eden to by-pass the French.* Churchill however persisted with the Weygand Plan, telegraphing to Lord Gort that it tallied exactly with the "general directions you have received from the War Office."

This evoked from Pownall the shocked observation in his diary that they had received *no* directions except for "the scribbled paper by Tiny [Ironside] telling us to do an impossible *sauve qui peut* to Amiens."

> Here are Winston's plans again. Can nobody prevent him trying to conduct operations himself as a super Commander-in-Chief? How does he think we are to collect eight divisions and attack as he suggests.

In an entry indicative of their mood Gort's chief of staff concluded, "The man's mad. I suppose these figments of the imagination are telegraphed without consulting his military advisers."[62]

* * *

Tough decisions also had to be made about Norway. Aware from intercepts of the enemy's plight at Narvik, Churchill had signalled to Lord Cork, "I should be very much obliged if you would enable me to understand what is holding you back." But now the chiefs of staff had to advise him to abandon Norway altogether as soon as they had captured Narvik. On May 23 he agreed: Britain would shortly need the weaponry and troops for her own defence.[63]

The news from France was a study in black. The War Room maps in the Admiralty showed the enemy panzers inside Boulogne and perhaps Calais as well. General Brooke was torn between despair ("Nothing but a miracle can save the B.E.F. now . . . the end cannot be very far off!") and admiration for their phenomenal opponents: "There is no doubt that they [the Germans] are the most wonderful soldiers."

Frustrated, Churchill telegraphed to Reynaud a demand for the "immediate execution" of the Weygand Plan. That afternoon he impatiently telephoned as well. Reynaud took note of Churchill's opening remarks, "Given the situation with the panzer divisions, he wonders if it wouldn't be better for the British army to beat a retreat to the ports."

---

*It was first monitored by German army Intelligence on May 22.[61]

The Frenchman replied haughtily, "Weygand is satisfied. We must not change anything now;" and, in English, *"We must go on."*[64]

Worried by the undertone to Churchill's remarks Reynaud had Weygand brought to the telephone at six p.m. to talk to London. The commander-in-chief assured Churchill that his planned attack *had* begun — indeed his forces had already retaken Amiens, Albert and Péronne in their northward drive.* Churchill told his colleagues at the Cabinet that he saw no choice but to conform to the Plan.

Word of the crisis reached Buckingham Palace. The King asked to see Churchill after dinner, and wrote down the prime minister's report that if the Weygand Plan "did not come off" he would order the B.E.F. back to England.[66]

But the great betrayal had already begun, effectively concealed from history. Without a word to Weygand, at about seven p.m. Gort had ordered the two attacking divisions, the 5th and 50th, to withdraw fifteen miles from Arras to the Canal Line. He gave a number of different reasons for this fateful decision. Their flank had been turned by "a number" of armoured fighting vehicles: he had no word of the French thrust from the south: he wanted the two divisions to hold the perimeter from the Canal Line to the sea: they could attack southwards later in conjunction with the First Army. Blanchard, unconvinced, accused the B.E.F. pointblank of ratting.[67]

Whatever the pretext, Gort had thus abandoned his half-hearted thrust towards the south — "For reasons to which history alone can apply an impartial judgment," as a chastened Reynaud would write, still baffled, after a year in captivity.[68] The effect on French opinion was annihilating: "Disobeying the orders of the GOC-in-C," wrote Admiral Darlan in July, "and obeying orders from London, Lord Gort had his divisions retire forty kilometres for no valid military reason whatever."

This, added Darlan, placed the French army to the east of him in a critical situation.[69]

The British lion [the admiral would write derisively to his wife] seems to grow wings when it's a matter of getting back to the sea.[70]

* * *

---

*John Colville, Gort's biographer, has termed this a deception, suggesting that Weygand was determined that *"we* should go under if *they* did." General von Bock's diary however shows the alarm caused by Weygand's offensive[65], and Reynaud's private papers confirm that at 4:20 p.m. Weygand had told Paul Boudouin that he was very satisfied with the development of operations since that morning. "He adds that our troops are touching Amiens, that he has been told of the message from Mr Winston Churchill and that he is happy to confirm once more their perfect community of views."

An odd mood now mantled the English people. Ambassador Kennedy informed Washington that they still refused to believe they could be beaten. "I honestly don't believe things will turn out as well as these people hope."[71]

CHAPTER 24

An Avoidable Disaster

EARLIER, HE HAD appeared as the champion of public liberties. In January 1939 he had told Kingsley Wood that Magna Carta and Habeas Corpus were indispensible to civilization. "Criticism in the body politic," he had once said, when he was the leading critic, "is like pain in the human body. It is not pleasant, but where would the body be without it?" Where criticism was crushed by concentration camp or firing squad, the dictator would be told only what he wanted to hear.

A less enlightened politician now ruled from Admiralty House. According to the security services there were 14,000 Communists, 8,000 fascists, tens of thousands of aliens in Britian, and all were potential fifth columnists. He cleared the decks: instructed the chiefs of staff to intern "very considerable numbers" including the leading Communists and fascists. He rolled up Magna Carta, suspended habeas corpus, incarcerated the bigoted, the cranky, the extremist and the influential. Mosley was cast into prison; his organization was "harried out of existence," its officers imprisoned, intimidated or "squelched."[1]

Scotland Yard rooted out a particularly nasty cell on May 20. In a shabby rooming house off Oxford-street they arrested Tyler Kent, an American embassy cipher clerk, and found a brown portmanteau stuffed with hundreds of stolen documents including the secret messages exchanged between Churchill and Roosevelt.[2] Planning to blow the lid off their "intrigue" he had squirreled away hundreds of documents since October and filed them under "Germany", "Turkey", "Czechoslovakia", "British Cabinet", "Churchill", "Halifax". He was also safeguarding the padlocked membership register of the Right Club.

For months MI5 had been running surveillance on the Club's officials. The wiretap on one South Kensington telephone revealed Kent regularly leaking embassy secrets to a suspected enemy agent, Russian emigré Anna de Wolkoff. Her subversive activity seemed harmless enough — it included starting the hissing in darkened movie theatres whenever Churchill's face appeared in newsreels. Among the secrets Kent leaked were Britain's real naval losses off Norway and confidential interviews between Kennedy and Halifax. On May 14 Wolkoff had telephoned him at the embassy, speaking Russian to foil the wiretappers. He told her later that Kennedy was warning Washington of coming internal unrest, and made what MI5 called "libellous remarks" about Churchill's behaviour at one unruly Cabinet meeting.

Wolkoff persuaded Tyler Kent to show the documents to Captain Archibald Ramsay, a Tory MP. On May 22, Ramsay was interned along with officers, clergymen, and professors — 1,847 of the more vociferous opponents of Churchill's War. Significantly, the embassy lifted Kent's immunity so that he could be tried in camera in Britain, rather than in public in America. Kennedy told the State Department on the twenty-second, "This case stinks to heaven." Sir Walter Monckton assured him it would be hushed up, and Wolkoff and Kent were tried in secret at the Old Bailey in November.

* * *

Roosevelt certainly engaged in remarkable dealings that spring of 1940.

Twice late in April, while Britain's expedition was floundering in Norway, he had invited the Canadian prime minister to secret meetings — at Warm Springs and at the White House. Trying to shock the pious, teetotalling Canadian, he remarked that Winston Churchill was "tight most of the time."[3] On May 24 he invited Mackenzie-King to send a secret emissary to Washington without telling Churchill and told that man that France and Britain were doomed: that he had it "on good authority" — which was an outrageous lie — that Hitler was going to demand Britain's fleet and empire: and that Canada should "line up the Dominions" to put pressure on Britain's inebriated leader to send her fleet across the Atlantic *now*. On no account, however, were they to let him know who was behind it.[4]

Seeing what big teeth the genial president now had, Mackenzie-King demurred: he indicated that Mr Roosevelt should put his proposition to Mr Churchill himself. He was repelled by any suggestion of turning over Britain's fleet to the U.S. "I would rather die," he wrote in his diary, "than to do aught to save ourselves or any part of this continent at the expense of Britain." Responding to an appeal by Churchill on May 23, on the very next day Canada sailed her three destroyers to Europe. This great Dominion's unselfish devotion to the Empire cause would endure throughout the war.

MIDST CONFUSION AND duplicity, by May 24 Lord Gort was pulling the B.E.F. back to the Channel ports. One thousand troops escaped during the night from Boulogne. Irked that Gort could not relieve Calais the PM spun off an angry minute ending with the observation — which he omitted from his published text — "Of course if one side fights and the other does not, the war is apt to become somewhat unequal."

He was surrounded by incompetents, many inherited from Chamberlain's administration, and knew it. Twice that day, Captain Edwards brought admiralty messages into the Cabinet — "a poor lot," he called them in his diary. "Most of them very ordinary & obviously out of touch with reality." In his presence they decided to abandon Narvik once they had captured it — "too late & at this time too! It's quite mad."

The strain of events told on Winston's frame. When he retired for his siesta that afternoon he donned a silken dressing gown since Beaverbrook's physician Sir Charles Wilson was to visit him. "I suffer from dyspepsia," the PM demonstrated, baring his midriff, "and *this* is the treatment" — indicating some medicine he preferred. Wilson was ushered out.

It had been a long night. On the day before, the King of the Belgians had given Admiral Keyes fair warning that if the B.E.F. withdrew, this could only result in his army's immediate capitulation; meanwhile, he had promised, Belgium would conform to the Weygand plan, the last Allied hope of pinching off the German armoured spearhead.

But at three a.m. on May 24 Keyes had telephoned Churchill that King Leopold had not received any orders from the army group commander, Blanchard. Churchill passed this complaint on at five a.m. to the French premier, adding that Gort had lodged a similar complaint.

"How does all this agree with your statement," Churchill challenged, "that Blanchard and Gort are hand-in-glove — *main dans la main*?" But he hastened to reassure Reynaud, "We are instructing him to persevere in carrying out your Plan."[5]

General Weygand looked in vain that morning for signs that Lord Gort was adhering to the Plan. "Accordingly," Reynaud stated in reply to Churchill, "[he] has this morning repeated his orders." Then he dropped the bombshell: Weygand had noted with surprise that, contrary to the Plan, Gort had evacuated Arras and that elements of his army were boarding ships at Le Havre. "General Weygand's orders," he concluded, "should be obeyed."[6]

Churchill hedged, and made inquiries. His ambassador had been present at that morning's Paris meeting where a shocked Weygand returned from the front and reported to Reynaud. The two Frenchmen, Campbell reported dryly, seemed "rather put out."

Weygand repeated several times that he was still pursuing his plan . . . and that he was convinced that the only hope for the encircled armies was to fight through and join hands with Frère coming up from the south.

He had taken the line that Winston no doubt knew what was going on.[7] Winston, however, did not. "We know nothing of any evacuation of Arras," he telegraphed to Reynaud. "It is entirely contrary to our wishes." The rest of his bulldoggish reply did not lack candour: "Believe me, my friend, until Weygand took control there has been no Command in the North worthy of the name since the retreat began."

Frère's counter-offensive made steady progress that morning. French wireless bulletins reported the recapture of Bapaume.

Lord Gort was not however attacking from the north; at B.E.F. headquarters, as his chief of staff wrote in an expressive diary, their spirits rose and fell. An early corps commanders' conference had been startled by false rumours that the Germans were coming and the resulting alarm had swamped the real news of the morning: at 11:32 a.m. the B.E.F. intercepted a German radio order *halting* the tank attack on the line Dunkirk - Hazebrouck - Merville. Pownall mentioned the intercept in his diary: so did Brooke. But it evinced no flicker of interest. For the next days their brains remained focused on the "dash to the ports" while the German tanks paused — "rooted to the spot," as General Franz Halder fumed in his diary.

We now know what had caused this dramatic order. Hitler, visiting his army group headquarters, had found General Gerd von Rundstedt concerned that his armour had gone too fast and too far; he approved Rundstedt's order. On June 1 he would spell out his reasons to his generals: "Gentlemen," he said, "you will have wondered why I stopped the panzer divisions outside Dunkirk. . . I was anxious lest the enemy launch an offensive from the Somme and wipe out our Fourth Army's weak armoured force." This was the offensive which Lord Gort had unilaterally junked.[8]

REYNAUD HAD CAUGHT a whiff of these curious events in Flanders. He hurled a furious protest at Churchill: in flagrant disobedience of Weygand's orders that very morning, as Blanchard had now reported, "the British army has decided on and carried out a withdrawal of forty kilometres towards the ports, at a time when our troops moving up from the south are gaining ground towards the north." Weygand had therefore abandoned hope of restoring the front. "It would be futile," Reynaud's telegram concluded, "to emphasize the gravity of the consequences that may ensue."[9]

Churchill ventured a reassuring reply — that "from everything we know here" Gort had not renounced the idea of the offensive. But the allegation vexed him: he called in his personal advisers — Churchill's new secretary John Martin found them at Admiralty House that evening, the "Crazy Gang of Prof Lindemann, Bracken and Morton," as he called them in his diary; Churchill packed off Dill to see Gort, and Spears to placate Reynaud. "I would propose," Winston suggested in the note he gave him for Reynaud, "that General Spears should normally live in Paris." But few days of normality remained to the Seine metropolis.

JOHN MARTIN HAD just become one of Churchill's six "operational" secretaries. Ushered in on May 23, he had been ordered to stand in the window, searched with one gaze then gruffly accepted: "I understand you're to be one of my secretaries." Martin was first apprehensive, then intrigued, then shell-shocked with fatigue. "Eels," Churchill would console him, "get used to skinning."

Capable, mild-mannered, a former principal secretary at the Colonial Office, Martin was aghast at the energy of this "superman". "Yesterday," he wrote on May 25, "began at a quarter to ten in the morning and ended at the Admiralty, where I was lucky to find a taxi, at three-fifteen a.m. . . The stimulus of the excitement seems to make up for lack of sleep."

He was assigned to a battery of telephones next to the Cabinet Room with two colleagues — Principal Private Secretary Eric Seal, and Anthony Bevir who handled patronage and general work; John Colville and another younger secretary shared another office with Edith Watson, who tackled the parliamentary and political matters.

Within a few days Martin had discovered the working system. A box of papers was left outside Winston's bedroom each night; he read these in bed each morning, dictating responses; he dressed quite late, went over to No.10 for a mid-morning Cabinet that might last until two. After lunch at Admiralty House and a siesta he would confer with ministers again at No.10 or in the House.

> He dines at Admiralty House and there sees a succession of ministers until bed-time. . . The chief difficulty is understanding what he says and great skill is required in interpreting inarticulate grunts or single words thrown out without explanation. I think he is consciously odd in these ways. Anyhow, he is certainly a "character" and I shan't soon forget an interview with him in his bedroom walking about clad only in a vest.[10]

Churchill had brooded all night about Arras, and that morning, May 25, he dictated this query to Field Marshal Ironside: "I must know at earliest why Gort gave up Arras, and what actually he is doing with the rest of his Army? Is he still persevering in Weygand's plan, or has he become largely stationary?"[11]

Ironside's reply was not encouraging: Gort had not even informed London that he was giving up Arras; it seemed he had indeed abandoned his part of the Weygand Plan; he might have taken as authority to do so a War Office telegram of the twenty-third, whose final sentence had talked of making "naval and air arrangments to assist you should you have to withdraw on the northern coast." Ironside concluded,

I think he will be lucky if he extricates himself from encirclement. I think he must move on the Coast ports and then face the enemy. We must prepare all air and naval help for partial evacuation if this becomes necessary.

Unable to dismiss Lord Gort, Churchill evidently pondered: someone must go.

GENERAL SPEARS HAD flown to Paris at eight that Saturday morning in a Blenheim bomber. He assessed in a private diary that there was "not one chance in a hundred" of the B.E.F. getting away, but when Reynaud now whined that British generals were "always making for harbour," Spears assured him: "Gort's one idea is to get South."[12]

Reynaud handed him a message for Churchill: Weygand had directed Blanchard to ensure that his northern group of armies could withdraw to the sea if the British retreat had wrecked the Plan: Dunkirk was "vital for their supplies." But, continued Reynaud, Blanchard had not given up the Plan yet: he had telegraphed Weygand since then, at one a.m., that he was going to counterattack southwards towards Cambrai, and then on towards Bapaume.

Meanwhile, at his Saturday morning Cabinet Churchill was conceding that the French had grounds for complaint. "He [Lord Gort] should at once have informed us of the action he took," he said. The Cabinet decided that since the B.E.F. had — "inexplicably, rather," as Cadogan affably put it — retreated forty kilometres it would be evacuated while a suicide garrison held Calais as a breakwater. Churchill signalled Brigadier Claude Nicholson: "The eyes of the Empire are upon the defence of Calais."[13]

No doubt, Winston postulated to his staff, the action had been forced upon Lord Gort. Shortly he dictated a message by telephone to Paris confirming it. He added, "As soon as we know what has happened I will report fully. It is clear however that the Northern Army are practically surrounded and that its communications are cut except through Dunkirk and Ostend."[14]

* * *

Counter-attack or final retreat? Lord Gort's confusion of mind at

Armentières was unenviable. By seven a.m. his chief of staff could see him feeling the situation keenly: "The least little thing that is helpful cheers him up and he clutches at it." He was toying again with the Weygand Plan. When, at two a.m., General Brooke (II Corps) had become alarmed that the Belgians might collapse and pleaded for reinforcements, G.H.Q. would grant him only one brigade, explaining that the "Rush for the Sea" was being abandoned. "Thank God for it," Brooke lamely inked into his diary, "I have always hated this plan." told of renewed plans to counter-attack southwards, Brooke was dubious, but drove over to the 4th and 3rd Divisions to discuss it.

During the day however Gort's pessimism had grown. If the Belgians collapsed, in Pownall's words, "we are bust." At five p.m. — the time is confirmed by Pownall's diary — without informing the French, Gort pulled the 5th and 50th divisions out of the southern perimeter and ordered the retreat.

This act, Gort's ultimate betrayal of his allies, was retrospectively camouflaged by a neat piece of historical sleight of hand that deceived Churchill — whose relevant chapters were ghosted by the same Sir Henry Pownall — as well as his biographer and the official Historian.[15] The legend was seeded that a "captured German document" had prompted Gort's retreat; that this had conveniently revealed the enemy Sixth Army poised to hurl two Armeekorps at a gap between Menin and Ypres; and that Gort had thereupon slotted in the 5th and 50th divisions at that point and thus "saved the B.E.F."

This was not true. While a patrol had indeed recovered a document wallet from the derelict staff car of Lieutenant-Colonel Eberhard Kinzel, a feckless liaison officer to Sixth Army, and this did contain the complete enemy Order of Battle,* the other document, vaguely described as referring to a Sixth Army attack on the morrow, can scarcely have influenced Gort's decision: Brooke picked it up from 3rd Division headquarters that afternoon; attended the seven p.m. conference at Armentières at which Lord Gort, to his relief, announced he had dropped the Weygand Plan; and only afterwards handed the German document to Gort's Intelligence officer for translation.[16]

In London, Winston dined at Admiralty House with the Prof, Beaverbrook and Bracken. At ten p.m. he called a Defence Committee meeting to pronounce the last rites over the Weygand Plan: an "advance" to the coast would begin twenty-four hours later. After all, he guiltily reasoned, Weygand's offensive in the south seemed unlikely to materialize for some time. No doubt Hitler would offer the French an armistice. If he were French prime minister, he said, he "would accept it."[17]

---

*Identified by MI14 as *Gliederung und Stellenbesetzung Fall Gelb vom 1.Mai 1940.*

Later still that evening, he invited Ironside to Admiralty House and secured his resignation.

CHURCHILL'S ADMISSION, telephoned to Reynaud, that the B.E.F. was pulling out shattered what remained of France's fighting spirit.

A mouse-eaten folder in Reynaud's papers contains the essence of his council of war held later that same Saturday. Could they honourably sue for peace without consulting Britain? Reynaud himself was bound by the London Agreement of March 28; but navy minister César Campinchi suggested that his signature would not bind a subsequent government.

"Suppose Germany," ventured President Lebrun, "offers us conditions that are relatively advantageous — ought we not give them very close and considered attention?"

Reynaud agreed, and declared he would fly to London the next day. He warned that Churchill might simply declare: "You're bound by your signature. You've got to fight, even if there's no hope."[18]

When London learned that Reynaud was coming over, Eden — obviously acting on Churchill's instructions — sent one of the less honourable signals of the Dunkirk affair. Claiming information that the French offensive from the Somme could not be made "in sufficient strength to hold out any prospect of junction with your armies in the North," he furtively directed Lord Gort to think only of the safety of the B.E.F. The navy would provide a fleet of small boats and the airforce would provide air cover. Gort was to prepare urgently all preliminary plans.

"In meantime," ordered Eden, "it is obvious that you should not discuss the possibility of the move with French or Belgians."[19]

That Saturday evening, May 25, the Italian ambassadors in London and Paris hinted that Mussolini was willing to sponsor a peace conference. Reynaud liked the proposal. So did Chamberlain, who trusted the Italians. So did Halifax who argued to the Cabinet, when it met on Sunday morning, that what mattered was not defeating Germany, but "safeguarding the independence of our own Empire."

Churchill disagreed.

THE PRIME MINISTER said that peace and security might be achieved under a German domination of Europe. That we could never accept. We must ensure our complete liberty and independence. He was opposed to any negotiations which might lead to a derogation of our rights and power.*

---

*Hitler wanted nothing at all from Britain, and this seems worth emphasizing.

Turbulent debate occupied the inner Cabinet over the next three days on this issue — whether or not to halt the carnage at that moment. Whatever his motives — and it is perhaps no coincidence that he received a sealed message from his old confrère at the French foreign ministry, the viciously anti-Italian Alexis Léger, this day[20] — the PM never wavered: Hitler, he declared over and over again, would show Britain no mercy: he was supported by Attlee, Greenwood (both Labour) and Sinclair (Liberal); and opposed by Chamberlain and Halifax, both of whom alone had met and sized up Hitler.

Thinking in ink, Winston drafted these lines "upon the realities of the case," and it seems fair to set them out.

> I fear that if we entered upon this pass we shd soon find that it lead to Mussolini being a mediator between us & Germany, & to an Armistice & conference under the conditions of our being at Hitler's mercy. Such a conference wd only end in weakening fatally our power to resist the terrible terms wh will almost certainly be imposed, if not upon France, at any rate upon Britain.
>
> We do not feel unable to continue the struggle & our people wd never allow us to quit until we have fought our fight. They are an unbeaten people & will never allow us to surrender. They know well that for us once under the Nazi domination there can be no mercy.
>
> Thus we do not see any way but to fight on, and we have good hopes of holding out until some deep change occurs in Germany or Europe. . . . [21]

REYNAUD ARRIVED AND lunched at the Admiralty. He too had jotted down some notes of what he intended to discuss: among them were, "Last straw British retreat." "My orders: fight on even if no hope." And, "Revolution both possible and probable — a factor ignored by your side."[22]

Marshal Pétain, Reynaud announced, favoured letting Mussolini mediate. He got short shrift. One of Reynaud's staff summarized: "Premier got nothing out of Churchill. Halifax was the only one to show the slightest understanding." Churchill prophesied that Hitler would now turn against Britain; Reynaud retorted that the dream of every German was to conquer Paris.

During an adjournment Churchill reported to his colleagues: Reynaud's conversation showed that he was inclined toward surrender. To avoid charges of leaving the French in the lurch Churchill now proposed to get him somehow to direct Weygand to order Blanchard to "authorize" the B.E.F. to march to the coast and embark. The document was drafted on a Downing-street typewrtiter; translated into French and handed to Reynaud to dictate by telephone to General Weygand at 4:05 p.m.[23]

This singular foreplay performed, Eden telegraphed to Lord Gort:

according to "reports received from the front" Weygand's plan had failed; in view of that, he was now "authorized to operate towards coast forthwith."[24] Of course, the operation had long begun.

Churchill reported all this to Spears in Paris: he was to resist any suggestion by the French of "cutting out." "Their duty," Winston defined, "is to continue in the war and do their best." The British would fight on: "I am advised by all our experts that we have power to do so."[25]

That same afternoon the Admiral Commanding, Dover, was ordered to commence the evacuation, Operation Dynamo. The liaison officer now sent over to him by the French C-in-C, Admiral Darlan was "stupefied" to learn that the British admiralty had prepared Dynamo days before, without notifying any of their Allies.[26]

* * *

Churchill had asked his military staff if Britain could fight on alone. They replied that it depended on whether the aircraft factory workers would carry on "in the face of wholesale havoc and destruction." True, Hitler held most of the cards. "The real test," they predicted, "is whether the morale of our fighting personnel and civil population will counterbalance the numerical and material advantages which Germany enjoys. We believe it will."

At the Admiralty that Sunday afternoon Churchill admitted to his Inner Cabinet that Hitler might offer to France "decent" terms. "There is no limit to the terms," he however asserted, "which Germany would impose upon us if she has her way."

He would leave this assertion studiously untested over the coming weeks. Lord Halifax expressed courteous but nonetheless firm disagreement, as the secret records show:

> THE FOREIGN SECRETARY . . . was not quite convinced that the Prime Minister's diagnosis was correct and that it was in Herr Hitler's interest to insist on outrageous terms.

After listening to wild speculation on Germany's possible demands — Somaliland, Kenya or Uganda — Halifax pointed out Britain might well be offered perfectly acceptable terms, which did not rob her of her independence: "We should be foolish if we did not accept them."

Shortly, Churchill was summoned to the telephone: Admiral Keyes was telephoning from France: King Leopold was staying in Belgium, with his army; the admiral added that he had witnessed the cheering at B.E.F. headquarters as Eden's orders to march to the coast arrived.

Churchill ended the Cabinet meeting, leaving everything in the air.

"Settled nothing much," wrote Cadogan, back at the F.O. "W.S.C. too rambling and romantic and sentimental and temperamental." Chamberlain was "still the best of the lot."

Churchill ordered a fresh signal to Brigadier Nicholson, to hold Calais to the last man. "Every hour you continue to exist," it began, "is of the greatest help to the B.E.F." That sent, the prime minister recalled betaking himself to the dining room. "One has to eat and drink in war," he would apologize in his memoirs; from time to time he had the tact to display, as Ismay observed during this meal, evident distaste.[27] As they folded their napkins, the B.B.C. was broadcasting an appeal for shotgun cartridges.

Churchill's signal to Nicholson was intercepted by a puzzled enemy. "It is probable," Hitler's Intelligence branch, Foreign Armies West, appreciated, "that the embarkation of the B.E.F. has begun." Incredulous that the British, his most feared adversaries, were ditching their allies, Hitler started his tanks rolling again.[28]

IT WOULD NOT be long before Belgium caved in; for Britain's purposes it was vital that King Leopold should escape while he could. Queen Wilhelmina of Holland had arrived in England two weeks earlier — though quite by accident: she had wanted to go to Flushing but the British destroyer *Hereward* brought her to exile in Britain instead: the flustered Dutch monarch had arrived at Liverpool-street station that afternoon clutching only a tin hat.[29]

The King of the Belgians proved less amenable. He had warned Britain explicitly that if the B.E.F. embarked he would cease fighting. Now the B.E.F. was quitting. At four-thirty a.m. on Monday, May 27, with Eden at his side, Churchill signalled Gort: "Presume troops know they are cutting their way home to Blighty. Never was there such a spur for fighting." Still hoping to persuade the Belgians to fight on, he asked the general to contact Leopold. "We are asking them," he said, "to sacrifice themselves for us." Admiral Keyes was to confirm to the monarch that the "British and French" were fighting their way to coast where they would embark; Keyes was to suggest that for the B.E.F. to be "hemmed in and starved out" would not serve Belgium's cause; and he was to ensure that Leopold escaped.[30] While this message lost its way, another did reach Keyes, telephoned directly by Churchill to Keyes some time before dawn.

King Leopold however had seen enough bloodshed and depredation. He would allege shortly that the retreating Allied troops had pillaged and ransacked his country as they withdrew.[31] By late afternoon rumours were reaching London about an armistice. Accepting that his messages might actually have undermined Leopold's will to fight on, Churchill suggested to his Cabinet that the King could hardly be blamed. That evening Spears telephoned: Leopold had indeed sent a plenipotentiary to the Germans.

It seems proper to set out these events in sequence because, for reasons of domestic policy, both Reynaud and Churchill would heap calumny upon King Leopold for his "betrayal". In truth, the Belgians had fought most gallantly, simplifying the embarkation that now began.

AUSTRALIA PLEDGED TROOPS: Canada's destroyers arrived: American aid was still conspicuously absent.

On May 27 a proposal arrived from Washington, passed on by the ambassador Lord Lothian, that Britain lease to the Americans airbases on Empire territories at Trinidad, Newfoundland and Bermuda. The Cabinet was indignant, and somebody remarked that Roosevelt seemed to take "the view that it would be very nice of him to pick up the bits of the British Empire if this country was overrun."

For a third time the War Cabinet considered approaching Italy; again they rejected it. The power of the minority Parties of Attlee and Sinclair depended, of course, on the continuance of the war. If peace came now, they — with Mr Churchill — would vanish into oblivion. Speaking "with emotion," Winston dismissed such an approach as futile. "Our prestige in Europe," he argued, "is very low. The only way we can get it back is by showing that Germany has not beaten us. If, after two or three months, we can show the world that we are still unbeaten, our prestige will return." Later he said, "if the worst came to the worst it would not be a bad thing for this country to go down fighting. . ."

Halifax listened to the rhetoric with mounting impatience.

> He could not recognize any resemblance between the action which he proposed and the suggestion that we were suing for terms and following a line which would lead us to disaster.

He reminded Churchill that only the previous day he had asked whether the PM would discuss terms if he was satisfied that Britain's independence was unaffected; and that Mr Churchill had replied that he would be thankful to "get out of our present difficulties" on such terms — "even at the cost of some cession of territory."

Overnight, continued Halifax, the PM had reverted to the view that Britain had no course but to fight to a finish. If it now proved possible to obtain a settlement, he announced, he for one would not accept Churchill's view. Two or three months, the PM had just said, would show whether Britain could withstand air attack. "This means," declared the foreign secretary, "that the future of the country turns on whether the enemy's bombs happen to hit our aircraft factories."

Lord Halifax was prepared to take that risk if Britain's independence *was* at stake; but not if it was not. "I would think it right," he concluded, "to accept an offer which could save the country from avoidable disaster."

Political oblivion looming ever closer, Churchill whistled up the familiar demons to prove Britain had no choice: "If," he argued,

> Herr Hitler was prepared to make peace on the [basis of] restoration of the German colonies and the overlordship of Central Europe, that was one thing. But it was quite unlikely that he would make any such offer.

The Cabinet minutes cast a discreet veil over what followed, but not the diary which Lord Halifax privately maintained. If this was how Mr Churchill felt, he declared, their ways must separate; he asked to see him alone, in the garden of No.10. Outside, Churchill mellowed, spluttered apologies. The foreign secretary was unconvinced. "I thought Winston talked the most frightful rot," he lamented in his diary. "It does drive me to despair when he works himself up into a passion of emotion when he ought to make his brain think and reason."[32] He seems to have imparted something of his irritation to the American ambassador. "Not realizing what difficulties may be in store for them," Kennedy reported to Washington, "people here are looking forward with joy to turning [Hitler's peace terms] down."[33]

IT CAN PERHAPS be said that victory was now becoming a far more dangerous obsession for Churchill than Catherine or Narvik had ever been. But the horizon now was dark whichever way he looked. Walking back to the admiralty, he murmured that he still could not believe that France would give in. A letter came from Spears — he had just left a Reynaud "rather yellow at the gills," predicting that others, willing to negotiate, would replace him. Spears had told him that his words in London had caused "grave concern." "Was I not right," Reynaud had replied, "to tell you the worst? What Weygand said?"

Winston read these documents quietly, called for Colville and bade him: "Pour me out a whisky and soda, very weak, there's a good boy," and then retired to bed. The fate of 300,000 troops now depended on Dynamo. But the R.A.F. was covering the beaches: its eight-gun fighter planes were outgunning the enemy: and that seemed to augur well.[34]

* * *

When he awoke it was May 28 and the Allied assault on Narvik, under the hard-bitten French general Antoine Béthouart, had begun. Eventually that forlorn Arctic township would be in Allied hands — a tiny victory at the cost of 150 more Allied lives. That battle won, against Béthouart's protests, the British would abandon Norway without a word to King Haakon, and evacuate him too to British soil.

Across the Straits of Dover, Dunkirk was under German air attack; bodies littered the streets. After hours of searching, Gort found General Blanchard, read out to him Eden's telegram ordering the B.E.F. to embark. Blanchard's visible astonishment baffled the British generals. "For what other reason," wrote Pownall in his diary, "did he think that we — he and Gort — had been ordered to form bridgeheads?" The French army group commander told them bluntly that if the B.E.F. withdrew it would be without the French First Army. "To which," recorded Pownall, "Gort replied that he was going." Gort moved his headquarters to La Panne, at the Dunkirk end of the telephone cable beneath the Channel.

Belgium had ceased fire at four a.m. In the confines of his Cabinet, Churchill conceded that Leopold might well obtain better treatment for his people thereby. "No doubt," he admitted, "History will criticise the King for having involved us and the French in Belgium's ruin." After speaking in the House that afternoon — with proper charity — about Belgium's misfortune, he invited his colleagues up to his private room.

FOR A FOURTH time they argued whether to approach Italy as Reynaud had yet again suggested. The voting was as before. Greenwood and Attlee now reasoned that any weakening would affront public opinion, particularly in the industrial centres.

Using what was to become a stock phrase, that the French were "trying to get us on to the slippery slope," Churchill suggested that the position would be very different once Germany had tried and failed to invade Britain.

Again Chamberlain and Halifax argued for peace. "We may get better terms *before* France goes out of the war and our aircraft factories are bombed," argued the foreign secretary, "than . . . in three months time."

To Churchill this was heresy — Hitler's terms, he repeated, would put Britain "at his mercy." "We should get no worse terms if we went on fighting, even if we were beaten, than were open to us now. If, however, we continued the war and Germany attacked us, no doubt we would suffer some damage, but they also would suffer severe losses."

Halifax did not share this enthusiasm for trading blows. He still did not see, he said, what the prime minister "felt was so wrong" in the French suggestion of trying out the possibilities of mediation. Neville Chamberlain also felt that to fight on involved a considerable gamble. He suggested they announce, "While we will fight to the end to preserve

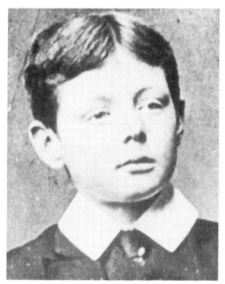

Churchill as a boy at Harrow School.

Right: 'And we lived happily ever after,' wrote Churchill in an autobiography, shortly after marrying Clementine.

Below: In August 1929 Churchill set off with his son Randolph and daughter Diana for a holiday in Canada.

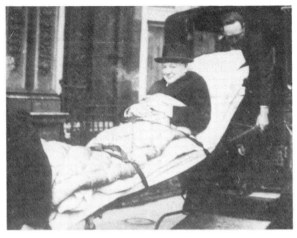

Above: Addiction to alcohol – an inherited weakness – left Churchill prone to a variety of illnesses including pneumonia and (picture) paratyphoid, for which he was hospitalized in October 1932.

Left: In February 1938 advice from his US millionaire friend Bernard Baruch (left) brought Churchill to the edge of bankruptcy. In desperation he put up for sale Chartwell, his beloved country mansion. Four weeks later, bailed out by a South African financier, Churchill took Chartwell off the market.

Often unsure in his early months of premiership Churchill turned to his former enemy, South African premier Jan Smuts, for counsel.

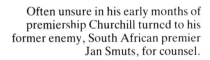

Wearing spurious naval costume
Churchill returned from his first
conference with Roosevelt in August
1941 to be met by his wife and Eden.

An effective and compelling orator, Churchill developed a style never
adequately copied by his admirers.

Right: Churchill's first wartime broadcast on October 2, 1939. In later months, as the strain began to tell, he had his famous speeches broadcast by a BBC actor instead.

Closely connected with the movie industry after Hungarian-born director Alexander Korda bankrolled his gambling debts, Churchill and his country home became a mecca for the world's film stars like Charlie Chaplin (here visiting Chartwell in 1931).

After attending Churchill's War Cabinet sessions in 1941 Australia's Prime Minister Robert Menzies put on a jovial face for photographers, then left to warn the other Dominion premiers that Churchill was running amok.

Above: What price Churchill? Is there some political move behind this giant poster in the Strand, London which has been mystifying Londoners for several days?

Unlike the rest of the big city populations Churchill was nearly always forewarned by British Intelligence of coming Nazi air raids, and fled from the capital, to return and show the familiar bulldog expression in the devastated streets the next day.

While London's wealthy and influential slept soundly in the bombproof cellars of the Dorchester Hotel, and Mr Churchill left by the back gate of No 10 Downing Street for his hideout in Oxfordshire, the working class took refuge in squalid conditions in the subway stations.

The secret underground headquarters of the War Cabinet and the Chiefs of Staff, in Marsham Street, Westminster, London. The building, designed to hold over 2,000 people, included radio and power stations. Lord Ismay in the Map Room of the underground H.Q. With him is Mr G. Ranse, to whom all correspondence was addressed during the war, when the War Cabinet Offices were a top priority secret.

MINISTÈRE
DE LA
DEFENSE NATIONALE
ET DE LA GUERRE.

RÉPUBLIQUE FRANÇAISE.

Original on Microfilm I76/123

Cabinet
du Ministre

(29)

Paris, le 24 5 1940

Copie du télégramme adressé par M.CHURCHILL
à M.REYNAUD pour le Général WEYGAND (Déchiffré
à 5 a.m.,le 24 Mai 1940)

-:-:-:-:-:-:-:-:-:-:-:-:-

Général GORT wires that co-ordination on the northern fr
is essential with the armies of the three different nations.H
says that he cannot undertake this co-ordination as he is alre
dy fighting north and south and is threatened on his lines of
communication.At the same time Sir Roger Keyes tells me that
to 3 p.m. today,May 23rd.,the Belgian Headquarters and the Kin
had received no directive.How does this agree with your statement that Blanchard and Gort are main dans la main? Appreciate
fully difficulties of communication but feel no effective concert of operations in the northern area against which the enemy
are concentrating.Trust you will be able to rectify this.Gort
further says that any advance by him must be in the nature of a
sortie and that relief must come from the South as he has no
ammunition for a serious attack.

Nevertheless we are instructing him to persevere in carryin
out your plan.We have not here even seen your own directive,and
have no knowledge of the details of your northern operations.
Will you kindly have this sent us throught the French Mission at
the earliest possible moment. All good wishes.

110042

After the defeat of France in 1940 the Nazis seized documents including
Churchill's damning messages at the time of Dunkirk. These are often still
withheld from the British archives.

our independence, we are ready to consider decent terms."

This attracted only derision from the PM. "Nations," he intoned, in full stormflood of his oratory, "which go down fighting rise again; but those which surrender tamely are finished."

"Nothing in my suggestion," Halifax corrected him, "could even remotely be described as ultimate capitulation."

Churchill said it again: "The chances of decent terms being offered to us are a thousand to one against."

It was six-fifteen p.m. Evidently worried by the simmering revolt, he ushered them out and invited in all twenty-five of their junior Cabinet colleagues. He motioned them to chairs around the long table, and harangued them under a lowering pall of cigar smoke, eschewing neither embellishment nor evasion. "He is quite magnificent," dictated Labour's Hugh Dalton for his diary that day. "The man, and the only man, we have for this hour."

Churchill spoke scathingly of the French — "hypnotized by the Maginot Line," he called them. He blamed the B.E.F.'s retreat on the French failure to push northwards from the Somme.

How many would get away we could not tell. . . . Calais had been defended by a British force which had refused to surrender, and it was said that there were no survivors.

Dunkirk, he continued, motioning with his cigar, was under a pall of black smoke. "On two occasions great flights of German bombers turned away and declined battle when they saw our fighter patrols."

It would be said, "and with some truth," that this was the greatest British defeat for centuries.

Attempts to invade us would no doubt be made, but they would be beset with immense difficulty. We should mine all round the coast; our Navy was immensely strong . . . our supplies of food, oil, etc., were ample; we had good troops in this island, others were on the way by sea, both British Army units coming from remote garrisons and excellent Dominion troops.

His main purpose was to discourage thoughts of peace.

It was idle to think that if we tried to make peace now, we should get better terms from Germany than if we went on and fought it out. The Germans would demand our fleet — that would be called "disarmament" — our naval bases, and much else. We should become a puppet state, though a British Government which would be Hitler's puppet would be set up — "under Mosley or some such person.". . .

"Therefore," he said, "we shall go on and we shall fight it out, here or elsewhere. And if at last the long story is to end . . . let it end only when each one of us lies choking in his own blood upon the field."

At this there was "a murmur of approval,"* primarily from his stalwart friends of The Focus — Amery, Lord Lloyd and Dalton himself. No one expressed dissent. Asked by the home secretary, Churchill said he was against all evacuation of London. "Mere bombing," he growled, "will not make us go."

He went to the fireplace. Dalton joined him, stooped and patted his shoulder. "You ought to get that cartoon of Low showing us all rolling up our sleeves and falling in behind you," he remarked, "and frame it."

"Yes," grinned Winston, "that was a good one, wasn't it?"†

"He is a darling!" added Dalton as a postscript to his diary.

When his inner Cabinet reassembled at seven Churchill referred to this demonstration — he could not, he said, recall "a gathering of persons occupying such high places" expressing themselves so emphatically. He might have added that their political fortunes too were closely linked with his own.

So the fight would go on. Shortly before midnight his message was telephoned to Paris, discountenancing any Italian mediation: Britain and France must display "stout hearts;" this would surely attract American support and admiration.[35]

True, the dissent was growing. The Australian High Commissioner submitted a seven page memorandum suggesting they invite Roosevelt to set up a conference "to formulate a peace settlement;" Winston crossed this out and scrawled *No*. Where Stanley Bruce had pleaded on the final page, "The further shedding of blood and the continuance of hideous suffering is unnecessary," Churchill violently scribbled it out and scratched *rot* at its foot. "The end is rotten," he amplified to his personal assistant, Desmond Morton.[36]

IN THIS ELDERLY prime minister, adrenalin had begun pumping. He savoured each ruthless decision.

He lectured the new C.I.G.S. that Gort must now slow his retreat to conform with French movements, "otherwise there would be a danger of getting no troops off." Weaponless and dispirited, two thousand

---

*Thus in Dalton's original diary; in Martin Gilbert's volume, "loud cries of approval." Sir John Reith noted in his diary only "humbugging and sycophantic" interpolations of *hear, hear* during the "dramatic, unreal, insincere" speech. The episode took its place in Winston's self-mythology and grew each time he recounted it, as in his memoirs: "Quite a number seemed to jump up from the table and come running to my chair, shouting and patting me on the back."

†In December Churchill suspected that Low was a Trotskyist and complained of his *Evening Standard* cartoons. Beaverbrook reminded him how often Winston had told him not to interfere. "I do not agree with Low," the press lord wrote him. "I have rarely done so. I do not interefere with Low. I have never done so."

British soldiers were now trickling onto the boats each hour, but as John Martin wrote, Churchill's confidence and energy were amazing.[37] There sprang to mind famous lines on William Pitt: "Nobody left his presence without feeling a braver man." As disaster overtook calamity, his mood brightened.

He telegraphed to Reynaud the promise to evacuate French troops on an equal basis. It was meant well, but when Spears delivered this telegram he saw the anger spurt into the Frenchman's face. If that were not so, Reynaud snapped, public opinion would be *dechainée* — "unleashed" against Britain. Churchill flashed a further message to Spears: "Continue report constantly. Meanwhile reiterate our inflexible resolve to continue whatever they do." He added however, "it would be inexpedient to give all the figures Reynaud wants at present."[38]

Over eight hundred boats and pleasure craft were now shuttling between England and the embattled beaches, braving air attacks. Vice-Admiral Jean Charles Abrial, the French commander at Dunkirk, was furious at having to hold the port's perimeter merely to enable the British to decamp: his government, he challenged Pownall at Dunkirk, had given him no such instructions. The British general quietened the Frenchman down, and embarked that night for England with Gort's ADC Lord Munster aboard a Thames pleasure steamer.

In London there was an air of tragedy and suspense. "A horrible discussion of what instructions to send Gort," wrote Cadogan, after the May 29 Cabinet. They decided to instruct him to choose his own moment to surrender. That evening Churchill, who had been "theatrically bulldoggish," opposed as usual by Chamberlain and Halifax, asked the War Office to despatch this cipher message to the B.E.F. commander:

> If you are cut from all communication with us, and all evacuation from Dunkirk and beaches had in your judgment been finally prevented . . . you would become the sole judge of when it was impossible to inflict further damage upon the enemy. His Majesty's Government are sure that the repute of the British army is safe in your hands.[39]

Shortly, he sent a message to Reynaud for the information of his generals: they had evacuated 50,000 and hoped to save 30,000 more during the night. "We shall build up a new B.E.F. from St Nazaire," he promised. "I am bringing regulars from India and Palestine. Australians and Canadians are arriving soon." He ended by assuring Reynaud, "I send this in all comradeship. Do not hesitate to speak frankly to me."[40]

Hours later, impatient to know if his telegram had gone off to Lord Gort, he telephoned his duty secretary to check up. John Martin found him pacing the bedroom, dressed only in an undervest: there was still no word from the War Office. Winston turned angrily away, picked up the chamber pot and made noisy use of it.

LORD MUNSTER ARRIVED at Admiralty House the next morning. He pleaded with Winston, still in his bath, to extricate Lord Gort.

Sir Henry Pownall came over to the morning staff meeting with the same plea. Winston pressed him for the latest figures, emphasized the need to embark French soldiers too. By morning, of 120,000 taken off the beaches, only six thousand were French. Only 800 troops had sailed with him on their pleasure boat — built for 2,000 — but Pownall suggested that each Frenchman saved meant one less Englishman. He also urged priority for the B.E.F.'s valuable commanders, staff officers and NCOs rather than its "tail."

After asking him to stay behind with Eden and Dill to discuss the hapless Lord Gort, Churchill drafted new instructions ordering Gort home as soon as his force fell below corps strength. It was an inspired, if uninspiring, solution. The message was sent over Eden's name at two p.m.: "No personal discretion is left to you in the matter." When the corps commander nominated by Gort considered further evacuation impossible, he was authorized "to capitulate formally to avoid useless slaughter."[41]

The afternoon Cabinet faced up to abandoning Norway. "I regard the operations at Narvik," minuted Churchill, "as a shocking example of costly overcaution and feebleness, all the more lamentable in contrast with German fortitude in defence and vigour in attack." "Ordinary Cabinet," recorded Lord Halifax wearily afterwards. "Winston was in combative and discursive mood. I have never seen so disorderly a mind. I am coming to the conclusion that his process of thought is one that has to operate through *speech*. As this is exactly the reverse of my own, it is irritating."

* * *

One day his son came on leave and, as Winston was shaving, commented in his forthright way, "I don't see how you can beat the Germans." Winston glared at Randolph. "I shall drag the United States in," he said.

The shrewd American president was not minded to be dragged anywhere, least of all in an election year. He hinted to Mackenzie-King that he might wage an undeclared war against Germany in the Atlantic, rather as America had fought France soon after 1776. Meanwhile his interest in the British fleet was growing. Churchill now received from the Canadian a message suggesting that sending it over the Atlantic might indirectly ease American entry into the war. Both the president and

Cordell Hull believed that if Germany threatened vicious action to punish Britain for allowing the fleet to escape "public opinion in the United States would demand active intervention."[42]

Churchill, for all his human failings in Roosevelt's eyes, was not befuddled by this convoluted offer: he correctly saw F.D.R.'s hand behind it, and replied to Ottawa in language strident enough to reach Washington. "We must be careful not to let Americans view too complacently [the] prospect of a British collapse, out of which they would get the British Fleet and the guardianship of the British Empire, minus Great Britain." And he allowed himself the pointed commentary: "Although President is our best friend, no practical help has been forthcoming from the United States yet."[43]

* * *

On the last morning of May he flew to Paris. Spears meeting him at Villacoublay found him in grand form — "Very sweet to me, poking me in stomach." Fortified by lunch at the embassy, Churchill entered the Supreme War Council with eyes aflame and cheeks aflush; the mood of the others was frigid. "By noon today," he boasted, "we evacuated 165,000 men from Dunkirk by sea."[44]

Reynaud pointed out the British had evacuated only 15,000 of the 200,000 French.

"The French are being left behind?" gasped Weygand.

Now it was Churchill who shrugged. "We are companions in misfortune," he responded. "There is nothing to be gained from recriminations." When Reynaud demanded that Britain throw in everything she had, Churchill hedged: "I cannot say if we will be able to send forces to France."

Since Reynaud insisted, he became blunt: "Do you recall when you asked me for ten fighter squadrons a fortnight ago? . . . Nobody knows what's left of them now. Now we've got to protect our factories — not so much our civilian population, who might almost be better off [*dont il vaudrait presque mieux*] if they were bombed. If we don't defeat the German airforce, it will be all over for us not long after."

"I'm well aware that you gave us one quarter of your defences," Reynaud politely summarised. "But *we* have thrown our entire airforce into this battle."

Reverting to Dunkirk, he suggested they now embark the rearguard, commencing with the British. Deliberately trading on Churchill's generosity [45] he introduced a draft telegram to Admiral Abrial at Dunkirk, ordering French troops to allow the British to embark first.

Churchill declared — "with tears in his eyes and a tremor in his voice," according to the French record — that he did not want further French sacrifice: the three British divisions would be proud to form the rearguard. The telegram was amended: the evacuation was to proceed on equal terms — "arm in arm."

He returned to the embassy: aware that he might never see Paris again, he tried in vain to persuade Louis Spears to motor him around its streets for one last time. "Winston magnificent," his old friend recorded that night, "and very moving: 'No recriminations; British will provide rear guards; better our civilisation should perish now and Finish be written at end [of] these grand chapters than that they should drag on for a while in slavery'."

"He means to say same thing in Commons on Tuesday."

CHAPTER 25

We Shall Fight In The Hills

A FTER HITLER'S ORGANIZATION chief Robert Ley strangled himself at Nuremberg the Americans removed his brain; they also borrowed the murdered Mussolini's brain, hoping to learn something about the chemistries of power. But for the workings of Mr Churchill's brain, we can only draw upon his observed behaviour: we can ask what impelled him to press on? What generated his mental troughs and peaks?

Undoubtedly he deliberately courted danger. His lifelong adviser Desmond Morton would see in him a "bogus maleness" — implying that Winston lacked those qualities of steadfastness otherwise known as "moral courage,"[1] that marked, say, a Claude Auchinleck. Modern psychiatrists would recognize in Winston a category familiar in the corporate world: the "harried over-achiever" — the man who has become addicted to stress. Stress gives him the high, the physiological arousal, that others derive from alcohol, caffeine or nicotine. In chemical terms, it rushes catecholamines like adrenaline into the bloodstream.[2] Leaders among these harried over-achievers are the "Type A" group — men who engage in chronic, continuous struggle against circumstances and against other people. Says Dr Paul A. Rosch, "The Type A individual has perhaps become addicted to his own adrenaline and unconsciously seeks ways to get those little urges."

Churchill displayed the characteristics of this type: if deprived of stress, he became irritable and depressed.[3] Speed was paramount. He glued specially printed red tags onto directives to his staff: ACTION THIS DAY. Chamberlain's secretary would write, "His policy is one of action for action's sake."[4] A.V. Alexander, Winston's successor as First Lord, observed: "Churchill [is] much better in health already since he became PM."[5] More than that: as his plight worsened, his mood brightened, his dynamism increased. Meeting him at Villacoublay on the last day in May 1940, General Spears spotted the startling freshness "generated by the sense of the danger inherent in such a journey." He added that the proximity of danger invariably acted as a tonic and a stimulant to Churchill.[6]

HE WAS UP at six a.m. in Paris that Saturday, June 1, flew back to London and stomped into No.10 toward mid-day. He relished the prospect of Nazi attack. "I believe," he red-inked on a memo on that day, "we shall make them rue the day they try to invade our island."[7]

By now nearly 200,000 British soldiers had been taken off the beaches; but only 34,000 French. Lord Gort arrived at Victoria station at 9:20 a.m., having crossed by motor boat. Anglo-French recriminations spewed out in his wake. At Dunkirk, Reynaud complained, Gort had refused boat passes to a French general and his ADC, saying "Two French going means two less British." Darlan later questioned whether it had been wise to entrust the defence of Dunkirk to the B.E.F. The British he opined, had only one thought: "To the boats!"[8]

As Gort walked into the Cabinet room the ministers rose and applauded. Churchill declared that Dynamo, the gigantic evacuation operation, would end that night. Justifying this in a message telephoned to Weygand, he explained that the crisis had been reached.

Six ships, many filled with troops, sunk by bombing this morning. Artillery fire menaces only practicable channel. Enemy closing in on reduced bridgehead. . . By going tonight much may certainly be saved, though much will be lost.

Since, the message continued, neither Admiral Abrial in the fortress, nor Weygand, nor those in England, could fully assess the situation, he had ordered Major General Sir Harold Alexander, commanding the British sector, to consult with Abrial on the best course to adopt.[9]

Before stepping into his boat Gort had consoled Admiral Abrial. "I am giving you my finest Alexander."

Darlan was unimpressed by Alexander. "The moment this military thunderbolt, this *foudre de guerre*, arrived at Dunkirk," he wrote scornfully, "he told Admiral Abrial that in his view the situation would not allow of his remaining and that he would therefore embark that same Saturday evening for England."[10]

Thus the French formed the rearguard after all.

* * *

In May the Zionists had resumed their haggling. They persuaded Churchill to lever their arch-enemy Malcolm MacDonald out of the Colonial office; it was his White Paper that had thwarted their plans to settle Jews in Palestine.[11] Six days after attaining office Winston sent his firstborn son to their leader, Chaim Weizmann, bearing a reassuring letter: it promised to accept Jewish help and to investigate the British army's oppressive searches for illegal Jewish arms in Palestine.

Britain had ten Regular battalions permanently stationed there. Weizmann now began demanding that Britain arm and mobilize the Jews there instead.

His long-term purpose was transparent. MacDonald's successor Lord Lloyd warned that to arm the Jews would stir up a Moslem hornet's nest. But on May 23 Churchill directed that in view of the impending danger to Britain, "At least eight Battalions of British Regular Infantry must come at once from Palestine." The Jews would be armed instead. Lloyd asked Churchill's P.P.S., Eric Seal, to see him immediately, and objected in the strongest terms: to give the Jews "arms to use with their own discretion against the Arabs" would have appalling repercussions, "even if ostensibly they are only given them for self defence." Seal reported this to Churchill, adding: "I must confess that I have a strong feeling that he is right."

Churchill scratched this out. "How can you remove all the troops," he scribbled, "and yet leave the Jews unarmed — & disarmed by us?" Lloyd refused to budge: he could spare the eight battalions, — provided only that there was no deviation from the White Paper that might inflame Arab feeling; above all, no steps whatever must be taken to raise "a Jewish military force for internal security purposes." Churchill scrawled: "*We must have the eight battalions*;" he invited Lloyd to talk with Weizmann, and commented crisply: "You know what I think about the White Paper."[12]

THE RICH AND influential reacted to the emergency in different ways: one titled lady wrote him offering £60,000 in pearls;[13] others tried to ship their children and themselves out to the New World. Churchill warned Ottawa that the Royal Family might be sent there soon.[14]

Like a major stockholder in a troubled company, ambassador Kennedy slept with one eye open throughout June. It worried him that Churchill had forbidden his ministers even to discuss the Canada plan with him. Halifax, asked point blank, ducked reply. "You'd better ask Winston," he said.[15] Then Churchill struck a different note: nothing, not even the National Gallery's collection, was to go abroad: everything was to be hidden in caves and cellars: "We are going to beat them."[16]

That Saturday, June 1, he drove to Chequers for his first weekend there as PM. Henceforth, come Friday afternoon he would bustle out of No.10, taking private secretary and shorthand writers down to the locked gate set in the garden wall where their car was waiting. The Daimler had been fitted with a police gong so that they could scatter other cars and run every red light between Downing-street and Buckinghamshire.

Chequers, the country estate of prime ministers for thirty years, had rated a mention in the Doomesday Book in 1086; work on the mansion had begun comparatively recently, around 1320. On one flank was a large terrace and rose garden; on the other a lawn, and beyond that parks and woodland to the horizon. With its sweeping lawns, century-old yew pines, sprawling terraces and brick chimneys it would have been a peaceful retreat were it not for the barbed wire, sentries and permanent police detail supervised by a Scotland Yard inspector.*

The twelve-hundred acre estate stood relatively high, so the summer heat did not disturb it. Inside the E-shaped three-storied Elizabethan-style mansion was what had originally been an open courtyard with a gallery along one side. The rooms were packed ·with museum piece furniture and Cromwellian relics. It was not an easy building to heat. Winston's ADC would discover one distinguished American visitor sitting in the toilet, reading the newspaper in an overcoat and trying to keep warm.

A distinguished painted audience of deceased English gentry frowned down upon the entrance hall, many with the bulbous noses typical of that species; the paintings of monarchs that enlivened this warren of panelled rooms revealed that several had the grubby necks that characterised former royalty — before their severance, that is.[17] At the entrance to the formal gardens were the words, "All care abandon, ye who enter here." The weekends were not always carefree: some of the grimmest news came to him here — but also the most uplifting, including news of the atrocity at Pearl Harbour.

REFRESHED, BY EARLY Sunday evening June 2, he was back at No.10.

He again ordered Dynamo ended. Taken aback, the French accused him of betraying their rearguard troops; Churchill relented. The French ambassador Charles Corbin had a frosty interview with him that evening and wired to Reynaud at seven-thirty: "I have just seen the Prime Minister who has given me a formal promise to continue during the night of [June] third to fourth all naval and air effort necessary to ensure that the remaining French troops are evacuated."[18]

Churchill performed this service in bad grace and sent a short-tempered telegram to Reynaud. "We are coming back for your men tonight," it read. "Pray make sure that all facilities are used promptly. Last night for three hours many ships waited idly at much cost and danger."[19]

Softening, Churchill felt that France should get the R.A.F. fighter squadrons that Reynaud again demanded. At a War Cabinet on Monday

---

*He kept a log of Mr Churchill's weekend guests: e.g., "Miss Roper, masseuse." Mrs H.M. Hyams placed this treasured 140-page volume of her late husband's at the author's disposal.

the third, he ran into violent opposition from the austere, pragmatic air marshals over this. Newall wanted everything but six bomber and three Hurricane fighter squadrons brought back from France. He scathingly pointed out that over 250 fighter planes had already been sent over against Air Chief Marshal Dowding's explicit advice. At one stage Dowding, who was present, rose from his seat, slapped on the table in front of the prime minister a graph showing the fighter wastage rate — some thought that he was handing in his resignation. The R.A.F. now had only 224 Hurricanes and 280 Spitfires left, and even fewer pilots; they were losing two dozen fighter planes a day. "If the present rate of wastage continues for another fortnight," he rasped, "we shall not have a single Hurricane left in France," and added, *"or in this country."* Exasperated, Dowding laid down his pencil and announced: "I have said my last word."[20]

The prime minister of course had to take a less insular attitude than the air chief marshal. He uneasily pointed out that it would look to the French as though Britain had five hundred fighter planes standing idle while France was making her supreme effort. But the Cabinet heeded Dowding's temper. For the coming battle on the Somme, the chiefs of staff agreed to send out two army divisons — Churchill even talked of three. He wired to his linkman Spears in Paris, staying at the Ritz: "You should prepare them for favourable response Army but disappointment about Air."[21]

THUS FAR HE had not had a good war. He had been outwitted in Norway and France; he was still trying to toss his airforce into the maelstrom of France's defeat. Several times during June the opportunity arose of ending this madness, but personal prestige demanded that he struggle on, like a punch-drunk boxer. "Britain always wins one battle," the pot-valiant Major Morton would reassure the French: "The last."

Superb oratory alone enabled Churchill to ride down the apprehensions of his queasier colleagues: few episodes illustrate his methods better than his address to a closed meeting of hero-worshipping junior ministers on Monday, June 3, when he wheedled out of them a demand that he should not contemplate peace with Hitler now. He promised that things were getting better; claimed that "the French [had] insisted on the post of honour" at Dunkirk and so, "after a seemly wrangle, we brought the Cameron Highlanders away" who would otherwise "have stayed and died at the end." He dwelt briefly upon Europe's likely fate — "Famine, starvation and revolt most of all in the slave lands which Germany has overrun."

The PM [Dalton recorded] wants to be able to say to the House tomorrow, "If I wavered for a moment, all my colleagues in the Government would turn and rend me."[22]

He detained his secretaries late at Admiralty House, preparing the next day's speech to the House and considering what support to render France.

That Tuesday afternoon — a sweltering hot day — was tense with an uncertain excitement. Before going to the Despatch Box to speak, he had ascertained the final figures on Dynamo: the final score was magnificent — 224,318 British saved, to which had now been added 111,172 Allied troops; the total was thrice that at Gallipoli.[23]

While warning the Members that wars were not won by evacuations, he lauded the heroism of the R.A.F. and the rearguard who had withstood the enemy's "eight or nine armoured divisions, each of 400 armoured vehicles" behind which had plodded the "dull, brute mass of the ordinary German army;" like splashes of oil colour he daubed words across the great canvas of his speech. A torrent of prose invoked a cavalcade of childhood images from the Knights of the Round Table to the Crusaders; he was in his element. "We are told" — he did not say by whom — "that Herr Hitler has a plan for invading the British Isles," he said, adding somberly: "This has often been thought of before."

He described candidly how the enemy panzer divisions had scythed around and to the rear of the Allied armies only to be halted just before Dunkirk — not by Hitler's order, which he did not mention, but by the heroic defenders of Calais and Boulogne. Four days of fighting had left only thirty unwounded survivors in Calais, he claimed, and these had been rescued by the Navy. It was a legend in the making, but it was both magnificently done and necessary: the re-born British army must look back on it as a heroic passage of arms, as a triumph despite the "treachery" of the Belgians. He accordingly reserved contumely for King Leopold. "With the least possible notice," he rasped, gripping the lapels of his jacket, "and without the advice of his Ministers," that King had sent a plenipotentiary to the enemy, exposing the whole Allied flank. The House rang with cries of Shame, Shame! Invited to form its own opinion upon "this pitiful episode," the House dutifully roared: "Treachery!" Taking their tone from this unseemly scene, the world's press labelled Leopold "coward," "deserter," "traitor" and even "the Rat King."*

---

*Tireless in his defence of the King's name, Admiral of the Fleet Sir Roger Keyes told Dalton. "It was a cowardly lie to say that the King ordered them to lay down their arms without having told his Allies."[24]

Now, Churchill promised, the British would rebuild their expeditionary army.

> We shall not flag or fail. We shall go on to the end. . . We shall fight on the beaches, we shall fight on the landing grounds, we shall fight in the fields and in the streets, we shall fight in the hills; we shall never surrender. And even if, which I do not for a moment believe, this island or a large part of it were subjugated and starving, then our Empire beyond the seas, armed and guarded by the British Fleet, would carry on the struggle, until, in God's good time, the New World, with all its power and might, steps forth to the rescue and the liberation of the old.

How often had the deliberations of the House been stifled by putrid, colourless verbiage — now Winston Churchill's tear-provoking, august prose reared like a moss-grown fortress out of its ceaseless blare, defying the scorn of commoner people for its pedantry and archaic form. By its rare beauty his language ennobled and sanctified the cause it was proclaiming.

That evening the BBC broadcast his speech after the News. The whole nation thrilled, not knowing that Churchill had refused to repeat it before the microphone. A BBC actor — "Larry the Lamb" of the Children's Hour — had agreed to mimick the prime minister before the microphone, and nobody was any the wiser.[25]

* * *

For months after the Dunkirk debacle Britain would remain on the defensive. While Ironside set about rebuilding the army, postmortems began into what Churchill had called the "unmitigated military disaster."

In retrospect, its seeds had been sown in February, with the provisional decision to ship three of the ten divisions (42nd, 44th, 5th) earmarked for Lord Gort to Scandinavia instead. Even at that time General Pownall had despairingly attributed this Norway/Finland plan to "those master strategists Winston and Ironside" — and had made comparisons with Gallipoli. Neither Georges nor Gort had been consulted about it, although it set back their build up in France by two months; in fact no ammunition at all was shipped to the B.E.F. during February in case it was needed "elsewhere." By April, Pownall was recording that Mr Churchill's Military Co-ordination Committee, responsible for the original "harebrained" plan, was known in the War Office as The Crazy Gang.[26]

Examination of the contemporary records cannot however exonerate the generals of the B.E.F. They were a poor match for Hitler's commanders, and knew it. While the nervous breakdown of one British corps commander was unexpected, the consequences of retreat should not have surprised them — the loss of morale, of heavy equipment, of prepared positions, and above all of intricate signals facilities. Their private papers reveal aristocratic, condescending attitudes; their ancient dislike of French and Belgians was resented and returned. The language barrier intensified the differences. French records tell of one farcical meeting between General Vuillemin "who can't understand English" and the British forward air commander Air Vice Marshal Sir Arthur Barratt "who talks *impossible* French."[27]

Churchill's mind was already roaming ahead to more glorious times. "How wonderful it would be," he wrote wistfully to Ismay, "if the Germans could be made to wonder where they were going to be struck next, instead of forcing us to try to wall in the Island and roof it over." They must shake off this "mental and moral prostration" to Hitler's will: special troops must create "a reign of terror" along Hitler's lengthening coastline with "butcher and bolt" tactics: tanks landed from flat-bottomed assault craft must make full-scale raids: Bomber Command must deliver ruinous attacks on the towns and cities of Nazi-occupied Europe. He displayed his impatience in a letter to the King that evening: "Better days will come — though not yet." And he admitted to old rival Stanley Baldwin, "I cannot say that I have enjoyed being Prime Minister very much so far."[28]

AT LUNCHTIME ON Wednesday June 5 the hand-lettered newsbills announced: GREAT GERMAN OFFENSIVE BEGINS — OFFICIAL.

Hitler's armies were lunging south across the Somme towards Paris. Weygand complained that morning to Reynaud that Britain was ignoring every appeal. Learning that France was pleading for planes Churchill was again overwhelmed by dangerous sentiment. "W.S.C. had meeting with Air Staff, Dowding and Beaverbrook," a top civil servant learned. "I do hope we're not uncovering ourselves to help a helpless France."

Again Dowding stood up to Churchill although closely cross-examined on how many planes and pilots he could spare.[29] Overruling him, Churchill telegraphed to Reynaud that two fighter and four bomber squadrons would stand by to help from British airfields.[30] But shortly he was shown an insulting letter written by the French airforce commander General Vuillemin jibing at the R.A.F. performance as "tardy, inadequate," and his sentiment ran out.[31] Two days earlier, Vuillemin had demanded the support of at least half of Britain's homebased fighters — wanting ten squadrons now and ten later; if Hitler should commit the "strategic blunder" of attacking Britain first, they could instantly return.[32] Vuillemin's language broke the camel's back. Echoing Churchill, Ismay called France's behaviour "outrageous — doing nothing but slinging mud at us."[33]

At Admiralty House he stayed in bed the next morning dictating fretful minutes: about new inventions, recruiting naval pilots to the fighter defences, mining Lulea, and disabling a Norwegian airfield. "This ought to have been thought of before," he dictated; on one Admiralty document he red-inked the comment: "We seem quite incapable of *action*." Shortly a minute arrived from the Prof, showing that his fertile brain was also working: "Ten thousand hot air balloons have been ordered. . . Delivery will be completed on July 14." Sir Henry Tizard, the Prof's jealous rival and scientific adviser to the Air Staff, visited the Prof at No.10, found that the PM had told him to "drive ahead" with anything new that might be of use that summer and noted, disgruntled, in his diary: "There is enough overlapping of responsibility to hinder almost anything useful being done."[34] But improvisation was now the order of the day. At the mid-day Cabinet on the sixth the news was that the B.E.F. had abandoned 7,000 tons of ammunition, 90,000 rifles, 1,000 heavy guns, 8,000 Bren machine guns and 400 anti-tank in Flanders, as well as 475 tanks and 38,000 motor vehicles.

A telegram came from Spears. Reynaud had telephoned President Roosevelt during the night, and gained "keen satisfaction." Roosevelt had claimed to be helping as far as U.S. neutrality law would permit. Spears had then attended that morning's Paris Cabinet: Weygand was proving difficult. "Mr Churchill," the French C-in-C had said, "may think General Vuillemin's demands unreasonable. Perhaps if he saw the condition of our army he would think we were unreasonable to go on fighting."[35]

The R.A.F. threw 144 fighters into the battle on June 7, an effort which Reynaud derided as inadequate. When Churchill promised five Hurricane squadrons for the morrow, and four more operating from British bases, the Frenchman protested that this was only a quarter of the British force. "It is my duty," he wrote the next day, "to ask that like us, you throw your entire force into this battle."[36] It was his final appeal, and it failed: Churchill smelt an alibi in preparation. As he pointed out to the Defence Committee, if Britain remained strong she could win the war "and in so doing, restore France to her position."

The French appeal was refused — Churchill's first draft being blunt to the point of injurious: "The score of squadrons or so," he would have written to Reynaud, "which you would like to have melted down in the next few days as a mere makeweight or episode in your splendid struggle will we believe if properly used in this country enable us to break his Air attack, and thus break him." Ultimately a more tactful message was sent: "We are giving you all the support we can in this great battle, short of ruining the capacity of this country to continue the war."[37]

GENERAL SPEARS RETURNED somewhat prematurely from Paris, and attended the afternoon Cabinet resplendent in red and gold and with a revolver holstered to his belt. As they trooped out, they glimpsed the *Pictorial*'s editor Cecil King sitting outside.

He and many other editors were concerned about the rising tide of discontent as a quarter of a million B.E.F. survivors found their voice. Fortunately, they were as yet blaming the presence in continued high office of Chamberlain and his "gang." On the sixth Churchill had put pressure on the editors not to disturb national unity, promising to ease out Chamberlain soon on the grounds of ill-health.

Cecil King had asked for a meeting and was ushered in at eight p.m. on June 7, as the harrassed air minister Sinclair was leaving — "the complete tragic actor," King wrote in his diary, a sort of "minor [Henry] Irving" with his long black hair, deepset hazel eyes and tragic pallor. Winston remained at the long table with his back to the fireplace; he was dressed in his rompers, his hair wispy, his face flushed. After warning that he would face down any serious criticism in the House with a vote of censure, he defended Chamberlain as head and shoulders above the rest of his "pretty mediocre" team. Only one year before some Tories had hated him, Churchill, enough to try and hound him out of his constituency, and they were still in the House. It did not escape him that Chamberlain still attracted the louder cheers. However unrepresentative of popular feeling, he lectured the newspaperman, this House was the ultimate source and arbiter of power. If he trampled upon it — as he could — the resulting internecine strife would afford the Germans their best chance of victory.

What use to be dictator, he asked, if he could not choose his own governmental personnel? After all, he had favoured with office every member who had opposed Chamberlain — men like Law, Boothby, and Macmillan. If he were to exclude everybody else where was he to stop? Only "a tiny handful" had been right. At a moment when Italy might declare war and France might quit, was this the time for bickering?

Spears came to dinner afterwards, and marvelled once again at "Winston's magnificent courage."

He needed every ounce of it to take the blow which misfortune bestowed on the eighth. In the final evacuation of Norway which had begun four days earlier the aircraft carrier *Glorious* had completed the remarkable feat of deck-landing a land-based squadron of Hurricanes for passage home to Scapa. Now the troopships and supply convoys were homeward bound, although neither Lord Cork nor the admiralty had advised Admiral Forbes of these movements. That omission now cost Britain dearly. An enemy battle cruiser squadron intercepted *Glorious* and her two destroyers, sailing alone to the south of the convoys, and

Scharnhorst sank all three with the loss of 1,470 lives.

DESMOND MORTON HAD always warned that the French army and airforce were rotten; at the time Churchill would have none of it. But now he must have wished many things unsaid. "Since the fall of the monarchy," he had declared on September 18, 1936, "the French Army has been the highest expression of the soul of France. No one can doubt its fine and enduring qualities." "The French Army," he had written on February 17, 1938, "from commander in chief to private soldier, from Monarchist to Communist, is a harmonious engine for the defence of France against aggression." Their chiefs, he had then claimed, could certainly watch the nazification of the German Army with composure.

Disappointed now in Georges and the older French generals, he was all the more enraptured by the lofty young cavalry officer who loped into No.10 on June 9 and proclaimed his country's will to continue the struggle "even, if need be, in her Empire." This was General Charles André Joseph Marie de Gaulle, recently appointed France's undersecretary for war — one of the few men not personally vetted by Reynaud's all-powerful mistress. The older diplomats mocked at this ill-proportioned tank officer; Sir Alexander Cadogan's sardonic *mot* galloped round the ministries: "I can't tell you anything about de Gaulle," he scoffed, "except that he's got a head like a pineapple and hips like a woman."[38]

The extraordinary romance with de Gaulle was to cause Winston more grief than any other matter in World War II. In the final year of war this Frenchman would swamp the cable traffic between London and Washington to the eclipse of matters of far greater moment: telegrams about de Gaulle outnumbered those about Poland by five to one.[39] An unexplained episode in April 1943 suggests that somebody even tried to do away with this power-hungry, amoral general.

Churchill detailed Morton to take de Gaulle under his wing.

HITLER HAD MADE no attempt to bomb London and, the intercepted Luftwaffe signals suggested, would not do so unless provoked. But to Churchill there seemed only one certain path to victory: and that was, he informed his old friend Field Marshal Smuts, that Hitler *should* attack, "and in so doing break his air weapon."[40]

On the same day, June 9, he briefed Britain's ambassador in Washington to talk to Roosevelt about the probability that a pro German government might surrender the British Fleet. "This dastard deed would not be done by His Majesty's present advisers, but if Moseley [sic] were Prime Minister or some other Quisling Government set up, it is exactly what they would do." Lothian was to discourage "any complacent assumption" by the Americans that they would "pick up the debris of the British Empire" by their present policy.

If we go down Hitler has a very good chance of conquering the world.[41]

Time was running out. Churchill could not expect United States intervention before the presidential election in November; asked that mid-day if the French were likely to hold on, Sir John Dill replied with a terse "No."

Churchill announced that he would fly to Paris after lunch.

All afternoon his party hung around, but nobody knew whether the government had left Paris or not, and they decided not to go until the next day. Spears detected that Reynaud was not very keen to meet Winston. To ease their meeting, Churchill sent a softer message hinting at aid and lauding the "undaunted courage" of the French armies.[42]

He took an afternoon nap and was wakened with news that Italy had declared war. "Am rather glad," sniffed Cadogan, over at the F.O. "Now we can say what we think of these purulent dogs." Churchill's language also rose to the occasion. "People who go to Italy to look at ruins," he tersely said to his secretary, sending for the American ambassador, "won't have to go so far as Naples and Pompeii again."[43] "Words fail me," reported Kennedy, "in repeating what he thinks of Mussolini." Churchill swore to him — as Lothian was no doubt also telling Roosevelt — that as long as he lived the navy would never be turned over to Hitler. But he again sought to stir fears about what a Mosley government might do to save the country from destruction — in which context he expressed vexation that Hitler had yet to bomb a single English town: "By his conversations," noted Kennedy, "I should judge that he believes that with the bombing of wellknown places in England the United States will come in."[44]

Roosevelt was too shrewd to hurry prematurely to either France's or Britain's aid. When an interventionist colleague urged him to send over aircraft, guns and destroyers, even if obsolete, the president replied candidly enough that the destroyers would be quite useless — they had only four guns each and no anti-aircraft armament. Moreover, what if Hitler should win? "I might guess wrong," explained Roosevelt. "They [the destroyers] might serve further to enrage Hitler. We cannot tell the turn that the war will take."[45] He was undecided whether to treat with a Nazi-installed regime in France or with Reynaud's. Thus Bullitt remained in Paris even though Reynaud's government was fleeing. Later that evening Kennedy warned Washington of mounting feeling in London. He could visualize the British people's "possible eventual acceptance" of a German victory; but they would never forgive America for not coming to their aid.

The gloom spread to Admiralty House. Beaverbrook described Winson in a letter as like Atlas, but with two worlds to carry. "With one hand," wrote Beaverbrook, "he bears up the British Empire; with the other he sustains the French republic."[46] Spears suspected that he ought to have remained in Paris. Over dinner the Churchills consoled him. Dill also joined the circle; the new C.I.G.S. impressed Spears as being already very tired. The War Office seemed happy to fasten responsibility for the disaster on the French, and leave it at that. That evening Spears gained "a very painful impression indeed." He left the PM at one o'clock profoundly unhappy. "He said several times," wrote Spears, "that we were losing everywhere in the field owing to lack of preparations." John Colville also sensed this lowering mood. "He was in a bad temper," ran his account, "snapped everybody's head off, wrote angry minutes to the First Sea Lord, and refused to pay any attention to messages given him orally.

Before he left for France on the eleventh, a German battle cruiser was reported at Trondheim, with two or three cruisers. The Cabinet turned down an Operations Division suggestion that the Fleet Air Arm go in and get them. "What the hell has the Cabinet to do with naval operations?" wrote Captain Edwards miserably. "Winston again! To put down the B.C. would be the best possible tonic for the Allied cause. It would reduce the risk of invasion 30%, go 15% of the way to win the war, restore morale in the Fleet. Why doesn't the 1st S.L. resign?"

DRESSED IN BLACK, Churchill sat in the Flamingo that afternoon as it lifted into the sunshine, escorted by twelve Hurricanes. He had promised his Cabinet to talk the French out of any armistice ideas. But in his file was a report by Lord Hankey on what to do if France collapsed — about her Gold, her fleet, her oil, and the new aircraft she had ordered off American production lines.

The French army had evacuated its headquarters to Briare, eighty miles south of Paris; Reynaud had arranged a seven p.m. Supreme War Council at the Château du Muguet.[47] Churchill found them all slumped around a dining table awaiting him: he recognized Reynaud, Pétain, Darlan, and de Gaulle. He spoke firmly — "forcefully, but retaining his magnificent composure," wrote an admiring Reynaud. "He interpolated only a few sentences in French in his remarks, as was his custom, but without much success." It was his "hope" that Hitler would turn against Britain, thus giving France a respite.* If France could hold on, by the spring of 1941 he could offer 20 or 25 more British divisions.

---

*Hitler would lecture Field Marshal Erich von Manstein in December 1943: "The enemy's not going to do what we *hope*, but what will damage us the most." —*Hitler's War.*

The French however were in despair. This became plain when Weygand spoke: France's entire forces were committed; her troops were dead tired — or dead. A cohesive defence was no longer possible. "If I was to say the opposite," he said, "I should be lying."

The sweat poured down Spears' face as he listened to Weygand:

> No reserves of any kind [Spears noted in his diary], troops been fighting for six days and nights without food or rest. Men fall back at night and have to be shaken to fire. The Germans are across the Seine. . . Nothing to prevent their reaching Paris.

Churchill flushed as Weygand continued the desolate tale. *"C'est la dislocation"* — the break-up, said Weygand "that is the position I've had to explain to my government." As for Reynaud, he just kept repeating: "If we lose this battle it's because we lack the airforce."

Churchill looked round for his old friend, inquired brusquely: "Oú est Georges?" The general was sent for; he only echoed Weygand.

> Winston obviously horrified [recorded Spears that evening] but splendid. He declared as he always does that whatever happens we fight on. . . Found words of fiery eloquence, both in French and English, but said that France could not expect us to destroy our only hope, air arm, in this battle. Winston was understanding and kind to the French . . . yet very firm. I have never seen anything to approach it especially as he was under stress, great emotion.

He tried to argue that Hitler's troops must be just as exhausted. This earned only fresh exasperation from the French.

Could they have seen into an American army docks in New Jersey that night, these unhappy allies would have witnessed the first supplies for Britain being loaded aboard merchant ships — 500,000 rifles, over twenty years old, accompanied by 250 bullets each; 900 field guns and 80,000 machine guns. Fight on! That was Churchill's plea to the French — fight on even within the streets of Paris. In his imagination he already perceived, as Spears would write, "the lurid glow of burning cities, some as beautiful as Paris, collapsing on garrisons who refused to accept defeat."

True, the French did not share his enthusiasm for fire; but he remained incorrigibly hopeful. "Perhaps the pressure will lessen in the next forty-eight hours," he suggested. He continued, fortified by his own fantasy, as the French minutes show:

> Mr Winston Churchill said he would not exclude the possibility of a rapid turn of the tide such as he witnessed several times during the last war, for example during the Battle of the Marne, when immediately after March 21 he was at Beauvais at Marshal Pétain's side. . . In a situation like this each day counts.*

---

*At this place on his French copy of the minutes Reynaud scrawled in the margin, *aucun rapport!*—"Quite out of touch!"

Pétain drily advised him not to press the analogy too far: in 1918 the French had had forty divisions in reserve. Reynaud pointed out that the enemy now was at the gates of Paris. It was, as Mr Churchill had said, an honourable page in French history — to which Britain could still contribute by throwing in fresh air power. "Without doubt," he said, "History will say that the Battle of France was lost for want of an airforce." Churchill snapped back, "For want of tanks as well!" He suggested holding at least a bridgehead on the Atlantic, or waging "a kind of guerrilla war" until the Americans intervened.

Pétain poured a douche on the idea. "That would lead to the country's destruction."

"Would the alternative be less terrible?" was Churchill's rejoinder. "Come what may, Britain will carry on the fight. If we are invaded, and if we experience all the horrors of war on our own soil, then that in itself must leave an impression on America."

In conclusion, he voiced his confidence in the ultimate downfall of Hitler. "Though Germany occupy the whole of France, That Man can not win the war!" "Britain," he added, "is ready and willing to face the same horrors. She is indeed anxious to draw on to herself the full malice of the Nazi's tyranny, and, however tremendous the German fury may prove to be, she will never give in."

The emotional conflagration damp'd down in this Pickwickian gentleman, the table was cleared for dinner. Ever pernickety about hygiene, he went off for a bath and change of clothes, and it was ten p.m. before the meal began.

Spears had watched General de Gaulle closely throughout the evening. "He never blinked an eyelid," he pencilled in his notes. "Smoking cigarettes *du bout des lèvres*, perfect demeanour." Churchill invited this junior general to sit next to him — a studied affront to the venerable Weygand that did not pass unnoticed. He cared little for Reynaud's generals now. At that moment, the local authorities were driving trucks onto the airfields at Sâlon, in southern France, to prevent R.A.F. bombers taking off against Italy.

* * *

He awakened with a start to the unfamiliar château surroundings, found his bath — after padding around the corridors in his red silk kimono and white silk pyjamas — and breakfasted heartily. The council resumed at eight a.m., but Pétain, Georges, and de Gaulle had already left. Reynaud asked outright for five more R.A.F. fighter squadrons, and defended Vuillemin's decision not to bomb Italy. Britain, he said, might do as she pleased but not from French airfields. As for Churchill's heroic vision of a Paris in flames, Weygand revealed that he had ordered the city surrendered as soon as its outer defences fell.

The gulf was widening. Speaking with emphasis, Churchill insisted that their prime minister notify him at once of any change in the situation so that he might return to see them "at any convenient spot".

With the conference dissolving on this unhappy note Churchill cornered the French fleet commander: "Darlan," he pleaded, "I trust that you will never surrender the fleet."

"There is no question of doing so," promised Darlan. "It would be contrary to our naval tradition and honour."[48]

THE SUN HAD clouded over. Back in London, Churchill reported to his Cabinet at five o'clock. It was time for Britain to withdraw within her watery frontiers. Even though it might spread ruin and starvation, he said, Britain must now intensify her blockade of Europe.

That evening Reynaud's Cabinet was meeting near Tours, taking ominous decisions. Reynaud wrote in his notes that General Weygand declared it was time to ask for an armistice. Pétain backed him up.

> The cabinet decided I should invite Churchill back tomorrow, to ask him the British government's attitude if France asks for an armistice.[49]

Unaware of this, Churchill sent a message to Roosevelt mentioning the young General de Gaulle and urging America to back France to the hilt. He had made clear to the French that Hitler could not win until he had disposed of the British, "which has not been found easy in the past."[50]

Kennedy however had submitted his own alarming prognosis to Washington. Churchill, he said, would stop at nothing to drag the United States in right after their presidential election. He was predicting that the American people would line up and demand war if they knew of the devastation of Britain's towns and cities "after which so many American cities and towns have been named." (No British towns it must be repeated, had yet been bombed.) That very morning, reported Kennedy, the American correspondent of an English newspaper had mentioned that it only needed an "incident" to bring in the United States: that was just what Kennedy feared. He warned Washington about Churchill, once again: "Desperate people will do desperate things if that is all that is needed."[51]

Mr Churchill recovered that evening in his accustomed manner at Admiralty House. Lord Beaverbrook came round to share and revive his spirits.[52] Some time past midnight, somewhere in that building, a telephone rang: the call was put through to Winston just as he was preparing for bed: it was Paul Reynaud speaking, indistinctly: could Mr Churchill return to France and see him at Tours that afternoon?

CHAPTER 26

Breakneck

THUS, ONLY ONE day after leaving him, Churchill would again
come face to face with Reynaud — this time at Tours, for a further
bout of their alliance: Reynaud with his powerful mistress the Countess
Hélène de Portes in his wake; Churchill — fearful of becoming
intoxicated by his own francophile emotions — bringing along his own
counsellors Lords Halifax and Beaverbrook.

He had got up late that day, June 13, 1940, and rushed off a
telegram to Roosevelt before driving through London's warm sunshine,
police gong ringing, to Hendon airport. "French have sent for me again,"
his message read, "which means that crisis has arrived. Am just off.
Anything you can say or do to help them now may make the
difference."[1] Escorted again by a dozen Hurricanes, the two Flamingoes
lowered themselves through clammy thunderclouds onto the rain-sodden
runway at Tours and taxied past red-flagged craters to the Air France
hangars.

It was two p.m.; clearly he was not expected. The only sign of life
was two airmen idly munching sandwiches; they ferried these unexpected
Englishmen downtown in private cars. Given Halifax's length and
Churchill's girth, it was a cramped and bumpy ride.

They made for Tours police headquarters. The drab préfecture was
besieged by equally hungry refugees who neither recognized nor
venerated their august visitors. Here too everybody was out to lunch.
Georges Mandel's aide, spotted outside by Tommy Thompson, said the
minister was about to move in. Up in his office they found engineers
installing telephones and a picnic luncheon waiting on a tray.

While Reynaud was fetched, Churchill's party went over to the
Hotel Grand Bretagne and lunched skimpily in a back room on cold
chicken and cheese washed down by an unprepossessing local wine.
Shortly Paul Baudouin, Reynaud's new under-secretary for foreign
affairs, joined them. He talked silkily of the hopelessness of fighting on
unless Roosevelt declared war too.

Back at police headquarters they found Mandel, minister of the interior, juggling two telephones and a chicken bone. When Reynaud arrived, he turfed Mandel out as he was not a member of the Supreme War Council, and perched on his chair. The eight Englishmen grouped around him in a semi circle and steeled themselves for the bad news: the French Cabinet had charged him, he announced, to ascertain Britain's attitude, given "the hard facts with which France is faced."[2]

His secretary Roland de Margerie arrived and took a note of Churchill's passionate reply:

CHURCHILL: We're asking you to fight on as long as possible, if not in Paris at least behind Paris, in the provinces or in your Empire. In our view such a resistance could last very long, above all if France could count on American promises of support. Maybe Hitler does meanwhile become for some time the absolute master of the European peoples. But that will not last and must not last. All his victories cannot destroy the natural forces of all the nations, large and small, which may fleetingly pass under his yoke.

He spoke of France's magnificent navy, her empire, and the rest of her army; he suggested large scale guerrila war, promised that the German airforce would be broken against Britain, and that there would then come the moment when the Hitler regime would quake, particularly if the United States decided to declare war: "Come what may, the British government means to continue the war. We are convinced that we shall break Hitler and his regime. . . The war will continue, it can only end with oblivion or victory."

But Reynaud returned doggedly to his own central questions.

REYNAUD: The United States can not adopt a position for many months before their presidential election, and suppose Roosevelt died? It is quite natural for Britain to continue, given that until today she has not suffered much: but we, the French government, do not believe that we ought to abandon our people without letting them see at least a light at the end of the tunnel, and we cannot see this light. . . Once the French army is hors de combat, we would have no means of preventing the Germans from occupying the entire territory. . . Hitler would be able to establish in France an authority with pretences to legitimacy, and the country would be prey to the most insidious propaganda.

He asked formally whether the British government would deem France justified, having now sacrificed the flower of her youth, in making a separate peace? "This is the question I have to raise."

"In that case," responded Churchill in steel-fisted language gloved in silken verbiage, "we should not waste our strength in reproaches. . . But that is very different from actually consenting to a separate peace concluded in direct contradiction of solemn engagements that you have entered into."

He suggested they both set out the situation to President Roosevelt and await his response. With tears forming in his eyes he continued: "The cause of France will always be dear to our hearts, and we shall restore her in all her power and dignity if we are triumphant."[3]

REYNAUD: The declaration that M Winston Churchill has just made is profoundly moving and I am very touched. The French government will therefore telegraph to M Roosevelt . . . that the French army, the vanguard of democracy, has gone down fighting in the front line. . . We have all committed many errors, as we French can well see. . . Hitler has killed France first, now he will attack Britain, finally America. It is both a moral and a material danger, and it threatens everybody alike.

In his reply, Churchill pointed to some questions that they should examine jointly if this terrible war was to continue. "We are moving towards a total blockade." Suppose Roosevelt's reply proved negative? "If our struggle should prosper and we survive the winter, the war will go on in increasing savagery. France will not escape the consequences of this duel. . ."

Reynaud was shocked by the prospect — "that if the war goes on Britain would find herself inflicting suffering directly on the French." He chose his words with delicacy. "If the French army and people continue to suffer," he continued, "without evoking from Britain the slightest sign that she recognizes how much we have already suffered, I should be very concerned for the future."

Spears slipped a note to Churchill suggesting they adjourn. Churchill led his team downstairs into the narrow garden. The undergrowth and branches were dripping from the drizzling rain. For twenty minutes they paced around this wretched garden. Beaverbrook's solution was the simplest: "Tell Reynaud," he exclaimed, "that we have nothing to say or discuss until Roosevelt's answer is received. Don't commit yourself to anything. We are doing no good here. Let's get along home."[4]

Upstairs Churchill announced that his opinion was unchanged.

REYNAUD: I am convinced that M Roosevelt will take one more step and that I shall therefore be able to agree conditions with the British government under which we shall continue in this war. . .

CHURCHILL: We shall say the same to the president in our most brutal manner. . . We cannot leave him many hours to reply. . . If he agrees to enter the war, victory is assured. It will become a war between continents, where we are in command of the oceans, and we shall liberate one after another of the different European nations, just as we did in the last war.

Gathering up his papers, Churchill mentioned one other urgent matter: "You're holding hundreds of German airmen prisoner in France, many shot down by the R.A.F. Let us transport them to safekeeping while there is still time."

"It shall be taken care of."

Churchill promised that Britain would continue sending troops to France to keep up the pressure.

Assuring him that he himself never wanted to raise these "certain eventualities" Reynaud however warned Churchill to make no mistake: "If President Roosevelt's reply is negative, this will create a new situation."

> CHURCHILL: I preserve my confidence in the ultimate destruction of the Hitlerite regime. Hitler cannot win. Let us await with patience his downfall.

> REYNAUD: I too keep faith in the future. Otherwise life for me would no longer be worth living.

Passing Charles de Gaulle in the courtyard of the préfecture, Churchill hissed three words to the impassive major-general — "*L'homme du destin.*"

His car was waiting. The Countess Hélène de Portes elbowed through the throng. "Mr Churchill," she cried emotionally, "my country is bleeding to death . . . you *must* hear me." She was evidently losing her head; and a few days later, she did.* The prime minister ignored her, told his driver to make haste for the airfield. Reynaud said his farewells there, then drove back to the countess who had, Churchill reflected contemptuously, succour to offer of the kind that was not in his gift.

He was aware that the long love affair with France was over. To cap the other indignities of this dreary day there were no batteries to enable the Hurricane pilots to restart their engines. He told his pilot to fly home without the fighter escort, above the cloud. But the cloud thinned out, they approached the English coast in dazzling sunshine; his Flamingo had to wavehop back to the shore. He landed at Hendon at eight-thirty that evening, having set foot in France for the last time for exactly four years.

His precipitous departure from Tours had unwittingly offended the French Cabinet, who had been waiting near by to hear him. Reynaud had forgotten to mention this to the British party. This added to the unfortunate impression burgeoning within the French ever since Dunkirk — that the British were leaving them in the lurch.[6]

IMMEDIATELY UPON HIS return, Churchill ordered Ambassador Kennedy to be ushered in.

He had Roosevelt's reply to Reynaud's earlier appeal, that of the

---

*Reynaud was an indifferent driver. Fleeing through France he crashed; she broke her neck.[5]

tenth. It read: "This Government is doing everything in its power to make available to the Allied Governments the material they so urgently require."⁷ The rest was platitudes, but Churchill was clutching at straws; he assured his colleagues at ten-fifteen p.m. that it was virtually an American declaration of war. Roosevelt, he triumphed, could hardly urge the French to "continue the struggle," if he did not intend to join in.

He stepped briefly out of the Cabinet Room and hectored Kennedy: the message must be published, to "buck up" morale in France — "The President's Note will do it."

Kennedy was dubious. He had booked a call to Washington, he said, and expected it "any minute." Shortly it came through: Roosevelt blithely agreed to publication, but then Cordell Hull came on the line and forbade it. Baffled, Churchill told his Cabinet the president did not realize how critical the situation was.⁸

As they rose at one a.m., a grim faced Churchill handed to Kennedy, waiting outside, a further telegram to Roosevelt arguing that it was "absolutely vital" to publish his message immediately so that it might play "the decisive part in turning the course of world history."⁹ For an hour after that, while Kennedy watched, Churchill sat at his desk drafting an heroic proclamation to the French people. "We shall never turn from the conflict," he had written, "until France stands safe and erect in all her grandeur, until the wronged and enslaved States and peoples have been liberated, and until civilization is free from the nightmare of Nazism. That this day will dawn we are more sure than ever. It may dawn sooner than we now have the right to expect."

Months later he would reveal to Eden that each day now he wakened with fresh dread in his heart.¹⁰ At nine-twenty the next morning Kennedy telephoned: Roosevelt had again refused permission to publish — "Not in any circumstances." He had also sent a Triple Priority telegram to that effect.¹¹ Kennedy spelt it out to the exhausted prime minister: only the U.S. Congress was authorized to declare war. The ambassador invited him to explain it to Reynaud, but this was a chore Churchill eschewed, accusing Roosevelt of "holding back." To convey this message to Reynaud now would merely dampen what little fire still burned within the French — "and I much doubt" added Churchill "whether it will be possible in that event for us to keep the French fleet out of German hands."¹²

German troops were pouring into Paris. Reynaud had left Tours that morning, received Roosevelt's second telegram at four-thirty and was at Bordeaux by eight. "For the first time this morning," reported Kennedy from London later on June 14 to Roosevelt, "many people here realize that they are in for a terrible time. . . They are beginning to say we have everything to lose and nothing to gain, and what is the use of fighting. If the English people thought there was a chance of peace on any decent terms an upheaval against the Government might come."

* * *

During the day, the Neville Chamberlains had moved out of the upper part of No. 10 Downing-street and the Winston Churchills moved in. The famous house — built in about 1665 by Sir George Downing, the second graduate of Harvard — was more spacious inside than it seemed, having an inner court; among the large, elegantly furnished rooms was a hall for state dinners. Winston's secretary John Martin hoped that life would be simpler now that they no longer had alternative headquarters at Admiralty House. But Winston still "thought it best" to sleep elsewhere. The Prof had warned him on the thirteenth that the Germans seemed to have developed some type of "ray device" to pinpoint their targets — perhaps radar, or radio beacons planted by spies.[13]

On June 14, keeping the promise he had made at Tours, Churchill had authorized the despatch of more troops.[14] But almost at once Dill warned that Weygand was talking of an end of "organized resistance" so Churchill stopped the movement.

At eight-twenty p.m. General Brooke, commanding the British force in France, telephoned Dill that he had already begun withdrawing the 52nd Division to the coast. Dill handed the phone to Churchill, who angrily told Brooke that he was supposed to be making the French army feel the British were supporting them. "It is impossible to make a corpse feel," was Brooke's succinct reply. Their conversation heated the wires for half an hour.[15] Finally Churchill ordered the necessary steps to evacuate the remaining British force from the Cherbourg and Britanny peninsulas.

Though he might harbour bold schemes to lure Hitler's bombers to London, Churchill was too prudent to sleep at No. 10 as yet. He crossed Green Park and slept at Beaverbrook's London mansion instead. This nightmare would probably last until the presidential election. "If we can hold on until November," he said, brightening, to his staff as he left No. 10 for Stornoway House, "we shall have won the war."[16]

He drafted a further plea to Roosevelt on the fifteenth, stating cruelly that if they could publish his message to Reynaud it "might save France," and reiterating what might happen if Hitler offered Britain easy terms: "A pro-German Government would certainly be called into being to make peace," Churchill prophesied, "and might present to a shattered or a starving nation an almost irresistible case for entire submission to the Nazi will." If Hitler could unite the fleets of Germany, Japan, France, Italy and Britain, he would have "overwhelming sea-power" in his hands. Churchill was becoming dangerously obsessed with the French fleet.

The War Cabinet endorsed a message to the Dominion prime ministers which he dictated there and then. New Zealand and Australia had cabled a pledge to remain with Britain to the end. Churchill's message encouraged the four Dominion Prime Ministers, "I do not regard the situation as having passed beyond our strength. It is by no means certain that the French will not fight on in Africa and at sea, but, whatever they do, Hitler will have to break us in this island or lose the war."[17] He liked that. He rolled it around his tongue and read it out to his staff that night. He sighed, and said with proper pride, "If words counted, we should win this war."[18]

AGAIN DUCKING No.10, he had driven out to Chequers that Saturday evening: there was a full moon.

Tin-helmeted sentries porting muskets with foot-long bayonets paced the lawns and mansion. The guest book shows that the Prof joined him here; in fact he counted as "family" — Mary totted up that Lindemann had signed the visitor's book at Chartwell 112 times since 1925. One of the crankier vegetarians, he refused to eat milk puddings, uncooked cheese, or eggs unless concealed in an omelette. But he was welcome, since he turned over his meat rations to Clementine. In return, Winston secured favours for him: among the Prof's papers is a certificate allowing his brother to send from Washington a gallon of pure olive oil "as an urgent medical requirement" for the Prof.[19]

Lindemann briefed him on A.I., the airborne interception radar being developed for Fighter Command. Once, the phone rang; it was the F.O. — their ambassador at Bordeaux was finding it difficult to obtain straight answers from the French, and ministers there were asking in "more brutal form" to be allowed to make a separate peace. Churchill slumped into a lugubrious gloom.[20] But then, as Colville recorded, "Champagne, brandy and cigars did their work and we soon became talkative, even garrulous." Churchill read out loud the telegrams he had exchanged with Roosevelt and the Dominions. "The war," he remarked cheerfully, "is bound to become a bloody one for us now. I hope our people will stand up to bombing and the Huns aren't liking what we are giving them."

He strolled in the moonlit rose garden with Duncan Sandys. There was no sign of the German airforce — they were still prohibited to attack towns. At one a.m. he went back inside, stretched out on a sofa, held forth on how to rebuild Fighter Command, told a few mellow stories, then bowed courteously and said: "Goodnight, my children."[21]

* * *

That Washington was refusing help clinched it for France. Reynaud read out to his Cabinet in Bordeaux Roosevelt's unhelpful — Pétain would even call it "evasive" — reply, brought to him by American ambassador Bill Bullitt at seven p.m. Pétain and others declared in favour of an armistice; Mandel and Campinchi opposed it. At eight Reynaud had sent for Spears and the British ambassador and drafted a telegram to Churchill announcing the end of the road. He was inquiring the enemy armistice terms through Washington. Seeing Bullitt again at midnight Reynaud told him this, adding without conviction, "I only hope the terms won't be too moderate."[22]

The dolorous telegram from Bordeaux reached Chequers by despatch rider in the early hours. Colville bore it into his master's bedroom. He found Churchill "looking just like a rather nice pig clad in a silk vest."[23] Moving with porcine swiftness, Churchill shifted a planned Sunday lunch engagement from Chequers to the Carlton Club and addressed an emergency Cabinet in London at ten-fifteen a.m. — stressing his alarm at the involvement of Washington in asking for the terms, lest Roosevelt appeal to *all* the belligerents to "call the war off," as he put it.[24]

The spectre of Hitler offering acceptable peace terms to Britain was one abiding obsession for Churchill: the other was the possibility that he might lay hands on the French fleet. Faced with Reynaud's resolve — or rather, lack of it — Churchill's colleagues refused to release France from her solemn obligation not to negotiate a separate peace, except on one condition: "That the French Fleet is sailed forthwith for British harbours pending negotiations." Sir Ronald Campbell handed this demand to Reynaud in Bordeax that afternoon.[25]

Reynaud had sent General de Gaulle to London to obtain the shipping France would need if she fought on from Africa. But in the British capital, de Gaulle plunged into an extraordinary intrigue. At noon-thirty he telephoned Reynaud in Bordeaux claiming to have seen both Churchill and the War Cabinet. Reynaud's papers contain the transcript.[26]

DE GAULLE: I've just seen Churchill, and there's something tremendous afoot on the lines of a union between our two countries. Churchill proposes we constitute one joint Franco-British government, and you, Monsieur le Président, can be the President of the Anglo-French War Cabinet.

REYNAUD: It's the only solution for the future. But it's got to be done in a big way and fast, very fast. It's a matter of minutes now. There's a big row going on here. I can give you half an hour. It would be *magnifique*!

Half an hour later de Gaulle again telephoned Bordeaux and asked for Reynaud. Margerie told him Reynaud was in Cabinet.

DE GAULLE: I wanted to tell him something tremendous is happening here. The War Cabinet's in session, preparing the text of a declaration joining our two countries into one common nation. I'm off to lunch with Churchill and I'll phone you again shortly. You can tell him [Reynaud] in strict confidence that he can become the President of the Anglo-French War Cabinet.

So far de Gaulle had impressed Churchill. He had proved very useful to the British cause, agreeing to divert to Britain war goods which France had ordered in America. Now, aided by the fine wine and Sunday luncheon offered by the Carlton Club, de Gaulle easily won him for the extraordinary idea for a political union between Britain and France.[27]

Some days earlier Desmond Morton had sent René Pleven to dine with Winston — Pleven had suggested the idea to Tory Chief Whip David Margesson: Pleven, a tedious government economist, had failed to inspire Churchill (although MI5 showed interest in his wife.[28]) When Chamberlain mentioned the idea in Cabinet Churchill had still seen only its propaganda value.[29] Now, lunching with de Gaulle, he suddenly warmed to the idea, agreed that the general should draft a Proclamation of Union, and emotionally commended it to his resumed Cabinet after lunch.

He hoped this scheme might yet avert the armistice. Indeed, he now instructed his ambassador in Bordeaux to "suspend action" on the telegram concerning the French fleet. On the copy in Reynaud's papers is a note, "handed to P.R. by Campbell and Spears forenoon of June 16, but withdrawn by them before five p.m. council of ministers, Gen. de Gaulle having meanwhile telephoned from London the text adopted by the War Cabinet on the Franco-British Union."

What had happened was this. Just before four p.m., Mr Churchill's Cabinet learned from a French radio broadcast that the Bordeaux government would decide in an hour's time whether further resistance was possible. At four-thirty, de Gaulle, still haunting No.10, telephoned to Reynaud — whom he privately termed "this frozen fish" — the final extraordinary text of the Proclamation, adopted by Mr Churchill's colleagues:

At this most fateful moment in the history of the modern world, the Governments of the United Kingdom and French Republic made this declaration of indissoluble union and unyielding resolution in their common defence of justice and freedom, against subjection to a system which reduces mankind to a state of robots and slaves.

The two Governments declare that France and Great Britain shall no longer be two nations but one Franco-British Union.

The Constitution of the Union will provide for joint organs of defence, foreign, financial and economic policies.

Every citizen of France will enjoy immediate citizenship of Great

Britain, every British subject will become a citizen of France.

Both countries will share responsibilities for repair of devastation of war, wherever it occurs in their territories, and resources of both shall be equal, and as one, applied to that purpose.

During the war there shall be a single war cabinet, and all the forces of Britain and France, whether on land, sea or in the air, will be under its direction. It will govern from wherever it best can. The two Parliaments will be formally associated. The nations of the British Empire are already forming new armies. France will keep her available forces in the field, on the sea, and in the air. The Union appeals to [the] United States to fortify the economic resources of the Allies, and to bring her powerful material aid to the common cause.

The Union will concentrate its whole energy against the power of the enemy no matter where the battle may be.

And thus we shall conquer.

Having dictated this to Reynaud in French, de Gaulle added his own blunt postscript: "In the United States they're asking whether you're going to be a man of war or whether you're going to chuck in the sponge like Queen Wilhelmina or Leopold — whether you're the kind who'll resign so that others can surrender?"

Prising the telephone away from him, Churchill spoke to Reynaud. "I hope you're happy," he glowed. "I want to see you in Brittany tomorrow mid-day. I'll telegraph to you where and when."

The rooms and corridors of No.10 glistened like the setting of a Gilbert & Sullivan opera. Birdsong twittered through the windows into the Cabinet room. They too had evidently luncheoned well. Churchill's staff watched with amazement as he milled around with his visitors, beginning speeches, clapping de Gaulle on the back, and promising that he would be the new commander-in-chief. "*Je l'arrangerai*," Winston cried to the Very Model of a Modern Major-general.

John Colville felt obliged to comment sardonically in his diary that meanwhile His Majesty did not know what was "being done to his Empire." While Chamberlain undertook to break it to King George that Britain might yet see the fleur-de-lys restored to the Royal standard, de Gaulle left to take the document to France.

They did not have long to wait for Act Two. In Bordeaux, Reynaud's sober colleagues dismissed the Proclamation with contempt. There were shouts of, "I don't want to become a British subject." In a private letter to Reynaud a year later Pétain would protest that it would have "reduced us to the rank of a [British] Dominion." "As for me," Reynaud tartly rejoined, "I prefer to collaborate with my allies rather than with the enemy." In London the scheme would unquestionably have been shipwrecked on the outer reefs of authority had it ever emerged from the safety of Mr Churchill's Cabinet. Lord Hankey wrote, greatly shocked, to Lord Halifax, "I should resist to the uttermost in my power any sacrifice of our nationality or any permanent fusion with France."[30]

ON THE EVENING of that exciting Sunday, Mr Churchill put on his naval uniform and prepared to leave for the solemn signing of the Proclamation. Labour and Liberal leaders Attlee and Sinclair were beckoned to accompany him, joining at Waterloo station. The cruiser *Galatea* was standing by at Southampton to carry them to the westernmost French peninsula of Britanny; the *Arethusa* would convey Reynaud's government from Bordeaux to meet them there the following noon.

It was this sense of drama and atmosphere that so distinguished Churchill from his predecessors. A year later he would meet a different statesman on a British battleship in an even more distant bay, to lay the Empire's future in one foreign statesman's hands.

But his journey was not really necessary after all. At one a.m., as they still sat in the train at mundane Waterloo, after Clementine had kissed him farewell, a telegram reached him from the ambassador, Sir Ronald Campbell: Reynaud had twice read out Churchill's dramatic offer to his Cabinet, but to no avail. He had accordingly resigned. Aged eighty-four, Pétain would replace him; Laval would be a member of his government.[31]

France was now determined to ask for an armistice, and no comic opera Proclamation could stop her.

CHAPTER 27

The Diehard

DISCONTENT FLARED UP again in Churchill's Cabinet after France's defeat. Lord Halifax was fearful that Winston was going to fight Britain into the ground. But what exactly did Hitler want? Halifax's capable under-secretary R.A. Butler had already extended feelers through Switzerland after the Norway fiasco.[1] On June 17, 1940 the F.O. began to probe through Sweden too. Mr Butler "chanced upon" the Swedish envoy Bjorn Prytz in St James's Park, and invited him back to the Office.

Prytz was half English and equally concerned about the bloodletting now in prospect. Perhaps on instructions, Butler made no record of their talk, but Prytz immediately telegraphed Stockholm: Britain, Butler had announced, would pass up no opportunity of compromise if Hitler offered reasonable conditions. "No diehards," he had added, "would be allowed to stand in the way." After being briefly called in to see Lord Halifax, the Swede reported, Butler then emerged with a postscript: "common sense and not bravado" would dictate the policy of His Majesty's government. This was not to be interpreted as "peace at any price," but the implication was clear to Prytz: if Mr Churchill got in their way, he would be forced to resign.

If Mr Churchill had now pocketed his pride, as the F.O. clearly felt he should, the war in western Europe would have ended — with Britain impoverished, but far from a pauper; with her Empire unravaged; and with Europe's great cities and populations spared, along with the millions of innocents whom the Nazis two years later began to liquidate under the cruel mantle of total war. But Churchill was determined, as he had so often said, to fight on, and smote down the hand of conciliation that he found his own colleagues cautiously extending.

The British archives on these two extraordinary days, June 17 and 18, are still closed; and twice after the war London prevailed on Stockholm to suppress Prytz's revealing telegram.[2] But Swedish, Italian, and German records reflect what was happening, as does a cryptic entry in Sir Alexander Cadogan's diary "Winston not there — writing his speech. *No reply from Germans*".*

While the Foreign Office awaited Hitler's response, on June 18 Churchill had made the tactical error of ducking the mid-day War Cabinet to draft a speech for the House. The relevant paragraphs of the minutes of the Cabinet presided over by Lord Halifax in his absence have been blanked out until 1990; but after the meeting the F.O. formally instructed the British envoy in Stockholm to investigate ways of extending official peace feelers to the Germans.[3] By the nineteenth, Germany had still not replied. But now, attending Cabinet, Churchill found out (those paragraphs are also closed) and forbade all further soundings. To torpedo the Stockholm manoeuvre once and for all, he adopted startling, autocratic means. He ordered the navy to seize four destroyers which Sweden had just purchased from Italy and were known to be passing near by. The naval staff, unaware of the political background, were astonished; on the twenty-second Captain Edwards would write that the Swedes were rabid about it and threatening to break off diplomatic relations. He could not understand all this trouble over "four elderly ships."

"It is the most extraordinary brain, Winston's, to watch functioning that I have ever seen," observed Halifax in utter resignation in his diary. "A most curious mixture of a child's emotion and a man's reason." A few days later the destroyers were released, but the act had the desired result on Sweden's future willingness to help. Still baffled, Edwards could only write: "What a blunder it's all been!"

Churchill's energetic postmortem into the Stockholm affair continued for several days. The Prytz telegram was quoted back to him;[4] it showed, Winston rebuked Halifax, that Butler had left a defeatist impression on Prytz or used "odd language" to him. "I was strongly pressed in the House of Commons in the Secret Session [on June 20]," he declaimed, "to give assurances that the present Government and all its members were resolved to fight on to the death."[5]

* * *

One afternoon he lunched at Lord Londonderry's mansion in the centre of London. As the brandy was served and cigars were lit he turned to the Hungarian ambassador György Barcza, a familiar gleam of mischief in his eye: "I'm glad to see you," he began. "I know of your work and I know you're a good Hungarian. I hope that whatever the Germans demand of you, you won't cross certain lines."

Barcza assured him that Hungary would not.

---

*Author's emphasis.

"You are on good terms with Hitler," continued Churchill, as the liquor suffused his veins. "You could do me a little favour. The British are still not aware of the danger they are in — the seriousness of their situation. We'll have to do something to wake them up. Would you tell Hitler to start a little bombing over *London* — that should wake up the most indolent Englishman!"

Taken aback by the burden of this message, Barcza murmured something about not being on any terms with Hitler at all; but he felt sure that air raids would soon start.

"Well," Churchill exclaimed, "the sooner the better! London is full of ugly buildings, at least we can build new ones."

Barcza reflected in his private papers afterwards that the prime minister was "stout, jovial, sometimes cynical and rude," but that there was no doubting that he spoke succinctly and was a man of action rather than words, and would be ruthless to anybody standing in his way.[6]

* * *

France had ceased to fight at noon-forty on June 17. Some saw the collapse as a blessing. After a talk with Churchill that afternoon Lord Halifax remarked in his diary that he was "very robust and almost convincing himself that we shall do better without the French than with them." "Well!" wrote Sir Hugh Dowding, chief of R.A.F. Fighter Command, to the prime minister, "now it is England against Germany, and I don't envy them their job." He had lost 250 Hurricanes in the last ten days in France, and only two were being manufactured each day. But he had saved enough for Britain. Months later he confessed to Lord Halifax, "When I heard the French had asked for a separate armistice I went on my knees and thanked God."[7]

"It is rumoured," wrote Captain Edwards, reflecting the prevailing nightmare in Whitehall, "that one of the German terms is surrender of the French fleet intact." After that day's Cabinet John Colville espied Churchill pacing the beautiful walled garden laid out by the Chamberlains: he was alone, head bowed, hands clasped behind his back. Later the PM drafted a stinging message, warning "the illustrious Marshal Pétain and the famous General Weygand" not to deliver their fleet to Hitler. "Such an act," he wrote, in awesome, untranslatable English, "would scarify their names for a thousand years of history."[8]

He asked the American ambassador to get the president also to warn Pétain about the fleet; at that moment a despatch arrived from Campbell reporting that the Marshal was now talking of scuttling it. "The old man's gaga," commented Churchill. He proposed to broadcast to America: Britain would fight on. "Why," he lisped to Kennedy, "if I don't say that, the people of England would tear me to pieces." Kennedy made no response, because he did not agree.[9] Newspapermen at the F.O. conference insisted that Churchill must broadcast that night.

The broadcast perturbed his information chief Harold Nicolson, who had bullied him into making it. It was plain that Winston hated the microphone. "He just sulked," he wrote, "and read his House of Commons speech over again." In the ancient chamber the words had sounded magnificent. *"We shall defend our island home,"* Churchill had roared at its end, the flames of his oratory licking around the rafters of the chamber, *"and with the British Empire we shall fight on unconquerable until the curse of Hitler is lifted from the brows of mankind."*[10] But, truncated and broadcast, it sounded ghastly. All the vigour seemed to evaporate. Cecil King, who had lunched with him so recently, summarized it as a "few stumbling sentences" — the situation was Disastrous but All Right. "Whether he was drunk or all in," he speculated in his diary, "I don't know. . . He should have produced the finest speech of his life."

That speech would come the next afternoon, June 18, one hundred and twenty-five years to the day since Wellington's victory at Waterloo.

When he sought new energy, Churchill returned to the fountainhead of his power; he communed with Parliament. Like Hitler, when he spoke, he needed live audiences. He needed a Box to pound with his fist — then to stand back, mechanically smoothing his paunch with his small white hands, tucking his thumbs into the waistcoat bridged by its unsightly gold chain, and stepping back and forth to pace his oratory.

His speech was taunting, unrepentant, defiant. Nobody was going to rob him of his vision — of Britain's skies darkening to the enemy hordes, of a pall of smoke enshrouding her capital, and then of his own crusaders rising with thundering horsepower to joust and save their country. The Battle of France was over, the "Battle of Britain" was about to begin.

Upon this battle depends the survival of Christian civilisation. Upon it depends our own British life and the long continuity of our institutions and our Empire. The whole fury and might of the enemy must very soon be turned on us. Hitler knows that he will have to break us in this island or lose the war. If we can stand up to him, all Europe may be free, and the life of the world may move forward into broad, sunlit uplands; but if we fail, then the whole world, including the United States, and all that we have known and cared for, will sink into the abyss of a new dark age made more sinister, and perhaps more protracted, by the lights of a perverted science. Let us therefore brace ourselves to our duty and so bear ourselves that if the British Empire and its Commonwealth lasts for a thousand years men will still say,

"This was their finest hour."

He had spent the whole morning writing this. Its delivery was indifferent. Again the loudest cheering came from Labour; Dalton found the subdued response of the Tories "sinister."[11] When it was broadcast that night the B.B.C. again asked a Children's Hour actor to mimick the drooling, slurring, lisping, elocution. (Later, Churchill begged the House to allow the B.B.C. to record his orations live; alert to its traditions, it wisely declined.) His personal staff remarked upon the broadcast speech's halting start; one listener, worried that the tired voice betrayed a heart defect, sent a telegram suggesting superfluously that in future Winston work "in a recumbent position."[12]

In fact his morning work was done a-bed, resplendent in silk kimono, dictating to Kathleen Hill and her silent typewriter.[13] The box of documents sagged open on the coverlet, a silver ice-bucket purloined from the Savoy waited at the bedside to receive the cigar butts. Nelson, the Admiralty's pampered tom, had evicted Chamberlain's black Treasury cat in the way that felines do to establish their own imperium, and now fondled the new premier's feet. The latter animal — the cat, not the prime minister — had become famous as the Munich Mouser and received a substantial fan mail including postal orders for catfood.[14] But Winston preferred Nelson's company: he found he could converse at any length with cats without fear of interruption, and once he would swear he heard one remark: "Humans are very intelligent — I believe they understand quite a lot of what we say."

During those June weeks the picture at No.10 was like behind the scenes at a circus — "every crank in the world" getting hold of the prime minister and extracting "half-baked decisions" from him, as Cadogan put it. Among them was Hore-Belisha: he suggested that Britain kidnap Marshal Pétain on a warship and force him to sign over France's fleet and colonies. Churchill, he told Hugh Cudlipp, was prepared to discuss it.[15]

As France collapsed, the Nazis captured her archives; Churchill's rude telegrams to Reynaud and Daladier about Norway and Dunkirk were found in a railway truck at Le Charité; compromising documents were confiscated from the private files of his friends Leon Blum and Yvon Delbos and in the Polish and Czech legations. The foreign ministry files, seized at Tours, revealed that France had been reading American diplomatic ciphers as recently as March.[16]

British ships rescued from Bordeaux Churchill's literary promoter Emery Reves* and ex-King Zog of Albania; by Most Immediate signal

---

*Hungarian born Imre Revesz had become a British subject in February. He fled to New York where he perpetrated the "autobiography" of German steel magnate Fritz Thyssen, *I Paid Hitler*. He purchased foreign rights to Churchill's war memoirs in 1946.

A.V. Alexander ordered the navy to evacuate hundreds of Red Spaniards too.[17] Ex-premier Paul Reynaud and his colleagues proved less willing to leave. Louis Spears and the British ambassador frogmarched them aboard a warship; Spears related to Hugh Dalton how he had even put aboard their mistresses — including Mandel's "fat cow" — to make sure their menfolk left for England. But they had all galloped ashore at dusk to ask the British consulate the latest news. The ship left without them.

Georges Mandel, tragically, would be put to death by his own countrymen. Reynaud evidently hoped to escape to Spain, as Spanish border police detained his two private secretaries and found in their baggage twelve million francs, several pounds of solid Gold, and the secret Anglo-French plans to invade Norway, enter Belgium, and bomb Russia, as well as the entire records of the Supreme War Council. The Madrid authorities illicitly copied six hundred pages for Hitler's amusement before returning everything to Marshal Pétain for his disposition.[18]

ONE VEXATION THAT now arose was of eggshell delicacy. It concerned the Duke of Windsor — still an admirer of the fascist dictators and still scornful of his Kingly brother. While First Lord, Churchill could afford to honour the young ex-King. In September 1939 he had sent a destroyer to carry the Duke back from exile and had greeted him at Portsmouth with a warm letter of welcome.[19] Neither the King, nor still less the Queen, had welcomed his brother's return; the King posted his brother back to France — to Gamelin's headquarters. Upon France's capitulation, no British warship having been made available to evacuate the errant Duke from Bordeaux, he headed for Spain instead "to avoid capture" and telegraphed plaintively to Winston from Barcelona on June 21.

Churchill had more important things on his plate. For a day he hesitated, consulted the War Cabinet, then sent him an urgent message: "We should like your Royal Highness to come home as soon as possible." The F.O. reserved him a seat on the flying boat that would leave Lisbon two days later.[20] But the Duke had now arrived in Madrid, and there he would remain for nine days while an unseemly tussle developed over this Spectre of the Feast — a tussle between Hitler, Churchill and Buckingham Palace.

Churchill had to make a hardnosed choice between satisfying an old friend and appeasing a new monarch who still had little liking for him as prime minister. Perhaps not realizing the weakness of his position, the Duke sent a personal cable declaring that he did not want to return as an unemployed refugee.

Churchill replied evenly, "It will be better for your Royal Highness to come to England as arranged, when everything can be considered."

The Duke's response was unyielding. "In the light of past experience," he stated, "my wife and myself must not risk finding ourselves once more regarded by the British public as in a different status to other members of my family."[21]

After a few days the prime minister sent a much sharper answer to Madrid, reminding the Duke of his military rank. "Refusal to obey direct orders of competent military authority would," he pointed out, "create a serious situation." In the draft he even hinted that there were some doubts as to how the Duke had left Paris, but he omitted this unflattering remark. The Duke continued to smoulder in the Spanish capital, and now cursed Churchill's name to anybody within earshot.[22]

* * *

"If Hitler," Churchill assured Parliament, meeting in Secret Session for the first time on June 20, "fails to invade or destroy Britain he has lost the war." Britain must survive the next three months; admittedly the United States had shown only lame interest so far, but he predicted: "Nothing will stir them like fighting in England," He ended on an alliterative note. "I . . . feel," he said, "we have only one enemy to face — the foul foe who threatens our freedom and our life, and bars the upward march of Man."*

The Tories were still unmoved. "There is always the quite inescapable suspicion that he loves war," Chips Channon commented afterwards — "war which broke Neville Chamberlain's better heart."

At about this time a placard appeared in the private secretaries' room, displaying Queen Victoria's words: "Please understand that there is no depression in this House and we are not interested in the possibilities of defeat. *They do not exist.*"

THE PRIME MINISTER certainly feared a pacifist trend. He could not intern everybody who opposed him. Once when somebody asked how the Public Schools were getting on, he growled, "Much as usual — Harrow has Amery†, Gort and myself, Eton has the King of the Belgians and

---

*Even the official *Hansard* reporters were traditionally "espied" and escorted from the House. But Mr Churchill retained his notes and sold three of the speeches to *Life* for $75,000 in 1945. Parliamentarians, irritated, claimed that the rightful place for these was in *Hansard*, not "touted" around the American press. Unrepentant, Churchill explained to the magazine: "It was like selling off my cuff links; the manuscripts belonged to me." To avoid tax, he represented it as a capital sale.[23]

†In July 1945 Leo Amery's son John — brother of Julian — would be flown back from Milan and arraigned for treason at the Old Bailey in November; he pleaded Guilty to spare his family the anguish of a trial and was hanged a few days later.[24]

Captain Ramsay, and Winchester has Oswald Mosley to their credit." He asked the Canadian prime minister to impress upon Roosevelt that though he would never enter peace negotiations with Hitler, he could not bind a future Government, "which, if we were deserted by the United States and beaten down here, might very easily be a kind of Quisling affair."[25]

Meanwhile, he fielded every peace feeler arriving from the Continent. One, through the Vatican's envoy in Berne, stung him to write: "I hope it will be made quite clear to the Nuncio that we do not desire to make any enquiries as to terms of peace with Hitler, and that all our agents are strictly forbidden to entertain any such suggestion."[26]

What terms would Hitler offer France? Churchill hoped they would be crippling; but so far Hitler had not put a foot wrong, and they might even be magnanimous.

His hope was that soon enemy air raids might come, putting an end to any British talk of peace. Churchill anticipated the coming ordeal with almost masochistic enthusiasm. "Steady continuous bombing," he suggested in his secret speech to the House, "probably rising to great intensity occasionally, must be[come a] regular condition of our life." He minuted the minister of information that when the bombing began media coverage must be careful not to damage public morale — people must learn to take air raids as if they were no more troublesome than thunderstorms.

As though on cue, scattered air raids on southern England now began. The targets lacked logic or symmetry; Churchill suspected their purpose might be to wear down his anti-aircraft defences. One of his staff mentioned in a letter that he had twice recently slept on a camp bed at No.10 and that on both occasions there were Yellow (preliminary) warnings.

The night of June 22 had been particularly unsettled:

> The PM had rashly gone down to Chequers but returned for a hastily summoned Cabinet, which went on till a late hour. Bevir and I were the only Private Secretaries there and we had a very hectic time, with a great many people coming and going and all the telephones (there are eight instruments) perpetually ringing. . . A tiresome, complaining letter from —. I wish he could see some of the pathetically brave and loyal letters we get from humble people in the PM's mail.[27]

Churchill had driven out to Chequers that Friday, June 21. His mood had been intractable for several days, perhaps a result of the Halifax-Butler-Prytz affair ("No diehards would be allowed to stand in the way.") Clementine noticed it — he was not as kindly as he used to be. A mutual friend confided to her unsettling details of his behaviour — "No doubt it's the strain" — and after much soul-searching she penned a letter to Winston warning that he was becoming generally disliked because of his "rough, sarcastic and overbearing" manner and his contemptuous way of dismissing ideas, good and bad alike. "It is for you to give the orders," she reminded him, "and if they are bungled . . . you can sack anyone and everyone." He must combine Olympic calm with this immense power. "You won't get the best results by irascibility and rudeness."[28]

But dining with a colleague, Winston's P.P.S. Eric Seal felt that their chief had in fact "sobered down" now — was "less violent, less wild and less impetuous." Evidently the prime minister believed he had a mission to get Britain out of her present troubles, Seal said.[29]

THAT SATURDAY GERMANY signed the armistice with France in the forest of Compiègne. Hitler's terms were said to be lenient beyond belief — "diabolically clever," as Sir Ronald Campbell, a fluent French speaker, called them in his telegram. Germany would leave over half of the country unoccupied, her forces would be demobilized, though not totally. But it was the future of the French fleet that worried the British. Marshal Pétain said he hoped to get the French fleet away to Dakar and Madagascar, but failing that it would be scuttled to prevent it falling into enemy hands. Campbell argued that the Germans, "who know something about scuttling," would find ways to prevent it.

An Italian wireless leak seemed to confirm Churchill's fears that the small print included German "control" of the French fleet. He summoned an emergency War Cabinet for nine-thirty p.m. Back in London however, he learned from the admiralty that Darlan had that very day ordered his fleet to fight to the last, surrender no ship to the enemy and obey only him; French officers at Toulon confidentially showed Darlan's signal to British naval liaison officers, and its arrival was confirmed by French units all round the Mediterranean (for example by the squadron based at Alexandria on the twenty-third.)

Uncertainty gripped the British Cabinet that evening. Pound trusted Admiral Darlan. They were old friends, and the French fleet commander had personally promised he would "never, never, never, never" allow the fleet to be handed to the Germans.

Half chewed cigar jiggling up and down as he spoke, A.V. Alexander pointed out that it would be easy for the Germans to "jump" the French ships.[30]

For compelling reasons, disregarding the weight of Intelligence evidence that Darlan could be trusted, Churchill wanted the French fleet sunk. While *Jean Bart* at Casablanca was only half completed, *Richelieu* at Dakar would soon be the most powerful ship afloat. Dramatic ideas were forming in his mind — British ships should go alongside those two battleships, parley with their captains and treat them as traitors to the Allied cause if they refused his demands. After a conversation with Halifax, Kennedy reported to Washington his own conviction that it was "not at all unlikely that . . . the first great naval battle may be between the French and the English."

* * *

The American Chief of Staff General George C. Marshall would be startled to find in mid-1942 that "an interchange of cryptanalytic information [with Britain] has been in progress for over a year."[31]

In January 1941 a new British battleship returning home from her maiden run to North America brought to England an extraordinary four-man American mission, armed with Mr Churchill's permission to inspect a secret establishment so closely guarded that for thirty-five years after that no British writer* was permitted to mention it: the Government Code & Cypher School at Bletchley Park fifty miles from London. In two closely guarded trunks the American mission brought their own dowry, Japanese ciphers and two hand-made copies of Japanese cipher machines; the Americans would spend ten weeks investigating the G.C. & C.S., with its radio intercept stations, computer systems and equipment laboratories. Chamberlain, they learned, had already had one hundred experts working on code-breaking before the war. Now there were eight hundred, in the one main building and eight huts at Bletchley Park. Officials proudly told the Americans that only four months earlier, in September 1940, Britain was on the brink of collapse: now they were confident of victory.

In crude terms, by early 1940 "the Park," was costing His Majesty's Government about two army divisions. But it was worth it: they had begun penetrating Hitler's "impregnable" machine ciphers. For six years his army had relied on the Enigma family of cipher machines; his airforce and navy used similar machines, capable of 160 trillion different cipher combinations. Using a pioneering valve-based computer, Bletchley had found how to resynthesize Enigma's daily keys, and the illicit decrypts had begun to trickle out during March, April and May 1940. By late March they had broken about fifty Enigma settings; on April 15 they were continuously breaking the special cipher allocated for Hitler's airforce and army operations in Norway.

While General Marshall showed only a languid interest in

---

*When the author drafted a chapter on G.C.& C.S. for *The Mare's Nest* (London and New York, 1964) the authorities prevailed upon him to remove it and detained the chapter and accompanying research notes.

cryptanalysis, Churchill worshipped it. It had already figured large at Jutland in 1916; after the Great War he had publicly eulogized Sir Alfred Ewing, the architect of British cryptanalysis, for his contribution to the fortunes of Britain and her admiralty.[32] Winston would do miracles for the G.C. & C.S., and Bletchley in turn provided the silent magic that underlay his success. By 1945 he would have five thousand working there.

From its sealed compound the intercepts were sent by car to the nondescript Secret Intelligence Service (S.I.S.) building in Broadway. To his uninitiated underlings he hinted that he had a super-agent, Boniface, in Berlin.[33] From Broadway the muffled voice of Boniface was carried in a buff box ("only to be opened by the Prime Minister in person") to No.10. Usually the head of the S.I.S., Brigadier Menzies, put in a covering note typed in his characteristic true-blue on unheaded blue paper, signed just "C." It was Mr Churchill's Most Secret Source in every sense: his own private secretaries never learned what was in that box; nor yet did some of his most trusted colleagues — among them A.V. Alexander and Anthony Eden.[34]

The G.C. & C.S. was evidently reading some Japanese ciphers to a higher command level than the Americans; they were also reading American ciphers. (Later, the PM would smugly assure Roosevelt he had personally ordered this must cease.[35]) Soviet, Italian and Vichy ciphers were an open book to them, as were those used by Spain and Latin America.[36] Churchill set up a unit out in Singapore, asked the American mission that arrived early in 1941 to supply Japanese translators, and undertook to cover Tokyo's cipher traffic with Berlin, London and Rome, in direct exchange for the Pacific traffic that was better monitored from America. Nor did the American mission leave empty handed. "The [British] material which was furnished by the Army personnel," they congratulated themselves, "will result in a saving of several years of labour."[37]

The codebreakers would give to the R.A.F. one important sword-edge, that summer of 1940 (the other was the supercharged Rolls-Royce Merlin engine.) On May 22 the trickle had swollen to a flood as the Park penetrated the operational Enigma cipher of the enemy airforce.

One breakthrough led to another. A navigation manual found in a crashed bomber refered to a radio *beam* of bearing 315°—aimed to the north-west, over England—and on about June 11 an intercepted airforce signal mentioned the "intersection of the Cleve Knickebein" at a certain map reference near Doncaster. This ominous discovery was the origin of the Prof's warning on June 13, which seems to have caused Winston to think twice about sleeping in No.10. A week later Enigma instructions on radio beams again coupled them with Knickebein (crooked leg).

An extraordinary row began between the professors. The air ministry's chief scientist Sir Henry Tizard argued that the earth's curvature made such beams impossible: besides, the R.A.F. was navigating satisfactorily by the stars. Lindemann disagreed, demanded an investigation. Churchill approved in red ink ("Let this be done without fail") and on June 21 found himself listening incredulously to Dr Reginald Jones, a young, solemn-faced scientist in Air Intelligence. Convinced by the Enigmas, though he could not say so, Jones argued to Churchill's Defence Committee that the beams did exist. He was asked to send a radio reconnaissance plane up at night to search for such beams.[38]

THE R.A.F. HAD been bombing Germany ever since Hitler's invasion of the Low Countries. On May 20, Arthur Greenwood had described the Ruhr as "a mass of ruins" but conceded that the Germans were somehow hiding the bomb damage from their public; however Churchill read an F.O. summary of Intelligence reports proving the "terrible effects of British bombing operations in the Ruhr."[39] He wondered when Hitler would retaliate but, although the sirens did sometimes wail, London remained unmolested.

As yet there were no signs of invasion preparations, but something akin to mutiny was growing in the naval staff over "the higher direction of the war." Their main concern was Sir Dudley Pound, the bumbling First Sea Lord. On June 17 several officers had privately taken their misgivings to Sir Walter Monckton, known to have close connections with the Palace. He revealed that Amery and Beaverbrook had also spoken to him; on the nineteenth he told Captain Edwards of the Operations Division that they were ready to act and would probably do so through the Queen — "The power behind the throne." Edwards suggested that Pound be replaced by Max Horton or Admiral Ramsay. On June 29 the King was told of the naval staff's "profound distrust" of the high command.

By this time Churchill's preparations against the French fleet were adding to the naval staff's unrest. Edwards heard that the King had sent for Winston and asked to see the navy's plans to meet invasion: they were "non-existent". In consequence on June 30 the prime minister called a conference on Naval Strategy which only dismayed the naval staff the more: "Why can't he get on with his job!" was Edwards' reaction. "W.C.," he wrote on the first day of July, "agrees that Sir D. is too old & promises action." But no action against Pound would ever follow. Edwards was probably correct in his assessment on the second: "The danger as I see it now is that W.C. has usurped the position of 1.S.L.!!"

That day, the admiralty ordered Sir Charles Forbes to submit plans for meeting an invasion.[40]

* * *

The Zionists and the Japanese, the Indians and Irish — all saw their chance in Britain's military embarrassment. Kennedy informed Washington on June 18, 1940 that the British were considering action very soon over Ireland. Shortsightedly, labour minister Ernest Bevin suggested they promise to Eire weapons and a united postwar Ireland if she would undertake to defend her territory against Hitler. But President Eamonn de Valera told Malcolm Macdonald that he would fight whoever attacked Eire, "whether it was Germany or England." On June 21 Churchill's Cabinet ruled out landing troops in Ireland as yet.[41]

A few days later they offered to de Valera a secret six point agreement — among them, a declaration for a united Ireland in return for Eire coming into the war, permitting the use of her ports and troops, and interning all aliens and Fifth Columnists. Fortunately for Ulster, from whom this offer was concealed, Chamberlain handled the negotiations and they went badly. "One reason," Chamberlain told Kennedy, "is that the Irish unquestionably believe that Britain is going to get licked." A Nazi invasion would bring about a united Ireland anyway, and that was all they were interested in.[42]

CHAPTER 28

A Misunderstanding Between Friends

IF LANGUAGE PROBLEMS had infected the alliance at Dunkirk, a muffed translation now led to an Anglo-French tragedy.

Mr Churchill could not be blamed for failing to notice the gauche error when it occurred. He was proud of his French — in fact he aired it whenever he could — but the pride was unjustified. ("Can anybody here speak French?" a gathering was once asked, and he volunteered: "*Je!*") His fractured French helped defuse awkward situations. At Casablanca in 1943 he would use it on the local French Resident-General: looking him sternly in the eye, he warned him not to tip off Pétain that he was there. "*Parce que si ils bomber nous,*" he threatened, jerking his thumb at the full moon, "*nous bomber vous aussi.*"[1]

When he conversed in French with the President of Turkey soon after, he paused in mid speech and heard Eden whispering a more intelligible rendering to the Turks. "Anthony," he grumbled, "will you please stop translating my French into French!"[2]

Once they had mastered his droll pronunciation, the French were flattered and amused, but more often foxed. Paul Reynaud dropped courteous hints that he should return to the safety of his native tongue, and once whispered *traduction* to the interpreter after Winston had obstinately finished.[3]

Until the end of June 1940 the only delicate linguistic problem had come at Tours on the thirteenth, when Reynaud had expatiated upon France's likely need for an armistice. Churchill grasped the point and nodded "*je comprends;*" the French however took it to mean that he "would understand." Paul Baudouin certainly heard it that way.* So did Pétain.

"Churchill promised," Darlan recalled a year later, "and the Marshal heard him, that if we had to seek an Armistice he would understand our

---

*He said so in de Gaulle's hearing; Spears hurried to Tours airfield and told the departing Churchill of the confusion. "Tell them," roared the PM, "My French is not so bad as all that."[5]

position and his friendship toward France would undergo no change." The admiral added bitterly, "The sequel was Mers-el-Kébir."[4]

THIS WAS NOT strictly true. Oran, as that tragedy became known in Britain, had its origin in another mistranslation, coupled with Churchill's obsession with the French warships coming under "German control." That menacing possibility had been examined at a small admiralty meeting on June 7: Pound had warned that the Germans must not get "control" of it — "The only way to do that properly," the meeting concluded, "was to sink the French fleet."[6]

It is now known that Hitler had ruled that France should retain her fleet. "You have not defeated the French navy," this quixotic dictator rebuffed Grand Admiral Erich Raeder on June 20: "You are not entitled to it!" He wanted a deliberately soft armistice. "*Armistice*," Raeder noted:

> The Führer wishes to refrain from taking any measures that would impinge upon French honour. The fleet is therefore to be interned [festlegen] at Brest and Toulon under peacetime disposition. The ships are to be immobilized.

France was even to be permitted warships to defend her empire in Indo-China.[7] Article 8 of the Armistice signed on June 22 provided that the rest of her fleet was to be "collected in ports to be specified, demobilized and disarmed under German or Italian supervision [*Kontrolle*].*" The document also contained a solemn declaration disowning any intention of applying the French warships to Germany's war purposes or of claiming them in the final peace settlement.[8]

Clumsily, in the paper submitted to the British Cabinet on June 23 the key phrase in Article 8 was translated from the German or French as "under German control," although neither *Kontrolle* nor *contrôle* means "control" except in special usages like Passport Control. Plainly a far smaller force was needed to *supervise* disarmament than to *seize* a fleet. But "under German control" was precisely the phrase that Churchill's ears had been attuned to: no matter that Darlan had assured the departing British naval attaché that no warship would be handed over, that the fleet would be scuttled if the enemy attempted to interfere with them; no matter that the foreign ministry had made the same assurances to Sir Ronald Campbell.[9]

---

*While we can appreciate the problems facing an authorized biographer of Churchill, there is no basis for asserting, "It became clear that Hitler had indeed insisted upon controlling the French Fleet" or that the Armistice defined that "all French warships were to come under German or Italian control" (Gilbert, vi, 589 and 628).

Churchill willingly believed that the French had signed a ruinous armistice. This slight translating error fuelled his obsession. It would cost the lives of twelve hundred French sailors, and poison relations between Britain and France for a generation afterwards.

* * *

It seems to be a universal failing of dictators that they cannot command the entire horizon of civil government and military activity, but must sweep like a searchlight across the darkened landscape, lighting upon each different subject which momentarily attracts them.

After France's fall, Churchill's towering obsession was that Hitler would get control of the French fleet. It overshadowed all three meetings of the Cabinet on June 24, held in the Cabinet room overlooking the garden behind No.10 — a garden that was a profusion of colour, and incongruous with birdsong that drifted into the room as though it were the library of a great country house. "We must at all costs ensure," Churchill declared, "that these ships either come under our control or are put out of the way for good."

Reassuringly, his codebreakers learned that during the day Darlan had signalled an order to all French warships to sail to the United States or scuttle if there was any danger of falling into enemy hands: the French naval mission in London had passed this signal to the admiralty. Darlan was keeping his promise. At the third Cabinet at ten-thirty p.m. it was also known that the two battle cruisers at Oran, Algeria, had moved into the adjacent naval base of Mers-el-Kébir where they were protected by shore guns.

We can reconstruct the thoughts that jumbled Churchill's mind. The wrong pall was forming over London — not of smoke, but the cloying pall of defeatism. The war was fizzling out before London had even been bombed. Roosevelt seemed unimpressed of Churchill's earnest. His leadership was under challenge both in the naval staff and Cabinet. Always sensitive to criticism, he was becoming arrogant, unapproachable.[10] The sullen Tory silences, the eager Labour applause troubled him. Opposition hardliners like Aneurin Bevan for their part could not understand why he kept Chamberlain and his "old gang" on: the last ten years had been the most disastrous in British history, yet Mr Churchill had retained every single foreign secretary of that era in high office.[11]

There were therefore several complicated reasons for Churchill to want some brutal, purifying course of action: political distraction was one of them. He told Beaverbrook, who sat through part of the discussion, that he had brought in Admiral Pound during most of the day—"Many objections were being raised to the policy," Beaverbrook later recalled him as saying, "and he wanted to keep Pound with him, in order to make answers to arguments." Six months later, sitting next to Cordell Hull at a Washington luncheon, Churchill himself confessed that he had wanted to raise Britain's low prestige throughout the world by showing "that Britain still meant to fight."[12]

It was one a.m. when the Cabinet dispersed. By that time he had decided: the warships collected in French ports would be neutralized; those that had taken refuge in Britain, seized.

He took the decision alone.

He marched up and down the lawn [Beaverbrook remembered] and a high wind was blowing — a very high wind. The night was dark, but he knew the garden well and it did not bother him. He was terribly disturbed and only recovered after a few minutes of aggressive and vigorous exercise.[13]

That decision taken, he just sat there with Bracken, glass in hand, anaesthetising his thoughts with alcohol. Several glasses of liquor later, according to Bracken,[14] sirens wailed London's first Red warning since September. The dreary and colourless Home Secretary, Sir John Anderson, led the way down to the air raid shelter where they joined Mrs Churchill, Mary and the domestic staff. As they settled on wooden benches it looked to one of the PM's secretaries, unaware of the awful decision just taken, like a village meeting. Knowing from the Bletchley oracle (his secret codebreakers) that London was not the target, Winston demonstrated the courage of the sapient, continuing to roam around the garden. "The searchlights were rather beautiful," wrote his secretary, "nothing happened and about three o'clock, with Duff Cooper and others, I walked home through the empty streets and went to bed, so sleepy that the All Clear failed to awaken." Lord Halifax, not privy to the Enigma intercepts, felt it more prudent to take shelter—already angry because, "owing to Winston's garrulousness," the Cabinet had lasted an hour longer than necessary with the result that he was caught by this air raid warning: "Once in [our Foreign Office war room] I sat till 4:15 gradually getting colder. I could not have been more bored. Dorothy [Lady Halifax] spent an entertaining evening in the Dorchester shelter with a mixed grill of George Clerk, the Vincent Masseys [Canadian High Commissioner], Diana Duff Cooper, [Chaim] Weizmann reading the Old Testament, and a lot more. She said it was the funniest thing she had ever seen."

On the following morning, the cruel decision about the French fleet hung over the prime minister. He announced in the House that he had read Article 8 — of which he rendered them the faulty translation — with grief and amazement: while he would not now state Cabinet policy on the French fleet, "neither patience nor resolution will be lacking in any measures they may think it right to take for the safety of the Empire."

On his orders, the admiralty devised an operation to appropriate the two French battleships and four light cruisers that had sailed into Portsmouth and Plymouth; simultaneously, a naval taskforce would seize or sink the French squadron concentrated at Mers-el-Kébir. Pre-empting the Cabinet's approval on June 27 Churchill ordered the latter operation, Catapult, executed six days later. Vice Admiral Sir James Somerville sailed in *Arethusa* to Gibraltar to improvise the taskforce. In Somerset dialect A.V. Alexander signalled to him, "Oi bee relyin on yu." The admiral replied, "Thank'ee zur. Doanee worree we got thay in the baag."[15]

* * *

Nothing, mused newspaper editor Cecil King privately as July 1940 began, could now avert defeat — "the country is already reconciling itself to the idea of a Nazi conquest." Even were Britain well led and really united it was hard to see how she could prevail against a larger airforce and more powerful army, an enemy occupying the whole coastline from Narvik to the Spanish border: "We are losing," he wrote in his diary, "because Germany does, and we do not, deserve to win." This accurately mirrored the mood that Churchill had to dispel: that was why he ordered Catapult, an act of war without parallel in modern history. It might yet inspire the sluggish Roosevelt.

Not one American-built aircraft or shell had yet reached Britain. Beaverbrook, perhaps more sanguine than Churchill, cherished few illusions. Roosevelt, he predicted, was motivated purely by patriotism, and certainly not by any desire to help the Empire; he would attend one meeting when Roosevelt, forgetting Beaverbrook's Canadian origin, declared, "Don't let Canada get Newfoundland. We want it."[16] Beaverbrook felt that Churchill should give him none of Britain's secrets "except for money value received."[17] Unhappy about the Empire's slide into a ruinous war, on the last day of June, Beaverbrook composed the first of many letters of resignation.

"At a moment like this," Winston replied on July 1, "when an invasion is reported to be imminent there can be no question of any Ministerial resignations being accepted."[18]

What Churchill could not accept was that the president was the slave of Congress, forbidden by the Neutrality Act to sell even obsolete weapons to Britain. Roosevelt's Treasury secretary Henry Morgenthau Jr. had earlier proven helpful but latterly had recoiled, disheartened by the debacle in France. General Marshall too predicted a British collapse and recommended a halt to all arms deliveries.[19]

On the same day, June 27, Cordell Hull urged the British ambassador to have the Navy sent across the Atlantic to safety. "Never cease to impress on President and others," reiterated Churchill in his scornful response, "that if this country were successfully invaded . . . some Quisling government would be formed to make peace on the basis of our becoming a German Protectorate. In this case the British Fleet would be the solid [sole?] contribution with which this Peace Government would buy terms." He added with perceptible bitterness, "We have really not had any help worth speaking of from the United States so far."[20]

"Am sure we shall be alright here," he reassured his veteran financier friend Bernard Baruch by cable, but carped: "Your people are not doing much. If things go wrong with us it will be bad for them. Winston Churchill."[21]

WHEN HE DROVE out to Chequers that evening, Friday, June 28, he was still brooding on the French fleet. More evidence had accumulated indicating that Darlan was keeping his promise. That very day every British naval liaison officer in the region had converged on Casablanca and agreed that the French fleet wanted to fight on the Allied side. The NLO at Mers-el-Kébir confirmed that the squadron there had received orders to tear up any signal from Vichy ordering its surrender to the enemy. On Wednesday June 26 Vice-Admiral, Malta, had reported seeing an order issued six days previously by Darlan: "Whatever orders be received," this read, "never abandon to the enemy a ship of war intact."

It was a ghastly weekend at Chequers. On Saturday Randolph came. Outsiders who witnessed the strange relationship for the first time winced at the son's "coarse and aggressive" treatment of his doting father. Randolph loudly demanded to be sent on active service. Winston refused, pointing out that if his son were killed it would impede him in his work. Vansittart had also come for dinner, bringing their old crony Alex Léger of the French foreign ministry. Churchill ruminated with utter candour about problems that would arise when he had to starve the French by blockade, and kill them by air raids, "being cruel in order to be kind."

Léger began talking of propaganda, but Churchill corrected him: "It is events that make the world."[22]

He returned to Downing-street late on Sunday the thirtieth. His fan mail at last outstripped the Munich Mouser's. One writer said he was a tonic for the nation; he directed his office to refer the letter to the Ministry of Health.

John Martin told him that six people had died of heart failure during the Red warning of June 24-25. "I am more likely to die of over-eating," Winston assured him. "But I don't want to die yet when so many interesting things are happening." The private secretary saw him later that evening wrapped only in a huge towel, "looking like one of the later Roman emperors."[23]

Churchill was eager for the coming passage of arms.

The admiralty had begun conducting an almost exaggerated search for loopholes in the evidence about Darlan's intentions: suppose the Germans had obtained his ciphers and faked these signals? Suppose he proved unable to stop the Germans? But even as signals expressing these doubts went out to naval commands, still firmer evidence of Darlan's integrity reached the British. A French submarine commander handed over to British officers at Malta the French naval ciphers: on July 1 Bletchley began reading Darlan's secret signals: there was no hint of treachery in them. The first intercept forwarded to the admiralty that Monday was his cipher signal transmitted the day before to the French naval mission in London, explaining that he hoped and fully expected to get permission to base the demobilized fleet in North Africa and at Toulon — both areas not occupied by the Germans.

That Monday evening the Cabinet decided nonetheless to send Somerville's new taskforce to Mers-el-Kébir with a list of "options" for the French squadron there. The signal to Sommerville went out in the early hours of July 2.

* * *

Given this Intelligence background, the steady preparations for Catapult aroused acute opposition in the naval staff. "As I see it," wrote Captain Ralph Edwards, the acting Director of Operations (Home), that Monday, July 1, "W.C. wants to take drastic action for the glorification of W.C. and the discomfiture of his erstwhile friends. He's always been the protagonist of France & feels their defection badly." He warned of all sorts of ugly possibilities. "Nothing however will shake W.C." Captain Cedric Holland, the former naval attaché in Paris, predicted that the assault would alienate every Frenchman.

"Against all the advice of the naval Staff," as Edwards learned on July 2, the taskforce was committed to the operation. Somerville was directed that if the French admiral in command, Marcel-Bruno Gensoul, failed to accept the alternatives, he was to be given six hours to scuttle his ships; failing that, Somerville was to blast the French squadron out of the water, and particularly the battle-cruisers *Dunkerque* and *Strasbourg*. In a signal to Somerville, Admiral Pound termed it "one of the most disagreeable and difficult tasks that a British Admiral has ever been faced with."

Somerville agreed — it was "a filthy job."

In London that July 3, Churchill convened his Cabinet at mid-day. It would sit throughout the next five hours. The French warships in British ports were seized without much bloodshed, in Operation Grasp. Meanwhile Somerville's taskforce had arrived off Mers-el-Kébir and began Operation Catapult: he had sent Captain Holland into the port to serve the ultimatum. Unhappy at the unfolding tragedy, Admiral Pound showed the Cabinet a draft signal, not yet sent, counselling Somerville to accept if the French offered to demilitarize their warships where they lay. But his draft was rejected lest it "look like weakening." When Gensoul did indeed make such an offer it was thus turned down.

Gensoul radioed his superiors in France, and played for time. Bletchley intercepted his signal. It over-simplified the ultimatum as "either-or:" either join the British fleet or scuttle. Admiral Darlan's response was angry and swift; his suppressed rancour toward Mr Churchill since the British "betrayal" at Dunkirk must not be overlooked in understanding this. He was shortly heard to make two distinctly ominous signals. The first ordered warships at Dakar in Senegal to show themselves "worthy of being Frenchmen." The second notified Gensoul at Mers-el-Kébir that he had ordered all French naval forces in the Mediterranean to join him immediately "in fighting order." It added: "You are to answer force with force. Call in the submarines and air force if necessary." Darlan also informed the joint Franco-German armistice commission of the forthcoming hostilities with Britain: knowledge of this must have rubbed salt in Churchill's obsessive wound.

At four-fifteen p.m. he sent an urgent signal over admiralty transmitters to Somerville's taskforce. "Settle the matter quickly," this read, "or you may have French reinforcements to deal with."

OVER AT THE ancient port of Alexandria, in Egypt, Britain's main Mediterranean naval base, the French had concentrated an elderly battleship and four cruisers under Admiral René-Emile Godfroy. When Churchill had first proposed their seizure three days earlier, Admiral Sir Andrew Cunningham, the C-in-C Mediterranean, had strongly objected: this squadron could hardly fall into German hands, and patience alone might bring it to the British side. Any seizure attempt would end in a shoot-out, and the harbour would be wrecked.

He therefore now made a tactful approach to Godfroy, who agreed to discharge his warships' oil. This diplomatic success scarcely satisfied Churchill's thirst for drama. Besides, a few minutes after six p.m., as the Cabinet was rising, the admiralty received from Bletchley the teleprinted intercept of a cipher signal made over six hours earlier by Admiral Darlan. This reported the terms of Somerville's ultimatum: announced that Gensoul had rejected it: and ordered all forces in the Mediterrannean to sail to Mers-el-Kébir.

At 6:24 p.m. the admiralty sent Cunningham a signal unmistakeably drafted by Churchill, defining that Godfroy's French crews were to be ordered off their ships "at once." "Do not, repeat not, fail." (Cunningham decided on balance to ignore it.) To report, no doubt, on all this Churchill drove off to the Palace at six-thirty p.m.

He had taken a spectacular gamble. Upon his return to No.10 he found Maisky, the Soviet ambassador, waiting. Looking fresh and cheerful, he told Maisky Britain's chances of winning were now good. Unaware of the extraordinary drama unfolding in the Mediterranean, Maisky asked how he viewed the future of the French navy. Churchill returned a look that the Russian could only describe as *artful*: "That question," he said through the cigar cloud, "is being attended to."Pressed further by the Russian, he amplified: "My strategy consists of surviving the next three months."[24]

BY THE TIME the squat, uncomely Russian had been shown out into Downing-street, the "battle" of Mers-el-Kébir was over. Just before six p.m. Somerville's guns had begun the massacre. After nine minutes they fell silent, as the port was blanketed in smoke. Beneath its swathes the *Bretagne* had blown up, killing over one thousand French sailors; the *Dunkerque*, with 210 of her crew killed, had run aground. But the battle-cruiser *Strasbourg* — the other primary target — unexpectedly emerged from the smoke escorted by three destroyers, charged out of the harbour, braved the magnetic mines laid across the entrance, and eluded the taskforce entirely: Somerville would regard Catapult as a failure.

Mr Churchill had burnt his boats. In reinforcing his political reputation, he had done lasting injury to Britain's; he had confirmed the image of Albion's endemic perfidy. Just before eight p.m. the French were heard ordering an all-out submarine and aircraft attack on Somerville's taskforce, followed by a further order to attack any British warship encountered and to seize merchant ships; the British were referred to as "the enemy." After that night's Defence Committee, General Dill uncomfortably remarked on the spectacle of two recent allies grappling at each other's throats while "the barbarians sat back and laughed." As for Churchill, he half expected to be at war with France on the morrow.[25]

However, the Marshal of France did not rise to the bait. Receiving U.S. Ambassador Bill Bullitt on America's national holiday, July the Fourth, Pétain frostily attributed Mers-el-Kébir to Churchill's "personal lack of balance."[26]

Only Admiral Cunningham's diplomacy prevented a repetition of the slaughter at Alexandria. The French admiral, alerted by Darlan's signals, had stopped the discharge of oil. Detecting this, Cunningham now demanded that he scuttle his ships. Godfroy refused and begain raising steam, clearly intending to fight his way out. Shortly after midnight Cunningham radioed to the admiralty a wan message fearing that in the sense of their Lordship's earlier order, he *had* "failed." But using purely diplomatic arguments, as one old seadog to another, Cunningham succeeded in talking Godfroy into accepting the inevitable. Late on the fourth Godfroy resumed the demobilisation of his warships. It was not as spectacular as blasting battleships out of the water; there was no pall of smoke: but it was a solution many times more satisfactory than Mers-el-Kébir.

The whole incident devalued Churchill's stock throughout the Navy.[27] At home, paradoxically, it raised it. On the fourth, the prime minister reported to the House. Its Members sat hushed, anguished, even ashamed at the day's news. But Winston spoke convincingly of the "mortal injury" to Britain if the French fleet had been handed over to German control. Heaping infamy on Reynaud, he recalled the unfulfilled promise to transfer to Britain the 400 Luftwaffe pilots taken prisoner in France. (It would have contravened the relevant Geneva Convention to do so.)

As for his own questionable deed, he told the House: "I leave the judgment of our action, with confidence, to Parliament. I leave it also to the nation, and I leave it to the United States. I leave it to the world and to history." It should, he said, dispose of the rumours of peace negotiations being spread by Hitler.

> We shall on the contrary prosecute the war with the utmost vigor by all the means that are open to us until the righteous purposes for which we entered upon it have been fulfilled. This is no time for doubts or weakness. It is the supreme hour to which we have been called.

As this "undistinguished little rotund figure," resumed his bench the House found its voice. Nodding off in the official box — he had spent the day helping his master draft the speech — Eric Seal was woken by the great shout that went up. John Martin thought that every man except for the three I.L.P. Members rose. The decorum of the Parliament vanished, wrote the American military attaché — everybody was shouting, cheering and waving order papers and handkerchiefs.[28]

Winston's cheeks pinked with emotion. Tears welled in his eyes, overflowed and tumbled down his cheeks.

Why were they cheering? Perhaps it was from relief that Britain had found a leader with the requisite ruthlessness to slay even his best friend. Yet from his own central vantage point, as he looked around, he saw he still had to win over the Tories.[29] The cheering was still loudest from the Labour benches facing him — to Dalton it seemed even deliberately so: they had given him a much finer ovation than the "old Corpse upstairs" — meaning Chamberlain — ever got.[30]

A victory mood settled upon his staff at No.10. That evening they made up a cinema party to the French film Neuf Celibataires; his private secretary found it "shriekingly funny."

The twelve thousand French sailors interned now in camps in Britain, seethed and smouldered. Whitehall forbade a memorial service for the dead, and only reluctantly agreed to compensate the officers looted by British ratings during Grasp. In September Admiral Muselier, de Gaulle's naval chief, would formally claim compensation for the wounded and next of kin of those killed in Catapult, and demand restitution after the war for the ships destroyed.[31] Softening, as de Gaulle began to recruit the matelots in the internment camps for his own Free French navy, the government permitted the French tricolor to flutter over Westminster Abbey on their national holiday.

* * *

On July 3, the day of the great tragedy, the Duke of Windsor had arrived, still sulking, in Lisbon. The American ambassador in Madrid telegraphed to Washington that before leaving the Duke had remarked to embassy staff that it was vital to end the war before thousands more were "killed or maimed to save the faces of a few politicians."[32] Churchill read this telegram either immediately as an intercept or when it was forwarded to him a few days later by Sam Hoare, now British ambassador in Madrid. It did little for his vanity. When he saw the King on the evening of the third, they hatched a plan to transport the garrulous Duke to the other side of the Atlantic, as governor of the Bahamas. There he would be out of harm's way.

The more petulant the Duke became about leaving, the more Churchill insisted. His codebreakers must have culled increasingly aggravating snatches of Windsor wisdom — the Duke asking the Spanish foreign minister to send an agent to Lisbon for a confidential message: the Duke advising that air raids would make Britain see reason: Ribbentrop directing his Madrid embassy to get the couple back "if necessary by force:"[33] the U.S. ambassador in Lisbon warning Roosevelt not to allow the press near Duke or Duchess since her private conversation showed her "by no means enthusiastic about Britain's prospects."[34]

FROM THE TENEMENT slums of the East End to Buckingham Palace itself, most of London's populace still had no cover against bombs other than flimsily shored-up cupboards beneath wooden stairs.

Scattered air raids were increasing, but a D-Notice forbade newspapers to give details. On July 5, Churchill noted to Ismay: "What has been done about air raid casualties? I understand that they were not to be published in any definite or alarming form, but I do not notice much difference in the procedure or any sign of measures being taken."[35]

The faint hearted had fled to Canada while they still could. The majority braved it out. "I would rather be bombed to fragments than leave England." wrote the child of one Labour MP to the *Times* on the fourth. Churchill congratulated the lad's father with a handwritten note: "We must all try to live up to this standard."

He and his colleagues would find it less hazardous than most, since the ministries had now built bunkers for themselves. Work had begun on the Central War Room beneath the ministries off Parliament Square during the Czech crisis two years earlier. Since it seemed an opportune moment, on July 5 the PM took Beaverbrook and Ironside with him across the F.O. courtyard to inspect this underground bunker.[36]

Perhaps these battlefield conditions were good for his adrenalin too. The rooms above the chosen basement area had been emptied, and engineers had poured in tons of steel girders and sixteen feet of solid concrete as a bombproof cover. A sentry opened the gas-tight door, and the prime minister was led into the complex by Royal Marines, who would guard the complex in an emergency. The underground passages were covered with burgundy red linoleum. The cabins where his ministers would sleep in an emergency were prison-like cells, shored up with balks of oak, and equipped with a simple camp bed.

Churchill's own cell was only about five yards long and three wide, and crowded with timbers to shore up the ceiling. It boasted only a small bed, a desk with three ivory bellpushes on a small wooden block, and the only carpet in the bunker, a cheap red fitted cord.

He did much of his work in bed — his dictum was, "If you can sit, don't stand. If you can lie, don't sit." For the chiefs of staff there were three buff chairs spaced along the wall next to the fireplace. (Of course they had their own conference room elsewhere in the bunker.) On a small table was a cigar-cutter made of gunmetal and a cannon shell, with the Star of David mounted on its wooden pedestal.

Cream coloured metal trunking clung like a rectangular serpent to ceilings and walls, entwined with the pneumatic tubes and lighting conduits. The air conditioning system hissed air through ball sockets. Indicators displayed the weather above ground and whether an air raid alert had sounded.

The Map Room had been staffed for weeks already. On one wall of the small, crowded room a painted sign read, "In case of Gas attack, Close this valve." Down the centre of a long table ran an elevated dais crowded with telephones manned by captains, colonels and wing commanders; three of the telephones were white — these could reach him instantly anywhere in London; two were green and one, standing on a table by itself, red. The walls were papered with charts — to his left Churchill saw the Naval Operations map, flagging the positions of merchant ships, escorts, U-boats and the fleet. The Eastern Mediterranean was almost bare of pinholes, indicating how Axis seapower was forcing the Allies to use the long route around the Cape instead of the Suez Canal.

Heaped on a cross table were several files and boxes, including a red leather despatch box embossed in gold THE KING. Beyond that was a floorspace surrounded by charts of the Far East and of Britain's immense Empire — now at its greatest ever extent.

The marines escorted him further into the maze, clanging shut each door behind them. At the tunnel's end a gastight hatch concealed a dark baize-covered door with a window slit of armoured glass, which opened into the Cabinet room, a windowless chamber perhaps twenty-five feet square. Two-foot girders, painted fire-engine red, spanned its ceiling. A telephone stood in a recess, with its scrambler in a small mahogany box. Charts covered the plasterboard soundproofing of these walls too.

This room was dominated by blue-baize covered trestle tables moved together into a hollow rectangle, with two dozen green-leatherette chairs of tubular steel. At each place was one white blotter, one Utility pencil, a polished silver ash tray, sheathed paper knife, and an inkwell; a polished wooden chair was provided for Churchill at the left of the table. In front was a tray of coloured pencils and the chromium hole-puncher he called his *klop* for tying documents together. Behind him as he sat at the desk was an electric fire and a red fire-bucket for cigar butts. There was another notice on the wall to his right. If enemy bombers were right overhead, it said, an alarm would ring.

Beneath it was a black box housing the bell. And on that was a white knob, so that he could turn if off.

CHAPTER 29

Gangster Methods

OUTSIDE THE IMMEDIATE compass of Mr Churchill's life — that is, outside the famous front door of No.10 — London was becoming dull and drab. The ornamental railings were ripped down around park and garden alike and fed into the scrap furnaces; none was spared, or almost none. In London, traffic was sparse; in the countryside, except on Derby Day, non existent.

Streets were barricaded against the expected paratroops; barbed wire and trenches serried the open spaces; every road sign referring to the Thames had been painted over. The shops were empty, the grand houses evacuated. The bourgeoisie had fled Eaton Square and Harrods alike, although the great store was about to open its summer sale. Nobody wanted to linger in a city expecting an inferno. So the streets were given over to French matelots and soldiers, and crowds of bored Anzacs who had arrived by liner. An American newcomer found the city as "dark as a pocket."[1] In the suburbs, the D'Oyly Carte was performing *Mikado*. A newcomer called Fonteyn was dancing *Sleeping Beauty* at Sadler's Wells to audiences clutching gasmasks in cardboard boxes.

The English, never fashionable, were now frumpy — the liveried doormen at the Dorchester and Savoy being the exception. The streets wore no flags, the girls no pretty frocks; women appeared in public in slacks, a few were even smoking cigarettes. Churchill's war was stirring a female migration to the factory bench, and this would have lasting social consequences.

It is unlikely that he noticed. He peopled a one-man world, friendless and alone. Like an absolute monarch, he never rode the bus, carried money, or went into a shop. In a sense he was living in the wrong century. In the fastnesses of No.10 he was as remote from the common man as "Tinskip," the silvery barrage balloon that wallowed up from Horse Guards Parade towards the clouds each time the sirens wailed. Once when he ventured up into the Midlands he would gaze perplexed upon a slum. "Fancy living in one of these streets," he exclaimed.

"Never seeing anything beautiful — never eating anything savoury — *never saying anything clever!*"[2]

His own sybaritic needs were certainly not those of the common English in the summer of 1940. "My idea of a good dinner," he once said, "is first to have good food, then to discuss good food, and after this good food has been elaborately discussed, to discuss a good topic — with myself as chief conversationalist." "Take away this dish!" he would thunder at the waiter who placed a nondescript pudding before him. "It has no *theme!*"

Now food and clothing were rationed, although this fact had yet to permeate the clubs. "Mr Churchill's tastes are simple," the first Lord Birkenhead once drawled. "He is easily contented with the best of everything."

Not everybody shared his sense of content. When he notified his requirements for the Quebec conference three years later — special trains, costly jaunts and accommodation for a princely entourage — Canada's frugal premier wondered how the man could square this with the rising toll in tax and sacrifice demanded from his people. "One cannot go about too humbly, it seems to me," this wise Canadian wrote.[3] To young John Colville, leaving the private office in 1941 to join the R.A.F., the prime minister would express anxiety about how he would find accommodation there for his *valet*. He had been out of touch with reality for half a century.

* * *

Surely Hitler would throw heavy air raids at London soon? Intercepts showed that his long range bomber force was to be ready by July 8, 1940; an enemy Flak (anti-aircraft artillery) corps was heard to clamour for maps of Britain as well as France.[4] Churchill called for the charts of tides and moons until mid-August and scrutinised them for clues as to Hitler's invasion intentions: but who could tell if the enemy would land at high tide, or at low; by darkness or by dawn? Moonless nights and a dawn high tide, they told him, would prevail in the first two weeks of July.[5]

For decades there had been a field marshal inside this gibbous politician, struggling to get out. Occasionally the former's voice escaped the latter's lips. Baldwin's secretary had remarked upon Churchill's negotiating with striking miners in the Twenties: "He is always deploying 'guns' or 'barrages' on the owners or the men."[6]

Like Hermann Göring, he had played only with tin soldiers as a child; as a youth he had hastened to every scene of bloodshed from Cuba, India and Egypt to South Africa. A German field marshal who chanced upon a copy of *My Early Life* in August 1945 would be struck by the obvious pleasure its author had derived from the adventure of killing. "I know," wrote this Nazi commander, "of no such enthusiasts among my own acquaintances."[7]

Winston's most intimate counsellor that summer of 1940 was the Prof — Professor Friedrich Lindemann.

Seemingly omniscient; austere; ascetic — intensely lonely, but loyal beyond belief, the Prof was the ideal foil for him; Winston was innocent of all scientific knowledge; when the B.B.C. developed a super-power transmitter, Aspidistra, he would believe it could be heard by the troops even without a radio set.[8] The Prof entranced him with his thumbnail calculations. After Winston was hit by the New York cab in 1931 he had dourly telegraphed that the impact was equivalent to falling thirty feet; or being hit by a brick dropped from six hundred feet. Even more flatteringly, Churchill's otherwise unenergetic person had absorbed the car's kinetic energy at the rate of eight thousand horsepower.[9]

The Prof too harboured an Ovidian disdain for the *profanum vulgus*; he regarded the working classes as a species of sub-human.[10] He rated politicians and rival scientists little higher. "Politicians?" he boomed over one dinner that summer. "They'd have done much better if they'd tossed a coin before every decision since 1932. Then at least they'd probably have been right half the time."[11] And he gave the little sniff that masqueraded for a laugh.

Churchill impelled him to start thinking about anti-aircraft rockets which could be guided by radar and detonated by proximity fuse, a new device.[12] Lindemann responded well to prompting and worked hard to better anti-tank weapons like "sticky bombs." He suggested Molotov cocktails too, which seemed to have proved effective in Spain and Poland.[13] Churchill promoted the Prof's favourite projects like the Naval Wire Barrage heedless of expert criticism. When Churchill suggested using giant ice floes as aircraft carriers, this Project Habakkuk would haunt the government departments throughout the war. Lindemann frowned on the idea: it would involve pumping 100m gallons of water a day, equal to the entire pumping capacity of the London Water Board, and freezing it three feet deep every twenty-four hours.

He suggested concrete instead — "A concrete Habakkuk would be very like a large skyscraper built on its side." It would be about 5,000 feet long by 1,000 feet broad and 100 feet deep. Churchill refused to be fobbed off. "I have long zested for the floating island," he would scrawl across one document. "It has always broken down. The ice scheme must be reported on first. Don't get in its way."[14]

Lindemann's fertile brain never wearied of new ideas. When Winston was still First Lord, the Prof had nagged the experts to develop a torpedo that would home onto a U-boat's own noise; they choked it off as impracticable. (Both the Americans and Germans succeeded.) Now he would suggest less likely projects: aerial mines dangled by slow aeroplanes along the enemy radio-beams, and myriads of "small magnets fitted with lights" cascaded into seas where a submarine was suspected. Between them, Churchill and the Prof did develop some schemes of great military vision, however: on July 7 Churchill asked the Minister of Supply what was being done about designing ships capable of transporting tanks for an invasion.[15]

If such an idea prospered, like these tank landing craft or the later artificial harbours, he would claim absolute paternity. Woe betide any scheme he had not fathered. Independently of him, Lord Hankey created the Petroleum Warfare Department and was igniting streams of petrol along possible invasion beaches and approach roads. Winston disparaged and obstructed the idea.[16]

"ON WHAT MAY be the eve of an attempted invasion or battle for our native land," stated the proclamation Churchill now circulated throughout his government, "the Prime Minister desires to impress upon all persons . . . their duty to maintain a spirit of alert and confident energy."

"The Prime Minister expects," he continued, with Nelson's famous flag hoist fluttering in his memory,

> all His Majesty's servants in high places to set an example of steadiness and resolution. They should check and rebuke expressions of loose and ill-digested opinion in their circles, or by their subordinates. They should not hesitate to report, or if necessary remove, any officers or officials who are found to be consciously exercising a disturbing or depressing influence, and whose talk is calculated to spread alarm and despondency.[17]

He half expected the invasion to begin that weekend: Hitler was known to favour Saturdays. Exasperated by his queries, Colonel Ian Jacob minuted to Ismay on July 2, "We really must leave the C-in-C to make his own plans." Saturday arrived, but not the enemy. Churchill obstinately minuted his staff to list every invasion indication[18], and left with Field Marshal Ironside to watch British and newly arrived Canadian troops conducting anti-invasion exercises in Kent. It gave him a happy excuse to weekend at Chartwell. He proudly showed off his pond and fed the golden carp. "He calls them all darlings," wrote a secretary who had accompanied him, "and shouts to the cat and even the birds."[19]

No warlord trusts subordinates to attend to detail. Hitler had scrutinized the demolition chambers on Dutch bridges, had reminded generals that sunrise in France was later than in Berlin, had peered at models of the Belgian forts. "The Playthings of the Empress," his staff officers had sniggered.

Churchill had always shown the same obsessive attention to detail. During the General Strike he had haunted the offices of the *British Gazette*, overseeing every comma. "He thinks he is Napoleon," wrote the responsible Cabinet minister ironically, "but curiously enough the men who have been printing all their life . . . know more about their job than he does."[20]

Now his inventive mind roamed the coming invasion battlefield, which he first took to be the East coast, and later the South; after donning an air commodore's uniform he would drive over to airfields in Kent and Sussex; in spurious naval rig he toured the Channel defences, asking probing questions about refugee control and the removal of untrustworthy people.[21] How could enemy agents fighting in British uniform be identified?[22] Had trenches been dug to prevent aircraft using open fields?[23] Had Britain prepared her own oil depots for demolition?[24]

He shared Hitler's fascination with gigantic artillery and the navy had installed at Dover on what Colville called his "caprice" a fourteen-inch gun capable of hurling one-ton shells at unfortunate France.[25] Around the coastline the Admiralty was emplacing torpedo tubes and 150 six-inch guns with seven thousand sailors and marines to man them.[26]

Ironside found him "in one of his go-getter humours."[27] Finding General Sir Bernard Montgomery's 3rd Division spread along the coast the PM demanded — flagging the note ACTION THIS DAY — that the War Office pull it back into reserve and requisition the omnibuses plying Brighton's summer seafront to make it mobile. The invasion battles should be fought inland; he suggested that the navy lay minefields to seal off the rear of an enemy seaborne landing.

A PM could take decisions that a colonel could not. He approved plans to drench invaders with poison gas, telling a major-general who lunched with him: "I have no scruples." He decided against apprising the United States; the necessary chemicals would be procured elsewhere.[28] When one Labour veteran from The Focus, Josiah Wedgwood, demanded that London not be declared an open city like Paris, Churchill, already fancying he saw a pall of smoke billowing above the capital as his troops fought the invaders in the streets below, replied with relish. "I have a very clear view," he advised Ismay, "that we should fight every inch of it, and that it would devour quite a large invading army."[29]

To the indoctrinated it was known that ever since the end of May Göring's messages to his commanders were being deciphered, and that

Hitler had emphatically forbidden any attack on London, which cannot have pleased Winston.[30] It was all rather an anti-climax. The Air Ministry had originally predicted six hundred tons of bombs a day on London, and 30,000 casualties. Re-assessing the enemy strength at 2,500 bombers in June, the Joint Intelligence Committee had increased this eightfold. The Prof pooh-poohed these estimates: and called for intercept data from Bletchley for his statisticians. On July 6 the Air Staff still predicted 1,800 ton attacks. The Prof pointed out that in the last nine days of June, each plane had dropped less than one-eighth of a ton and none of these bombs fell on London.[31]

THE PRIVATE SECRETARIES were unaware of the intercepts. They wilted throughout that summer as the despatch boxes were borne in and stacked up on Winston's desk or around his bed. Humans, he lectured them, needed change, not rest. John Martin, summoned before breakfast to Winston's bedroom, wrote: "Some day I propose to sleep for a week without stopping."

Churchill revolutionized methods at No.10. Telephone operators throughout Britain uttered the code "Rapid Falls 4884" and were put through to him immediately. He issued orders only in writing, accepted responsibility for no others.[32] His terse Prayers multiplied. "Pray let me have," they might begin, "by this evening, on one sheet of paper. . ." "One sheet" became a requirement throughout Whitehall, though the wordier ambassadors writhed under the irksome rule. He would red-ink "Why worry? W.S.C.,30.3." on a report by the Prof on casualties in the British and American armies in the final battle for Germany; the two words were solemnly typed out as adequate reply.[33]

As the more onerous matters silted down through the boxes, the staff devised an urgent "top of the box" category; when that too clogged the really vital documents were taken in by hand.

Those officials he could not tolerate, those who failed to succumb to his spell, were sacked, and without ceremony. Sir John Reith would learn of his dismissal from his morning newspaper. "Believe me," Beaverbrook would reminisce three years later, "No man is more ruthless . . . more bitter and unforgiving."[34] Churchill was displeased when the permanent head of the Foreign Office included a kind remark in the telegram dismissing one wretch at his behest that summer. Cadogan was shocked, but kept his feelings to his diary: "After all, the man had given the whole of his life, and we are sacking him on hearsay evidence." "Winston," he added, "is very babyish in some ways."[35]

Nobody stood up to him. When Lord Halifax again ventured the idea, in Cabinet on July 10, that at least they might *ascertain* Hitler's peace terms, he camouflaged his courage with the weak excuse that this would win time to rearm.

On the twentieth he put General Brooke in command of Home Forces, retiring the bumbling Ironside. Brooke, like Halifax and Cadogan, was canny enough to confine his distaste of their prime minister's verbosity, meddling and occasional alcoholic fuddle to private, padlocked, leather-bound diaries.

Admirals followed generals into retirement. While Captain Edwards' diary entries should be treated with the reserve that all clandestine writings merit, they indicate how far Churchill's prestige had sunk in the Royal Navy since Mers-el-Kébir. As he predicted, Winston had not taken off the First Lord's cap and began a lengthy wrangle with Admiral Forbes over the distribution of the Home Fleet between anti-invasion and Atlantic convoy protection duties; Forbes refused to believe that the Germans either could or would invade.[36]

On July 15 Edwards wrote with evident sarcasm: "Winston over at the Admiralty telling us how to dispose the fleet." Two days later, seeing the appointment of Lord Cork as C-in-C, Shetlands — "Another Old Codger for a job. . . Another of Winston's ramps." On the eighteenth, seeing Roger Keyes nominated Director of Combined Operations — "Are we all balmy? — God preserve us from the old Gang."[37]

The First Sea Lord took a more comfortable view. Writing to another admiral in December he would find mitigating circumstances for what Cadogan had called the PM's "babyish" ways.

> The PM is very difficult these days, not that he has not always been. One has, however, to take a broad view, because one has to deal with a man who is proving a magnificent leader; and one just has to put up with his childishness as long as it isn't vital or dangerous.[38]

Such patience in the First Sea Lord was remarkable: there was not one seagoing admiral whom Winston would not try to dismiss. Neither Pound nor A.V. Alexander objected. The Board of Admiralty, whose prerogative dismissals had always been, was widely referred to as Alexander's Ragtime Band; the First Lord himself, as Churchill's toady.

Over Mers-el-Kébir, Winston had flouted the advice of all three competent admirals — Cunningham, Somerville, and Admiral Sir Dudley North, the Flag Officer at Gibraltar.

North protested in writing about the whole ungallant incident.

The admiralty sent a chilling response, deprecating comments on any policy already decided; shown a copy by Alexander, Churchill ominously wrote back on the twentieth that Admiral North had evidently not got "the root of the matter" in him: "I should be very glad to see you replace him by a more resolute and clear-sighted officer."[39]

But it would take another episode to break Admiral North finally.

* * *

During July 1940, England waited for Hitler's long expected peace proposals. Churchill occasionally went to the Channel coast, hoping to see air battles, or drove out, dressed "rather self-consciously" in airforce uniform, as Martin thought, to the Hurricane airfield at Kenley, and splashed around in gumboots among the fighter pilots.

His cheeks pink with exuberance he toured the southern defences using a special train of whose comfort Lord Birkenhead would certainly have approved. The Midland Railways had installed two Royal suites in it for the PM and his V.I.P.s, with a lounge in the centre, Pullman sleepers for his staff, and a diner and the usual boxcars.

His appointment card at No.10 and the Chequers guestbook reveal him lingering with his old friends from The Focus, including his millionaire benefactor Sir Henry Strakosch. But he now needed little encouragement to hate Germans. Everywhere he preached the "coming invasion" and spoke of the atrocities which the Nazis would perpetrate — the only way, he explained to his private staff, to get every man, woman and child to fight desperately. After one dinner engagement at Chequers with three generals he laughingly told his staff that he had enjoyed a "real Hun hate" with them. "I never hated the Hun in the last war," he smiled, "but now I hate them like an earwig."[40]

By 1941 they would have fifty-five divisions — enough to execute raids of the "butcher and bolt" variety. Whether or not Hitler ever invaded, as he told them with surprising candour, this "invasion scare" was serving a useful purpose: he intended, he added, to broadcast about it that Sunday evening, July 14, and give a deliberate impression of "long and dangerous vigils."[41]

"Here in this strong City of Refuge," he proclaimed into the microphone, with that easy grandiloquence of his, "which enshrines the title-deeds of human progress and is of deep consequence to Christian civilization; here, girt about by the seas and oceans where the navy reigns; shielded from above by the prowess and devotion of our airmen — we await undismayed the impending assault. Perhaps it will come tonight. Perhaps it will come next week. Perhaps it will never come. We must show ourselves equally capable of meeting a sudden violent shock or — what is perhaps a harder test — a prolonged vigil. But be the ordeal sharp or long, or both, we shall seek no terms, we shall tolerate no parley; we may show mercy — we shall ask for none."

Once again he boasted that the capital could devour an army — "We would rather see London laid in ruins and ashes than that it should be tamely and abjectly enslaved."

Phonograph records of these broadcasts went on sale. The proceeds went to a charity set up for Londoners whose homes were shortly laid in the ruins and ashes of which he had spoken.

At the same time he took measures to deal with possible emergencies if Hitler's proposals proved irresistible. Bevin declared strikes illegal; special courts would order the summary execution of disaffected citizens found guilty of treason, sabotage or looting.

That Monday, his buoyant mood was perceptible to John Martin, lunching en famille with the Churchills and Attlee. "He likes his food," wrote the private secretary. He chuckled at Churchill's remarks about the rationing ideas of the food faddists — they would have Britain fed on oatmeal, potatoes, and milk, "washed down on gala occasions with a glass of lemonade."

> He is in a very confident frame of mind, more so now than ever . . . he seems very playful in his family and fond of animals, playing with a little dog and making absurd remarks to it.

BY THE END of July the prime minister had become privately convinced that Hitler was not going to invade Britain — or at least not yet.

Inspired probably by the "feel" of the Enigma intercepts, he took the decision to send Britain's armoured forces out to Egypt. "He has seemed," wrote one of the servants of the Bletchley oracle, "as bold as the Senate of ancient Rome when it sent an army to Spain while Hannibal was still at the gates of the city." In fact, Winston knew rather more about his enemy than the Roman senate did. A newcomer at Bletchley that summer was given as his first job the role of avocatus diaboli, proving that Hitler's invasion operations were genuine and not deception.[42]

The signs of Hitler's hesitancy were there. On July 16 he had added to his main directive ("I have decided to prepare a landing operation against England") the eloquently indecisive afterthought — *"and, if necessary to carry it out."*

Whether or not this signal, or the secondary echoes of it, were intercepted, Churchill had already deduced Hitler's ultimate intent to crush the Soviet Union. Cripps had just returned briefly from Moscow with word that Stalin expected such an attack.[43] "Even if that Man reached the Caspian," Churchill had remarked to John Colville on July 13, using a motif that was to recur many times over the coming months, "he would return to find a fire in his backyard."

BEFORE HITLER DARED turn east, he had to quieten England one way or the other. For this reason Churchill acted firmly to pinch off each German feeler that came through, like ivy creeping through a wall, via Stockholm, the Vatican, Berne and Washington.

More than one high official showed profound disquiet at his

obstinacy. In Berne the British ambassador revived an earlier contact with Hitler's emissary Prince Max von Hohenlohe; meeting him in secret in mid July, Sir David Kelly had agreed with the unflattering description of Churchill as being unreasonable and often under alcohol but had pointed reassuringly to Halifax and Butler as being still amenable to logic.[44]

On Friday the nineteenth Hitler delivered his famous Reichstag speech, calling upon Britain to see reason. Cripps, who had returned to Moscow, described it as "outstanding" and "very clever."[45] Britain, the German leader said, now had a choice between peace or suffering — not that Mr Churchill, he scurrilously added, would be among those to suffer, for he would have betaken himself to Canada where the wealth and children of "those principally interested in the war" had already gone before.

> I consider myself in a position to make this appeal since I am not a vanquished foe begging favours, but the victor, speaking in the name of reason. I can see no reason why this war need go on. I am grieved to think of the sacrifices it must claim.

Halifax was disappointed that the speech contained no concrete terms. In his diary he regretted that little could be made of it. The BBC broadcast an immediate rebuff one hour later, spoken in sneering German by Sefton Delmer of the government's Black Propaganda agency. Churchill believed he had scotched Hitler's final attempt.

That Saturday however a telegram jolted him: an American Quaker in Washington had brought a message from the British embassy from his German counter-part. "German chargé d'affaires," Lord Lothian said, "sent me a message that if desired he could obtain from Berlin Germany's present peace terms."[46]

Lothian revealed to the American intermediary that dissidents in the War Cabinet — which can only have meant Halifax and Chamberlain — felt it was time to negotiate a fair peace, and had asked him to find out from the German embassy what Hitler had to say about the kind of peace that "a proud and unconquered nation" could accept.

Hans Thomsen, the German chargé d'affaires, had reported the gist of this by cipher message to Berlin on July 19. If, as is probable, Bletchley intercepted this[47] it must have stunned Churchill to see it described as a "British approach."[48] He knew that Lothian had met Hitler and admired him. Hitler moreover authorized Thomsen to widen the Washington contact.

Annoyed at this hiccup in his strategy, Churchill fired a sharp telegram at the F.O. "I do not know whether Lord Halifax is in town today," this said, "but Lord Lothian should be told on no account to make any reply to the German chargé d'affaires' message."[49] Halifax, notably, did nothing.

IT WAS NOW all the more urgent to light that "fire in Hitler's backyard." A timely bombing of Berlin would put an end to his yammering about peace.

True, in calmer years Churchill had declared that when nations began to wage war on their enemy's civil population, they were doomed. Neville Chamberlain had opposed mass bombing — "I do not believe," he wrote, "that holocausts are required."[50] On September 1, Hitler too had appealed for an embargo. Roosevelt had warned that America would not aid any nation that initiated the bombing of civilians. That September, Winston told colleagues he wanted world opinion to see beyond doubt that "Messieurs les Assassins" had begun this bloody exchange.

As First Lord, Churchill had nonetheless urged intermittently that they "bomb the Ruhr" — a term showing no understanding of how verdant and farflung the Ruhr is. He felt that such a blow might destroy Germany's "brittle morale," that it would prove "mortal" (he meant *fatal*.)[51]

Two days after becoming prime minister, he again advocated bombing the Ruhr; after obtaining Labour approval he began a few days later. To justify it, he would shortly propagate the myth — which he maintained even in his memoirs — that "many thousands" had been slaughtered in the enemy's tactical air strike at Rotterdam on May 14.[52]

Three months had passed since then, and there was little sign of morale cracking. Impatient to do more, on July 8 he had asked Beaverbrook, minister of aircraft production, when Britain could obtain sufficient air mastery to launch "an absolutely devastating, exterminating attack by very heavy bombers" which, he felt, was "one sure path" to victory.

We have no continental army which can defeat the German military power. The blockade is broken and Hitler has Asia and probably Africa to draw from. Should he be repulsed here or not try invasion, he will recoil eastward, and we have nothing to stop him.[53]

R.A.F. BOMBER COMMAND had now passed into the hands of Charles Portal, a tall, ice-cold air marshal destined for the highest post in the airforce, a man who may readily be judged from his application to the air staff for a directive that bomber crews might resume machine-gunning people seen rushing out of enemy factories, although many might be women.[54]

On the weekend of Hitler's peace speech and of Lord Lothian's mysterious feelers in Washington, Churchill suddenly invited "Peter" Portal down to Chequers for the night.

The invitation was evidently unpremeditated, for he had written to Portal and his minister Sinclair earlier that Saturday, July 20, suggesting that if Hitler bombed "the centre of Government in London" it seemed important "to return the compliment" the next day on Berlin. The new generation of heavy bombers, the Stirlings, would soon be ready: but would the nights be long enough to reach Berlin? "Pray let me know."[55]

In conversation that night with Portal it became clear that Winston intended to strike at Berlin anyway, and he named a target date: September 1. Portal agreed that the nights would then be long enough to reach Berlin with bombers carrying about 100 tons.[56]

Meanwhile to prevent, as he said, Dr Goebbels branding him a warmonger he decided not to reply himself to Adolf Hitler's speech — "Not being" he jocularly informed his staff, "on speaking terms with him."[57] The Cabinet decided, with more than a little irony, that Lord Halifax should perform that historic deed in his routine ministerial broadcast on Monday evening. Churchill invited him to join Portal at Chequers, bringing a draft retort to Hitler.

The lugubrious foreign secretary lacked Winston's facile pen and laboured hard over the distasteful script. At one point he wanted to declaim that Hitler could not win, whatever Hitler might achieve elsewhere, unless he disposed of the British army, navy and airforce. Churchill paced the room, then asked: "Why not say, Unless That Man can sap the might of Britain"?[58]

Halifax marvelled at such talent. "I have never met a greater artist in language!" he recorded. "The only fly in the ointment was that he kept me talking till 1:30." Later, when John Martin took a message in, he found the foreign secretary in blue velvet slippers, reading his Bible before the fire.

Worrying voices reached the PM upon his return to No.10 that Sunday night, demanding a moderate response to Hitler. On Monday the Chief Whip told him that forty-eight MPs had tabled a resolution calling upon him to state Britain's war aims. But that would mean telling the Poles and Czechs, for instance, sad home truths about the future of their territories.[59]

ONE LAST TIME, Churchill's War hung in the balance as the debate flared up anew that Monday morning. Once more, the relevant War Cabinet paragraphs have been blanked out.[60] Once again, he carried the day: outnumbered, or outflanked, Halifax inserted the terse rejection of Hitler's "appeal to common sense" into his B.B.C. script that evening.

(He showed it beforehand to Kennedy; the ambassador's only comment was that "the God stuff" sounded all right.)

Even so, it was touch and go. Berlin's official response to Lothian's feeler had now reached Washington: Berlin, Hans Thomsen was directed to say, would welcome a fair peace — one which Britain could properly accept — but Mr Churchill's bellicose broadcast of the fourteenth, implying warfare from city to city, was a stumbling-block. Thomsen was to ask whether the PM had spoken purely for "home and colonial consumption." If so, Berlin would not take it amiss; otherwise it would change the face of the war.

At seven p.m. that Monday, just before Halifax was due to broadcast, Lothian *telephoned* from Washington, an appeal not to close the door: a further approach had arrived from Thomsen. "Lord Lothian," Halifax scribbled, "[said he] could get the information as to what he means if we want it."

Evidently Hitler was willing to disclose his terms. "We ought to find out what Hitler means," Lothian had pleaded, "before condemning the world to one million casualties."[61]

London's reply was simple: Lord Lothian should tune in to Halifax's broadcast that evening.

In the event, one million was to prove an under-estimate.

A FURTHER, POLITICAL consideration underlay Churchill's stubbornness. "At this moment," he argued, reading a suggested F.O. reply to the Swedish King's renewed offer of mediation, "when we have had no sort of success, the slightest opening will be misjudged."

Four years later Hitler would use the same stubborn arguments for fighting on. Even so, Halifax's rude reply was a shock to Berlin. The Nazi propaganda agencies were ordered to take the gloves off and brand the rejection a "war crime."[62] Moderates had been optimistic that, faced with the alternative — the bankruptcy of her Empire — Britain would see reason. "Churchill," Baron von Weizsäcker privately assessed that Tuesday, "has gone out on a limb and can't get back." That day, Britain jacked up income tax to 8s.6d. (43p.) in the £. On Wednesday Walther Hewel, link man between Hitler and Ribbentrop, wrote to an intermediary: "The Führer does not desire further attempts made to build bridges for the British. If they crave their own destruction, they can have it."

* * *

In mid-May 1940 it was already clear that Britain might have only three weapons of offence: economic warfare; bombing; and the fomenting of unrest in enemy occupied territories.[63] "[For the Germans] to try to hold all Europe down," Churchill had reassured his venerated friend, the South African prime minister Jan Smuts, "in a starving condition with only Gestapo and military occupation, and no large theme appealing to [the] masses is not an arrangement which can last long."[64]

Churchill decided to set up a British fifth column to organize Special Operations — strikes, propaganda, terrorist acts, boycotts, riots, bribery, industrial and military sabotage, assassination. A civilian should run this dirty war, ideally a radical intellectual from the Left, since most agents would be recruited from the underground. His choice fell on the minister of economic warfare.

It was going to be a distasteful job, but then Hugh Dalton was a distasteful man — booming of voice, towering of physique, with eyes of Mephistophelean pale blue.[65] He was also a fervent advocate of "all those ungentlemanly means of winning the war," as he described them to a queasy Attlee, "which come so easily to the Nazis." Throughout occupied territory, he wrote, they must agitate — "one might as well admit it" — like the networks of Nazi agents all round the world.[66]

Churchill had asked him to come over to No.10 on July 16.[67] "I was just writing to you," he said, looking up. He was minded to ask Vansittart to help with this task. Would they get on together? "Why yes," replied Dalton, "we are very old friends and all through these years he, you and I have thought the same." On the twenty-second the PM introduced him to the War Cabinet in his new role. "And now," he said, turning to Dalton, "go and ....".*

Desmond Morton's files suggest that he, Vansittart and Dalton would also have a hand in a hitherto unknown department, identified only as M.U.W., directing strategic bribery.[68]

Meanwhile, Special Operations spread tentacles across the Continent. Available documents are patchy, Dalton's diaries being more eloquent for their omissions. Trawling through the archives turns up glimpses of its work — including assassins ordered to dispose of dangerous enemies like Rommel: inexpedient French officers like Huntziger and Darlan: American isolationists like William Rhodes Davis: and at least one friendly statesman, to render credible British allegations about an international Nazi conspiracy.†

* * *

---

*Dalton inserted the missing words in handwriting in his dictated diary — *"set Europe ablaze."*

†See page 526.

Lord Beaverbrook felt that Mr Churchill's judgment was still unsound. He later recalled months of "decisions taken at 1:30 a.m. — always bad," of nobody standing up to Winston except Herbert Morrison and himself, and of people agreeing only because they were desperate for bed. He watched the PM switch his attention to the Middle East that July, and realized that Churchill had been obsessed with that region since Omdurman in 1898: on that occasion, attached to the 21st Lancers, his horse had rather galloped him into that battle. Now, in mid July Churchill warned Eden that the storm might soon break in the Middle East.[69]

He was unhappy with the C-in-C out there, Wavell. Eden disagreed, and over dinner on the twenty-fifth they flew at each other in front of General Dill, while Beaverbrook and Lord Lloyd listened in silence.[70] Dill and Beaverbrook were at Chequers on the next evening, which impressed itself upon General James Marshall-Cornwall as the Mad Hatter's dinner party.

After champagne the Prof conjured forth a Mills grenade, toyed with it, lectured his bilious companions on its inadequacies. Churchill invited the general to talk about his corps and its deficiencies. His figures differed from the War Office tables which Winston produced and when the general denounced them the PM hurled the papers at Dill in a rage.

Retiring to an adjoining room with brandy and cigar, Churchill unfurled a map of the Red Sea and outlined a capricious plan for an immediate descent on Massawa, presently in Italian hands.[71] General Dill was increasingly disinclined to indulge him: only recently the PM had ordered Marines in Northern Ireland to stand by to seize Portuguese islands in the Atlantic, alternatively to invade Eire and reoccupy the naval bases.[72] Those bases were in danger of becoming a typical obsession even though all convoys now approached Britain by the northwestern route anyway, which made them irrelevant.

Churchill was irked by Dill's relentless professional opposition; he intimated to Eden that the General was disappointing the hopes they had vested in him after Dunkirk — he seemed "tired, disheartened, and over-impressed with the might of Germany."

This was unjust to the General. His vision sharpened by years of soldiering, the C.I.G.S. had decided that this war was foolish and opportunist. He remarked over dinner with Sir John Reith that Winston was "cashing in" on a war which was all his own fault. He left no doubt what he felt about their PM and his present *galèrie*.[73]

* * *

Still lingering at Lisbon, the Duke of Windsor was delaying his exile to the Bahamas as long as he could. Churchill had good reason to suspect his motives. Bletchley Park was reading many foreign diplomatic ciphers, and these now rang with Hitler's attempts to procure the former King's services, and with the Duke's language about Churchill and his war. The Duke's Madrid friend, the brother of Jose Antonio, repeated to the German embassy that the Duke dismissed King George as "altogether stupid" but feared the "clever" Queen Elizabeth and her intrigues against the Duchess; he was toying with publicly dissociating himself from Britain's policies and "breaking with his brother."

Similar vapourings bubbled forth from Lisbon. The Italian minister radioed that the Duke had no intention of leaving Portugal until October.[74] On July 24 the Duke told the Spanish ambassador — General Franco's brother Nicholas — that he was "ready to return to Spain."[75] Worse still was the German cipher report from Lisbon on the twenty-fifth. A Nazi intermediary had told him he might yet ascend the British throne. The Duke had displayed surprise and disbelief.[76]

Small wonder that Churchill's messages to the Duke of Windsor during the next few days were garnished with a caustic imperative which the mere exile of a friend would hardly warrant. On the twenty-fifth the Italian minister radioed to Rome that the Duke had applied for a Spanish visa and that he had told a friend that the King had "demonstrated much feebleness."[77] On the twenty-sixth the German ambassador quoted the Duke as calling the war a crime, and Halifax's speech rejecting Hitler's peace offer shocking. "The Duke," the telegram read, "is said to be delaying departure. . ."[78] Meanwhile Mr David Eccles, an Intelligence Officer operating in Lisbon, flew back to London with despatches furnished by Franco's brother. These confirmed that the Duke was planning to return to Spain.[79]

When Halifax reported to Churchill the next day there was turmoil. The PM's first action was to send for Sir Walter Monckton, a friend of the Duke's, a former lawyer steeped in secret service rituals as head of British Censorship. He came round to No.10 at 5:45 p.m., and Churchill told him to fly out to Lisbon. His precise instructions other than to brief the Duke on "various matters" are shrouded in mystery. What is known is that Churchill sent to the Duke a peremptory telegram on July 27, ordering him to sail for the Bahamas five days later as arranged. Fearing quite reasonably that the Duke might even then return, he drew attention to the monarch's archaic rules forbidding his Governors to quit their islands "on any pretence whatever" without first obtaining "leave from Us for so doing under Our Sign Manual and Signet."

The evidence that Churchill had been reading other people's telegrams is in the letter which Monckton carried, counselling the Duke to hold his tongue. "Many sharp and unfriendly ears," he wrote, "will be pricked up to catch any suggestion that your Royal Highness takes a view about the war, or about the Germans, or about Hitlerism which is different from that adopted by the British nation and Parliament." The Duke's various Lisbon conversations had, he said, been "reported by telegraph through various channels" to his disadvantage.[80]*

Despite the pressure from Monckton the Duke was still loath to leave. Churchill knew why. On the twenty-ninth the Italian minister radioed to Rome that, still playing for time, the Duke had become less cautious the last few days in conversations with his intimates and that one of them — a Spaniard of Falangist tendencies — had told a colleague: "The Prince [sic] thinks like us."[81] On July 29 Monckton telegraphed from Lisbon asking for a Scotland Yard detective to be sent "to accompany our friend for voyage to destination." A plausible reason for such an armed escort was concocted. On the eve of his departure for the Bahamas the Duke secretly visited the Spanish ambassador and revealed that he had fears "that old Churchill, who had given such clear proof of his unscrupulousness, would have him assassinated if he did not decide to leave." "And so," reported the Spaniard's Italian colleague Bova Scoppa to Rome, in a telegram that cannot have endeared the Duke to the British prime minister, "in spite of . . . his personal conviction that he might be able to pull his country back from the precipice by hurling Churchill and his gang into the sea, the ex-King took the road to political isolation and exile."

The Duke drafted an angry missive to Churchill, hurt by his "gangster methods," but sailed from Portugal on the first day of August, the appointed day, aboard an American merchantman.[82]

There were two epilogues to this extraordinary story. In August he wired his Lisbon linkman to the Nazi foreign minister Ribbentrop to let him know when he should "act."[83] After the war the Americans found a German file with this and all the other highly compromising messages despatched by the German embassies in Madrid and Lisbon. The Foreign Office accessioned the file — "with the contents, of which," Attlee minuted Churchill, using the routine circumlocutions used to deal with codebreaking references, "I think you should be familiar." Dropping the broadest hint, Churchill replied: "I earnestly trust it may be possible to destroy all traces of these German intrigues."[84]

The Americans however, had already microfilmed the file at Marburg. Their ambassador in London pressed their supreme commander to track down every copy made "without delay." Prime minister again in 1953, Churchill suppressed official publication of the documents. The microfilm was destroyed.[85]

---

*Such documents have been well used by Martin Gilbert. Unhappily the Churchill files in Royal Archives are reserved exclusively for Dr Gilbert's perusal.

ON THE LAST night of July 1940 the first convoy of American rifles, guns and ammunition reached a British port. Churchill ordered special trains to rush the rifles to his new army. Until then they had had to drill with wooden imitations.

But it was in the revival of the fighter defences that the miracle occurred. From January to April they had received only 638 new fighters. But now Beaverbrook had taken over. By cannibalizing aircraft, by raiding squadrons and factories for hamstered stores of spare parts, by deciding which plane types should be produced, he had multiplied production.

New concepts had not frightened him. Against all advice he had installed cannon instead of .303 machine guns. Dowding had backed him: the manufacturers had agreed: it was done. Later, he would put his shoulder behind jet engine development, the ten ton earthquake bomb, and the dambusting weapons known as Highball and Upkeep. Incorruptible, ambitious, insensitive, neither Beaverbrook nor his senior officials drew government salaries: they were paid by industry or by his own newspaper group.

Justifiably proud of this man he had appointed, Churchill never tired of showing off his achievements. "Beaverbook," he triumphed to the editor of the *Manchester Guardian* at the end of July, "has done miracles."[86] Told that Beaverbrook was a magician, the jealous labour minister Ernest Bevin would say, "Magic is nine-tenths illusion."

But it was no illusion, what Beaverbrook had done. From May to August his factories produced 1,785 fighters, and repaired 1,872 more. This extraordinary Canadian would write to Winston boasting that thanks to him the R.A.F. had now been able to draw upon nearly one thousand new operational aircraft. "In addition," he bragged, "all casualties had to be replaced. And 720 aircraft were shipped abroad."

"Nobody," he ended, "knows the trouble I've seen."[87]

"I do," replied Churchill.

CHAPTER 30

The Eagle Never Landed

FOR SIX WEEKS after the French collapse, Churchill would recall, the Americans treated Britain in that "rather distant and sympathetic manner" that one adopts towards an old friend dying of cancer.[1]

Hitler did not invade, however. He had other fish to fry. On June 20, 1940, the day when the Armistice took effect in France, his private secretary wrote: "I think it still hurts him to have to get tough with the British. He would obviously far perfer them to use their commonsense. If they only new the Boss doesn't want anything at all from them other than our former Colonies, they might be more approachable. . ." This was the unfortunate truth that Mr Churchill would withhold from the British people. In fighting Hitler, Britain would quintuple her prewar debt, forfeit her world position, bring the Red Army to the Elbe, and collapse her Empire. But we now know from captured documents that despite all the sabre-rattling Hitler probably never intended to invade. Jolted by Soviet expansionism towards Romania, late in June 1940 he had reverted to his primary ambition, a German empire in the east, trusting that the British would see reason. He refrained from inflicting real pain on them: they had rescued their army at Dunkirk; he had vetoed all air attacks on London.

Only Hitler's closest advisers were aware that he did not plan to invade Britain. General Hans Jeschonnek, chief of air staff, refused to attend to lower echelons' queries about invasion plans, explaining: "In my opinion the Führer does *not* have a Channel crossing in mind." "Sea Lion," he snapped to a staff officer, "won't take place and I've no time to bother about it." Significantly, Hitler's high command (O.K.W.) had simultaneously issued a directive ordering its Intelligence agency to dupe Britain into expecting an invasion and, in collusion with Italy and Russia, an attack on the Middle East; the latter was to provide cover for the steady eastward movement of the Eighteenth Army from France.[2] The O.K.W. colonel who countersigned this directive had already begun mapping out a Russian campaign for Hitler.

In the first week of July Hitler disclosed his decision to attack Russia to his chief adjutant (Schmundt) and his army's commander-in-chief (von Brauchitsch), who in turn briefed the chief of general staff (Halder).[3] Henceforth Hitler continued the dispositions for invasion only as a deception, codenamed Sealion.[4] He had hornswoggled Churchill before, he believed he could do it again.

A month later his staff issued a directive codenamed Aufbau Ost, Eastern Buildup; the O.K.W. war diary defined this on August 8 as "our order to camouflage the preparations against Russia."[5] By that time the army's own Russian campaign plan, drafted by the Eighteenth Army's chief of staff, was also ready.[6]

The deception would continue throughout the summer. Barges were converted into "assault craft;" stores were brought up, maps of England noisily procured. Hitler's field commanders wondered why he vacillated; the more astute realized what he was up to. "The Führer wants the *threat* of invasion of Britain to persist," the German naval staff learned on August 14. "That is why the *preparations*, whatever the final decision, must continue." Unhappy about the cost to the economy, the chief of naval operations suggested calling off Operation Sealion altogether — "In its place a special deception operation should be mounted to maintain the threat on the enemy."[7]

A few days later Hitler expressed his frustration to Major Vidkun Quisling. "I now find myself," he excalaimed, "forced against my will to fight this war against Britain. I find myself in the same position as Martin Luther, who had just as little desire to fight Rome, but was left with no alternative."[8] Two weeks after that, although Churchill's bombers had just singed Berlin for the first time, Hitler sent his adjutant to scout a location for his headquarters against Russia.[9]

THIS TIME CHURCHILL was not outwitted. Thanks to his codebreakers at Bletchley, he now commanded a total, indeed Olympian, view which his subordinates were denied. Armed with immense wartime and political experience he interpreted the auguries more accurately than his soldiers. By the end of July he certainly recognized that Sealion was bluff. Colonel Menzies, head of the secret service, believed however in the invasion: on the twenty-ninth for example he circulated a typical intercepted Luftwaffe signal reminding bomber crews not to damage certain South Coast ports.[10]

That seemed a bit too obvious even to the diplomats. They too, albeit slowly, grasped what Hitler was up to. Halifax referred in his diary of July 25 to evidence that Hitler was hesitating; Sir Alec Cadogan also remarked on the "funny pause" across the Channel. "What are they doing," he mused on the thirtieth, "with these costly and half-hearted air-raids?" Both he and Halifax concluded by the end of July that Hitler was not going to invade. R.A. Butler, under-secretary at the F.O., would brief a newspaperman on August 20 that the invasion was hooey — "There had never been," he said, "sufficient concentrations of troops in Northern France." Hitler's troops were going East, he said: "They are going to attack Russia."[11]

Churchill had deduced this too, but kept his comforting deduction to himself, because what he himself had privately termed the "invasion scare" was bringing him overwhelming support — Gallup now polled eighty-eight percent backing him as prime minister, twenty percent more than Chamberlain at his most popular. Besides, Roosevelt still had to be gulled into entering the war.

In Grosvenor Square, Kennedy found the shift in Churchill's stance, from Cassandra to optimist, somewhat perplexing.[12] Kennedy also fancied he heard rumbles of discontent from the munitions workers and poorer classes — they had begun comparing the liberty which Churchill *told* them they enjoyed, with the security that Hitler gave his people.

Churchill had a stranglehold on public opinion. The Socialists were now the dominating group in his Government, but those Englishmen with insight had begun to ask, he said, "Where is all this doing to end?"[13]

* * *

Whitehall that summer became accustomed to the sandbags and barricades, the barbed wire and the pocketful of passes needed for even the shortest walk between Ministries. Winston yearned for real air raids to begin: he talked about them ceaselessly: he had been predicting them ever since 1934, but still they had not come. Instead, all that summer he found himself contending with enemies more malevolent to Britain's interests than Hitler.

There were the Japanese: In mid June the Japanese had demanded that Britain close down the Burma Road — the supply route for the Chinese — as well as the frontier with Hong Kong and the military base at Shanghai. Meeting Lord Halifax briefly on July 6, he had remarked that he had no desire at all to get into a war with Japan. "Nor do I," observed Lord Halifax in his diary, "but I am more disposed to think they are bluffing than he is." Unwilling to be seen as an appeaser, Churchill instructed the ambassador, Sir Robert Craigie, to negotiate a compromise. The Japanese refused: Churchill agreed to close the Burma Road. "Cabinet," recorded Cadogan on July 10, "led by Winston, evidently bent on surrender."[14] On balance, the prime minister felt that Britain must play for time in the Far East.

That included India. When the Cabinet had discussed India's claims in October he had protested against yielding to parties "exploiting the dangers with which Britain was faced." Genuinely proud of the Empire, he had flung some of his fieriest epithets at its enemies. Earlier in his career he had slighted Hindu leader Mahatma Ghandi as "a seditious Middle Temple lawyer now posing as a fakir of a type well known in the East, striding halfnaked up the steps of the Vice-regal palace." When Sam Hoare's India Act was passed in 1935 Churchill had warned that it was bound to dislodge India from the Empire. Two years later Ghandi's Congress party triumphed at the elections. In the ensuing turmoil the subcontinent divided along religious lines.

Within that cause, the British Empire, his methods were more profane than humane. He opposed any attempt at religious reconciliation, cynically telling the Cabinet in February 1940 that he "regarded the Hindu-Moslem feud as the bulwark of British rule in India." He wrote to Chamberlain in the same vein, complaining about the Viceroy's policy of "running after Ghandi and the Congress."[15] Now that he was himself prime minister, the Socialist minority held the Whip hand, as Kennedy had remarked: beholden to them in the fight against those who favoured a negotiated peace with Hitler, he had to shape his tactics over India accordingly.

The Labour party and *Tribune*, the newspaper founded by Sir Stafford Cripps, backed Ghandi. Cripps visited India and befriended Jawaharlal Nehru, the leader of Congress. Labour's policy was simple — in return for Indian collaboration now, Churchill should promise independence afterwards. Thus he played for time: Churchill had Cripps posted out of harm's way to Moscow, and there he would languish as ambassador for the next twenty months, a "lunatic in a land of lunatics."

In a sense, Churchill was hoist by his own petard: for reasons of high policy, he was portraying Britain's peril as dire and immediate. After the fall of France the Viceroy, Lord Linlithgow, had promised Ghandi, with no authorization from London, that Britain would "spare no effort to bring about Dominion status within a year after conclusion of the war." Fortunately, Ghandi held out obstinately for independence and Churchill refused to utter any promises. "Not now," he wanted the Indians to understand, "not yet;" but what he meant was: "Not ever."

"You must remember," he wrote sternly to the Viceroy, "that we are here facing constant threat of invasion." If such an immense issue as India were put to the Cabinet now it must be "to the detriment of matters touching the final life and safety of the State."

He tried to send this off on July 26 without consulting the India Office. Blistering with anger, the Dominions Secretary Leo Amery, came round to No.10 to remonstrate.

Churchill promised to redraft it, but the version finally sent off still avoided either commitments or promises.

THROUGHOUT THAT VIOLENT summer Churchill also had to contend with the singleminded badgering of British and American Zionists, to mobilize and arm the Jews in Palestine; when he obdurately refused to offer more than oral expressions of goodwill Chaim Weizmann stepped up the campaign he had resumed after Dunkirk.[16] "If we go down in Palestine," he cried in June, writing from the Dorchester, "we are entitled to go down fighting." Privately believing that England was in fact in the more immediate danger, in mid June the Zionist Office began shipping its archives out to Palestine.

After France collapsed this hubbub over Palestine arose anew. Churchill received a letter from the Board of Deputies of British Jews, which had sustained The Focus during his wilderness years (the letter is missing from the official files.) In Washington American Jewry pressured Lord Lothian into telegraphing him on June 21 about their concern that Palestine might be overrun: Britain must arm and organize the Jews there under her command; Lothian warned of "a most deplorable effect" on Jewish opinion in America if Britain did not comply.

Churchill passed this to the Colonial Secretary. He reminded Lord Lloyd of his greatest interest in the matter, and added that the "cruel penalties" imposed by Lloyd's predecessor for illegal arms had made it necessary to tie up forces for the Jews' protection now. "Pray let me know exactly," concluded the PM, "what weapons and organization the Jews have for self defence." Lloyd replied that substantial sealed armories had been provided, and that of 21,411 Palestinian police all but five thousand were Jews — an enormous force for so small a country.

Taken aback, Churchill huffed in his reply that Colonial Office policy on Palestine had failed — otherwise they would not need to keep 20,000 trained infantry there to protect the Jewish settlers and native Arabs from each other.

Refusing to admit the strength of Moslem feeling in the Middle East and India, he could not help letting off steam about this "scandal:"

> This is the price we have for the anti-Jewish policy which has been persisted in for some years. Should the war go heavily into Egypt, all these troops will have to be withdrawn and the position of the Jewish colonists will be one of the greatest danger.

There was no danger of "properly armed" Jews ever attacking the Arabs, he felt, since they were dependent upon Britain and her command of the seas. In further justification he argued that the Levantine Arabs were "very poor representatives, and are only a small part" of the Moslem world. "We have treated them with the greatest consideration and as you know, the settlement I made with them on the basis of the Zionist policy commanded the full assent of [T.E.] Lawrence."

The Colonial Office refused to budge. Lloyd had no political objection to the enlistment of Jews and Arabs in Palestine, he assured Churchill on July 20 — but only on the basis of absolute numerical equality, and "provided that nothing in the nature of a Jewish army should be created for service in Palestine." Precisely this was the ultimate Zionist objective however — a cohesive Jewish army, fighting under its own emblem. Nothing of course prevented Jews from volunteering singly for active service with the British forces; many did and fought with distinction, as did individual Americans and Irishmen.

Heedless of the air battles now beginning over England's countryside, Weizmann wrote again to Churchill on August 6 ("Loth as I am to take up your time.") "In a war of the magnitude now proceeding," he reasoned, adopting a scarcely flattering argument now, "it is impossible to say what the strategic disposition of the British fleets and armies may be before victory is attained. Should it come to a temporary withdrawal from Palestine — a contingency which," he added, "we hope will never arise, the Jews of Palestine would be exposed to wholesale massacre at the hands of the Arabs." He now held out the prospect of an army of 60,000 Jews — "No negligible force if properly trained, armed and led."[17]

Churchill endorsed this proposal — "arming the Jewish Colonists sufficiently to enable them to undertake their own defence" — in a letter to the chiefs of staff and General Wavell on the twelfth. But they were not keen; his proposal got nowhere, and the haggling continued.

At one Zionist luncheon with members of The Focus on September 3, Winston emotionally gushed that he was "in favour" of a Jewish Army.

"Everybody," Weizmann cynically replied, "even Lord Beaverbrook, seems to be in favour of it." He produced a memorandum and asked if he might carry it straight round to the War Office. This ambush evoked chuckles around the table. Churchill read it and *verbally* approved.

Weizmann suggested that Churchill's intimate friend Bracken accompany him in case of "difficulties."[18]*

---

*Beaverbrook's files C57 and D447 reveal Bracken's increasing anti-semitism over the years — squashing 1929 campaign rumours that he was a German Jew by publishing his Irish birth certificate; writing in 1933 of a certain cinema group as being "as crazily constructed as those of their co-religionist Mr Elias of Odham's'" writing in 1952 to Beaverbrook about certain "tarbrushed American Hebrews;" and referring to the Savoy Hotel's attempts to "purge itself of the invading Israelites" Samuels and Clore (whom he called "the Jewish terrorist.")

His triumph ("As great a day as the Balfour Declaration!" he called it at the Dorchester that evening) was shortlived.[19] After sober reflection Churchill slithered out of this noose too, and welshed on his convivial lunch-time commitment.

Mid December would find Weizmann complaining to the Prof that the War Office was showing "scant enthusiasm." Several times over the next year he would hark back to Mr Churchill's "broken promise."[20]

* * *

A regular pattern emerged in Churchill's routine which exhausted his friends and defeated his subordinates. He could climb into pyjamas each afternoon and sleep, but not they. The records testify to meetings of his Defence Committee, in the clammy Central War Room bunker, often lasting until two a.m. When it rose he would sometimes insist that the unhappy Beaverbrook, clutching his chest and gasping with asthma, join him upstairs to carry on the discussion in his sitting room.

After one 1941 weekend at Chequers, General Pownall would write, "We went to bed at two a.m. *He* gets some sleep in between lunch and tea — others can't do that and he is wearing them down in consequence." This officer regarded it as a serious failing that the captain could not care for his crew better. "Other people," Pownall repeated two months later, "have not the opportunities for afternoon naps that the PM has got. *They* have got to go on all day and every day."[21]

Everybody lamented the verbosity that choked these proceedings — one girl who had worked at No.10 since Lloyd George's time described them as Winston's Midnight Follies. In April 1944 the First Sea Lord would write, "Never has the PM been so discursive and wasted so much time." And on July 6 of that year, "PM is in no state to discuss anything — too tired and too much alcohol."[22]

AT ONE INTERMINABLE meeting after the 1940 French collapse he had run probing fingers over the Canary Islands, Casablanca, and even Oran. "W.S.C.," wrote Sir Alec Cadogan, describing the confusion of those days, "endorses any wild idea."[23]

De Gaulle bulked large in them, although by hiring him the British had offended more Frenchmen than they pleased. But there was no going back and Winston authorized substantial sums for bribery and covert operations against Marshal Pétain. General Georges Catroux was bribed to leave Saigon and head the Free French in Egypt; de Gaulle also recommended purchasing anti-Pétain coups in Syria and Morocco; Mr Leo d'Erlanger, who owned property in Tunis, advised that most French officials in North Africa had their price. "He strongly advocates,"

Desmond Morton reported, "an intensive campaign of propaganda and bribery." Churchill approved in red ink.[24] In December one Daniel Dreyfus would even offer to buy Pierre Laval for Britain, claiming to have bribed him in the past. Sir John Anderson suggested that Dreyfus, while otherwise "thoroughly unscrupulous," could be relied on because of his religion. But by the time Halifax put the idea up Pétain had dismissed his prime minister and Churchill red-inked that Laval was "no longer worth buying."[25]

Winston trusted Morton — one of his pre-war informers inside the S.I.S. and his neighbour at Chartwell — implicitly. In 1919 Winston had appointed him to the secret service; he had created the Industrial Intelligence Centre. Now the bluff and somewhat pompous Major alone had a key to Winston's buff box of Most Secret documents; he kept it attached to his person. Some idea of his position is given by Winston's memorandum constituting his liaison staff in June: his son-in-law Duncan Sandys to liaise with Home Defence and the Air Raid Precautions; Oliver Lyttelton, with the Ministry of Supply; and Morton, to handle enemy war production data, relations with the F.O. and the French Committee, and "Secret Service and fifth column activities."[26] Now pushing fifty, Morton had a pre-dilection for pink gins that made Winston feel at home with him, and an Irish impertinence as well: he successfully put himself forward for a KCMG in the 1945 New Years Honours List.[27]

In June 1940 Morton had formed a small committee to manipulate de Gaulle. Churchill had formally recognized this extraordinary General as leader of the Free French on the day after the Armistice, and had invited him to broadcast a declaration to France. (It had taken quite a tussle at the F.O. to persuade this headstrong Frenchman to amend the declaration and take out names — "In particular *his*," as Cadogan observed in his diary.) Admiral Cunningham, close to the disgruntled French in the Middle East, warned the First Sea Lord that "no one has any opinion of him." But Churchill had, and Eden found him late in July in the garden of No.10 "anxious to let de Gaulle loose somewhere."

With Churchill's approval, Morton gave a City public relations expert a big budget to "sell" de Gaulle in Britain as well as in France's colonies and the Americas: Morton had argued that they could switch off his publicity at any moment.[28]

On July 5, Churchill directed the admiralty to allow him access to the French sailors interned after Grasp so that he could raise a small navy of two or three ships, perhaps even a battleship, to fly the Free French flag. "These ships," he suggested, "may be of use in parleying with French Colonies and in getting into French harbours on one pretext or another."

He was already eyeing Dakar in Senegal, a port of strategic importance in West Africa. Officials there had suggested that taking it would be easy; on July 5 he had asked Spears to discuss it with de Gaulle. The French General warned frostily that in view of Catapult any British force would be received with the utmost hostility.[29] The corollary was obvious — he and his troops should occupy Dakar.

Planning went forward all summer. Over lunch with de Gaulle at Chequers on August 3, Churchill approved a plan to put ashore three battalions of French troops.[30] The British were to keep a low profile: their ships would ferry the Gaullist troops but would ideally even stay out of sight of land. The chiefs of staff were uneasy about accepting an unlimited liability in a non essential theatre. Churchill tore into them over their lack of enthusiasm. His vehemence shortly persuaded them to approve a more ambitious plan.

By mid August the plan had significantly changed in character: British troops were to secure Dakar, following which de Gaulle's troops would come in from beyond the horizon and take over, to "impart a French character" to it. Churchill's added interest now was in grasping the new French battleship *Richelieu*, damaged in July by Royal Navy attack, and the Polish and Belgian Gold reserves which he believed the French had spirited away to Dakar.

Later in August the plan hit snags. Admiral Cunningham stipulated that tides and moon would not be favourable until September 12. The chiefs of staff suggested Conakry and an overland march to Dakar. Churchill disagreed, insisted that de Gaulle be master of Dakar, if need be by force, by nightfall of the first day.

All too lightly de Gaulle accepted the decision, and was shortly observed buying tropical equipment at a Piccadilly store for use in "West Africa." Free French security was not good. At a public dinner in Liverpool his officers toasted "Dakar" by name.

THE FREE FRENCH was one of several ad hoc exile movements managed by Desmond Morton's committee. The Norwegians, Poles, Dutch had been allowed these privileges; but not the Austrian, German or Italian emigrés who might equally argue that their countries had been overrun by the fascists; nor the Baltic states which Stalin had annexed in cahoots with Hitler.

If Churchill stolidly refused to hand over the London-banked Gold of the Baltic states to Moscow, there were cogent economic reasons; exile leaders who mentioned their Gold balances found him afflicted by sudden deafness. Since 1939 a committee under Lord Hankey had kept tabs on Europe's Gold — urging Oslo, Copenhagen, The Hague,

Brussels and Paris to ship theirs to the safety of London, and keeping track if the Gold was sent elsewhere.

On June 7, Hankey had briefed Churchill,

> Every [French] warship larger than a destroyer which crosses the Atlantic [to the U.S.A.] to bring back aeroplanes is taking as much Gold as possible; and practically the whole will have left France by the 15th or 20th June.[31]

In June the cruiser *Vincennes* alone transported $240m of Gold from Bordeaux to buy arms in America. On the twentieth, Intelligence learned, a French warship left Lorient carrying all of Poland's Gold and much of Belgium's. The French refused to impart its destination to their British Allies, but part was believed to be bound for Dakar. A few days later Intelligence learned that the *Emile Bertin* was leaving Nova Scotia to carry France's Gold to her Caribbean colony, Martinique. Major Morton's committee recommended persuading these ships to take the Gold to Canada instead.[32]

"What a wonderful thing," wrote the American military attaché with unconscious irony, "if these blokes do win the war! They will be bankrupt, but entitled to almost unlimited respect."[33]

That was not the same as unlimited credit, and less starry-eyed Americans wondered how Britain was going to pay for the war. Sir Kingsley Wood suggested the Treasury requisition everybody's wedding ring to replenish the Gold reserves; Churchill did not need a Gallup poll to know where that would leave his popularity. He suggested they defer such a step until Britain needed "some striking gesture for the purpose of shaming the Americans."[34] Meanwhile he took the less painful alternative of separating Britain's foreign guests from their Gold in the cause of liberty.

Among the earliest arrivals had been the Czechs. His Treasury had cast covetous eyes on their National Bank's Gold deposits in London; in October their former president Dr Eduard Benes would agree to lend the entire £7.5m worth to Britain for "increased expenditure on aircraft and munitions in America."[35] But another year would pass before Churchill would even recognize his government in exile. He dismissed the teetotal "Dr Beans" as a lightweight and found meals with him particularly trying, since the wronged Czech politician held authoritarian views on everything from sex to religion, having been agnostic since he was eighteen.

Churchill paid only lip service to Czechoslovakia's cause. After one luncheon with the PM on August 8, Benes reported in code to his agents in Czechoslovakia: the prime minister had been incisive and firm, he was determined to "fight to the end," since anything less would spell the end for Britain. "Our restoration is self evident," triumphed Dr Benes, "and like Poland's is a war aim." "Churchill," he dictated to his secretary afterwards, "expects the German offensive against the British Isles to begin in the next few days. He is full of optimism concerning this great battle, but he thinks that the war will go on for quite some time."[36]

THE TOWNS WERE not yet bleeding. The enemy airforce was still attacking mainly ports and shipping. But in a new directive on the first day of August, Hitler ordered the airforce, starting on or after the fifth, to knock the British airforce out of the skies — both literally and by marauding its ground organization, supply lines, and aircraft factories. Hitler reserved strictly to himself the right to order "terror raids" — meaning air raids on city areas — even in reprisal.[37]

Thus London was still not bombed. On Sunday August 4, de Gaulle found the prime minister on the lawn at Chequers shaking his fist at the sky, and shouting in strange fury, "So they won't come!"

Seeing his puzzlement, Churchill explained his deadly rationale. The bombing of cities like Oxford and Canterbury would cause such indignation in the United States that they would have to come into the war. De Gaulle was sceptical. Roosevelt, he observed, had not come in for France.

Churchill knew how close he was to inveigling the Americans. So did Berlin. Rumours were filtering through from Washington of an extraordinary deal whereby Churchill was offering Roosevelt bases in the Caribbean in exchange for American destroyers. On August 7 Ribbentrop exclaimed to Dino Alfieri, the Italian ambassador, "Churchill is crazy and the British are imbeciles!" The ambassador radioed this message to Rome in a cipher which the British could read.[38]

After lunching that Sunday with Spears and Morton, Churchill went over with Dowding to see Fighter Command's new operations bunker at Bentley Priory, Stanmore. Work had begun here, on the outskirts of London, three months after Munich. By March 1940, when it began operations, 60,000 tons of earth had been dug out of the pit, and over 20,000 tons of concrete poured to reinforce the deep shelter. Over the next few weeks the magnetism of the unfolding drama repeatedly drew Churchill to this command centre.

Chequers that Sunday evening was enlivened by the arrival of the chief of Bomber Command. Clementine had returned to London, which left only Winston, Portal and the Prof in the house party.

> Winston was in a very good form [a private secretary wrote.] I only wish I hadn't such a sieve-like memory and could remember all the talk afterwards. He always talks very freely on these occasions and is extremely good company.

CHURCHILL HAD NOW streamlined the flow of Intelligence. That Monday August 5, he directed that all intercepts were to be submitted to him undigested, in the raw. "Major Morton will inspect them for me," he ruled. "He is to be shown everything."

Göring optimistically asked for three fine days to fulfil Hitler's requirement for the destruction of Britain's air defences. Day 1 would be "Eagle Day." He issued these orders to his three Air Force (*Luftflotte*) commanders on the sixth. Bletchley intercepted the directive and forwarded it to No.10. The enemy plan was for strongly escorted bombers to approach targets around London in broad daylight and overpower the fighters that rose to engage them. Göring favoured August 10 for Eagle Day, but the weather did not. He postponed it first to the eleventh, then fixed Eagle Day for the thirteenth.[39]

A buff box evidently brought this news to Mr Churchill immediately: a bracket was inked across three days on his appointment card beginning late on the thirteenth; since Hitler had forbidden attacks on London itself he made no plans to leave the city.*

* * *

R.A.F. fighter losses began rising steeply. Eighteen had been shot down on Thursday the eighth. That summer, the callowest youth in the English countryside could tell from its sounds, without a glance, which aircraft was pirouetting thousands of feet above, tracing vapour trails that tangled briefly and occasionally withered away as one or the other was hit and spiralled down.

Worried by the narrowing margin, Winston had driven out to Chequers that Friday evening, August 9, for a weekend with his generals.

Eden brought Generals Dill and Wavell down to see him. Churchill was growing disenchanted with Wavell. He felt that the army in the Middle East was farflung and supine. At the end of July he had detained Eden after one meeting in the Cabinet bunker and disparaged the General.[40] This nagging did not abate, because Churchill was oppressed with the future of the Middle East. He told Benes that the enemy might well score in Egypt, because Wavell had only fifty thousand soldiers and the Italians two hundred thousand.

This is why Eden had ordered Wavell home: but Wavell was a grim, taciturn soldier — he spoke in single syllables. To a politician, to whom flummery was everything, such inarticulateness was almost a mortal sin.

---

*Martin Gilbert states (vol.vi, 735) that 1,419 civilians were killed during the second week of August 1940, 1,286 of them in London; this is an error for September. No bombs fell in London before late August 24.

Over dinner Winston talked eagerly: how Britain would have ten armoured divisions in a year, how they could raid Holland, thrust into the Ruhr, seize the Cherbourg peninsula. Venturing out of the monosyllabic, Wavell added Norway to this euphoric list. "We've had enough of that," winced Churchill.[41]

That Saturday two more generals were at dinner — Pownall and Sir Robert Gordon-Finlayson who had returned from Egypt to take over the Western Command. Churchill knew how to handle generals, he told them affably — rather as a country farmer herding pigs along a road, for ever poking and prodding them so that they would not stray.[42] His generals may not have liked the comparison with swine, but it was hard not to like the way that Winston had said it.

That Saturday, August 10, "C" sent word that Bletchley expected no invasion this month either.[43] Thus encouraged, Churchill decided to take the risk of shipping out to Egypt over half of Britain's tanks to reinforce Wavell. Back in London on Monday evening, using his familiar method, Churchill wrangled with Dill, Eden, and Wavell until two a.m. The navy, he felt, should risk fighting a fast convoy of tanks through the Mediterranean, under the open jaws of the enemy; his admirals were understandably more cautious.[44]

These further meetings with Wavell hardened Churchill's bad impression of him. He began gloomily pawing over the General's plans, moving battalions across the map; on the thirteenth he remarked to his staff that Wavell seemed short in mental vigour and resolve. Eden stood up for him, and marched into No.10 that evening bringing Wavell and the C.I.G.S. to point out that what the Middle East lacked was equipment, not men.

Churchill still took a dismal view of Wavell: he was "a good average colonel" who would make a good local Tory chairman: which said little for the prospect of holding Egypt against a numerically superior enemy.[45]

TUESDAY, AUGUST 13: this was Reichsmarschall Herman Göring's Eagle Day, the day when the three-day bracket on Churchill's appointment card began.

The card shows that he regularly lunched at the Palace on Tuesdays. King and first minister were warming to each other. It might ruffle royal feathers when Churchill was down for an audience at six: postponed it by 'phone to six-thirty, delayed by de Gaulle: and then arrived at seven.[46] King George would soon admit to greater confidence in him, confess that there was "no one even remotely as competent" as Churchill.

On this Tuesday the thirteenth he took Dr Benes with him. Knowing of the former relations between Prague and Moscow, the King thoughtfully asked Benes which he thought would prove the greater menace, Germany or Russia? "I thought Russia would eventually be," he wrote in his diary. His guests disagreed, suggesting that she could be "organized." Benes described Churchill as "emphatic": the United States would enter the war immediately after the presidential election: Russia would eventually come in too.[47]

As they emerged, London was still decked in insouciance: there was nothing to be seen of the aerial killing match that had begun: the combats were over England's southern countryside and Channel. Since six in the morning the heavily escorted enemy bombers had been marauding across the southern counties. Their offensive was only at half strength, because worsening weather had forced the recall of Field Marshal Albert Kesselring's Second Air Force. Even so, by nightfall the enemy had flown 1,500 sorties against which Fighter Command had managed barely 700.

At dusk the enemy airforce retired. Their losses were substantial — forty-five, compared with thirteen of the R.A.F. Churchill again visited the Palace, returning to No.10 for a further argument with Pound about convoying those tanks through the Mediterranean.

Something of the temper of that meeting emerges from Sir Dudley Pound's private letters on the fourteenth: General Wavell, he wrote, had faced a "pretty stiff" argument with the PM who tried to "impose some amateur strategy on him."

"At the moment I am not quite sure," admitted the First Sea Lord, "how the argument ended." Churchill wanted to risk sending the tanks straight through the Mediterranean to Alexandria, to arrive on about the third of September, since the Italians might invade Egypt at any moment. The navy preferred the longer Cape route, to arrive on the twenty-second. "We have had a great battle today," wrote Pound again on August 14, referring to the same argument — Hats or Bonnet, as the two routes came to be known; Wavell had been subjected to "rather a rough and trying time" as the PM disagreed with his troop dispositions: Winston wanted to put everything in the front line, even though Wavell pointed out that many units were not fully equipped.[48]

In the skies the battle for air supremacy had continued, though the scale of the enemy effort on this day had been smaller. Göring lost nineteen planes, Dowding eight. Knowing what the former had planned, the latter had good cause to be pleased.

Hitler was loath to continue this pointless battle. In Berlin that day, issuing the bejeweled, velvet-upholstered batons to his new field marshals, he made this quite plain.

Germany [he said] is not striving to smash Britain, because the beneficiaries will not be us, but Japan in the east, Russia in India, Italy in the Mediterranean and America in world trade. That is why peace is perfectly possible with Britain — but not so long as Churchill is prime minister. That is why we've got to see what our airforce can do, and await a possible general election.[49]

The intercepts still mirrored Hitler's resolve not to invade. Churchill did not ease up on the scare-stories when Kennedy called round at four-thirty that afternoon, but the ambassador had heard it all before. His own feeling, which he cabled to Washington that evening, was that the Germans would not attempt any invasion until they had achieved greater supremacy in the air.[50]

IN FACT THE scare-story was no longer needed. Kennedy had brought a personal message from Roosevelt. It was the one Winston had been praying for ever since he had stepped up his campaign to "drag the United States into the war."

"What would I not give," Pound had written to Cunningham, "for another 100 destroyers." Eight more had been lost at Dunkirk. Now Churchill had Roosevelt's response. The president, the message said, now agreed that it might prove possible to furnish him immediately with the fifty destroyers, motor torpedo boats and aircraft.[51]

Churchill summoned his colleagues to discuss the immodest price that Washington was asking: the freedom to use Newfoundland, Bermuda, certain Caribbean islands and British Guiana in the event of an attack on the American hemisphere — in fact the right to establish U.S. bases there right now. Moreover — and this hurt — Roosevelt wanted a written assurance that Britain would send her fleet overseas in the event of collapse.

His junior secretary John Colville remarked quite pertinently that these rather smacked of Stalin's recent demands on Finland.

Churchill disagreed. "The worth of every destroyer," he replied with solemnity, "is measured in rubies."[52]

CHAPTER 31

In A Single Gulp

WHAT HE WANTED, of course, was a token American commitment. By the time the first of the American destroyers arrived, it would be late autumn and they would have lost much of their purely naval relevance. They turned out to be barnacled with age, useless; they mounted one obsolete gun, and no Flak at all. By the end of 1940, after extensive refits, only nine would be operational. The only one ever to see active service would be the *Campbelltown*, blown up as a blockship at Saint-Nazaire in March, 1942.

Roosevelt moreover was striking a tough bargain. He would set terms so oppressive that Mr Churchill went to lengths to keep them from becoming public. True, as the PM declared to his colleagues that afternoon, August 14, 1940, the president was taking a long step towards coming into the war.

His colleagues had heard those words before, but now they were nervous, bemused by the very invasion psychosis that he had conjured up to entrap Roosevelt. "We *must* give a very easy quid for the quo," was how Sir Alec Cadogan expressed his relief, hearing of the deal, "and I understand Winston now agrees."

Since it was to prove a remarkable deal — allowing the first real, permanent inroads into Empire territories, to help ward off an imagined (and indeed non-existent) threat by Germany — the history of the Churchill-Roosevelt deal, Destroyers for Bases, deserves closer scrutiny from both the Washington and the London viewpoints.

Churchill had first asked for the destroyers a few days after taking office. Apprehensive of another Tyler Kent, he by-passed Kennedy and dealt through Lord Lothian, his ambassador in Washington. As France crumbled he stepped up the pressure, spelling out Britain's destroyer losses in mid June in a telegram to Lothian: in 1918 the British had had 433 destroyers in commission; they now had only 133, of which only sixty-eight were fit for duty. Thirty-two had been lost since the war began, he said, twenty-five of those since the beginning of February.

"Unless we do something to give the English additional destroyers," Henry Morgenthau minuted in Washington, impressed, "it seems to me it is absolutely hopeless to expect them to keep going."[1]

That Roosevelt waited a clear month before even replying alarmed Churchill. Those destroyers became a touchstone of American intent. But the war had awakened new interests in the Roosevelt administration which lay athwart Britain's. Washington could not see how Britain was going to pay. Informally, officials began to suggest that she relinquish her West Indian possessions to the Americans.

Churchill drafted a cable to Lothian on July 5 warning that unless he got these boats he could not defend the Channel against Hitler. The draft telegram talked of the "grievous responsibility" the United States would bear if she "failed Britain," and claimed inventively that Eire was about to make common cause with the Germans "who they think are bound to win." Halifax gave Kennedy an informal glimpse of this draft. The ambassador discouraged its transmission, and Churchill scrapped the telegram altogether.[2]

Roosevelt could hide behind his country's Constitution and neutrality legislation. His next gambit was to argue that he was not permitted to send the destroyers unless the U.S. navy certify that it would serve America's defence.[3]

CHURCHILL GRIEVED THAT despite Mers-el-Kébir Roosevelt still discounted Britain's chances. He adopted an equally dog-in-the-manger stance. Roosevelt, he knew, also wanted to get his hands on Britain's most advanced military hardware. Broadly speaking, the scientists on both sides of the Atlantic were greedy for an unrestricted exchange; Sir Henry Tizard, the air ministry's principal scientist, had first suggested such an exchange late in 1939 but the admiralty had opposed it, lest the enemy also get hold of Britain's secrets. When the Prof had put the idea up again on June 20, Winston decided to treat it as part of the "larger issue."[4]

In the second half of July, Roosevelt urged that a technical mission be sent, and soon; apprehensive that Britain's secrets might go under with Britain his officials began to harry Churchill to hand over the most advanced inventions. On July 17 Winston inquired in a note to General Ismay, "Who is making a fuss? And what happens if we do not give an immediate decision?"[5]

It was at this stage that he made the acquaintance of a man shortly destined to head the American Foreign Intelligence Service. On July 21, Desmond Morton told him that an influential friend of Roosevelt, the Republican lawyer William J. Donovan was in London, charged with a somewhat nebulous mission — ostensibly to promote an exchange of naval inventions; Mr Churchill "might wish to find time to see him." In fact Donovan had been singled out a month previously by the new head of British covert operations in North America, William Stephenson; his trip had the political and financial backing of the secretary of the navy, Colonel Frank Knox.[6] According to what Stephenson told "C" in December, Donovan had even more influence on Roosevelt than Colonel E.M. House had had on President Woodrow Wilson.[7]

Donovan was ushered into No.10 at five-thirty on July 25; he was fifty-seven, blue eyed, muscular. Incongruously, he had been something of an isolationist, and no champion of the Empire. Meeting Winston evidently stirred him: by the time a British flying boat bore him away a week later he was putting Britain's chances above fifty-fifty.[8] Churchill had instructed that he be shown everything: "C" had even taken him round Bletchley Park. Shortly, Arthur Purvis, the remarkable Canadian handling Britain's arms purchases in Washington, telephoned London that Britain now had a firm friend in the Republican camp.[9]

Softened by Donovan's visit, Churchill approved the departure to Washington of a secret technical mission; he agreed that Tizard should head the mission and summoned the eminent scientist to his presence.[10]

They had last met at the June meeting where the Prof, backed by his young air ministry protégé R.V. Jones, had predicted that the enemy airforce was using radio beams for target finding. Nettled by Churchill's reliance on Lindemann, Tizard had scoffed, left the meeting and written out his resignation. "The fact is," he explained to a colleague, "that Winston is trying not only to be Prime Minister and Commander-in-Chief, but also, through his pets, to control in detail all the scientific work."[11] Lunching with an editor at the Athenaeum after that, he ridiculed Churchill. "He sees himself as another Marlborough," he observed; he described how with a theatrical gesture Winston had cried to his staff, "I command that this be done."[12]

Unhappily for Tizard, the command referred to was that Jones conduct an airborne search for the controversial radio beams: by nightfall they had been found: Tizard discredited, and the Prof triumphantly vindicated.

After that episode the back-stabbing scientific community declared war on the Prof, declaring him in one circular to be "completely out of touch with his scientific colleagues", and branding his judgment as "unsound" and his influence as dangerous. There was a lingering odour of antisemitism in this campaign, although Lindemann did not regard himself as Jewish. Even Beaverbrook was heard to sneer about the Prof's French Jewess mother.[13] The main charge against Lindemann was that he wasted time and resources on harebrained schemes like aerial mines and incendiary pellets to destroy enemy crops; the chiefs of staff pointed out that no planes were capable of carrying the former, and if the latter were used, Hitler would merely starve his subject peoples and blame Britain for the consequences.[14]

On the first evening in August, Churchill sent for Tizard to brief him — the unsightly little scientist being in his fifties, with untidy graying hair that would have seemed dyed auburn, if the moustache were not of the same reddish hue. Churchill made him wait, explaining through a minion that an archbishop had dislocated his timetable.[15] Tizard adjusted pince-nez, unhappily suspecting that this mission was the Prof's neat way of levering him out of the country (it is worth noting that Churchill would make no attempt to see him on his eventual return.)

The prime minister competently dispelled such thoughts.

> The PM [was] quite emphatic [the scientist wrote in his diary] that the mission was important and that he particularly wanted me to lead it. I asked if he would give me a free hand, and would rely on my discretion. He said 'of course' — and would I write down exactly what I wanted. So I said I would go, and went into the lobby and wrote out a paper which I left with his secretary.

ON THE PREVIOUS day Churchill had resumed his nagging about the destroyers.

"It has now become most urgent for you to give us the destroyers, motor boats and flying boats for which we have asked," he reminded Roosevelt in a rambling cable. "I am confident, now that you know exactly how we stand, that you will leave nothing undone to ensure that 50 or 60 of your oldest destroyers are sent to me at once." He concluded, "Mr President, with great respect I must tell you that in the long history of the world this is a thing to do *now*."[16] Meanwhile he toyed with the idea of blackmail. "In view of the holding-back on the American side which has manifested itself in the last three days," he counselled his staff, "the question of the date of the departure of the [Tizard] Mission should be reviewed."[17]

But in Washington things were moving. Navy secretary Frank Knox assured Lord Lothian that they would help, in return for proper consideration — naval bases in Empire possessions close to the American coast. But when Knox raised the issue at the White House on August 2, his Cabinet colleagues decided to add a second "consideration." — "that the British fleet be sent over here if Great Britain could not beat back the Germans."[18]

Four more days passed before this was put to Mr Churchill in a telegram. His reaction was petulant and inconsistent. He was not averse to leasing bases in the West Indies: but he was angry at the demand on the British fleet.[19] He lectured Halifax on the seventh, "We must not discuss the question of what to do with the Fleet in the event of invasion." He wired to Lothian that any such "defeatist announcement" would have a disastrous effect.

Roosevelt, enjoying Britain's predicament, again took his time to reply. He finally settled the details of the cynical bargain with his principal Secretaries — State, War, Navy and Treasury — on August 13. The resulting telegram handed to Lord Lothian at nine p.m. included rather more than the West Indies. "The plan on the destroyers," summarized Henry Morgenthau Jr., who had helped in the drafting, "is to give us land in Newfoundland, Bermuda, Trinidad, and some other places in exchange for the fifty destroyers."

Elated by these acquisitions, Roosevelt had gone further and suggested that they also let Britain have twenty speed boats and some long range bombers. This was agreed, but there were limits to American generosity: when Morgenthau suggested throwing in the secrets of the highly prized Norden bombsight he found that his colleagues "didn't seem to think well of that;" and, when someone mentioned sending 250,000 ancient Enfield rifles Henry Stimson, Roosevelt's secretary of war, objected that they must go to the Philippines.[20]

THIS WAS THE telegram which Kennedy had brought to No.10 at four-thirty on August 14. Simultaneously, British gifts of incomparably greater value left for North America, as a flying boat skimmed across Poole harbour in Dorset with Tizard and his mission, bound for Washington. In a cheap black japanned metal footlocker the scientist was carrying the distillate of British genius — secrets that would give the more backward reaches of American science the means to make a quantum leap forward into the Twentieth Century.

Whether inspired by scientific ignorance, or impelled by selfless altruism, Mr Churchill had authorized Tizard to give the Americans blueprints of Britain's microwave radar including the new air-to-surface vessel (ASV) radar and an actual specimen of the cavity magnetron developed by Sir James Randall and H.A.H. Boot — the sophisticated device that increased radar power by one thousandfold at a stroke. (American radar development was in the stone age — no American plane had ever carried even airborne radar.) In Tizard's locker too were chemical warfare formulae; details of the new RDX explosive; data on the rocket defense of ships, on Bofors pompom predictors, on the proximity fuze, on Frank Whittle's jet engine, and on the enemy's magnetic mines. With the samples of the latest miniaturized valves went a pious wish from General Electric that Tizard consider the company's interests if ordered to lift the veil on these industrial secrets to the ravenous Americans.

It was the beginning of a torrential leak in Britain's scientific resources to the Americans, which would reach full flood a year later when Mr Churchill voluntarily surrendered Britain's secrets of the atomic bomb.

* * *

Bases for destroyers. One Cabinet member remarked to Joe Kennedy as he left No.10 on the fourteenth, "Is it not rather a hard bargain for you to drive?" Kennedy retorted that Washington was only asking Churchill to live up to his promise in the House on June 4 — to send the fleet abroad if the Germans invaded British waters.

Churchill was uneasy about possible bad publicity. Kennedy cabled his superiors, and the State Department replied assuring him that the president did not contemplate making anything public. The PM thanked him for his "untiring efforts to give us all possible help."

> You will I am sure send us everything you can, for you know well that the worth of every destroyer that you can spare to us is measured in rubies. But we also need the motor torpedo boats you mentioned and as many flying boats and rifles as you can let us have. We have a million men waiting for rifles.

He added that as regards the bases, he agreed to the proposal to lease them to the United States for ninety-nine years "which is easier for us than the method of purchase." He mentioned, almost as an afterthought, that he would now have to consult Canada about Newfoundland.[21]

Roosevelt now had to announce to Congress the dangerous step he was taking. On August 16, he conferred with attorney general Robert H. Jackson and Harry Hopkins on the best way of doing it. Morgenthau pencilled this note on the discussion.

> It was finally R's idea to do it at his press conference and only handle what we were to receive, namely air bases etc. . . Jackson and I persuaded not to include the 20 speed boats at this time as Congress had turned it down once.

For understandable political reasons, Churchill wanted the destroyers to look like a gift. For procedural reasons, Roosevelt wanted a clear legal connection between the two halves of the deal — the bases and the destroyers. He had to establish that the bases were for America's protection. Lothian telegraphed to Downing-street that Roosevelt was insisting on a formal "exchange of letters." When Cadogan saw him on August 23 he found the PM at his surliest. "Won't have an exchange of letters," recorded the F.O. official. "Says he doesn't mind if we don't get destroyers. Won't expose himself to a wrangle with Americans, having made us definite gift, haggling over the extent of ours."

Churchill dictated a draft message to Roosevelt as he drove down to Chequers that evening. But he received a further message from Lothian reporting that Roosevelt had explained to Sumner Welles that he could only send over the destroyers in return for what he called "molassess" — evidently some American jargon. And he wanted a binding contract. "The constitutional position made it 'utterly impossible' for the President to send them as a spontaneous gift but only as a quid pro quo."[22] In fact, the bases must become sovereign American territory. He had the British over a barrel and knew it.

From Chequers, Churchill telephoned Cadogan to say that this message put a different complexion on things, but Cadogan persuaded him to send the original draft.

In it, he grumbled to Roosevelt that in exchange for the war materials Britain was being asked "to pay undefined concessions in all islands and places mentioned from Newfoundland to British Guiana 'as may be required in the judgment of the United States'." But suppose Britain found she could not agree? "Your commitment is definite, ours unlimited," he pointed out. Despite the anticipated destroyer gap over the next months, he now felt that Britain would not be justified in giving the United States "a blank cheque on the whole of our trans Atlantic possessions," merely to bridge this gap, "through which anyhow we hope to make our way though with added risk and suffering."

This confident tone differed markedly from the vulpine wails with which Churchill had until recently plagued the White House. He had, of course, now deduced from the intercepts that there was no longer an invasion risk, but he could hardly divulge that to Roosevelt.

Churchill had in mind a looser bargain, more like an informal exchange of gifts. He suggested a sly formula: "Could you not say that you did not feel able to accept this fine offer which we make unless the United States matched it in some way?"[23]

The Americans would not budge from their terms. Two mornings later Churchill formally offered to Roosevelt ninety-nine year leases on the bases.

THE VOICES IN his Cabinet were divided. Some welcomed the deal as entangling the United States in Britain's war. Others saw it in a harsher light. "If we are going to make a gift," groused Beaverbrook to Joe Kennedy, "all well and good. If we are going to make a bargain, I don't want to make a bad one and this is definitely a bad one." Reporting this to Roosevelt in a cable, Kennedy cheerily commented: "England never gets the impression that they are licked, and consequently can not understand why they should not get the best of a trade."[24]

At 6.15 p.m. on August 29, after formally accepting Roosevelt's harsh terms, Winston received Kennedy and told him bitterly that Roosevelt had every right to be cockahoop. With those bases, he said, Britain had given America a ring of steel, and Roosevelt could always answer his critics in private by saying, "At least I have carried on the affairs of the United States in such a way that we are able to get these necessary bases for ninety-nine years with no loss to America of anything worthwhile."[25] He pleaded with the ambassador not to allow Washington to make public the humiliating terms — particularly the one speculating on a British defeat — as they would have a "disastrous effect" on morale in Britain.[26]

Even now, years later, there are those who maintain that Mr Churchill's deal was the "ultimate triumph" of British policy.* This view is hard to sustain in the unflattering light of archives across the Atlantic. Discreet celebrations over the boondoggling of Churchill continued in Washington until the end of the month. Cordell Hull whooped at the State department that "obviously" fifty destroyers worth perhaps three hundred thousand dollars each were "no proper compensation" for very many valuable British bases. "The British," he explained, "were therefore very anxious that it should not appear as a bargain."

Listening to Hull's remarks was Assistant-Secretary Adolph A. Berle Jr, a man so anti-British that, according to one F.O. source, he took Dominion ministers to the window, showed them the White House and foamed, "The British burned it in 1812." Berle now allowed himself a cynical commentary on the deal.

In a single gulp we have acquired the raw material for the first true continental defense we have had since the sailing ship days.[27]

Those in the know in London kept an ashamed silence. Fleet-street was uneasy but did not criticize.[28] One editor, reading off the tickertape what little Churchill did vouchsafe to the House, reflected that it marked the first step in Britain's retreat from the Western Hemisphere, just as her withdrawal from Peking, Tientsin and Shanghai had heralded her departure from the Far East. "Don't let us deceive ourselves," he added, "They are withdrawals. And they are permanent."[29]

Perhaps a government with less American blood flowing through its veins would have had second thoughts. Churchill now made the public assurances that Washington had asked for, about the future of the fleet.

In Washington, F.D.R. announced the bargain, and the terms, at a triumphant press conference on September 5. A journalist asked if Mr Churchill's announcement about the fleet was part of the deal.

"No," said the president, smooth as an eel. "It happens to come along at the same time."

*Martin Gilbert, vol. vi, 733.

CHAPTER 32

The One Sinless Man

NEVILLE CHAMBERLAIN HAD once reassured a colleague that Baldwin would never risk making Winston foreign secretary — "He would find himself waking up nights with a cold sweat at the thought of Winston's indiscretions." The colleague, Leo Amery, had charitably defended Winston as being not so much rash as "picturesque."[1]

Now, in mid August 1940, Chamberlain was weakening to a cancer diagnosed two weeks earlier; and Winston had adopted towards him that rather distant and sympathetic manner that the United States was manifesting towards Britain. Behind the sympathy was a lingering contempt. "History will deal severely with Chamberlain," he would rasp, toward the end of the current war, and add, after a well timed pause, "I know — because I shall write it."

It was now August 15, 1940: Through a series of his own indiscretions he had become prime minister of a country upon which an unwilling enemy would soon direct his combined airforces. That enemy's cipher indiscretions alone enabled him to avoid defeat in the air, although neither he nor "Stuffy" Dowding could later admit it. Bletchley was often reading the precise orders, naming actual airfields to be attacked — names which would be graven in the Battle's history, like Warmwell, Little Rissington, Abingdon.[2]

By Thursday August 15 Göring was clearly baffled; he recalled his Second, Third and Fifth Air Force commanders to headquarters and censured them for their failure to reduce the British defences. He suggested precision attacks on aircraft factories at Birmingham. "Cities as such," he reminded them, "are not to be attacked yet — particularly not London."[3]

That day, Thursday, brought the climax: from morning until dusk the rival squadrons brawled across the southern counties. Göring's pilots flew 1,786 sorties. To exhaust the fighter defences, they threw seven great raids at southern England, staggered throughout the day, coupled with a Fifth Air Force punch at the north. The purpose was to catch half the fighter squadrons on the ground refuelling. Knowing this, the austere, wordless Dowding ordered restraint, and thus mastered the situation.

Aware that London itself was not on the menu, Churchill had stayed in town, on hot coals all that day. A secretary noted in his diary that he was perpetually telling them to ring up Dowding for the latest reports.

All three enemy Air forces operated; from Norway one hundred bombers escorted by seventy fighter planes bore down on factories and harbours in northern England while the Second and Third Air Forces tied down all twenty-two R.A.F. fighter squadrons in the south. But, forewarned, Dowding had retained seven squadrons in the north-east to ward off precisely this blow. Months later, Churchill recalled this as "the decisive incident in the campaign."[4]

He met his Cabinet at noon, drove out once more to Fighter Command's operations bunker at Stanmore to savour the narcotic excitement there, returned to his Cabinet at five-thirty. Beaverbook, now a member, was blue: the damage to aircraft factories was growing serious.[5] The evening score was telephoned to No.10: Dowding had lost thirty-four; he still had 235 Hurricanes and Spitfires as replacements, and his pilots were claiming one hundred enemy destroyed.

Churchill bade a secretary inform the convalescent Chamberlain of this victory. "The Lord President is very grateful to you," the secretary told him, putting the phone down.

"So he ought to be," was the prime minister's reply. "It is one of the greatest days in history."

The remaining August air battles were inconclusive. On the morning of the sixteenth the sirens sounded in London, but without event. Churchill was not surprised, having been telephoned routinely by Fighter Command around eight a.m. reassuring him that London was not due for attack. "We had an air-raid warning at 12:20 as I was going to the Cabinet," recorded Lord Halifax, unaware of the PM's secret information, "but . . . I found that the Cabinet was to be held as arranged. Winston thought that it was time enough to take cover when the guns started going off." This was probably the afternoon that he drove out to the command bunker at Stanmore and watched from the gallery of this underground theatre as the tide of battle ebbed and flowed across the chart of southern England.

By duskfall the coloured lamps indicated that every fighter squadron had been thrown in. Pug Ismay was ashen faced, but the raiders withdrew, the coloured lights gradually flickered out, and the girls raked the squadron markers off the table in the manner of roulette croupiers on the Riviera. The enemy had flown seventeen hundred sorties and lost forty-five planes; Dowding claimed 161, and was invited to dine at Chequers.

Climbing back into his Humber, Churchill made no attempt to hide the tears flowing down his cheeks.

"You're a cold blooded fish, Pug," he reproached Ismay, sitting next to him, "a typical office-stool soldier who can't appreciate the great moments of history."* Ismay began a reply, but Churchill silenced him. "I have never been so moved," he said, and after a few minutes murmured something about so much never having been owed to so few.[6]

The margin was narrowing. Accompanying Churchill to a fighter station, Ismay watched the eager young men clamber into their Merlin-engined steeds, a strand of the Old Testament tugging at his memory: "And they shall be mine, saith the Lord of hosts, in that day when I make up my jewels." [Malachi: iii: 17]

Churchill recognized the danger now — that the enemy airforce was methodically wrecking Dowding's sector and radar stations. But he was devising the salvation: he would divert the attack onto London proper by deliberately striking at Berlin — Hitler's capital and one of Germany's biggest industrial centres. He invited Sir Charles Portal to Chequers for dinner on the seventeenth to discuss it. It would be a cynical step, fraught with the utmost danger for the Londoners. Hitler had ten times as many bombers, and their bases were only one-sixth as far from London as the British were from Berlin.

Bomber Command had nearly triggered the deadly exchange that morning: Portal had ordered an attack on the Siemens factories, in the heart of Berlin. While willing to wound, however, Churchill was still afraid to strike — or at least to strike *first*. He wanted to win American public opinion, not alienate it. Thus at 6:25 p.m., while Portal was still at Chequers, a cipher signal went to his headquarters postponing the Berlin attack indefinitely.[7] Hitler must seem to throw the first punch.

Some time after midnight, a lone German plane droned high over Chequers, unaware that with one bomb it could have disposed of Mr Churchill, the chief of his Bomber Command, and their plan. That hot and summery weekend he had all his "family" there — including the Prof, Beaverbrook and Bracken.

For General Sir Alan Brooke, now commanding Home Forces, Beaverbrook was "an evil genius, who exercised the very worst sort of influence on Winston." It was Brooke's first weekend spent at Chequers. He savoured the boundless hospitality offered by the government mansion but found the weekend excruciating, recalling in his private notes the desperate longing for bed as the PM yarned on.

Beaverbrook's presence did not alloy his enjoyment. "After dinner,"

---

*Hitler also liked to call Halder a typical office-stool(*Drehschemel*) general. *Hitler's War*.

Brooke recorded, "he sat at the writing-table, pouring himself out one strong whisky after another, and I was revolted by his having monkey-like hands as they stretched out to grab ice cubes out of the bowl."[8]

Private secretary John Martin had twisted his ankle running to have the guard's wireless switched off — Churchill was hypersensitive to sounds. Martin's diary shows that the Halifaxes came for Sunday lunch, with de Gaulle and his twin keepers, Spears and Morton. But Churchill did not show himself after that as he was dictating a brilliant new speech for the House.

DURING SUNDAY THE eighteenth the enemy badly mauled the fighter defences; as Churchill dined with Clementine and Sarah, his oracle reported that the Nazi airforce commander Hermann Göring had warned his commanders to prepare "a large scale operation" on Monday.

Bad weather closed down air operations that Monday. "C" reported that Göring had summoned every commander down to squadron level to a meeting where, the British learned, he ordered the ratio of fighters to bombers increased and authorized a night attack on Glasgow. It cannot have pleased Mr Churchill to see that London was still embargoed.[9] He retired to bed and was still there when Lord Halifax arrived at eleven a.m. — "surrounded," the foreign secretary found, "by papers, secretaries, and all the appurtenances of writing and working, with a large cigar and a beautiful many-coloured gaudy silk dressing gown." Halifax marvelled: "It is amazing how he gets through the work."

Later that Monday, August 19, Churchill reported on the Battle to the House — a memorable speech, dazzling with the facets and bezels he had been polishing all weekend. "Never," he declaimed, "in the field of human conflict was so much owed by so many to so few." He praised Lord Beaverbrook too, whose genius had produced their planes — "It looks like magic," he admitted. He talked of rapidly overtaking Germany in the air.

As a secret American military mission — two generals and an admiral — listened in the gallery, Churchill talked of Britain's own attack on Germany. The R.A.F., he said, was bombing targets "with deliberate, careful discrimination." Reverting to what he privately called "the fire in Hitler's backyard," he dropped a hint that Germany might yet turn against Russia. "Even if Nazi legions stood triumphant on the Black Sea," he declared, "or indeed the Caspian, even if Hitler were at the gates of India, it would profit him nothing if at the same time the entire economic and scientific apparatus of German war power lay shattered and pulverized at home."

Defending the bargain over the Caribbean bases, Mr Churchill assured the house that sovereignty would not be transferred. It was all part of the process of mixing the two English speaking democracies, a process which no man could stop. "Like the Mississippi," he declared emotionally, "it just keeps rolling along. Let it roll. Let it roll on full flood, inexorable, irresistible, benignant [*sic*], to broader lands and better days."

As the Humber drove him from Parliament back to No.10 — he never walked those few hundred yards — he carolled Ole Man River to the private secretary sitting with him, as though to underline that peroration.[10]

* * *

He viewed the "mixing process" without misgivings. Had he been a British admiral who dined at the White House some months later, perhaps he might have felt misgivings after all. "Oh yes," Roosevelt would drawl, "those West Indies islands; we're going to show you how to look after them, and not only you but the Portuguese and Dutch. Every nigger will have his two acres and a sugar patch."[11]

Churchill's own attitude to His Majesty's coloured subjects was no less old-fashioned. He had opposed Indian sailors joining the navy, arguing that "theoretical" racial equality would in practice cause great inconvenience, so "not too many of them, please."[12]

His interest in Britain's paupered and neglected colonies was limited; on the day that France collapsed it occurred to him that a West Indies Regiment might be raised "to give an outlet for the loyalty of the Negroes, and bring money into these poor islands."[13]

When Lord Cranborne reported that a Black member of the Colonial Office could no longer lunch at a certain restaurant because it was patronised by U.S. officers, he would look up from the papers he was reading, and suggest unhelpfully that he take a banjo with him — "they'll think he's one of the band!"[14]

* * *

On the evening of his speech he invited the American mission to a stag dinner, provided cigars and victuals, but failed to impress: the military attaché found him "little, fattish, un-handsome, stoop-shouldered, baldish," but jotted in his pocket diary:

10 Downing Street = powerhouse. Churchill knows people better than Chamberlain. Tells them facts: trouble, work, anguish. After nothing but defeat they are in better spirit.

This was true: With the realisation that the enemy was not invincible his popularity soared. He professed himself puzzled by it — he had brought only disasters, and promised nothing but blood, sweat and tears.[15] The Spanish ambassador reported that a wind of optimism was blowing. "The military measures adopted," the Duke of Alba stated, "the sturdy defense put up by the British airforce, the propaganda personally inspired and directed by Churchill have all had remarkable results."[16] He would cable to Madrid on the twenty-sixth a further flattering picture of Churchill with his eccentric hat — of a type that a doctor might have sported thirty years ago — touring suburbs, ports and airfields. "Churchill's prestige," he reported, "is increasing all the time." "As viewed from Britain, the figure of Churchill bulks larger every day."[17]

THAT WEEKEND A turning point in the life and death of a million Europeans arrived.

During Saturday August 24 the enemy began using the new fighter-saturation tactics, with bombers taking part only as bait to lure the defences into combat. Warned in advance, Dowding refused to be drawn.

That evening the bombing continued. The targets included oil tanks and airplane component factories on the very periphery of London. One bomber overshot its target, oil tanks in Rochester, and its stick of bombs fell inside Greater London; nobody was killed, but a hundred people lost their homes in the working class East End.

Churchill learned of this on Sunday morning. It was the break he had been waiting for, as his immediate intervention — revealed by Bomber Command's telephone records — shows. By-passing both Sinclair and the chief of air staff, he telephoned Bomber Command just after nine a.m., learned that Portal was away, told the Senior Air Staff Officer there, Air Commodore Norman Bottomley, that he had discussed with Portal "a certain projected attack on a target in the East of Germany" and was anxious that it be bombed that night.

> The order when given [Bomber Command recorded him as saying] would come through the Air Ministry in the usual way; but he wished us to be fully prepared and hoped we had adequate resources "in the bag" and that there would be no difficulties. He felt that it was no good tackling this job with small forces and was averse to administering "pin pricks."[18]

The three Group commanders, who took seriously their responsibility for their young aircrews' lives, contemplated the unhelpful weather conditions forecast for Berlin that night, and reported from their respective headquarters that it might "go off at half-cock." Bottomley warned them that Mr Churchill was "most anxious" for a really heavy attack as an immediate reprisal for "the attack on London." But then the Chief of Air Staff intervened: Unaware of Portal's private discussion a week earlier with Churchill at Chequers, Sir Cyril Newall decided the Command must go ahead with its long-prepared attack on Leipzig instead. Ordering this by cipher telegram at four p.m. he postponed Berlin by twenty-four hours, even ordered his crews to avoid "indiscriminate bombing of the civil population."

This was not what Winston wanted at all. Air Vice Marshal Arthur Harris, standing in that day for Portal, felt that this night was likely to be as favourable as any other and in a telephone conference with the other commanders at four p.m. argued strongly that this opportunity to attack Berlin was unlikely to return for some time.

Newall approved, reluntantly, at 4:25 p.m.

As feared, the raid went off at half cock. Eighty bombers were sent that Sunday night, less than thirty claimed to have found Berlin; nobody was killed, the Flak put up a noisy barrage.

On Monday morning Newall assured Bomber Command that he would not tolerate any more such last minute changes of plan and target. He proposed that on Tuesday night they attack Leipzig as planned.

Churchill disagreed. "Now that they [the Germans] have begun to molest the capital [London]," he told the chief of air staff, "I want you to hit them hard, and Berlin is the place to hit them."[19]

Newall telephoned Bomber Command at 5:40 p.m.: The PM, he said, had demanded a renewed attack on Berlin that night —

> the Prime Minister had pressed him for these attacks to be repeated but . . . he has resisted the demand for a change of programme at a late hour of the day. It was likely however that we shall be required to undertake the operation on the night of 27th/28th.

Winston's staff were becoming accustomed, as one wrote on the first day of September, to ceaseless air warnings. They lost count of their number. By day they yielded little except an occasional distant and muffled explosion; by night the lone planes were more of a nuisance, prowling overhead aimlessly with only very rarely "a dull boomp" as a distant bomb fell.[20] The private secretaries, not privy to the utterances of Bletchley's oracle, did not know that London was still on Hitler's embargo list for attack. They quietly marvelled as their master stalked out into the garden at No.10, when the sirens sounded, to pace the lawn, helmet in hand, before retiring to his bunker for the night.

PERHAPS IT IS a truism that the successful warlord has to be an artful liar too; but even at the admiralty Mr Churchill's record had shown no deficiency in this respect.

Not everybody grasped the importance of this. On August 28 Mr Frank Pick, the new director-general of the Ministry of Information had visited No.10 to urge the importance of truthful reporting.

To the amusement of his colleagues, Churchill walked round the Cabinet table and put out his hand to the dazed civil servant.

"To-day," he announced, "I'm going down to Dover to watch the air battles. Perhaps tonight I shall be in Hell, and if so I should like to tell the people there that I have shaken hands with the one sinless man since Jesus Christ."

Sarcastically, he demanded, "Shake my hand, Mr Pick!"[21]

That day he did indeed go down to Dover, after ordering the chief of air staff to lay on "a large scale of attack" on Berlin that night.[22] He joined the visiting American military mission at Victoria, sporting bowler and cigar; sipped sherry, retired for an hour, emerged for a "real" drink, and orated until they reached the Channel coast.

One American suggested that the Germans might slip ashore under cover of fog. "With mists," the PM pointed out, "come storms and rough seas."

They scoured Dover for signs of devastation but in vain, because "Hellfire Corner" was a product of American journalism; after a while he drove on alone to Ramsgate, returned angry, described how small traders were losing their livelihoods in the bombings. He was going, he said, to hammer Berlin again that night; to the visitors he seemed not to care if London was bombed in reprisal.

At nine p.m. their train pulled back into Victoria. The platforms were in darkness. The visitors heard the top-hatted stationmaster announce to him, "There's an air-raid warning on, sir. Will you take cover?"

"Not at all," said Churchill, plucking the cigar from his mouth. "It's only a Red, isn't it?"

A Red alert indicated enemy bombers right overhead. They were not, and he knew it. Winston may well have stagemanaged this harmless drama for the naive, unblooded Americans, just as their arrival in London a week earlier had been met with the fruitless wail of sirens.

Summarising impressions one of them would note that he was an unscrupulous "rough-and-tumble" fighter. He added the ambiguous tribute: "He is perfectly at home in his dealings with Hitler and Mussolini."[23]

HITLER, NO GREAT respecter of the truth either, a man whose patience had been readily exhausted in the past, had not flinched as the first raids hit Berlin. His airforce had continued to batter the R.A.F.'s sector and fighter stations, but on the twenty-ninth, as Churchill had promised the American mission, his own bombers returned to Berlin and this time they drew blood. Ten people were killed, the Nazi leader flew north to his capital. He ordered Goring to prepare — but not execute — massive retaliation. Thus, while Churchill was fortifying himself with 1911 Bollinger at Chequers on the last day of August, the Reichmarschall attacked southern England with the largest force of bombers yet — 380 by day and 260 by night.

But still the city of London was embargoed.[24]

Evidently the new bombing policy hatched between Churchill and Portal, over whisky and victuals at Chequers, evoked consternation among the air marshals at intermediate levels between them. But Portal now had the higher authority he needed to start a holocaust. "We have not yet reached the stage of desiring to burn down a whole town," he coolly wrote to those intermediate officials on Monday, September 2. "But when this stage is reached we shall do it by dropping a large quantity of incendiaries first and then [following with] a sustained attack with High Explosive to drive the firefighters underground and let the flames get a good hold."[25]

Hitherto, the death of civilians and destruction of hospitals, churches and cultural monuments had been regarded as a by-product of bombing; but, in the opinion of the official Historians, in Portal's mind these now became a desirable end-product.[26]

Churchill echoed this new heroism. "The Navy can lose us the war," he summarized in a treatise circulated to the Cabinet on Tuesday, September 3, "but only the Air Force can win it." Narrowing the strategic focus still further, he added: "The Fighters are our salvation, but the bombers alone provide the means of victory."[27]

* * *

His chiefs of staff knew of other alternatives. Issuing their first strategic review since June they would add to bombing the methods of economic warfare and subversion.[28] Dr Dalton, the tall, forceful minister who handled both, came round to No.10 to report that evening, September 3. But Churchill wanted to talk, not listen. He was fulminating against the secret service for declining to convey a clandestine message to his old friend, the bumbling General Georges, under house arrest in occupied France. "It would be quite a short letter," Winston grumbled, misquoting famous words of Leon Gambetta spoken in 1870: *"On penser toujours! On parler jamais!"*

Dalton tried later to recall the pearls of Winston's wisdom, uttered as he paced the floor. "This is a workman's war," was one, "the public will stand everything except optimism." Even in their rough-cut form, his pronouncements still glowed and sputtered incandescently: he muttered about not being like the knight "who was so slow in buckling on his armour that the tourney was over before he rode into the ring."

Comforted by the familiar sound of his own rhetoric, he commanded John Peck, one of his more able secretaries, to darken the room and throw onto a screen the latest aerial photographs of dockyards in northern Germany and Hitler's big guns at Cap Gris Nez. On one photograph he espied a car travelling the road to a gunsite, and jabbed a childish finger on the screen as if squashing an insect. "Look," he cried. "There's a horrible Hun! Why don't we bomb him!"

"Peck," he exclaimed, "you must get some new photographs every day and show them to me every evening."[29]

ON THE FOLLOWING day his foreign secretary expressed private surprise at the German restraint in the air. "I cannot understand," he mused in his diary, "why Hitler, if he has the immense reserve Air strength that we are told, doesn't throw it in?"

But Hitler's temper was fraying. That night, September 4, he delivered a major speech in his capital. After a sarcastic mention of "that noted war correspondent" Mr Churchill, he suddenly referred to the repeated British raids on German cities.

> For three months I did not answer because I believed such madness would be stopped. . . We are now answering night for night. If the British airforce drops two or three or four tonnes of bombs, then we will in one night drop 150, 250 or 300 tonnes. [*Hysterical applause.*] If they declare that they will increase their attacks on our cities, then we will raze their cities to the ground.

A few hours later he secretly lifted the embargo on London; flare aircraft illuminated the English capital that night as a warning of things to come.

Portal's bombing offensive against Berlin continued.

In full view of British watchers, German barges massed and other munitions of war were rattled on the far coast of the Channel. In the first six days of September the barges at Ostend multiplied from eighteen to 205; Churchill did not take them seriously. On the seventh day, four Dutchmen landed by dinghy, and were arrested.

When, after the war, the government was asked what proof there was that Hitler had ever planned to invade, Mr Attlee would solemnly refer to the capture of these four spies.[30]

MR CHURCHILL HAD withdrawn to Chequers on Friday the sixth, inviting General Brooke to dine with him there again. After an all-evening snooze he went downstairs at nine to polish his wit on the owlish, bespectacled General. In Brooke's description, he was "most entertaining" for several hours: "He placed himself," he wrote that night, "in the position of

Hitler and attacked these shores while I defended them."

Fortunately, they were still at Chequers on Saturday September 7: only a few days before, Winston had remarked to Dalton that the nation was finding the war less unpleasant than feared. "The air attacks," he had explained, "are doing much less damage than was expected before the war began."

At five p.m. the unpleasantness began: the sunlit estuary of the Thames filled with the roar of three hundred enemy bombers escorted by twice that number of fighter planes, droning in at high altitude from the east to the docklands, where the river begins to snake.

This was Hitler's reprisal for the Portal raids on Berlin — the first mass attack on targets in London. For once, Dowding, his communications tattered, his radar systems damaged, his fighter airfields cratered, fumbled the response.

Bombs began falling on the Royal Arsenal at Woolwich and munitions factories.

More formations were approaching from due south, over the Channel; running battles could be seen over the city itself as the massed bombers clawed their way forwards to the Millwall and Commercial docks.

Londoners who had never seen such a thing before crowded into the streets, craned their necks to follow the thunderous spectacle, then broke for cover as the bombdoors opened right overhead and the first dark spots hurtled down.

Immense blazes raged through the dockyards and the adjoining East End slums, fires too vast to douse by duskfall. Off duty that weekend, John Martin found himself among crowds on the Thames embankment at Charing Cross, hypnotized by the smoke rolling upwards from the dockland.

Around eight-thirty, as flickering searchlights fingered the darkening pall, the bombers returned, beaconed by the glowing inferno in the East End. The city was an easy target — its famous ribbon of river fringed by flames.

Bombs bracketed Battersea power station, plunging the West End into darkness; another power station was hit at West Ham. Martin, returning from early dinner to the back entrance of No.10, heard the Red alert, and almost immediately the shriek and dull thud of a bomb not far away.

> The cat was waiting at the garden gate to take refuge with me. Things became too lively to remain upstairs, so we all went down to our underground shelter and I spent the night there in my clothes on a bunk. We had occasional explosions and at one moment the light went off for a while.

THUS AT THE crucial moment Churchill had tricked Hitler and Goring into shifting their aim from the fighter defences to the capital city. We have no eye witness account of how he responded to this deadly triumph. "Each night," he admitted to his duty secretary, "I try myself by Court Martial to see if I have done anything effective during the day. I don't mean just pawing the ground."

This time he had not just pawed the ground. He had saved Fighter Command. Five forward airfields and six of the seven sector-stations had been seriously damaged; London would soon have been defenceless.

There were added bonuses: American newspapermen were already reporting the bombing to their editors; and this Nazi Schrecklichkeit would hammer into a frustrated silence all those Englishmen who voiced doubts about the wisdom of his war. For the first time, moreover, he had forced Hitler to dance to his tune. It was just as he had wanted, though he could hardly tell his public that.

This first attack had killed 306 Londoners. It was the first lurch towards the holocaust. Now Churchill and Portal needed no further justification for what they proposed — to unleash a new kind of war, in which ultimately one million civilians in Germany as well as hundreds of thousands of French, Poles, Czechs and others would die under the trample of the Allied stragtegic bomber forces.

CHAPTER 33

Good Ole Winnie

UNTIL NOW HE had scarcely known personal popularity. Now, with each new ordeal, it soared. Newsreels showed him touring troops, stumping warship gangplanks, inspecting gigantic guns, acknowledging with flamboyant upward sweep of square porkpie hat the cheers of bystanders. Recently, enemy transmitters had begun to rouse the workers against him. But these violent air raids gave him the chance to drive to their stricken suburbs and show himself to the newly bereaved and homeless, flicking Havana ash onto glass-strewn sidewalks and waving his walking stick; 7,000 would die during the remainder of September 1940, including seven hundred children.

He had gauged the British mood exactly. By October Gallup pollsters would see his popularity soar to eighty-nine percent.

Of course this stoical, suffering people could not know that for reasons of grand strategy he and Bomber Command had done their utmost to induce this very outrage; nor that there was worse to come; nor that the carnage would last for four more years.

Until that first Saturday, September 7, Londoners had had little contact with war, a single tank rattling down the Strand had brought gaping crowds to the kerbside.

But for the rest of the winter the capital was a nightmare by day and an inferno by night. The grinding, unsynchronized drone of Daimler-Benz and Jumo aeroengines clashed with the smoother Rolls-Royce Merlins; this was punctuated by the scream of bombs and the shower of broken glass as windows were sucked into the streets; this curtain of sound was riven by the crack of the anti-aircraft guns. Braver souls crowded rooftops watching the Flak shells flash two or three miles above them, heard the fragments rain down with a vicious hum, striking flinty sparks wherever they impacted, and then the clangour of fire-engines passing through the streets. The fireman became Britain's first real hero, together with the elderly air raid warden who patrolled the streets with only a tin hat between him and eternity.

The summer's hit was A Nightingale Sang in Berkeley Square; but the nightingales had flown. A typical London dawn, as autumn came, found cranes, mechanical shovels and ambulances foregathered around new ruins and disposal squads digging down to unexploded bombs. Freshly erupted craters might be closing Park Lane and Oxford Street.

A time bomb closed Regent Street for two days. Selfridges lost its windows, John Lewis burnt out. Everybody was at risk. The richer homes collapsed into larger heaps of rubble — that was the only difference. Their Majesties no longer slept in town but in Windsor Castle; which was as well, because on September 9 the first bomb hit their London palace. Most nights, a fresh draw was held in this lethal lottery, and it unified those brave enough to remain in London.

A newfound courage in adversity pervaded them, transcending class barriers and obscuring the old Party distinctions.

Through this rising chaos came, lisping and snuffling, the familiar voice of Mr Churchill, broadcasting bravely to the nation, steady and reassuring, promising victory and crying revenge. "It would take ten years at the present rate for half the houses of London to be demolished," he calculated. "After that, of course, progress would be much slower."

EVEN THE AMERICAN ambassador, wiser than most to Mr Churchill's methods, was swept up by the spirit of bravado. He climbed to the roof of his chancery, blinked through circular, hornrimmed glasses into the London night. "On Sunday night," he reported to Roosevelt after the first four days of the ordeal, "a high explosive made a direct hit on a house twenty yards from [First Secretary] Herschel Johnson's house, killing six people, but he is well and hearty. Today, coming back from the Foreign Office, a delayed time bomb near Bond Street and Piccadilly blew up about fifty yards from my car. Boy, this is the life!"[1]

Churchill's colleagues — happily unaware of the private arrangements which he had reached with Portal at Chequers two weeks earlier — took a dimmer view. Shocked at reports that the bombing had been "quite indiscriminate," his Cabinet decided on modest retaliation. Bombers attacking Germany, they decided, must "not return home with their bombs" if aborting an attack.[2]

The bombing was widely covered in American newspapers. The *New York Times* headlines were: 1,500 NAZI PLANES BOMB LONDON; INDUSTRY AND SERVICES DAMAGED on Sunday, and MIGHTY NAZI AIR FLEET AGAIN BOMBS LONDON — DOCKS AND PLANTS HIT, FIRES RAGE, 400 DEAD on the day after.

Visiting the South Coast seaside resorts with the American military mission Churchill's heart had bled briefly for the widowed landladies who had sunk their savings into little hotels, only to see the beaches mined and closed, their families killed, and their properties wrecked.[3] Believing that money — awards of up to £2,000 — would redeem the injury he announced a compensation scheme in the House on the fifth.[4] It smacked perhaps of the Anatole de France minister who advised his monarch that a particular war would cost £5m. "But what about the cost in human lives?" the King had asked. "Your Majesty, they are included in the £5m," was the reassuring reply.

Raids on this scale faced him with new problems. The very first had closed Victoria and a dozen other London railroad stations, as well as Vauxhall bridge and a highway tunnel under the river. But they also gave a pretext for delaying the American mission's departure: he wanted them to get an eyeful of the Nazi frightfulness.

Ancient London, the London of Christopher Wren and John Adams, was collapsing in ruins. Churchill arranged for the paintings — including his own — to be removed from No. 10 and stored beneath the National Gallery. "I do not think much will be left of Downing-street after a few weeks," he observed without perceptible regret on the twentieth, and on the following day he sent the rest of his personal property to safety.

"I propose," he wrote to the worried wife of the former prime minister, Neville Chamberlain, "to lead a troglodyte existence with several 'trogs'."[5]

* * *

On Sunday the eighth, the evening after that first raid, he deemed it safe to return to London. Accompanied by carloads of photographers and his brother Jack — who had moved into No. 10 — he toured the stricken docklands. The Humber was a big car to manipulate in these narrow Dickensian slums and it was slow going but worthwhile, because he drew fresh chemical strength from the guileless enthusiasm of the simple people.

Ragged looking neighbours were raking over the rubble where forty people had been killed in a shelter, and they mobbed him as he stepped out of his Humber.

There were shouts of, "Good ole Winnie! We thought you'd come! We can take it! Give it 'em back." Of course, there were other shouts as well — "You've got to make them stop it!" was one — but he turned on them the same ear he had earlier applied to the late Countess de Portes.

Propaganda officials had handed out paper Union Flags shortly before the PM's arrival. Lump a-throat, he marched through the slums and found this pathetic bunting fluttering everywhere from the powdery heaps. Tears moistened his eyes. Pug Ismay nearly cried as well, although the PM had perhaps larger grounds for remorse than he. "You see," the general heard one old biddie say, "He really cares. He's crying."[6]

"What fellows they are," he declared to Ismay. "D'you hear them! They cheered me as if I had given them a victory, instead of getting their houses bombed to bits."[7]

HE MADE ANOTHER journey that day, to Dollis Hill in North London. Here, bombproof arrangements had been made for his own safety.

Archie Sinclair, who had fawned shamelessly on Winston — his battalion commander in the Great War — had privately written to remind him how in 1916 Churchill had insisted on having "the best shelter that was available" at their farmhouse headquarters on the Western Front; he demanded that Winston now again put his own safety above all else.[8]

It was a theme never far from Mr Churchill's mind. Up here in Dollis Hill he had prepared a suite of rooms at Neville's Court for his family should Whitehall become uninhabitable, while in the General Post Office's new research centre nearby he had installed an underground command bunker, with twenty-five rooms for himself, his closer Cabinet colleagues and their staffs.

On September 9 and 10 there were more attacks, killing four hundred more Londoners. After touring the City on the morning of the tenth, he invited Halifax and Cadogan to come and discuss the situation with him while he was taking his afternoon rest. "I must say," noted the foreign secretary afterwards, "he is a person of wonderful courage and determination. He says the scientists are very hopeful indeed of getting on to the secrets of night interception." Belatedly, he set up a Night Air Defence Committee with himself in the chair. By the eleventh the capital's gun defences would have been doubled at the expense of the provinces.

After the Germans again attacked that night, killing 235 Londoners, his private secretary wrote, "There was an intense and continuous barrage from the AA guns which had hitherto seemed oddly inactive, and this had an immense effect on people's morale. Tails are up and, after the fifth sleepless night, everyone looks quite different this morning — cheerful and confident. It is a curious bit of mass psychology, the relief of hitting back." On the following morning, he drove into the City with the prime minister: both were surprised to see how localized the damage was. "There was great enthusiasm," the secretary observed, "from the crowds."

MINOR INVASION SCARES continued to bubble to the surface throughout September and October, mostly at weekends — the Führer was known to favour Saturdays.

Churchill was nonchalant. More than usually clairvoyant, thanks to his oracle, he spent leisurely weekends at Chequers, displaying an aplomb that Sir Francis Drake would have admired.

Once A. V. Alexander, the First Lord (who was not trusted enough to receive all of Bletchley's "golden eggs") nervously telephoned with word of German ships approaching from the Dutch coast — this might be the invasion. It wasn't.[9] Air Intelligence dutifully reported every straw that floated in the æther — preparations at fifteen airfields across the Straits from Dover to accommodate divebomber and fighter squadrons from September 4, the transfer of Stukas from Norway to France on the sixth.[10]

On the seventh the Joint Intelligence Committee felt that, given the favourable moon and tides, these intercepts and the increase of invasion barges might indicate invasion within twenty-four hours. After all, it was Saturday again.

The chiefs of staff met that evening as the violent air raid began and General Sir Alan Brooke sounded the Invasion Alarm a few minutes after eight p.m. But on Sunday the War Office concluded from the raw intercepts that the enemy's training was incomplete and that there was no "hard and fast decision" to invade.[11]

The naval staff remained nervous. "Invasion information," Captain Edwards wrote on the tenth, "has assumed most alarming proportions. Ships in vast numbers moving down the enemy coast and concentrations of barges everywhere. . . An intercept shows German troops are about to embark at Ostend."

Intercepts like this should subsequently have been subjected to rigorous analysis: since no German troops ever embarked, the signal can only have been intended to deceive the British: and this in turn implies that the enemy suspected that at least this cipher had been broken.

Churchill was sure the invasion talk was bluff. (While we have no proof, he may have been privy to signals *like* one just issued by General Jodl ordering the Nazi Intelligence service to camouflage troop movements to the East "as the impression must not be allowed to arise in Russia from these deployments that we are preparing an eastern offensive."[12]) Of course he concealed this from the American ambassador. After talking with him on the eleventh Kennedy reported to F.D.R. Winston's belief that Hitler was about to invade; but the astute diplomat was puzzled nonetheless — "He does not usually tip off his punch before he delivers it." Kennedy also referred to the movement of German divisions to her eastern frontier. Eden, he said, anticipated that they would roll through Romania, Bulgaria and Turkey "to sweep into Syria and Irak and hit Egypt on the other side." As for Churchill's popularity, Kennedy explained that the media were keeping the public ignorant of Britain's plight. Churchill and his men were just "holding their breath," as he put it, until the presidential election. Again he warned that the United States must not "sign a blank cheque" to help Churchill out of his difficulties.[13]

WITH THE ONSET of mass air raids Churchill's political difficulties shrank. He could turn the blandest gaze on fresh peace emissaries like the one — behind which the British legation correctly detected Hitler's hand — that now arrived in Sweden.[14]

A Berlin lawyer, Ludwig Weissauer, had travelled to Stockholm to contact Sir Victor Mallet through a senior judge and friend of the Swedish monarch, Professor Lars Ekeberg. But now Churchill was running Britain's foreign policy.[15] Through Halifax, he forbade Mallet to meet Weissauer. The British envoy, who sincerely desired a negotiated peace, ascertained Berlin's terms nonetheless. They were as before — for Germany, the continent; for Britain, her overseas empire. Ekeberg asked for an answer by the eleventh.

Halifax and Cadogan brought the resulting Stockholm telegram over to No.10 on the tenth and left Churchill to think it over. "If you want any more questions asked," Mallet had promised in it, "I can easily get them put by Ekeberg, again without committing anyone and as though coming from me alone."

Churchill tossed the telegram aside. When the F.O. mandarins returned at seven-thirty p.m. he had drafted a rejection, and was sprawled in bed in his flowered Chinese dressing gown, drawing on a Havana cigar.[16]

Kennedy learned of this episode and revealed it to former president Herbert Hoover. Told Hitler's terms, the former president gasped: "Why didn't the British accept?"

"Nothing but Churchill's bullheadedness," replied Kennedy.[17]

THE INVASION SCARE had served its purpose. While he divulged to Kennedy his firm opinion that the armada photographed by the R.A.F. indicated "imminent invasion," in private he deployed more double-negatives than Hitler was deploying barges. He told his Cabinet colleagues on Wednesday September 11 that it was "by no means impossible that the Germans would in the end decide not to launch an attack on this country because they were unable to obtain the domination over our fighter force."

General Brooke believed that Saturday the fourteenth was Hitler's D-day. His headquarters now ordered a Lanchester armoured car and driver to Chequers, equipped with special orders and a pass that would get him through any roadblock outside London: "You will be responsible for getting him through. You will ride in front, show your identity card at any road block where it is required. . . Do not say the Prime Minister is in the car."[18] "This order," the pass stated, "will be valid from 14th to 16th September inclusive."

Mr Churchill did not share these invasion fears, although he certainly intended to proclaim that he, with the assistance from "the Few," had momentarily thwarted Hitler's invasion. He would confide to Hearst journalist H.R. Knickerbocker two weeks later that the enemy had planned to invade on the thirteenth, but had been frustrated.[19]

He carefully bricked-in the foundations for this propaganda claim in a broadcast on the eleventh. "We cannot be sure that in fact they will try at all," he admitted, "but no one should blind himself to the fact that a heavy full-scale invasion of this Island is being prepared with all the usual German thoroughness and method, and that it may be launched at any time now."

To put his own achievement in historical perspective he compared the coming week with the greatest moments in Britain's history. "It ranks," he claimed immodestly, "with the days when the Spanish Armada was approaching the Channel, and Drake was finishing his game of bowls; or when Nelson stood between us and Napoleon's Grand Army at Boulogne." Through the loudspeaker grills of wireless sets behind the barricaded and blacked-out windows growled the voice of Churchill calling on every man and woman "to do his duty."

He went centre-stage to the Channel Coast on the twelfth, taking generals and admirals with him. Like his opponent he had succumbed to the fascination of big guns. He inspected twelve-inch railway guns and 5.5-inch coastal batteries. Hitler might have his Todt Battery in Calais; but Churchill's newspapermen could admire the erection of his 13.5 inch monsters, Winnie and Pooh, capable of firing into France. He had ordered them himself, when minister of munitions in 1918.

Brooke sighed at these guns. They were Winston's "pets", but the trained military mind despaired at the manpower they wasted. The PM's popularity continued to astound him. Several times local people rushed forward and cheered him: "Stick it!", which he took to be a sign of encouragement.[20]

IN HIS BROADCAST on the eleventh he had dwelt upon the blitz.

These cruel, wanton, indiscriminate bombings of London are, of course, a part of Hitler's invasion plans. He hopes, by killing large numbers of civilians, and women and children, that he will terrorize and cow the people of this mighty imperial city, and make them a burden and anxiety to the Government and thus distract our attention from the ferocious onslaught he is preparing. Little does he know the spirit of the British nation, or the tough fibre of the Londoners, whose forebears played a leading part in the establishment of Parliamentary institutions and who have been bred to value freedom far above their lives.

"This wicked man," he contined, "the repository and embodiment of many forms of soul-destroying hatred, this monstrous product of former wrongs and shame, has now resolved to try to break our famous Island race by a process of indiscriminate slaughter and destruction.* What he has done is to kindle a fire in British hearts, here and all over the world, which will glow long after all traces of the conflagration he has caused in London have been removed."

The American ambassador remained unimpressed. "First of all," he cabled secretly to Roosevelt, "I don't believe that the bombing of the Germans is all indiscriminate. . . They are principally after railroad installations, docks and power plants and regardless of what anybody writes or says they are doing a terrible lot of damage."[22]

But Churchill had assessed the mood of the British well: London could take it.

Lady Spears watched one Cockney woman pick over the wreckage of her home, and heard her exclaim: "I don't fink much of them Germans. Why, if one of 'em should land right 'ere in this street with a parachute, I don't believe I'd even offer 'im a nice cup of tea."[23]

One Whitehall witticism was that the Air Ministry had protested that the Germans were hitting "non-military targets" like the War Office. On Friday the thirteenth the Palace was again dive-bombed: King George glimpsed the two bombs hurtling past his window.

"A magnificent piece of bombing, Ma'am, if you'll pardon my saying so," the duty constable remarked to the Queen.

FEARING THAT THE enemy might have similar designs on No.10, Mr Churchill had taken some precautions since Chamberlain's departure.

Having seen blitzed dwellings in the East End where the whole fabric had pancaked into the basement, the PM was not sanguine about No.10, despite the tiny air raid shelter built below stairs and the reinforced lounge and dining room that had been converted from old offices by putting steel shutters on the windows and shoring up the ceilings. He

---

*Hitler rejected repeated requests by General Hans Jeschonnek, his chief of air staff, to authorize "terror bombing." The most restrictive orders bound German crews. On September 14 the Führer again prohibited "terror attacks" on London's population.[21]

ordered his living quarters shifted to the Annexe — a street level apartment converted from two typists' rooms in the solid government building at Storey's Gate, right above the C.W.R. bunker.

Clementine began to decorate this apartment, with its drawing room, dining room, and study, in pastel shades, and hung paintings and cosy furnishings. Winston began to live here on the sixteenth.

Part of the urgency for the move was inspired by Bletchley. That Friday, September 13, they had intercepted orders for nine hours of very heavy attacks on "a target believed to be London" beginning at six p.m. "If the weather permits," Intelligence warned, "long range bombers will be employed." Shortly a further intercept revealed that the bombing offensive would continue into Saturday morning and probably afternoon as well.

Since the Annexe would not be ready by then, Mr Churchill felt it would be appropriate to leave London; it was nearly the weekend anyway. He again visited Dollis Hill on the way, and upon arrival at Chequers he ordered the evacuation prepared of the first three hundred officials, including the War Cabinet, its secretariat, chiefs of staff committee, and General Brooke's headquarters to this bunker. "Publicity must be forbidden."[24]

Nothing much came of the predicted air raid. Thirty-one Londoners died in scattered bombing. Saturday was also ominously quiet. General Brooke suspected that the invasion scare was a bluff to pin troops down in this country, since Italy's invasion of Egypt had just begun. Churchill drove back to No.10 that afternoon, and spent his first night in the Central War Room bunker.

* * *

His first amphibious landing operation since Namsos was about to begin. A British naval taskforce with General de Gaulle would, he hoped, shortly put ashore 6,000 British marines and French legionaries at Dakar. But there were bad auguries. The British Governor of Nigeria, Sir Bernard Bourdillon, had warned that "General de Gaulle's name cut no ice in West Africa." And six French cruisers loyal to Marshal Pétain had left Toulon on September 9, and steamed out of the Mediterranean.

In fact they were bound for Gaboon, carried no troops, and had no connection with the Dakar operation. The French admiralty had even formally notified the British attaché at Madrid of the sailing, and his "Immediate" signal reached London at 11:50 p.m. on the tenth. It was not drawn to Admiral Pound's attention until the eleventh.

Later, searching for scapegoats, the prime minister would make capital out of this delay. That morning, he presided over the chiefs of staff meeting, and learned that the French squadron had been sighted off Gibraltar. Pound ordered *Renown* to raise steam. At noon-thirty on Thursday the twelfth the Cabinet ordered that a naval squadron confront the cruisers off Casablanca and impede their advance on Dakar — wrongly presumed to be their final destination.

For the next three days Churchill had other occupations on his mind. It was not until he returned to Chequers at four-thirty on Sunday afternoon, September 15, that the bad news hit him: this powerful French cruiser squadron had put into Dakar undetected. *Ark Royal's* aircraft had sighted them there.

It was pure coincidence, of course. But seizing a map of West Africa, Churchill telephoned Downing-street around five-fifteen p.m., ordered his trusty Major Morton to convoke the military staffs: cancel Dakar: and replace it with a landing further south at Conakry, followed by an overland march to the north-east; de Gaulle could then invest Dakar from land while the British blockaded it by sea.[25]

THAT CLEAR, BRIGHT Sunday afternoon 1,000 enemy planes — two hundred of them bombers — had attacked London. Again Churchill must have had warning, because he hurried out to Uxbridge taking Clementine and a private secretary to follow the battle from No.11 Group's bunker.

From a gallery of this totally silent underground room, he watched as Air Vice-Marshal Kenneth Park marshalled twenty-five fighter squadrons for London's defence. Cigar unlit, he thrilled at the vibrant gadgetry — the multicoloured bulbs, the duty officers plotting the avalanche of reports from the fifty thousand members of the Observer Corps and the radar stations tracking the inward march of the enemy formations. The controller that day was a deceptively young-looking R.A.F. officer, Lord Willoughby de Broke.

Park told him afterwards that more than once the switchboard had been overwhelmed; every reserve squadron had been thrown in.

But at 3:50 p.m. the unwavering tone of the All Clear had relieved southern England. It was on Churchill's arrival back at Chequers at about four that he was shocked by the admiralty's report that the French cruisers were inside Dakar. After telephoning his instructions to Morton, he went upstairs for his afternoon siesta.

After three hours of troubled sleep he was wakened by John Martin with an up-date on the war. As he peeled the black silk mask off his eyes he heard Martin's concluding words, spoken in a conscious parody of his own style.

—However, all is redeemed by the air. *We have shot down one hundred and eighty-three.*

Churchill did not investigate that figure too closely. It was a great victory. Hours later he emerged from his study and found his bodyguard, Inspector Thompson, still draped against the door.

"You're tired Thompson," said the PM, putting his arm affectionately round the Scotland Yard man's shoulder. "It will be worth it in the end. We're going to win, you know."

Out in the darkening countryside, England was picking up the pieces of that shattered Sunday. Delayed trains were being slotted back into timetables: unexploded bombs defused: crowds watching as the cadavers were gingerly prised out of a Dornier bomber which had hurtled down onto the roof of Victoria station. True, R.A.F. investigators could find the wrecks of only thirty-five German bombers and twenty-one fighters, which did not add up to 183. But to Churchill it was enough. Back in London on Monday morning he decided he did not like Dollis Hill after all; he sent a note to Sir Edward Bridges, his overworked Cabinet secretary, saying: "The time has not yet come to move."[26]

He also released the cooped-up generals of Roosevelt's secret mission, adjudging that they had seen enough. At four p.m. Sinclair bade them farewell at the station on their way back to Washington DC.

* * *

Churchill's initial instinct to abort Dakar had been right, though for the wrong reasons. On Monday September 16, he drafted an instruction to the commanders of the taskforce, Admiral Sir John Cunningham and General N.M.S. Irwin, to reconsider the whole position with de Gaulle.

"Arrival of French cruisers," he explained, "possibly with troops on board, seems to me to destroy hope of a bloodless capture of Dakar."

Having written this however he retained the draft. "Show me later," he scribbled on it. In Cabinet at mid-day he expressed the hope that this "fiasco" would escape attention. Not anxious to offend Vichy further his colleagues agreed. "The French have forestalled us in Dakar," noted Cadogan afterwards, "and so [it] is off! I cannot truly say I am sorry!"

In the event, Churchill never sent off the signal because the taskforce commanders radioed their opinion that they should go ahead.[27] More tellingly, de Gaulle insisted "personally and formally," in a message which reached Churchill at noon on Tuesday, that the plan proceed. For him, even more than for Mr Churchill, it had become a matter of prestige.

The matter went back to the Cabinet at nine p.m. Cadogan warned that they might be risking another Mers-el-Kébir, even a bloodbath. Recent Intelligence from Senegal was clear: de Gaulle would not be welcome. Eden backed the taskforce commanders, as did a gaunt and ailing Neville Chamberlain.

Mr Churchill, encouraged by this unusual line-up, had the face to remind his colleagues that they had lived to bless the day on which "they had decided" on Mers-el-Kébir. He was appalled by the derision that would greet an expedition returning "with its tail between its legs."

In this vainglorious mood he appointed a new D-day six days hence, and authorized the taskforce to land wherever they thought best.[28]

De Gaulle realized that there would be shooting — that he would be killing fellow Frenchmen — but recklessly accepted this responsibility.

A few doubting voices were heard, pointing to signs that Vichy opinion was tilting in Britain's favour. Churchill dismissed them. "The odds," he cabled to General Smuts on the twenty-first, "are heavily against any serious resistance." Nor was he overlooking the £60m of Belgian and Polish gold "wrongfully held" in Senegal: nor the fine French battleship *Richelieu*. He advised Roosevelt: "We have decided to accept the risk . . . of such action leading to declaration of war by Vichy France."

When Churchill wrote "we", he meant himself: if his Cabinet colleagues were at odds with him they seldom showed it. On the twentieth, the First Sea Lord had written privately, "I have pretty difficult times with W.S.C. occasionally as he is quite impervious to arguments and sweeps them aside as if they did not exist." he mentioned the controversy over the armoured reinforcements being rushed out to Egypt as one such instance. "I felt that it was so vital that these tanks should reach the Middle East that I held out against their going through the Mediterranean." Here, Pound had prevailed. "However," he mistily added, explaining why he so seldom rebelled, "W.S.C. is so magnificent in many ways and the ideal leader of the Nation in these times that one must put up with his idosyncrasies."[29]

STEPPING UP THE bombing, the Germans had begun dropping chunky eight foot naval mines over London. Since these drifted down on parachutes — whatever Hitler's veto on "terror bombing" — they could hardly be aimed with discrimination. Their blast sucked windows and walls outwards, toppling buildings into crowded lower floors. One typical air mine in Battersea blasted fifteen hundred people out of their homes.

Churchill, receiving these reports in his War Room bunker, declared that Hitler was trying terror; he challenged whether the German morale would withstand terror as well as the British. "My inclination is," he minuted Ismay, "that we will drop a heavy parachute mine on German cities for every one he drops on ours;" he suggested they single out

German towns hitherto undamaged.[30]

By so doing, of course, he was returning the strategic initiative to Hitler's hands, but the primal hunger for venegeance was greater than the cool power of logic. As he drove down to Chequers for another weekend he was still mouthing Freudian malevolence towards the Germans, and talked of "castrating the lot."[31]*

Throughout that summer, Churchill had telephoned the Commander-in-Chief of Fighter Command at 7:45 each morning for a briefing on the night's battle and the coming day's prospects. He defined that the C-in-C, Air Chief Marshal Dowding, had a "personal responsibility" for his protection. On September 19 Churchill issued a blanket directive to Fighter Command that during daylight hours there was to be no (Red) air raid alert if just one enemy plane was approaching; London areas were regarded as "sensitive" only when Parliament was sitting — which was not at present the case.[32] The Government and its members were thus in a privileged position now that the raids had begun. Unable or unwilling to flee their city, London's artisan population and their families now surged helplessly into the underground Tube stations, basements and warehouses every night. From four o'clock they stood in line waiting to get in. The shelters were wet, lice-infested, dark; they stank of excreta and urine.

"Saw and smelt the horrible conditions inside," wrote one lady of Churchill's circle who did not usually venture this far east of the Savoy. "It was like a scene from Dante's Inferno." But morale seemed good and, contrary to expectation, "enquiry elicited no sign of anti-Semitism."[33]

A week later, Ambassador Kennedy rendered an uglier picture. "The Government tells me," he told Washington, "they have discovered definite Communistic propaganda being spread during the last three nights in the air raid shelters, and again there is great criticism of the Jews."[34]

His military attaché found out about a "select" shelter under the Dorchester "reserved for Lord Halifax, Duff Cooper and others." The modern hotel was considered bombproof, with shatterproof windows. When the sirens sounded the upper classes assembled in its lower tiers — noble foreign secretary and squinny-eyed minister of information rubbing shoulders with Lord Melchett, Chaim Weizmann, and other wealthy notables like Somerset Maugham, Cicely Courtneidge, Leslie Howard (the film actor and S.I.S. agent), Oliver Stanley and their ladies,

*In May 1945, considering Soviet demands for slave labour from the Germans, Roosevelt's legal adviser Sam Rosenman disclosed that at Yalta the president "even discussed sterilization and more or less in fun had devised a machine to perform the operation on a mass production basis." — Justice Robert H. Jackson's diary, May 12, 1945 (in author's possession.)

all in night attire. "Apparently a lot of jittery people . . . have moved in there," observed Cecil King. "At eleven p.m. [an] astonishing mixed grill of people, mostly women with knitting, assemble in the hall to spend the night."[35]

After being trapped once in their august company the Director of Naval Intelligence would write that — if one did not mind being "thoroughly nauseated by the ways of the rich" — there was no better education than to visit the Aldwych deep Tube shelter, crowded with men, women, and infants, some sleeping slung between the rails in tiny hammocks: and then proceed at once to "the luxurious basement rooms of the Dorchester, where those who could afford it continued to rough it on the softest settees in pleasantly warmed rooms."[36] During the next months it became a public scandal, and lent to the phrase "the Few" a meaning about which Mr Churchill's colleagues — given their own shelters, the War Room bunker and Dollis Hill — could scarcely complain.

THE DAKAR OPERATION was launched at first light on September 23.

It was a humiliating fiasco. The assault forces never got off their troopships. De Gaulle's aviators landed on the airfield and were arrested by the local gendarmerie. His emissaries were fired upon as their boat entered port, and turned back. The *Richelieu*, which Churchill had covetously described to Smuts as "by no means permanently disabled," opened fire through the gathering fog with her new fifteen inch guns, as did the Dakar fortress batteries which hit the cruiser *Cumberland* amidships and put her out of action.

A gloomy Cabinet in London considered these reports at mid-day. De Gaulle was attempting an alternative landing at Rufisque, just to the right of Dakar, but Vichy's cipher messages revealed that the defenders "had been ordered to resist."

By eight p.m. Churchill had word that his taskforce was withdrawing. It was Gallipoli, Namsos, Dunkirk all over again. Frantic at the thought, he wirelessed his commanders that night: "Having begun, we must go on to the end. Stop at nothing."[37] He scrawled a muddled telegram to the White House too. "It looks as if there might be a stiff fight," he told Roosevelt. "Perhaps not, but anyhow orders have been given to ram it through."

The next day's brawling off Dakar was equally messy. The British sank a French submarine, the shore guns savaged *Barham*. On the day after that General Spears, accompanying de Gaulle, radioed that the latter had thrown in the sponge and would proceed to Bathurst, a British colony one hundred miles down the West African coast. At nine a.m. a

French submarine slapped a torpedo into the battleship *Resolution* and she too beat an undignified retreat. Morale among the French defenders was high. Churchill dithered, his ministers demanded they cut their losses.

Just before one-thirty p.m., frustrated and furious, he called the operation off. To Roosevelt he offered an invented excuse for failure: "Vichy got in before us and animated defence with partisans and gunnery experts. All friendly elements were gripped and held down."

He made a similar claim to the House on October 8 — that the six French cruisers had "carried with them a number of Vichy partisans . . . sent to overawe the population, to grip the defences and see to the efficient manning of the powerful shore batteries."

Both claims were lies.[38] The naval staff was shocked, Captain Edwards recorded privately that Winston had blamed "some unspecified naval authority" for the failure.

> There is very little truth in any of his statement. The expedition was ill-conceived & therein lies the whole trouble. W.C. is really the evil genius of the party.

Knowing Churchill as he did, Cadogan wondered where the buck would stop this time. He considered both F.O. and S.I.S. to be blameless as Winston had taken the decision without consulting or informing either. Churchill's reaction to the fiasco was savage and vindictive. He found the first scapegoats in the admiralty. First to feel the lash was the Director of Operations (Foreign) duty officer on the night that those French cruisers had passed through the Straits: Captain Robert Bevan had delayed showing the Madrid attaché's signal to Admiral Pound. True, even when shown it the next morning, Pound had not taken it seriously. But Churchill regarded it as the origin of the disaster.

He demanded exemplary action, but now learned that their Lordships had already notified this officer of their "displeasure."[39] No doubt Pound had issued the mild rebuke to preclude further punishment; but Churchill demanded that nonetheless.

At this even Alexander demurred, fearing, as he warned Churchill, "a sense of injustice in the fleet." Churchill insisted, replying in biting language on October 23: "I consider the officer should be placed on half pay and trust you will be able to meet my wishes."* There was no legal way of penalizing the man twice, and the First Lord put this to Churchill while applying soothing libations of oily words. "I am sure," he wheedled, "you know that there is nothing that I would like to do more than to meet your wishes at all times."[40]

---

*There was an identical scene at Hitler's headquarters in November 1942 when a plea for help from Rommel was withheld from him overnight; he equally unjustly ordered the dismissal of the O.K.W. general concerned, Walter Warlimont.

Thwarted here, Churchill hurled his barbs at Gibraltar instead, at Admiral Sir Dudley North, Flag Officer commanding North Atlantic — known to the Lower Deck as "Don't-do-it Dudley." Churchill blamed him for letting the French cruiser squadron through.

In mid-October the First Sea Lord notified Admiral North that he had lost "their Lordships' confidence," and dismissed him. True, the same Admiral Pound had written him earlier that year in terms of the warmest confidence;[41] true, he had thwarted Winston's recent desire to dismiss North for daring to criticize Mers-el-Kébir. True, moreover, North could argue that after that massacre the admiralty had specifically directed him that, "if and only if" Britain became involved in war with France, were inferior forces to be stopped and ordered into British controlled ports;[42] true, also, that as recently as September 22, *after* the French cruiser incident, Pound had written him a further amiable letter. If somebody had now prevailed on him to make a scapegoat of North, that can only have been Churchill.

North was dismissed. But that was not the end of the story. He pressed repeatedly to be honourably court-martialled. In November 1943 he wrote to Pound's successor asking for the case to be reopened. A.V. Alexander intercepted and halted the letter. After the war, supported by five admirals of the fleet, North called for his name to be cleared.

During Churchill's second administration in 1954 the Official History magnificently lifted the slur from the Admiral's name, but it was not until 1958 that Sir Winston's successor discharged him entirely of the allegation of dereliction of duty.

* * *

From Australia's far-sighted prime minister Robert Menzies came a vehement protest at the manner in which Churchill had authorized Dakar without consulting the Dominions.[43] And the fiasco rendered American intervention less likely than ever. Journeying to Dover with H.R. Knickerbocker two days after he called it off, Churchill admitted that it had been "unfortunate."

Their conversation turned to American isolationism. "Your entry into the war," remarked Churchill to the American journalist, "would change history."

"I should have liked it a little better," admitted Knickerbocker, "if the bargain over the destroyers had not been so one sided."

"The vessels are so old," admitted Churchill, off the record, "they would not be used by anybody except in extremity such as ours . . . dire extremity."[44]

At nine p.m. that evening Ambassador Kennedy cabled his dismal views to Washington. "The Dakar situation," he informed Roosevelt, "is a bitter pill for the entire Cabinet." Newspapers had not spared with criticism. "It is the first real break in the Churchill popularity."

Kennedy warned that production was falling, regardless of what reports the president might be getting. Churchill was "hoping and praying every minute that something will happen that will bring the United States in."

> I cannot impress upon you strongly enough my complete lack of confidence in the entire conduct of this war.

"If by any chance," the ambassador continued, "we should ever come to the point of getting into this war we can make up our minds that it will be the United States against Germany, Italy and Japan, aided by a badly shot to pieces country which in the last analysis can give little, if any, assistance to [the] cause. It breaks my heart to draw these conclusions about a people that I sincerely hoped might be victorious but I cannot get myself to the point where I believe they can be of any assistance to the cause in which they are involved. Kennedy."[45]

CHAPTER 34

The Fixer

BRENDON BRACKEN WAS a self-educated Irish bachelor with carrot red hair and a tongue and temperament to match. Brash and ambitious, he had wormed his way into Churchill's confidence at twenty-two and clung on through the wilderness, earning Winston's undying loyalty while harvesting Clementine's disdain.

The two men had much in common: both sought solace in the bottle, both were bold and imaginative liars, both were driven by the same lust for power over the lives and destinies of their fellow humans. They inspired fierce hatreds too. When Bracken lost his seat after the war, Hugh Dalton would smirk to an American diplomat that Labour had got rid of him, a "most malevolent influence upon Mr Churchill" and a "force for evil" who was "not even good enough to black his boots." Like Winston's other enigmatic aide Desmond Morton, Bracken would leave no papers: he gave orders to burn them on his death.

He talked with an unstoppable booming voice, though never about his past. We know that he entered Sedbergh after writing out his own cheque for the first term's fees and claiming to be of school age, and we know that he died a viscount in 1958. By twenty-eight he had founded one banking newspaper and bought two more — *The Economist* and *Financial Times*. A year later he was an MP.

By the time of the Battle of Britain he was turning forty but the venom lingered on. He was "Winston's jackal" and rumoured — to the distress of Mrs Churchill, whom he nonchalantly addressed as "Clemmie" — to be Winston's bastard son as well, a fiction which Winston took pains not to deny. He included Bracken in his favours; he had unsuccessfully pressed Chamberlain to appoint Bracken to the ministry of information[1] and upon becoming PM he had bullied the King into appointing Bracken to the Privy Council although he had held no office of state — Churchill claimed that Bracken's unswerving support was service enough and he had his way.

Brusque and dogmatic, Bracken seldom came out to weekend at

Chequers — it was Clementine's domain. But he ministered to Winston with something like the wiles of a spouse, taking care to delay the breaking of bad news until after the PM had spent a restful night. He won powerful influence over him, being a fount of boisterous optimism even when the PM's spirits were at low ebb; he would chide him, "Now you are behaving like Mr Sparrow," a petulant bird featuring in a Sunday newspaper. He was a connoisseur of his own wit, and did not care who knew it. He heartlessly mocked even Churchill's most intimate companions. He dubbed Anthony Eden "Robert Taylor," meaning this comparison with the film actor unkindly. On making Bracken's acquaintance one Canadian statesman was struck by his evident knowledgeability. "He talked straight ahead all the time," wrote that observer in a diary, "having I think at least five if not six different drinks of Scotch."[2] Another noted that Bracken was rarely sober after eleven p.m.; was "partly alcoholic"; and was "another victim of the PM's passion for late hours and alcohol."[3]

He had become Churchill's right hand man, tirelessly managing internal affairs while Winston directed his war. Drawing on Bracken's encyclopædic memory Churchill turned to him when he had to appoint, patronize, promote or honour. While Churchill rigged his ministerial and military apparatus, Bracken was the fixer of Church and Civil Service. Bracken would reveal to the startled Canadian premier that he was the one who made ecclesiastical recommendations and drew up the honours lists.

"D'you want to make the whole honours list a joke and farce?" snorted Churchill, seeing that he had marked a BBC announcer for the Order of the British Empire. "I'll see this never happens as long as there's an England. Announcers!" Then, after a pause — "Well, I suppose I can't be responsible for what happens when I'm gone, but I'll take very good care to leave a paragraph about it in my last will and testament."[4]

* * *

To Winston, Bracken was as much "family" as his four grown up children. And like many dictators he bestowed a shameless favouritsm on his kin which provoked incredulity and anger among the less fortunate. Clementine long-stopped the worst excesses — like when she prevented one infant Churchill from being evacuated to Canada at the height of the blitz.

Except for the youngest daughter Mary, all his children suffered from this patronage. Mary was sent out of London to the Norfolk countryside, and then more permanently to Chequers. But Sarah's marriage to comedian Vic Oliver was already steering toward distant rocks: her Viennese-born husband had opted for American citizenship to avoid nationality problems. Diana had married an able artillery officer, Duncan Sandys, who as an MP had fought in the House on Winston's behalf before the war. Sandys suffered little from having a powerful father-in-law, accompanying him on his foreign trips as First Lord, although neither he nor Randolph had real cause to be in Paris, when Winston was attending the Supreme War Council.

Winston had spoiled his only son rotten: by 1940, Randolph was pugnacious and articulate, but wilting in his father's reflected glory. A handsome man with clever gray eyes and thinning, sandy hair, he would pay for his father's indulgent folly for the rest of his life. He became a raucous know-all, a strident and often alcoholic critic of government policy and strategy whenever at his father's table. Winston smiled on his son's unmannered bickering, but every guest at Chequers or No.10 winced at it anew.

Since Randolph had split the Tory vote at one pre-war election and supported Sandys' opponent at another, he had not been acceptable as a Tory candidate until now. But in 1940 his father was PM, and the son was given Preston and returned unopposed to Parliament. Winston introduced him on October 8 to loud if not unanimous applause.

The muttering was often audible. When he shortly announced a further appointment for his son, a Conservative who had won his seat the hard way challenged his qualifications for the job and added under his breath to loud titters, "And what has Mr Vic Oliver done to be left out!" Churchill purpled with anger and bore down on him afterwards. A Labour legislator saw the PM's knuckles whiten as his tiny fists clenched, then be brought himself under control and stumped out.[5]

HITLER'S ANGRY SWITCH in target strategy had saved Britain's fighter defences, but had cost seven thousand lives in London during September. Low in spirit, grumbling about de Gaulle, and still smarting from Dakar, Churchill retreated to Chequers and reconstructed his government. Bracken now emerged more clearly as Winston's "fixer," often blueprinting the changes, and leaving Churchill to rubber-stamp them. The PM provided the personal touch: he invited the fast fading Neville Chamberlain to accept the Order of the Garter as a parting flourish to this old friend and enemy. But the peace-loving politician stood on his dignity, remarked modestly that he preferred to die "plain Mr Chamberlain" like his famous father, and rejected this honour just like the peerage Winston had previously offered.[6]

It was Chamberlain's resignation as Lord President of the Council that had permitted this reshuffle. For a while Churchill tried to shoehorn Anthony Eden back into the Foreign Office; he would prove more complaisant in Cabinet than Halifax. (Attlee, appraising Eden dismissively, would later say, "He's got no status of his own. He's only a Private Secretary to the PM."") Churchill suggested to Halifax that he transfer to Chamberlain's former office: Lord President was, he suggested unconvincingly, the second position in the government.[8]

Undeceived, Halifax recommended the present home secretary instead, remarking that Sir John Anderson had the same kind of orderly mind as Neville — "which I don't think Anthony has." It was true that the East End population disliked Anderson, feeling that he was a dry old stick; besides, in their present plight, they wanted a man of their own class. Beaverbook had the idea of giving the Home Office to the Cockney politician Herbert Morrison, currently minister of supply. Winston had little liking for this Socialist minister but agreed.

At Bracken's suggestion he now offered Morrison's old job to Beaverbrook; but the minister of aircraft production declined with the usual pathetic recital of woes — his crippling asthma brought him a procession of sleepless nights.

When the music stopped, the game left Halifax and Eden in the same ministerial chairs as before. On the last day of September Churchill sent for Eden and apologized; knowing what really mattered to the young man, he reassured him however, that Anderson was not in the running for the succession as PM. Eden sent over two hopeful messages brimming with higher aspirations but heard nothing more until after midnight when Churchill sent for him again. Eden arrived hotfoot in pyjamas only to hear Winston dismiss his two "very sweet letters, generous and worthy of the occasion" and order him to stay on at the War Office.

Before letting him out into Downing-street again, Churchill reassured the young pretender: "We shall work this war together."

* * *

Everybody had joined in the game — Bracken, Lindemann, even Churchill's secretaries. John Colville recorded on October 2 that there would also be changes in the plodding chiefs of staff, and in the navy because of the unchecked merchant shipping losses. Eric Seal talked with the Prof and wrote to Winston on the third about ways of counteracting the "menace of night bombing." By this he meant personnel changes, and mentioned one officer by name: "Dowding," said this secretary, "has the reputation of being very conservative, and of not being receptive to new ideas." That said, Seal referred to the Admiralty as needing "galvanizing" in the anti-submarine campaign."

I do hope that you will forgive this note, but I always said that I would speak plainly when I felt strongly.[9]

Disgruntled air marshals and a small number of fighter pilots had begun campaigning against keeping the over-age "Stuffy" Dowding at Fighter Command. It had been a long battle.[10] Since August 1938, when the Air Council first notified him that he was due to retire a year later, he had four times been informed that he was to leave and four times reprieved. In July 1940 Newall formally proposed he retire at the end of October. "Before the war," replied Dowding haughtily, who now asked to stay on until 1942, "I should have been glad enough to retire; now I am anxious to stay." Nobody would fight like him, he said (recalling the fraught Cabinet meetings of May and June) when "proposals are made which would reduce the defence forces of the country below the extreme danger point." Newall however felt obliged to lever the more senior officers out of office, in order, as he apologized to Dowding on July 13, to maintain an adequate flow of promotions.

This was what Churchill very aptly called Buggins' Turn. "Personally," he had written to Sinclair, "I think he is one of the very best men you have got." He had invited the commander down to see him on the thirteenth. "Last night the Prime Minister asked me to dine at Chequers," Dowding wrote triumphantly to Sinclair. "He was good enough to tell me that I had secured his confidence, and that he wished me to remain on the Active List for the time being without any date for my retirement being fixed." He assured the seething politician that he had done nothing to bring this about. Another month passed, and it would be the very eve of Eagle Day, August 12, before Newall grudgingly wrote him that circumstances had changed in his favour. "It has been decided," he wrote, "to cancel the time limit to the period of your appointment as C-in-C, Fighter Command."

This unleashed a political witchhunt against Sir Cyril Newall. In mid-August a woman MP sent to No.10 an anonymous report accusing the air chief marshal of weakness in tolerating Dowding despite his slow brain and mental inadequacy, and for procrastinating over the replacement of Ludlow Hewitt by Sir Charles Portal at Bomber Command. Churchill gingerly forwarded this ugly document* with a scribbled minute instructing Archie Sinclair, "Let me have this back."[11] Sinclair did nothing. He was completely in the PM's pocket, a weak and loathsome Liberal subaltern, and Churchill treated him with only bantering levity and bullied him mercilessly to get his way. Not receiving,

---

*It was probably originated by Beaverbrook — there is a copy in his papers. After one Dorchester dinner party in September an American colonel made a note of the "dwarfish and prickly" Beaverbrook's obvious dislike of both Newall and Sinclair. When Newall was posted to New Zealand as Governor General, the same colonel wrote: "I am sure the moving spirit in ousting him is Beaverbrook, to whom Newall never conceded an inch; and he is a violent, passionate, malicious and dangerous little goblin."[12]

any reply the woman MP sent a further copy to Bracken on the day of the first September mass air raid on London, and this time she urged Newall's replacement by Sir Charles Portal. Bracken took the matter up, and his influence was evidently the clincher, because Sinclair had only recently told the nagging MP that Newall enjoyed Churchill's confidence. On October 4 Portal would replace him as chief of the Air Staff.

"Peter" Portal would remain effortlessly in this position until the end of the war. This beaky air chief marshal was ineffably boring and unsociable, but had undoubtedly impressed by his willingness to fall in with Churchill's grand strategy. He was a decade younger than Dill or Pound and a beaver for hard work. He avoided small talk, as though he had no family or private life at all. He was unreasonable, callous and inconsiderate. He barked orders at his female secretaries as though they were squaddies paraded before him. But he had a clinical efficiency which appealed to the prime minister. Like Chaim Weizmann, Duff Cooper and others deemed irreplaceable, Sir Charles Portal was found a billet in the bombproof Dorchester.

The reshuffle virtually complete, on October 3 Churchill invited his junior colleagues to meet him at Dollis Hill, to see the bunker accommodation. "A meeting of Ministers, to whom PM explains present situation," dictated one, Hugh Dalton into his diary afterwards.

> Invasion "menace" still remains and will, so long as Germans have in that long row of ports transport enough to put half a million men on board and in the Channel and North Sea on any night they choose. But, as the weather breaks and the season advances, the invasion must surely seem to them more and more difficult. (It seems clear that it was definitely projected for September 15, but that at the last minute they decided that they had better not.) As my driver says his daughter says, "Hitler's got the words, but he can't get the music right."

"I had a date with the PM after this Ministers' meeting, at which I wished to speak to him on S.O.E. . . . and then leave documents with him. But he asks me to 'let him off' until next week, being pressed and weary, though smiling and friendly."[13] They celebrated this rare visit to the bunker with what the PM called "a vivacious luncheon," then he returned to No.10. In his absence a sense of calm had descended which historians can compare with the equal tranquillity which enveloped Hitler's headquarters each time he too departed for the front. "John Martin and I remained alone at No.10," Colville recorded that day, "dealing placidly with our business." They missed the ringing of the PM's bell and the general "atmosphere of rush."

In the seven days prior to October 21 Hitler's airforce had killed 1,700 in London in response to Bomber Command's attacks on

Germany. Even the Dorchester now offered little luxury. Dining with a blissfully hard-of-hearing Lord Halifax on the sixth floor, Cadogan deprecated the accompaniment of 4.5-inch guns which, he wrote with uncustomary hyperbole, "knock the glasses off the table, tear your eyebrows out and snap your braces."[14] Numbed resignation descended on the less privileged, even though shelter conditions were improving. Scouring the Tubes with the *Daily Mirror* editor, a newspaper proprietor found them now orderly and odour-free — "Not many children," he wrote privately, "a good many Jews and a few youths." Most of the occupants were middle-aged, middle class women, "surprisingly steady and almost contented."[15]

CHURCHILL EXPLOITED this perverse contentment, intoning ceaselessly against Hitler's barbarism and visiting the provinces to display his own portly presence to the people there. The newsreels show him stumping through the shattered streets acknowledging cheers and perching on the back of a car, the better that the crowds might see him. Despite the unhappy circumstances, he was enjoying the limelight. When he hoisted his headgear aloft on his walking stick he was in his element.

His hats were his trademark: they were fitted by the best hatter in town. Like a jealous woman, he would rather die than appear in a hat that anybody else was sporting. At the historic siege of Sidney Street everybody had worn top hats or army headgear — Winston wore a bowler. Motoring out in 1926 he and Baldwin had both chosen gray trilbies — Churchill turned his back to front. For his visit to the Monterey peninsula in 1929 he had bought a *ten* gallon Stetson. He had tried five kinds of trilby, three of topper, two each of bowler and Panama, a naval cocked hat, an Irishman's "Paddy" hat with claypipe, an Oxford degree cap, an army pillbox, a Hussar's busby, caps with and without peaks, an artist's beret, and now a tin hat too.[16]

Now that he was PM and Britain was "in peril" he became downright flamboyant. A strange new fashion in outer apparel was added to the hats: When the foppish Eden — no Mrs Grundy himself when it came to haute couture — arrived for dinner in the newly strengthened basement at No.10, Winston strutted in wearing his new airforce-blue siren suit. With its full-length frontal zipper it was like a baby's giant rompers. (Once, the zip fly came undone, but he reassured an alarmed visitor: "Madam, a dead bird never falls out of its nest.")

Something — perhaps the impending resignation of Chamberlain as Party leader — had evidently pleased him because he was in a rare humour. He harangued the cat he had shanghaied from the admiralty and evoked roars of laughter from Eden and secretary Colville when he rebuked Nelson for jumping at the gunfire. "Try to remember what those boys in the R.A.F. are doing," guffawed Churchill to the apprehensive feline.[17]

"This exhilarates me," he confided to General Sir Frederick Pile that month, touring the experimental rocket and searchlight sites. "The sound of these cannon gives me a tremendous feeling."[18] London's ancient acres were being methodically wrecked. The factories were tangled ruins, the workers' graveyards filling. Winston demanded that his Londoners like this kind of war. "Sitting in his siren suit," recorded Colville, straightfaced, on October 12, "and smoking an immense cigar, he said he thought this was the sort of war which would suit the English people once they got used to it." They preferred, he claimed, to be in the front line of battle in London than to look on passively at "mass slaughters" like Passchendaele.[19]

After one nocturnal tour of Pile's gunsites he returned to Downing-street at five a.m. — frisky from the boom of the cannon and the inadvertantly neat whisky which a colonel had pressed into his hand — rapped on the door of No.10 with his walking stick, and announced to the butler: "Göring and Goebbels coming to report!" followed by a stentorian aside: "*I* am not Goebbels." Like a schoolboy in a dormitory feast, he plied the General with Bovril meat extract and sardines, and then showed him out.[20]

NEVILLE CHAMBERLAIN HAD succeeded Baldwin as Party leader in 1937. Now that he was resigning, Churchill agonized over whether to claim the leadership or remain above Party. He asked Clementine. She loathed the Party, and warned that accepting would alienate the working class. But Beaverbrook counselled against letting the leadership fall into the wrong hands and on October 9 he was formally elected Tory leader. The newspapers reported his speech of acceptance the next day.

> My life, such as it has been, has been lived for forty-five years in the public eye, and very varying opinions are entertained about it and about particular phases in it. I shall attempt no justification. I have always faithfully served two public causes which I think stand supreme — the maintenance of the enduring greatness of Britain and her Empire (*applause*) and the historical continuity of our island life.[21]

Like Hitler, he devoured newspapers. They were brought down to Chequers by despatch rider, even flown out to him at Cairo by plane. A Berlin newspaper report on a man who swindled soldier's widows would result in a swift decision by Hitler upgrading the mild penalty to death; a Fleet-street item about firemen convicted of looting, would produce the opposite reaction in Churchill, perhaps since liquor was involved.

"Five years' penal servitude for stealing whisky . . . seems out of proportion," he rebuked the new home secretary. His biographer tells us without comment that a few months later Mr Churchill protested at a five year prison sentence imposed on a woman for observing that "Hitler was a good ruler, a better man than Mr Churchill." This seemed to him "unduly harsh" punishment for expressing an opinion, "however pernicious."[22]

Nor was the press spared the PM's displeasure. To him all journalists were "filthy Communists" and as dangerous as the fascists he had locked up. True, they had raucously applauded those arrests, but soon he would have offending columnists transferred to the colours and close down recalcitrant publications. Fleet-street was contemptuous about Dakar, and on October 6 the *Sunday Pictorial* powerfully attacked the recent reshuffle. At Monday's Cabinet Churchill, still casting about for scapegoats, boiled over onto the "scurrilous" tabloid press. Brandishing the *Pictorial* and a column by Cassandra, the immortal, incorruptible William Connor, from the *Daily Mirror*, he blared that these attacks on him were a dangerous and sinister attempt to prepare the country for a surrender peace. He wanted to prosecute the editors but the Attorney General poured cold water on his urge, warning that the government had no case.

Churchill winced. He considered he was of almost papal holiness if not infallibility. It was not right, he grumbled, that someone bearing his responsibilities should have to put up with attacks like these. Willing to wound but afraid to strike, he prodded Attlee — whom he himself would later dub "that sheep in sheep's clothing" — into giving Fleet Street's editors a verbal dressing down.[23] Attlee summoned the proprietors and with the utmost sheepishness hinted at a possible censorship of news *and* views. A few months later Churchill, still writhing, would return to the attack.

* * *

At that Monday morning Cabinet Churchill fulminated against the navy too. The First Lord had remarked, according to Dalton's notes, that he was superseding Dudley North.[24] "Since 1923," Desmond Morton related to Dalton a few days later, echoing Churchill, "every sailor who made even the slightest mistake was axed. The result is that now all the senior officers are men who have never made a mistake and are therefore quite incapable of action!"[25]

Sir Charles Forbes, Commander-in-Chief of the Home Fleet, would be the next to go. He was one of the soundest admirals, but Admiral Cunningham would write later: "Winston and Brendan Bracken disliked him."[26] Some said that he was too old, others that he was a bad tactician.[27] He seldom put to sea escorted by fewer than eight destroyers, while the luckless *Glorious* had been provided with only two.[28] Pound believed that Forbes had lost the confidence of the Fleet.[29]

Forbes's final downfall was disagreement that summer over the big ships. It was obvious that there would be no invasion, but Churchill wanted them stationed to the east and south because of the invasion scare; Forbes refused to denude the Atlantic convoys and made a "final appeal" to this effect on September 28. In mid October he was replaced by Jack Tovey, and the fifty-five year old new Commander-in-Chief, Home Fleet, was invited down to Chequers for the weekend. After this extraordinary encounter with the PM Tovey wrote two letters describing it. The first was to the First Lord, violating all the rules, on October 9, attempting to explain what he had said "when undergoing the test in agility of intellect and resoluteness of spirit" at Chequers. "One or two of the Prime Minster's remarks," Tovey wrote to A.V. Alexander, "particularly when he said during the after-dinner discussion on developing our offensive in the Near East that like everyone else I was all for one of the other services doing the job, showed very clearly a complete misunderstanding of our ideas in the Mediterranean. . ." A few days later he wrote to Admiral Cunningham, still expressing astonishment at the PM's remarks. "He made some such astounding statements about naval warfare [that] I still don't know if he was wanting to find out if I was prepared to applaud everything he said or whether he really believes half what he says." At one point the PM referred to Admiral Cunningham's "pussy-footing" around with the French admiral at Alexandria in July. Tovey found that raw but made no comment. Churchill said he liked outspokenness, but when Tovey pluckily rejected his accusation that the heads of the armed forces were to blame for their sorry state in 1939 he rose and swept out with a tongue-clucking First Lord in his wake. Winston was so taken aback that for a few days he reconsidered his decision and even ordered Tovey back to the Mediterranean. But he relented, and Tovey assumed command a few weeks later.[30] The Battle of the Atlantic was entering a painful phase. The Germans had sunk two million tons of shipping since Britain declared war on them. In October they sank fourteen ships in one convoy and sixteen in another and losses like these preyed on Winston's mind.[31]

* * *

General Sir Alan Brooke had also been invited to "dine and sleep" at Chequers that remarkable weekend. After sitting up with Winston until two a.m. he wrote: "PM in great form," and marvelled at his vitality and the way he bore his heavy burden. "It would be impossible to find a man to fill his place at present."[32]

Something of Churchill's greatness came out in the case of Major-General P.C.S. Hobart. Hobart was slated for retirement, charged with being hot-tempered and narrow minded, despite his wide expert knowledge and drive. "Such prejudices," Churchill wrote, perhaps thinking of his own past fortunes, "attach frequently to persons of strong personality and original view." Hobart's controversial views on tank design had now been confirmed, he pointed out. "We cannot afford to confine Army appointments to persons who had excited no hostile comments in their career."[33] "Remember," he would rebuke General Dill when the Hobart case came up again, "it isn't only the good boys who help to win wars. It is the sneaks and stinkers as well."[34] Hobart was reappointed, raised two armoured divisions, and commanded them with great distinction. To a family friend visiting Chequers on his return from Dakar Churchill would give this advice — even if he did not always follow it himself: "Carry a little slate with you and wipe it regularly clean of all grudges."[35]

That Saturday evening, October 12, Chequers teemed with Churchills. Clemmie was showing off their first grandson, born to Randolph the day before. Winston was visibly nervous about air raids. "Probably they don't think I am so foolish as to come here," Colville quoted him, writing in his vivid diary. "But I stand to lose a lot. Three generations at a swoop." Hearing of more heavy bombing of London and of damage done to the War Office, he commented that frequenting Chequers was tempting providence. He decided to spend future weekends, when air raids seemed likely, at some other country estate.

* * *

With less than his usual honesty, Winston had announced to the House in October that Bomber Command was attacking only military targets. In secret he pressed Portal for more widespread attacks. "Remember this!" he lectured his staff, "Never maltreat the enemy by halves. Once the battle is joined let 'em have it."[36] Six months later his colleagues would endorse his deceit, ruling that the government need never reveal that their bombing was killing German civilians. "It was better," the Cabinet minutes recorded, "that actions should speak louder than words in this matter."[37] After Sunday lunch on the thirteenth, puffing his cigar and sprawling in his new rompers, the PM pontificated to Sir Charles Portal and "Stuffy" Dowding: "A Hun alive," he defined, "is a war in prospect."[38]

The corollary was to kill as many as possible. With his own role in the bombing of London clearly uppermost in mind, he adivsed Lord Halifax to discourage the International Red Cross from monitoring the British and Nazi air offensives. "It would simply result," he claimed, "in a committee under German influence or fear, reporting at the very best that it was six of one and half-a-dozen of the other. It is even very likely they would report that we had committed the major breaches." And he added, "Even if Germany offered to stop the bombing now, we should not consent to it. Bombing of military objectives, increasingly widely interpreted, seems at present our main road home."[39]

He returned reluctantly to Downing-street on the fourteenth. Dining that night in the fortified rooms, behind windows protected with steel shutters, he heard a bomb detonate in the Horse Guards Parade. On an instinct, he left the table and directed the cook and downstairs servants to the shelter. His secretary John Martin galloped down and jumped in on top of them just as a second bomb hit the Treasury next door. The kitchen's plate-glass window which had not been provided with shutters was blasted inwards in a shower of glass, timber, masonry and the sooty grime of centuries. The blast left the doors dangling drunkenly on broken hinges and curtains and chairs hurled about the rooms. The bomb had killed one man in the Treasury. Donning a tin hat, Bracken went over in a dressing gown to ascertain his name, and in a typical act of generosity anonymously sent the widow money.[40]

Standing on the roof that night, Churchill watched the fading dazzle of incendiaries replaced by the flicker of flames rising from Pall Mall and Piccadilly. Clubland was in flames, not that he was a clubbable man. His secretary telephoned the Reform. "The Club is *burning*, sir," the hall porter evenly replied. Afterwards, Winston visited the charred wreckage of the Carlton. The severed marble head of William Pitt the Younger, his predecessor at the time of Waterloo, lay tumbled on the threshhold. The dining room tables were littered with unfinished meals and wine. It was like Pompeii, or perhaps less civilized.

* * *

Eden would have hated the scene had he been in England. Still secretary of war, he had left for Egypt, bitten by the travel bug, and it would be November before he returned. He toured the Empire reinforcements and conferred with General Wavell at Cairo. Worried at the weakness of the desert airforce he cabled asking for reinforcements, and added in the message which reached Churchill on the sixteenth, "Politically [the] whole situation here would be immeasurably improved if you were able to gain some military success."

Churchill had nothing planned just yet. He was happy to have Eden out of the way. "We are considering how to meet your needs," he replied. "Meanwhile continue to master the local situation. Do not hurry your return." Eden dutifully took his time, dawdling in the Western Desert, attending to his suntan and bathing in the clear blue sea; he wondered how long they could bluff the Italians opposing them in the Middle East. Meanwhile other ministers were learning of the reason for Churchill's confidence. "The rumour grows," wrote one minister with access to Intelligence, "through various telegrams and other agencies, that the Germans may attack the Russians in the spring."[41] The F.O. considered it now "*very* doubtful" that England would be invaded.[42]

Since July Churchill had sat on his private Intelligence that the invasion was bluff. He needed it to entrench his position. There was enough fluff floating over the Channel to feed the woolly minded, and it remains enigmatic that the Germans should have used high level ciphers to carry deception material. Less perplexing is Churchill's misleading of his own public and the Americans. As the Director of Naval Intelligence would observe, "There is nothing new in a dictator seizing an exclusive source of Intelligence, using it as his own, and producing it in a spectacular way at his selected moment — or even withholding it."[43]

Military Intelligence continued to fatten its file on "German preparations for Invasion" with intercepts reporting the enciphered queries, movement orders, embarkation exercises, and timetable instructions that showed that preparations for invasion were being pursued.[44] The director of Naval Intelligence discounted them. The Germans had always backed up deception plans with something that could be observed, like bombers shifted to Bremen or divebombers to Belgium and the barges along the Channel coast were no exception. The invasion was off, he would later write, and "we knew it in October." This certainty is reflected in F.O. documents. Lord Halifax notified a British embassy on the twenty-fourth, "Though Hitler has enough shipping in the Channel to put half a million men on to salt water — or into it, as Winston said the other day — it really does seem as if the invasion of England has been postponed for the present."[45]

Churchill periodically brandished the Nazi invasion threat at Roosevelt, and he used it to turn aside Dominion anger at lack of consultation too. In one angry riposte to Robert Menzies, he wrote, "We have had to face the threat of invasion here."[46] He cajoled the president that the danger was still not past. "The gent has taken off his clothes," he said, "and put on his bathing suit, but the weather is getting colder and there is an autumn nip in the air."[47] Three weeks later he routinely upheld the illusion, telling Washington: "I do not think the invasion danger is yet at an end."[48] On January 28 he would still be saying it to Roosevelt: "All my information shows that the Germans are persevering in their preparations to invade this country, and we are getting ready."

A painful affair momentarily diverted Churchill's attention. His former private secretary Robert Boothby, who had represented East Aberdeen for the Tories since 1924 and was now a junior minister, had recently come under scrutiny for accepting in 1939 what looked like a dishonest payment from a Czech financier of "dubious character."[49] He was a close friend and banker of this man, Richard Weininger, until the latter's arrest — in Boothby's apartment — and internment as an alien under Regulation 18b. Boothby protested to Churchill, but Weininger's files disclosed cash inducements that he had offered to the MP. Boothby had subsequently delivered a powerful speech on the Czechoslovakia (Financial Claims and Refugees) Bill in January 1940, arguing against repatriating Czech assets held in London to Prague.

The background was this: by 1938 the flamboyant politician was in the clutches of moneylenders but had obtained a five thousand pound loan from Sir Alfred Butt. That summer he had visited Dr Benes and urged him to fight; on the morning after Munich, Weininger and a Dr Jansa of the Czech legation had consulted him about raising a loan for their country. In the following January Weininger had sought more personal help in getting payment of his claims against Prague from Czech assets frozen in London. He promised Boothby a percentage and handed over one thousand pounds on account of expenses. That was all that Boothby would ever receive from the Czechs, although in one letter found in Weininger's files Boothby had grandiloquently reassured Butt: "I am, at the moment, the possessor of assets amounting to approximately £20,000 in the form of cash and bonds in Prague."

Subsequently he had become ensnared in a committee representing similar Czech claimants in London.[50] One of the largest claimants, Dr Walter Petschek, complained that this committee's lawyer had written implying that they were acting for the Treasury and threatened penalties if he declined their help. Petschek showed the letter to the authorities, and it was Boothby who got the blame.

It was a disturbing case. To make it worse, Boothby had recently written Churchill indelicately telling him how to run the war. The PM summoned him to No.10 and savaged the document so aggressively that Boothby interrupted. "You are a bully," he said, "and you've always been a bully. But there's one person you'll never bully and that's me." He left slamming the Cabinet room door.[51] Lloyd George buttonholed him afterwards. "Winston's trying to destroy you," he said. "You're not the first, and you won't be the last."

On October 17 Churchill moved that a Select Committee investigate his old friend's conduct. Since his own pre-war Focus had been partly financed by the Czechs, he might well reflect that there but for the Grace of God went he, were he not now drawing substantial emoluments from His Majesty instead.* Defending himself before the House a few weeks later the MP argued that he had dealt no differently than many other members. Churchill dropped a powerful hint that he leave the public gaze. "There are paths of service open in war time," he declared, in his speech, "which are not open in times of peace; and some of these paths may be paths to honour."⁵² Boothby declined to relinquish his seat, but joined the R.A.F. as adjutant of a bomber squadron.

* * *

In the second week of October, enemy bombing had killed 1,500 Londoners. There was no sure defence for those without country retreats. In a typical incident, an apartment block in Stoke Newington collapsed, burying several hundred people; water flooded the basement and drowned the survivors.

On the sixteenth a bomb wrecked more of the Treasury killing four men, and concussing No.10. The hallowed Cabinet room was untouched and the reinforced basement still seemed strong enough, but Bracken prophesied that No.10 was doomed. Several minor colleagues wrote begging Winston to take care.⁵³ He was undaunted. Members that day espied him in his second home, the smoking room at the House, sipping port in a leather armchair and burbling greetings to all who passed. Harold Nicolson asked himself whether it was just a pose, but concluded it was not. Another member, Robert Cary, approached him about the public outcry for reprisals against German cities. Churchill took another swig of port, and glared at Cary. "My dear sir," he said, "this is a military and not a civilian war. You and others may desire to kill women and children. We desire — and have succeeded in our desire — to destroy German military objectives." As an afterthought, he added, taking another swig, "My motto is business before pleasure."

In pleasant ignorance of the Cabinet's less august decisions, the Lobby-fodder marvelled. "That was a man!" reflected Nicolson as he sauntered out.⁵⁴

Dining at Chequers that weekend was Sir Richard Peirse, Portal's successor at Bomber Command. They planned their new offensive against Germany's cities. Churchill could write to Chamberlain that Sunday, accurately enough, that in switching the attack to London Hitler had made a "tremendous mistake." In endeavouring to intimidate the

---

*His pay as PM was £10,000 p.a. or £3,873 post-tax.

population the enemy had "only infuriated" them.[55] But he missed the obvious corollary that what was a mistake for Hitler must be a mistake for Churchill too. That same day he ordered Portal — without reference to Sinclair as secretary of air — to attack enemy towns and morale. He demanded raids on Germany regardless of accuracy, utilizing training and other substandard crews. "The Ruhr, of course, is obviously indicated." he suggested, "The object would be to find easy targets, short runs and safe conditions."[56]

Portal baulked at this proposal. But he did command the Air Staff to devise new bomber tactics, attacking civilian morale more directly for the next few months. At the end of the month they issued to Bomber Command a new directive: in future fire-raising planes would lead the attack, followed by regular bomber squadrons who would prevent the fire services from extinguishing the conflagrations and give them "every opportunity to spread."[57] Still Churchill was not satisfied. On the first day of November he sent to Portal three stinging notes expressing "extreme regret" that the bomber force was not being expanded fast enough, and that even more bombs were not being "delivered overseas and particularly on Germany." "It is the rising scale of delivery of bombs," he wrote, "which must be taken as the measure of the success of our policy."[58]

Understandably he pondered his own safety. Talking with the secretary of the Cabinet, Sir Edward Bridges, he predicted on October 22 that the enemy would wreck Whitehall and demolish the capital's other older buildings. Dollis Hill had displeased him and he decided to carry on from the Cabinet War Room bunker; its ceiling would now be reinforced by an extra concrete slab, as would Brooke's Home Forces headquarters in the modern Board of Trade building. For living quarters Churchill would move permanently into the Annexe above the C.W.R., and this Annexe would also have to be bombproofed.[59] Carpenters and builders moved into No.10, repairing the damage and inserting extra timbers. Unwilling to linger there until this was complete he moved office to "The Barn," a deep shelter at the former Down Street underground station a few yards from Piccadilly. Nelson the cat was whisked off to Chequers, whither Mary and other junior members of the Churchill family had been evacuated.

It was a crushing work load, but on the twenty-second it was marginally lightened. Ambassador Joseph P. Kennedy finally left England, his scepticism undimmed and still threatening to torpedo Roosevelt's re-election campaign. After a meeting at the White House, however, Kennedy would mysteriously drop all opposition, and he endorsed F.D.R. in a nationwide broadcast. When no high office was forthcoming he reverted to his uncompromising views. Visiting

California he spoke "off the record" at the film studios for three hours, urging that America never get involved in this war. "He apparently," one famous filmstar wrote secretly to the president, "threw the fear of God into many of our producers and executives by telling them that the Jews were on the spot and that they should stop making anti-Nazi pictures." Kennedy added "that anti-Semitism was growing in Britian and that the Jews were being blamed for the war." The film industry, he said, was a malign influence on public opinion. "The Jews, in particular, would be in jeopardy if they continued to abuse that power."[60] Speaking on the last day of May to graduating students at Notre Dame in Indiana the former ambassador would unfashionably describe the Führer as "the greatest genius of the century," and his diplomatic and military ability as superior to anything the British could muster. "Britain," Kennedy concluded, "is hopelessly licked and there will be a negotiated peace within sixty days."[61]

In October 1940 the prospects of American intervention seemed remote. Mr Wendell Willkie, Roosevelt's opponent, mocked: "If his promise to keep your boys out of foreign wars is no better than his promise to balance the budget, they're already almost on the transports!" At Boston on the thirtieth the president proclaimed with a grinning Ambassador Kennedy at his elbow, "I have said this before, but I shall say it again and again and again. Your boys are not going to be sent into any foreign wars!"* When November 2 came, a reassured America re-elected him.

Churchill disliked those words but was relieved at F.D.R.'s victory. He telegraphed congratulations. "I prayed for your success," he revealed. Roosevelt vouchsafed no reply, a silence which the former naval person found frankly disquieting and queried with his embassy in Washington.[62] Roosevelt wanted to squeeze the British lemon still harder, as time would show. The unequal partnership was about to begin: Roosevelt's star was ascendant, Churchill's would soon be past its zenith. Gallup pollsters found confidence in him topping eighty-nine percent in October. He knew well why: "I represent to them," he said, "something that they wholeheartedly support: the determination to win." Realistically he added, "For a year or two they will cheer me."[63]

If his life had ended now he would have been hailed as Britain's saviour — the man who had rallied an almost defeated nation and led her out of that despondent slough. The burden of the later toil, across the seas and deserts and beaches, would have fallen upon other

---

* The sentence was omitted from the official text shortly published by Samuel I. Rosenman, *The Public Papers and Addresses of Franklin D. Roosevelt*; but it was in the recording, and in the *New York Times* two days later.

shoulders; and others would have earned the obloquy for ultimately bankrupting the Empire. But fortune plays a straight hand, and to Winston Churchill would now fall the duty of ploughing the same furrow he had set, one which would drag his country into ruin and disqualify her as a world power.

CHAPTER 35

Britain Can Take It

W HEN THE WAR ENDED and D-notice restrictions were lifted Lord Beaverbrook's newspapers revealed that while the King and Queen had left London by car every evening during the blitz to join the Princesses at Windsor, and while the Queen Mother had spent the war years at Badminton, Mr Churchill had been "living throughout his premiership at No.10 Downing-street, and spending week-ends at Chequers."[1] This appealing legend was enriched over the years. Readers learned that Second Lieutenant John Watney had been detailed to drive the PM around bomb-torn London in his armoured car. "But," puzzled this soldier, "he never got into it. I would call at the front door in Downing-street with the car, and Churchill would go out of the back." Until every citizen had an armoured car he pledged he wouldn't use one.[2]

His was a robust image. To junior ministers soon after taking office in May 1940 he had declared himself against any evacuation from London, unless life became impossible. "Mere bombing," this indomitable man had said, "will not make us go."[3] By "us" he meant the Londoners. In October he decided that even Chequers was not safe. He feared that the knavish Göring might lay a *Knickebein* beam across Chequers and blast if off the map of Buckinghamshire. He began to cast about for an alternative country retreat.

In October over six thousand Britons had been slain. In November 4,500 more would die. Movie theatres were running the film "Britain Can Take It," but propaganda alone could not patch the Londoners' fragile morale. One neutral observer reported a growing ferment in the lower classes against "the very differing plights of car owners who are able to betake themselves to safety, and those who have to spend the night in improvised shelters or Underground stations." He recognized that many officials still clung to the hope of an early negotiated peace. As the raids worsened, a clamour began among the PM's friends like Josiah Wedgwood who urged him to seek a deeper shelter. "Eventually I agreed," Churchill would write. "One felt a natural compunction at having much more safety than most other people; but so many pressed me that I let them have their way."[4]

Another neutral, an American who had dallied six months in London, meeting men like Spears and Duff Cooper, gave the Germans in Lisbon this picture a few weeks later: devastated docks, dwindling food supplies and a stultified public opinion — people did whatever Whitehall commanded. Commenting on de Gaulle, Spears had said: "We bet on the wrong horse." Meanwhile, the American added, Churchill was trying to find ways of restoring contact with Vichy.[5]

De Gaulle's prestige was at low ebb; he was "a loser."[6] Shortly after the Dakar fiasco, on October 1 Lord Halifax had persuaded the Cabinet to face up to the general problem of Britain's relations with Marshal Pétain and his Government at Vichy. "I still think," Halifax dictated into his private diary, "that with the German behaviour in France, if we could play our cards, French opinion is likely to turn more and more our way. . . The ultimate alternative is something like hostilities with Vichy." They gnawed over the Vichy problem in Cabinet that day, and the foreign secretary found Churchill not unhelpful — "much as it goes against his natural instinct for bellicosity." Halifax reminded him that Britain's purpose was to defeat Germany, and not to make new enemies.[7]

Fortunately, Churchill was not committed to "any exact restoration of the territories" of France and he felt after Dakar that losing Morocco might be a suitable penalty for France's "abject" attitude. He asked Halifax to let the Spanish know that Britain would be "no obstacle to their Moroccan ambitions."[8]* But when the foreign secretary suggested that they also hint at handing back Gibraltar after the war, the PM put his foot down: "Does anyone think," he inquired, "that if we win the war opinion here will consent to hand over Gib. to the Dons? And, if we lose, we shall not be consulted."[9]

Churchill's hostility toward de Gaulle grew during October. In private remarks he showed an inclination to deal with Pétain, whatever the public vilification of the Marshal. "Vichy is being bad enough," he had told the journalist Knickerbocker at the end of September, "but not as bad as it could be; for instance, they could turn over their ships to Germany if they wanted to be nasty." Writing to Roosevelt a week later the PM mentioned that Vichy was trying to enter into relations with

---

*In 1946 Franco staggered Randolph Churchill by revealing this — that in 1940 "the British ambassador offered me part of French Morocco if I promised to remain neutral." Sam Hoare (Lord Templewood) denied this as "entirely untrue and without any foundation." (*Daily Telegraph*, February 18, 1946)

London, "which," he suggested, "shows how the tides are flowing in France now that they feel the German weight and see we are able to hold our own."[10]

What he did not tell Roosevelt was his decision to embark on clandestine conversations with Vichy aimed at reaching a *modus vivendi*, a gentleman's agreement. Broadly speaking, once he was sure that Pétain was moving the right way he was prepared to relax the naval blockade he had announced at the end of July.[11] He put out his secret feelers through Madrid, asking Sam Hoare on the twentieth to convey to the French ambassador there two root ideas, as he called them: that Britain could always let bygones be bygones; but that failing that "we shall stop at nothing."[12]

On the following evening he broadcast to France — first, ignoring professional advice, in French and then in more intelligible English. The British were waiting for Hitler's invasion, he said: "So are the fishes." "Never," he added, "will I believe that the soul of France is dead."[13]

* * *

Out of this developed two extraordinary and controversial meetings with a Vichy emissary, Louis Rougier. Equipped with credentials signed by Marshal Pétain, this French-Canadian professor of philosophy arrived in London via Madrid on the day after Churchill's broadcast.[14] The F.O. forbade him to contact either de Gaulle or the American embassy.

Before he was brought over to No.10 there was an unexpected interlude: on the twenty-fourth Hitler met both Prime Minister Pierre Laval and Marshal Pétain, and during the night rumours reached London that at Montoire the aged Marshal had agreed to hand over Toulon naval base to the enemy.

Churchill had taken fitful refuge from the bombs in his private Down Street deep shelter, The Barn. A secretary woke him with the news; he hurried back to No.10 and drafted a disapproving message for the King to send Pétain. It spoke of Britain's resolve to fight on to the end and restated the promise to restore "the freedom and greatness of France" — though not mentioning her territories.[15] The rumours about Toulon worried him, and he asked his military staff to consider a purely British assault on Dakar — proof how far de Gaulle had fallen in esteem.

Lord Halifax's diary of October 25, 1940 renders an amusing picture of that day:

Dorothy and I had slept in the [Dorchester Hotel's bombproof] dormitory and at 5:30 a.m. I was woken up by the night waiter who said that the Foreign Office wanted to telephone me on the Prime Minister's instructions.

I could not have been more annoyed and came upstairs wondering whether Alec [Cadogan] had been hit by a bomb or the Germans had gone into Spain or Anthony Eden had been assassinated in Egypt. It turned out to be a message from Sam Hoare giving some side-lights on the Vichy conversations with Hitler [at Montoire], in regard to which Sam suggested certain prompt action might be helpful.

When I got to the [Foreign] Office after breakfast I went over to No.10 where I found Winston in his dugout, having drafted one or two telegrams which he invited me to improve. He was . . . in what I understand nurses are accustomed to call a "romper suit" of Air Force colour Jaeger-like stuff, with a zip fastening up the middle, and a little Air Force forage cap. I asked him if he was going on the stage but he said he always wore this in the morning.

Lord Halifax, who had been the Reichsmarschall's guest three years before, concluded, "It is really almost like Göring."

It was later this day that the first meeting with Pétain's emissary took place. Churchill and Rougier mapped out a gentleman's agreement.[16]

After Rougier left No.10 there was a further shock. Fleet Street falsely reported that Pétain had signed a peace treaty with Hitler. Outraged at this apparent treachery, Churchill shouted at Rougier the next day: "I will send the Royal Air Force to bomb Vichy!"*[17] With some difficulty, the professor calmed him down and they settled the terms of the agreement. Before Rougier left London on the twenty-eighth Sir William Strang asked him to draw up a memorandum of the kind of statements he proposed to make to Pétain; two copies in the professor's flawless native French were brought across to No.10. Churchill added marginal alterations and returned one copy fifteen minutes later to the F.O. On November 10 it was in Pétain's hands.[18]

* * *

What *was* agreed? Five years later, with de Gaulle in power and Marshal Pétain on trial for his life the very notion of such dealings was abhorrent enough to deny. Thrice in 1945 Mr Churchill would do so. On February 28, 1945, two days after Pierre-Etienne Flandin revealed to astonished Gaullist judges that Pétain had shown him a secret treaty concluded with Churchill "at the time of Montoire," he denied it through Reuter's; he denied it again on All Fool's Day. On June 8, 1945, the defendant Pétain confirmed Flandin's testimony. "It is correct," the

---

*Churchill echoed this to Attlee and Halifax: Britain must emphasize in communicating with Pétain "that in the event of any act of hostility on their part we should immediately retaliate by bombing the seat of the Vichy Government, wherever it might be."[19]

Marshal wrote to the instructing judge, "that I caused a treaty to be settled with Mr Winston Churchill that was supposed to remain secret. This treaty — whose negotiation began on the day of Montoire — gives Montoire its true character; it was what guided my policies, even if the British now seem to dissociate themselves from it." When Rougier shortly published a book with the documents on the case in Canada, Churchill was embarrassed, and again denied it, this time in a White Paper.[20] Even now, parts of the F.O. file are closed until the year 2016 and all the papers relating to Rougier and the Churchill-Pétain deal have been physically removed by the British Government from the late Lord Halifax's papers.

Rougier appears to have told the truth. While guest of Walter Lippmann in Washington later in 1940 the noted commentator introduced him to Judge Frankfurter, and the summary which Rougier drafted for the White House is among the judge's papers. Paul Baudouin would testify that the professor returned to Vichy with "a document I myself held, corrected in Churchill's own hand."[21]

Among the terms reliably recalled by Baudouin and Rougier were that Britain agreed to restore France provided she gave the Axis no quarter; to ease the blockade; and to oblige the BBC to take the heat off Pétain as he had become a symbol to the French. Vichy promised not to recapture the dissident colonies or to cede bases in Provence or Africa to Germany.[22] Admiral Fernet saw Rougier report to Pétain on the secret meetings with Churchill and Halifax. "These talks," Rougier had said, "permit of big hopes." Later Baudouin asked the Portuguese ambassador to have Dr Salazar forward word of Vichy's unconditional acceptance of these terms to Mr Churchill. In his July 1945 White Paper Churchill would nonetheless maintain: "His Majesty's Government never received any communication from Marshal Pétain or his Government suggesting that they considered themselves under any commitment as a result of M Rougier's conversations."

Be that as it may, in 1940 he immediately put the "gentleman's agreement" into effect. The BBC dropped its attacks on Pétain, and the blockade was eased.[23] All operations against Vichy France's territory and fleet ceased.[24]

Subsequently, Churchill would imply that Rougier was used only as an emissary to General Weygand, Governor-General of Algeria.[25] He was certainly anxious for Weygand to raise the standard of rebellion in North Africa, because behind Rougier's back he drafted a rousing message to the General.[26] He had also given Rougier an oral message to deliver to Weygand when he passed through Algiers. The professor called on Weygand at the Palais d'Hiver on November 5, chancing to arrive at the same moment as the PM's clandestine letter, which proposed a Vichy-British staff meeting at Tangier. Weygand was not pleased by this: German agents, he pointed out, would certainly detect any such move and Hitler would insist on his recall. He knew of only one set of instructions, this loyal servant of France told the professor: to defend her empire against everybody.

After the emissary's departure, Churchill was pricked by conscience. "In view of our relations with de Gaulle, and engagements signed," he suggested to Eden, "he has a right to feel assured we are not throwing him over." But actions spoke louder than words. While still awaiting Pétain's response he ordered Admiral Pound to stay any naval actions against Vichy forces. If Vichy interferred with de Gaulle, who had landed a small force at Duala and obtained the French Cameroons' adherence, Britain must not defend him: so Churchill ruled. On the first day of November 1940 he was heard to mutter that the Free French General had become an embarrassment to him in his dealings with Vichy and the French people.[27]

HIS WAR CABINET now met regularly in the bunker Cabinet War Room as did the specialized committees on night air defence and tanks. He harried and pressed and badgered, calling for progress reports and deciding priorities: radar-controlled guns and searchlights were coming into use, and the top-secret airborne interception (A.I.) radar was undergoing trials. He was pleased at reports that German aircraft were aborting their missions because of increasingly accurate gunfire even through cloud. "We are getting our cat's eyes, it seems," observed a minister.[28]

Professor Lindemann stood watchdog over these inquiries, growling like a Cerberus over each fued or folly perpetrated by more mortal subordinates. Electronic experts were designing transmitters to interfere with *Knickebein*; by mid November three would be ready and eighteen more under construction. Now Churchill was told that deciphered messages showed the enemy was using an even more accurate radio-beam device, the *X-Gerät*. Shortly he received angry news from the Prof: an enemy Pathfinder plane carrying this vital apparatus had belly-landed on the beach only to be washed out to sea while officers bickered over whether it was naval, army or airforce property.[29]

It was going to be a long war, but Churchill was confident that British science would outclass the enemy's. Knowing perhaps more than he ought of his opponent's industrial Four Year Plan — to prepare the Wehrmacht for war ("with the Soviet Union") by 1940 — he elucidated to his private staff that it took four years to reach maximum war production. Germany, he said, had attained that peak, while Britain was still at Year Two.[30] Reviewing strategy at the end of October he asked the crucial question: "How are we to win?" Bombing seemed the only answer.

He knew that Hitler's main offensive would be against the convoys supplying Britain. During 1941 Germany might in theory campaign in Spain and Turkey and simultaneously, Churchill predicted to the Defence Committee, Russia: Hitler would probably turn covetous eyes on the Caspian and the Baku oilfields.[31] Bletchley proved that his airforce was installing a ground organisation in Romania and Bulgaria. Seen from No.10, it seemed that Hitler was planning to thrust through the Balkans and Turkey to the Suez Canal.

Each day saw the conflict widening, and it affected Churchill's health. He was sleeping badly, and when John Martin woke him at Chequers early on October 28 with news that Mussolini had invaded Greece he just grunted, rolled over and dropped off to sleep again. "Never do that again!" he lectured him later that morning. Martin apologized that the PM might have wanted to summon the Cabinet. "What could they do?" asked Churchill dismissively. "Just gape round the table." He never wanted to be wakened again "just because Hitler had invaded a new country." (Usually he knew from his Bletchley oracle anyway.) Back in London, he siesta'd in his bunker bedroom next to the C.W.R. but, meeting Greenwood and Dalton later that day in what the latter irreverently called "his boudoir," he still looked haggard and had not pondered the minor point that bothered them at all. "I have just had my sleep," he apologized.[32] To the home secretary he sighed that this was the "most unnecessary war in history."

A few days later he had a gastric complaint. He turned aside the doctor's castor oil, refused dinner, and as the sirens wailed entombed himself again in The Barn seventy feet below Piccadilly instead.[33]

He hated this troglodyte existence. Clearly it was not unreasonable for Winston to wish to preserve himself in the nation's interest — "of which," he shortly told Hugh Dowding,* "I am the judge." But his previous braggadocio was proving brittle. At the end of July he had announced that all ministers were to be at their posts when the bombing began, and urged Halifax to move back from the Dorchester to the F.O. Now his own senior staff ascribed his frequent exchange of capital for country to "the full moon and the fear of night attacks." When Dr Dalton suggested they bomb Rome but spare the Pope, Mr Churchill replied with feeling, "I should like to tell the Old Man to get down into his shelter and stay there for a week."[34]

Others contemplated their own mortality with sang-froid. Sir Alan Brooke resolutely bedded down each night on an upper floor of the

---

*See p. 462 of this Chapter.

Army & Navy club, reposing his trust in God. Mr Churchill had invoked the Lord's name too liberally in the past, and in the present extremes he trusted more religiously to distance, putting as much as possible between himself and the enemy's target whenever it was known to him from the Engimas. London could take it; he could not.

* * *

The Secretary for War was still out in Egypt as November began. Churchill drove out to Chequers that Friday evening, buoyant again; he was leaving the nightmare behind him, and he was going to see his family. Eden had telegraphed that he had sent a battalion by cruiser to the Greek island of Crete, and a squadron of Blenheim bombers; but he urged against going overboard in aiding Greece as this would jeopardize "plans for offensive operations" being laid in Egypt.[35]

Winston also briefly had second thoughts. Just as before Dakar, a cautious instinct tugged at his sleeve. Halifax was talking of injecting British planes into Greece. Should he do more? To Churchill, investing in Bomber Command still seemed the more flexible means of helping. He had written to Portal suggesting an attack on "the morale of the Italian population;" he justified this diversion from precision targets as "in the nature of an experiment."[36] When he spoke to Peirse, chief of Bomber Command, he again warned: "We must be very careful not to bomb the Pope. He has a lot of influential friends!"[37]

On Saturday November 2 he changed his mind. Freed from the shackles of Cabinet restraint he threw caution to the winds; he decided to do everything possible, "by land, sea and air," for the Greeks. "Greek situation," he replied to Eden, "must be held to dominate others now. We are well aware of our slender resources." He expressed concern at the effect on Turkey if Britain welshed on yet another guarantee. Urging Portal to send four bomber squadrons over to Greece, he wrote: "Please try your best."[38]

Telegrams flew back and forth, but still he did not consult his colleagues. In the Great War, Lloyd George would never have attempted even to browbeat let alone bypass the elder statesmen like Balfour, Milner or Bonar Law. But Churchill had a Cabinet of shadows. Even the Service ministers were sycophants.

Eden was restless to return home — Churchill urged him to stay on in Cairo. He took the big decision at Chequers that weekend, far from moderating influences: Britain would shift one Gladiator (fighter) and three Blenheim (bomber) squadrons into Greece. Nor did he consult the Dominions. Scrutinizing a telegram notifying their prime ministers of his resolve to accept the risk of rushing aid to Greece, Churchill objected to the draft: "Who is responsible for drawing it up and sending it out?"[39]

That Sunday morning he sent a sharply worded telegram to Eden:

Trust you will grasp situation firmly, abandoning negative and passive policies and seizing opportunity which has come into our hands.

Sipping soda and reclining in a silken kimono on a chintz-curtained four-poster bed, he dictated a scowling finish to the telegram. "Safety First," he said, "is the road to ruin in war, even if you had the safety, which you have not. Send me your proposals earliest, or say you have none to make."[40]

The first British troops were disembarked on Greek soil. Until now Hitler had had no plans to invade Greece; but fearing that British bombers might soon be within range of his Romanian oilfields, he would now order contingency invasion plans prepared.

Pale-faced, the C.I.G.S. left Chequers on Sunday with the PM's exhortation in his ears — "Don't forget, the maximum possible for Greece!"[41] A new Churchill fiasco was beginning, of which he was the unquestioned architect.

Was it just the sentimental Churchill, seeing himself as the saviour of Greek civilization? Was he turning a greedy eye on Suda Bay, the fine naval anchorage on Crete's northern shore? Perhaps the word *opportunity*, used in Sunday's telegram to Eden, held the key. Was he illicitly reading frantic Italian messages as their brash offensive into Epirus came unstuck? Was he hoping to reap the triumphant harvest with the Greeks? Certainly among the visitors he received after he returned to No.10 on Monday, November 4, was "C", head of the Secret Intelligence Service, at 6:15 p.m.

Early in October he had again insisted on getting every Enigma message deciphered by Bletchley. He guarded his oracle jealously and was vexed to learn that digests had even circulated to the American embassy. He very properly ordered that this practice cease — to the enduring ill-feeling of the Grosvenor Square diplomats who considered that the prospect of a $3,500m loan entitled them to more.[42] Shortly, the three Bletchley women who allocated daily priorities — which of the dozens of ciphers was to be run through the computer (*bombe*) first — began each producing a weekly digest for him of their expert knowledge, since they had to read every single document deciphered; this identified the cipher from which each item had been culled.[43] This all-embracing knowledge added a fearsome dimension to his burden: it gave him insight into events which he would not always be able to hinder.

Early in November it yielded evidence that Hitler's Sixteenth Army, along the channel coast, was finally returning its invasion gear to store.[44] The PM had expected as much since late July anyway. On November 5 he told the House, adopting his most theatrical stance —

rubbing his hands up and down his coat front with every finger extended as he searched for the right phrase, "conveying almost medicinal poise," as one member put it, and dressing up the news as a great victory.

The plain fact that an invasion, planned on so vast a scale, has not been attempted in spite of the very great need of the enemy to destroy us in our citadel; and that all these anxious months, when we stood alone and the whole world wondered, have passed safely away — that fact constitutes in itself one of the historic victories of the British Isles and is a monumental milestone on our onward march.[45]

It gave him little joy. He was to lunch at the Palace, but he slouched into the Smoking Room instead and buried himself in an afternoon newspaper with some liquor until a harrassed minion found him. "Luckily," noted the Member who found him, "I had just seen him boozing in the Smoking Room." Churchill grunted ungraciously and shuffled off to the Palace.[46] That evening he again lowered himself in the little two-man elevator into the bowels of The Barn. He was accustomed now to the Tube trains that thundered past his bedroom, only the thickness of a freshly-bricked wall away; but the ticking of the ancient clock, screwed to the wall, unnerved him and he ordered it permanently stopped.

The blitz was getting on everybody's nerves. Little heroic spirit remained at ministerial level. Churchill had not visited the blitzed areas for weeks. Dalton, privileged like the PM with access to Enigma, jotted two cryptic lines one evening in November: "Revelations! I therefore leave early in the afternoon instead of risking anything by staying the night."[47] It was difficult not to become edgy or mercurial. Churchill could plunge into a Stygian gloom in an instant. Kingsley Wood, now a Cabinet minister, came to see him on the eighth, and found him more depressed than ever before.

"Cabinet in the morning," dictated Dalton, to whom he told this,

very ragged and much depression, principally owing to heavy naval sinkings and decline in various indices of output. . . In the Midlands, e.g. Coventry, the morale of munitions worker is affected by raids.

Production was falling. That evening Churchill again sought refuge in The Barn, calling in the Prof and Sir Andrew Duncan, a businessman who had taken over the ministry of supply to sounds of relief from Beaverbrook. But then a shaft of light penetrated this gloomy scene. The secretary for war had just returned from the Middle East by flying boat, arrived dramatically in this disused Underground station, and announced that Wavell was preparing a bold counter-stroke in the Western Desert — it would be the first great offensive of Churchill's war. The PM purred, he later admitted, "like six cats" as his young Pretender elaborated this plan.

His opinion of Italians was low. On first hearing in September that Italian troops had invaded Egypt he remarked that he did not fear the outcome — "unless our men behave like skunks and the Italians like heroes."[48] Accurately gauging the British humour he let it be known that in one antiquated Italian flying machine his crash investigators had found a loaf of bread, a bottle of Chianti and some cheese. He betrayed a residual envy only of Mussolini: In 1935 he had called him "so great a man, so wise a ruler;" in 1937 he had said, "If I had been an Italian I would have been on Mussolini's side fifteen years ago when he rescued his country from the horrible fate of sinking into violent communism," or from "incipient anarchy into a position of dignity and order," as he put it even in 1939. Once he had scoffed to Ribbentrop that Germany was welcome to the Italians as allies. "It's only fair," he said, "we had them last time."[49] Speaking of the Italian navy he mocked that there was "a general curiosity in the British Fleet . . . whether the Italians are up to the level they were at in the last war or whether they have fallen off at all." When Admiral Sir Andrew Cunningham wanted, early in October, to mention Italian sailors' gallantry in attempting to salvage a crippled destroyer under fire Churchill condemned the tribute: "This kind of kid glove stuff," he wrote, "infuriates the people who are going through their present ordeal at home."[50]

Some of his brooding envy was also reserved for Hitler. On November 8 he sent Bomber Command to Munich to disrupt the Führer's annual speech to Party veterans. He himself lingered in town that night — unusual for a Friday, but he had to address the Lord Mayor's luncheon on the ninth. As he had notice of a coming raid he planned then to escape London — not to Chequers this time, but to Dytchley* in Oxfordshire, a sprawling estate which Bracken had recommended.

His speech was platitude: not for the first time, he guaranteed the allied nations their future freedom.†

> Since we have been left alone in this world struggle [he said], we have reaffirmed or defined more precisely all the causes of all the countries with whom or for whom we drew the sword — Austria, Czechoslovakia, Poland, Norway, Holland, Belgium, greatest of all France, latest of all Greece. For all of those we will toil and strive, and our victory will supply the liberation of them all.

That said, he drove out to the country to weekend with greater

---

*Thus the spelling on its notepaper.

†On September 5 he told the House: "We do not propose to recognize any territorial changes which take place during the war, unless they take place with the free consent and good will of the parties concerned."[51]

serenity than the dockers in their squalid firetrap terraces. Later that day Neville Chamberlain died, a brave but unpleasant death over-shadowed by the knowledge that his image had been falsified beyond repair by his enemies. Upon Lord Halifax's farewell visit two days earlier Chamberlain had croaked a warning to him not to place much trust in Russian promises. ("I am sure," Halifax had softly whispered, "that you will be trying to help us — wherever you are.") "I think History," Halifax entered in his diary, "will be more just to Neville than some of his contemporary critics." Churchill dictated a eulogy with customary facility — not an insuperable task, as he commented to his host, since he admired many of Neville's qualities. "But I pray to God in his infinite mercy that I shall not have to deliver a similar oration on Baldwin. That indeed would be difficult to do."[52]

Dytchley, a manor set in three thousand acres north of Oxford, was the domain of a wealthy benefactor from the Focus, the ruddy-faced Ronald Tree. It had a lake and a spread of lawns shaded by tall trees. There was little sign of war except the tramp of sentries on the flagstones, and Bofors guns in the grounds. The building dated back three hundred years but had been rebuilt in 1720. Inside, the decor was in faded greens and blues, but there were splashes of red and yellow too; the furniture and wall coverings glittered with gilt. The walls of the dining room were plaqued with the antlers of ancient deer, one slain by King James in 1608. The quiet, high-ceilinged rooms were hung with old masters, ancient prints, and paintings of King Charles II: the first owner Sir Henry Lee had married the monarch's bastard daughter; Winston had nothing against bastard daughters — he had married one himself.

He was assigned to a room with an eighteenth century mahogany bed fashioned after Chippendale. Ronald Tree and his comely Virginian wife were perfect hosts; and since Churchill took a liking to Air Chief Marshal Portal, and since his wife was as beautiful as her husband was homely, they were invited too when London was about to be bombed. Dytchley was a pleasant retreat in both senses of the word.[53]

From Churchill's desk calender we know that he was back at Downing-street on Monday the eleventh for a mid-day meeting on night air defence. He slumbered after that until the sirens startled him awake and drove him to the garden shelter, where he again went to bed. But here the shriek of the bombs seemed even louder, and he retired to his bunker room.[54] He presided over Tuesday's Cabinet down here in the bunker. That night's bombs hit the new Sloane Square station and pancaked it on top of an Underground train with heavy loss of life.

More ominous events were augured. On Monday Bletchley had deciphered signals instructions radioed by the Senior Signals (*Luftnachrichten-*) Officer of the First Air Corps at two p.m. on Saturday, about the time the PM was speaking at the Mansion House, for a future moonlight attack of "very considerable dimensions." Call-signs indicated that both air fleets would participate, led by a fire-raising force of KG.100 — some 1,800 planes under direct control of Hermann Göring; the squadron commander of KG.100, the Pathfinder squadron, would fly himself.[55] Four target areas were mentioned: the first was uncertain but was "possibly Central London." As for the actual date of attack, at one p.m. on the day KG.100 would check the weather and the beams, and if the weather report from KG.100 was unfavourable the codeword MOND MOND would be transmitted three times and *Knickebein* realigned onto the night's alternative target.[56]

Churchill was immediately notified. His secretaries were of course not privy to this secret data. Colville recorded only that the operation was known in advance "from the contents of those mysterious buff boxes which the PM alone opens, sent every day by Brigadier Menzies."[57]

The PM had learned from the codebreakers precise details of Hitler's appointments too — the Soviet foreign minister was about to arrive in Berlin. Bomber Command was ordered to see that the Russians were left in no doubt that Mr Churchill's arm was neither short nor weary.

MEANWHILE CHURCHILL KEPT his daily routine.

He delivered his obituary oration on Chamberlain on the twelfth to the parliamentary colleagues now assembling in the less vulnerable setting of Church House, Westminster. A velvety spirit of final reconciliation seemingly inspired his words, yet they slid the last nails into the failed premier's coffin as surely as if he had spewed forth gall. "Whatever else History may or may not say about these terrible, tremendous years," he declaimed — profoundly conscious that he intended to write that History himself — "we can be sure that Neville Chamberlain acted with perfect sincerity according to his lights and strove to the utmost of his capacity and authority, which were powerful, to save the world from the awful, devastating struggle in which we are now engaged."

He mocked at Hitler's recent Munich protestations that he had only desired peace with Britain. "What," he cried, "do these ravings and outpourings count before the silence of Neville Chamberlain's tomb?" The answer is one that even now History cannot render: fifty years later, the official record of the peace feelers between his less bellicose colleagues and Hitler is still closed to public scrutiny.

ON THE THIRTEENTH, Air Intelligence unravelled more evidence on the coming mighty air raids: "the same source" had indicated that there would be three attacks, on three successive nights. At seven p.m. the source revealed that there was a code word for each attack: the first was Regenschirm (Umbrella), the second Mondschein Seranade (Moonlight Sonata). The third was not known. The most likely target was still Central London.[58]

The next full moon would be three hours after midnight on the fourteenth. On Churchill's desk calendar a bracket appeared, pencilled in from dusk on the fourteenth to dawn on the eighteenth; he left that three-day space free of appointments in London.

To this codebreaking information from Bletchley — primly euphemized as "a very good source" — the air ministry added the lurid boasts of a Nazi airman shot down on Saturday to an S.P. (stool pigeon) planted in his cell. The blitz had led to rioting in London, and "Hermann" thought the time ripe for this colossal raid. True, this bragging airman had also mentioned Birmingham and Coventry, a city of a quarter-million souls; but the Enigmas indicated London and, as the Operations Orders now issued for the counterattack (Cold Water) showed, that was the air staff's bet too.[59]

* * *

On Thursday November 14 the three-day, four-night bracket pencilled on Churchill's desk card began. "?No Cabinet" had been entered for the morning: at mid-day he and his unwilling colleagues had to be in their pews for Chamberlain's funeral.

Several windows of the Abbey had been blown out and the November air gusted in from outside, cold and bleak. Bevin looked bored, Duff Cooper disdainful. One man observed the irony of this overcoated, mufflered congregation — "all the little men who had torpedoed poor Neville's heroic efforts to preserve the peace and made his life a misery: some seemed to be gloating. Winston, followed by the War Cabinet, however, had the decency to cry as he stood by the coffin."[60] The ceremony could not have been staged to provide Chamberlain with a more undignified exit — the mourners found the fullsize coffin already in position in the Choir, so there was no solemn procession behind it; as the ceremony ended, the coffin was opened and a little oaken casket was plucked out, as though in a conjuring trick, and this — containing the ashes — was "put in a hole in the ground," as Lord Halifax recorded with evident indignation.

The clock ticked on. At 12.45 he presided over a Defence Committee. Entered on Churchill's card at one-fifteen was "C-in-C Fighter Command." He was going to replace Dowding after all — a Party caucus had again complained that the airforce lacked confidence in him. Churchill offered the air chief marshal a mission to the United States — his standard way of disposing of ill-fitting critics. Dowding demurred, Churchill told him curtly it was "in the public interest, of which I am the judge."[61] To Dowding it must have looked like banishment from the kingdom which his Command had so recently saved; and so indeed it was.

Winston lunched with the minister of shipping; he even forgot the man's name, his mind was on other things.[62] The Air Ministry had summarized their findings on Moonlight Sonata in a seven-paragraph report and sent it round to him. "The whole of the German long range Bomber Force will be employed. The operation is being co-ordinated, we think, by the commander-in-chief of the G.A.F. [Göring]. It is probably reprisal for our attack on Munich." The target would probably be London "but if further information indicates Coventry, Birmingham or elsewhere, we hope to get instructions out in time." In reprisal, Bomber Command would simultaneously raid Berlin, Essen or Munich, on a "knock-for-knock" basis, and other countermeasures had been planned.

Churchill read in the report that Air Intelligence expected to learn the actual date and target of Moonlight Sonata in good time because at one p.m. on the day KG.100 would reconnoiter the target areas and transmit a weather report. "This will be our signal that the party is on."

In the margin was scrawled: "*This unit sent the approved codeword at 13:00 exactly. 14/11.*"

THUS SOONER THAN expected, the drama was upon them. Even as Churchill finished his luncheon, radio monitors across southern England found the Nazi beam transmitters warming up, heard reconnaissance reports, intercepted messages from the special Central Control set up for Moonlight Sonata at Versailles, and picked up the chaotic traffic as hundreds of enemy bombers switched on and tested radio gear.

It would be dark at six. Normally he would nap until three or four, then take visitors. But today was different — he would clear out of town as soon as he had cleared his appointments: his card shows them as 2:45 p.m., Lord Halifax; three p.m., Mr Attlee.

He certainly saw the former, because the foreign secretary afterwards poured out his heart to a fellow minister about "a great row which he has just been having with the PM."[63] Churchill had recently intercepted some general's letter to Eden containing the sentence, "So far as I can make out the Prime Minister's *scribble* —" and now it had happened again: the ambassador in Cairo had sent a private telegram describing any further transfer of R.A.F. squadrons to Greece as "quite crazy." Through a typical F.O. blunder, this telegram had gone to everybody from the King downwards.

"The PM," recorded Dalton smugly, "is furious."

Winston had insisted on a reprimand. Halifax wrote back refusing, pointing out that the message had never been meant for his eyes. The PM exploded, and sent for him: he wanted to haul him over the coals for disobedience. But Halifax came over to No.10 in no mood of contrition toward Winston. "Always stand up to him," was his advice. "He hates doormats. If you begin to give way he will simply wipe his feet upon you." He again reminded the PM that he had merely nosed into a private letter addressed to somebody else. Of course, he concluded, if Winston insisted, the rebuke would be sent.

The PM pouted. "I don't wish," he snorted, "to hear anything more about the matter."

"A most extraordinary man!" remarked Halifax, after relating this to Dalton.

After Attlee also left, Churchill summoned the Humber to the garden gate to take him out to Dytchley, and slipped out by the back door; soon it would be dark and the inferno would begin.

Down at the gate John Martin handed him an urgent message. As the car gathered speed Churchill slit open the buff envelope, gasped, and at Kensington Gardens told the driver to turn back.[64] The target was not Central London at all. In his pocket notebook Martin entered afterwards: "At No.10. False start for Dytchley (Moonlight Sonata - the raid was on Coventry.)"

* * *

According to the shocked investigations carried out three days later by the air ministry's Directorate of Home Operations, which surely had little cause to bring forward the timing, by three p.m. 80 Wing's radio countermeasures organisation "was able to report that the enemy River Group [*X-Gerät*] beams were intersecting over Coventry," hundreds of miles to the north of London. "All R.A.F. commands were informed, and Home Security and Home Forces put into the picture."[65]

This matches the recollections of Group Captain Frederick Winterbotham and officers working at the intercept stations. All agree moreover that the radio monitors briefed to listen for the codeword to abort the primary target — MOND MOND — heard it as anticipated between one and two p.m. and that Humphreys of Hut 3 immediately phoned Winterbotham's office at Broadway.[66] The latter goes further, claiming that the message from Humphreys also named Coventry. His secretary typed a note in the treble spacing which Winston required and sent it over to No.10.[67]

Professor R.V. Jones, whose early reputation was closely identified with Mr Churchill's premiership, disputes this. He maintains that he alone could work out the beam tangents that identified each target; that first Bletchley had to decipher the relevant signals; and that on the fourteenth the necessary break did not occur until far into the night. He also insists, despite the evidence, that 80 Wing had *not* located the beams by the time he left his Broadway office at five-thirty. Perhaps the Wing simply could not contact him; perhaps Wing-commander E.B. Addison did not even try. Jones will not accept either possibility. What is sure is that by the time the watch was changed at Fighter Command headquarters at four p.m., the WAAF officer bringing on the new watch was detailed to transfer her most able plotters from No.11 Group (covering London) to No.10 Group, covering the route to Coventry.[68]

* * *

The Humber had returned to Downing-street. The buff envelope in Churchill's hands had told him that the London raid was off; and that the beams had been found intersecting over Coventry.[69]

Noticing the curiosity at No.10 about his unexpected return, he explained to his staff with perhaps less than utter candour that "the beams" indicated a colossal air raid on London that night, and he was "not going to spend the night peacefully in the country while the Metropolis was under heavy attack."[71] He sent the female staff home to their lodgings, then packed off Colville and Peck, the two private secretaries still on duty, to The Barn. "You are too young to die," he said. He himself mounted to the air ministry roof, "waiting for Moonlight Sonata to begin," as he told Colville afterwards.[72]

He felt little anxiety about Coventry. He had ordered its defences strengthened after Ernie Bevin, now in the War Cabinet, had reported its vulnerability to him on the seventh. Although the first bombs would not fall for several hours there could of course be no question of alerting the whole population (and that is not the point at issue in this narrative.) But since four p.m. the teletypes had gone out from the air ministry to the Commands and ministries concerned, issuing the pre-arranged code-signal: "Executive Cold Water."[70] This triggered immediate counter-measures including bomber attacks on Berlin, the enemy airfields and beam transmitters, and extra fighter cover.

By-passing London, Göring's bomber armada hit Coventry at seven p.m. Fighter Command scrambled 121 fighter planes; twelve thousand rounds of flak ammunition were expended, but neither they nor the fighters injured the attacking force. The diary of General Hoffmann von Waldau, chief of Luftwaffe operations staff, betrays his delight:

Coventry attack proved to be biggest Luftwaffe operation ever and biggest success. Giant fires, 458 planes dropped bombs in good visibility. British report thousands of dead and injured. . . Pleasing results of our own flak particularly at Berlin, altogether ten bombers shot down.

Churchill went back to The Barn to sleep. Archie Sinclair admitted baldly the next day that the result was "thoroughly unsatisfactory." Sir John Anderson described the surviving Coventry workforce as "shaken" and "bitter."[73] Over five hundred and fifty had been killed and fifty thousand homes rendered uninhabitable; twelve aircraft factories — the pilots' allotted targets — had been brought to a standstill. The enemy had lost only one plane, a Dornier. It was not a good beginning for the post-Dowding era.

CHAPTER 36

All Very Innocent

FRIDAY, NOVEMBER 15, 1940: soldiers cordoned off all access roads to Coventry; nobody was allowed through, even with ministry passes. That day the Bletchley oracle spoke again. London was definitely to be the target. The air ministry flashed this secret message to all Commands: "Beams laid from Cherbourg to West of Surbiton station, Olympia, Paddington area, Westbourne Grove."[1]

There had been a time when bombing did not worry Churchill: "I take refuge," he would say, quoting Raymond Poincaré, "beneath the impenetrable arch of probability." He had long since decided that probability needed a tilt — that there was something to be said for spending the night in the country while the Metropolis was under attack; so he had gone again to Dytchley, and summoned Sir Alan Brooke to join him there at five p.m. next evening.

The General was not keen. He had spent a poisonous night in his club with only blankets between himself and eternity, listening to bombs falling all around St James's and fire engines clanging past; he dreaded the bombers far less than the prospect of being kept up until two a.m. listening to the PM.[2]

Returning to Whitehall the PM doublechecked the safety of the Cabinet War Room. While a secretary held a torch he clambered among the new girders and stanchions being inserted beneath the Annexe.[3] He decided to continue living in The Barn.

WITH SUDA BAY NOW a British naval base, he had great plans — he contemplated attacking Abyssinia, campaigning in the Balkans, even re-entering France in 1941. In his imagination he seized the Portuguese Azores and Cape Verde islands, and the Spanish enclave of Ceuta. It was down in this disused Underground station that he called a staff meeting to urge a project which had now become an obsession — the seizure of Pantelleria, an islet seeming to dominate the narrows between Tunisia and Sicily. He wanted a victory, however minor. Only one man was enthusiastic, Admiral Keyes, Director of Combined Operations. He offered his five thousand Commandos for this assault. But Sir Andrew Cunningham demanded a postponement. He loathed Keyes and hated the whole idea — how could the navy supply a garrison on Pantelleria as well as its other duties? Churchill accused the admirals of "negativism" and woeful ignorance of the time factor.[4] Down in The Barn he blistered at the Joint Planning Staff for wet blanketing the fiery Admiral Keyes. "I tell you frankly," he promised, detaining the Admiral afterwards, "I am not going to have anything to do with it unless you lead it."[5]

* * *

The PM risked staying in the Metropolis that night. His oracle had revealed *Regenschirm* as the target for destruction: an obvious reference to Mr Chamberlain's umbrella, and hence to Birmingham, the late premier's constituency. He seemed in better health — his cheeks ruddy, firm and lean — as he drove back to No.10 next morning, November 20, for an hour with Cecil Beaton, photographing him across the Cabinet table.

On the morrow the Monarch would re-open Parliament. Today Churchill invited his ministers to the House for the traditional preview of the King's Speech. They stood self-consciously around his panelled room clutching sherry glasses while Churchill read the text. "It is cu*th*tomary to *th*tand up," he lisped, "when the King*th* *th*peech is read." They stared curiously — they did not often set eyes on him. His lids did not droop, nor were there bags or black lines. One minister found himself fascinated by the eyes — "glaucous, vigilant, angry, combative, visionary and tragic."[6] He was running his war almost single handed, and barely needed ministers.

Anxious for Wavell's offensive to begin, Churchill harried the taciturn General with inquiries. After he drafted one telegram over Eden's head the secretary of war telephoned an acrimonious protest.[7] But he told Eden and Dill on the twenty-second that if Wavell could win a victory in Libya it might impress Turkey to enter the war. A few days later he invited Eden into his bedroom to feast with him on oysters; Winston washed them down with glass after glass of champagne, continuously sipped from an outsize wine glass whose stem he held between the first two fingers, until a healthy pink suffused the unnaturally pallid cheeks. Like father and son, together they looked forward to the time after Wavell's offensive: Eden said they must not leave his army idle — perhaps they should reinforce the Greeks? Bitten by the old unhealthy wanderlust, he suggested flying out to Wavell again.[8]

General Dill, the C.I.G.S., was excluded from such conversations. Churchill found it easy to dominate him. Dill was not getting enough exercise; one attaché found him charming but very pale.[9] He was burdened by a slow domestic tragedy — his wife was fading away at his Westminster apartment, paralyzed and unable to speak. Moreover, Beaverbrook had begun poisoning Churchill's mind against him in favour of the Ack-Ack General Pile. Once Churchill taunted Dill that he wished he had General Papagos to run the army. Dill was a thoroughbred, too finely tuned to handle the "gangster transactions" of politicians, as he called them; he poured out his heart to Brooke about how difficult he found the PM to deal with, and Brooke wrote, "I feel he is having a miserable life."[10]

Churchill thrived on friction; he wanted his lieutenants to be at each other's throats, not his. Beaverbrook squirmed, but toed the line. "In Cabinet meetings," learned one observer, referring to the Canadian, "he crabs the plans laid before them and is the one dissentient in almost everything. His close tie-up with Churchill is a thing of the past."[11] On December 2, Beaverbrook wrote once again tendering his resignation. "When the reservoir was empty," he grumbled, sour that he was no longer getting his way, "I was a genius. Now that the reservoir has some water in it, I am an inspired brigand. If the water slops over I will be a bloody anarchist." He suggested Churchill hand over aircraft production to somebody who would "inspire confidence" at the air ministry. The PM replied sharply. "You are in the galleys," he wrote, "and will have to row on to the end."[12]

Beaverbrook was not an easy horse to ride. Altogether he submitted half a dozen such resignations. Months later he would write cheekily to the prime minister that he had deduced what was wanted of him: to stay in office, but "to storm, to threaten resignation — and to withdraw again."[13]

AS THOUGH TO ASSERT his potency, Winston thrived on cutting short majestic careers; his own ruthlessness rejuventated him. His baleful eye had settled again on the navy in the Mediterranean, despite the daring exploits which had recently tilted the balance firmly in its favour. By hit and run tactics Admirals Cunningham and Somerville had gnawed at the Italian navy's superior strength. A spectacular Fleet Air Arm attack had crippled three of Mussolini's biggest warships in harbour at Taranto. Despite these triumphs, Churchill was out for Somerville's blood: in fact he had wanted revenge ever since Somerville had dared criticize the massacre at Mers-el-Kébir.

On November 27 the PM saw his chance. Escorting a convoy from Gibraltar the Admiral had briefly tangled with the Italian battle fleet off

Sardinia but gave up the chase when they outran him. To Churchill this smacked of a dearth of "offensive spirit" and he rushed Admiral Lord Cork out to investigate. But hearing jubilant Italian propagandists claim that Somerville had "run away" he had second thoughts — a court-martial now would confirm the propaganda — and suggested they merely tell Somerville to haul down his flag. He would put Admiral Sir Henry Harwood in his place, the victor over the *Graf Spee*. He had entertained him recently at Chequers and liked his style.

But Cork was already out at Gibraltar, so it was too late to call off his investigation; Churchill expressed confidence that Somerville could nonetheless be relieved within the week — unless of course found blameless, which seemed to him hardly likely.[14] To the PM's chagrin Cork not only exonerated the admiral but called the investigation a "bloody outrage" while privately urging him not to bear hard feelings against the admiralty: there were, he apologized, people inside and out — which the victim took as an aspersion to Tom Phillips and Winston Churchill — ready to "raise their voices without any knowledge of the facts."[15]*

While this row was blazing, in Defence Committee on the fourth he asked impatiently about Wavell's offensive, and was indignant that Eden could not say when it would begin. He criticised the generals, ranted that the army should "do something," and sulked when Eden suggested leaving Wavell to do as he thought best; the normally whitefaced Dill coloured with anger at the PM's attitude.[16] Winston was unrepentant. "If with the situation as it is," he wrote to the C.I.G.S. a few days later, "General Wavell is only playing small and is not hurling in his whole available forces with furious energy, he will have failed to rise to the height of circumstances. I never worry about action, but only about inaction."[17]

Churchill revived his current obsession Pantelleria. He put it to Chiefs of Staff and Keyes on the third. But two days later it was finally shelved in Defence Committee. Eden poured cold water on the project, though carefully attributing to Wavell the blunt opinion that the islet seemed "an insufficient prize." The First Sea Lord agreed, alarmed at the sidetracking of warships he urgently needed for convoy duties. "Pantelleria," he quietly murmured, "has so far caused us very little trouble." Roger Keyes did not attend, and the plan was shelved, to Churchill's enduring discontent. "It is really a terrible business having

---

*Readers already dubious about the Official Histories may compare Capt. S.R. Roskill's bold 1977 narrative in *Churchill & The Admirals* with his anodyne 1954 account in the official *The War at Sea*. The latter narrative published during Mr Churchill's second premiership makes no mention of his part in this episode.

R.K. mixed up with the business as DCO," Admiral Pound lamented later. He is a perfect nuisance. . . The only thing he cares about is the glorification of R.K."[18]

* * *

That day, December 5, he drove over to the Spanish embassy to lunch with the Duke of Alba. When the civil war broke out in July 1936 the traditionalist in him had swayed him to General Franco's cause against the Republicans. He became a fervent advocate of non-intervention during August and insisted that the majority was on the rebel side. On October 2, 1936, moved by the atrocities committed by the communists and anarchists, he had declared: "It would be a mistake alike in truth and wisdom for British public opinion to rate both sides at the same level." He was initially unmoved by news that German and Italian "volunteers" had begun slaying Russian Bolshevists and French Communists in Spain. "When I search my heart," he announced on January 7, 1937, "Even if all these armed tourists to Spain were to transfix each other with the simultaneous efficiency of Ivan the Terrible and Bulbul Amir, till there was no one left except the press representatives to tell the tale, I cannot feel that the interests and safety of Britain would be in any way endangered." Only in April 1938 had he reversed his public stand and spoken out against Franco.

But in private he liked the Spanish and had urged Roosevelt to ship victuals to them. There were sound political reasons for alleviating their suffering. Germany had to be kept away from Gibraltar.

"In your civil war," the Spanish ambassador reported Churchill as saying at this luncheon, "I at first took your side, and if I were a Spaniard I would have served Franco without hesitation.

> Subsequently, when I saw Germany and Italy intervene, I believed as a good British patriot that a Nationalist triumph was not in our interests and for this reason I went so far as to write articles against you. Later still I persuaded myself that it was not certain that you were in the wrong, and I tried to demonstrate this by my speeches to the House. It pained me, to be sure, that my words were not published in the Spanish press.
>
> We have decided — and I have intervened personally now in this matter — to facilitate supplies to Spain as much as possible. Will Spain be able to resist Germany's pressure? We ourselves desire to maintain the best and most cordial relations with you, and if these change you can be certain that we shall not be to blame. I detest Communism as much as you do yourselves.[19]

Hitler had sent his Chief of Intelligence, Admiral Canaris, to pressure Franco in Madrid. If Churchill was reading the German diplomatic cables he could follow the admiral's progress. Two nights after the London banquet Franco rebuffed Hitler: in both countries' interests, as he put it, he declined to approve of Felix — the proposed entry of German troops into Spain scheduled for January 10; he did not want Spain to become a burden on the Axis.[20]

The self-effacing cryptanalysts at Bletchley were the unsung heroes to Churchill's strategy. The strain on these men and women was seldom less than on their comrades in combat. One professor — who would eventually crack Brown, the cipher used by the Hitler's secret weapons establishments — was slowly cracking up himself. His colleagues saw him storm out slamming doors or wrapping an imaginary gown about himself. How many German deaths were already on their minds, how many British lives? Churchill longed to magnify and sing their praises, but could do so only in the utmost privacy. Visiting these rare people once, he complimented them: "You all look very, uh," he began, groping for the right expression of what was passing through his mind, "*innocent.*"[21]

* * *

Churchill would have found time for an embassy luncheon even if Hitler was not wooing Franco: eating was his second major pleasure. Told in Cabinet that sardine imports would have to cease he had quietly vowed out of earshot, as he thought, "I shall never eat another sardine."[22] The noises of uninhibited digestion added to his eating pleasure — if not of his neighbours. After one Chequers dinner a supreme commander secretly demonstrated to his incredulous staff "how the PM eats his soup — if 'eats' is the word:"

> Being short and blockily built his mouth isn't very much above the soup plate. He crouches over the plate, almost has his nose in the soup, wields the spoon rapidly. The soup disappears to the accompaniment of loud and raucous gurglings.[23]

"On the first sip of clear turtle soup," wrote the Ivy League host of a Churchill banquet years later, "his head bobbed up and down in vigorous approval. He was firm about having no sherry in the soup, pushing away the heavy silver ladle which the waiter almost reverently proffered; but the soup in its unboosted state disappeared into the Marlborough throat with a smacking of lips and hissing inspirations which, had they been broadcast to the nation as an example of table etiquette, would have undone in a single stroke the entire theory of polite eating as now applied to American children." When the terrapin was brought in he lowered his mouth and forked in the rare fish with the "businesslike thrust of the grab bucket of a steam shovel."[24]

* * *

In the distance that Sunday evening, December 8, 1940, he could hear London again being bombed. Four hundred bombers were over the capital. But the news from Madrid was good: a visitor noticed that he looked vigorous and bright of eye and confident.[25] He had another reason too: General Wavell had begun slowly advancing into the western desert. For five weeks Winston had had one nightmare — that "some sandstorm" would give the generals a chance to cry off the offensive.

The next morning, he pulled on a fur-collared topcoat, drove to Westminster and picked over charred wreckage in Parliament escorted by Eric Seal and a policeman. "Horrible!" he observed, without plucking the cigar from his mouth. Bombs had demolished the wing where Oliver Cromwell signed King Charles's death warrant.[26] He went back to his bunker to preside over a night air defence meeting and sent Clemmie out to tour the shelters. She had a realistic understanding of the common people's problems, as her recommendations showed — models of logic and humanity, which Winston passed on without amendment to Herbert Morrison.

The news was that British troops were now engaging the Italians south of Sidi Barrani. In Cabinet he apologized for having taken the decision to authorize this offensive with only Defence Committee approval. As Lieutenant General Sir Richard O'Connor's two divisions rolled westwards into Libya they took thousands of prisoners and killed or captured several Italian generals. With visions of corn falling before the sickle, Churchill reported this victory to the house on the tenth. Eden telephoned that O'Connor had taken Sidi Barrani. Unable to sleep for excitement he even telephoned Eden on the twelfth to complain about not pursuing the Italians hard enough, and rasped about "missed opportunities." It was a symptom of his continuing distrust of local commanders.[27]

He basked in reflected glory, not all of it unjustified. To the Dominion premiers he preened himself for having run the risk, "in the teeth of the invasion menace," of reinforcing the Middle East.[28] It was a bald untruth but he had come to believe it himself, and repeated it to his duty secretary who was not aware of Bletchley's achievements. With unconscious irony he predicted how future History would have written of this "gamble" had it failed — of his criminal folly in exposing Britain to invasion, compounded by sending to Greece the very squadrons that might have brought victory in Egypt. But it had not failed: he had brought this offensive to brilliant fulfilment — "unlike Narvik," he sighed, "which of all [the] fiascos had . . . been the worst — except for Dakar."[29]

Flushed and jubilant, he carried the tidings to his junior ministers assembled in the bunker for the purpose. His earlier obloquy about the

Cairo generals was forgotten. "In Wavell," he announced, "we have got a winner." The victory would send ripples around the Mediterranean and as far as Moscow. One minister dictated afterwards:

> The PM says that he is quite sure that Hitler cannot lie down under this. Perhaps within three weeks, and certainly within three months, he must make some violent counter-stroke. What will it be? An attempt, at long last, to invade us? Perhaps a gas attack on us on an immense scale, drenching our cities with mustard?

The British, Churchill continued, must be prepared for worse to come. There was nothing to stop Hitler advancing through to Salonika. As for American aid, he expressed perennial optimism. "They will soon be in the war in fact," he hinted, "if not in form." His message to Washington would be this: So you want to watch us fighting for your liberties? Then you'll have to pay for the performance.[30]

AFTER BEING LAID UP for decades the fifty destroyers which he had wrested from the U.S. Congress had proven of such questionable seaworthiness that he was loath to put British sailors aboard them. Two of the destroyers turned turtle and sank. The Director of Naval Intelligence learned that they were unstable.[31] Dining at Chequers with Churchill and Lord Louis Mountbatten an army lieutenant gathered that the ships' designer had been sacked. "They roll 70°," he wrote a few days later. They would be useless until refitted, in the spring.[32]

Unofficial Washington jeered that having cried out for the ships now Churchill was not manning them. The truth was more unpleasant but in the current state of play he could hardly complain to Roosevelt. Britain would shortly need massive financial aid and he spent two weeks drafting an appeal to Roosevelt. No doubt gritting his teeth, he praised the destroyers as "invaluable."[33] Anticipating further jeers, he confidentially asked the admiralty for data on the destroyers — when each had arrived and "defects that had to be remedied."[34] In Cabinet he confessed that he was chilled by the American attitude since the presidential election.[35] Worried, Churchill tried to coax some response: a typical telegram began temptingly, "You may be interested to receive the following naval notes on the action at Taranto. . ."[36] Viewed from Downing-street, Roosevelt's was the silence of the sphinx.

Britain was now buying hundreds of fighter planes, aircraft and aero engines from America; billions of bullets, tons of explosives, a million rifles and machine guns. When there were delays the PM would telephone to the British Purchasing Commission in Washington, to inquire; its director, Arthur Purvis had direct access to the White House. Purvis had reported to him in person late in November; Churchill liked his eagerness and invited him down to Chequers to work with him on the latest dramatic appeal to Roosevelt.[37]

The fifteen page document was cabled to Lord Lothian, the ambassador in Washington, on December 7, "a statement of the minimum action necessary to achieve our common purpose." Churchill referred in it to Britain's "perhaps unexpected" recovery, but predicted that the decision for 1941 would lie upon the high seas, across which the supplies had to be brought.

> We can endure [he wrote] the shattering of our dwellings and the slaughter of our civil population by indiscriminate air attacks, and we hope to parry these increasingly as our science develops, and to repay them upon military objectives in Germany as our Air Force more nearly approaches the strength of the enemy.

After discussing other ways in which the United States could help he turned to the underlying nightmare: how to finance all this. "The moment approaches," wrote the PM, "when we shall no longer be able to pay cash for shipping and other supplies. While we will do our utmost, and shrink from no proper sacrifice to make payments across the exchange, I believe you will agree that it would be wrong in principle and mutually disadvantageous in effect if, at the height of this struggle, Great Britain were to be divested of all saleable assets so that after the victory was won with our blood, civilisation saved, and the time gained for the United States to be fully armed against all eventualities, we should stand stripped to the bone."[38]

* * *

Uncertain about the future, he had resumed his flirtation with Vichy. He told General de Gaulle only in part — about the prospect of winning over General Weygand. The Free French General was careful not to agree to serve under this rival.[39] Shortly impressive secret assurances reached London from Vichy: Professor Rougier sent a written statement.[40]* The Canadian chargé at Vichy, Pierre Dupuy, confirmed the terms orally with Pétain and his ministers. Churchill asked Halifax to circularize details to the Cabinet in utmost secrecy.[41] A few days later Dupuy came down to Chequers and reported over dinner that Pétain, Darlan — now prime minister — and Huntziger, the minister of war, had suggested they co-operate with Britain behind a fake "smokescreen" of

---

*Rougier had gone on to Washington. Churchill proposed they buy his silence. The F.O. instructed the Washington embassy to "discuss Rougier's financial position with him," and added, "We are rather apprehensive of his indiscretions. One report states that he is incapable of holding his tongue."

apparent hostility. Even Darlan had agreed, while huffing that after Mers-el-Kébir he would never shake hands with a British officer again.[42]

Fate would reward these three Frenchmen poorly: Pétain was sentenced to death by de Gaulle for treason; Darlan, assassinated by an S.O.E. hired gun; Huntziger, liquidated by de Gaulle's agents.[43]

ALONE AMONG CHURCHILL'S colleagues, Lord Halifax was quite underawed by the PM. Rather proud of the fact, the foreign secretary had noted in his diary on the last day of April, after Churchill had been "rather cantankerous" at the Cabinet meeting: "It is a source of amusement to me to watch John Simon slightly mesmerized by him, and his look of surprise if I venture, as I often do, to butt into Winston's tirades; the latter doesn't really mind, but grunts a bit over his cigar and is as friendly as ever afterwards." With Winston now prime minister, that friendliness had worn thin, and their relations had smouldered all that autumn on a shortening fuse.

According to some the devout Catholic insisted on starting Cabinet with a prayer. He was a knobbly, gangling aristocrat who wore ancient leather-trimmed tweeds as a conscious mark of superior breeding. He fled most weekends to Yorkshire to escape the PM's verbosity, but was pursued even there by the PM's lisping, snuffling voice, calling him by telephone; he found he could kill this irksome long distance verbal floodtide ruthlessly, by interrupting: "What's that, Winston. I can't pwoperly hear you!" (He could not pronounce his r's.)

After one late November Cabinet had dragged on wholly needlessly Halifax blamed it on Winston's infatuation with his own voice. Worse had followed — a Defence Committee "at which Winston turned up in a grey romper suit," as Halifax disrespectfully termed the siren suit. "It was all I could do to keep my face straight." The PM talked from nine-thirty until midnight, "round and round and across."[44] Sometimes, commented one colleague approvingly, Halifax could "give the PM the unmistakeable impression that he regarded him as a very vulgar and ignorant person."[45] Churchill allowed it to be noised around that Halifax was having the F.O. flat elaborately redecorated, and chortled at the resulting contumely heaped upon the minister. (Halifax never used the flat.) The elaborate building works on Churchill's own "Annexe" never became known.

The differences with Halifax shortly came to a head. After seeing him briefly on Thursday the twelfth Churchill drove to Chequers. He had arranged a private preview of Charlie Chaplin's new movie, The Great Dictator. But unexpected news reached him: Lord Lothian, the ambassador in Washington, had died. He had become increasingly drowsy, fallen ill, and being a Christian Scientist had refused treatment. Thoughts of man's mortality oppressed Churchill; only a few days ago Lothian had lunched with him. Brooding over dinner, he reflected on the future — of both Europe and himself. The one should become a confederation, the other retire to Chartwell to write a book about the war; he knew its ending, and he had its outline in his head.* The thankless task of reconstructing Europe would be best bequeathed to his successors.

Washington was the plum embassy posting. Churchill contemplated sending the even drowsier Pound; considered Vansittart, who had aroused American disquiet by asinine broadcasts about Germany; looked at Lyttelton, and opted for David Lloyd George, the fiery Welshman. Wrapping a rainbow coloured kimono around his siren-suit, he phoned the ex-premier's son to sound him about his father. Lloyd George declared himself still willing: Winston returned to the Great Hall and planted himself beaming in front of the fire. He invited Halifax down to lunch on Saturday and told him. But this solution was soon shot down. The Welshman's doctor opposed it; and the embassy in Washington advised that Lloyd George was regarded as an appeaser and "not unwilling to consider making terms with Germany."[47]

Then Eden, still secretary for war, came down to Sunday dinner. Together they watched Gone with the Wind, then sat up late talking. Eden had long resigned himself to Churchill clinging on to the premiership until the war was over. But he spread the flattery as thick as butter every time he could. After the PM's sixty-sixth birthday he had forced himself to pen a fulsome letter about how heartened he had been to hear Winston remark that he had never felt more equal to his work than now. "All the same," he had written ingratiatingly, "take care of yourself." Somehow between them, in the warm afterglow of Clark Gable and Vivian Leigh, the ideal solution occurred to them: that Halifax should be moved three thousand miles to Washington, while Eden moved into the Foreign Office — only a few yards from No.10. Churchill saw Eden again on the sixteenth before lunching with Lloyd George, and by next day he had made up his mind.

A multitude of reasons underpinned the choice: True, Halifax was as much an appeaser as Lloyd George — and Lothian for that matter. In Britain, Winston quietly told his staff, he had "no future." But he

---

*Hitler expressed similar ideas after Franco let him down: "We sat for a long time," wrote one listener, "with the Führer around the fireside. He talked about his pension — that of a middlegrade civil servant! He is going to write books — a third volume of *Mein Kampf* . . . entitled *Collected Broken Promises*, and books on Frederick the Great, Luther and Napoleon." He would give Churchill "leave to paint and write his memoirs."[46]

could yet restore his name if he could bring America into the war.[48] Appointing the foreign secretary to the embassy might seem like a demotion to him: but it would flatter the Americans. Halifax cursed Eden for stabbing him in the back. Eden told him, "In wartime everybody must go where they are sent." Over dinner with Eden on Thursday, Churchill said that Halifax had suggested that Eden take Washington instead. Eden turned that down and on Friday the PM wrote to Halifax insisting. "You are," he said, "I am sure, the one person best qualified for this paramount duty."[49] Lady Halifax was furious at seeing her husband shunted into this Washington cul de sac. She rampaged into No.10 at her husband's side and asked bluntly what the emoluments would be: "When they had been promised plenty of money," wrote Beaverbrook maliciously, "all was well."[50]

Headaches plagued Churchill when he listened to these tiresome squabbles. Later that Friday Eden came down to Chequers, handed his rakish hat to the butler, and sat up with the PM. Winston reassured him that he would make a marvellous foreign secretary. "It is like moving up from fourth form to Sixth," he suggested.[51] In fact he was appointing a nonentity, and deliberately. While every poll demonstrated his immense popularity, Eden was admired by nobody at Cabinet level except himself. "I should hate to have in [Halifax's] place," wrote one minister, "that wretched Eden, posing before the looking-glass."[52] Americans might dub him "Miss England," but he was oblivious to his reputation for vanity. Winston might call him his "Princess Elizabeth," and did; Eden took it as a compliment.[53] One of his staff at the Dominions Office recalled that Eden had asked outright for "as much publicity as possible."[54] Nor did the new foreign secretary impress foreign notables. He had rather liked Hitler, but the Führer had dismissed him as a "brilliantined dandy."* The American military attaché meeting him at a dinner party with the C.I.G.S. would make a note of his "extreme collegiate manner — rather limp and inclined to flop about." "He was the only one," commented this general, "who sat at table feeding himself like an untrained child."[55]

A few days later an intimate emissary sent by Roosevelt met the new foreign secretary: "The words," he reported to the President, ". . . carried no conviction, for I am sure the man has no deeply rooted moral stamina. A goodly number of soft Britishers must like him and his hat and I fancy Churchill gives him high office because he neither thinks,

---

*In February 1934 he told Jan Masaryk the Führer made an excellent impression on him. "He considers Hitler an honest fanatic who does not want war," noted the Czech diplomat. "My own impression is that Eden's promotion to Lord Privy Seal and tour of Europe right afterwards have gone to his head."[56]

acts — much less say[s] — anything of importance."* For an hour Eden dilated on the Balkan war and the desert. "I gained the impression," his visitor secretly wrote to Roosevelt that day, "that Mr Anthony Eden had little more to do with the prosecution of the war than the Supreme Court. . . . Mr Eden took [me] to my car where the photographers were conveniently and no doubt spontaneously waiting."[57]

Churchill's future ambassador to Washington was a different breed altogether. Just as those who worked with horses or dogs might come to resemble them, observed one envious colleague at this time, so Halifax was "touched with a distant semblance of stags and the like." The same American visitor commended him to Roosevelt. "A tall, stoop shouldered aristocrat with one hand in a gray glove greeted me," he described, and summarized: "I liked him."[58]

Lord Halifax had tried even harder than Chamberlain to halt this ruinous war. But he had the grace to concede defeat. Before giving him a triumphant send-off to Chesapeake Bay aboard the new battleship *King George V*, Winston proposed his health at the farewell Pilgrims' luncheon. Here, he said, went a man of deep religious conviction; and an ardent supporter of the chase. "And thus," he followed, with a gentle twinkle in his eye, "he has always succeeded in getting the best of both worlds."

Halifax rose drily to the occasion. As Viceroy of India, he said, he had once thanked the stationmaster at Delhi for the excellent arrangements for his journey. The turbaned Indian gentleman had bowed low and replied, "It has always been a very great pleasure to see you off."

He ventured a mirthless smile. "No doubt many of you here to-day are animated by feelings no less kindly."[59]

*　*　*

Still visited by doubts about his own longevity, Churchill passed an afternoon on a twice-postponed call at his old school, his first in thirty years. Once during the wilderness years, hoping to wallow in nostalgia, he had driven out to Harrow with Lord Birkenhead only to be espied and booed by a multitude of pupils; he vowed never to darken Harrow's door again. But the school had had its share of bombs and casualties, and he softened. Together with his Harrovian colleagues he joined in the lusty songs remembered from half a century before, and tears rolled down his cheeks to the concealed merriment of the boys.

---

*From the handwritten original in the Harry Hopkins papers in New York. Robert Sherwood, *The White House Papers of Harry Hopkins*, 238, imperceptibly omitted these lines. One more example why it pays to eschew printed sources.

After the memorial service for Lothian, Dalton came over to No.10 and spoke with Churchill who had not attended the abbey, sending Bracken in his place. Being partly responsible for psychological warfare, Dalton's people had drafted a script for Churchill to broadcast urging the Italians to get rid of Mussolini. Given his recent setbacks the time was ripe. Dalton said his agents would make hay when the Fascist leader visited Milan.

Churchill remarked, "They will all be killed."

"No doubt," said Dalton without feeling. "But that is war. If they can add to the confusion and loss of morale, they will help us to a victory." In his secret diary he observed that they must offer "a fair price" to Italians willing to get rid of "M[ussolini] and his gang." He added however, "There is no place today for stupid doctrinaire prejudices against Fascism as such. If some Fascist toughs will murder M. and a few more, and then join with others representing the royal family, the army, industry, the Italian workers and peasants, we must not reject them for the sake of some thin theory."[60]

The PM broadcast the desired text on the twenty-third from his bunker. One American journalist remarked, "It is the best thing that Winston has ever done."[61]

One thing puzzled him on reflection: retaliation against Germany — what the Air Ministry had alluringly called "knock for knock" — was not working. The enemy raids were getting worse. After Coventry, Bomber Command was ordered (on December 4) to deliver an area attack with the town centre explicitly stated as aiming point for the first time. The Cabinet approved this order retroactively on the thirteenth and the first such attack was executed three nights later on Mannheim, an inland port and a chemical centre. Experienced crews went in first as fire-raisers. But now Photographic Reconnaissance was available for the first time; and the photographs taken five days later showed that despite bright moonlight the 134 bombers had caused no damage to the town. The P.R. unit then photographed oilplants allegedly attacked by hundreds of bombers. They had not been damaged either. Seemingly Mr Churchill's night bombers, lacking navigation aids, had so far released most of their munitions into countryside or open sea.

It was a sobering revelation, and certainly untimely: On his resolve, the war economy was being geared to an immense bomber programme (it was not a Cabinet decision). The discovery that humans cannot see in the dark was not new. But there was no way back now.

Two or three times over the next three weeks the Canadian defence minister Colonel James L. Ralston called on Churchill and expressed concern about how he proposed to employ the Canadian contingent training in Britain. "I mentioned," Ralston reported to Ottawa after seeing the PM in the Cabinet Room on December 17, "that in Canada already there had been newspaper reports intimating that it was proposed to send Canadians to the Middle East." Ralston reminded Mr Churchill that such a proposal had never even been put forward: "We assume," he said, "that employment of our troops outside of the United Kingdom will be left for our suggestion."

"Of course," replied Churchill, and mentioned in his next breath that there was "always a very real threat" of Nazi invasion.

> He was confident [reported the Canadian minister] that notwithstanding [Hitler's] apparently great military superiority we can survive and eventually defeat him. Victory might, however, take years.

In his private diary Ralston described a Churchill conference on gun production that day with the minister of supply. "Churchill," he wrote, "completely dominated the situation. They were all assembled and Churchill was writing something. They all sat around and spoke in whispers. No one took liberties and the atmosphere was only lightened when he made some Churchillian remark."

Ruling that Germany was not to be bombed over Christmas — an act of charity that under these circumstances seems of only academic interest — Mr Churchill drove down to Chequers. (He had probably been warned by Bletchley that Hitler had already issued identical orders.*)

"Wonder whether the Germans will fall into the trap!" wondered an F.O. official. They did not. Afterwards, he heaved a sigh of relief. "Thank Goodness we decided not to bomb," he wrote. "We should have looked fools talking what Joe K[ennedy] would call all that 'God stuff,' if we had bombed and the Germans had not."[62]

As Papa Winston joined his family that Christmas, Mary observed that everybody was in good spirits. "No reports," she entered carefully in her teenager's diary, "of any air, land or sea activity."

True, her Papa made a point of working on, and exhorted his staff to do the same: but after the Christmas turkey the necktie was loosened, and Sarah sang while husband Vic Oliver strummed the piano. Everybody joined in until far into the night — the PM singing lustily and occasionally in tune; and when their Viennese family pianist hammered out some waltzes Winston trod what one secretary called "a remarkably frisky measure of his own" on the centre of the floor. "This," wrote Mary that day, "was one of the happiest Christmases I can remember. . . I've

---

*After visiting German airforce headquarters, Görings deputy Erhard Milch recorded in his pocket notebook: "From 24th till 26th, a.m., no attacks on England on Führer's orders." (In author's possession.)

never before seen the family look so happy — so united." They were all there, son, daughters, spouses and now even a grandson. "No one but the family," Winston told Halifax in a proud letter, old enmities forgotten. "And oddly enough the whole of it." Christmas one year later would find them both three thousand miles away.

He had invited the clever and perceptive Canadian, Colonel Ralston, to weekend at Chequers together with Canada's ambassador to Vichy, Dupuy. Ralston's diary gives a vivid picture of that weekend:

Saturday, December 21, 1940: The Prime Minister did not come down so we chatted until dinner time, 8:40 p.m., with Mrs Churchill, very kindly and agreeable, and Miss Mary, most attractive and unspoiled.

At dinner the Prime Minister was vigorous and intensely interesting and told us the story of . . . Dunkirk and . . . his conferences with Gamelin and others. He described graphically the rearguard battles to enable the withdrawal to be made at Dunkirk. . . I was in no position to check the facts but it did seem to me that the story upheld almost too wonderfully, and that it might be that there were rough edges which had been smoothed off in the telling.

It was however an outstanding demonstration of vitality, clearheadedness . . . the story of a man who would not simply sit by and allow the staff to work things out, but had night and day taken a direct hand in the policies being carried out.

More than once during the evening he gave evidence of his fighting quality and his confidence in the indomitable spirit of the people of England. He described their fighting with pitchforks and hoes and shovels. He was asked what England would do if Hitler attempted to invade. He said that they would drown as many of them as they could on the way over and knock the rest of them on the head when they got there. He said the Hun had to be fought with everything we have.

"I shall stop at nothing," Churchill said. The Canadian defence minister continued his diary the next day:

Sunday, December 22, 1940: While Churchill was working (in bed), Howe, MacQueen and I went up to say goodbye. . . He had a big mahogany board with legs on it on the counterpane. On the right hand side was the despatch box with the lid up and all the papers and whatnots; left on the table were clips, extra supplies of paper, general stationery sundries.

Churchill was busy pasting red stickers, which he was wetting with a moistener held in his left hand, onto documents from the box. Ralston saw that they were printed with big black letters, ACTION THIS DAY.

He smoked the regulation long cigar, which by the way only seems to get smoked now and again. His practice (I saw him at dinner) is to chew the fuller end of the cigar, the cigar having gone out, then finally to cut down both ends and get a fresh grip. He then lights the fuller end and most gradually consumes the cigar, more by chewing than by burning. . . He is to see Dupuy again. . . I must say that I came away with a deep impression of his robust courage, force and resourcefulness.[63]

Churchill drove down again to Chequers for the following weekend.

Invisible, five thousand feet above London's empty streets that Sunday night, December 29, the *Knickebein* radio beams intersected in the pitch darkness above the University tower. At seven p.m. the enemy arrived at that crossroads in the ether, and began dropping explosives and incendiary canisters. It was only on a moderate scale, with 136 bombers — two more than Churchill had sent to Mannheim. But the City buildings were locked, deserted and inaccessible; and the river was at low ebb. When the all clear sounded two hours later, fifteen hundred fires were burning; and these multiplied to four thousand. A fifty-knot wind fanned eastwards across the City until the blaze was out of control. Wren churches, the Guildhall, County Hall, bastions of the Tower itself — masterpieces of London's architectural history — folded into the unfeeling flames.

The newspapers needed to penetrate no cordons to visit the wasted streets. They were on their very doorstep. "Near the office," wrote Cecil King, footsore after picking his way for hours through the wreckage, "there was one big fire.

It stretches from Usher Walker's premises, just off Fetter Lane, through Gough Square (Dr Johnson's House is apparently not touched after all) to Eyre & Spottiswoods (completely gutted) and Shoe Lane. St Bride's was destroyed . . . almost every building round St Paul's, including the old Chapter House, the whole of Newgate Street, both sides from the Old Bailey to St Martin's le Grand, including one of the three huge blocks comprising the G.P.O.. . . One side of Moorgate is badly burnt as far as Finsbury Square. Then I turned west again through Bunhill Fields — two sides of the three built up are gutted, and all around the City Road, Old St and Goswell Road. . . There is another bad area near the Tower and another in Cannon Street and Queen Victoria Street and I heard London Bridge Station is burnt down. In all it is obviously the greatest disaster to London since the Great Fire.

"It gives us a grand chance of building up a fair city," he concluded — over-optimistically, it would turn out: "But . . . the City of London as I have known it for twenty years has gone."[64]

Churchill had tuned in to hear Roosevelt's fireside chat as bomb flashes lit the distant skyline like the flicker of sheet-lightning over London. "There is no demand for sending an American expeditionary force outside our own borders," the president was saying, in that tone of ringing sincerity that had become so familiar now. "There is no intention by any member of your Government to send such a force. You can therefore nail — *nail* — any talk about sending armies to Europe as deliberate untruth."

But after that disappointment came a phrase which uplifted Mr Churchill's stout heart: President Roosevelt talked of America becoming "the Arsenal of Democracy."

CHAPTER 37

The Unsordid Act

ON THE DAY THAT President Franklin D. Roosevelt died, Churchill telegraphed to a mutual friend that he understood the depth of his grief. "We have lost one of our greatest friends and one of the most valiant champions of the causes for which we fight," he said. "I had a true affection for Franklin."[1] From first to last, he had not understood Roosevelt's imperatives; he had been unable to penetrate the wall of implacable American self interest.

Seen from the banks of the Potomac river, Roosevelt was the most illustrious American of the century. He gave his ragged nation a sense of empire. Ten millions were unemployed and his New Deal was in disarray, but by plugging into Churchill's war at the most judicious moment he would bring wealth and prosperity to his great nation. With eleven millions under arms, and by ruthless power politics and financial huckstering, he made it a great Power. He blackjacked his allies into parting with their Gold. Loaded with new richesse he contemplated taking over Britain's colonies, and offered cash on the nose for defeated France's two latest battleships, *Jean Bart* and *Richelieu*.

Twice by late 1940 contemporaries had benevolently applied the label "gangster" to Mr Churchill. But in a century of gangster statesmen, he and Roosevelt were not on the same side; they were not playing the same game; they were not even in the same league. "I never let my right hand know what my left hand does," the president told his Treasury secretary as he settled into his third term. "I may have one policy for Europe and one diametrically opposite for North and South America. . . And furthermore," he bragged, unwittingly echoing Hitler's words, "I am perfectly willing to mislead and tell untruths if it will help win the war."[2]*

He ran rings around the British and boasted that he was better at

---

*On June 2, 1941 Hitler told his staff, "As a private person I would never break my word. As a politician for the sake of Germany, if need be, one thousand times!" — *Hitler's War*.

it than President Woodrow Wilson.[3] He regarded Churchill as a pushover — unreliable and "tight most of the time."[4] He turned a deaf ear on all Churchill's pleas: when the PM suggested he send American warships to Britain's Imperial outpost at Singapore to keep the Japanese in line — since he was about to reopen the Burma Road to let supplies into China — he got no joy from the White House.[5]

This is not surprising. The survival of the British Empire did not figure high on Roosevelt's priorities. "I would rather," said Roosevelt in 1942, "lose New Zealand, Australia or anything else than have the Russians collapse."[6] A few weeks later he repeated this. England was, he said, "an old, tired power" and must take second place to the younger United States, Russia and China.[7] Later this sly statesman conceded, "When there are four people sitting in at a poker game and three of them are against the fourth, it is a little hard on the fourth." Vice President Henry Wallace took this as an admission that Roosevelt, Stalin and Chiang kai-Shek were ganging up against Mr Churchill.[8]

France's humiliating defeat and Britain's threatening bankruptcy gave Roosevelt the opportunity to clean up these old empires. At Teheran in 1943 he would confide to Joseph Stalin, "I want to do away with the word Reich." He added, "In any language." Stalin liked that. "Not just the *word*," he said.[9] Roosevelt's policy was to pay out just enough to give the Empire support — the kind of support a rope gives a hanging man. When his Treasury secretary confirmed after visiting London in 1944 that Britain was penniless, the cynical man in the Oval Office would prick up his ears and snicker. "I had no idea," he said, "I will go over there and make a couple of talks and take over the British Empire."[10]

This inspired American statesman would pursue his subversion of the Empire throughout the war. He might lead the crusade for democracy, but he expected the frontline nations to foot the bill. During the Munich crisis, he had predicted to his Cabinet that the United States would be enriched by any resulting war. Sure enough, Gold from the beleaguered nations had begun to flow in payment for American war materials. The 1939 revision of neutrality legislation, which legalized this sale of war goods to belligerents, and the Johnson Debt-Default Act required that such purchases be for cash. So the great blood-letting began. Britain donated £2,078m of aid to her own minor allies during the war years, but the United States extorted from her every moveable asset in return for acting as the Arsenal of Democracy. During the war Britain would sell off £1,118m of foreign investments; in addition, her foreign debt would increase by £2,595m from 1938 to 1945.[11] Formerly the world's major creditor, Britain became an international pauper and even forty years later she had not permanently recovered.

A FAVOURITE POEM OF Churchill's ended with the rousing line: "But westward, look, the land is bright!" The transatlantic incandescence in 1940 was the glow of Europe's Gold, as it was carted to America by cruiser and battleship. Britain too had snapped up what Gold she could — Britain had impounded the Romanian, seized the Czech, and, to use one F.O. official's word, "snaffled" the Dutch and Belgian.[12] As France collapsed, a benign Roosevelt offered safekeeping to her Gold too; Reynaud had shipped 500 tons across the Atlantic.[13] Later Roosevelt tried to obtain the Soviet reserves as well and called their ambassador Constantine Oumansky "a dirty little liar" when he demurred.[14]

Mocking the president's Wagnerian lust for this precious metal, Churchill chided an American special emissary after one dinner, when liquor had loosened his tongue: it would serve Franklin right if the world struck back and decided that Gold was only of value for filling teeth. "Well," replied his visitor, unabashed, "We shall be able to make use of our unemployed in guarding it!"[15]

What was no joke was the deeper purpose underlying Roosevelt's foreign economic policy. Under Morgenthau, but particularly after June 1941 when Cordell Hull called the shots, American aid was conditional on Britain dismantling the system of Imperial preference anchored in the Ottawa agreement of 1932; to Hull, aid was "a knife to open that oyster shell, the Empire."[16]

Roosevelt went further than either Hull or Morgenthau. He wanted to dismantle the Empire altogether. "Winston," he would lecture the PM, "this is something which you are just not able to understand. You have four hundred years of acquisitive instinct in your blood. . . A new period has opened in the world's history, and you will have to adjust yourself to it." Briefing his staff for a mission to London in 1944, he authorized them to broach the Colonial problem, and recalled to them with warmth how he had once sent American troops to seize a British island in the Pacific.* "The British," he told them, "will take land anywhere in the world — even if it is only a rock or a sand bar." Ultimately, a trusteeship agreement had been hammered out for that island, and he regarded that as a model for all former colonies.[17]

Britain and France had invested millions in expanding and modernizing American industry as war approached. "Generally," the director of the U.S. Bureau of the Budget would testify, "they have paid

---

*The Americans had sequestered the unoccupied Canton island in the Phoenix group (although Britain had only just reiterated her sovereignty over it) transferring troops there from Howland island. The Secretary of the Interior observed at the time, on August 14, 1937, that Roosevelt favoured making "wide claims" of unoccupied British islands in the Gilbert and Ellice groups in the Pacific. British archives on the extraordinary Canton incident are closed for 75 years.

twenty-five percent cash when orders were placed, in addition to [subsidizing] capital investments required."[18] According to Morgenthau's files Britain invested $550m in this way. Roosevelt nonetheless made Britain sell off assets, while the United States used her capital and inventions to build up aircraft and arms industries which would guarantee their own postwar domination of civil aviation and related fields.

Britain had entered the war a wealthy nation, but her assets were not limitless. At the end of 1940 they were about to run out. "We have been milking the British financial cow," confided this outstanding president to his Cabinet, "which had plenty of milk at one time but which has now about become dry."[19] The war was costing Britain $1,500m each month.[20] By the end of 1940 Arthur Purvis's purchasing commission had placed orders worth $2,700m in the United States, and had advanced about $1,300m on them. There was no way that Britain could pay the balance, or stand this drain much longer, despite having raised $2,000m from Gold production in South Africa and from her dwindling exports.

Financially, Britain could keep going only a few months longer by selling off her foreign assets. At the end of 1940 Morgenthau assessed her holdings in the United States at $616m of marketable securities and $900m of direct investments; Britain had also invested $2,000m in Canadian enterprises — which had however been earmarked to pay for her purchases from Canada — and over $3,500m in Latin America.[21]

But that was all. To his Cabinet on November 8, Roosevelt put the saleable British assets at about $2,500m. Morgenthau's experts believed they could squeeze Britain into spitting out even more — $3,000m; but after that any squeeze would just be breaking ribs. They would have to make some other arrangement. Roosevelt suggested to his Cabinet a kind of "leasing arrangment" for the supplies to Britain.[22]

* * *

The threatening bankruptcy hung like a pall over Churchill's war strategy. As the blitz intensified in November he had begun drafting that fifteen page letter to Roosevelt, and had invited his Washington ambassador Lord Lothian, visiting England, to come out for lunch on the tenth to help. The message would lay Britain's cards on the table. It took four more weeks to write, and Lothian had dropped a hint about its content when he returned to New York on the twenty-third: "Well, boys," he said, as flashbulbs popped, "Britain's broke; it's your money we want."

Britain's orders placed with American factories for deliveries due up to August 1941 already totalled $9,000m. Her Gold and dollar balances combined had sunk to $574m. Morgenthau wanted her to start using the Allied, Dominion and French Gold. Suspicious that she was not trying hard enough to sell off her assets — and might even be concealing information about them — on December 9 he had complained to Britain's senior Treasury representative in Washington, Sir Frederick Phillips. Phillips had recommended to Lord Lothian that they must help Roosevelt make up his mind on how to address Congress: Britain must start selling; otherwise, he said, the Roosevelt administration "will wash its hands of us."[23] Churchill drafted a hurt reply to Roosevelt direct.

> If you were to "wash your hands of us," i.e., give us nothing we cannot pay for with suitable advances, we should certainly not give in, and I believe we could save ourselves and our own National interests for the time being. But we should certainly not be able to beat the Nazi tyranny and gain you the time you require for your re-armament.[24]

Roosevelt had yet to reply to Churchill's fifteen page message of the eighth. But he dropped a broad hint at his press conference on the seventeenth. He talked about lending a neighbour a garden hose if his house was on fire, and not being too particular about when and how the neighbour paid him if the hose got damaged.[25] Reflecting perhaps that half a loaf was better than no bread Churchill filed away his draft telegram, unsent.

But sensitivity was not Roosevelt's forte. In a few days' time Britian's Gold would run out. He proposed that an American battleship visit South Africa to collect £50m of British Gold there. "There is nothing for it," Phillips felt, "but to acquiesce."[26] To the wincing PM, reading this message on Christmas day, the battleship proposal sounded like a loan shark collecting on a debt. He minuted the Chancellor that day, amidst the family festivities: "I do not like it." Lord Beaverbrook wanted it resisted to the utmost. "Our financial relations with the Americans," he wrote to the PM, "have been so loosely handled that it is necessary, now and forthwith, to take up a firm policy . . . even to the extent of a rupture."

> They have conceded nothing. They have exacted payment to the uttermost for all they have done for us. They have taken our bases without valuable consideration. They have taken our Gold. They have been given our secrets and offered us a thoroughly inadequate service in return.

Arthur Purvis, declared Beaverbrook, had nothing to show except "a kindly disposition on the part of Mr Morgenthau," easily purchased at such a price. The time had come for showdown. Britain must retain a tight grip on the Empire's Gold.

> These are the last resources of the British people and should be held intact to provide us with essential means in the case of a compelling necessity to obtain foodstuffs for our people.[27]

Sir Kingsley Wood shared his concern, but warned Winston that if Roosevelt prevaricated in obtaining Congress approval for his Lend-Lease scheme, Britain was liable to be "stripped bare." He suggested they offer to load £10m of Gold aboard the American warship.[28] Hearing of this halfhearted measure Phillips was terrified, as he cabled to Churchill, of its effect on the president: "You did ask him urgently for help and as a favour to us, he is doing most unusual thing in sending a Cruiser." After all, Britain was expecting interest-free aid to the tune of £800m a year.[29]

The PM smouldered for several days. On the twenty-eighth he began drafting a biting reply to the battleship proposal, rasping that it would look to all the world like "a sheriff collecting the last assets of a helpless debtor."

> It is not fitting [he dictated in this draft] that any nation should put itself wholly in the hands of another, least of all a nation which is fighting under increasingly severe conditions for what is proclaimed to be a cause of general concern. If I have some word from you showing us where we stand, and that the United States is going to supply us with the thousands of millions of dollars worth of munitions which we shall need in 1941 and 1942 if Nazi-ism is to be beat, I will gladly give directions for any Gold in Capetown to be put on board any warships you may send or do anything else that may be just and fair. I feel however that I should not be discharging my responsibilities to the people of the British Empire if, without the slightest indication of how our fate was to be settled in Washington, I were to part with this last reserve from which alone we might buy a few months' food.[30]

He chewed over this text all day, neutralizing the acid and letting off steam; he liked its masculine tone and would eventually publish it in his memoirs.[31] In fact he never sent it, on the lame excuse that he wanted to hear first what Roosevelt said in his "fireside chat" the next day.[32] During this, Roosevelt comfortingly announced, "We must be the great Arsenal of Democracy." But how much longer would Churchill have to wait for Roosevelt's terms? His staff could see his growing concern lest their American cousins' nose for business led them to strip Britain of every asset before acting Good Samaritan.

On the last day of that ruinous, triumphant year, Churchill sent for Eden, perched Kingsley Wood on an armchair and, occasionally consulting Beaverbrook, drafted a more mellow reply to Roosevelt. Sending "the warship" (no longer "battleship") to Capetown might, he argued, "produce embarrassing effects." It would certainly upset Empire opinion and probably encourage the enemy. If Roosevelt felt this was the only way, however, direction would be given for the loading of the "available" Capetown Gold.[33] Afterwards, he took his party up onto the roof; but there was little gunfire to be seen and his adrenalin remained unreplenished.

* * *

The upshot was Lend-Lease. President Roosevelt mentioned it almost in passing in his traditional opening address to the Congress on January 6, 1941. To Churchill it was a milestone. Later, he would write of Lend-Lease as "the most unsordid act in the history of any nation." His colleagues aided in the deceit. They could hardly blazon forth how much their war would cost unborn generations of their countrymen. On October 1, 1941, Kingsley Wood would hotly deny in the House that Britain was being "bled to death." Mr Churchill also kept silent: once, he had quailed at the prospect of asking his people to surrender wedding rings to the nation's Gold reserves; in August 1944, when Henry Morgenthau lunched at No.10 in the role of Roosevelt's avuncular bailiff, Churchill had to admit to him that he had no intention of telling the House about Britain's insolvency until after the war.[34]

He had learned to pocket his pride. One month later, he would ask Roosevelt for an extension of Lend-Lease, while a smiling Morgenthau and his mysterious assistant Harry Dexter White looked on. "What do you want me to do," Winston exclaimed, nervous at some minor delay: "Get on my hind legs and beg like Fala?", a reference to the president's odios dog.[35]

The rakish progress — of selling the Empire down the Potomac river — had begun with the bartered bases. By December 1940 Churchill knew that the U.S. destroyers were worthless heaps (though Phillips begged him not to be so indelicate as to mention this). Few political benefits had accrued. Roosevelt remained as remote as ever, playing his cards at leisure; a general sent to London to observe the Battle of Britain reassured him that there was scant real danger to the country. The enemy had no secret weapons; so there was no need to rush in to save "British culture and civilization."[36]

The view from the White House was very different from the view from No.10: angry contrasts were drawn between Britain's "stinginess" and her rumoured wealth. Morgenthau assured Roosevelt that his agents, burrowing everywhere, had now located all Britain's worldwide Gold and assets; he had spied upon her account in the Federal Reserve Bank and his agents there were supplying regular Intelligence on Arthur Purvis's billion-dollar purchases. When Britain reluctantly began to liquidate her investments, Sir Edward Peacock, the Whitehall official sent over to supervise this painful auction, would also be shadowed on Morgenthau's instructions.[37] His crackdown aroused vestigial sympathy for Britain. "These same people seem to agree," wrote one uncomfortable colleague after a White House cabinet, "that our own safety depends upon Britain's ability to withstand Hitler, and yet . . .

they wanted to be perfectly sure that England was fighting naked, with bare hands, before they would be willing to go to her aid under the pending Lend-Lease Bill."[38]

Mr Churchill's begging telegram reached Roosevelt on the second day of 1941 at his Hudson riverbank estate. The president turned to Cordell Hull for advice: the face value of Britain's worldwide assets might be $9,000m (Hull had suggested $18,000m); and perhaps $1,500m of this was in the United States; but Britain could probably raise only $1,000m of this at short notice. Clearly worried about security for any loan F.D.R. mused, "There is always the possibility of their putting up [as collateral] their sovereignty to and over certain colonies, such as Bermuda, the British West Indies, British Honduras and British Guinea." But he dismissed this possibility. "If we can get our naval bases," he reasoned, "why for example, should we buy with them two million headaches." Their Blacks would be a drag on the economy and their new American citizenship would "stir up" questions of race. Taking over Britain's Pacific possessions on the other hand, the islands south of Hawaii, would be worthwhile, "as stepping stones in the control of the Central Pacific area."[39]

The Lend-Lease Bill would authorize Roosevelt to advance to the democracies war materials initially worth $7,000m. In the spirit of making Britain "get on her hind legs and beg," his legislators ironically numbered the bill 1776. Generations of his fellow countrymen still breathed the independent aroma of that year. Most Americans perceived that Mr Churchill was inveigling them into war. Anti-British feeling was running high. The grudges against Britain were ancient but all-embracing — upper class arrogance, colonial government, penal settlements, the Hessians, the Boston Tea-party; her peccadillos included 1812, the Civil War, the China Wars, the Indian mutiny, the Boer War, Ireland, and now "this King business" — coupled with a demand that Britain restore the Duke and his American Duchess to the throne. The Hearst newspapers had a hue and cry about hordes of British propagandists on the loose; British speakers were drummed off the lecture-circuits. When novelist Somerset Maugham asked the pained question in the *Saturday Evening Post*, "Why d'You Dislike Us?" his mailbag burst with answers — less than one in ten favourable to Britain's plight. Only Mr Churchill's steadfastness during the blitz had earned his country admiration.

All Americans, whether their ancestors had arrived on the Mayflower or they themselves had barely dusted the mud of Eastern Europe off their boots, grasped at this opportunity to liquidate Britain's wealth and Empire. When Roosevelt's Cabinet examined on January 16 Mr Churchill's creditworthiness, former vice-president John N. Garner — "flushed of face and loud of voice, and at least half full of whiskey"

— reminded them of Britain's immense American assets. "Why, Mr President," he boomed,

> you told us that the British had three or four billions of dollars in this country that could be spent here. The British, per capita, are the richest in the world, and if they care anything about their freedom, they ought to be willing to spend all that they have.

The Secretary of Agriculture chimed in that the Mid West farmers had told him the British had unlimited wealth. But Roosevelt shook his head and Morgenthau said flatly that the British were broke — they had spent everything they had. "When the British pay off what they have now contracted for," he said, "they won't have a dollar left."[40]

CHAPTER 38

There Goes The Empire

THE OLD BRAVADO was wearing thin. People plodded into work that winter through streets strewn with broken glass, but they began to notice missing faces. Drab became dreary. The meat ration had been cut. London's smile had faded except where the high-heeled strumpets strutted Mayfair in their short fur coats and silk stockings.[1] Army engineers ushered in 1941 with the mournful thud of demolition charges levelling ancient buildings that had survived one Great Fire but been engulfed by the next. Rush hour in the darkness became a stampede each time the sirens sounded. The proletarian East End was a wasteland; but now the praetorian West End was also looking gawky.

Dinner guests leaving hotels stepped around the burning incendiary bombs and used the sand bags provided at lamp posts to douse them. One January night the enemy torched the Law Courts and Fleet Street with equal contempt; tin helmeted newspapermen told each other it was the worst raid so far.[2] For those who stayed in London, each night brought excitement and danger; socialites and journalists crowded rooftops, and there was a strange beauty in the air. "While I was on the roof," scribbled an editor around midnight on the eleventh, "another two bombs whistled over and then two more that sent us diving for cover." Walking up Ludgate Hill he glimpsed the dome of St Paul's rearing through billowing clouds of red-hued smoke; Cheapside and St Martin's-le-Grand had been gutted and a gas flame was geysering from a crater.[3] A canyon marked Bank subway station — it had taken a direct hit.

The damage was more than material, as London filled with foreigners and the Englishmen went forth. "Women give themselves freely," one grimacing American notable observed, "and men take just as freely. Even the 'war widows' are willing to grant their favours."[4]

BEHIND THE SHUTTERS and sandbags protecting his frayed home in Downing-street, Churchill nursed a stubborn cold. He was putting on weight too. As he went over to inspect damage to the House — now corseted in scaffolding — and exchange a few whispered remarks with the Speaker, one witness remarked that his double chin had swollen as if a goitre.[5] Newspaper executive Cecil King looked him up and down and decided he looked more lined than in June — but tougher.[6] "Churchill," he wrote, "*is* wartime England —"

> England with all its age, its waning virility, its dogged courage, its natural assumption that Instinct is more valuable than Intellect. In Churchill the country feels it is personified and for this reason there can be no question of Churchill's departure until after complete defeat. From his point of view he has done, is doing and will continue to do all anyone could, to win the war. He feels this, and so attacks on his Government mystify and bewilder him.

His speeches were popular only because "they are the articulate expression of what is in most Englishmen's hearts."

> He has no contribution to make to our future, but he personifies our present and our past.[7]

Impatient for American Lend-Lease to pass into law, he became cantankerous and unjust. Bevin explained that he was incapable of delegating authority and grossly overworked.[8] The Defence Committee on the thirteenth demonstrated this. "PM in the Chair gives the impression of being mentally completely exhausted," wrote one minister afterwards. "Almost alone, he argues against the proposals of the Chiefs of Staff and the Hankey Committee. He goes round and round the same point and is, for him, terribly slow in the uptake and most pig-headed."[9]

He even questioned whether bombing could win the war. A year ago everybody had produced cut and dried calculations proving it could. After Hitler attacked Holland and Belgium they had bombed the Ruhr. Result? Barely any interruption of production.[10]

Once again, his instinct was sound; but he lacked the energy or willpower to act upon it. He was tired, and no wonder. Only liquor and contact with the humbler orders replenished his vital juices, and he drank often from both cups. Lingering at Dover with an American emissary for a baleful glint at the Nazi-held coastline he heard one artisan remark as he passed by, "There goes the bloody British Empire." Winston took it as a compliment, and his face wreathed in smiles. "*Very* nice," he lisped to the secretary sitting next to him.[11]

LIKE A BADLY DIGESTED repast, the Dakar fiasco kept throwing up bubbles of foul-smelling gas by a kind of peristalsis in his gut. In the first days of 1941 his Falstaff, Desmond Morton, brought mortifying evidence that none other than Vice Admiral E.H. Muselier, commanding the Free French navy, had betrayed Dakar to the enemy. Seething with anger, Churchill ordered the Frenchman's arrest: Muselier was discovered pleasuring a woman of easy virtue, stripped of his epaulettes, and tossed into Brixton Jail. MI5 searched his apartment and claimed to have found documents and tens of thousands of pounds. The Gallic Admiral screamed that it was a preposterous frame-up: "If I had that kind of money," he argued, "would I have been in bed with a common woman?" Never short in sense of history, Churchill had him removed to Greenwich — where Admiral Byng had been put to the firing squad "pour encourager les autres" — and invited a judge, Mr Justice Singleton, to review the evidence.

The case collapsed as inevitably as it had against Somerville. Singleton found that the Admiral had indeed been framed. The humiliating story, better than Gilbert & Sullivan, ran round Whitehall. Who had prematurely ordered the arrest? "That baby dictator Winston!" chortled Sir Alexander Cadogan. The episode illuminated the chronic frailty of Churchill's colleagues too. The First Lord had wanted to ease the imprisoned Admiral's lot — until he realized whose hand was behind it, and then he went all "wankly," as Cadogan put it. Muselier was brought back to Carlton House Terrace, the Free French headquarters, in his powder gray Rolls Royce, and his treasured epaulettes were handed back. *Daily Mail* journalist G. Ward Price concluded that the Admiral may not have been pro-Vichy before, but he certainly must be now.[12] Churchill snarled — "When I'm in the wrong," he explained to Eden, "I'm always very angry" — and issued a D-notice prohibiting press mention of the ludicrous affair.[13]

Churchill's strange dealings with Vichy surfaced again in his farewell conversation with the Canadian defence minister, as Colonel Ralston's diary shows:

*January 7, 1941:*Had a half hour with Churchill in the Cabinet Room. . . I spoke of the Dupuy incident. . . He said Dupuy had done a very useful service and that he was anxious to have him go back and see Weygand and Pétain if possible. He said, "You know, I suppose, that we have offered Pétain six divisions?" I told him I knew we offered help but I did not know to what extent. He said they had done that as the reply [from Pétain] had indicated that the door was not closed. I said to him that probably there might be some criticism of Canada appearing to flirt with the German-controlled Government at Vichy, and that I felt we should be able to say that it was at the suggestion of the U.K. He said, "You certainly can do so and you can use my name if you want to."

He put out a further D-notice forbidding editors to ventilate his furtive talks with Vichy.[14] It was true that he had written to Pétain through American diplomatic channels offering an expeditionary force of six divisions if his Government crossed to North Africa and resumed the fight against Germany. There was no reply.

* * *

Roosevelt had not yet replied to his fifteen-page letter either.

Anglo-American relations were in disorder. Since Lothian's death and Kennedy's return neither country had an ambassador in the other's capital. But on January 9 an unkempt and unlikely emissary arrived at Poole from Lisbon aboard the British Overseas Airways Corporation flying boat: Harry L. Hopkins, the president's intimus and confidant. Bracken who had met him some years earlier announced that this was a most important American, and hurried down to fetch him taking the finest Pullman train that Southern Railways could assemble at such short notice, staffed with white gloved attendants; this brought the shy American wearing a battered hat and untidy necktie back to London just as the sirens howled at 7:25 p.m.

Hopkins' mission was something of a mystery. Roosevelt had evidently instructed this quiet, unassuming native of Iowa to report on Britain's needs and morale. He and Hopkins had become intimates through the intrigues of a mutual lady friend.[15] Of these Hopkins had enjoyed many — one had jumped to her death after he jilted her in 1940.[16] Hopkins' installation at the White House badly upset Bernard Baruch and other jealous satraps of the president.[17] He sold White House influence: Baruch had stumped up a large annuity for him, and when he stopped paying, industrialist Averell Harriman and car rental magnate John Hertz replaced him as benefactors.[18] He was a rare friend, and the president liked him enough to hire him as personal librarian at Hyde Park. Moving into the White House he soon became as popular with Eleanor as Bracken and Beaverbrook were with Clemmie Churchill.

Roosevelt congratulated himself on having sent Hopkins to London — he was just the person to impress somebody of Mr Churchill's pedigree and breeding. "According to the president," noted one colleague as Hopkins left England on his return, "the deeply laid plot had worked out even better than he had anticipated."[19] He would become intimate adviser of both statesmen — a "spider sitting in the centre of the net."[20] A year later Hopkins would remarry, and would brag about the wedding gift that Lord Beaverbrook gave his bride — one million dollars in emeralds.[21] It looked like barefaced bribery: but since Hopkins became Lend-Lease administrator, the million dollars may have been well spent for England.

* * *

Workmen were still swarming over No.10 repairing bomb damage when Bracken brought Hopkins round for lunch with Churchill on the tenth: it was a Friday, and Churchill would soon be leaving for the country. He went downstairs in his Pickwickian striped pants and black jacket, and extended what Hopkins called a "fat but none the less convincing hand." The American was a sallow, shrivelled, frail, whimsical looking man, his face gaunt from his recent illness, but with all his wits about him.[22] Studying him over soup and cold beef in the tiny basement dining room, Winston's private secretary liked the visitor's quiet dignity.

Hopkins found the PM a "rotund, smiling, red-faced gentleman," mushy of voice but clear of eye. He mentioned straight away that Roosevelt was hoping to meet Winston in April. A remark about Churchill's rumoured anti-American sentiments provoked a tirade about Joe Kennedy; he flourished the congratulations he had sent Roosevelt on re-election. He proudly displayed photographs of his grandson and no less proudly reviewed his other accomplishments, beginning with Dunkirk; Hitler could not invade, he declared, even if he used poison gas: "We too have the deadliest gases in the world."

The American talked little and listened much — which left on the loquacious an agreeable impression of his sagacity — and afterwards jotted down these impressions of what Churchill had said:

He thinks Greece is lost — although he is now reinforcing the Greeks — weakening his African Army — he believes Hitler will permit Mussolini to go only so far downhill — and is now preparing for the [German] attack which must bring its inevitable result. He knows this will be a blow to British prestige and is obviously considering ways and means of preparing the British public for it. . . The debacle in Greece will be overcome in part by what he considers to be the sure defeat of the Italians in Africa.

"Make no mistake about it," was the message from Roosevelt which Hopkins conveyed to the British, "He will carry you through, no matter what happens to him."

Hopkins lingered three hours here. At four o'clock, an hour late, he drove to a press conference in Grosvenor-square. "I have never had such an enjoyable time as I had with Mr Churchill," he declared to the newspapermen, lighting a cigarette. "But God, what a force that man has!"[23]

CHURCHILL HAD TOUCHED upon his surreptitious offer of six divisions to Vichy in Africa. He was, he had told Hopkins, "in close touch with Pétain on this point."[24] He had sent Pétain a message via Admiral William D. Leahy, U.S. ambassador to Vichy. Vichy offered no reply. Puzzled by this, Churchill wondered whether the elderly Marshal had

had failed to grasp what was being offered. On Saturday the eleventh he wrote a rather plaintive telegram to Roosevelt. "It seems," he wrote, "from [Admiral Leahy's] report . . . that the Marshal may not have realized that the message was one from myself and that it involved considerably more than a suggestion of assistance in the event of the French Government deciding to cross to North Africa." He wondered whether the presence of the collaborationist M Flandin had inhibited Pétain, and suggested that Leahy try conveying the message to Pétain again.

> I do not want to press Marshal Pétain to cross to North Africa; I would not press him for any further answer; I only want to be sure that there has been no misunderstanding and that the Marshal would be fully aware of the nature and origin of the message.[25]

On the thirteenth Churchill sent another oral message for Leahy to deliver, stepping up the offer to Pétain: if the Pétain government crossed to Africa, Britain would allow the French fleet to sail from Alexandria.[26] Nothing came of this, except for an indirect reply that eventually filtered back: Pétain was "anxious for a British victory."[27]

As usual that Friday afternoon Churchill had driven down to Dytchley for the weekend. While German bombers again blitzed London, and the empty buildings blazed fiercely, in Washington Bill No.1776 was published.

Bit by bit Britain was being burnt and bankrupted. Sir Kingsley Wood warned that the Bill would "strip us of everything we possess;" such was Roosevelt's intent, for Hopkins confided to staff at the embassy that the president was stubbornly insisting that Britain cough up first — for example, they must vacate all their commercial shipping routes and confine British shipping to the North Atlantic route. Deaf to the roaring dangers, Churchill welcomed Lend-Lease, and proclaimed it the next best thing to an actual declaration of war.

Hopkins had come down to Dytchley with him. In the afterglow of these weekends Churchill's guests often found they could not reconstruct his monologues in their memory. "I feel quite peeved," John Martin regretted after one dinner conversation, "that I haven't the sort of memory that could treasure up the PM's obiter dicta to chuckle over afterwards."[28]

It was the language that mattered, and that was as difficult to capture as the splash of a sunset on a mountain range. Churchill treated Hopkins that Saturday to his customary recital of events. The American flattered him that the president brought a radio into Cabinet to listen to the historic speeches, but to Winston 1940 was a blur. The only speech he recollected was one to junior ministers after Dunkirk: he had realized even as he spoke that they *wanted* to hear him say that Britain would fight on.[29] Once the phone rang: the night's target was Portsmouth and refugees were fleeing the city. Wearing siren suit and bulldog mien, and puffing at a larger than usual cigar, he paced the floor or stood at the hearth declaiming until four a.m.; Mers-el-Kébir, he claimed, was the "turning point" — after that the world accepted Britain was in earnest.

Around two a.m., the phone brought further ill-tidings: down in the Mediterranean, German dive bombers had sunk a cruiser and damaged the new carrier *Illustrious*. The news could hardly have been better timed. Churchill betrayed neither shock at this German debut in the Mediterranean nor dismay at the loss of life. He and Roosevelt, he said, reverting to a familiar theme, could field 120 million Whites against Germany's sixty millions, and that was what this war boiled down to. Hopkins wrote to Roosevelt afterwards, "The people here are amazing from Churchill down, and if courage alone can win — the result will be inevitable." "*Churchill,*" he emphasized, "is the gov't in every sense of the word — he controls the grand strategy and often the details." Organized labour and the armed forces all backed him. "He is the one and only person over here with whom you need to have a full meeting of minds."

The PM did make one tactical mistake. He begged his guest to stay out of the blitz. The frail American defiantly drove back to Claridges Hotel. "This is no time to be out of London," he told Roosevelt, "so I am staying here." "I have been offered a so-called bombproof apartment by Churchill," he added, "a tin hat and gas mask have been delivered."[30]

Hopkins had won the confidence and intimacy of the prime minister. "I am most grateful to you," Winston cabled to the president, "for sending so remarkable an envoy."[31] And Roosevelt told his staff, delighted:

> Apparently the first thing that Churchill asks for when he gets awake in the morning is Harry Hopkins, and Harry is the last one whom he sees at night.

The rest of Washington took a more jejeune view. "The attachment of Churchill to Harry Hopkins may be entirely genuine," observed one cynic. "I suspect that if as his personal representative the president should send to London a man with the bubonic plague, Churchill would nevertheless see a good deal of him."[32]

One source of friction was the famine spreading across Europe under British naval blockade. Churchill imperturbably argued that this was Hitler's weakness — "to be in control of territory inhabited by a dejected and despairing people."[33] Promoting insurrection had been a British objective ever since November when the chiefs of staff directed the Special Operations Executive to prepare "co-ordinated and organized revolts" in occupied Europe as a preliminary to action against Germany.[34]

Roosevelt had discussed the famine with the late Lord Lothian, but Churchill refused to lift the blockade so that the American Red Cross could transport even limited quantities of dried milk for French children. The president urged him to relent "for humanitarian and also political reasons."[35] Churchill however had been brought up in the belief that it was cruel to be kind: and he was a very kindly man. Perhaps war is never so harsh as when an unforgiving enemy or woolly-minded friend can credibly portray its machinery as being levelled against non combatants. Given the larger issue at stake — Lend-Lease — he grudgingly yielded but pleaded with Roosevelt to present the British case, in any announcement to be made, in "as favourable a light as possible."[36] In fact, famine was as necessary as Lend-Lease to his war plan, and he urged Hopkins orally to persuade his boss not to go "too far in feeding any of the dominated countries."[37]

As yet, he showed little interest in Special Operations and obstinately left it to Dr Dalton. At the Defence Committee on January 13, their attack on Hitler's Romanian oilfields was up for discussion. Churchill was too tired to listen. "You needn't go into any detail," he told Dalton. "Provided the F.O. and the Treasury and the Service Departments agree you can do what you like." Dalton failed to see how they were ever going to win the war like this. Alone, his staff began mapping out an assault on the Lofoten islands where Norwegian fish processing plants supplied Germany's most vital vitamins.[38]

CHURCHILL'S MIND WAS with his beloved navy. On Tuesday the fourteenth he was going to take Hopkins up to the great Home Fleet anchorage at Scapa Flow in the Orkneys to see off Lord Halifax. He was sending him over to Washington in style aboard the newest battleship; he correctly guessed that Roosevelt would be curious enough to want to meet the ship at Annapolis. Such attention to detail was typical of the PM. In fact he pored over the passenger list, called the First Lord over to No.10 and insisted that two would be passengers in particular be dumped ashore with bag and baggage. Thus on Tuesday he was not in Cabinet. Attlee announced why, and everybody sighed with relief.[39]

As the endless snake of warm Pullman cars hauled northwards out of the frosted capital, Churchill bathed, exchanged his spurious nautical garb for a dinner jacket and tottered into the dining car. Clemmie was educating the new ambassador on how the White House got its name — it had been ignited by the British and painted white to conceal the blackened scars; Halifax looked shocked, and one pained American diplomat gathered that he was unaware that the war of 1812 had ever happened.

A moaning wind was driving snow horizontally across the darkened moors when Churchill awoke. The train stood still for three hours while a derailed wagon ahead was cleared from the line. His throat was sore, and the seas off Thurso were reported to be rough, but a large brandy revived spirits. "I'll go and get my Morthersills," he croaked at breakfast, and began talking about a new anti-aircraft missile which they were to see fired — in fact he expected to fire it.

"It costs about £100 a minute to fire it," the Captain of the Fleet said rather drily. The smile faded from the PM's lips and the corners of his mouth turned down like a baby.

"What, not fire it?"

"Yes, darling," Mrs Churchill added quickly, "You may fire it just once."

"Yes, that's right, I'll fire it just once. Only once. That couldn't be bad."

Halifax's former private secretary, recording this in his diary, observed that nobody had the heart to say that it would be bad, and Winston was soon beaming again.[40] Oblivious of his doctor's warnings — Clemmie had insisted that Charles Wilson accompany them — he marched aboard the minesweeper as the sun lifted above the horizon, and declared that he for one was going on up to the Flow.

From the little minesweeper, rolling and pitching in seas whipped up by a bitter north-easter, they transferred to the destroyer *Napier*. "It was a beautiful scene," wrote his own secretary, "the mainland and low islands covered with snow, the sea extraordinarily blue and bright sunshine turn about with lashing blizzards."[41] The American military attaché looked at the freezing hills and was not surprised that the sheep there had to grow Harris tweed. Hopkins was too miserable to enjoy the bleak scenery — he had all but fallen overboard during the transfer while Churchill had prattled on heedlessly about Wavell's triumphs in Libya.

Clearing the anti-submarine booms guarding the Flow the destroyer made fast alongside *King George V*. Touring the battleships, this pudgy politician wedged in the hole as he squeezed into her fourteen-inch turret. Despite one withered and useless hand Halifax slithered up into the turret with agility. Churchill said farewell to him and to the officers who were to open secret staff talks in Washington, then crossed over to the *Nelson* to watch it test the anti-aircraft rocket. The missile fouled the rigging and blew up, catapulting an object the size of a jam-jar at the bridge where it detonated five feet from Hopkins: Churchill did not share the American's roars of laughter.[42]

Throughout his stay so far, Hopkins had offered no inkling of his thoughts. It unsettled Churchill, but the canny American planned to make no speeches. They inspected Rosyth dockyards, but still Hopkins kept his thoughts to himself. Over lunch in his train on the seventeenth, Churchill quietly asked Tom Johnston, editor of *Forward* and a former Scots miner, who had joined them as Regional Commissioner for Scotland, to arrange a small dinner party in Glasgow that night: they would try to draw him out.

The dinner was at the Station Hotel. At Churchill's whispered bidding Johnston proposed their guest's health. Hopkins had no option but to rise to his feet. "I suppose you wish to know what I am going to say to President Roosevelt on my return," he teased. "Well, I'm going to quote you one verse from that Book of Books in the truth of which Mr Johnston's mother and my own Scottish mother were brought up: "Whither thou goest I will go; and where thou lodgest, I will lodge; thy people shall be my people, and thy God my God."

He added softly, "Even to the end."[43]

Tears frolicked down Churchill's cheeks. At eleven-thirty p.m. they were back aboard the train, returning to Chequers.

HE ALWAYS REMEMBERED those warm words; Hopkins never forgot that ice-cold weekend. His victory gift to Britain, he vowed, would be central heating for Chequers.[44] With an overcoated Hopkins huddled near to him, Churchill telephoned the White House late on the nineteenth. ("Mr President, It's me — Winston speaking!") No record has been released of any Roosevelt-Churchill telephone conversations. On this occasion he probably touched on the possibility of a meeting. "Before Hopkins could deliver the message," Roosevelt later minuted, "Churchill expressed exactly the same thought to Hopkins."[45]

A new week began. Winston's cold had not improved. Back in London, Eden found him tired and resigned. The inevitable Greek tragedy was crowding closer, as the oracle at Bletchley showed: Hitler was bound to invade Greece soon. The German airforce was preparing to move into Bulgaria: their mission in Romania had that very day transmitted a cypher message about fuel logistics in Bulgaria.[46] On Saturday, Bletchley had decyphered a signal about German airforce huts being moved down to Bulgaria. When the Defence Committee met that Monday night in the bunker Eden predicted that Hitler was going to invade Turkey. Churchill was more immediately concerned about Greece: Hitler was obviously about to move into Bulgaria, probably with the King's connivance. "The Germans would gain a dominating position from which to threaten Salonica."[47] But Athens was confident that Hitler was only acting defensively and General Metaxas declined Britain's offer of reinforcements.

Churchill felt sick. He snarled and snapped at imaginary enemies.
He growled at Eden that the Tories hated him, and he talked of willingly
yielding to anybody prepared to face problems like Australia's obstinacy
and the constant, almost unendurable "nagging" in the House.[48]
Sensing communists and fifth columnists everywhere, he suddenly shut
down *The Week* and the Communist *Daily Worker* on January 21. (The
Daily Mirror had got wind of this four days before and printed a malign
cartoon and comment.[49]) Fleet-street did not even whimper. When the
home secretary briefed the editors, only the great Frank Owen, editor of
the *Evening Standard*, protested. The rest squealed approval, the
Liberals louder than the rest: the *Manchester Guardian* bayed that the
Communist daily believed in neither the war nor democracy: "We can
well spare it." "It was given a lot of rope," echoed the *News Chronicle*,
"and it has now hanged itself."[50]

Their complaisance was fortunate, because Churchill could not bear
criticism. Shown the *Mirror*'s cartoon all his ugly suspicions about its
"hidden backers" bubbled forth, and on Thursday he fired a broadside
at it: he complained particularly of the columnist "Cassandra" who had
recently reported an alleged rebuff by him to Eden — "Your report
contains every cliche except 'God is Love' and 'Adjust your Dress Before
Leaving'." Two days later Churchill wrote again, accusing the *Mirror*
and its sister *Sunday Pictorial* of paving the way for "naked defeatism
and a demand for a negotiated peace."

Fearful of being closed down, editor Cecil King saw Churchill at
No.10 on the last day of January. He arrived at three p.m. as an air raid
was beginning:

> I waited ten or fifteen minutes by a big coke fire just outside the Cabinet
> room where I waited the last time I saw Churchill. I was then ushered in
> by a secretary — tall, blue-eyed, fair and of the pansy brand. . . . Winston
> went into the Cabinet room by another door and was standing up by the
> fire when I came in.*

He motioned King to a table on his right. King saw on it a green
telephone labelled "Admiralty." The wallmaps had changed since June
— Europe, the Mediterranean and the world. Once or twice enemy
bombers droned overhead and through the mist he heard Bofors guns
firing in the park. "When a plane came very near," King noticed, "he
stopped his talk and listened, and twice seemed on the point of retreating
to his shelter but did not do so."

---

*The author relies upon the late Cecil King's voluminous pocket diaries at Boston
University, Massachusetts, rather than the published text which was edited for tact and
brevity.

He started off with a great tirade. . . . Our policy constituted a very clever form of Fifth Column'ism: praising the PM, pressing for an intensification of our war effort, but at the same time magnifying grievances, vilifying ministers and generally creating a distrust by the nation for its leaders. . . . I protested that . . . we supported many of his ministers, but others we thought unworthy of high office and said so.

Churchill flared up. Did the *Mirror* arrogate to itself the right to appoint ministers? "No," replied King evenly, "but surely loyalty to him as PM did not carry with it loyalty to Attlee as Lord Privy Seal?" The PM, who found his deputy small-minded and a bore,[51] conceded this point. He revealed that there had been discussion about the *Mirror* group and that "research had been undertaken into the ownership of our shares."

I said there was nothing — there were five executive directors, of whom I was one. . . The politics were largely left to me.

"Well," he said, "you look innocent enough!"

Churchill stressed that it was the malignancy of the attacks that annoyed him; he had contemplated prosecution and even denouncing the *Mirror* in a broadcast, but decided that would be "out of proportion." King asked why the PM had not telephoned the newspapers to "pipe down"? Churchill huffed that he "would not ask for favours." King replied that it would have been an order, not a favour: he recalled Churchill only making one such request since becoming PM, in fact — that newspapers refrain from attacking Chamberlain; the *Mirror* had obliged, temporarily.

Churchill then turned to the criticism of some of his ministers:

He said that he had never taken back what he had said about the appeasers, but that the MPs who had supported Chamberlain still formed a majority of 150 in the House and that he was not going to fight them as they were too numerous. He had, however, moved away the old bunch bit by bit, keeping Chamberlain on for a time to minimize the shock of the change.

Throughout their rambling seventy-minute conversation Churchill had been "very difficult to talk to," wrote King,

He reminded me strongly of Rothermere — getting up and striding about, shooting remarks at me that often had nothing whatever to do with his last remark or anything I was saying, sitting down again, leaning on the fire-guard or lighting his cigar.

*   *   *

With General Wavell's triumphs in Libya, something of the old exuberance returned. Answering one MP's criticism in the House, Churchill slipped in a Latin phrase; and when Labour members shouted,

"Translate!" he agreed smilingly that he would do so — "for the benefit," he added with the barest pause, "of any Old Etonians present."[52]

Two days later, on Friday January 24, he was back at Chequers wrestling with top secret papers on Libya and Greece. As was his custom he turned over one of the foolscap-sized Cabinet papers to Harry Hopkins as bedtime reading. It reproduced on seventeen green pages — with no reference to intercept Intelligence — the dramatic telegrams that had passed between himself and Wavell.

"This morning," wrote Hopkins on Saturday, dazed by those amazing messages,

I have awakened on a cold, dreary morning — and the formal garden of this lovely old place seems very unhappy under the onslaughts of wind — and snow and cold — I have just finished my breakfast in bed — of kidney and bacon and prunes —

He picked up the document again, and marvelled at those directives written at the height of the September blitz. Ignorant of the oracle which allowed Mr Churchill his strategic insights, he jotted down his feelings on the daring and determination they displayed:

Italy invades Greece — precious planes must be taken away to bolster the Greeks — and guns too — but the PM even urging Wavell to press on — planes desperately needed in England rushed to Wavell's support by the PM's insistant orders — the PM impatient — prodding Wavell — but ever giving him his confident support — but Greece must be supported for political reasons and Wavell grudgingly agrees for these are explicit orders from the Minister of Defence.[53]

Since early January, the Greek tragedy and Libyan triumph had become entwined. With his Russian campaign only weeks away, Hitler had tried desperately to avoid involvement in Mussolini's Balkan quagmire; but, concerned by the menace to Romanian oil resources, he had reinforced his airforce mission there and reluctantly prepared to move through Bulgaria to Greece to rescue the Italians. Germany's moves — faintly reflected by Bletchley's uncertain mirror — were closely followed by Mr Churchill and on January 6 he recommended that Libya take "second place" to Greece.[54] On the ninth there was an Enigma message about German airforce telephone lines being laid through Bulgaria to the Greek frontier.[55] The indications were that Hitler was going to slam two Panzer divisions through Bulgaria into Greece on or about the twentieth; two hundred dive bombers would support the attack. Churchill had been outwitted over Norway, and did not want it to happen again.[56] This time he hoped to push airforce and mechanized units into Greece at once, and asked Wavell to consult with Athens. But in his eyes Greece was already doomed, and he told Hopkins so, while ordering a reluctant General Wavell to comply with "our decision, for which we bear full responsibility."[57]

Ignorant of the intercepts the Greek authorities refused the offer of army aid, anxious to avoid provoking the Germans. Until then, Churchill had planned to divert Wavell's main effort to Salonika (northern Greece) as soon as he captured Tobruk. Now he shrugged. "Prince Paul's attitude," he had written to the Cabinet before entraining for Scapa Flow with Hopkins, "looks like that of an unfortunate man in the cage with a tiger, hoping not to provoke him while steadily dinnertime approaches."[58]

In Libya, Wavell's victorious army had swept the Italians before it. Bardia had fallen with 462 guns and 45,000 prisoners including two corps commanders, 4 divisional commanders, three nuns and a bishop. "The general has now telegraphed that all resistance has ceased," Winston had reported to Roosevelt — without specifying whether this included the ecclesiastical captives.[59] On January 22, the Australian and British troops over-ran Tobruk. Given Greece's uncooperative attitude, the Defence Committee had however authorized Wavell two days earlier to continue from Tobruk to Benghazi.

There seemed little to be done for Greece. On the twenty-sixth, Churchill reiterated that the enemy was now in Bulgaria and preparing to attack Greece. "We must expect," he warned Wavell fatalistically, "a series of very heavy, disastrous blows in the Balkans and possibly a general submission there to German aims."[60]

As the last hope he turned to Turkey. Hitler would no doubt tell Instanbul to keep out or be bombed. In a letter to President Ismet Inönü, the PM proposed a pact allowing Britain to put planes and ground personnel into Turkey immediately, to menace Hitler's oilfields in Romania and, if need be, Stalin's at Baku — a nostalgic echo of the Anglo-French planning heyday twelve months previously. Over-generously he offered Turkey ten squadrons of bombers and fighters.[61] It dawned on him that he had offered most of these to Greece as well and he inquired of Sir Charles Portal, "Have we not in fact promised to sell the same pig to two customers?"[62] Fortunately, Turkey rejected this naive proposal out of hand. Inönü had a written guarantee from Hitler too, and that evidently counted for more in his eyes.

CHURCHILL, SURE OF THE impression he had made on Hopkins, became sunny, almost benign. The hangdog air had gone. Roosevelt's rival Wendell Willkie had also come over and arrived at Chequers on the twenty-seventh bringing a few lines by the poet Longfellow copied out in Roosevelt's hand: "Sail on, O Ship of State! /Sail on, O Union, Strong and Great! /Humanity with all its fears, /With all the hopes of future years, /Is hanging breathless on thy fate!"

Winston overwhelmed him easily, as he had won Hopkins. On Willkie's return home he too pressed the urgency of getting aid to Britain. At first he called Churchill a much greater man than F.D.R. but on reflection, after further British humiliations, he changed his tune and declared that self-assured men made poor planners. The trouble was, he told the vice-president, that Churchill "came from the most aristocratic bloodlines from Britain, that he had been subject to flattery from early youth, that the women had always adored him." Even so he admitted that Churchill was gifted with the ability to "speak like a Demosthenes and write like an angel," that in conversation he was scintillating, and "that he was an excellent raconteur of stories, couched in the most correct English language." Roosevelt's first question to Willkie on his return was, "Is Churchill a drunk?"

"Mr President," replied Willkie. "I had as many drinks as Churchill all the time I was with him, and no one has ever called me a drunk."[63]

When Churchill visited the southern naval base of Portsmouth, touring the blitzed streets, he took Hopkins with him. On February 2 they dined at Chequers, and the PM even danced a bit, mellowed by the meal and the music of records that Hopkins had brought with him. "He feels a great bond of sympathy for America, and in particular for Roosevelt," wrote one secretary on February 2. "He had an American mother. . ."[64] They dined and journeyed together that first week of February like friends who had known each other for a lifetime.

Down at Chequers again, late on Saturday the eighth, Churchill learned that the House of Representatives had passed Bill No.1776 in Washington. It still had to clear the upper house. As Winston was pacing up and down, dictating a broadcast for Sunday evening, a securely overcoated Hopkins arrived to bid farewell.[65] The dampness of winter England had chilled him to the marrow and he was feeling poorly. Churchill handed him a bottle of tablets, saying he took them three times a week.* Hopkins pocketed them, scribbled a note on Chequers notepaper wishing "confusion to your enemies", and left at ten-thirty p.m. by Pullman train for Bournemouth.

The broadcast went out worldwide that Sunday night — the PM's first in many months. Waiting down in a Bournemouth hotel for flying-boat weather, Harry Hopkins listened to it with Bracken. Churchill

---

*Months later, Hopkins had them analysed. The medicine was harmless: "It is a conglomeration of everything," Hopkins noted for his records in December, "that couldn't do anybody much harm. They tell me it couldn't possibly do them very much good either."[66]

spoke of the tragic indifference of the little Balkan nations in face of the stealthy German encroachment:

> Of course [he said] if all the Balkan people stood together and acted together, aided by Britain and Turkey, it would be many months before a German army and airforce of sufficient strength to overcome them could be assembled in the south east of Europe.

As things were, he expected them to be dismembered one by one and share the fate of Denmark, Holland and Belgium. Later in his broadcast he turned to Britain's immensely strengthened position. "In order to win the war," he declared, repeating a familiar argument, "Hitler must destroy Great Britain."

> He may carry havoc into the Balkan States; he may tear great provinces out of Russia, he may march to the Caspian; he may march to the gates of India. All this will avail him nothing. It may spread his curse more widely throughout Europe and Asia, but it will not avert his doom.
>
> With every month that passes the many proud and once happy countries he is now holding down by brute force and vile intrigue are learning to hate the Prussian yoke and the Nazi name as nothing has ever been hated so fiercely and so widely among men before.
>
> And all the time, masters of the sea and air, the British Empire — nay, in a certain sense the whole English-speaking world — will be on his track, bearing with them the swords of Justice.

Conscious that Hopkins and perforce, the president as well were listening, he answered that verse of Longfellow, addressing himself across the ether to "this great man," the "thrice-chosen head" of a nation of 130 million souls.

"Put your confidence in us," he cried. "Give us your faith and your blessing and, under providence, all will be well. We shall not fail or falter; we shall not weaken or tire. Neither the sudden shock of battle, nor the longdrawn trials of vigilance and exertion will wear us down.

"Give us the tools, and we will finish the job."

CHAPTER 39

Against His Better Judgment

ON HIS RETURN TO New York, Wendell Willkie privately uttered this warning about Mr Churchill as conversationalist: "He can thrust," he said. "He can take, appreciate, and acknowledge your thrusts. He is subject to no doubts about his own greatness and importance — his supreme importance as the greatest man in the British Empire. But he cannot endure bores." Therein he saw the danger — that at some critical moment "slick presentation" might prevail over "the man of substance who bores him."[1] Others had long criticized his judgment. "He is the sort of man," one Tory had written, "whom, if I wanted a mountain to be moved, I should send for at once." But: "I should not consult him, after he had moved the mountain, if I wanted to know where to put it."[2] Neville Chamberlain had also remarked on his "furious advocacy of half-baked ideas."

In his time Churchill had been with equal vehemence both pro and anti North America; Germany; France; Finland; Franco; Home Rule for Ireland; the Gold Standard, and the House of Lords. He had changed colour with a facility that the chameleon could envy. Once (in 1901) he had announced, "I am not such a vain and foolish creature as to be seduced from my allegiance to the Conservative Party by the fulsome and gushing flattery of the radical press." Three years later he had crossed to the Liberals.

It was not irresponsible buffoonery. He enjoyed a lifelong love affair with the sound of his own voice. In 1903 he had declared, "The cruel and clanking struggle of armaments is drawing to a close, and with the New Century has come a clearer and a calmer sky." Through this New Century had flowed golden rivulets of such Churchillian nonsense prose, of a ripeness obscured by its undeniable eloquence. The instances were endless: As recently as October 1939 the BBC had carried his prediction into the ether: "An Eastern Front has been created which Nazi Germany does not dare assail."

Such idle prophecies would matter less, if he was not so often seduced by his own emotional prose into taking decisions against his better judgment. Years before, Chamberlain had noticed how Winston might pass casual comment on a topic and then, as though waylaid by a sudden image springing across his mind, become seized with animation, his face suffused with impetuous pink, his language accelerating until shortly he would not tolerate opposition to this idea which had only just occurred to him.[3]

These were serious faults, and deeply pertinent to the history of 1941: they explain why he pressed Britain's suit upon a reluctant Greece, against his better judgment. Britain's prestige could not take the abandonment of Greece, but it was not just that: half forgotten lessons at Harrow stirred within him; an illogical affection for the Cradle of Civilization blinded him to realilty, just as he had emotionally declared in May the year before his "invincible confidence" in the French Army and its leaders.

The auguries about Greece were as clear as the writing on Belthazar's wall. From airforce cyphers Churchill knew that the enemy was moving into the Balkans. Göring had earmarked twenty-two of the fifty-four airfields in Romania and a similar number in Bulgaria.[4] But neither Turkey nor Greece would see things his way. "Last year's history in North-West Europe," wrote one Cabinet minister, "is likely, the PM thinks, to repeat itself this year in South-East Europe." Germany was devouring the little nations one by one.[5]

Who took the fateful decision during February to divide Wavell's army of the Nile to help Greece? It aroused heated controversy. When Colonel Truman Smith of U.S. military intelligence shortly described it as the most disastrous political interference in a military strategy "since General Halleck in the civil war," he was roasted for "this dangerous statement." The very safety of the United States, defined Henry Stimson, depended on Mr Churchill's preservation in office: he alone had promised to keep the British fleet from Hitler.[6]

But the truth was that in the first instance it *was* Mr Churchill who decided to help Greece. He was unworried about North Africa. Broadcasting on February 9 he boasted that the triumph in Libya had "broken irretrievably the Italian military power on the African continent." Nobody raised his voice against the decision, least of all the generals who knew the fate of dissidents. As minister of defence Churchill dictated his whims to Pound, Dill and Portal directly. In Cabinet he acted as though their ministers were not even present.

The Service ministers were now all awestruck figureheads. In the December reshuffle he had made Captain David Margesson secretary for war, the fourth incumbent within a year. Margesson was a clean-cut, florid Party official who had once sold cutlery on New York's Lexington

Avenue; he had served eight efficient years as Chief Whip to Chamberlain and Churchill. But his appointment raised eyebrows: antisemites whispered that Lord Bearsted paid his expenses; giving the War Office to a Party hack smacked of Caligula. One editor scoffed, "The papers are so pleased about the victory in Libya they would applaud if Winston made his horse minister of transport."⁷ But he had already given *that* post to a retired army colonel, John Moore-Brabazon.

Eden ran diplomatic errands for Churchill just as Ribbentrop ran them for Hitler. He had no real power. Unlike Cadogan his permanent under-secretary, Eden was not trusted with Ultra, the codebreaking output of Bletchley Park. He penned peevish minutes or stalked languidly around exclaiming, "I can't imagine what Edward [Halifax] did with himself all day!" By telephone he clung to Winston for diplomatic decisions.⁸ On February 10 he drafted a long, muddled minute addressing the claims of Tripoli *versus* Greece. Churchill probably ignored it: the only way to get a clear line from Foreign Office memoranda, he had once said, was to skip alternate paragraphs; they usually started "on the other hand —." The Defence Committee also tackled the question that night. Under Churchill's guiding harness — he pleaded that the Greeks were "putting up a magnificent fight" — they decided to halt Wavell in Libya and to help Greece instead. He cabled this decision to Wavell on February 11.⁹ While that brave General now fished around for reasons establishing the correctness of Churchill's decision, the PM ordered Eden and the C.I.G.S. to fly out to him bearing sealed instructions.¹⁰ Since these confirmed the decision to aid Greece, while leaving minimum forces in Africa at El Agheila, Colonel Truman Smith's information was substantially correct. The decisive interference was political: Mr Churchill's.

His two emissaries Eden and Dill set out from London at mid-day on the twelfth. At that very moment, unbeknown to any Englishman, another newcomer was arriving not in Greece but in North Africa. At Tripoli airfield a slight, shortsighted German general clambered out of a Heinkel aircraft — General Erwin Rommel.

Hitler was about to outwit Churchill all over again.

* * *

Britain had scored some success in small-scale covert warfare. Five Norwegian freighters laden with ball-bearings and machinery had been extricated from Gothenburg in an operation devised by the First Lord and Hugh Dalton. Churchill, worried by larger issues, contented himself with giving Special Operations a blank cheque. Dalton used this freely in bribing the necessary Swedes, and the ships reached Britain safely on on January 24.[11] He was also planning murkier missions. Savanna was one, a plan to parachute agents into Britanny to liquidate the pilots of the KG.100 radio-beam squadron outside their Vannes airbase. Portal refused to supply a plane, priggishly calling the agents "assassins." Dalton gasped, agreed to use uniforms, and went ahead. He rather liked the inevitable comparisons between himself and Himmler, noting that one intercepted Spanish message showed "the Duke of A[lba] thinks he has made a discovery," namely two certain agents had been appointed by "a certain minister engaged on some sort of S.S. work."[12]

Rarely did Churchill intervene in Special Operations. At one Cabinet in February Dalton asked for the navy to stop a Japanese ship carrying machinery and Oerlikon guns from Europe to Japan. But, his colleagues argued, the Japanese might be hoping to provoke an incident. Churchill, seemingly less concerned, dropped a "broad hint" to Dalton to get on with it.[13]

THE PACIFIC WAR SCARE that gripped Whitehall that February has still not been explained. Mr Churchill put it about that "drifting straws" suggested that Japan was spoiling for a fight with Britain. There is however no sign of this in Japanese telegrams or records. Again according to Mr Churchill, indiscreet chatter indicated that Tokyo had signalled embassy staff in London to be ready to pack immediately. "Wait for *the* cable next week," one message had said. And, "Cut off all social contacts and hold yourselves aloof."[14] Again the Japanese files do not help us. But London advised Washington of the danger with remarkable speed.[15] Churchill undoubtedly saw a possible way of involving Roosevelt: The British navy was weak in the Far East; so the United States must lean on Japan. He passed on to Washington a digest of "the machinations of these beastly little monkeys."[16] On the seventh Eden summoned the baffled Ambassador Mamoru Shigemitsu and railed at him — a "last warning" that Britain would defend her Empire.[17]

Churchill shortly learned from his oracle that the scare was unfounded. Under an agreement signed at highest level several weeks earlier, his Intelligence had just received two American-built MAGIC machines, capable of breaking the Japanese diplomatic cipher known as Purple.[18] They reached Britain aboard the returning *King George V.* Churchill would also receive all American MAGIC intercepts. He guarded this new material as religiously as the Enigma intercepts.*

---

*Although the key 1941 Japan files in the Public Records Office remain closed, Purple messages transmitted between Tokyo, London and Washington have now become available in the United States.[19]

But he relentlessly pursued his main priority — to ensnare the United States in war. On February 15 he expressed well feigned concern about Japan to Roosevelt: while he did not think the Japanese ready to attack Singapore, they might be coveting the Dutch East Indies. "Everything that you can do," he suggested, "to inspire the Japanese with the fear of a double war may avert the danger."[20]

The Japanese were perplexed by this British bellicosity. Foreign Minister Yosuke Matsuoka ordered an investigation. Meanwhile he reassured London that Japan regarded the Axis pact signed with Germany and Italy purely as a means of limiting the spreading war. He voiced misgivings about the warlike posturing by Britain and America in the South Pacific, and pointed to the risk of escalation. He even appealed to Churchill to help put Washington's mind at rest. Recalling pre-war meetings with Eden at Geneva, Matsuoka continued "in this connection" that Japan's motto was "no conquest, no exploitation," suggested that a prolonged war would leave Europe in "chaos and confusion," and offered Japan's services as a mediator "not only in Greater East Asia but anywhere the world over."[21]

Whatever Mr Churchill's feeling about receiving yet another unsolicited offer to end the war, he probably shortly read a MAGIC intercept of Matsuoka's inquest on the war scare: British diplomats in Tokyo had mistranslated official statements. "Thus," the foreign minister cabled to his ambassador in London, "England seems to have been greatly shocked." That in turn explained Mr Eden's inexplicable "last warning" to Shigemitsu on the seventh.[22]

Evidently the straws had drifted away. Rather disingenuously Churchill claimed to his staff that "further chatter" had shown the Japanese "climbing down."[23] When a "friendly and deprecatory" Mr Shigemitsu came to Downing-street on the twenty-fourth he reiterated that Japan was not about to attack Britain or the United States.[24]

For some unfathomable reason the PM preferred to conduct such interviews alone; when his secretaries asked him afterwards to dictate a note for the record he found he could remember his own remarks, but never his visitor's.[25] Fortunately the ambassador transmitted his own record by Purple that day, and this shows that Winston did the talking anyway:

He traced the history of Japanese-British relations, with which he has personally been in touch since the time of the conclusion of the Tokyo-London Alliance [of 1902], up through the Russo-Japanese War and the World War. He went into great detail and told me how, as Prime Minister, he is greatly interested in his country's relations with Japan.

As his second point, he went on to state: "Relations between our two countries have gradually been growing worse and worse. I am very sorry to see this happening. If our two nations clash, it will be a tragedy indeed. That is just what it will be! Now, our bulwarks principally about Singapore are purely defensive. Great Britain has not adopted the policy of attacking Japan."

Thirdly, he impressed upon Shigemitsu Britain's determination. "I know that his is not going to be an easy war for us," he said. "I do not think it will be over this year; nevertheless, I do feel that ultimately we will win. Therefore," he continued, "I do not think the question of the mediation of another country will be brought up."[26]

That said, Churchill handed over a leisurely and hectoring reply to Matsuoka's message. Britain was going to extirpate the "system of lawlessness and violence abroad and cold, cruel tyranny at home, which constitutues the German Nazi regime." She sought only the satisfaction of ridding the earth of "a hateful terror and of restoring freedom to the many insulted and enslaved nations." Accordingly she had no need for Matsuoka's implied offer to mediate.[27]

This coarse rebuff annoyed Tokyo and Matsuoka now denied having so offered.[28] The scare had outlived its purpose, and Churchill poured oil on the waters. On March 3, after a weekend at Chequers, the Australian prime minister Robert Menzies would speak to the Foreign Press Association and urge friendlier relations with Japan. Meeting Shigemitsu again the next day, Mr Churchill blandly remarked upon this speech and used the French term *détente*. "Well," wired the ambassador, relieved, to Tokyo, "I think that we can take this speech of Menzies' as a gesture of friendship from Great Britain."[29] MAGIC unravelled his telegram a few days later.

* * *

On February 14, 1941 Hitler's first troopships for North Africa sailed past the sunken hospital ship at the entrance to Tripoli harbour. A grinning General Rommel was there to greet them. Unaware that German units were now joining the Italians in Libya, Churchill was still resolved to divert troops from there to Greece whether Athens wanted or not. He felt honour bound. If Hitler did overrun Greece then Britain would just have to salvage what she could from the wreckage; and that might well happen, he somberly told Cadogan, standing in at the F.O. while Eden was away.[30] But shortly — perhaps it was because he had read the first intercepts about Luftwaffe units in Africa — Churchill's instinct began bleating warnings. He cabled Eden on February 20:

Do not consider yourselves obligated to a Greek enterprise if in your hearts you feel it will only be another Norwegian fiasco. . . But of course you know how valuable success would be.

Bletchley had now begun sending its intercepts out to Cairo direct. But Eden had evidently not seen the news. He sent a message listing the armour, anti-tank and flak troops that Wavell proposed to ship over to Greece. It would be a gamble but, he reminded Churchill, "when we discussed this matter in London we were prepared to run the risk of failure, thinking it better to suffer with the Greeks than to make no attempt to help them."[31] "A[nthony]," observed Cadogan with profound misgivings, "has rather jumped us into this."

Among the guests at Chequers on the twenty-third was Mr Robert Menzies, the genial, backslapping Melbourne barrister who was nursing a one-vote majority as Australia's prime minister. His pencil diary recorded their "momentous discussion" about diverting troops from Libya to defend Greece, "largely with Australian & New Zealand troops." "This kind of discussion," reflected Menzies, "which may mean thousands of lives, is not easy."

The Cabinet discussed the diversion late on the twenty-fourth. "You have read your file, gentlemen," said Churchill, "and the report of the Chiefs of Staff Committee. The arguments are clear on each side. I favour the project."

Menzies, an almost silent observer, wondered if the speed with which the decision was approved indicated "great clarity and directness of mind" in all these ministers — or had Winston merely taken charge of them? "I was the only one to put questions," Menzies wrote in his illuminating diary, "and felt like a new boy who in the first week of school commits the solecism of speaking to the Captain of the School."

Privately, the ministers were not without misgivings about helping Greece. "It's a nasty decision," wrote Cadogan, "but I *think*, on balance, I agree with it." Squashing the instinct buzzing around his own head, Churchill also commended it, but only weakly because he asked his colleagues for a show of hands: nobody dissented: democracy had its uses.

"Full steam ahead," he wired to Eden that night.

YUGOSLAVIA'S STANCE, stratigically wedged between Nazi Germany and Greece, thus became crucial, and S.O.E. played a major role. Instructed by Churchill in July 1940 to "set Europe ablaze," Dalton had spread subversive tentacles throughout the Balkans. Where Britain had few friends, he procured them by old fashioned means. His agent in Crete disbursed £400,000 monthly.[32] While Brigadier Menzies ("C") scoffed at S.O.(2)'s "sheer waste of money" in Yugoslavia, Dalton had assiduously bribed the new Serb Peasant party since July to oppose Belgrade's pro-German tendency.[33] The British legation housed a powerful S.O.(2) mission consisting of George Taylor, Tom Masterson and Julian Amery;

they had established financial relations with the leader of the Peasant party, Milos Tupanjanin, and the older parties in opposition to the Prince Regent, Paul. S.O.(2) also channelled funds to the National Associations, the Chetniks, and veterans' bodies: by 1941 the British were able "to ask and obtain virtually anything we wanted" from them.

This now had its uses. Hitler wanted facilities to pass troops through this rugged country to Greece. On the day that his troopships arrived in Tripoli, he invited prime minister Dragisa Tsvetkovitch to Berchtesgaden and suggested that Yugoslavia join the Axis Pact. A tug-of-war began between Hitler and S.O.(2) with Yugoslavia as the prize.

* * *

On February 27 Mr Churchill was to address the House.

Anguish still oppressed him before every speech. It hung above him "like a vulture," he once said.[34] An American statesman would also write eleven years later of how much Churchill's recent speeches had preyed on his mind. "He referred several times to them as vultures which were hovering over him and depriving him of all power to relax and enjoy himself."[35] This speech was no different. Dictated line by line to a secretary he laboured until three a.m. The notes were typed downstairs, revised, then retyped in "Chinese" — the abbreviated and echeloned script he read from.

Oratory without a script was a gamble he had long abandoned. "It is too easy to come a cropper," he once explained, and illustrated the point. "All went well," he recalled, "until a certain day when I arrived at the phrase, 'The decision rests with the men who. . .' As I came to the word *who* my memory went over a precipice. There was nothing beyond, absolutely nothing, a desert. I took another run at it, 'The decision rests with the men who. . .' Once more everything went blank. I sat down, to receive one of the greatest ovations of my long career in the House."[36]

Tomorrow's speech was to justify MPs retaining their seats even when taking up government duties abroad — Cripps was in Moscow, Hoare in Madrid, Macdonald in Ottawa, and his own son Randolph had now flown to Cairo with No.8 Commando, equipped by his doting father with letters of recommendation to Smuts and Wavell.

As he worked on the script that night the admiralty telephoned No.10: a supply convoy had been massacred in the North Western Approaches. John Colville kept these ill tidings from his chief until three-thirty a.m.: but then Winston asked him outright what news from the admiralty. "It is very distressing," Colville sympathized.

"Distressing!" exclaimed the PM. "It's terrifying. If it goes on it'll be the end of us."[37]

The debate could not be put off. Seal feared it was a grotesque ordeal, but for Winston the skirmish set his adrenalin pumping and he felt quite invigorated.[38] But then toward the end he faltered, and Nye Bevan torpedoed his peroration with a sly interruption; all exhilaration gone, the PM stumped off to the Smoking Room with tears of exhaustion in his eyes. A veteran MP bearded him there but only offended him. How difficult it was to say anything that did not upset him when he was in this mood, the MP noticed.[39]

Grim-faced at the shocking shipping casualties the PM drove to Chequers. Convoys were the lifeline which the New World was holding out to the old. When the jovial Australian prime minister Robert Menzies arrived, evidently to discuss the Pacific War Scare, the PM steeped him in gloom about the convoy losses — but went on, to the amazement of Menzies, to "fight his way out," pacing the floor of the ancestral hall with growing light of battle in his eyes.[40] Engrossed in his own oratory, he always stood with his head thrust forward and his thumbs tucked into the armholes of his waistcoat, or strode up and down as if "trying to keep pace with his own eloquence," one man had remarked.[41]

That Sunday Dalton came down to talk about S.O.E. but Churchill could not put convoys and rations out of his mind. Charts were spread out and sinkings marked in. The troops were eating too much, he growled to the minister. "They could do with less rations," he added, "They are using too much cotton and wool."

During lunch he tried to get a rise out of the now silent Australian premier. "Hitler says," he remarked, methodically forking food from plate to mouth, "that sixteen million Jews ought to go and live in Australia. What d'you say to that?" The Socialist minister Dalton — whose private views were plain from uncompromising tidbits about Jews in his diaries* — pricked up his ears.

Menzies affected not to hear the remark. He was reflecting how much Churchill grew upon one: "He has amazing grasp of detail," he wrote after retiring to his room, "and by daily contact with the Services' headquarters knows of dispositions and establishments quite accurately."[42] Hitler had the same grasp. A few days later Churchill translated his distilled wisdom into a written directive, announcing "The Battle of the Atlantic."[43]

HE FELT NONE too good. He had stomach pains, and on February 24 his

---

*Bigoted and antisemetic, Dalton privately referred to one MP as "that most displeasing rich black Jew" and noted with interest Desmond Morton's information that Georges Mandel was "a Jew, whose real name is said to be Rehoboam Rothschild."[44]

appointment card had showed: "?3:15 Treatment." The mortal danger to Britain's lifelines "gnawed my bowels," he later wrote.[45] His malaise probably had a less picturesque origin in his sybaritic lifestyle. X-rays found nothing wrong. "But what about the stomach pains?" he asked. The doctor asked what he had eaten or drunk recently and the Ritzy recital that followed was enough for him to fold away his stethoscope: so Major Morton related with a guffaw a few days later.[46] Afflicted with a bad cold, he was scolded by the ENT specialist that it was because of the snuff he was taking *against* colds.[47] He disliked doctors, and had the habit of summoning several until one yielded the diagnosis he had in mind. His medicines were equally bizarre: he kept a cupboard full, and used them regardless of the malady against which they had been prescribed.[48]

After lunch that Sunday, Dalton talked to him for an hour about Special Operations and its officers: only Brigadier Colin Gubbins seemed to register slightly. He pressed for more aircraft. "We are now ready," he urged, "for more tools." But the needs of Bomber Command were already paramount.

"I am not dissatisfied," Churchill consoled him. "I know that you are a very able man." Urged to meet more S.O. chiefs, Churchill said: "No, I see no-one."* But he had pushed through Dalton's plan for a Commando raid on the Lofotens. "The admiralty," he sniffed, "didn't want to do it." As for the rest, he approved of Savanna and Josephine — a project to sabotage a power station near Bordeaux. Turning to Roosevelt's tedious insistence on allowing dried milk through the blockade to France, Churchill quietly told the minister that they must prevaricate, delay, and diminish all such maudlin aid.

About three-thirty, Dalton observed, Winston wandered off for his afternoon nap.[50]

* * *

"Give us the tools. . ."

Words like these bedazzled many, but Robert Menzies for one was unimpressed by eloquence. True, supreme office had "improved and steadied" Churchill. "His real tyrant," feared the Australian, writing up his diary, "is the glittering phrase — so attractive to his mind that awkward facts have to give way."[51]

---

*Dr James Conant, president of Harvard, told Churchill over lunch on March 6, 1941 how valuable the Tizard mission had been. "I was glad to hear this," Sir Henry Tizard jealously wrote in his diary, "as the PM, who sent me there, had not found time to see me since my return, and had not even acknowledged a preliminary report that I sent him."[49]

Neither Roosevelt nor Morgenthau was going to "give" Britain the tools. The price of Churchill's war would be paid by Britain — in the Caribbean base leases, in the end of Imperial preference, and in higher taxes. The taxes on income and cigarettes had doubled since the war began; even the tax on whisky, the PM's staple drink, had gone up by 50 percent.[52] Canada began remorselessly selling off Britain's $1,924m investments to pay for raw materials bought in the United States. Washington journalists howled that if Canada found nothing "irregular, mean or grasping" in forcing Britain to sell, the United States should not adopt "a more altruistic" policy.[53] India too was billing Britain heavily for her contribution.[54]

The United States had by now accumulated $22,000m in Gold. Economist John Maynard Keynes pointed out that Gold was of value only so long as nations accepted the convention: "The convention," he warned, in language reminiscent of Churchill's "Gold teeth" remark to Hopkins, "depends on not all the Gold being in one hand."

> When in the game of 'beggar my neighbour' [Keynes wrote] all the cards belong to one player, that is the signal for the game to come to an end. The pack becomes worthless pasteboard: the fun is over.[55]

Bankrupt and unable under American law to place further orders until the Lend-Lease Bill, No. 1776, passed into law, Britain's financial plight was blessedly secret, but none the less terrible for that. Roosevelt procrastinated. Blasé about Britain's difficulties, he laughed at one press conference, "They are not going to be solvent next Monday and insolvent the week after."[56] Morgenthau unfeelingly remarked on January 9 that the British were getting "hysterical."[57] On the next day the American cruiser *Louisville* picked up £42m of British Gold at Simonstown naval base, South Africa.

Roosevelt's austere eyes turned to the Allied, Dominion and French Gold. France had £284m of the metal in trust in Canada (including £70m deposited there by the Bank of England); legally it belonged to Vichy. While this did not impress Churchill he was unable despite the nagging by Morgenthau to switch it to Washington for fear of French-Canadian disturbances; besides, Nazi propaganda would exploit the theft in France. Instead, Mackenzie-King generously agreed to purchase increasingly worthless sterling for hard dollars.[58] The Dutch and Norwegians refused outright to sell Churchill their gold for sterling; on February 4 he tackled the Belgian prime minister and he reluctantly agreed to lend $300m in Gold if Britain guaranteed to replenish it postwar.[59]*

---

* At this time $100 = approximately £20.

It was an unholy financial mess. There were those who failed to understand why Britain should pay anything for the defence of American freedoms. On February 19, Lord Beaverbrook soberly totted up for Churchill twenty years of grievances with the United States. Ever since World War I their American cousins had kept upping the ante — demanding recognition of their twelve-mile limit, prohibition of Empire liquor exports to the United States, peace with Ireland, a settlement of the war debt, and breaking the alliance with Japan. "And look where it has taken us!" exclaimed the minister. "The Japanese are our relentless enemies. And the Americans are our unrelenting creditors."[60]

The End-of-Empire Sale had begun. The first stage had been relatively painless, the gift of British technological secrets to America. In Washington, experts told Henry Stimson that American science had been lagging years behind the British until the Tizard mission came: it had brought "infinitely more" than the Americans could offer in return.[61]

The next stage was more painful: the liquidation of Britain's real-estate and property.

Worried about Roosevelt's agreement to appropriate $7,000m for Lend-Lease, Morgenthau harried him over lunch on March 10: "What do you expect in return?"

> I asked him if he was thinking in terms of taking over the English Fleet or the British isles in the West Indies.

Roosevelt feigned lack of interest. "I don't want the British Fleet," he said, "because by the time we got it it would be too antiquated." As for taking over the British West Indies, he said, they seemed to be in revolutionary turmoil. That left Britain's assets in North America. Morgenthau promised to keep piling on the pressure until Roosevelt told him to stop. "I may be mistaken," dictated Morgenthau after their luncheon, "but I don't think that the President has in mind to do anything very dramatic to help England at this time."[62]

It was a buyer's market. First to go under the hammer was the wealthy British-owned Viscose Company, worth $125m. Jesse Jones later admitted that he would have lent up to $75m against it. Instead, it was liquidated. To handle it the House of Morgan called in Dillon & Reed, a firm of which James Forrestal — Roosevelt's close friend and later Navy secretary — was president. Viscose had no debts except current accounts; it held government bonds worth $40m. "It was sold to the Morgan people," recorded Harold F. Ickes with distaste, "at an initial price of $37m." After re-sale the British eventually received a total of $87m.[63]

Belying his simulated lack of interest in the British Caribbean, Roosevelt had sent an economic mission there and had raised steep demands on Bermuda, St Lucia and Trinidad, involving huge garrisons for the proposed American bases. Bermuda and the West Indies — the oldest Crown possessions — protested. "Early in December," the president wrote to King George in his first letter after re-election, "I hope to get a bit of a holiday by going over to the Bahamas and several other prospective bases. That destroyer arrangement seems to have worked out perfectly." Only now did His Majesty learn details of the "arrangement," which Churchill had evidently struck in part by transatlantic telephone, perhaps to avoid creating records on paper.* Alarmed by Roosevelt's proprietorial tone, the King registered profound concern. "The Americans have got to understand," he wrote to his private secretary, "that in leasing the bases the question of Sovereignty does not come in. These islands are part of the British Colonial Empire and I am not going to see my West Indian subjects handed over to the U.S. authorities."[64] On February 25, Roosevelt showed impatience: "I have been very much concerned at the delay in reaching an agreement in respect to the naval and air bases," he notified Churchill, and he hinted that Lend-Lease could be affected.[65] There was resentment at every level in London. The demands on the islands amounted, observed Colville, "to capitulation."[66] The secretary of the Cabinet warned that if the demands became public knowledge they might bring down the government. But Churchill could not go back. In a note to Lord Moyne, his new Colonial Secretary, he explained that a "first class row" would only aid the opponents of Lend-Lease in the Senate.[67]

Moyne was no match for Winston. Over sixty, the former Walter Guinness appeared to some long past his prime, but critics whispered knowingly. One afternoon at Cherkley, his country estate near Leatherhead, Beaverbrook jealously told a close friend that the appointment was further proof that Churchill put personal friendships before Britain's interests. He remarked upon Moyne's "gifts of cigars and alcohol" to Winston and more specifically upon the fact "that Moyne kept him regularly supplied with champagne."[68]

Churchill dined with Moyne and Gil Winant, the new American ambassador, on March 4. John Gilbert Winant was fifty-two, Republican, and a shy homespun Liberal. Thrice governor of New Hampshire, he was not a trained diplomat, and had few useful British contacts. But he had money, having literally struck oil in his youth; and he was a New Dealer. As a speaker his delivery was hurried in public and inaudible in private. People said he had Red Indian blood — he was the

---

* When Henry Stimson telephoned Roosevelt on August 3, 1940 at Hyde Park about the destroyers-for-bases deal, the president outlined to him "several other talks he had had with other people on the same subject—notably Winston Churchill and Lothian." (Diary).

ghost of Abraham Lincoln in both looks and outlook.[69]

Churchill met this silent but agreeable man again more formally with Moyne and Lord Cranborne, the Dominions secretary, on Wednesday March 5 at No.10. Moyne told Cranborne that he feared Churchill would "in the heat of the conflict" cede too much to Roosevelt in the West Indies. Cranborne saw it all as the first ugly move by Washington towards hemispheric defence. But Churchill reassured them both. "America," he reminded them, "is providing us with credits that will enable us to win the war, which we could not otherwise do." With unbecoming cynicism he warned, "We cannot afford to risk the major issue in order to maintain our pride and to preserve the dignity of a few small islands."[70]

* * *

Bulgaria had signed the Axis pact that Saturday, March 1, and Hitler's troops swarmed down to the Greek frontier and began feverishly laying airfields and reinforcing bridges.[71]

The foreign secretary was still in Cairo. Churchill telegraphed Eden to turn his "main appeal" now to Yugoslavia, on the flank of Hitler's approach to Greece. He hoped too that Turkey might now declare support of Greece — a rather tenuous hope given the centuries of enmity between them. (He received both ambassadors on February 24, though safely separated by lunch.) A timorous Prince Paul — whom he dubbed "Prince Palsy" in conversation with Dalton — refused even to see the itinerant Eden and travelled in secret to Hitler's lair at Berchtesgaden three days later.

As prince regent and dictator conferred, the first Australian and New Zealand troops arrived on the Aliakhmon line in Greece. But now there was a snag: Athens was becoming alarmed, Eden reported on the fourth, awkward, and even "defeatist." At the War Office Captain Margesson was growing queasy about Greece and told Churchill's secretary so. "Many others," the latter noted, "feel the same." Nobody had the courage to argue with Winston. Looming ahead, Colville saw another Norway, Dunkirk and Dakar "rolled into one."

Churchill also resigned himself to the inevitability of tragedy in Greece. After seeing Winant and sleeping off a rich lunch at the Savoy with Oliver Lyttelton on the fifth, whom he had appointed to the Board of Trade in October, he pulled off the bedclothes and stifled a yawn. "The poor chiefs of staff," Colville heard him mutter, "will get very much out of breath in their desire to run away."[72]

Eden's forlorne advice was that they see it through. But luncheon and siesta had fortified Churchill's judgment and he began to argue at that afternoon's Cabinet that to desert a *halfhearted* Greece could surely not damage British prestige? A few hours later, with barely suppressed relief, the Defence Committee agreed. Churchill immediately cabled Eden: losing the Balkans might not be a catastrophe after all; but Britain's "ignominious ejection from Greece" would. He hinted that Eden should liberate Athens from the obligation to reject a German ultimatum.[73]

A remarkable change of mind, but it was too late. During the night London received the agreement which General Dill had signed in Athens on the fourth. Britain was committed to the hilt. In Cabinet that evening, March 6, Churchill put a good face on it: Dill would surely not have signed if the operation was hopeless? Dill now reported that the two ground commanders in Greece, Generals Blamey (Australia) and Freyberg (New Zealand) were willing to take the risk.

The Cabinet met at noon on the seventh, but Eden was now reporting that everybody at Cairo was unanimous that they could see it through. The material damage to Greece, if the battle into which Britain had urged her proved hopeless, briefly occupied the ministers; and Robert Menzies, attending this Cabinet, expressed quiet concern about the political damage in the Dominions if New Zealand and Australian troops paid heavily for a "commitment entered into by a British Cabinet Minister in Athens." He was uneasy at how readily the Cabinet was swayed by Churchill's eloquence. Clutching at straws — for example, the hope that Yugoslavia might enter on the British side — Churchill ruled, "We should go forward with a good heart."

"Cabinet accepts for itself the fullest responsibility," he telegraphed to Eden, and drove over to the Savoy for luncheon, taking this time Captain Margesson.

WHO COULD SAY? Greece might yet prove a British triumph. After lunch, more bountiful in mind, he left for Chequers early; no doubt the oracle had told him what the Luftwaffe had in store for London that night. The raid was the first in two months. The crowded Cafe de Paris received a direct hit which slew many revelers who had believed the structure to be impregnable.

Out at Chequers, the PM appeared witty and entertaining.[74] His cold was becoming bronchitis, but the awful burden of decision no longer preyed upon his mind. He had retired to bed unusually early when a call came through from Washington — it was Harry Hopkins reporting that Bill No.1776 had just cleared its final hurdle, the Senate. Churchill cabled him the next morning. "The strain has been serious," he said, "so thank God for your news."[75] That Sunday evening, General Alan Brooke came down from London, and was convulsed like so many others before him by the spectacle as Winston appeared for dinner in his light blue siren suit, "like a child's romper suit."

> He was in great form, and after dinner sent for his service rifle to give me a demonstration of the 'long port' which he wanted to substitute for the 'slope'! Then he followed this up with some bayonet exercises![76]

For a while the hall at Chequers — a covered former courtyard — echoed with Winston's clattering footsteps. With the passage of Lend-Lease, a load was off his heart.

Roosevelt formally signed it into law on Tuesday — "An ocean-borne trumpet call that we are no longer alone," as Winston triumphed in a speech on the eighteenth. It was another of those phrases that sounded so fine at the time. Three days later, with Britain's Empire entering liquidation and her armies embarking on a disastrous adventure in the Balkans, the agreement on the West Indies bases was signed.

CHAPTER 40

The Midas Touch

ONCE OR TWICE A small, steely eyed visitor was let into No.10, so secretly that the private secretaries were unaware of his presence. He was William S. Stephenson, a quiet Canadian who had made millions from electronics. Churchill had sent him in June 1940 to New York, officially as Passport Control Officer, with orders to establish a secret service there. Behind his outward mission of preventing sabotage to Britain's war supplies was an ulterior one of the highest priority: to lure the United States into Britain's war.

Operating from the thirty-fifth and thirty-sixth floors of the Rockefeller Center on Fifth Avenue, Stephenson acted for both S.I.S. and S.O.E.[1] At the behest of J. Edgar Hoover of the FBI his office was designated "British Security Coordination." This title aroused suspicions: the State Department complained that it was "not particularly revealing." They questioned his officials [2] and sent an agent to investigate, but he reported that local anti-sabotage officials had never heard of BSC. "Mr Stephenson," railed the agent, "has so far refused to reveal the exact whereabouts of his office."[3] By late March 1941 they learned that BSC was fashioning "a full size secret police and intelligence service." It all sounded highly irregular to Adolph A. Berle Jr, the State Department official concerned. Unaware that BSC had the very highest sanction, Berle even wanted the president warned: suppose, he asked, Stephenson attempted to subvert American decisions or to "make trouble" for individuals to whom the British took exception?

At that time there was no American foreign Intelligence service. It was a gap which Churchill effectively filled through Bill Donovan, the Wall Street lawyer who had twice since July 1940 come under his spell.[4] Stephenson provided Donovan with the secret data he needed to impress Roosevelt with his ability. Donovan had just spent two months visiting Spain, Britain and the Mediterranean, and returned to Washington convinced of the rightness of Churchill's strategy. In May the PM sent over to the White House his Director of Naval Intelligence to impress

Donovan's suitability upon Roosevelt and on June 18 the latter appointed Donovan "Coordinator of Information."

Thus during those crucial months of 1941 it was the delicate hand of Mr Churchill that controlled the embryonic United States Intelligence Service. There can be no questioning this "most secret fact," as Major Desmond Morton termed it. He boasted later that summer that the PM was fully aware that the U.S. Intelligence services were "being run for them at the President's request by the British." In fact Stephenson's deputy, the S.I.S. career officer Colonel Charles H. Ellis, was sitting with Hoover and Donovan, and reporting regularly to the president.

It is of course essential [noted Morton] that this fact should not be known in view of the furious uproar it would cause if known to the isolationists.

Berle did learn of it. "In other words," he expostulated in a choked letter to his superior, Sumner Welles, "Stevenson's assistant in British Intelligence is running Donovan's Intelligence service."[5]

THROUGHOUT 1941 BSC refined and developed methods of doing what Berle had called "making trouble" in the United States. Stephenson's three hundred agents (he admitted to only 137 employees, but Berle minuted that obviously Stephenson had shuffled far more of his men onto Donovan's payroll) intercepted mail, tapped wires, cracked safes, kidnapped, and rumour-mongered. They whispered that the anti-war campaigner Charles Lindbergh's abducted and murdered son was alive and training in Nazi Germany. Other tricks were evidently dirtier. After the untimely death of isolationist lobbyist William Rhodes Davis at age fifty-two, BSC requested the FBI not to investigate.[6]

Churchill assigned highest BSC priority to panicking Washington into believing that Hitler had designs in America's backyard, Latin America. Here Hoover had retained control of counter-espionage, so BSC faked documents to plant on the FBI. To "prove" that Hitler was masterminding a coup in La Paz, BSC forged a letter from the Bolivian military attaché in Berlin.* Roosevelt, who may have been unaware of the deception, called it "this astonishing document" in his next broadcast.[7] BSC furnished similar documents about Franco's Spain: this time the forgery was detected, and Berle huffed to his superiors that the British had even approached "our people" to collaborate in "certain other forgeries." Stephenson, he warned, was using manufactured

---

*Dated Jun 9, 1941 the letter read: "Friends in the Wilhelmstrasse tell me that from information received from you the moment is approaching to strike in order to liberate my poor country. . . I go much further and believe that *el golpe* should take place in the middle of July." Written in Spanish the letter was "signed" by the military attaché Major Elias Belmonte.

incidents to influence public opinion via the *New York Tribune*.[8] But even the watchful Berle was suckered by another BSC product: "The FBI," he wrote in April 1942, "has intercepted and given me today a copy of the German plan for the invasion of Colombia." And he added admiringly, "These Germans are thorough."[9]

Just how thorough, became evident a few weeks later. From the U.S. ambassador at Bogotá he learned that Stephenson's station chief Fred Stagg had blandly requested co-operation in assassinating Dr Luis Lopez de Mesa, the Colombian foreign minister.[10]* This unfortunate gentleman was commendably pro-British but due to retire in May and hence expendable. No doubt the Nazis would be blamed. The U.S. ambassador, noted Berle, declined to co-operate.

Almost certainly, BSC had another function: to provide an informal "secret channel" between White House and No.10, circumventing noisome embassy and Cabinet officials. Using a special cipher, Stephenson sent thousands of code messages from the FBI transmitter on Chesapeake Bay. They were picked up and deciphered at S.O.E. headquarters in London's Baker-street. The president began availing himself of this channel to Churchill in 1941; since the files of messages that flowed through the other channels make no reference to ULTRA and MAGIC, the oracles that certainly guided Mr Churchill's destinies, it is fair to speculate that these messages were exchanged by some such secret channel.[11] Hoover noted in July that Stephenson was proffering this clandestine traffic as his reason for denying access to his special cipher. When Hoover's superior the attorney general Francis Biddle learned of this later he was perplexed and furious. "Several thousand cables a month," he protested, "and in code, are being received and sent through the FBI radio station in Maryland."[12]

Hoover voiced concern about the growth of BSC, and Berle joined him in insisting that the hundreds of agents now operating for Churchill on American soil register under the Foreign Registration Act; William Stephenson retaliated in his own way, telling an agent to "get some dirt" on Berle.[13] Hoover's G-men caught the BSC agent redhanded and gave Stephenson twenty-four hours to remove him from the country.[14] Many Federal officials thought Stephenson should follow. Biddle told Lord Halifax that Roosevelt's Cabinet wanted Stephenson replaced by a different type of man. Halifax retorted amiably that Stephenson was on the best of terms with Hoover. To Biddle, Hoover afterwards exploded

---

*Traced and interviewed by this author in Paris, Stagg admitted requesting American assistance for ditching a refrigerator containing a German agent from a chartered plane — after he had first been relieved of a suitcase of dollars — but denied any recollection of the episode referred to in Berle's files.

that Stephenson "tapped wires and shangaied sailors." The FBI wanted his wings clipped too.[15]

Berle, Biddle, Hoover and the other Federal officials were way out of their depth in the game now being played between No.10 and the Oval Office. They had become pawns, with neither voice nor authority. Another meeting was held, this time in the British embassy. Biddle challenged the BSC claim that the FBI channels were carrying clandestine Churchill-Roosevelt messages. Halifax countered that Stephenson denied ever making "any such statement." In vain Biddle brandished Hoover's written statement to the contrary.

Stepping out into Massachusetts-avenue afterwards, Biddle glimpsed a smile flickering across Halifax's skeletal features. "Somebody," he scowled to Berle, "has been doing some tall lying here."[16]

* * *

Like some inverse Midas touch, everything that Churchill touched still seemed to turn to ashes. His moods swept by as suddenly as sunshine on a gusty day. Only the hopes he vested in his maternal America sustained him. Australian prime minister Robert Menzies wrote after one March weekend at Chequers, "Winston is completely certain of America's full help, of her participation in a Japanese war, and of Roosevelt's passionate determination to stamp out the Nazi menace from the earth." And he lamented, "If the PM was a better listener and less disposed to dispense with all expert or local opinion, I might feel a little easier about it — he's a holy terror. I went to bed tired."[17]

Increasingly the radiant bursts were clouded by sudden gloom and Churchill took refuge, as old men do, in ill health: his cold had become bronchitis by that Monday March 10 and he funked returning to London — where a Cabinet had been marked down for the bunker at Dollis Hill — and stayed at Chequers until his Tuesday luncheon at the Palace.[18]

He was worried about Africa, but did not show it. Bletchley had broken into the airforce cipher used by the new Fliegerführer Afrika: this revealed that a German Africa Corps was out there, and that Rommel was commander. More than one Cabinet colleague now quietly regretted that Wavell's antitank guns, armour and troops were being shipped across to the Piraeus in southern Greece, and murmured that he should have mopped up North Africa while he could.[19] "War Cabinet," Robert Menzies recorded on March 5. "The Middle East proposal is going bad. Why the devil should Eden purport to commit us on facts which he must know are most disturbing and which have Empire significance?" The next day Menzies spoke "plain words" about the need for Mr Churchill to consult the Dominions before taking grave decisions affecting them.

Churchill decided to let Eden stay out there for a while. Ambassador Winant, viewing the Whitehall scene through a newcomer's eyes, could see why the PM preferred to handle things by himself. "Outside of Churchill," he would tell Washington, "the people in the government seem to be mediocre."[20]

LADEN WITH TANGERINES from Lisbon a further Roosevelt emissary arrived — William Averell Harriman, with F.D.R.'s orders to keep Britain afloat. At forty-nine Harriman was handsome, wealthy and — what mattered more — a protégé of Harry Hopkins. Baruch enviously called him a "spoiled rich man's son." But Churchill knew this banker and society mogul from chance encounters on the Riviera and having met him at Barnie Baruch's around the time of the Wall-street crash.

His family took an instant shine to him. At Chequers in mid March, the American revealed that F.D.R. undertook to build merchant ships and even convoy them to Britain. Churchill knew what that meant, and liked it: Harriman and Winant, he confided after that heady weekend to his Cabinet, were hoping to trap Hitler into commiting "some overt act" of war.[21] "I am all for trusting Mr Harriman fully," the PM wrote to the indefatigable Cabinet secretary Sir Edward Bridges, "and working with him on the most intimate terms."[22] But, astute enough to recognize that Roosevelt would use Harriman to bypass Purvis, Churchill decided to continue in secret correspondence with Purvis's purchasing commission. Perhaps recalling the secret channels he had employed at Narvik and Dunkirk, he urged Bridges: "It should not be difficult to devise methods."

Churchill had been driven to this jaundiced view of Roosevelt's motives by the hard line adopted by Morgenthau over Britain's interim payments for war supplies pending the signing of Lend-Lease. Refusing to be "hustled and rattled," he recommended Halifax to deadlock and remind the Americans that "their lives are now in this business too." "Morgenthau," he wrote tersely to the ambassador, "may have a bad time before his Committee, but Liverpool and Glasgow are having a bad time now."[23]

His anger was evident, though never in outgoing messages to the president. "Are we," he reminded Kingsley Wood, "going to get our advances for building up factories in the United States repaid to us?" "A small crash" was his proposed remedy — a show-down preceded, as he put it, by "a lie-down": Britain should put on a "dumb and immobile" act for the Americans:

As far as *I* can make out we are not only to be skinned but flayed to the bone. I would like to get them hooked a little firmer, but they are pretty well on now. The power of the debtor is in the ascendant, especially when he is doing all the fighting.[24]

Hitler's bombers had levelled more of the City that weekend. The new vista of St Paul's was one which Wren would have given his soul to achieve. Churchill dourly double-checked the arrangements for his safety, ambling over with his mousey P.P.S., Eric Seal, to see a new bunker being constructed in the government quarter. Paddling through wet concrete and clambering down ladders he asked the bystanding labourers: "Are we downhearted?"[25]

With his porkpie hat and outsize Havana cigar, he put on a brave face, but it was not easy, burdened with his awesome insight into the future from the oracle at Bletchley: the ineluctable defeat of Greece; the defection of Yugoslavia; the devastation of ports, and decimation of shipping. "I'm not afraid of the air," he blurted out, baring his thoughts at the close of one Cabinet: "I'm not afraid of invasion, I'm less afraid of the Balkans — but — I'm anxious about the Atlantic."[26]

The disciplines of discretion and the impulses of death-wish fought within him for control. He took immense pains over security. Even on the scrambler telephone he used guarded language. He pruned the lists of those receiving the codebreakers' intercepts — not even Anthony Eden was privy to the oracle. He treated its products as gingerly as nitroglycerine, as one example shows: on April 2 he told Roosevelt that "entirely authentic secret information" showed that the enemy had given Vichy permission to transfer *Dunkerque* to Toulon for "disarmament." Since Mers-el-Kébir he knew he could not trust Admiral Darlan, and he begged the president to lean on Vichy to cancel this transfer; for otherwise Britain would have to intercept the battlecruiser. In a frantic after-thought Churchill sent a second telegram warning that on no account must Admiral Leahy use the phrase "permission of the Armistice Commission" since this would compromise his source.[27]

And yet in major strategy the PM was distressingly indiscreet. We have already remarked upon how Churchill's and Reynaud's indiscretions in March 1940 had prompted Hitler's rapid invasion of Norway. Churchill also indirectly ensured that the R.A.F. and American bomber crews would have to contend with the Flak nightmare over Germany: "We have Churchill to thank that we got so much flak," said the commander of Germany's air defences, Lieutenant-General Beppo Schmid, in July 1945. "In one of his speeches in the House of Commons he explained, after being attacked over the poor showing of the anti-aircraft artillery, 'I need the A.A. if only for reasons of population morale.' Our Flak people rushed off to the Führer and said, 'You see, Churchill also says it!' "[28]

Now, in March 1941, Churchill began speaking all too frankly about Britain's shipping crisis: formally welcoming Winant at a London luncheon he underscored this "potentially mortal" challenge,[29] and over the following months he missed no opportunity of referring to this chink in Britain's armour. Hitler pricked up his ears, and directed his airforce and U-boat commanders to complete the task by attacking ports and supply convoys. A year later he pointed out to Grand Admiral Raeder: "Time and again Churchill speaks of shipping tonnage as his greatest worry."[30]

On March 19 the PM called the first regular Wednesday meeting of a new Battle of the Atlantic committee.[31] Restlessly searching for ways of bringing America in, he cabled to Roosevelt an invitation to police the Central Atlantic where the battlecruisers *Scharnhorst* and *Gneisenau* were marauding: the Americans, he hinted, could at least report what they saw.[32]

Five hundred planes attacked the Port of London that night. After dining at No.10 with Harriman and Anthony Biddle, American ambassador to the governments in exile, Churchill handed out helmets and invited them to join him on the air ministry roof, climbing up through a manhole to watch the spectacle. The bombing had stopped, but it exhilarated him — his secretary heard him quoting Tennyson above the distant gunfire — and nor were these two hours without effect on his transatlantic cousins.[33] By the time they retraced their steps and went down to the C.W.R. to see night duty officers marking up war maps among the ventilators, girders and stanchions, 1,700 fires had been kindled and 504 Londoners had paid the ultimate price for the night's "fun" (as Colville heard Winston call it.)

IN THE BALKANS his Midas touch appeared again. Diplomacy having failed to win the Belgrade regime as a whole, S.O.(2) decided to topple it instead. They confided their plot to the Serb opposition factions behind closed doors at the British legation on Wednesday the nineteenth. They won round three ministers; when their colleagues approved the draft Nazi-Yugoslav pact on Thursday these three resigned.[34] From Chequers, Churchill telephoned all that Saturday morning with the F.O., drafting a letter which went to Prime Minister Tsvetkovitch. It drew up the now familiar balance sheet — of 65 million malignant Huns, already holding down other "ancient races," confronted by nearly 200 million Whites of the British Empire and United States — and warned Yugoslavia not to become an "accomplice in an attempted assassination of Greece."[35]

The warning fell on deaf ears: Tsvetkovitch wanted, and Hitler promised, to leave Yugoslavia alone in reward for her signature to the pact.[36] On Monday March 24 Tsvetkovitch left for Vienna to sign with Hitler. On Tuesday Baker-street suggested to S.O.(2) that they wreck the train bringing him back to Belgrade. Casting about for action Churchill rasped to Cadogan something about a man whom he helplessly called "Sonofabitch." The F.O. official took this to be Tsvetkovitch (Churchill had meant Dr Milan Stoyadinovitch, the former prime minister.) Feeling helpless, with so little time to act, the PM could only urge his minister in Belgrade to "continue to pester, nag and bite" the regime. "This is no time for reproaches or dignified farewells." The legation, he hinted, should resort to alternatives if the "present government" were beyond recall.[37] With precious few days left, S.O.(2) had approached army officers without success; but the British air attaché had found support in the airforce: "This was a comparatively small but united body of men," reported station chief George Taylor, "intensely anti-German, solidly against the policy of the Pact and the Prince, led by an enthusiastic and energetic man, Bora Mirkovitch, the deputy chief of air staff."[38]

That Wednesday rumours of a coming airforce putsch gripped Belgrade.[39] They were not without foundation, and conferring in secret that morning with Simovitch the attaché had outlined what help Britain would offer. During the night the regime collapsed like a rotten puffball, more swiftly than S.O.E. had dared to hope. Tanks took over the government area. Tsvetkovitch was arrested, Simovitch was brought from his surburban villa and installed in power.

At four a.m. on Thursday the S.O.(2) telegram bearing these tidings reached S.O.E. headquarters at No.64 Baker-street. It was rushed to Churchill. He had instructed Dalton to "set Europe ablaze." Here was the first triumph. In Belgrade the seventeen year old Peter was proclaimed King. Excited crowds stormed the German tourist office, burned swastikas, and manhandled German diplomats. "The money we have spent on the Serb Peasant party and other opposition parties," Dalton reflected that morning, "Has given wonderful value."[40] S.O.E. had ignited its first European blaze — one that would shortly engulf 17,000 citizens of Belgrade and would in time kill two million more in the grimmest of civil wars.

More concerned with purple prose than human tragedy the PM addressed a long-planned Party conference at noon. "Early this morning," he announced, "the Yugoslav nation found its soul."

His bronchitis was forgotten. He was uplifted by this news. In his imagination he drew a new Balkan front with seventy divisions — if Turkey came in — confronting the thirty of the Axis.[41] But he was viewing the Balkans through the wrong end of a telescope: suppose Belgrade did not share his enthusiasm for fire and steel? At a joint luncheon given by employers and union leaders an hour later he revealed something of this naiveté: "Though I don't know what will happen," he confessed, "and one cannot be sure of anything, I believe that it is reasonable to expect that we will have a government in Yugoslavia which will repudiate the pact . . . and will be ready to defend the honour and frontiers of Yugoslavia against aggression. If that be so, Great Britain will recognize that government."

At one p.m., even as Churchill was lowering his chin to the soup plate at No.10, a most displeased Adolf Hitler was announcing to generals hastily summoned to his Berlin chancery his resolve to "smash" Yugoslavia. Previously he had not planned to pass his armour through that country at all. Later that day, even as Churchill was stepping forward under arc-lamps to sign the Bases Agreement with the American ambassador, in Berlin the Führer executed Directive No.25 spelling out his new plan.

It would be unjust to point to Churchill alone for being outwitted once again. Even that wise statesman Jan Smuts shared his lack of foresight. "The Germans," he announced on hearing of the putsch, "have lost the Battle of the Balkans," and he fulsomely declared the new boy King Peter the Great. But now the real Belgrade crises began. The new Cabinet retained most of the ministers and much of the flavour of the old; appalled at having already offended Germany they declined Britain's offer of assistance. Simovitch even asked Britain to tone down the strident propaganda. Whitehall could not have predicted how swiftly Hitler's general staff was capable of regrouping its forces against a new target. By opening Yugoslavia to Hitler's tank columns after all, Mr Churchill had turned the Anglo-Greek line of defenses and rendered Greece indefensible.

* * *

The putsch sealed one nagging problem in Churchill's mind. Its aftermath convinced him that Hitler was going to attack Russia.

On the one day that lay between Yugoslavia's signing the pact in Vienna and the putsch in Belgrade, Bletchley had deciphered German airforce signals proving that significant Wehrmacht units including three Panzer divisions had been ordered north from Romania toward Cracow. (Hitler was regrouping Panzer Group Kleist, XIV Corps and some Twelfth Army units for Operation Barbarossa, his campaign against Russia.) But a few hours *after* the putsch the astonished Germans halted the transfer and ordered the trains held in the sidings; moreover, Göring had ordered the chief of air staff Hans Jeschonnek and the commander of the Fourth Air Force Alexander Löhr to consultations in Berlin.[42] It was from these clues that Churchill reached his remarkable conviction.

We now know that Hitler had reiterated in a staff conference on

January 9 his intention of invading Russia in the first half of May.[43] While Whitehall — the F.O. and Military Intelligence — had consistently rejected this possibility, Churchill somehow possessed an overview that these floundering Intelligence services did not. The files do not reveal the origin of his certainty, but Stephenson's reports from New York, together with still unreleased intercepts, may hold the key. One thing is certain: while Churchill's ponderous and slow witted Intelligence experts were effectively duped by enemy deception schemes and had expected Hitler to invade Britain throughout the summer of 1940 and the Middle East from October onwards, and while early in 1941 the War Office still regarded the build-up on the Soviet frontier as quite normal,[44] ever since late June 1940 the PM and his ambassador in Moscow, Sir Stafford Cripps, had unwaveringly predicted an attack on Russia; they couched their statements in such categorical terms that mere speculation or "gut feeling" can be ruled out.

On the last day of October 1940 the PM had reaffirmed his view orally to the Defence Committee: Hitler would attack Russia in 1941 for her oil.[45] He restated this on January 6. "A great campaign in the east of Europe," he said, "the defeat of Russia, the conquest of the Ukraine and an advance . . . to the Caspian would none of them, separately or together, bring him victorious peace."[46] Reinforcing his knowledge was what the oracle told him: in December Bletchley had begun reading the manual cipher used by Hitler's military Intelligence, and this reflected a predatory Abwehr interest in Russia as well as the Middle East.[47] In February 1941 the War Office had organized a major anti-invasion exercise. After dinner at Chequers on February 2 General Brooke lectured an impatient Winston with an epidiascope on the "invasion" and how he had countered it. "Winston's reactions were very typical," wrote Brooke. "He was quite flattering . . . but considered that the umpires had exaggerated the German threat of invasion."[48]

By that time Washington — and possibly No. 10 too — had obtained remarkable confirmation of the German plan. A Nazi traitor leaked to the commercial attaché at the American embassy in Berlin the actual Barbarossa directive signed by Hitler on December 18, and a record of his staff conference on January 9.[49] Intercepted Japanese messages — which Churchill was also getting from Bletchley and in the diplomatic pouch from the United States — provided background confirmation. One such MAGIC intercept on March 20 indicated that Hitler would attack Russia within two months.[50]

When later the more poorly informed F.O. obtained rather less coherent reports from Washington, Desmond Morton could afford the acid comment: "The Book of Revelations read backwards would be more helpful."[51]

Hitler's sudden change of mind — the signals following the Belgrade putsch — clinched it in Churchill's mind.[52] On the twenty-ninth he delivered a little homily to his staff on other notables who had invaded Russia down the ages, and particularly on Charles XII of Sweden who had been trounced at Poltava in 1709.[53] Telegraphing Athens, Churchill tested the opinion of Eden and Dill: "The moment he [Hitler] was sure Yugoslavia was in the Axis," he suggested to Eden, setting out his own reading of the oracle,'"he moved 3 of the 5 Panzers towards the Bear, believing that what was left would be enough to finish the Greek affair." The sudden reversal of orders could only indicate that Hitler intended to attack Yugoslavia. "It looks," he said, "as if heavy forces will be used in Balkan peninsula and that Bear will be kept waiting a bit."[54]

Military Intelligence remained incorrigible. Lacking Churchill's background information, whatever it was, they dismissed the intercepts as "of interest." The F.O. applauded their "sane view."[55]

Winston let them stew in their own juice. It was remarkable how this autocratic old gentleman continued his lonely swim against the stubborn tide. He knew what he knew, and it was enough.

* * *

The Japanese foreign minister Yosuke Matsuoka had arrived in Berlin. Through MAGIC, Churchill in effect eavesdropped on his luncheon with Hitler on the twenty-eighth. Having sagely assured his visitor that the Kremlin was behind the Belgrade putsch, Hitler added these measured words:

> If the Soviet Union were to attack Japan, then Germany would not hesitate to launch an armed attack on the Soviet Union.

Ribbentrop echoed that this was an "absolute guarantee."[56]

When Matsuoka returned a few days later through Russia and the Trans-Siberian railroad to Japan, Churchill arranged for a letter to await him in Moscow: it asked eight mildly sarcastic — but prophetic, as it turned out — questions which he suggested that Tokyo consider before becoming embroiled with the Axis Powers against Britain. Seven concerned Germany's relative air and naval power, and the respective strength of Japan and the United States. The eighth gave the tenor of the rest:

> Is it true that the production of steel in the United States during 1941 will be 75 million tons, and in Great Britain about 12½, making a total of nearly 90 million tons? If Germany should happen to be defeated, as she was last time, would not the 7 million tons steel production of Japan be inadequate for a single-handed war?[57]

THAT WEEKEND AT Chequers had been brightened by a spectacular achievement of those innocent-looking cryptanalysts at Bletchley. They had established that the Italian fleet was preparing a raid into the Aegaean or Eastern Mediterranean on Thursday the twenty-seventh.[58] This information was swiftly signalled to Admiral Sir Andrew Cunningham at Alexandria. He put to sea. At noon-thirty a plane from Malta sighted the Italian force. Off Cape Matapan the next day he sank three Italian cruisers and two destroyers, and saved the vital British convoy to Greece which had been their intended target.

Never again did the Italian fleet seriously bother the British. Small wonder that Winston passed much of the weekend striding and even dancing up and down the Great Hall while a table gramophone tinkled marches and vulgar waltzes. But all the while he was sunk deep in thought, as his staff could see.[59] He was now certain that Hitler would shortly attack Russia. That weekend he decided he must notify the Kremlin. He telegraphed Cripps in Moscow, and commanded him to deliver a cryptic warning message to Stalin in person — his first as PM to the Soviet head of state — telling him of "sure information from a trusted agent" about the sudden halting of the move of the three Panzer divisions. The message concluded portentously, "Your Excellency will readily appreciate the significance of these facts."[60]

It was *too* cryptic. Without the supplementary Intelligence available to Churchill, it meant nothing. Churchill later explained that he left it cryptic because of its "deadly" content, hoping that its very brevity would "arrest Stalin's attention."[61] It did not arrest Cripps', in the Moscow embassy: he scratched his head, and filed Churchill's message away — undelivered.

All the more inexplicable was the Intelligence failure that allowed Rommel, on the last day of March, to launch an all-out attack on the British forces remaining in Libya. By April 2 he was in Agedabia; Churchill sent an alarmed message to Wavell. To withdraw from Benghazi would, he said, "appear most melancholy." But by late on the third Wavell was evacuating Benghazi, and Rommel's offensive was gathering momentum.

Churchill's oracle had let him down partly because the German army Enigma ciphers were still secure. The lack of evidence from airforce Enigma had produced a false sense of security: that Rommel would test the British defences was half expected, but not that he would attempt a major offensive beyond Agedabia, let alone Benghazi. The evidence pointed the other way. Hitler had directed that Rommel's "main task" was to hold his current line and tie down enemy forces; Keitel had forwarded this directive to the Africa Corps on the third — Rommel was to restrain his troops until the 15th Panzer division arrived: accordingly

"Further major offensive out of the question until autumn."[62]

Churchill's oracle produced Enigma intercept CX/JQ 829 on April 5 proving that Rommel was flouting Hitler's instructions. Churchill immediately notified Wavell that Rommel was not under orders to conquer Egypt — quite the contrary. But Rommel was a disobedient, impulsive general and this was a lesson that Churchill and his generals still had to learn. Violating Hitler's directive, he continued the attack: on the seventh he took Derna, and at the end of the month he would hold the Halfaya pass on the frontier of Egypt.

HITLER NOW PUT THE torch to the Balkans.

Churchill watched it happening with a sense of fatalism. A decoded telegram from the Italian legation in Sofia had revealed that Greece and Yugoslavia would be attacked on April 5.[63] On Wednesday the second, Bletchley told him about a German operation codenamed Judgment Day, scheduled for April 6. Late on the fourth he passed a vague warning to Simovitch — all he could safely say — that German airforce formations were arriving "from all quarters."

Helpless to do more, with the eyes of Bletchley he watched as Hitler moved up reinforcements from France, Sicily and North Africa. Early on Saturday the fifth the codebreakers discerned that the enemy air attack would be sprung on Yugoslavia at five-thirty the next morning. Dalton, with some of S.O.E.'s best men still in Belgrade, noted that day: "Our best information is that the balloon will go up to-morrow at dawn when the Germans will attack both Yug[oslav]s and Greeks and launch the most terrific blitz of which they are capable."

The PM had invited Harriman for the weekend. An hour before midnight they telephoned the White House. Churchill spoke to Harry Hopkins, indicating that "there would be very vital moves in the Balkans." He also spoke of "the urgency of the situation by sea." Evidently their mutual friend was not well, because when he asked to speak to Roosevelt, the call was put through to the president in his doctor's office.[64]

Judgment Day struck Belgrade at dawn on Sunday. Germany's airforce killed seventeen thousand people in the capital — Hitler's first and only strategic air raid of the war. Simultaneously, his Wehrmacht attacked Greece. Bombers hit the shipping in the Piraeus. The British freighter *Clan Fraser* blew up with 200 tons of high explosives, devastating the port.

For Churchill, the Balkan nightmare was beginning.

For his adversary in Berlin, it seemed in retrospect that the Belgrade putsch had come at just the right time. Had Churchill waited until mid-May, the Wehrmacht would have been embroiled in Barbarossa and sorely vexed for a military solution in Belgrade. "Luckily the enemy unmasked themselves now," crowed Hitler on the day of the S.O.E. coup, " — while our hands are still free!" And he reflected to the Hungarian envoy in Berlin, "I can't help believing in a Higher Justice."[65]

CHAPTER 41

Mr Optimist Frog

GETTING AMERICA INTO the war remained Churchill's highest priority throughout 1941. Keen to influence Washington opinion, he steered every American notable out to see the beleaguered ports and devastated cities for himself. Thus Thursday evening, April 10, found him aboard his train bound for the West Country, taking Ambassadors Winant and Harriman, on the pretext of conferring honourary degrees on them at Bristol university.

Regularly informed by his oracle of the *Knickebein* beam settings, he may well have known that this port was Hitler's target for that night.[1] They passed the hours of darkness in a railroad siding outside Bristol until the raid, by nearly two hundred bombers, had ended. As they drove into the city outskirts the next morning troops were still fighting fires and the citizenry was visibly shaken. Fortunately the Grand Hotel had escaped damage and kitchen staff volunteered to carry hot water up to fill a bath for Winston.

Bathed and refreshed, he led his dishevelled transatlantic friends out to feast their eyes on a Bristol bruised and still noisy with time bombs, but going about its business. Like Mr Pickwick on a stagecoach, he clambered on top of the open car to wave his porkpie hat, then dismounted and walked rapidly through the freshly rubbled streets. News spread rapidly ahead by word of mouth, and crowds flocked round shouting, "Hello Winnie!" "Good ole Winnie!" "You'll never let us down!" "We'll never let you down!" or just, "What a man!"

Flags stuck out of the ruins. Amidst one such heap the gas cooker still worked and neighbours were lining up to make breakfast as he walked past. He hid the anguish that gripped him well, but Winant did not fail to note that he changed the Cheerio, spoken when leaving Swansea and Aberport the night before, to God Bless You, here in Bristol. What impressed the young ambassador was the determination and enthusiasm of Bristol's middle-aged women, particularly when these matronly home-makers glimpsed Clemmie at her husband's side. "The look which flashed between her and these mothers of England was something far deeper and more significant than the casual newspaper accounts of friendly social interchange," wrote Winant privately to the president. "The whole town," he added, "was back on its feet again and cheering within two hours of his arrival although no one had got any sleep during the night."[2]

The mayor had been rescued by boat, his house flooded by a fractured water main. His wife was fainting from the strain. But nothing would deter immense crowds from packing the front of the university as Mr Churchill, its chancellor, arrived. A nearby building was on fire, and the choking fumes of burning wood drifted into the hall through the gaping window sockets. Against this cruel backdrop the smoke-stained medieval procession of academic and civic worthies laden with ceremonial maces and gold chains swayed down the aisle to hear Mr Churchill, robed in his father's finery, bestow the honorary degrees. As he spoke, he glimpsed beneath more than one robe in his audience the sodden uniforms or gumboots of a civil defence worker.

He ducked behind a newspaper as his train left Bristol, trying to hide the tears in his eyes. All these people, both inside the hall and out, showed such childlike confidence in him: the responsibility was almost too much to bear. He turned to Winant, still seeing all those trusting faces in his mind's eye. "I am going to see to it," he said, "that the necessary tonnage is allotted for foodstuffs to protect them from the strains and stresses they may be subjected to in a period of great emergency."

HE KNEW THAT THINGS were going to get worse before they got better. Rommel's forces in Libya had turned out to be twice as large as anticipated. "Only tonight," wrote Robert Menzies on April 8, "I was horrified to hear Churchill saying à propos of Tobruk, to which we are retreating and where we [Australians] hope to make a stand, 'if stout hearted men with rifles and machine guns cannot hold these people until the guns come up, I must revise my ideas of war.' " By the tenth Rommel, this barely known Nazi general, had taken two thousand British prisoners including three generals (O'Connor, Neame and Combe); but he was about to fail, despite several bloody attempts, to capture Tobruk. The C.I.G.S General Dill was despondent, privately saw no way of victory, and told a visiting American general that their only hope was a repeat of 1918 when enemy morale "cracked for no real reason."[3]

Worried by Rommel's seemingly unstoppable advance to Egypt, the PM ordered Admiral Sir Andrew Cunningham to accept major risks to cut the enemy supply line, even if it meant taking "heavy losses in battleships, cruisers and destroyers." It was a remarkable signal. Alerted by the oracle that an enemy convoy was carrying units of the 15th Panzer division to Tripoli, naval forces sank two merchantmen and three Italian escort destroyers on the sixteenth; five days later Cunningham reluctantly sailed a bombardment force to Tripoli and shelled the port, but pleaded not to have to take such "unjustifiable risks again."[4]

By the end of April Churchill's latest debacle, in Greece, would be complete as well and he began to cast about for scapegoats. Anthony Eden provided one scapegoat. The foreign secretary had now returned from his peregrinations. Churchill, in a recalcitrant mood, told him he had never wanted to help Greece anyway.[5]

Wavell made another easy scapegoat. Ungraciously the PM remarked to his nodding entourage that the general had been "very silly" and should have been prepared for Rommel's attack.[6] Now he reminded Wavell by telegram that Tobruk had been well fortified by the Italians, and suggested it be held to the death — "without thought of retirement." Pug Ismay was ordered to procure a model of Tobruk without delay.

It did not help Churchill's mood that he had been scheduled to propose the House's congratulations to Wavell for recent victories. He was due to make that speech on the ninth, but now events had overtaken him. "If there were enough good and strong men in Parliament outside H.M.G.," observed one worried minister, "there would be danger of an upset. But there aren't and so there isn't — yet."[7] As he entered the famous chamber on the ninth, sympathetic cheers greeted the familiar figure, with the ugly gold chain strung across his runaway paunch; he scowled as he waited between Labour ministers Arthur Greenwood and Clement Attlee, looking, as Lord Beaverbrook would later remark, like a bird of paradise perched between a sparrow and a jackdaw. He made a final alteration with gold pencil to the notes clutched in one heavily ringed pink hand, then delivered his speech.[8] It was uninspired and he knew it.

> At War Cabinet [wrote a seething Robert Menzies in his diary on April 14] W.C. speaks at length as the Master Strategist — Tobruk *must* be held as a bridgehead or sally port, from which to hit the enemy!"
> "What with?" say I, and so the discussion goes on.
> Wavell and the Admiralty have failed us. The Cabinet is deplorable — dense men, most of whom disagree with Winston but none of whom dares to say so. . . . The Chiefs of Staff are without exception yes-men, and a politician runs the services. Winston is a dictator; he cannot be overruled, and his colleagues fear him. The people have set him up as something little less than God, and his power is therefore terrific.

That day the Australian leader decided to remain in London for two more weeks, because grave decisions would now have to be taken about the Australian forces in the Middle East — "and I am not content to have them solved by 'unilateral rhetoric.' "

ON EASTER SATURDAY, as German forces began entering a Belgrade over which the stench of spent cordite and death hung no less than over Bristol, Churchill drove out to Chequers with the Americans, Winant and Harriman.

There was some good news here — a telegram from Roosevelt announcing that he was pushing the American security zone far into the eastern Atlantic.[9] "We will want in great secrecy," the telegram said, "notification of movement of convoys so our patrol units can seek out any ships or planes of aggressor nations operating west of the new line of the security zone." Roosevelt's intention was to report to Churchill, the "former naval person," the position of these ships and planes. It was perhaps a bigger stride towards belligerency than the president appreciated: because, armed with his knowledge from the oracle, Churchill would soon be able to route convoys *deliberately* so as to put American warships at maximum risk of confrontation with the Germans.

But that was the only good news that week. His appointment card for Wednesday April 16 was crowded with conferences. At 11:15 a.m. it listed the Director of Military Intelligence, Davidson, with "C" — Brigadier Menzies. Bletchley had now revealed that Hitler's troops had broken through the last Greek defences on the day before and were advancing down the coast. An hour later Churchill met with his chiefs of staff and First Lord, then lunched with the Polish president, recorded a message to Australia — whose troops were at that moment fighting a heroic defence of Tobruk — and conferred on the Battle of the Atlantic at five. A few hours later a shocking telegram arrived from Wavell — the Greek General, Papagos, had formally invited Britain to remove her expeditionary force from Greek soil to avoid further "devastation." The Cabinet agreed that the Empire troops should be withdrawn to Crete.

With so much on his plate, it was small wonder that when the sirens sounded that night — the Luftwaffe was attacking London in reprisal for his raid on Berlin one week earlier[10] — Mr Churchill was, uncharacteristically, still in London. There were many who quietly welcomed this, feeling that the PM's attitude toward reprisal and counter-reprisal raids was altogether too sanguine. General Sir John Kennedy, the Director of Military Operations, expressed private pleasure that this time Churchill himself would get a taste of the "kind of retaliation the Germans are capable of." To continue harrassing Hitler's distant capital, and against such odds, he argued, was like putting a middleweight boxer into the ring against a heavyweight with a longer reach.[11]

It was the enemy's heaviest raid on London so far. Railroad stations including Paddington were hit, and a bomb had struck the Thames embankment behind the Savoy exposing the subway tunnel underneath and ripping thousands of windows out of the hotel. Oxford-street was blocked by avalanches of masonry released by two mines. Christie's auction house had burned out; Selfridge's, John Barker's and Derry & Toms department stores had been hit. Wealthy Mayfair was tattered, elegant Jermyn-street in ruins. Gas mains were flaring all the way down Piccadilly. Official photographers recorded grisly spectacles including a woman stripped naked and scalped by the blast, and a fireman with both legs torn off. As a lovely spring day dawned elsewhere, the sky over a bleary-eyed London was blotted out by smoke. John Colville strolled behind No.10 and found Averell Harriman out walking with Winston's comely daughter-in-law Pamela — her husband Randolph was now out in Cairo — inspecting the new ruins.

The admiralty had been gashed by four heavy bombs, but Churchill, who had spent the night in the deep shelter, was unmoved by the fresh ruin. Taking his seat at the Cabinet table at eleven-thirty he drily commented on the improved view that Hitler had given him of Nelson.

News from Libya that the Australians were still holding out in Tobruk prompted him to talk of the weakness of the Germans in Libya. "Then how the hell did they get there?" carped Cadogan in the safety of his diary, echoing what newspaper editors had been asking all week.[12]

This was the morning when another American, General H.H. ("Hap") Arnold, commanding the U.S. army air corps, was due to arrive. His plane came down to Hendon airfield through veils of rising ash and smoke. "Signs of bombing everywhere as we drove to the Dorchester," he pencilled in his diary. "People salvaging what they could from wrecked stores. Glass all over the streets. Buildings flattened. Fire departments working everywhere. Traffic re-routed where streets were impassable. . . Report that Selfridges destroyed. Four bombs dropped within 150 feet of hotel. Two houses flattened. Glass everywhere but hotel unscathed. . . Britain back at work in a determined sort of way. Fires still burning this p.m." Later Archie Sinclair showed the visitor the night's bomb-plot — "In most cases," noted Arnold, "close to railroad stations, switching points, power stations, or transformers, bridges, arsenals, docks, warehouses. But a lot that was not."

Encouraged to stroll around the blitzed streets, General Arnold jotted down his impressions of Churchill's London in April 1941: "Glass, glass everywhere. Shops with crockery and beautiful nicknacks and glass on shelves but windows and doors blown out. Baker shop with no front — women selling delicious hot bread and rolls. Antique shop with furniture, almost priceless, spread all over street and sidewalk. . . Pathetic sights of people trying to gather such of their belongings from wrecked homes. . . London is smiling only a little, in a grim sort of way. Hundreds of people killed and injured. . . The fire at Selfridges is still burning but steps are already being taken to open up on the ground floor. . . Six thousand bombs dropped last night, six hundred people killed, four thousand injured. . . Back of it all, a determination not to be wiped off the map."[13]

* * *

From the German airforce Enigma cipher Churchill could see that Hitler had been moving hundreds of gliders and towing aircraft down to the Balkans throughout March and April. The German chief of air staff Hans Jeschonnek shifted his headquarters there too, evidently preparing some major airborne operation. Even without the oracle, it was obvious that it might be against Crete. But there just was not enough strength to go round. On April 18 Churchill decided to work up that island's defences later because the evacuation of Greece and the defence of Libya must come first.[14]

That afternoon he did what he had never done before: he summoned a dozen Fleet-street editors to No.10 and prepared them for the disaster in Greece. British troops would be evacuated, he said, as soon as "honour was satisfied." It would be more difficult than Dunkirk: the distances were greater, the shore line less favourable. Hoping to avert criticism, he strongly implied that the fateful decision to switch Wavell's troops from Libya to Greece, snatching defeat as it were from the jaws of victory, had been taken "by general agreement of the whole Cabinet" and had been backed wholeheartedly by the generals on the spot.[15]

Not to be outdone by Hitler, he had again ordered Berlin bombed the previous night. Berlin, not to be outdone by him, announced that they felt free to take reprisals against Athens and Cairo. Churchill, in staff conference when he heard of this broadcast, had instructions telephoned to the B.B.C.: if Hitler bombed either town then he, Churchill, would "commence a systematic bombing of Rome." That bold threat announced, he left for Oxfordshire, undoubtedly with foreknowledge that Göring had laid on seven hundred bombers to attack London that Saturday night.[16] Hap Arnold admitted in his diary that he was thankful to be accompanying the PM out to Dytchley.

Churchill had invited seven others to share Friday dinner with them at this refuge including Harriman, Brendan Bracken, and several ladies. Arnold talked with Churchill until two a.m. and was struck by one cryptic reference to the Soviet Union. "Russia," Winston had said, "is like an immoral crocodile waiting in the depths for whatever prey may come his way."

Their talk touched many continents. "The German army can roam at will over Continental Europe," admitted the PM. He underlined that Britain must win the battle of North Africa, but added that it would take American aid; he was frankly worried about Roosevelt's indifference to the Mediterranean. He himself was planning for a long war — for 1943 and beyond: they must build bases in Greenland, the American navy should seize bases in the Portuguese Azores. "Britain may not win many battles," Arnold recalled the prime minister as saying, before he himself retired to bed in an ancient wing overlooking the garden, "but she always wins the war."

While the rain poured down all that Saturday Churchill mapped out to his American visitors his grandiose plans: he would build a base for them at Basra on the Persian Gulf, and an air depot a thousand miles from Cairo, to which he was sending 2,500 men. With coloured pencils he drew rings around places they could not afterwards recall in Norway, Morocco, Greenland and Iceland, and spoke of the need to win over the American public by cunning propaganda — as in fact British Security Co-ordination had already begun to do from New York.

The little square-headed Czech president Benes had joined them for lunch before they drove over to review Czech troops. In the car Churchill was still talking, his imagination charging and marching about Europe and the Middle East, projecting his listeners now into Spain, then Portugal and Persia, Tripoli, Sicily and Italy.

* * *

It was his first visit to the resurrected Czech army, two thousand troops looking keen and alert in British uniforms. When they ended the visit by singing Rule Britannia the PM joined in, his eyes moist with tears. He let Benes into his innermost thoughts, and a few days later the Czech president cabled his agents in these terms: "Mr Churchill thinks that Germany will invade the Ukraine within two months at the latest." Admitting that he himself was doubtful as to that, Benes urged: "If it does happen don't expect miracles, and try to restrain our people." He predicted that the Russians would fight as they had always done — "They will retreat as far as they can, and the Germans will occupy vast Russian territories." The PM anticipated further reverses in the Balkans, but was sure he could hold Egypt and the Middle East. Churchill's strategy was simple: "The bombing of Germany will be intensified," reported Benes. "He is expecting real help from America late in the summer, and until then it is necessary to hang on. The real offensive war against Germany will start, according to him, in the spring of 1942. . . Any peace offer will be refused."[17]

On Sunday morning, dictating letters in bed, Churchill sent for Arnold before the general left Chequers. "Tell the President that with you we win!" he barked at the American general.

Arnold drove back to London. There had been another raid: Waterloo Bridge had been hit and was blocking the Thames. Two more tunnels had caved in. Beaverbrook's famous wine cellar at Stornoway House had been blown away by a direct hit in the kitchen. "I notice that people don't smile as they walk along," wrote Arnold that Monday, still completing his word picture of Churchill's city.

Seeing the damage to London that Monday morning appears to have strengthened Churchill's resolve. Worried by indications from the oracle that Rommel was getting his second Panzer division, at mid-day he decided to ship three hundred tanks to Egypt immediately — Operation Tiger — and to take the risk of running the convoy straight through the Mediterranean. At four p.m. that afternoon, April 21, a telegram came from Wavell urging him to evacuate as much as he could from Greece. With gathering memories of Dunkirk the PM cabled back: "Get the men away. We can re-arm them later."

As the embarkation of the fifty thousand men began on the twenty-third, Churchill set up, like Hitler, indeed simultaneously, a Tank Parliament to boost production. He wrote to Eden, the Prof, Margesson and others summoning the first for May 5. "I myself," he wrote across the invitation sent to Lord Beaverbrook, "should like to discuss the organization of Armoured Divisions and the present state of their mechanical efficiency, as well as the larger questions wh[ich] govern 1943."[18]

At Cabinet and staff level criticism of Churchill, hitherto muted, grew in volume throughout April and May. Lord Hankey was registering dismay from every quarter at their new PM's unfortunate record so far. "It is Norway all over again," reflected Hankey on April 22. "Just the same mistakes. The vital need for air forces overlooked. No-one seems to have realized that there were not enough aerodromes in Southern Greece."[19] The origins of the disaster had been kept closely secret until now, but top general staff officers revealed that Wavell, the C-in-C, had warned all along that the Australian and New Zealand divisions were still inadequately equipped; General Macready, assistant chief of staff, described to Hankey how Menzies had held out for several days against the Australians going into Greece — but might now lose office in Australia in consequence of the debacle. "The root trouble is," General Haining, deputy C.I.G.S., complained to Hankey, "that Churchill is running the war as a Dictator." The War Cabinet rubber-stamped his decrees. Churchill had deliberately reduced the Chiefs of Staff to cyphers: Pound had never asserted himself anyway, Portal was bemused by the PM, and General Dill — the C.I.G.S. — was with Eden in the Middle East. "So it looks as though Winston," recorded Hankey on April 22, "who as I always thought was mainly responsible for the Norwegian fiasco, was responsible for this also. And it looks as though it was going to put our whole position in Egypt and the Eastern Mediterranean in jeopardy. What will happen to Churchill if and when all this leaks out?"

Six days later Hankey wrote this troubled passage in his diary after lunching with General Haining: "He was very anxious about the complete subservience of the chiefs of staff to Churchill and gave an appalling account of the meetings of the War Cabinet he had attended."

> I had some experience of this this evening [recorded Hankey] as I was summoned to a meeting of the War Cabinet about Turkish policy. . . I spoke for ten or twelve minutes. . . Except for a very short statement by Eden, and long harangues by Churchill, no one spoke at all, and they all seemed very bored and tired. Winston eventually drifted into a long monologue on the situation in the Mediterranean in general and Libya in particular, which left me very anxious indeed — but seemed to have no effect at all on the members of the War Cabinet. They struck me as a set of "yes" men, leaving the running of the war to Churchill. He struck me as a very tired man, and he has worn out his Chiefs of Staff by his late meetings ending long after midnight.

After that day's War Cabinet, Robert Menzies also wrote an acid diary entry. Winston had assured them, "We will lose only five thousand men in Greece." Menzies knew that the true figure was closer to fifteen thousand. "As usual," he wrote, "Beaverbrook supports me but 'the rest is silence.' "

He attended the Defence Committee on the twenty-ninth to ask the pertinent question, "What next, if Egypt falls?" Churchill fobbed him off with a trite retort: "Let us keep our minds on *Victory*." Menzies argued alone, the others remained silent.

> Menzies [recorded Lord Hankey, learning of this the next day] had gone there to find out about intention if things went wrong in Libya, where the largest forces are from Australia & N.Z. Apparently Churchill burst out into one of his fervid orations as to how nothing would induce him to make plans or order preparations for such a contingency. . . They had to contest every inch and fight to the last and sacrifice their lives if necessary to defend Egypt & Palestine and so forth. No one else spoke a single word.

"Menzies," Hankey was told, "at first had fallen for Churchill, but gradually he had changed. He admitted now that it was dangerous to go to Chequers and spend an evening, because Churchill was so persuasive." Lord Hankey — administrative genius of the interwar period — now realized that Churchill had deliberately smashed the Cabinet system that he had created "to increase his own power."

* * *

Churchill was at his most incorrigible when he had just orated, whether in the House or by radio. From his study at Chequers, he broadcast about the Greek debacle that Sunday. Into the B.B.C. microphone he decanted fiery phrases about the "exaltation of spirit" which he had found in the blitzed cities of the north-east, and he spread a verbal rainbow across the dismal misfortune that Britain had suffered or was visiting on others.

"The Huns," he reassured the unseen millions, knowing what he knew, "may lay their hands for a time upon the granaries of the Ukraine and the oil wells of the Caucasus. They may dominate the Black Sea. They may dominate the Caspian. Who can tell?" To win the war, however, they must "cut the ocean life-line" joining Britain to the United States, and here he repeated the arithmetic he had variously tried out on Matsuoka and the Fleet-street editors. "There are less than seventy million malignant Huns — some of whom are curable and others killable — many of them already engaged in holding down Austrians, Czechs, Poles, French and the many other ancient races they now bully and pillage. The peoples of the British Empire and of the United States number nearly two hundred millions."[*]

Dinner, delayed by the broadcast, became acrimonious when Major General Sir John Kennedy ventured rather indelicate views on future strategy — speculating all too freely on possible Empire plans to evacuate Egypt. The PM flew off the handle, but the D.M.O. relentlessly suggested that Britain had more important things to lose than Egypt.[21] His words festered in Winston's mind all night, and on Monday he issued from No.10 a brusque directive forbidding all talk of withdrawal. "The life and honour of Great Britain depends upon the successful defence of Egypt," he defined, and ordered all plans for evacuation called in: "The Army of the Nile is to fight with no thought of retreat or withdrawal."

A naval officer summoned to meet the PM after dinner that month wrote this disturbing contemporary record of Mr Churchill's councils of war: "Rendezvous was the underground Cabinet War Room. It was like a nightmare without emotion. The news from Greece and Yugoslavia and Libya was bad and the PM came in ten minutes late very depressed. He was puffy and very pink and white — pig like. Dressed in a grey siren suit, one hand clasping a cigar, the other, beautifully manicured, tapping the table impatiently, bearing a large four banded ring on the fourth

---

[*]Describing one lunch with Churchill in February newspaper executive Cecil King noted: "[He] calculated that there were 45 million of us here and 20 million Whites in the Empire, which exactly matched with 65,000,000 real Germans — the others under German control being Czechs, Poles, Austrians, and what-not. So we start level," King heard him say, "and if we get American help with her 110,000,000 Whites, we shall be at an enormous numerical advantage!"[20]

finger. He was very depressed and desperately tired — in a sort of coma almost. His speech was rather slobbery and very slow." The officer found their interview depressing. "The general atmosphere," he wrote in a letter afterwards, "of sycophancy, and the old man's lack of grasp and understanding apparently, made me leave to walk home convinced for the first time that we could not win the war."[22]

THE EVACUATION OF Greece was completed. One Cabinet official wrote, "That's all that we're really good at! And we anticipate that five thousand German airborne troops are going to wipe us out of Crete! Our soldiers are the most pathetic amateurs, pitted against professionals." A minister found himself now steeled for the loss of Egypt, Syria and Palestine, as well as North Africa, Spain and Portugal and probably part of the Mediterranean fleet. "We are perhaps now in for a Twenty Years' War."[23]

There was not much doubt about Hitler's next move. On April 25 the oracle had supplied Churchill with intercept CX/JQ 889, revealing that Göring's Fourth Air Force was talking about an "Operation Crete," and that the Eighth Air Corps commanded by Wolfram von Richthofen was requesting maps of that island. There were some — Wavell among them — who thought this blatant camouflage for another target, perhaps Cyprus or Syria, particularly now that an anti-British uprising had begun in neighbouring Iraq. Churchill disagreed. "It seems clear from all our information," he telegraphed to Wavell on April 28, "that a heavy airborne attack will soon be made on Crete."[24]

He did briefly waver, writing to Pug Ismay on the next day, "We must not exclude the possibility that Crete is a blind, and Syria or Cyprus the quarry." But on the first day of May he was reading the secret orders to Richthofen not to bomb Crete's airfields or mine Suda Bay; that seemed to clinch it. It was going to be an ugly battle — the Allied commander on the island, Major General Bernard Freyberg VC, had only one divison, while his air power consisted of six Hurricane fighters and seventeen obsolete planes.

Attention had been drawn to Syria after ex-premier Rashid Ali staged an anti-British coup in neighbouring Iraq on April 3. Local S.I.S. agents in this oil-rich country had given due warning but this had not been passed to Downing-street. Berlin and Rome were equally startled, but, on the fifth Bletchley deciphered an Italian diplomatic message from Teheran, revealing discussions about funneling German arms to the Arab insurgents in Iraq through Syria.

Churchill decided on maximum force. Since Wavell was reluctant to spare troops for Iraq, he called upon India to divert a division earmarked for Malaya to Basra. Recalling the fiasco in Romania, where they had failed to destroy the oilfields, the Prof warned meanwhile that they must act at once to wreck the three hundred oil wells in Iraq.[25]

Indignant about the unauthorized British troop disembarkations at Basra, on the last day of April, Rashid Ali's ragged army massed to attack the main British base at Habbaniya west of Baghdad. Churchill felt confident. Bumping into Sir Alexander Cadogan at that evening's Defence Committee, he said with a chuckle, "So you've got another war on your hands tonight!"

He was at his most infuriating now. Robert Menzies, whose contempt for his former idol was now complete, waded into Churchill at the War Cabinet on April 30 for having dared to ask President Roosevelt to move the Pacific Fleet to the Atlantic "*without* reference to Australia, though I was in London!" (as Menzies noted angrily in his diary.)

Churchill however was in one of his inexplicable buoyant moods. That day he had hosted a diplomatic luncheon at No.10. After the white gloved butler and parlormaid had removed the plates and two Johnny Walkers, chased by two generous brandies, which had mellowed the prime minister, the Swedish minister felt it safe to ask him outright how Britain planned to pull through.

The reply that their host had lisped was in this vein: "Once upon a time there were two frogs, Mr Optimist Frog and Mr Pessimist Frog. One evening the two frogs hippety-hopped across the meadow enchanted by the smell of fresh milk from a dairy. They hopped through the dairy window and plopped right into a pail of milk."

The PM applied a fresh match to his cigar, enjoying the attention that his fable was attracting. "The pail's sides were too steep," he continued. "Mr Pessimist Frog soon gave up and sank to the bottom. But Mr Optimist Frog took courage and began thrashing around, hoping to get out somehow. He didn't know how, but he wasn't going to give up without a fight. He churned around all night, and by morning — oh joy! — he was floating on a pat of butter."

Taking a long puff at his cigar, Churchill ended, "I'm Mr Optimist Frog!"[26]

CHAPTER 42

The "Telephone Job"

NO OBLOQUY STUNG MORE than that heaped on Churchill by the triumphant warlord who addressed the Berlin Reichstag on May 4, 1941.

"A man who is as miserable a politician as soldier," so Hitler characterized him, "and as wretched a soldier as politician." He invoked the shades of Narvik and Dunkirk, and blamed Churchill for Greece and Yugoslavia as well. "If ever any other politician had met such defeats," he rasped from his swastika-decked podium, "if any soldier had encountered such catastrophes, he would not have kept his job six months. Unless, of course, possessed of the talent that distinguishes Mr Churchill: to lie with devout mien until in the end the most crushing defeats turn into the most glorious victories."

Churchill was out at Chequers, from where he had broadcast a week before. He heard Hitler tell his cheering audience that parts of that broadcast could only be explained as the fevered outburst of a chronic drunkard. Many of Hitler's barbs like this one cut deep into his skin, because he quoted them over months to come.

In Whitehall there were many who nodded silent approval.[1] British generals privately confirmed to foreign diplomats what they already suspected, that the decision to go into Greece had been political, not military.[2] Americans like Harriman and Lee noticed "growing apprehension" among Churchill's colleagues. Beaverbrook, still expecting an invasion, tackled the American Airforce General Arnold one day and asked: "What would you do if Churchill were hanged and the rest of us in hiding in Scotland or being overrun by the Germans? . . We're up against the mightiest army the world has ever seen."[3] Later in May, Churchill sent Pug Ismay over to the U.S. embassy to reassure the nervous Americans; but both Ambassador Winant and Military Attaché Lee were disturbed by blatant falsehoods in the reassurances.[4]

Beaverbrook could no longer take the strain, and adjured Churchill to let him go. His physician warned the PM that the minister had no health reason to quit, and quoted to Beaverbrook from his diary about how, as a battalion medic, he had kept sending a shell-shocked infantryman back to the trenches in the Great War until he was killed. "We do not count," he rebuked Beaverbrook. "Our own lives are nearly over." Beaverbrook's real complaint was that Winston "does not ask my advice," indeed regarded him as quarrelsome. "The PM," he argued, "needs tough men around him." Instead, "old Bottleneck," as he called Winston, wasted time inspecting defences or sitting up all night drinking.[5] Churchill accepted Beaverbrook's resignation on May 1, appointing him a Minister of State — a meaningless new title — with little power but some responsibility for supply.*

The rising criticism of Churchill was not unfounded. Oliver Stanley blamed Greece on his "vain and unreliable" foreign secretary as well: Eden had been cheered in Athens and bombarded with roses. "How," asked Stanley, "could he keep his judgment clear?"[7] To Lloyd George the whole direction of the war seemed haphazard — the Cabinet endorsed whatever Winston suggested.

Policy differences erupted between No.10 and the ministry of information. Duff Cooper — Churchill belittlingly called him "Duffy" — seemed incapable of discipline. Downing-street announced that three U-boats had been sunk: the M.O. warned editors that the third was a figment of Churchill's imagination.[8]

The dishonesty extended to shipping statistics: April's losses were the worst ever — over one hundred ships, half a million (581,251) tons. Labour MP Emanuel Shinwell accused Churchill of lying when claiming only five percent of Britain's tonnage had been sunk; he pointed out that that was twenty-six percent of Britain's *useful* tonnage. Shortly Winant learned that Churchill had not included the 187,054 tons sunk in the evacuation of Greece. Meanwhile, many of the merchant ships purchased from America proved unserviceable; filled with cement, they were sunk as block-ships.[9]

Former prime minister Lloyd George did not mince his language about Churchill. He had picked him out of the political gutter, he commiserated with Shinwell, but wished now he had left him there.[10] Together with the rumbustious Nye Bevan, Hore-Belisha and Lord Winterton, he and Shinwell cast about that Spring for ways of preparing a negotiated peace with Hitler. Like Beaverbrook, Lloyd George had met and liked the German leader, and compared him shamelessly with

---

*"I never wanted to leave the Ministry of Aircraft Production," Beaverbrook admitted brokenly at a newspaper luncheon on June 5 after several whiskies. "I loved that job. Don't believe anyone who tells you I left it of my own free will. I wanted to have a Department that would help to win the war." Dabbing his eyes, he rushed from the room.[6]

Napoleon — a genius, "one of those men who appear once in a century out of the forest and can see beyond the well-rubbed field where we and they stand, into the green grass beyond."

One day in May they found a note "from the British workers" in the pocket of a new siren suit made for Mr Churchill: "May God grant you the very best of health and strength to carry us through our Greatest Ordeal in History to keep the British Empire Free."[11] It reflected what one Dominion representative called "under-currents of anxiety" in British society. Morale was low, absenteeism high even in the well-paid aircraft industry. "Mr Churchill," this envoy explained to Ottawa, "has never been particularly concerned with social and economic matters and has little experience of problems relating to the organization of industry and man-power."* That said, he added that never had a prime minister experienced "such immunity from criticism." The British felt they owed him a debt. It had become almost disloyal to criticize him.[12]

Accurately gauging the rising anxiety and realizing that he could no longer browbeat the editors, on May 1 the PM, looking pale and drawn, drove over to the Dorchester for a luncheon in honour of Sir Emsley Carr's fiftieth anniversary as owner of the News of the World; Winston's contract to write for the newspaper still had several years to run. The 150 newspapermen gave him an ovation; but he still left sunk in thought after two hours.[13]

Further up Park Lane, at the Grosvenor House hotel, Menzies arrived late at the Iron & Steel Federation's luncheon, and began his speech with caustic remarks about Mr Churchill's War Cabinet. "As Adeline and I walked away down Park Lane," noted Lord Hankey afterwards, "we heard someone running and, lo and behold, it was Menzies himself. He burst out at once about Churchill and his dictatorship and his War Cabinet of 'yes-men'." "There is only one thing to be done," puffed Menzies breathlessly, "and that is to summon an Imperial War Cabinet and keep one of them behind, like Smuts in the last war, not as a guest but as a full member."

To Hankey it seemed that the mutiny was coming to a head. He consulted the Lord Chancellor, highest legal authority in the Empire, that afternoon. Sir John Simon suggested that Menzies should tackle Winston — "If he will not play," continued Simon, "there is nothing for it but for you, Hankey, to see Winston yourself." He advised Hankey however to wait until the big Debate, due next week in Parliament, was over.

---

*This view was echoed by newspapers. "It is not practical," suggested "Scrutator" in the Sunday Times on July 20, "that Mr Churchill, while putting the last ounce of his energy and brilliance into the conduct of the war, should exert a peace time Premier's control over home Departments. Yet such a control is more needed in war than in peace."

The Australian PM bearded Churchill in private on May 2. He got nowhere with him. "You see the people by whom I am surrounded," Churchill said, excusing his manner in Cabinet: "They have no ideas, so the only thing to be done is to formulate my own ideas." (He had deliberately got rid of all the men with ideas, observed Hankey upon hearing this.) "I am desperately afraid of the future in Great Britain," Menzies pencilled in his diary as he left London that day.

THE AIR RAIDS WERE approaching a vicious climax. Many regarded the night bomber as the biggest menace facing Britain. "I don't think," one official would write, "the PM realizes its supreme importance."[14] Plymouth had just been savaged five times in nine nights by the bombers, and on May 2 Churchill toured the devastated town. If he was seeking a psychological high as at Bristol, Plymouth offered only the reverse: the naval dockyard rang with hammering as coffins were nailed down all around. Shaken, he kept murmuring. "I've never seen the like."

How much longer before the Americans came in?

"With Hitler in control of Iraqi oil and Ukrainian wheat," he mused out loud, "not all the staunchness of 'our Plymouth Brethren' will shorten the ordeal.[15] Pathological despair choked him as his train pulled out of Plymouth. John Colville had never seen a mood like it before.

Out at Chequers that Friday evening there was a distasteful telegram from Roosevelt, discouraging Winston's perennial ambition to seize the Portuguese Atlantic islands. In perhaps ill-chosen words, the president voiced the belief that "even if you have to withdraw further in the eastern Mediterranean" surely the PM would not allow "any great debacle or surrender," and he suggested that "in the last analysis the naval control of the Indian Ocean and the Atlantic Ocean will in time win the war." As for Hitler's gains, Roosevelt showed little concern: "Personally," he wrote airily, "I am not downcast by more spread of Germany to additional large territories. There is little of raw materials in all of them put together — not enough to maintain nor compensate for huge occupation forces." And he closed on an avuncular note: "Keep up the good work."[16]

Already depressed beyond measure by the carnage he had witnessed, Churchill was stunned by this easy anticipation of "additional withdrawals." It seemed, he remarked in a message to Eden, that there had been a "considerable recession" in Washington: "Quite unconsciously we are being left very much to our fate."[17] It bothered him all night and on Saturday afternoon he telephoned Winant about it: the ambassador could see he was sad and discouraged after Plymouth and tried to soothe him, saying that Roosevelt had only meant to send a message of support; Churchill suggested they lunch on Monday and talk over a response. Unable to get it off his mind however he drafted a reply spelling out what the loss of the Middle East would mean to the Empire. "Therefore," it read in part, "if you cannot take more advanced positions now, or very soon, the vast balances may be tilted heavily to our disadvantage.

> Mr President [it continued] I am sure that you will not misunderstand me if I speak to you exactly what is in my mind.

The United States, he insisted, must range herself with Britain *immediately* as a belligerent. "We are determined to fight to the last inch and ounce for Egypt, including its outposts of Tobruk and Crete."[18]

He sent it off before Winant or Eden could stop him. The ambassador protested over lunch on Monday, and Churchill and Eden apologized. "It will not happen again," they said, but there is no doubt that sending it made Winston feel better.[19]

BY SATURDAY NIGHT, May 3, his mood had mellowed anyway: a buff box from the oracle had brought proof that the Australians had inflicted a real defeat on Rommel at Tobruk. It was remarkable how soon Churchill cast off the "Black Dog," as he called his fits of depression. He stayed up talking until three-thirty, comparing Tobruk with Acre in the wars against Napoleon: it was "a speck of sand in the desert which might ruin all Hitler's calculations."[20]

What had been in that buff box? Berlin had flown out deputy chief of general staff General Friedrich Paulus to the western desert, alarmed by rumours of Rommel's disregard for casualties. On Friday the second, Paulus had issued this binding directive to Rommel: given the "exhaustion" of his troops he was to hold Cyrenaica, regroup, and refrain from further attacks on Tobruk unless the defences caved in; moreover, he was not to advance beyond Sollum into Egypt without sanction. Before flying home Paulus signalled a copy of this directive ahead to Berlin, using the airforce Enigma cipher; the intercept CX/JQ 914 was in Churchill's delighted hands soon after.[21]

If it made more sense to him than to Rommel, this was because Churchill knew that Hitler was husbanding every ounce of strength for his attack on Russia. But Wavell also failed to grasp the directive's significance (Bletchley had sent it out to him direct.) "[I] presume," Churchill cabled him on Sunday, "you realise authoritative character of information?"[22] It betrayed his waning confidence in Wavell that he reminded the General that Tobruk's defenders must harry Rommel and force him to expend ammunition and fuel.

Wavell had more problems on his mind. Iraqi rebels were beseiging the British airbase at Habbaniya. Though outnumbered the airmen put up a stout defense. Hitler could only aid Rashid Ali through Syria, and Churchill read intercepts proving that Vichy had agreed to allow this. Churchill briefly suspected that the German airborne troops massing in the Balkans might swoop into Syria.[23] He urged Wavell to smash the Iraq uprising rapidly. Wavell was loath to take on any new commitment. "Your message takes little account of realities," he admonished the PM on May 5. "You must face facts."

The general recommended a political solution; but the very notion was anathema to Mr Churchill. Deeply disturbed, he inevitably compared Wavell's tone with the brisk helpfulness of General Claude Auchinleck, commanding the troops in India. "He seems," the PM advised Ismay on the sixth, "to have been taken as much by surprise on his eastern as he was on his western flank." Wavell seemed "tired out," he concluded. Perhaps he was unjust in uttering these criticisms, since he had possessed substantially more evidence of Rommel's movements and events in Iraq than any general. New intercepts showed German chief of air staff Hans Jeschonnek in Athens, preparing a minor airforce operation from a Greek airfield, and thirty German planes being flown with Iraqi markings to Rhodes. But under Churchill's urging, British troops advanced on the Iraqi capital from Basra. "Every day counts," he warned Wavell, "for the Germans may not be long." Soon Rashid Ali faced collapse. A Japanese diplomatic intercept from Baghdad showed this. Churchill sent it out to Wavell to bolster his resolve, adding tersely: "Burn after reading."

It was unusual for Churchill to reveal the Japanese intercepts. Like Admiral "Blinker" Hall in World War I, he kept his special Intelligence close to his chest: it was his source of power — and glory. Probably he alone in Whitehall was reading the MAGIC Japanese intercepts — whether independently deciphered by Bletchley, or supplied by Henry Stimson's War Department in Washington. They told Churchill what Berlin was up to, because Hitler trusted the Japanese and kept their embassy closely informed of his intentions. But they also let him keep an eye on Washington. Only when Stimson now read the MAGIC intercepts himself did it dawn on him that they exposed the U.S. State Department's "double dealing" with Japan and "very equivocal position" towards the British. Horrified, he noted in his diary, "I fear they [the British] will not very much like the terms of the negotiations." He frantically reminded the Secretary of State of the late 1940 agreement over "exchange of cryptology with the British" under which his G-2 was routinely forwarding MAGIC to London. Cordell Hull was furious, because this gave Churchill the opportunity to read "some of his messages."[24]

ALONE POSSESSING THE key to those vital buff boxes, Churchill faced the domestic carping in England with complacency.

Rommel's wings had been clipped. Britain's fighter defences were equipping with night radar. Operation Tiger was rushing three hundred tanks to Egypt (the convoy would arrive with the loss of only one ship.)

Above all, on May 6 Bletchley deciphered the complete operational orders for Hitler's forthcoming assault on Crete.[25] On or after the seventeenth, this intercept revealed General Kurt Student's paratroops would land in the Maleme-Khania area and at Heraklion and Rethymnon; flak and mountain troops would follow by sea.[26]

"Ten million pounds!" triumphed Churchill: that was what this intercept was worth to him.

It was flashed to Wavell in Cairo; but for security reasons it could not be sent to Freyberg himself in Crete. A subterfuge was adopted. "On the Prime Minister's decision," recorded one of Bletchley Park's senior officers, "the B.P. 'U' Air Intelligence Section produced a paper purporting to be a compendium of German documents obtained through Secret Service channels from General Headquarters in Athens." This was sent to Freyberg.[27]

When Parliament met on May 6 and 7 to pass judgment on Churchill's leadership, he could therefore afford to speak with rising confidence and elation. The pale, drawn look had gone. He waded two-fisted into Lloyd George and Hore-Belisha. A glowering Lord Beaverbrook watched the brilliant performance, and made a note of Churchill's boast that Crete and Tobruk would be defended "to the death and without thought of retirement." Napoleon too had won initial victories, the PM recalled, knowing what he knew, and it might well be that Russia would shortly furnish "new chapters to that theme." That said, he chivalrously offered to accept the blame for their reverses. "I am the one whose head should be cut off if we do not win the war." The vote of confidence showed 447 in favour, three against. Tears of triumph in his eyes he walked out on air between cheering MPs standing on their seats. For better or for worse, they had Churchill for the duration – the mutiny had been stifled at birth. He went to bed early, elated by this victory.[28]

While going about his business — dining with Mr Deakin, debating in the House, receiving James Forrestal, banqueting at the Savoy — he pondered on ways of saving Crete. In a little over one week the Nazis would attempt to seize the island. On the ninth he suggested to Wavell that concealed troops and guns ambush the gliders and paratroops: after all, they now knew precisely when and where they were going to land. Briefly he toyed with sending over the actual intercepts for General Freyberg to read and burn afterwards.[29] But generals might be captured: and the oracle was too important to put at risk like that.

ON FRIDAY THE NINTH he drove out to Dytchley. A dazzling full moon was climbing into the sky, and he needed no whispering oracle to tell him of the danger. A few minustes after seven p.m. on Saturday, Fighter Command was warned, "There is reason to believe KG.100's target tonight will be London," and at 7:45p.m. this information was hardened to: "KG.100's target will be East of Regent's Park. Attack will be from 2300 hrs till 0130 hrs and there may possibly be a second attack at 0230 hrs." Sure enough, that Saturday London's sirens wailed as the Luftwaffe made a farewell visit before removing to the eastern front.

It was the heaviest blitz ever. Over five hundred planes attacked, killing fourteen hundred people, destroying railroads and termini, and levelling entire streets in the City and Westminster. Westminster Abbey, hall and school were scourged, and the main chamber of the House where Churchill had just won that vote of confidence was destroyed. Colonel Josiah Wedgwood, who had called on him after Question Time, sent him a letter offering cynical consolation: "Such ruins are good assets — all round the globe, and especially in America!" Big Ben was damaged but still chimed the quarter hours: Fleet-street was in flames, Odhams Press burnt out, the Temple and St Clement Dane's both gutted. Queen Victoria street was ablaze, Regent street blocked by unexploded bombs, a landmine had crumpled a corner of Bond street, and Park Lane was blocked by craters. "All this is hearsay," wrote the PM's secretary John Martin on Sunday, "for we have been here since Friday in peace and sunshine, though still not in summer warmth."

* * *

An hour before the sirens had sounded, a Scottish airfield detected a lone enemy fighter plane approaching Glasgow. The Observer Corps identified it as a Messerschmitt 110, which perplexed the wing commander on duty, the Duke of Hamilton, as it would not have the range to return to Germany. He scrambled a Defiant, but soon after eleven o'clock the Messerschmitt crashed. Later the police telephoned the astonished Duke — the Luftwaffe pilot was saying that he had come on a "special mission" to the Duke and had intended to land at his nearby estate, Dungavel. The wing commander visited him a few hours later at a Glasgow barracks. The German pulled out a snapshot of himself and his infant son. They had met, he said, in Berlin at the 1936 Olympic Games.

"I don't know if you recognize me," he prompted, "but I am Rudolf Hess."

As deputy Führer of Nazi Germany, Hess was second to Hitler himself. He had taken off at Augsburg at six p.m., flown singlehanded eight hundred miles, arrived off Scotland while still light, circled ninety minutes, jettisoned the drop tank, reached his target area and made his first-ever parachute jump after giving up the idea of landing in the dark.

Unlike the other Nazis he was modest, retiring and fanatically pro-British, as his pre-war letters to his parents in his native Alexandria — intercepted by Intelligence[30] — showed. His record was clean: his office had issued emphatic instructions forbidding anti-Jewish outrages on the Night of Broken Glass in 1938. He had attended none of Hitler's planning conferences. Touring the French battlefields with Hitler in 1940 he had heard the latter voice admiration for the British; later that summer he had endorsed Hitler's peace attempts and shared his dismay at the bombing raids that began early in September. Like Hitler he was contemptuous of orthodox diplomacy, and secured permission from him to put out direct feelers to Britain.* At the end of August he talked over ways and means with the doyen of geo-politicians, Karl Haushofer, his former teacher.[31] It was Haushofer's son Albrecht who had recommended the Duke — they had corresponded in July 1939 about German war aims. Albrecht Haushofer had signed the first letter that went on Hess' behalf to Hamilton on September 23; it was posted to the Duke via an Englishwoman in Lisbon, and suggested a meeting there.

British Censorship intercepted the letter and handed it to the security services. In October 1940 Hess had begun planning to fly over. He made three or four attempts, frustrated by bad weather. Meanwhile the security service embarked on a leisurely Intelligence "game" to find out who was behind all this. Faking Hamilton's signature, they replied to Haushofer.[33] Not until mid March was the Duke shown Haushofer's letter. On April 25 the air ministry instructed him to arrange the meeting with Haushofer in Lisbon, but the canny Duke demanded written orders.[34] More weeks passed. Frantic to stop the slide towards a bloodbath, on April 21 Hess had meanwhile sent the younger Haushofer to meet veteran League diplomat Carl Burckhardt in Geneva and the British ambassador in Madrid; an appointment with Samuel Hoare was actually scheduled for Monday May 12, but by that time Hess had taken matters into his own hands: he had pocketed visiting cards of both Haushofers and flown by Messerschmitt to Scotland.

Churchill was still at Dytchley when his wiretapping service brought word of the gatecrasher and his message to the Duke: "Hitler wants to stop the slaughter."

---

*This was probably on September 4, 1940. Twelve months later Hess would say within the hearing of British Intelligence, "I went to the Führer one year ago and I told him."[32]

Who can say what thoughts inspired Churchill on hearing this, on Sunday May 11, 1941? He had an unbroken string of disasters to his name. He believed himself on the brink of his first tactical victory in Crete. If the war were to end now his name would vanish into oblivion.

The Duke flew down by fighter plane, and arrived by car at Dytchley while Churchill was dining before a private showing of a movie.[35] The Duke handed Churchill the snapshots and said Hess had asked "if I could get together leading members of my party to talk over things with a view to making peace proposals." These embraced the familiar spheres of influence — Europe for Hitler, the Empire for Britain. Hess, added the Duke, had come unarmed — evidently believing he was to parley secretly with the highest officials; Hess was also expecting the King to guarantee his return to his own lines.[36]

"Well," growled the PM, "Hess or no Hess, I'm going to see the Marx Brothers." Churchill was floundering. Perhaps it was not Hess at all? He phoned Eden to investigate, then turned to more mundane matters — the appointment of a new principal private secretary — until his secretary John Martin put him to bed around two a.m.

Back in London on Monday he lunched with Lord Beaverbrook. After a while he pulled out the photograph and said, "Who's that?" Beaverbrook recognized Hess, and said so.[37] He had seen those bushy eyebrows often enough at the Reich Chancery each time he visited Hitler.

The Foreign Office chose more laborious methods, flying a diplomat who had worked for the S.I.S. at the Berlin embassy, Ivone Kirkpatrick, up to Glasgow with the returning Duke; it would be nearly ten p.m. on Monday before they landed at Turnhouse airfield, and meanwhile the news could not be released.

At eight p.m., Berlin announced the disappearance of Hess, coyly suggesting that he had been behaving erratically of late.[38] Exasperated, Churchill phoned Eden, and Eden phoned Glasgow, but Kirkpatrick had decided to dine out before even visiting the prisoner. The B.B.C. lamely repeated the German communiqué at the tail end of its main nine o'clock bulletin, commenting with less than utter objectivity that Hess had either committed suicide or been liquidated by the Gestapo.

If the propaganda exploitation so far was unimpressive Mr Churchill was partly to blame: his minister of information knew nothing of Hess' arrival until the German broadcast; not until ten p.m. did Churchill confirm it to him.[39] In an unguarded moment of candour, the PM proposed announcing that Hess had flown to Britain "in the name of humanity;" but Eden, shown this draft towards midnight in the C.W.R. bunker, stopped him. Cadogan also objected. "It looks like a peace offer," he remarked in his diary, "and we may want to run the line that he has quarrelled with Hitler." Thus truth was the casualty, and over at *The Times* the next day's main headline was set up: HITLER'S DEPUTY ESCAPES TO BRITAIN.

Hours later, Eden telephoned Kirkpatrick who was still reeling from a lecture by the deputy Führer. It was Hess alright, he confirmed. He had come "without the knowledge of Hitler" but swore that he knew the latter intimately and that the Führer "would sincerely regret the collapse of the British Empire."* Hess knew less than Kirkpatrick did himself about Hitler's intentions towards Russia. There was one snag, which Hess had delivered as a parting shot to him as he left: "Mr Churchill who had planned the war since 1936 and his colleagues who had lent themselves to his war policy were not persons with whom the Führer could negotiate." This detail was passed on to Mr Churchill, who could scarcely have cared less.[41]

Kirkpatrick's report from Scotland was dynamite. Churchill stamped it Most Secret, and restricted it to Attlee, Eden and Beaverbrook. A D-Notice on Tuesday warned Fleet-street not to mention the Duke. At mid-day Cadogan brought Kirkpatrick's interview reports to Churchill — who was just off to lunch with the King — and discussed the ugly possibility that Hess had indeed brought proposals: Hess was again saying that Hitler just wanted a free hand in Europe. Churchill busied himself only with the histrionics of the affair — what to call their visitor. "I want him to be a State prisoner," he said and ordered him brought down to the Tower.

At a special meeting with Eden, "C" and "Duffy" on Wednesday evening he mulled over the Parliamentary statement he proposed to make the next day. Cadogan sighed: it was all wrong — it would have tallied exactly with what the Germans had just announced. "Then it *is* true, what our dear Führer has told us," the Germans would say. "Our beloved Rudolf has gone to make peace." No: the Nazis must fear that Hess had turned traitor. Churchill threw a tantrum and decided to make no statement at all. He refused to give any directives — only that the media must not make a hero out of Hess.

On the other side of the Atlantic, the bold night flight of Rudolf Hess had — in the words of a worried White House adviser — "captured the American imagination" no less than that of Charles Lindbergh. But that also suggested how Hess could be exploited. "No amount of conversation about economic penetration of South America or Nazi trade wars," suggested this official, "or even the necessity for survival of

---

*"At this point," reported Kirkpatrick facetiously, "Hess tried to make my flesh creep by emphasising that the avaricious Americans had fell designs on the empire."[40] The author's history of the Rudolf Hess affair, based on unpublished documents, will be published by Macmillan (London) Ltd.

the British navy seems to have convinced the American people particularly the middle and far West, that this country is in danger from the Nazis. But if Hess were to tell the world what Hitler has said about the United States, it would be a headline sensation."

Given our present knowledge of German archives, this might appear naive. But for nearly a year British Security Co-ordination had been planting forged evidence of "Nazi plots" against the Americas. It was natural for the gullible White House to hope that Hess could flesh these plans out. Urging his idea on FDR's private secretary the official unconsciously provided an important clue as to how Roosevelt and Churchill were, by May 1941, accustomed to do business outside the regular channels. The idea, said the official, would get nowhere with the career men in the British embassy or State department —

It is a "telephone" job between the president and Churchill . . . because time is of the essence.[42]

Perhaps the hour was too far advanced to telephone London decently. Roosevelt sent an overnight telegram to Winston instead:

If Hess is talking, or does so in the future, it would be very valuable to public opinion over here if he can be persuaded to tell your people what Hitler has said about the United States, or what Germany's plans really are in relation to the United States or to other parts of the western hemisphere, including commerce, infiltration, military domination, encirclement of the United States, etc.

The notion that Germany could "encircle" the United States reveals the extent to which William Stephenson had succeeded in unbalancing American opinion. Roosevelt urged that the story be kept alive. "If he says anything about the Americas . . . it should be kept separate from other parts and featured by itself."[43]

Hess was questioned along these lines that same day. Mystified, he volunteered only that Hitler had no designs on the United States or the Empire. "If we made peace now," he confided to Kirkpatrick that Thursday, "America would be furious." Roosevelt wanted to "inherit the British Empire." Churchill kept this unhelpful riposte to himself, and — neatly twisting the president's arm — informed him that the deputy Führer had rather disparaged the United States and cast doubt on "the degree of assistance that you will be able to furnish us." He had decided how to use Hess — as a silent pawn in international power politics. His very presence in Britain would put pressure on Washington and, in due course, Moscow: a reminder that at any moment Britain could end the war — the enemy spokesman already being on the threshhold. That same Thursday Beaverbrook summoned the editors to lunch with him at Claridge's and instructed them to *speculate* about Hess as much as they liked; the PM, he assured them, would do nothing to end such speculation.[44]

The Kirkpatrick interviews were kept going.[45] By mid-May however, Hess wanted to speak with the organ grinder and not the monkey; he demanded to see a Cabinet minister and named a German prisoner to act as adjutant in the forthcoming "talks". Stringing him along, Churchill decided that the Lord Chancellor Sir John Simon should visit him. Visiting Hess at an S.I.S. villa near Aldershot he concluded that Hess was telling the truth: he had come on a peace mission. "We must decide how best to exploit H.," recorded Cadogan, and proposed: "mendaciously."[46]

Desmond Morton, Winston's liaison officer to the security services, suggested that since the villa was bugged they publish the transcripts. "The longer we wait," he warned, "the rottener the apple." The texts would reveal the "ignorance, stupidity, falsity and arrogance of the Nazi leaders."[47]

Hess knew he had failed. Alternating between hope and despair, and fearful that the S.I.S. would use truth drugs on him, he made a suicide leap at the villa, but only broke a thigh.

"Mum's the word!" said Churchill, referring to the Hess mission.[48] It has been ever since. When Dr Benes made an incautious Czech broadcast about the mystery, based on what S.I.S. friends told him,[49] Churchill was challenged in the House to make some authoritative statement. He declined. Hess remained in captivity, effectively silenced*, from that day on. "He firmly believes," Morton guffawed in a note to Churchill late in July, "that the Government will one day wish to send him back to Germany with an offer of peace terms."[50]

Cleared of war crimes but convicted of conspiring against the peace, Rudolf Hess would be sentenced in 1946 to life imprisonment. He served forty-six years in captivity, the last twenty-one of them in solitary confinement.

---

*At the time of his death in August, 1987, Hess was forbidden to speak about the past. His letters were censored, his daily diary regularly destroyed. Aged ninety-four, he outlived Churchill and his entire Cabinet, as well as all the Nuremberg judges and defendants.

CHAPTER 43

Turning Point

FOR A TIME LATE in 1940 Churchill had eyed the islands in the eastern Mediterranean, and he had ordered models made of Leros and Rhodes, the fortress island between Crete and Turkey.[1] January 27, 1941 saw him inspecting the models in his bunker. Subsequently he had sent two thousand Commandos round the Cape to spearhead an invasion force; but after the Greek fiasco all his attention was devoted to Crete instead.

Ten thousand Greeks and 32,000 British and New Zealand soldiers with six or ten years' service had been evacuated to the island. But although Britain had been in occupation for six months little had been done for its ground or air defence; the costly lessons of Norway in 1940 had not been learned.

Crete had had five commanders, and now he suggested a sixth: His old New Zealand friend, the much wounded and much decorated Lieutenant General Bernard Freyberg VC, should command the island's defences.

Freyberg took fright when he saw the defence plans. On May 1 he urged his own government to "bring pressure to bear" on Whitehall, either to improve the defences or to evacuate the island while they still could.[2] It was a realistic view, but Churchill could not take another humiliating retreat. Knowing the enemy plans as he did, he did not see how he *could* be defeated in Crete? He did what he could to impart this confidence to Freyberg, and on May 12 a courier took the enemy plan out to Crete. The general's confidence grew. "With help of [the] Royal Navy," he reported after touring the island, "I trust Crete will be held."[3]

The S.O.E. had also laid its plans in Crete. Since 1940 its station chief Captain John Pendlebury had been bribing every newspaper; he had paid fortunes to procure the thick-skulled Cretans for the British cause; and he had established cells throughout the island. "Our captains," he wrote to his wife on May 5, "will fight in the hills and so will the women and girls if necessary."⁴*

On Thursday, May 15, Bletchley Park reported that the enemy's D-day for Crete had been postponed to Monday. Churchill left for the country that weekend satisfied he had done all he could. "The PM himself has been most affable," wrote John Martin, now his principal private secretary, in a letter home, "and gave me a friendly poke in the ribs when he went off to the country."⁵ He made no secret of the political moment of this operation — exhorting Wavell on the Sunday eve of battle that victory in Crete would affect the entire world situation. "May you have God's blessing" he signalled to the Commander-in-Chief, "in this memorable and fateful operation, which will react in every theatre of the war."⁶

General Sir John Dill, the C.I.G.S., watched the exchange of signals between Churchill and Wavell with silent anger. Lunching with Lord Hankey on the thirteenth he had expressed himself "profoundly disturbed" about the PM.

> He confirmed [recorded Hankey in his diary] that [Churchill] sends all the telegrams to Wavell & drafts them himself, but said that in fact they were always shown either to him or someone in his confidence before. What bothered him was not Winston's direction of policy so much as his meddling in matters of detail down to such questions as supplies of maps. . .
> He asked me what a C.I.G.S. could do if he thought the PM was endangering the safety of the country. . . "Can one resign in war?" he asked.

PERHAPS HE HAD BEEN too confident about Crete. Even after the island had been identified as Hitler's next target he had still fretted about Syria — that vast, sparsely populated area through which Hitler might march to Suez. On May 14, alarmed by intercept evidence that Damascus was permitting thirty German planes to reach rebellious Iraq, Churchill took the far reaching decision to allow General de Gaulle's Free French forces into Vichy-controlled Syria.

Latterly he had seemed disenchanted with both the quixotic general and his British Sancho Panza, Louis Spears. Britons freely described the latter as "a born intriguer" and "unscrupulous," while de Gaulle's French

---

*Pendlebury may sound like a Bernard Holloway character from an Ealing film but German Intelligence took a dim view of him in their 236-page report on his work. J.D.S. Pendlebury had been a Cambridge high jumper. He had gone to Crete as an archeologist in 1934, became a curator at Knossos, and returned after S.O.E. training in 1940. His account books showed that he doled out 302,000 drachma for agents and 100,000 to every Cretan newspaper. Ten days after the British defeat German Intelligence warned: "As long as he is at large the subjugation of the island cannot be guaranteed;" his files proved that "war crimes" against the paratroops by the Cretans had been prepared well ahead by "the British secret service," long before the military took an interest in Crete. Pendlebury was wounded in a shoot-out and subsequently shot out of hand by the Germans.⁷

opponents called him "bent" (*louche*).[8] Dakar had left bitter memories,[9] and Churchill had recently let Marshal Pétain secretly know that the General had been "no help to the British cause."[10] But de Gaulle's growing following in occupied France could not be ignored, and on March 7 he had been invited to Chequers. Pétain was perplexed by this evident reconciliation and told an American he failed to understand why Churchill did not "eliminate him from the problem."[11]

De Gaulle did all he could to torpedo Churchill's flirtation with Vichy. It was his agents who furnished evidence of Nazi "activities" in Damascus. Although Bletchley warned him that there was no supporting evidence from the Most Secret Sources Churchill fell for it and briefed Wavell on May 19 to improvise an invasion; General Catroux, the Free French leader in Trans-jordan, claimed that the Damascus French would welcome the British. Told on May 20 that German planes had landed in Syria, which was untrue, Churchill approved an immediate "political" intervention. (He decided on this new commitment while driving from the House to No.10) Wavell rightly disbelieved Catroux: he knew that blood would flow if Britain invaded; when London ruled against him, he offered to resign. Churchill, already unhappy with Wavell, was about to accept when Catroux climbed down: he now accepted that the Vichy troops *would* fight any Anglo-French intervention.

It was too late, however, to call off the intervention: once laid, such plans gain a momentum of their own.

SINCE SYRIA BORDERED onto British-mandated Palestine, a third party declared an interest. In February 1941 the Jewish Agency had used the hiatus created by Lord Lloyd's death to invite Churchill to allow into Palestine the Romanian Jews in danger of being massacred. Jewish Agency director Chaim Weizmann reminded him that even if the policy of the 1939 White Paper were adhered to, there were still forty thousand certificates available. In a scarcely veiled threat, while apologizing for adding to the PM's burdens, he hinted that if the refugees were not allowed into Palestine peacefully every shipload might give rise to "painful incidents which we all would wish to avoid."

Churchill strung him along, referring to "practical difficulties."[12] Seeing Weizmann for a few minutes in March, the PM silkily amplified that there was "no need" for a long conversation, as "their thoughts were ninety-nine percent the same."

> He was constantly thinking of them, and whenever he saw Dr Weizmann it gave him a twist in his heart. As regards the Jewish Force, he had had to postpone it, as he had had to postpone many things.

He promised not to let the Zionists down, but advised them to curry favour with King Ibn Saud. Even if Saud became Lord of the Arab countries, or "Boss of the Bosses," as Churchill termed it, "he will have to agree with Weizmann with regard to Palestine."

He led Weizmann to the door, "I will see you through."[13] In a Cabinet paper on Syria on May 19 he argued that Britain too should negotiate with Saud over a Jewish State of "Western Palestine" with "the fullest rights of self-government, including immigration and development, and provisions for expansion in the desert regions to the southward, which they would gradually reclaim."[14]

* * *

The German D-day arrived. Early on May 20 thousands of paratroops swooped on Crete after an hour's bombardment. It was a matter of deadly prestige for Hitler no less than for Churchill. The paratroop division was the flower of German manhood — an elite among elites. But Churchill was confident that he had the edge on Hitler this time. He had read Hitler's plans, and he was not going to be outwitted again.

"Dead on time!" triumphed Freyberg, as the first Nazi paratroops spilled out of five hundred low-flying Junkers transport planes over the airfields in western Crete.

In London Mr Churchill went to lunch with the King. Meanwhile, in Crete the killing began. The paratroops found the ground defences at Maleme and Canea neither old nor derelict, but well camouflaged and viciously efficient. True, Freyberg had no planes and little anti-aircraft defence. But his troops outnumbered the attackers by over four to one, and were hidden at the very points selected as dropping zones.

Only seven planes of the first wave failed to return, and the Germans flagged off the second wave to Crete all too blithely. The planes arrived over Heraklion and Retimo badly scattered; half of the paratroops were dead withing seconds of landing. But Freyberg was in trouble too. The bombing had shredded his communications, and his officers were not familiar enough with the tactical plan. There was no front line, just soldiers digging in like ants, and killing where they could. The island was a slaughtering ground. At ten p.m. Freyberg sent an ominous signal to Cairo — the margin was "a bare one," this said; and: "It would be wrong of me to paint [an] optimistic picture."

* * *

Some hours after Churchill returned from Buckingham Palace to No.10, he received a chilling message from Sweden. The enemy's battleship *Bismarck* was out. The danger was acute. Eleven Allied convoys were at sea.

Brand new, with 2,300 sailors on board, *Bismarck* was the most powerful battleship in the world; she and the eight-inch cruiser *Prinz Eugen* had marched proudly out of German waters on the day before, wearing the black and white flag of Admiral Günter Lütjens.

She was heading north. Unsinkable, rakish and arrogant, *Bismarck* displaced fifty thousand tons when fully oiled and armed. Grand Admiral Erich Raeder was sending her on a three month raiding cruise in the Atlantic. Units of the Swedish navy had sighted her heading north, and British naval attaché Captain Henry Denham reported the grim news from Stockholm at nine p.m. Some time after midnight it was passed by telephone to Admiral Sir Jack Tovey, commanding the Home Fleet in the new *King George V*. As recently as the seventeenth Bletchley had picked up airforce signals showing that the enemy was reconnoitering the iceline off Greenland and to the north-west of Iceland.[15] That suggested the planned route. Nor could there be any doubt as to *Bismarck*'s predatory intention because the oracle had just deciphered, with some weeks' delay, messages in the intractable naval Enigma, and these revealed that the battleship had embarked prize crews to bring home captured merchant ships.[16]

For two days, while the cruel fighting raged in Crete, there was nothing new on this threat. There was one aircraft sighting which suggested that the battleship would break through the Denmark Strait between Iceland and Greenland. That would take her into the newly announced American-controlled zone. Churchill cabled to Roosevelt on Friday May 23: "Should we fail to catch them going out your Navy should surely be able to mark them down for us." To this he added buoyantly, "Give us the news and we will finish the job."[17]

HIS HOPES FOR A rapid triumph in Crete had been frustrated. Surprised by the unexpected vigour of the defenders, on Wednesday the Germans re-focused their effort on Maleme airfield alone, leaving the other lodgements to fend for themselves. Churchill's oracle could not help in a fast moving situation like this. That afternoon Junkers transport planes loaded with mountain troops began landing recklessly on the cratered airfield, regardless of machine gune fire and shells smashing all around; each plane disgorged forty or fifty fresh troops into the battle.

Nothing made up for Freyberg's lack of air cover. He counter-attacked but too late. He could not dislodge the Germans. A few hours later he pulled out of the bomb-blasted defences — the only hard-topped positions he had prepared — and began a retreat that would end on the southern coast a week later.

There was an important psychological reason for the erosion of morale among his troops. Churchill would maintain in the House that Crete was a battlefield where there was no retreat for either side. But this held true only for the German paratroops: they were outnumbered, trapped like rats and fighting for their lives. But — short of victory — Freyberg's defenders knew that personal survival equally lay in retreat by land and evacuation by sea. Late that Thursday a destroyer had already discreetly evacuated the King of Greece and the British Minister from Crete.

In the waters north of the island, disaster befell the navy. Anticipating a major seaborne invasion, Admiral Sir Andrew Cunningham had stationed his Alexandria fleet out of enemy aircraft range, but where it could intervene north of Crete if need be. The Germans had planned only to send over reinforcements in two groups of caiques — unarmed motor schooners robbed from the Greeks. Two-score of these little ships had been organized to carry 2,250 mountain troops to Maleme on day two, and nearly forty more were to ferry four thousand to Heraklion on day three. The admiralty got wind of this audacious plan on Tuesday the twentieth, and Cunningham ordered up two cruiser squadrons from south of Crete to thwart it.

One squadron intercepted the first schooner group on Wednesday, mauled it like a pack of wolves in a sheep pen, and reported it totally destroyed. In fact ten schooners were sunk, and just under three hundred soldiers drowned; the rest were picked up by German and Italian rescue boats.[18]

These were meagre pickings given the casualties which the navy now sustained, exposed to German air power. Early on Thursday Admiral Cunningham's second squadron chanced on the other German schooner convoy; this made smoke, scattered and escaped. The British force came under heavy air attack and Cunningham's battleship group had to hurry to assist. The battleship *Warspite* was bombed and badly damaged. By May 23 the British had lost two cruisers and three destroyers with shocking casualties. Unable to fathom the frenzied importance that Churchill attached to securing victory in Crete, that day Cunningham concluded a signal to Whitehall with asperity that it was perhaps fortunate that the carrier HMS *Formidable* was immobilised at Alexandria, "as I doubt if she would now be afloat."[19]

Churchill insisted that Cunningham risk his ships regardless of enemy air supremacy; the admiral did so, but the price was rising — it would finally total two thousand British sailors' lives. In his post-war memoirs Churchill would suggest that the costly attacks on the schooners had been justified: "It was estimated that about four thousand men were drowned that night."* In fact the two skirmishes had merely postponed the final defeat in Crete by two or three days.

By Friday May 23 that defeat was in sight, though Churchill would not admit it. He was bitterly shocked at this outcome. All the auguries had been favourable, but now the German command was landing, or crash-landing, troop-carrying planes on the shell-pocked Maleme airfield at three minute intervals.

Plagued with remorse for not having insisted earlier on more tanks for the island Churchill streamed imperious signals out to Crete and Cairo.[21] To Freyberg: "The whole world is watching your splendid battle, on which great events turn." To Wavell: "Crete battle must be won," and: "Fighting must be maintained indefinitely in the island." But Freyberg was pulling his troops back from one improvised line to another, only to see each outflanked by the enemy's mountain troops.

Dispirited and thoughtful, the PM drove out to Chequers for the weekend: It was indeed a "turning point."

That was the phrase he himself had used.

SINKING THE *BISMARCK* might be his last chance but until late this Friday she and *Prinz Eugen* had eluded observation.

Then that fickle God of Fortune that had smiled alternately on the opposing war leaders seemed to turn his way again. At seven-fifteen p.m. a lookout in the cruiser *Suffolk*, followed shortly by *Norfolk* too, sighted the battleship: she was in the Denmark Strait plunging south towards the open Atlantic. Alerted three hundred miles away by radio signal, the elderly but mighty battle cruisers *Hood* and *Prince of Wales* began converging at speed on the Germans, heading into the teeth of a rising north wind.

Churchill brightened. There seemed an excellent chance of catching *Bismarck* at dawn in the Strait. For a while he sat up, glass in hand, talking quietly with Averell Harriman, his ears cocked for the ring of the telephone. But no call came by three a.m. and he went to bed drained by the day's events. "I awoke," he later recalled, "in peaceful Chequers about nine a.m. with all that strange thrill which one feels at the beginning of a day in which great news is expected, good, or bad." Towards nine a.m. that Saturday morning a private secretary came into his bedroom. "Have we got her?" the PM asked. But the news was not good.

In the Arctic twilight some time while he slept, lookouts aboard the

---

*Churchill, *The Grand Alliance*, page 255. German records give the real figure as 297. While Playfair wrote in *The Mediterranean and the Middle East* of 800 drowned, Roskill in *The War at Sea* was more circumspect: "The exact enemy losses in this action are not known but were certainly heavy."[20]

rival battleships had spotted each other's squadrons almost simultaneously at a range of seventeen miles. Like mounted knights in armour levelling their lances at their rival's breastplates, they had charged into the gloom closing head on at sixty knots or more. *Hood*'s fifteen inch guns had bellowed first, then *Bismarck*'s: as at Jutland, the German gunnery had been superb: within seconds *Hood* had been grazed by one hit, then pierced by a shell that touched off her main magazine. The volcano of molten steel and fire killed all but three of her 1,500 sailors — as many as the French who had died under her guns at Mers-el-Kébir. That left the *Prince of Wales*. Moments later a fifteen inch shell swept through her bridge killing everybody on it except captain, chief yeoman and navigating officer. Reeling from four hits by *Bismarck* and three by *Prinz Eugen*, she fled trailing a cloud of angry black smoke.

When the stunning news reached the admiralty, the First Lord went down to the admiralty shelter and fingered the harmonium, playing Oh God our Help in Ages Past.[22]

The skies were leaden and a gale was sweeping southern England. Rain lashed down.

At Chequers, Churchill stumbled into Harriman's bedroom and told him what had happened. He was taut and silent when he went downstairs, unable to break the awful news to his family. Sensitive to all Winston's moods, Clemmie poured him a glass of port. Less sensitively, Vic Oliver — Sarah's Vienna-born comedian husband — strummed a few bars of Beethoven's Appassionata on the piano until Winston shouted to him to stop. "Nobody plays the Dead March in my house," he cried.

Only one hope sustained him that day: that *Bismarck* had not escaped the gun-duel unscathed. There was a report that she was trailing oil. The admiralty ordered counter-measures — an ancient battleship from Nova Scotia, an even older one from Newfoundland, two cruisers from the Azores, a battleship from the Clyde: all were ordered to converge on the German's probable position. But where was she heading?

Throughout Saturday they shadowed the scurrying, victorious Germans through the North Atlantic mist and rain. By afternoon *Victorious* was moving up to launch torpedo planes: *King George V* and *Repulse* would probably be within range the next morning. Irritably pacing the Great Hall, glass in one hand and cigar in the other, Churchill dictated a signal ordering Admiral Wake-Walker in *Norfolk* to continue the pursuit even if it meant running out of fuel. Later, he ordered the Admiral to be asked for his intentions about re-engaging the Germans. Hundreds of miles away, the Admiral took the hint, crept up on *Bismarck* and attacked her from astern. Under cover of this firefight

Admiral Lütjens managed to detach *Prinz Eugen* to continue the Atlantic sortie which he himself was now being forced by loss of oil to abort. A few hours later *Victorious* was within aircraft range: but a torpedo from one of her brave biplanes merely grazed the paintwork on *Bismarck*'s armourplate. She seemed impregnable.

Early on Sunday the cruisers lost their quarry completely. But Lütjens seemed unaware of this and instead of imposing radio silence he transmitted three lengthy messages between nine and eleven a.m. to Germany. The admiralty got fixes on these signals, and these showed that *Bismarck* had moved south and east during the night. Evidently she was running for France.

GOING TO BED THAT night he would remark that these were the worst days he had ever spent. His mental turmoil must be born in mind when examining his actions on this particular weekend. But out at Chequers he was waylaid by temptations as well as torments, for here in the country he was perilously free from the constraints and bridles that London imposed on him with its constantly hovering ministers and staffs. Out here he could take independent decisions, and often did.

In his eyes extreme actions were justified. He was going for broke. Crete seemed lost and he was mortally afraid that the sacred, mighty *Bismarck* was slipping away too. He pored over maps, made calculations, rasped orders down the telephone to London. His intuition told him that Admiral Lütjens was returning north, to Germany. Far out to sea Tovey believed that too, and had begun heading north. On Churchill's orders[23] a signal went to *Rodney* to conform with Tovey's movements towards the Iceland—Faroes gap, and *not* to steer for France. Tovey in turn read this signal and assumed that London knew things that he did not.

Thus for most of this Sunday Tovey was galloping away from the limping Lütjens. At 4:21 p.m. he uneasily signalled London. "Do you consider the enemy is making for the Faroes?" Perhaps Pound had to consult Chequers for a reply: After waiting nearly two hours for this, Tovey turned back of his own accord to the southeast, toward France, at 6:10 p.m.

Five minutes before that, the admiralty had suddenly cancelled Churchill's instructions to *Rodney* and told her to assume that *Bismarck* was heading for France.[24] Once again the oracle at Bletchley Park had provided the vital clue: We now know that Hans Jeschonnek, Göring's chief of air staff, was in Athens directing the Nazi assault on Crete. From there he had signalled an anxious inquiry about where the damaged

Bismarck was heading — his son was aboard the battleship.*
In airforce Enigma code Berlin replied, "Brest."[25]

* * *

Not satisfied with acting as unofficial "First Sea Lord" that Sunday, Churchill watched the battle in Crete and wished that he was Commander-in-Chief in Cairo too. "I would gladly lay down the premiership," he told his secretaries, "Yes, and even renounce cigars and alcohol!"[26]

But at Chequers both commodities abounded, and extraordinary orders winged into the ether that weekend. In one, despatched over the admiralty's signature — a familiar Churchill expedient — he contermanded an order by Admiral Cunningham to the fast troop transport *Glenroy* to withdraw from Crete to the south (Cunningham ignored the London signal.)[27] Envious at reports of the enemy's "blind courage," fearful that Hitler was shipping still more reinforcments into Crete, (he wasn't) and apprehensive that his craven admirals might hesitate to risk their warships against them, the PM lisped that Sunday: "The loss of half the Mediterranean fleet would be worth while in order to save Crete." Again he ordered Cunningham to intervene north of the island, even in broad daylight. "Only experience," the admiralty's wounding signal; initiated of course by Churchill, suggested, "would show how long the situation could be maintained."

Knowing whose hand had drafted this, Cunningham retorted: "Their Lordships may rest assured that [the] determining factor in operating in Aegean is not fear of sustaining losses, but need to avoid loss which, without commensurate advantage to ourselves, will cripple Fleet out here."[28] Taking a less sanguine view of losing half his fleet, Cunningham would shortly write to the First Sea Lord, again offering his resignation.

* * *

Jeschonnek's paternal inquiry about his son had settled the fate of *Bismarck*. A Catalina — piloted in fact by an American — was immediately sent out to search the Atlantic off Brest; it sighted the fugitive battleship at ten-thirty on Monday morning May 26, seven hundred miles from the port, still leaking oil but seemingly too far ahead

---

*His son survived. Jean Howard, the Bletchley Park analyst who handled the decrypt of Jeschonnek's signal, vividly recalls the thrill as it arrived.

for *KGV* or *Rodney* to catch. Admiral Somerville's Force H was moving an aircraft carrier between her and Brest.

Back in London for his five o'clock Cabinet Churchill was edgy and despondent. The Cabinet handled him roughly, ganging up on him and forcing him to abandon notions he had adopted without consultation. Only labour minister Ernie Bevin supported him, over conscription in Ulster. Beaverbrook was pugnacious as a stuck pig, and Dalton noted the "general sense of gloom." The convoy HX126 had been sunk by U-boats in the Atlantic; and news of the heavy Mediterranean losses in the battle against the schooners had arrived. "Thus," lamented Churchill, "the Germans have established a unit superiority over us." *Hood* was sunk, and *Bismarck* had evidently escaped. "This," he cried, "is the most injurious and distressing naval incident since we missed the *Goeben*."[29]

"Poor Winston will recover all right," assessed one witness of that Cabinet, "if we get a bit of good news. Tonight he was almost throwing his hand in. But there is a bit of the histrionic art in *that*."

Afterwards, the PM found a warm and human note from Anthony Eden: while this might be a bad day, the foreign secretary reminded him, on the morrow they would enter Baghdad, and *Bismarck* would be sunk. "On some date the war will be won," he encouraged the PM in this note, "and you will have done more than any man in history to win it."[30]

Just now, Winston could not see how. Tears of mortification in his eyes, that evening he read a signal from Admiral Tovey warning that he would have to break off the pursuit to refuel unless Lütjens reduced speed by midnight; *Rodney*'s fuel was also running out. Shortly Admiral Somerville signalled Tovey curtly, "Estimate no hits" — that was the Swordfish attack by *Ark Royal*. (They had fired their torpedos at *Sheffield* instead, shadowing *Bismarck*, without hitting her.)

FOR SOME REASON CHURCHILL was incapacitated that grim evening, May 26. Perhaps it was his old curse, "Black Dog."

News reached London on which he took no action for several hours. Left to his own devices in Crete, General Freyberg decided that evening to evacuate the bloody island. "The limit of endurance," he signalled to Cairo, "has been reached." Perhaps Churchill could not bring himself to read the signals. "Your glorious defence," he would signal to Freyberg the next day, "commands admiration in every land. We know enemy is hard pressed. All aid in our power is being sent." And to Cairo, "Victory in Crete essential at this turning-point in the war. Keep hurling in all aid you can."[31]

His mood was suicidal. His appointment card that Monday evening, May 26, shows a dinner at eight-thirty with the Winants. Whatever it was that happened there, the U.S. ambassador's concern was profound enough for him to make immediate plans to fly back secretly to Washington on Wednesday to report to Roosevelt at first hand. Ripples lapped as far as the State department, where Cordell Hull was heard to murmur over and over again: "Everything's going hellward."[32]

It looked like the end of the road. Frantic at the thought that Tovey's two battleships might soon break off the pursuit, at some time during those dark hours Churchill drafted this extraordinary signal to the admiral:

> *Bismarck* must be sunk at all costs and if to do this it is necessary for *King George V* to remain on the scene, then she must do so, even if it subsequently means towing *King George V*.[33]

Given his mood, it would be uncharitable to criticise him for having penned this signal. But that Admiral Pound sent it on without remonstrance is surely the final proof how far he was beholden to his master. As has been pointed out [34] enemy submarines were gathering in the area: the order if obeyed, would have signed the death warrant for *King George V* and her crew.

Six hundred and fifty miles out in the Atlantic, the pursuit had entered its final stage. At nine p.m. the seemingly puny Swordfish torpedo planes had repeated their attack on Hitler's fifty-thousand ton naval giant. They seemed to have missed, but after a while something strange was seen happening: *Bismarck* had begun turning a huge, aimless circle. Her steering must have been jammed. She was doomed after all.

Five destroyers closed in as daylight failed and loosed off torpedos for several hours; none actually scored hits in the darkness. But as day returned on Tuesday May 27, the battleships *King George V* and *Rodney* arrived and opened fire at twelve miles. Just before nine a.m. the first hits were scored on the German, now blind, crippled and hopelessly outgunned. An hour later, battered by hundreds of tons of shells and torpedos but still flying her battle ensign, *Bismarck* was a blazing hulk, the screams of the dying mercifully masked by distance and the towering seas.

The biggest battleship in the world was no longer a fighting machine, but she was unsinkable. Her guns fell silent by ten a.m., their last ammunition spent. A message from Admiral Tovey arrived in London: the battleship could not be sunk by gunfire. It did not matter, because even as Churchill's Cabinet met at ten-thirty a.m. to accept the loss of Crete, engineer officers aboard *Bismarck* were blowing open her seacocks to scuttle her. She went down at eleven a.m.[35]

Moved at the infernal spectacle and by the death of 2,000 German sailors Admiral Tovey, the British Home Fleet's Commander-in-Chief, signalled to London this chivalrous request: "I should like to pay the highest tribute for the most gallant fight put up against impossible odds", meaning by the *Bismarck*. Churchill forbade it, citing "political reasons."[36]

Thus was lifted the curse of defeat from Churchill's brow. In an hour he was to address the Commons — now at Church House since Parliament had been bombed — and this would allow the kind of staged drama in which he excelled. To the restless Members he recounted, as only he knew how, the whole epic from the sinking of the *Hood* right up to the disappointments of the previous evening: even at this moment, he continued, the great warship was, he said, steering in uncontrolled circles while our own fleet bore down on her. Shells were without effect on her, and torpedoes would be the only finish — "That process is in action as I speak."

That said, he tantalizingly deferred to other speakers.

Shortly a slip of paper was handed John Martin in the official box, and he passed it forward to the front bench. Aware that every eye was upon him, Churchill unfolded the paper. "Mr Speaker," he said rising to his feet, interrupting another Member. "I crave your indulgence. I have just received news that the *Bismarck* is sunk."

As wild cheers lifted to the roof, the PM shot a triumphant glance across at the Opposition benches: Shinwell winked broadly at him. Bevan scowled with chagrin.[37] It looked like Churchill was going to be prime minister for a long time.

CHAPTER 44

Beaverbrook, Battleaxe and Barbarossa

THE BULLDOG FACE with its familiar folds and dewlaps was almost a caricature of itself. Somebody once remarked on Winston's "knack for looking crumpled," and on his "self satisfied smile that trembles between a grin and a pout." The face was memorable, but it was hard to say why: the ears were unobtrusive, the chubby features neither aristocratic nor "English"; but the mouth was soft and effeminate, the lower lip protruding in a permanent moist pout. The eyes were small and twinkling, with pouches that underlined their mood. Clemmie (whom he called the "Cat") dubbed him "Pig." Worried at the load he was carrying, this marvellous woman would confide to Harry Hopkins: "I can't bear his dear round face not to look cheerful and cherubic in the mornings, as up to now it has always done."[1]

Winston was beginning to regard it as a "most unnecessary," "obstinate" war. Once a month he could escape from it when he dined with The Other Club. He and F.E. Smith had founded it one Thursday thirty years before. It was here in June 1941 that he cornered H.G. Wells and chaffed him: "Well, H.G. — how're your 'war aims' getting on?" He continued, barely pausing for the reply, "There's only one war aim for the present. — K B O."

The great novelist harrumphed and raised his eyebrows.

Churchill happily translated for him. "Keep B*ggering On!"

"Ay yes, Mr Prime Minister," the writer called out, "but ye can't go on fighting rearguard actions all the time!"[2]

There were powerful voices who felt that now he should admit failure and accept Hitler's very favourable peace terms. Among them was David Lloyd George, who justified his views in a furtive talk with Lord Hankey in Kensington on May 29: "We agreed all along the line," Hankey wrote that day: "Churchill has great gifts of leadership, and can put his stuff over the people, Parliament, his Cabinet colleagues and even himself. But he is not what he thinks himself, a great master of the art of war. Up to now he has never brought off any great military enterprise. However defensible they may have been, Antwerp, Gallipoli and the expedition to help the White Russians at the end of the last war were all failures. He made some frightful errors of judgment between the two wars in military matters, e.g. obstructing the construction of new ships in 1925; the adoption of the Ten Year Rule ('no major war for ten years') in 1928; his false estimates of the value of French generals & French military methods. . . It was he who forced us into the Norwegian affair which failed; the Greek affair which failed; and the Cretan affair which is failing."

Lloyd George astonished Hankey by revealing that he had rebuked Churchill in private a few days earlier for "his constant reiteration that he would never make peace with Hitler or any of his gang."

> The war [as Hankey noted his words] was likely to be long in any event, but this attitude made it interminable because Hitler & his crowd had rescued Germany from the Slough of Despond and raised it to the strongest military Power. In the circumstances it was inconceivable that the Germans would overthrow the Nazis. Besides, the Germans were entitled to have the Government they want. . . When Ll.G. had said this kind of thing to Winston, the latter had replied, "Nothing would induce me to treat with these fellows." Whereat Mrs Churchill had piped in with, "Well, Mr Lloyd George, we can all change our minds, can't we!"

In June 1941 the PM still had more reason to pout than grin. Among the few in whose company he sought solace was the restless Lord Beaverbrook. Bracken would declare with more than an ounce of justification that "Max" took up more of Winston's time than Hitler;[3] another minister would surmise that overthrowing Asquith in 1916 had gone to his head — "He has been trying to repeat his success ever since."[4] But Churchill admired Max as a troubleshooter, and he had recently appointed him Minister of State to increase arms supplies to the services.

Beaverbrook was also deputy chairman of the Defence Committee (Supply). His office was two doors from No.10. He soon found Churchill's interventions tiresome. The PM had set up a "Tank Parliament" of generals and production experts, and asked Beaverbrook to chair it. It held only three meetings — Beaverbrook chaired the first, the PM the other two.[5] This was only one example. Early in June Beaverbrook itemized the prime minister's meddling in a letter.[6] Churchill drafted a reply jealously pointing to his wide powers as Minister of Defence, but decided not to send it.

At the root of Beaverbrook's unhappiness was a fundamental opposition to this war. Britain had come to a pretty pass, he would blurt out a few weeks later to Rudolf Hess. "I was very much against the war," he recalled, "I [hoped] greatly that we wouldn't be involved in this terrible world crisis." Out of minor events had grown a major tragedy which could no longer be stopped. "It bothers me a great deal," he added. "I used to go to Germany quite often before Hitler came to power. My newspapers always gave him a good hearing."[7]

At the end of February 1940 his evening newspaper had leaked details of peace talks between Lord Tavistock and the Germans. On March 5, 1940 he had invited John McGovern of the Independent Labour Party and two colleagues to dinner and, confiding to them that he saw no sign of Germany's defeat, he had offered £500 and newspaper backing for every peace candidate they fielded.[8] During the Crete crisis, a disenchanted McGovern blew the gaff in a by-election speech.[9] Beaverbrook, embarrassed, would only comment that the dinner had lasted until two a.m. and that they had quaffed two bottles of 1911 Pommery as well as port and brandy. He soothed his irate prime minister with ten cases of Deidesheimer Hofstück 1937 from his own cellar. Winston found the liquid gift "exhilarating" and forgave him; asked in the House on June 25 about Max's 1940 misdemeanor he dismissed the allegation as "Communist vapourings." McGovern was furious about what he called the PM's "vicious and false" answers.[10]* But Beaverbrook was indispensible and knew it. A few days later Churchill promoted him to Minister of Supply.

* * *

Thirty-two thousand troops had been defending Crete. "I don't see how we can expect to get any of them out," a haggard C.I.G.S. had gasped to the American military attaché as the evacuation began. "Freyberg was left with no air support at all."[12] But in four nights 16,500 men including General Freyberg, too good a man to lose, were embarked from the island's southern fishing ports. Five thousand more were authorized by Wavell to surrender — "a shameful episode," in Churchill's view. He felt troops should not surrender with less than thirty percent fatalities.

On May 31 Churchill drove down to Chequers to reflect. The dispirited tone of Wavell's telegrams unsettled him. He muttered about "defeatism" — "He sounds a tired and disheartened man," he remarked to his secretariat.[13] Then he turned to his weekend guests. Harriman had brought his daughter, Kathleen, with him; she found Winston smaller than expected, and less plump. In his airforce blue rompers he looked

---

*In 1942, U.S. Censorship intercepted a supportive telegram from Beaverbrook, then in Washington, to an anti-Churchill candidate at Rugby; Churchill's candidate was defeated.[11]

"rather like a kindly teddy bear," she wrote to her sister. Harriman, worried about the Middle East, obtained his permission to fly out and investigate the situation for himself.

CHURCHILL SUFFERED THE SAME weakness as Hitler: he would grumble volubly about the most senior commanders for many months before summoning up the necessary resolve to replace them. Thus he now grumbled to his staff about the Wavell's caution and pessimism and wrote to Dill about the General's reluctance to launch armoured offensives: Wavell, he suggested, should do so "while his fleeting authority remains."[14]

Perhaps the Mediterranean crisis bore more heavily on Wavell in Cairo than on Churchill in the serenity of Chartwell, whither he repaired that Whit Monday evening, June 2. Denied effective air cover, the British ships evacuating Crete had been attacked without mercy and hundreds more were killed — 260 in the cruiser *Orion* alone. Churchill, after grumbling for months about Air Chief Marshal Longmore, the Middle East airforce commander, now replaced him with Air Vice-Marshal Sir Arthur Tedder.*

Tedder was one of Winston's most felicitous appointments: he rapidly earned the affection of the desert airmen and would prove a real asset when North Africa became an Anglo-American theatre of war.

The naval disasters at Crete had cost Churchill the supremacy in the Eastern Mediterranean which Cunningham had won for him at Taranto and Cape Matapan. But Hitler had burnt his fingers too: capturing the island had cost him more than in his entire Balkan campaign — five thousand troops, and 150 Junkers transport planes including twenty crews; the operation had broken the back of his only paratroop division. While Hitler vowed never to use paratroops again, Churchill, casting about for new initiatives, decided to raise an airborne division on the German model.

Crete finally taught Churchill the importance of air supremacy in invasion operations. He even decided to relinquish Cyprus to Hitler, if he decided to invade.[16] Fortunately Hitler remarked petulantly that if Mussolini wanted Cyprus he should get it himself. "Occupying Cyprus would have some point for us only if we wanted to influence Syria from there," he said, "otherwise there's no point at all."[17]

The Axis had no interest in Syria. On May 31 Bletchley issued categoric reassurances to that effect.

---

*For a time he considered Sir Hugh Dowding instead of Tedder, but neither Sinclair nor Portal would hear of it.[15]

In Iraq, Hitler ordered a last stand by the Arabs at Baghdad, only to reverse the decision hours later upon learning that the uprising had been crushed; he diffidently dismissed Iraq as a "blemish" to his grand strategy.[18]

Churchill read Hitler's secret orders about Baghdad on June 1, but — we shall never know why — refused to heed Bletchley's reassurances about Syria and decided to invade it, regardless of his secret agreement with Marshal Pétain.

Perhaps he was impressed by the assurances of General Georges Catroux, de Gaulle's commander in the region, that Britain could stage an easy coup in Syria. He called a Staff meeting, ostensibly to discuss the pros and cons, on June 4. "Actually," recorded Cadogan resignedly, "there was only desultory conversation about anything that came into the PM's head — in that order."

To invade a strongly garrisoned Vichy territory one week before Battleaxe, Wavell's major summer offensive against Rommel, was surely tempting Providence. To his Defence Committee later that evening Churchill adopted a frivolous argument: he might as well invade Syria now, since he had to face the Commons music over Crete anyway on the tenth: he could ride out both storms in Parliament together.

* * *

To some advisers it looked like studied nonchalance. To others, it seemed that he was floundering: but he was treading water to a purpose. The optimist in him was waiting for America to come in; and more immediately for Hitler to attack Russia. He alone was 100 percent certain that this Event was imminent.

Even after Belgrade, the F.O. remained adamant that Hitler had no such intention.[19] Military Intelligence, seeing no Panzer divisions moving eastwards yet, also insisted that his main enemy was still Britain.[20] On May 6 the C.I.G.S. sent a paper to No.10 stressing "on the highest professional authority" the danger to Britain, and not mentioning Russia at all.[21]

Churchill had sources not available to either Eden or the War Office, and had taken a different view since July 1940. Even his own chief of staff seemed unaware of these sources: "The night before," Pug Ismay remarked to the Canadian prime minister in August (and some wonderment), "one would never have thought that Germany would attack Russia."[22]

This perhaps explained why the diplomats were curmudgeonly when Churchill had first tried to warn Stalin. Eden had advised him on April 3 not to do it; Cripps, the ambassador in Moscow, had not bothered to forward Churchill's cryptic warning to Stalin. Mortified by Cripps's insensitivity but unwilling to unmask his sources, Churchill had lectured his youthful foreign secretary: "The Ambassador is not alive to the military significance of the facts. Pray oblige me." Stalin had made no reply to his warning.[23] Considering how Stalin had treated Britain in 1939 and 1940, Churchill had decided to let him stew in his own juice and made no further approach.

On April 24 the oracle detected further creakings as Hitler's assault circus lumbered eastwards. This time it was a pivotal Luftwaffe signals unit being transferred from the Channel coast to Poland. The airforce and railroad Enigmas now bulged with cipher traffic as elite units were shifted east, including bridging units and the Hermann Göring Flak Regiment. Eden, with only diplomatic evidence to go by, remained convinced that this was just the paraphernalia of Nazi blackmail: his instinct had been blunted by weeks of incestuous rumours — whispered from one diplomat to another and back again — that Hitler was merely black-mailing his Soviet allies for concessions, possibly German control of the Ukraine.

Churchill kept his sources to himself. The raw intercepts told him all he needed to know. On May 5 cryptanalysts noticed a P.O.W. guard unit being moved from Zagreb to Poland. Later they would underscore this: "The quiet move . . . of a prisoner-of-war cage to Tarnow looks more like business than bluff."[24] On the eighth they deciphered a German airforce signal linking the Fourth Air Force to an unidentified operation Barbarossa; and on the twelfth, one linking Twelfth Army to *Fall B* — "Case B." All Hitler's offensives had been "Cases" — White against Poland, Yellow and Green against the Low Countries and France. What clinched it was evidence that General von Richthofen's Eighth Air Corps and the First and Second Flak Corps — the combat-hardened spearheads of the western and Balkan campaigns — were being rushed to Poland.

On May 14 the buff box submitted by "C" to Churchill contained Bletchley's firm conclusion that Hitler was planning a surprise attack on the Soviet Union. "A ceaseless movement," he telegraphed to General Smuts in South Africa two days later, "of troops, armoured forces, and aircraft northwards from the Balkans and eastwards from France and Germany is in progress."[25]

A week later the Joint Intelligence Committee — a ponderous body on which all three services were represented — belatedly addressed the question. Churchill, scornful of "collective wisdom", had long before prudently demanded to see original intercepts himself.[26] By studiously ignoring these, the JIC concluded that Hitler was bluffing. The Japanese ambassador in Berlin was heard speculating that Hitler's real interest was in India. (Hitler had not yet initiated him.) Echoing the wholly incorrect "economic blackmail" theory, on the last day of May the chiefs of staff advised General Wavell that Germany was making drastic demands on Stalin and would march if he refused them.[27]

By then the codebreakers had heard Göring's commanding generals asking for maps of new operational zones — all areas still under the Russian heel: the Baltic States, eastern Poland, north-east Romania. "It would no doubt be rash," assessed Bletchley Park on the last day of May,

for Germany to become involved in a long struggle on two fronts. But the answer may well be that the Germans do not expect the struggle with Russia to be long. An overwhelming eastward concentration, a lightning victory, an unassailable supremacy in Europe and Asia — such may be the plan behind this procession of troop trains from the Balkans to the eastern frontier.

It was as though they had been reading Hitler's mind: and, in a sense, they had.

On June 3 German ambassador Count von der Schulenburg assured his Italian colleague in Moscow that *no* negotiations were going on. Churchill read the Italian's cipher telegram. That ruled out "blackmail." On the fourth Göring summoned his commanding generals to a conference. Orders went to Richthofen not to move forward "for Case B" before the sixteenth. "It looks to me more and more likely," Churchill wrote privately on June 8 to his son Randolph, who had telegraphed to him a disturbing report on the British set-up in Cairo, "that Hitler will go for Stalin."[28]

Washington was also in the picture, though from different sources. In 1940 Hitler's former chief economist Dr Hjalmar Schacht had tipped off the U.S. chargé in Berlin about Case Yellow one week in advance. Now he told the same diplomat that it was a *feststehende Tatsache* (established fact) that Hitler would invade Russia on about the twentieth.[29] Churchill may well have been told. He certainly learned of Göring's indiscretions. Late in March the Reichsmarschall had told a Swedish industrialist friend about Barbarossa;[30] in June he would add the date, and on the eighteenth or nineteenth the Swede would pass it to London. The Polish exile leader in London learned from this source that Göring was stating that Germany would "launch an attack against Russia on Sunday, June 22."[31]

* * *

Churchill's address to the House on Tuesday June 10, 1941 would be crucial.[32] He began dictating it at No.10 as the week ended. The first draft was cantankerous and even smug — he claimed that no error had been made in Crete "from this end."[33] He tried out this line on the senior Fleet-street editors after they trooped in through the famous front door for a private briefing on Saturday morning. Conciliatory, even jocular, he revealed secretly that he had known of Hitler's airborne plan a fortnight in advance. He had felt sure that Freyberg could hold off both this and the seaborne invasion to follow. Freyberg, he claimed, could have had more tanks if he had asked. He voiced genuine surprise at the public anger over what was, after all, "only one episode" in the Middle East: it was unreasonable to call him to account each time "any little thing" went wrong. Besides, he claimed, Britain had destroyed four hundred enemy planes and killed fifteen thousand Germans for only ten thousand British killed and missing; and this, he argued trimphantly, was why Hitler had been unable to spare more than forty planes for Iraq.

The red meat of this confidential briefing was his revelation of Barbarossa. Hitler had, he suspected, demanded oil from Stalin, and part of the Ukraine. If he was asking for Baku and its oilfields as well Stalin would have to refuse — "even though he knows his army could not stand up to the Germans."[34]

WITH TUESDAY'S ADDRESS still hovering over him — he expected Hore-Belisha to snivel about the lack of Flak on Crete — he drove out to Dytchley, looking forward to the nightly movies and other reliefs from the grinding mills of war. He instructed that General Dill, who was wearying of the whole business, should come too. "A man of simple tastes," Lord Hankey learned two days later, "he had to partake of an enormous dinner with quantities of champagne. After dinner, instead of discussing business, he had to see a cinema, which lasted until midnight. *Then* the business. He did not get to bed until three a.m. Characteristic."

Churchill had just completed his King's Birthday Honours List: a welcome chance to rebuff and outrage his critics. He had put down the Prof for a peerage and A.V. Alexander as a Companion of Honour; Morton and Seal would become Companions of the Bath. Reading the smoke signals correctly, *Mirror* editor Guy Bartholomew commented, "Evidently Churchill realizes this will be his last Honours List!"[35]

His family was now far flung. Offended by her husband's surliness, young Pamela had farmed out baby Winston to Max Beaverbrook so as to spend more time with the visiting Americans.[36] Randolph, when in England, treated her like a pasha. "I want you to be with my son," he shouted, and when Pamela retorted that he was *her* son too he rudely snorted: "No, my son. I'm a Churchill."[37] Everybody except the prime minister could see what was happening to the marriage.

Harriman was leaving for Cairo. Churchill wrote to his son out there, commenting ingenuously on the friendship that Harriman's daughter had struck up with Pamela. "I hope," he added, "you will try to see Averell Harriman when he arrives." The bunkered Annexe was now complete, but he rarely took shelter there (as he knew from the oracle the blitz on London was over anyway.) "Your Mother," he explained to Randolph, "is now insisting upon becoming a fire watcher on the roof, so it will look very odd if I take advantage of the securities provided."

Some 2,500 miles away, that Sunday June 8 his assault on Syria began. "No one can tell," he wrote to Randolph, "which way the Vichy French cat will jump and how far the consequences of this action will extend." He was on tenterhooks next day, as his field commander Jumbo Wilson sent no word. Churchill, still anxious about the Commons speech he had to make, grumbled: "It's damned bad manners."[38] The news was bad: Syria was not going to be a walkover. There were 25,000 Vichy regulars and ninety tanks there. Ten thousand Allied and Vichy soldiers would be killed or wounded in the following five weeks. The military benefits of this unwanted new front were negligible; the political ramifications vast. In particular Churchill had violated the "gentleman's agreement" with Pétain, and from now on their relations were marked by unremitting hostility.

* * *

His "largest problem," as he described it, remained embroiling the United States. In mid April Canada's prime minister deduced from a visit to his southern neighbours that they would not willingly go to war: Roosevelt talked only about his people's defeatism, Morgenthau about Canada's refusal to turn over French Gold, and Hull about his daily homilies to the Japanese ambassador on the wisdom of peace. "If a fight came at all," Mackenzie-King remarked to Lord Halifax, "it would probably come at the outset between Britain and Japan, not the U.S. and Japan."[39]

But there were moves in the right direction. Iceland was one. In 1940 British troops had occupied key points there; now Roosevelt agreed to replace this garrison, since Iceland was in his newly defined western hemisphere. The British division could be released to the Middle East.[40]

There were other possibilities. Churchill tried to persuade Roosevelt to transfer elements of his fleet from Pearl Harbour into the Atlantic; for a time he nearly succeeded.[41] After *Bismarck*'s destruction and the escape of her consort he sent a new idea over to the admiralty in a locked box. "The bringing into action of *Prinz Eugen* and the search for her," his secret suggestion read, "raises questions of the highest importance." In short, an American warship should be invited to find and shadow her.

"This," he explained, "might tempt her to fire upon that ship, thus providing the incident for which the United States Government would be so thankful."[42]

A further method suggested itself in June, even as the U.S. Marines began moving into Iceland. He now revived an earlier plan to stage an Allied propaganda summit in London (it had been thwarted in December by Greece's pettifogging refusal to attend, not being at war with Germany.) "At a time when the Germans are trying to declare peace in Europe," he telegraphed to Roosevelt from Dytchley, inviting America to participate, "it will be useful to show that the inhabitants of the occupied countries are still alive and vigorous."[43] Roosevelt declined because of "domestic considerations."[44]

The banquet went ahead, and Churchill spoke before the microphones at St James's Palace. If the exile leaders expected him to state his war aims, at long last, they got no more than H.G. Wells. He used them as a sounding board for crashing arpeggios of rhetoric, thundering at these innocent exiled statesmen about concentration camps and about German firing parties working every dawn. "Such is the plight of once glorious Europe," he cried, "and such are the atrocities against which we are in arms." His message was simple: Hitler was doomed: "It is here, in this island fortress, that he will have to reckon in the end." "Our airpower will continue to teach the German homeland that war is not all loot and triumph."

"Lift up your hearts," he concluded in his hymn-like peroration. "All will come right. Out of the depths of sorrow and sacrifice will be born again the glory of mankind." They were great and often moving phrases but they boiled down to the same prosaic strategy: Keep B*ggering On.

THE TIGER CONVOYS HAD shipped more tanks — Churchill called them his "Tiger Cubs" — to Egypt, and munitions were arriving direct from American production. On the fifteenth, Battleaxe would begin. But he was worried: Rommel now had his 15th Panzer division, and Wavell seemed to be losing his grip. After hearing a first-hand account of Crete Churchill complained to the chiefs of staff of the lethargy displayed in acting on the very precise intelligence he had furnished to Wavell.[45]

He would face the House on Tuesday June 10 with little enthusiasm. "People," he had grimly observed to his Cabinet on the eve of this debate, "criticise this Government. But its great strength — and I dare say it in this company — is that there's no alternative!" "I don't think it's a bad Government," he continued. "In fact there never has been a Government to which I have felt such sincere and whole-hearted loyalty!"

Underlying the forced joviality was a deeper worry about his own political survival: John Martin saw him labouring on his speech until three a.m. that night.[46]

AT THAT CABINET CHURCHILL had broached the Barbarossa issue: should they risk telling the Soviet ambassador now? It was still "a big if," felt Eden, unaware of the decrypts from the oracle.[47] But in Cabinet he finally conceded that the political benefits that Hitler might expect from a crusade against Communism might outweigh the economic disadvantages. "All the evidence," he agreed, "points to attack." The chief of air staff suggested, to general approval, that if Hitler did invade Russia, Britain undertake to "draw off German air forces" by bomber action in the west.[48]

Whitehall had cold shouldered Ivan Maisky since the Nazi-Soviet pact, and he was flattered to be summoned to the Foreign Office on the tenth. Looking the perfect stage foreigner with his goatee beard this affable diplomat earnestly denied to Eden and Cadogan that Moscow and Berlin were conducting talks.[49] Eden outlined to him the troop movements eastwards, adding that if Hitler attacked — which possibility Whitehall "could not ignore" — Britain was willing to assist Russia with air action, a combat-experienced military mission for Moscow, and economic aid.[50] Across Downing-street on that same day Churchill was reading intercept CX/JQ 1048: Göring had summoned all airforce commanders to his private estate Karinhall in five days' time.

The picture was clearing fast. Now Bletchley's Japanese section, covering the Purple traffic between Tokyo, Berlin and Rome, belatedly deciphered a message which Baron Oshima had sent to Tokyo on the fourth, after seeing Hitler at Berchtesgaden.[51] Hitler had told him that he had resolved to eliminate Communist Russia; if he postponed it by five or ten years it would cost twenty times the sacrifice; he would always be first to "draw his sword" against a hostile opponent; Romania and Finland would join in. "If Japan lags behind when Germany declares war on Russia," the Führer had said, "that will be up to her." Ribbentrop was chillingly precise: it would all be over in two or three months — he did not say when the campaign would begin, but he did advise that Japan prepare "in as short a time as possible."[52] This shook even the Joint Intelligence Committee. "Fresh evidence," they announced, "is now at hand that Hitler has made up his mind to have done with Soviet obstruction and to attack."[53]

These final days of waiting frayed Churchill's lonely nerves. The official Soviet news agency might dismiss the rumours as "absurd."[54] But everything pointed the same way in mid June: The airforce Enigma carried cipher signals about a "Chief War Correspondent" arriving in Kirkenes in northern Norway, data about Russian camouflage, and

Notes And References

FAITHLESS BUT FORTUNATE: Page 1

1. Harold Nicolson, MS: Portrait of WSC, 1947: Longwell papers: Columbia Univ., New York.
2. Cecil King diary, Feb 19, 1941: Boston Univ.
3. General Sir Hastings Ismay, cit Nicolson diary, Aug 7, 1942.
4. Letter from Nigel Nicolson, Mar 23, 1978.
5. William Lyon Mackenzie-King diary, Aug 11, 1943: Public Archives of Canada, Ottawa.
6. N. Chamberlain (Min of Health) to Ld Irwin, Aug 15, 1926: Gilbert, *Winston Churchill*, v, 180f.
7. WSC to Ld Hugh Cecil, unsent, Oct 24, 1923: cit R. Churchill, *Winston Churchill* (London 1969), ii, 70f.
8. Roskill, *Churchill and the Admirals* (London, 1977) 21.
9. Roskill, ibid., 33, remarks that Martin Gilbert, in *Winston Churchill* iii, 40ff, "glosses over" WSC's role in this.
10. Mackenzie-King diary, Aug 16, 1943.
11. From WSC, "My Life." First publ. in Chicago *Tribune*, Feb 4, 1935: Orig MS at Oregon Univ., Eugene, Oregon.
12. Interview of Kay Halle, Washington, May 1978.
13. Hankey cit in Liddell-Hart: notes, May 23, 1945: Liddell-Hart papers, King's College London.
14. WSC to Baldwin, Dec 13, 1924: Gilbert, v, 75ff; Ltr Ld Beatty to wife, Jan 26, 1925.
15. Naval Staff memo Mar 5, 1925: Gilbert, v, 103.
16. Cf. Gilbert, v, 290ff.
17. Ibid.
18. Memo on Anglo-American relations, Nov 19, 1928: Gilbert, v, 308. The Chartwell quotes are from the diary of Henry Scrymgeour-Wedderburn, later an MP: Sep 21, 1928: ibid, 301.
19. WSC to CSC, Nov 7 and 15, 1928: ibid, 306ff.
20. Gilbert, v, 315.
21. WSC to CSC, Sep 9, 1929: Gilbert, v, 346.
22. WSC to CSC, Sep 29, 1929: Gilbert, v, 348.
23. Maurice Ashley, *Churchill as Historian* (London, 1968), 18.
24. Mackenzie-King diary, Aug 1941, and Aug 24, 1943.
25. Chamberlain to Irwin. See Note 6.
26. John Davidson, diary, Mar 6, 1929: recording luncheon with Sir William Berry, later Lord Camrose: Gilbert, v, 316.
27. Interview of Kay Halle, (See Note 12): she was at Chartwell that evening. FDR's son was present.

* * *

KEEPING IT UNDER HIS HAT: Page 14

1. Douglas had first published his infamous attack, "The Murder of Lord Kitchener and the Truth about the Battle of Jutland and the Jews," in his obscure weekly *Plain English*, Jan 1921: the Attorney General had at the time advised WSC to ignore it. WSC had of course left the Admiralty in 1915, one year before Jutland.
2. Halifax, cit in Dalton diary, Dec 18, 1940.

3.   Prince Otto von Bismarck, Aufzeichnung, London den 20. Oktober 1930: German FO papers: NA film T120/5540/K567887ff.

4.   WSC to Beaverbrook, Sep 23, 1930: Beaverbrook papers, C86.

5.   WSC to Randolph 8 Jan. 1931, Gilbert, v, 379.

6.   WSC to Baruch, Nov 1, 1931: Baruch papers.

7   Washington *Star*, Jan 10, 1932; and see John Wheeler, *I've Got News for You* (E.P. Dutton, New York 1961), 163. He also sold it to the Daily Mail.

8.   CSC to Randolph, Jan 12, 1932: Gilbert, v, 423.

9.   C. Murphy MS, Mar 1945: FDR Library, Winant papers, box 190, W Churchill.

10.   Speech in New York, 28 January, 1932, Gilbert, v, 425.

11.   WSC, "Zionism versus Bolshevism: A Struggle for the Soul of the Jewish People," in *Illustrated Sunday Herald*, London, Feb 8, 1920.

12.   WSC speech, Jan 27, 1926: PRO: TREASURY 172/1505

13.   WSC to Clementine, Jan 6, 1927: Gilbert, v, 224

14.   Cit in *Current Biography*, 10ff.

15.   WSC's original typescript in Univ of Oregon, with his MS corrections.

16.   WSC article Mar 31, 1931: Gilbert, v, 408f.

17.   See WSC's speech to the House on Nov 23, 1932: H of C Deb.

* * *

WUTHERING DEPTHS: Page 23

1.   Interview of Kay Halle, May 1978.

2.   Beaverbrook to Sir Robert Borden, Jan 7, 1931.

3.   Beaverbrook to Arthur Brisbane, Oct 20, 1932.

4.   Beaverbrook to Sir Robert Borden, Jan 7 and Mar 28, 1934.

5.   Beaverbrook to Theodor Fink, Nov 19, 1934.

6.   T.E.B. Clarke, *This is Where I Came In* (London, 1974), 87.

7.   Christopher Hassall, *A Biography of Edward Marsh* (New York, 1959), 575f.

8.   *The Times*, reviewing *The World Crisis*, ii, on Oct 30, 1923.

9.   Prof. A.J.P. Taylor, in *The Observer*, May 17, 1970; cf R. Rhodes James, op.cit.

10.   Ltrs WSC to E. Marsh, Aug 31, 1922; June 24, 1934; Aug 30, 1947: Berg Library, New York.

11.   Gilbert, v, 333; M. Ashley, *Churchill as Historian* (London, 1968.)

12.   Gilbert, v, 303.

13.   WSC to CSC, Nov 15, 1928: Gilbert, v, 307.

14.   Colville diary, Nov 3, 1940.

15.   L. Amery diary 5 Nov 1928; Gilbert, v, 306.

16.   WSC to Spears, Mar 22, 1930: Spears papers: 1/76b.

17.   Gilbert, vi, 961.

18.   Ltr Aubrey Neil Morgan MP to author, Dec 9, 1977.

19.   WSC to Prof, Feb 26, 1931: Cherwell papers.

20.   WSC speech to the US Congress, Dec 26, 1941.

21.   WSC to Camrose, Aug 2; and to CSC, Aug 8 1929: Gilbert, v, 339.

22.   C. Murphy: memo on dinner party of Mar 16, 1946: C.D. Jackson papers, box 32: DDE Library.

23.   C. Scribner to WSC, Mar 11, 1932: Gilbert, v, 427. They sold 4,000 of the final volume of *Crisis*.

24.   Ltr Thornton Butterworth to WSC, Nov 19, 1931: Gilbert, v, 416.

25.   Jack Churchill to WSC, Sep 16, 1932: Gilbert, v, 438.

26.   Correspondence between Curtis Brown and Chicago *Tribune*, Sep 19, 1932 to Feb 13, 1933: University of Oregon, Eugene. And see Dr J. Richard Heinzkill and Martin Schmitt, "Sir Winston's Potboilers," in *Imprint: Oregon*, Fall 1974, 3ff, and note in The Papers of the Bibliographic Society of America, vol.72 (1978) 359.

27.   Curtis Brown to Chicago *Tribune*, Feb 13, 1935.

WILD MAN IN THE WILDERNESS: Page 30

1. C.D. Jackson, memo: Churchill speaking during cruise with Henry Luce: DDE Library; Jackson papers, Apr 14-17, 1955, box 32, Churchill.
2. Lord Birkenhead, *The Prof in Two Worlds,* (London 1961) 126f.
3. Hoare to Willingdon, Apr 6, 1933: Templewood papers.
4. WSC to Lord Burnham, Apr 9, 1933: Gilbert, v, 477.
5. Hoare to Willingdon, Apr 20, 1934: Templewood papers.
6. WSC to Cyril Asquith, Aug 8, 1934: Gilbert, v, 584.
7. Gilbert, v, 457: WSC speech Feb 17, 1933.
8. Cabinet meeting, Mar 15, 1933.
9. WSC speech at Devonshire Club, Nov 14, 1933: Gilbert, v, 498.
10. "His thirst for talking military strategy is unquenchable." Colville diary, Sep 20, 1940.
11. Hore-Belisha to Liddell-Hart, diary, Mar 10, 1944.
12. Cecil King diary, May 10, 1941: quoting W.J. Brown, Sec. of Civil Service Clerical Association.
13. Tel. Masaryk to Prague, London Mar 15, 1934: Berber, op.cit, No. 23.
14. Hitler's first reply to Lord Rothermere was on Dec 7, 1933. See the photocopies retained by Rothermere's go-between, Princess Stephanie von Hohenlohe, in her papers, and the two original Ribbentrop files in the Louis P. Lochner collection, Hoover Library.
15. WSC to CSC, Aug 22, 1934: Gilbert, v, 559.
16. Alexander Korda told Ladislas Farago (a reporter on *News Review*) over lunch at the Korda home in Swiss Cottage. Interview of Farago, Jun 1979; ltr Michael Korda to author Jun 1979.
17. Ltr Bracken to Baruch, May 21, 1947: Baruch papers.
18. See for instance Kapt. von Puttkamer's telegram to Raeder from the Berghof, May 24, 1938: in German naval file PG/36794: "The Führer must now assume that Britain and France will rank amongst our enemies."

* *

SIXTY: Page 41

1. From WSC, "My Life," MS first published in Chicago *Tribune*, Feb 4, 1935: original MS in Univ of Oregon.
2. Liddell Hart related this to E. Wingfield Stratford, ltr, Apr 12, 1942: Liddell Hart papers: Kings College.
3. D. Longwell memo, Oct 15, 1953: Longwell papers, Box 2: Columbia Univ, New York.
4. Arthur Krock MS, May 22, 1969: Krock papers, Princeton Univ.
5. WSC to CSC, Feb 23, Mar 2 and Apr 13, 1935: Gilbert, v, 612.
6. Morton to Thompson, Aug 20 1960: in R.W. Thompson, *Churchill and Morton* (London, 1976) 71.
7. WSC to Hankey, Jan 31, 1936: Gilbert, v, 702.
8. In December 1940 WSC would appoint Mr Justice Singleton to review the secret information: Air intelligence at that time estimated the enemy front line at 5,710 planes, while MEW put it at 3,000. WSC to Sinclair, Dec 9, 1940: Cherwell papers.
9. WSC to Cherwell, May 2, 1947: ibid.
10. WSC to Spaatz and reply, Jul 17, 1947: Spaatz papers, Library of Congress. Spaatz supplied figures from British ADI (K) report 352/1945 on captured GAF Equipment Branch files suggesting that in Sep 1938 Germany had a first line strength of 3,200 mobilized planes, and in Sep 1939 4,300.
11. Hinsley, i, 53. This, says Prof Hinsley, remained the best source on the subject "when other sources were providing conflicting and only tentative assessments."
12. Erhard Milch diary, Aug 20, 1938: in Irving Collection, film DJ-59.
13. Milch diary, Feb 1935.
14. Bruce Lockhart diary, Sep 5, 1943.

15. WSC to CSC, Apr 13, 1935. Londonderry never deviated from his view that WSC had grossly exaggerated the German airforce and attributed Britain's troubles to the attitude which developed after Simon returned from Berlin. "Our first line strength at that date was 897 machines, and as I calculated at the time and verified from subsequent information which I received, the first line strength of the German Air Force was *12* machines." Winston's "delusion" about the German airforce had "disastrous results" on foreign policy. Ltr to Halifax, Dec 2, 1939. Ld Halifax papers, FO800/328.

16. Ld Rothermere to Hitler, Apr 29; and reply, May 3, 1935: Hohenlohe papers: Hoover library, Stanford Univ, Calif.

17. Milch diary, Jan 12-15, 1935. In Aug 1935 they began planning the 1936 budget. The airforce claimed 4,300m Reichsmarks; Hitler said 3,100m was possible, but Göring warned Milch that they would probably get only 2,000m. Later the 1936 budget (without *SA*) was set at a total of 7,200m (army 4,200m, navy 680m, airforce 2,300m.)

18. Rose Kennedy memo, 1940; and WSC to J.P. Kennedy, Oct 12, 1935: JPK papers, Kennedy Library. WSC had cabled to Ld Beaverbrook on Oct 10 inviting him to dine with Kennedy in Oct at Claridges; B declined. Beaverbrook papers. C86.

19. WSC: "Zionism versus Bolshevism: A Struggle for the Soul of the Jewish People," in *Illustrated Sunday Herald*, London, Feb 8, 1920.

20. Rothermere to Hitler, Dec 6 and Dec 16, 1935; reply, Dec 19, 1935: Hohenlohe papers.

21. W.C. Bullitt to FDR, Feb 22, 1936. In Orville H. Bullitt: *For the President* (New York, 1972) 144.

22. E.g., WSC to Flandin, May 15, 1936: his estimate, "drawn from a variety of sources," was 1,200 first line German machines, and 2,000 by the end of 1936; Flandin replied on May 16 giving French estimates of 1,236 and 2,000 respectively.

23. Leo Amery to Beaverbrook, Nov 7, 1936: Beaverbrook papers, C5.

24. WSC to Londonderry, May 6, 1936: Gilbert, v, 732.

* * *

THE HIRED HELP: Page 54

1. WSC to Randolph, Nov 13, 1936.

2. Eugen Spier, *Focus - A Footnote to the History of the Thirties* (London, 1963). — Credit is due to Dr Dietrich Aigner of Mannheim Univ. for his research into the Focus in *Das Ringen um England. Das deutsch-britische Verhältnis*. (München, 1969) and particularly his unpublished bibliography, *On Producing Chaff. Materials for an Inquiry* (Weinheim, 1980).

3. Ld Citrine, *Men and Work - An Autobiography* (London, 1964), 347ff.

4. E.g., ANC to Spears, Sep 19, 1935: Spears papers 1/55: Churchill College. Vice chairman was Sir Robert Mond of ICI. *Vice Presidents* were Nobel peace prizewinner and fellowtraveller Angell, Herbert Morrison, E. Sylvia Pankhurst, Canon F. Lewis Donaldson, Eleanor Rathbone; *Chairman,* George Latham; Hon Sec and Treasurer, C.Q. Henriques; *Council:* Monica Whately, A.M. Wall, V. Adams, P. Guedalla, A. Conley, P. Horowitz, F. Rodgers ("organizing secretary"), L.W. Carruthers, and M.H. Davies.

5. WSC to FDR, undated, Nov 1940: FDR film 1/0148.

6. The fund was controlled by foreign propaganda chief Jan Hajek. In 1923 he paid Steed £10,000, ostensibly for advertising in his *Review of Reviews*, although it could never handle so much advertising; he paid Steed £8,000 on Nov 27, 1923 and £5,000 six months later, acknowledged by Steed to Dr E. Mastny on Mar 27, 1924. Payments continued through the 1930s. He was receiving 8,000 crowns monthly in 1936 (£1 = 200 crowns) and collected £3,000 in 1938. T. Masaryk gave him 120,000 crowns — half from the foreign ministry. Czech funds flowed freely to writers like Machray and Poliakoff; Laurence Lyon was slushed with 100,000 crowns for an unpublished book. Newspapers like the Canadian *La Presse*, Montreal *Daily Star*, *The Gazette*, Toronto *Star Weekly* and *Globe* were also on the Czech payroll. Prague was even subsidising

Alexander Kerensky's anti-Soviet newspapers like *Dni* and *Volja Rossiji* and making payments to intellectuals "for their service rendered to our legions during their conflict with the Soviets." Stefan Osusky, MS: Benes and Soviet Russia, in Osusky papers: box 14: Hoover Library, — Dr R. Urban, *Tajne fondy III sekce, Z Archivu ministerstva zahranici Republiki Ceskoslovenske*, Prague, 1943, proves that Hajek on Dec 11, 1935 ordered 15,000 crowns paid quarterly to Kerensky in London.

7. Leon Poliakov, in *Histoire de l'Antisemitisme*, vol.iv: *L'Europe suicidaire, 1870-1933* (Paris, 1977) 230ff, even has Steed instrumental in propagating the "Protocols of the Elders of Zion."

8. *Christian Science Monitor*, Boston, Dec 4, 1936.

9. Sir Robert Bruce Lockhart, diary, Aug 17, 1936.

10. Urban (note 6).

11. Gilbert, v, 739, citing ANC minutes in Churchill papers, 2/282-3, closed to other historians.

12. Spier, 20.

13. See note 8.

14. Citrine (note 3).

15. Gilbert, v, 739: quoting Churchill papers 2/282.

16. In 1940 Arthur Harris, cdr of No 5 Bomber Gp discovered that Anderson was reporting directly on his two bomber squadrons to WSC. When he ignored warnings Harris sacked him and posted him to Canada. Anderson protested to the Prof that the real reason was "because I am regarded as a personal friend of the Prime Minister's and of other serving Ministers. I am therefore regarded as a potential danger." (Sinclair to WSC, Aug 24; and Anderson to Prof, Oct 29, 1940. Cherwell papers.) Beaverbrook took him on as personal assistant at MAP despite Sinclair's warnings. In 1942 WSC told him that a number of Sinclair's top secret minutes and copies of all the PM's minutes to Beaverbrook had been found in Anderson's possession. Anderson was invalided out of the RAF; Beaverbrook referred to him sympathetically as "the poor fellow who went mad." B. to Sinclair, Jun 29 and Jul 13, 1942: C311. He died in 1982.

17. Tel Franckenstein to Vienna, Jun 25: NA film T-120/1447/D568395.

18. Hankey to Inskip, Jun 29: Gilbert, v, 757.

19. Swinton to Hankey, Jun 26: CAB 21/426.

20. Wigram memo, Jun 30: FO 371/19946.

21. See note 18.

22. WSC to Randolph, Nov 13, 1936.

23. Steed, "The United States and British Policy", address at Chatham House on Nov 25, 1937: in *International Affairs*, London, vol. xvii, No. 1, 1938, 51-3.

24. Spier.

25. Robert Henriques, *Sir Robert Waley-Cohen 1877-1952. A Biography* (London, 1966) 362.

26. It was published in the *Sunday Chronicle*, Jul 4, 1937, and in *Collier's*.

27. S. Roskill, *Churchill and the Admirals*, 27.

28. Swinton at Cab. Joint Planning Cttee, Sep 15, 1936: AIR 2/1873.

29. Verbatim transcript of Parlt. Deputation, Jul 28-29, 1936: PREM1/193.

30. *Evening Standard*, Aug 10, 1936. Similar articles followed on Aug 21, 1936 and Jul 7, 1938.

31. Spier; and see note 8.

32. WSC to A.H. Richards, Oct 21 and 26, 1936.

33. Adams to WSC, Oct 20: cit in Gilbert, v, 790.

34. Spier, 53ff.

35. WSC to Randolph, Nov 13, 1936.

36. Ltr Sarah to CSC, May 19, 1950: unpubl.

37. Arnold diary, Jun 16, 1944: Library of Congress, MS Division

38. Ltr Sarah to CSC, Oct 12, 1936: unpubl.

39. Ltr WSC to Baruch, Jan 1, 1937: Baruch papers.

40. Lothian to WSC, Mar 30, 1940: FO371/24263.

* * *

OVER-REACHING HIMSELF: Page 66

1.   WSC: My Life, typescript in Univ of Oregon.
2.   C. King diary, Feb 19, 1941: Boston Univ.
3.   Deputation of Nov 23: PREM1/193.
4.   WSC to E.L. Spears, Nov 17, 1936: Spears papers, Churchill College.
5.   Cummings, cit in German emb. despatch, Dec 3.
6.   Naomi W. Cohen: *Not Free to Desist — The American Jewish Committee 1906-1966* (Philadelphia, 1972), 183f. And ltr WSC to Baruch, Jan 1, 1937.
7.   Ltr Ital Consul General at Cannes to Ciano, Dec 16, 1936: Ital emb. (London) file 963, Rapporti politici; and Gran Bret 1: Reali Inglesi Questioni Dinastiche: Conflitto tra Corona-Governo. This file includes telegrams of the Finnish minister in London George Gripenberg to Helsinki, of interest since his American wife Peggy was a friend of Mrs Simpson. Ital. FO archives, Rome.
8.   Tel Gripenberg to Helsinki, Nov 6.
9.   Ditto, Dec 15, commenting on this and on Hoesch's hold over Edward VIII; cf Bruce Lockhart diary, May 27, 1935.
10.   F. Hesse memo, London, Mar 11: Hesse papers: Bundesarchiv Koblenz: K1.Erw.262-1. He died in 1980.
11.   Chamberlain diary, Nov 25: Chamberlain papers, Birmingham Univ.
12.   Ld Citrine: *Men and Work* (London, 1964)
13.   Ltr Beaverbrook to Guy Ross, Dec 11.
14.   Blanche Dugdale diary, Dec 5.
15.   Gilbert, v, 817.
16.   John Parker, MP, interview, Apr 1978.
17.   Nicolson MS: Longwell papers: Columbia Univ, N.Y.
18.   Dugdale diary, Dec 8. Amery diary, Dec 7. *Hansard,* H of C Deb, vol.318, col.1643f.
19.   Ilse Hess to Rudolf's mother, Nov 3, 1937: FO371/26566: PRO.
20.   Naomi Cohen, op.cit., 183f.
21.   Joseph Kennedy, cit in Forrestal, James V.: *Diaries,* ed. W. Millis (New York, 1951), 122. Kennedy's own antisemitism was notorious.
22.   WSC to Baruch, Jan 1: Baruch papers: Princeton Univ; Steed left via Canada in Sep 1937, was interviewed by the Montreal *Star,* which like him was being funded by the Czechs, met the Governor-General in Ottawa; crossed into the U.S. on Oct 5, met Sulzberger, Swope and Baruch. He reported to The Focus on Oct 28, and had this to say at Chatham House on Nov 25: "I spoke confidentially to the Council on Foreign Relations, to the Foreign Policy Association, to the New York Jewish Committee, to the Harvard Club and various other gatherings. I met also some responsible executive officers of the United States." *International Affairs,* xvii (1938) No.1, 51-3.
23.   WSC to Baruch, Jan 1.
24.   WSC to CSC, Jan 7: Gilbert, v, 835; and Feb 2, 1937: Mary Soames, *Clementine Churchill,* 274.
25.   Curtis Brown Ltd to Chicago *Tribune* Syndicate, Mar 29; reply, Oct 29, 1937: Univ of Oregon.
26.   Gilbert, v, 835n..
27.   Others included "A Stand against Aggression" in Mar 1938, and "For a Pact with Russia," in May 1939.
28.   Churchill, i, 203.
29.   H.V. Johnson to FBI, Mar 11, 1941: US emb. (London) secret files: Box 6, file 820.02, Military activities: RG-84: NA, Suitland, Maryland. Guy Liddell's original MI5 report of Mar 5 was removed from this file on British instructions in 1975.
30.   J. Kuczynski: *Memoiren* (East Berlin and Weimar, 1975), 325-7.—In Aug 1939 the Left Book Club published 50,000 of his *The Condition of the Workers in Great Britain, Germany and the Soviet Union 1912-1938.*
31.   Mackenzie-King diary, Aug 12, 1943: Public Archives, Ottawa.

* * *

PEOPLE ARE BUYING "CHURCHILLS": Page 78

1. Ironside diary, Dec 6, 1937.
2. Milch, Gedenken für den Luftkrieg: returned by Karl Bodenschatz, Feb 1, 1937: Milch papers (deposited by the author at IfZ, Munich.)
3. Sir Herbert Creedy (War Office) commented on Steed's Memorandum on Germany, "The value of this report is much reduced by the great exaggeration in it as to the strength of Germany's air force and army. Thus the source estimates that Germany has between 2,000 and 3,000 war 'planes ready for service (i.e. first line): but the Air Ministry estimate is about 1,000 first line and this agrees with the strength given them by the Germans." FO371/19446.

   In FO371/19914 is further evidence of how avidly Churchill swallowed Steed's data. In October 1936 Steed reported a (fictitious) Hitler speech at Würzburg on September 18; warned that Hitler was about to invade France through Switzerland; advised that the Nazis had established a submarine base off the coast of Portuguese Guinea; and talked about the (in fact diesel-powered) German battleships being under orders to raise "a good head of steam". Sending this report to an F.O. official on October 20, Wickham Steed wrote: "I mentioned some of it to Mr Winston Churchill last week and he said it 'ought to go also to the Government'." Steed added that since his own financial resources had come to an end, "a wealthy friend" had placed money at his disposal "for this 'research work' " in the summer of 1936 (the Board of Deputies, it will be recalled, had first funded The Focus in July 1936). He continued, "I have now six or seven non-Jewish informants on my string."
4. Wigram, minutes, May 12 and Jun 16. WSC's and Wickham Steed's memoranda on German air power; air ministry responses; British papers on Swinton's discussions with Milch and Wenninger, and Wigram's exchanges with Wing Cdr Medhurst: FO371/19446.
5. Sir E Phipps to FO, Tel. No.1344, and reply, Jan 16, 1936. FO371/19946.
6. CID mtg, Jul 10: FO371/19946. Wenninger talk with WCdr Medhurst, Jul 6. Ibid.
7. Cab Mtg, Feb 3, 1937: FO371/20734.
8. Their mission lasted from Jan 17-23; report in FO371/20733.
9. For German documents on this mission see Milch files, vol.56, pp.3003ff: now at BA Freiburg. Swinton discussed the results in Cabinet on Feb 3, 1937.
10. Mary Soames, *Clementine Churchill* (London, 1979) chap.15.
11. F. Owen MS in Beaverbrook papers, C86.
12. H. Rauschning, *Hitler m'a dit* (Paris, 1939). Cf ltr Steed to Kingsley Martin, Aug 6, 1939: "I have got a number of German Aryans working on this very problem [of making the Germans understand encirclement] — Rauschning and Hollermann among them . . . last week I put Rauschning into touch with Benes." On Rauschning, cf FO371/26581.
13. M.J. Creswell to WSC, Dec 22, 1937: Gilbert, v, 890f.
14. H. Wilson to P.J. Grigg, Jan 31, 1938: Grigg papers, Churchill College.
15. H. Channon diary, Apr 14, 1937.
16. Mackenzie-King diary, Aug 30, 1941.
17. Cf ltr King Saud to FDR in Mar 1945 (Leahy file 56), in Adm. William Leahy's words (diary, Oct 2, 1945) an excellent refutation of Jewish claims to a historical right to ownership of the Holy Land.
18. WSC, "Zionism versus Bolshevism: A Struggle for the Soul of the Jewish People," *Illust. Sunday Herald*, London, Feb 8, 1920. He argued that the Russian post-revolutionary experience confirmed the case for a national Home for "the political conceptions of the Jewish race."
19. Ltr Blanche Dugdale to Lord Cecil, Feb 17, 1936: Cecil Papers, MS 51157: Brit. Museum.
20. Ltr Weizmann to Meyer W. Weisgal, his NY agent, Jul 9, 1948; and WSC to Weizmann, Nov 1951: Weizmann archives. WSC's Zionist fervor has been properly noted by biographer M. Gilbert and by monogrpahers like O. Rabinowicz (1956) and A. Ade (Zurich, 1972).

21. Peel Commission, Mar 1937: CO733/344.
22. Prof Norman A. Rose, *The Gentile Zionists* (London, 1973) 131f; Dalton diary Jun 18, 1937. Weizmann wrote to WSC, Jun 14, "I have followed your advice and have made it clear, both to members of the Commission and to [Colonial Secretary] Mr Ormsby-Gore . . . that they should not assume that I am in any way committed to . . . partition." Weizmann archives.
23. Spier, op.cit.
24. Ashton-Gwatkin — Waley corresp, Jun 24—7; A.E. Barker, memo, Jul 4: FO371/20733, fols 261ff; Leith Ross conv with Goerdeler, Jul 6: T188/288. Another clandestine German visitor to Churchill from 1937 was Dr Richard von Kühlmann, former *Staatssekretär* in the German F.O. (Affidavit, Dec 29, 1947 in U.S. *vs.* Körner et.al.)
25. Sheila Grant Duff to WSC, rec'd Jun 19: Gilbert, v, 863.
26. WSC to CSC, Jul 25, 1937.
27. WSC to Feiling, Feb 26, 1938: Gilbert, v, 907.
28. Ltr WSC to Beaverbrook, Oct 20, 1937: C86.
29. WSC to Eden, Oct 1937: Gilbert v, 870.
30. Tel Ribbentrop to Hitler, May 18, 1937: No. 277.
31. C. Murphy, MS. J. Ribbentrop, *Zwischen London und Moskau* (Leoni, 1953.)
32. US War Dep interrog of Bohle, Jul 26-27, 1945.
33. FO371/20733.
34. Milch diary, MS, and ltr to Trenchard, Dec 12, 1945; Trenchard to H. Elmhirst, Feb 19, 1946: Trenchard papers, MFC 76/1-565: RAF Hendon.
35. WSC to Hankey, Oct 16, and reply Oct 19: Gilbert, vi, 877f: and Hankey papers.
36. WSC to Hankey, Oct 21: Hankey papers.
37. CAB24/273. Up to that time no German contingency plan against the Low Countries had been prepared.
38. Pearman to A.H. Richards, Jan 8, 1938: Gilbert, v, 894.
39. Ribbentrop, memo of Dec 28, 1937 (listed by *DGFP* as "lost," but found by the author in FO files; and subsequent Note for the Führer, Jan 2, 1938: ND, TC-75; original in Loesch papers, NA film T120/622/339ff.

* * *

THE GRAND ALLIANCE: Page 92

1. Vollbrunner, Franckenstein's colleague in Paris, was arrested on his return to Austria for destroying legation files wanted by the Gestapo; Ribbentrop assured F. he had nothing to fear. Loesch papers, T-120/617/0289ff.
2. *Los Angeles Times*, Mar 18, 1939.
3. Churchill, i, 263; Maisky, 405.
4. On Oct 27, 1938 Oliver Harvey urged Halifax to curb such activities. FO800/311.
5. Mussolini papers, esp. files of Ministry of Popular Culture, NA film T-586/15 et seq, and of Ital. press attaché in Paris, Amadeo Landini, T-586/148.
6. Dr Fritz Hesse, note on propaganda possibilities in Britain, Nov 23, 1938: Hesse papers, BA Koblenz, Kl.Erw.276-1.
7. Examples of PRO files closed for 75 yrs are T210/12 of the Treasury's Czech financial claims office (on the Weininger claim) and T236/729-31 general files on Czechoslovakia, 1939-49.
8. *Hansard,* H of C Deb., Jan 28, 1941, cols. 445-461. Indignant Liberal MP Geoffrey Mander complained: "Many of us are not aware of anything that has been 'going on for years'."
9. BBC Mon Report: Munich broadcast, Jan 19; ltr FO Central Dept to Prague and Paris, Jan 21; and reply, Feb 10, 1939: FO371/22903. Re *Cyrano*: T-586/145.
10. As Lady Spears (Mary Borden) put it: diary, Oct 3, 1938. Boston Univ. Library.

11. So Chargé d'Affaires Karel Lisicky informed Prague by 'phone on Mar 1, 1939. Dr R. Urban, *Tajne fondy III sekce*. ["Secret Funds of the Third Section"], *Z Archivu ministerstva zahranici Republiki Ceskoslovenske* (Prague, 1943); and Stefan Osusky, MS: Benes and Soviet Russia: Osusky papers, box 14: Hoover Library.

12. Eden diary.

13. H. Wilson MS, Oct 1941: "Munich, 1938," CAB127/158; Eden, i, 580; WSC spoke on Feb 17 to the Foreign Affairs Cttee of MPs, officered by Emrys-Evans, Nicolson and John McEwen (all covert Focus members.)

14. Grandi Tel to Rome, Feb 18: Ciano papers.

15. Sir John Simon, who put this to J.P.L. Thomas: Eden, i, 585.

16. Churchill, i, 231.

17. Beaverbrook to Bracken, May 11, 1948: Beaverbrook papers (C57).

18. Hankey to Phipps, Feb 21, cit Gilbert, vi, 904; Mrs Chamberlain to Lady Chamberlain, Feb 23: Templewood papers.

19. A.H. Richards to Spears, Feb 25, 1938: Spears papers.

20. Nicolson to wife, Mar 1.

21. *Daily Express*, Feb 25.

22. Kennedy to State, Tel. 184, Mar 4; embassy files. Given his central role in 1938-1940, the author has built up a comprehensive set of his unpublished despatches, from the FDR Library, the Cordell Hull papers (Library of Congress) and particularly the confidential, secret and top secret files of his embassy deposited at the Federal Records Center, Suitland, Maryland. His private diaries at the JFK Library are closed; Michael Beschloss, author of *Kennedy and Roosevelt: The Uneasy Alliance* (New York, 1980) was given access; as was JPK's friend James Landis: Landis papers, Library of Congress.

23. Morgenthau diary, Dec 8, 1937: FDR Library; Beschloss, 157.

24. Ernest Lindley, in *Liberty*, May 1938.

25. Kennedy to State, Tel. 185, Mar 9, 6pm: embassy files.

26. Tel Berlin to Ribbentrop, rec'd London Mar 10, 9a.m. The ballot text was: "Mit Schuschnigg fur Österreich. Wir wollen ein freies und deutsches Österreich. Ein unabhängiges und soziales Österreich, ein christliches und einiges Österreich. Wir wollen Brot und Frieden am Land, die Gleichberechtigung aller, die zu Volk und Heimat stehen." Loesch papers.

27. Churchill, i, 243. And interview of Frau Annelies von Ribbentrop, 1975.

28. See e.g., Ribbentrop to Hitler, London Mar 10, 1938: Loesch papers, T-120/622/318.

29. Ribbentrop note, Conv with PM Chamberlain after luncheon on Mar 11, 1938. (With no mention of WSC.) Loesch papers: NA film T120/622/323ff and T120/619/15ff. Cf Cadogan diary, Mar 11.

30. Bracken to Baruch, Mar 11: Baruch papers.

31. WSC to Unity Mitford, Mar 12: Gilbert, v, 911.

32. Chamberlain to sister, Mar 20: Chamberlain papers, and cf Feiling, 347f.

33. COS 697 (JP), draft, Mar 19: "The Military Implications of German Aggression Against Czechoslovakia." Cf CAB16/183; and COS 698 (revise) Mar 28 in CAB53/57.

34. Feiling, 347; and Cadogan diary, Mar 16.

35. Maisky Tel No. 103, Mar 24. A private Soviet source obtained for me Russian copies of Maisky's dispatches to the People's Commissariat of Foreign Affairs, from Soviet foreign ministry archives.

36. Published between Dec 5, 1937 and Feb 13, 1938 as "My Life and Times." In 1938 Harrap published his political pamphlet, *Arms and the Covenant*. Later in 1938 Harrap and Scribner declined to make any offer for his *History of the English Speaking Peoples*.

37. Baruch to WSC, Feb 8: Baruch papers.

38. Nicolson diary, Mar 16.

39. *Daily Telegraph*, Apr 14.

40. Maisky Tel. No.103, Mar 24.

41. Maisky Tel. No.121, Apr 8.
42. Beaverbrook to A.J. Cummings, Mar 16: Taylor, 381.
43. Ltr Prince Max von Hohenlohe to Hewel, Jul 25, 1940: Hewel papers. T-120/776/371063.
44. Beaverbrook to Herbert Swope, Mar 9, and to Frank Gannett, Dec 9: Beaverbrook papers. Prof Taylor (p387) calls this letter "deplorable."
45. Gilbert, vi, 919f: cit Churchill file 1/328. The actual debt was of £18,162, to stockbrokers Vickers, da Costa. When Strakosch died in 1943 he left Churchill £20,000 in his will: *The Times*, Feb 6, 1944, thereby effectively wiping the slate clean.

* * *

"LET'S WAIT AND SEE," SAID MAISKY: Page 105

1. A Nazi document reveals those methods: SR1787D, in Box 20: D Lerner papers, Hoover Library.
2. Cadogan to Henderson, Apr 22: FO800/269.
3. Grandi to Ital FO, Apr 2: Ital emb file 1272, Telegrammi per corriere: FO archives Rome.
4. Phipps to Cadogan, Mar 24 and 28, 1938: FO800/311.
5. Phipps to Halifax, Mar 28: FO800/311.
6. Phipps to Halifax, Mar 27: FO800/311.
7. See note 28.
8. Phipps to Halifax, Apr 25: FO800/311.
9. WSC to Cadogan, May 27, 1940; reply May 28. FO800/312.
10. Maisky to Moscow, Tel. No 111, Mar 31.
11. Gilbert, v, 898f.
12. See note 26.
13. Grandi to Ital FO, Nov 2, 1937: Ital emb file 1007.
14. *Evening Standard*, Oct 15; *Sunday Chronicle* Oct 17, 1937: cf Grandi to Ciano, Oct 15 and 18, 1937: ibid.
15. Spears to WSC, Mar 19, 1942.
16. Spears invited WSC to accompany him to Prague in April. Replying on Apr 25, WSC hesitated: "It might be embarrassing from several points of view. Let us have a talk about it when we meet." Spears papers 1/76b.
17. Spears memo, Mar 14: Spears papers 1/41; he sent it to Halifax too, FO800/309.
18. WSC to Deakin, Apr 4: Gilbert, v, 930.
19. FO371/22902; and Ashton-Gwatkin, memo, Feb 13, 1939 in Treasury file T210/236.
20. Steed to Spears, Apr 13: Spears papers.
21. Dalton diary, Apr 8.
22. Richards to Spears, May 21: Spears papers, 1/103; Steed to Spears, Apr 13: 1/316. Cf Henriques, 364; Spier, 141. *Headway*'s new editorial board in Aug 1938 was: Viscount Cecil, Lord Lytton, Lady Violet, Waley-Cohen, Angell, Gilbert Murray, Wickham Steed, and A.M. Wall. They published their first issue in Oct 1938 with a message from WSC wishing success.
23. Knop's material came from the Jewish Central Information Office in Amsterdam. This shifted in 1940 to London, as the Wiener Library, with subsidies from Waley-Cohen and H.M. Government: minute of Mar 2, 1940, FO371/24423; Wiener Library *Bulletin*, (London, 1964) No. 1.
24. Werner Knop, *Saturday Evening Post*, Nov 2, 1946. He identifies one sponsor as wealthy Labour MP George Strauss. Cf Knop, *Beware of the English!* (London, 1939) and *Germany's Economic Situation in 1939 and Her Challenge to the World*, published by Friends of Europe with a foreword by Capt Oliver Lyttleton — later Churchill's Cabinet minister Ld Chandos.
25. Grandi to Ital FO, Nov 2, 1937.
26. Journalist Dr Hubert Ripka, note in Czech FO, Apr 21, quoting ltr from Sheila Grant Duff, Apr 12.: in Václav Král (ed.) *Das Abkommen von München 1938: Tschechoslowakische diplomatische Dokumente 1937-1939* (Prague, 1968), 116f.

27. Grandi to Ital FO, May 10, 1938: London emb file 1007, rapporti politici GB.
28. Maisky, Tel.176 to Moscow, May 13.
29. Himmler note, Jun 17, 1943: "Habe dem Führer auf den Verdacht §175 aufmerksam gemacht." NA film T-175/94/5107.
30. Henlein quoted by Hungarian MilAtt in Prague, Eszterhazy, to Budapest, May 24: Budapest archives.
31. Lindemann's note is in PREM1/249. Henlein "offered to give his word of honour that he had never received orders or even recommendations 'Weisungen' from Berlin."
32. WSC to PM, May 15, reply May 16 (ibid); and WSC to Lindemann May 19. Cherwell papers.
33. R[ibbentrop], note for Führer, May 18: Adjutantur des Führers, BA file NS10/92.
34. CAB64/9.
35. WSC to R. Acland, May 26.
36. Thus Masaryk said to a British editor on Jun 22: "Don't forget that we, the Czechs, heard of these movements first from your people!" W.P. Crozier, *Off the Record — Political Interviews 1933-1943*(London, 1973) 75; and Gen Frantisek Moravec, chief of Czech intelligence: *Master of Spies* (London, 1975), 124ff. A Czech agent in London reported that the original "exaggerated" information on May 21 came from Capt Kettering, an SIS agent in the British consulate in Vienna (probably the S.I.S. station chief Capt. Thomas Kendrick); Kettering had reported to the MilAttache in Prague an increased movement of the German V Corps towards the Czech frontier, and sent a copy to London too. Prof F Dvornik report No.3469/38 to Prague Cabinet, London Oct 20: Dok 270, in Král, 286ff. Cadogan emphasized to Maj H.R.S. Massy on Oct 27, 1939 the "close relationship" between the SIS and Czech General Staff. FO371/22949.
37. Summary for Cab mtg on May 22: CAB23/93, fol. 325.
38. General Alfred Jodl, chief of the German high command operations staff wrote in his private diary on 30 May: "The Führer's plans have been changed as a result of the Czech mobilization of May 21, which occurred without any German threat or even the most threadbare pretext."
39. Nicolson diary, May 20.
40. Masaryk to Prague, Jul 14: Král, 150; and cf Krofta circular, May 22: ibid., 131.
41. Dirksen to Berlin, Jun 10: NA film T-120/914/382769ff.
42. German navy/airforce conf in Berlin, May 4: German naval staff file PG/33272.
43. Puttkamer Tel to OKM, May 24: PG/36794.
44. Order of May 27: note in German army 10th Branch files, Jul 23: T-78/300/1029f.
45. Capt Fritz Wiedemann note Feb(?) 1939: Wiedemann papers, box 604, fols.43 and 65: Library of Congress. Cf Beck note, May 28: BA-MA, N28/3.
46. Milch diary, undated but Jun 2-16, 1938: They would have some 3,051 Maschinen, including 867 fighters, 1,134 bombers, 162 transporters, 252 dive bombers, and 195 ground attack planes.

* * *

CHOOSING BETWEEN WAR AND SHAME: Page 117

1. WSC to A. Crossley, Jul 4: Gilbert, v, 953.
2. WSC to Halifax, Aug 20: FO800/309.
3. WSC to Spears, Jun 3: Spears papers, 1/76b.
4. Baruch to WSC Apr 28: Baruch papers.
5. Bracken to Baruch. Baruch papers.
6. Author's interview of Jack Leland, senior reporter of the *Evening Post*, Charleston, South Carolina, Nov 1979. He has the tape-recorded memoirs of the Madam at Georgetown. When she asked who the girls were for, Baruch's major domo advised: "Read the newspaper!"
7. Baruch to WSC, Mar 30, 1954: Baruch papers.
8. Ibid.
9. Ibid., Jul 22, 1947.

10. *Manchester Guardian*, Jun 3, 1938.
11. MS in Liddell Hart papers; and Cecil King diary, Feb 19, 1941 (lunch with WSC.)
12. Ripka is identified in FO371/30826 as connected with the Czech "information service" in Paris in 1939/40; he became acting foreign minister in exile. Bericht über Géspräche in London, June 21-23.: Král, 144.
13. *Daily Telegraph*, Jul 6.
14. Spears appointment book: in possession of Col J.A. Aylmer.
15. Masaryk memo, Jul 14: Král, 152.
16. Lindemann's note on WSC's Talk with Herr Forster, Jul 14: FO800/314; a 1943 translation is in Herbert von Dirksen's files: Nr.13, *Dokumente und Materialien aus der Vorgeschichte des Zweiten Weltrkrieges, 1937-1938,* (Moscow) 144ff.
17. WSC to Halifax, Jul 16. FO800/314.
18. WSC to Lloyd George, Aug 13: Lloyd George papers.
19. [Randolph Churchill]: Conv between "Monsieur de K." and WSC: FO800/309, fols 241ff.
20. WSC to PM, Aug 24, 1938: PREM1/249.
21. Adams spoke to them about the persecution of the Jews in neighbouring Germany and Poland. "It does not seem to me," he wrote Halifax on Apr 5, "to lie in the mouth of the Germans to talk about the wrongs suffered by their minorities in Czecho-Slovakia." FO800/309.
22. Steed to WSC, Halifax, Vansittart, Chamberlain, Apr 28 and May 5: ibid, and PREM1/249; to Halifax Jun 18: FO800/313.
23. Hore-Belisha denied the remark, but not convincingly: FO800/309.
24. Chamberlain to Halifax, Aug 19: FO800/314; cf Halifax at Cab Mtg Aug 23: CAB 23/94.
25. Cab Mtg, Aug 30: CAB23/94.
26. Maisky to Moscow No. 321, Aug 31; cf WSC to Halifax, Aug 31: FO800/314.
27. Cf Krofta's note on visit from Alexandrovsky, Prague, Sep 3: Král, 211f.
28. Maisky, 412f; WSC to Halifax, Sep 3 and reply, Sep 5: FO800/322.
29. Brüning to Daniel Longwell, Feb 7, 1948: Longwell collection, Columbia Univ.
30. Ltr Bergmann to Hull et al., Sep 9, 1938: PPF 5237, FDR Library.
31. Templewood, *Nine Troubled Years*, 301ff; Halifax at Cab Mtg Sep 12: CAB23/95.
32. WSC to Lord Moyne, Sep 11: Gilbert, v, 972.

* * *

HERE TODAY, GONE TOMORROW: Page 126

1.   Kennedy to State, Aug 31: US emb files.
2.   Harold Ickes diary, Sep 18, 1938: re Cabinet, Sep 16: Libr of Congress MS Division.
3.   Benes cit in General Lev Prchala diary, Oct 8, 1940: FO 371/30826.
4.   W.C. Bullitt to State Sep 15, 11am: Box 26, PSF, FDR Library.
5.   Luftflotte 2 study, Planning Case *Green*, Sep 22: in Dr K. Gundelach, "Gedanken über die Führung eines Luftkrieges gegen England bei der Luftflotte 2 in den Jahren 1938/39." On Nov 7 Göring called for an expansion by April 1942 to a front line of 14,600 planes including 7,300 bombers, 1,500 dive bombers, 4,000 fighters.
6.   Hinsley, i, 79.
7.   Nicolson diary, Sep 4; Duff Cooper's letters to Halifax, Aug 1938, are in FO800/309-10.
8.   Ronald Tree learned this. James Margach, *The Abuse of Power* (London 1978).
9.   E.g., in Cadogan diaries, Apr 29, 1938; May 3, 1939; May 25, 1940; intercepts of Joe Kennedy's remarks are hinted at in FO371/22827 and /24251; of Italian and US embassy lines, in the Tyler Kent file, NA, RG-84.
10. Dalton diary, Sep 19.
11. Dugdale diary.
12. Ibid., Sep 25.
13. On the afternoon of Sep 27 Göring's aide Karl Bodenschatz handed to British embassy official Ivone Kirkpatrick the blue-mimeographed Forschungsamt intercepts of Masaryk's conversations with Prague. Officials lined every reference

to Churchill in the margin, but the Central Department found no evidence of improprieties by Masaryk. Krofta denied the Nazi assertions as "typical of the method used by the German government." Masaryk called them "utterly untrue." FO371/21742, fols 223ff. From interrogations of FA officials it is clear that these transcripts are authentic.

14. Hitler, speech to Nazi editors, Nov 10: BA file NS11/28: cf his words quoted in German FO files, T120/32/29044ff: "There's one other good representative of his own country, and that's Jan Masaryk in London. He also put up a brave fight for his country."

15. Hoare to Halifax, Oct 17: FO800/309.

16. Ltr Duff to Diana Cooper.

17. O. Harvey diary, Sep 15.

18. See note 4.

19. Ltr Phipps to Halifax, Sep 10: FO800/314. Bonnet had exclaimed, "Toute de même il ne faut très pas que les anglais nous poussent à la guerre." Phipps to Halifax, Sep 16: FO800/311. Masaryk found out, and told Osusky; he also told Benes on Sep 17, and Massigli on Sep 15: Král, 227.

20. Phipps to Halifax, Sep 16.

21. NA films T586/148; and T175/124/9424.

22. Masaryk gave £300 to the Czech Committee in London, and mysteriously disbursed no less than £3,987 in the last six months of 1938. On March 16, 1939 (the day after Hitler invaded Prague) Dr Cerný, sent to London to investigate, reported that Masaryk had claimed to have spent the money "financing official obligations," had no written receipts, and refused further details. − Stefan Osusky, Benes and Soviet Russia: Osusky papers, box 14, Hoover Library; and Dr. R. Urban, *Tajne Fondy III Sekce* (Prague, 1943).

23. Gilbert, v, 976.

24. Kennedy to State, Sep 19: 6:00 p.m: US emb file.

25. Gilbert, v, 976f.

26. Král, 231f, 233.

27. Masaryk to Prague, rec'd Sep 20, 2.04 a.m.: ibid., 236.

28. Masaryk to Halifax, Sep 19: FO800/309; cf Harvey diary, Sep 19.

29. Cadogan diary, Sep 19; Masaryk to Prague, Sep 20.

30. Dalton diary.

31. Boothby to Spears, Sep 23: Spears papers.

32. Dalton diary, Sep 20. They were not pleased at this stiffening.

33. MS quoted by Gilbert, v, 978.

34. Osusky, testimony to Czech State Council, London, Mar 11, 1942; introduced as evidence in Prchala, Osusky vs. Bohus Benes and Another, FO371/30826; his hostility to President Benes is plain from his private papers, Hoover Library. Records in Czech state archives bear this out. Osusky first learned of this version on Sep 22, and challenged Benes for an explanation that day; he further challenged the Prague foreign ministry on Oct 10, 13 and 14, without getting either reply or denial. Documents Nr. 262, 265, 267: Král 280ff; cf *Le Temps*, Oct 11-12.

35. Osusky's testimony: see note 34.

36. WSC/Benes conv, in Taborsky diary, Apr 4, 1943: Taborsky papers, Hoover Library; Reynaud diary, Sep 21-2, 1938, Reynaud papers: NA Paris; Spears to Vansittart, Sep 23; Spears papers 1/245.

37. Reynaud MS for *News Chronicle,* Reynaud papers, 74AP27.

38. Nicolson diary.

39. Dalton diary, Sep 22.

40. Boothby to Spears, Sep 22: Spears papers, 1/245; Nicolson diary, Sep 23.

41. Walter Elliot, cit in Blanche Dugdale diary, Sep 23.

42. Krno note, Sep 23: Král, 249f; Dugdale diary, Oct 1.

43. Benes conv: see note 3.

44. Eden diary.

45. Eden diary; cf Cadogan diary, Sep 24.

46. Phipps to Halifax, Sep 24, *DBFP*, (3rd), ii, 510.
47. Dalton diary, Sep 24.
48. The others were A.P. Herbert, Boothby, A.A. Somerville, Gunston, Crossley, and Strauss. FO800/309.
49. Harvey diary, Sep 25.
50. Dugdale diary.
51. Ibid., Sep 25.
52. Lady Spears diary: Mugar Memorial Library, Boston Univ.
53. Carruthers to Spears, Sep 25: Spears papers 1/245; he suggested WSC, Cranborne, Nicolson, Boothby, Cecil, Emrys-Evans, Ld Lloyd, Duchess of Atholl.
54. Nicolson diary, Sep 26.
55. Lady Spears diary. One went to Crossley, who wrote that WSC had described his position as very simple: "Only a joint declaration by England, France & Russia could possibly save peace with honour." Cit Gilbert, v, 983.
56. Smutny memo, Sep 26: Král, 257.
57. Baruch papers.
58. Nicolson diary, Sep 26.
59. Nicolson, Ld Cecil, Ld Lloyd, Sir E. Grigg, Sir R. Horne, Boothby, Bracken, R. Law; Amery mentioned in his diary Ld Lytton and Sinclair too, while Nicolson noticed Macmillan and Spears.
60. R. Harrod, *The Prof* (London, 1959) 169ff; J. Wheeler-Bennett, Munich — Prologue to Tragedy (New York, 1948) 150; Corbin to Bonnet, Sep 30, in *Documents Diplomatiques Francais*, 2e., xi, 720; Harvey diary, Sep 26: "Preparations are being made for a broadcast in German of our point of view."
61. Lady Spears diary, Sep 27.
62. Grant Duff, cit Gilbert, v, 985f.
63. *Evening Standard* Sep 28.
64. Rendel memo, Nov 8, 1937: FO371/20733.
65. Nicolson diary, Sep 28.
66. Walter Elliot, heard it: Dugdale diary, Sep 28.

*   *   *

OUTCAST: Page 143

1. In 1937 Prague had sent Father F. Dvorník, a professor of theology, to conduct political intelligence in the west. His report and recommendations Nr. 3469/38 dated Oct 20 are Doc 270 in Václav Král (ed.) *Das Abkommen von München 1938: Tschechoslovakische diplomatische Dokumente 1937-1939* (Prague, 1968), 286ff
2. Chamberlain to sister, Oct 9: Templewood papers. When details of Benes' similar attempts in October 1940 to bribe Czech general Lev Prchala threatened to surface in court documents the FO refused to order the case held in camera, minuting on Nov 11, 1942 that it did not much matter if the attempt came out: "I do not think anyone will be very surprised. . ." Prchala diary, Oct 8, 1940, and the "dirty linen" file on *Prchala, Osusky vs Bohus Benes and Another,* FO371/30826.
3. Hankey diary, Oct 2.
4. FDR to Chamberlain Tel No. 572, Sep 28, 1:00 p.m.
5. H.S. Truman to Marshall, Mar 12, 1948; Acheson to HST, Dec 4; Elsey to Acheson, Dec 11, 1950: HST conf file, 37: HST Library.
6. Ltrs cited by Gilbert, vi, 987.
7. Ld Lytton, cit in Dugdale diary, Sep 29; Lady Spears diary; Lady Violet, Foreword to Spier op cit.
8. Nicolson diary.
9. Colin Coote, *Editorial*; Spears and Dugdale diaries.
10. Eppstein to Spears, Oct 7. Funded — apart from one 10 shilling donation from an unsuspecting subscriber — entirely by Masaryk, a "Czech Association" had begun operating on May 25 fronted by Spears, Eppstein, Steed, several Tory MPs, and other Focus worthies. Spears papers, file 1/95.
11. Nicolson MS, Portrait of WSC (1947): Longwell papers.

12. Masaryk to Prague Tel 1015/38, Oct 1: Král, 276; Cadogan diary, Oct 1.
13. R. Harrod, *The Prof*, 171f.
14. Masaryk to Prague, Oct 20: Král 298.
15. Dugdale diary, Oct 1. Also present were Ben-Gurion, Locker-Lampson and Namier. By 1941 Sieff was non gratissima to the Min. of Inf.: Ltr Smithers to Eden, Jul 22, 1943, in FO371/34198.
16. Dugdale diary, Oct 1; Dalton diary, Oct 2.
17. Bracken cit in Bruce Lockhart diary, Mar 4, 1943. Writing to Raczynski on Oct 7 Churchill called these events "squalid." See Raczynski diary, Oct 20.
18. Dispatch by Count Jerzy Potocki to Warsaw, Jan 12, 1939: Doc No.6 in German FO, *Polnische Dokumente zur Vorgeschichte des Kriegs—Erste Folge* (Berlin 1940), 15f.
19. Baruch to Potocki, Jul 18, 1944: Baruch papers.
20. Lady Spears diary, Oct 3.
21. Dalton diary, Oct 3.
22. *Hansard,* H of C Deb, vol. 339, cols 365ff.
23. The pupil was Eden, cit in H. Butcher diary, Jan 27, 1945: DDE library.
24. Nicolson MS: see note 11.
25. Boothby to WSC, Oct 10: Gilbert, v, 1003; and to Spears, Nov 2: Spears papers.
26. Gilbert, v, 1005.
27. Chamberlain to sister, Oct 15: Templewood papers.
28. Dalton diary, Oct 6. WSC and Duff Cooper were "out for Chamberlain's blood, and inclined to join with anybody else to get it."
29. Dalton diary, Apr 29, 1941 - confidential annex, a conv with O. Stanley.
30. Dalton diary, Oct 12.
31. Benes arrived on Oct 22. FO371/21588.
32. FO371/24292.
33. Nevertheless the F.O. discreetly investigated: Lloyds confirmed that S. was a well-established customer; that he had told them the box contained £3m; and that its size was consistent with such a sum. Hodza had sent the £3m out through Switzerland to a Mrs Stern, a mutual friend, who handed the box to S. to deposit; a few days later Mrs Stern withdrew it from the bank. FO371/21588.
34. Cf FO memo of Sep 25, 1939: Benes was unpopular in Slovakia, Hungary and Poland. FO371/22949.
35. Ltr WSC to Dafoe, Oct 11 (Dafoe papers, MG.30 D.45, Public Archives of Canada, Ottawa); Lady Spears diary, Oct 4; ltr Nicolson to wife, Nov 9; ltr WSC to Richards, Nov 12, 1938; ltr Beaverbrook to WSC, Apr 23, 1949: C88.
36. Beaverbrook to W.R. Mathews, Nov 10: Taylor, 386.
37. Reichspropaganda-Amt, circular of Oct 28: IfZ, 235/52.
38. Bracken to Baruch, Nov 22, 1938; *The Week*, cit. in Ickes diary, Jul 2, 1939; FBI files cit. Beschloss, 187.
39. Landis to JPK, Jul 2 and Aug 2, 1948: Landis papers: Library of Congress.
40. *Hansard,* H of C Deb., vol. 341, cols. 1987-2107.
41. Mary Soames, 279.
42. Bracken to Baruch, Nov 22: Baruch papers.
43. Sir J. Langford-Holt MP, interview, Feb 20, 1978.
44. Pownall diary, Jun 27; Dr Fritz Hesse, note, The Sandys Case, Jul 6: Hesse papers; Simon to Chamberlain, Jul 14: PREM1/283.
45. Nicolson diary, Dec 5; interview of J. Parker MP, Apr 12, 1978.
46. Col Hon Arthur Murray note on conv with FDR, Oct 16-24; Halifax to PM, Dec 14: PREM1/367; Murray to FDR, Dec 15 and 20, 1938: Box 53, GB-Murray.
47. *New Statesman*, Jan 7, 1939; *Picture Post*, Mar 11, 1939: the interview was at Christmas.
48. Halifax to Hull, Jan 24: *FRUS*, 1939, i, 2-6. Cf diary of Col Martin F. Scanlon, Asst Mil Att. at U.S. Embassy London, Feb 1: "For the last two months very startling reports have been received about Germany's preparations for a coup

between the middle of this month and first part of March. Holland, Belgium, France and G.B. greatly alarmed." US airforce archives, Maxwell AF base, Alabama.

49.   WSC to CSC, Jan 8.
50.   WSC to CSC, Jan 18.
51.   Scanlon diary, Jan 9.
52.   WSC to CSC, Jan 18.
53.   Vincent Shean, *Between the Thunder and the Sun.*
54.   Spears diary, Feb 10, 1940: he noted in the margin, *"Omit."*
55.   Gilbert, v, 1038.
56.   O. Harvey diary, Apr 3.
57.   Picture Post, Feb 25, Mar 4,11.
58.   WSC to Spears, Feb 15: Spears papers, 1/76b.

* * *

STILL HIBERNATING: Page 157

1.   Kennedy to State, Tel. 290, Mar 3, 1939: US emb file; and RG-59, Office of European Affairs.
2.   [General] Frantisek Moravec, *Master of Spies* (London, 1975), 151.
3.   That Maurice Hankey was informed about the telephone intercepts is evident from his diary on Oct 2, 1938. "There have been efforts," Hankey recorded, commenting on Churchill's Paris visit, "to give both the French and Czech Governments the impression that Chamberlain's Government was about to fall. "Bonnet, the Foreign Minister . . . has also protested against being rung up by Churchill and Spears from London for information. . . Van[sittart] remains in charge of all propaganda and is almost certainly in touch with Churchill, Eden, the Labour leaders and with Léger in the Quai d'Orsay, who is playing the same tricks over here." (Hankey Papers, 1/8: Churchill College, Cambridge).
4.   Forschungsamt report N.140098, g.Rs., Zu der englischen Politik vom Münchner Abkommen bis zum Kriegsausbruch: in Woermann papers, T120/723/323510ff; translated in Irving, *Breach of Security* (London, 1968).
5.   Reichspropaganda-Amt directive, Mar 13: ZSg101, Sammlung Dertinger: BA Koblenz.
6.   Osusky refused, saying he did not know Moravec. Testimony to Czech State Council, London, Jul 1, 1941: in *Prchala, Osusky vs Bohus Benes and Another*, FO371/30826.
7.   FO memo, Mar 16: FO371/22904. Among those listed by Steed was General Alois Elias; he was arrested as PM on Sep 27, 1941, confessed to spying for London, and was executed in May 1942.
8.   Leith Ross memo, Mar 23: FO371/22902; cf Treasury file T210/236.
9.   The government had made a £10m loan to Czechoslovakia, including £6m for economic reconstruction and £4m for Czech refugees; this resulted in one Czech family receiving £753,000 and another £537,000. T210/20 and FO371/24292.
10.   Weininger's bank statement is in T210/5. A Treasury letter of Sep 26, 1940 (FO371/24292, fol. 208) describes his compensation claim as fraudulent. File T210/23 is still closed. A handwritten note of Oct 21, 1938 in FO371/21588 links Churchill's Intelligence source Desmond Morton with Jan Masaryk, and Weininger, who "put Mr Morton in touch with the Czech Legation."
11.   *Hansard*, H of C Debs, Mar 22: vol. 345, col.1317. On Apr 1 he wrote to Weininger that he would be weekending with the Financial Secretary to the Treasury to apply further pressure.
12.   Dugdale (diary, Mar 22) was present at the luncheon. On Mar 18, in consequence of Tilea's warning, the Cabinet decided to make approaches to Romania *and* Poland: CAB53/10 and 23/98.
13.   Tilea told this to Milanovic, the Yugoslav minister: Forschungsamt intercept, Mar 21: see note 4. At the WO, General Pownall wrote in his diary, Mar 20: "It appears that the Romania story of the weekend was a big exaggeration on the part of M Tilea . . . No doubt he had instructions to keep us up to the mark but overdid it!"

14. Papers concerning Tilea's application to emigrate in Jul 1942: FO371/33265; one document closed until 2013. Citing his "anti national attitude" while in London, Bucharest withdrew his Romanian citizenship in Feb 1941. FO371/30016.
15. Ltr Chamberlain to sister, Mar 19 and 26, Templewood papers; Feiling, 402f.
16. Ltr Ismay to Wilson, Mar 31, 5:45 p.m., enclosing report by MI2(b), the German section of SIS, "Germany's Intentions Regarding Danzig, 30th March 1939." PREM1/331a.
17. E. Bridges to Cadogan, Mar 19, 1943: FO371/34482.
18. Colvin to WSC, Jan 4, Nov 22, 1938: Gilbert, v, 896f, 963. Through Churchill's personal influence, Colvin was commissioned in the Royal Marines. Morton to WSC, Nov 11, 1940. PREM7/3.
19. Oberst Curt Siewert, Aufz., Mar 25: ND, R-100.
20. Harvey diary, Mar 29; Colvin, *Vansittart in Office*, 303ff; and DBFP, iv, No. 566.
21. Iverach McDonald, *A Man of the Times* (London, 1976) 60f.
22. Nicolson diary, Apr 3.
23. H. Wilson study, Oct 1941: CAB127/158. Neville Henderson had written to him on May 9, 1939: "The blind faith of the Labour leaders in Russia is pathetic - or tragic. One is almost led to believe that they want a war for the sake of their own internal purposes and the Socialism which war, successful or unsuccessful, will spread." PREM1/311a.
24. Ltr Chamberlain to sister, Apr 13: Templewood papers.
25. See note 4.
26. Halifax also attended. On May 12 Ld Davies wrote him: "I hope I may be wrong, but at Winston's lunch the other day, you gave us the impression that you were not happy in your job." Surely Halifax's feelings had been outraged by Chamberlain's policies? Davies suggested he resign. "Do not lose the first opportunity of taking this step before the sands run out." Halifax replied that on the contrary he agreed with the PM on foreign affairs. FO800/328.
27. Weizmann to WSC, Apr 26: Weizmann archives, Rehovot, Israel.
28. Boothby to WSC, May 27: Gilbert, v, 1072.
29. Dalton diary, May 4.
30. See note 32.
31. Col Malcolm Christie, memo May 25: Spears file 1/74.
32. Ltr Grigg to father, Jul 1939: Grigg papers 2/4; Reynaud diary; Spears file 1/53.
33. Lippmann's notes cit in Gilbert, v, 1075; Nicolson diary, Jun 14.
34. WSC to Chamberlain, Mar 27: PREM1/345.
35. *The Times, Daily Telegraph, Yorkshire Post*, Jun 29.
36. Daniel Longwell pressed WSC for an explanation: ltrs, May 18 and Jun 29, 1954; in vain. Longwell collection, Columbia Univ.

* * *

TWO FISTED: Page 167

1. Bruce Lockhart diary, Jan 9, 1946, quoting G.M. Young.
2. Max Freedman (ed.), *Roosevelt and Frankfurter: Their Correspondence 1928-1945* (Boston, 1967); see James Leutze, The Secret of the Churchill-Roosevelt Correspondence, in *Journal of Contemporary History* (London, 1975), vol.10, 465ff.
3. Minutes of meeting, Apr 10, 1939: File 2621, Antisemitism: box 126, Frankfurter papers: Library of Congress. One participant argued that fighting a war of defence justified Jewish secrecy; another, that audiences would disregard certain anti-German films (identified in this document) if they learned that the AJC had financed them.
4. Cf Frankfurter to Prof Lindemann, Jul 18: Bowra wrote to the Prof Jul 13 that FDR was "almost our only friend in the world worth cultivating." Social Corresp., 1939: Cherwell papers; and Ickes diary, Oct 26: Library of Congress. Frankfurter's Oxford Ll.D. ceremony was on June 21; he dined at No. 10 on Jul 10.

5. Ltr Brandeis to Flexner, Jul 12, in Melvin I. Urofsky (ed.) *Letters of Louis D. Brandeis* (New York, 1978). Frankfurter noted to FDR on Aug 30 that the crisis had developed "by the clock," and reminded him that he had reported "that in London they had definite word it was to begin about the 21st." PSF box 150, Frankfurter: FDR Library.

6. Churchill, i, 321.

7. Ltr Henderson to Halifax, Aug 1. FO800/316; H.V. Johnson report, Jul 22: US emb file: Dirksen Tel. Nr. 227, Jul 3: Weizsacker papers, T120/234/169617. According to a US embassy report on the British Press in 1942, Kemsley shared Chamberlain's conviction that Hitler had no quarrel with England: "He opposed the Eden school as being pro-French and fought against Churchill's inclusion in the Cabinet to the end." FDR papers box 53.

8. Dirksen Tel. Nr.231, Jul 7: T120/234/169629; the Churchill archives declines to confirm whether he corresponded with Negrin.

9. Camrose notes, Jul 3: cit Gilbert, v, 1081f.

10. Still seething five years later, WSC ordered Bracken to investigate Henry Brooke, a director of Truth Publishing Company, suspecting an enemy plot behind these 1939 articles. Bracken to WSC, Jul 11, 1944: Beaverbrook papers, D422.

11. Ltr Rothermere to WSC, Jul 17: Gilbert, v, 1088; and Kennedy to FDR, Jul 20: PSF Safe File, Kennedy: FDR Library.

12. Ltr Hoare to W. Astor, Jul 11: Templewood papers.

13. Ltr Chamberlain to sister, Jul 23.

14. Kemsley, Notes of the Conversation with Herr Hitler, Bayreuth, Jul 27: FO800/316; Paul Schmidt's German record of Hitler's prewar meetings with leading Englishmen (Sir Thomas Beecham, Lds. Beaverbrook, Rothermere, Kemsley, etc) vanished from the captured German files: cf BA Koblenz, Kl. Erw.501.

15. Ironside diary, Dec 5-6, 1937.

16. Ibid, Jul 24-27, 1939. The disparaging views about him are in Kennedy to Welles, Tel.1140, May 8: US emb file; and Cadogan diary, May 17, 1940.

17. Ltr A.H. Richards to Spears, Jul 21 on paper headed "Defence of Freedom and Peace." Spears papers.

18. Czech memo, Jul 27: box 14, Osusky papers; and box 3, Taborský papers. Both in Hoover Library.

19. Ltr Chamberlain to sister, Aug 5.

20. Ltr WSC to Wood, Aug 5: Churchill, i, 344f.

21. Channon diary, Easter 1939.

22. Hans-Heinrich ("Johnny") Herwarth von Bittenfeld, 35, second secretary in the German embassy in Moscow, called U.S. diplomat Charles Bohlen round to tell him the secrets of the pact. Bohlen, *Witness to History* (New York, 1973), 69ff; cf Tel Bohlen to State, Jul 1, and Adolph A. Berle Jr, diary, Aug 24 ("We have pretty clear information" of the "secret arrangement") and Pownall diary, Aug 23.

23. Ltr WSC to Wood, Aug 30; curiously, WSC (vol.i, 357) dates his return from Paris three days later, Aug 26.

24. Diary, Aug 23.

25. Kennedy to State, Tel. 1221, Aug 23: US emb file.

26. Karl-Heinrich Loesch memo, Hitler-Henderson conv. Aug 23: Loesch papers, T120/622/405ff; cf *ADAP* (D), vii, No.200.

27. Raczynski diary, Aug 30.

28. Ibid., Sep 2.

29. Dugdale diary, Sep 1; ltr WSC to Chamberlain, Sep 2: Feiling, 420.

30. Raczynski note, Sep 6: op. cit, 29.

31. Ltr WSC to Chamberlain, Sep 2: Churchill, i, 362f. The author has also relied on the private diary dictated by the Chancellor of the Exchequer Sir John Simon, (MS Simon 11: Bodleian Library, Oxford.)

32. Churchill, i, 365.

* * *

A FOOT IN THE DOOR: Page 179

1. Eden diary.
2. Spears diary, Sep 3, 1939. The author has used the original text.
3. Dalton diary, Sep 15 and 25: London School of Economics Library.
4. WSC to Halifax, Sep 10; and Sep 16, Gilbert, vi, 31.
5. WSC to Pound, cit Gilbert, vi, 158; the warship was HMS *Baralong*; we do not know if the culprits were punished.
6. ADM116/4239. Sir William Malkin was legal adviser to the FO.
7. WSC paper, Dec 16: CAB66/4.
8. Colville diary, Aug 11, 1940.
9. WSC to Ismay, Jul 6, 1944: PREM3/89.
10. WSC to Halifax, Jan 16, 1940: FO800/328.
11. Alanbrooke papers, 3/A/111: King's College, London.
12. Adml. Godfrey, MS: Naval Historical Branch, London.
13. Churchill, i, 415, and 626ff.
14. Godfrey MS.
15. ADM199/1928.
16. Churchill, i, 416; Godfrey MS, vii, 365.
17. WSC to Secretary, Sep 9: Churchill, i, 663: and Godfrey MS, v, 111. cf Harrod, *The Prof*, 179.
18. Gilbert, vi, 59f.
19. Godfrey MS, vii, 303.
20. Pownall diary, Jun 13, 1938; Sep 3, 1939.
21. C. King diary, Jul 7, 1941: lunch with Frank Owen.
22. CAB 92/111.
23. Kennedy to State, Tel.1518, Sep 8: RG-84, U.S. emb (London) secret files: Box 2: 711-War.
24. Hoare to Beaverbrook, Oct 1: Beaverbrook papers.
25. Hore-Belisha, cit in Kennedy to State, Tel. 1666 Sep 15: U.S. emb secret files.
26. O. Stanley, cit in Hoare diary, Sep 8: Templewood papers.
27. Camrose note, Sep 11: in Gilbert, vi, 24.
28. Dalton diary, Sep 13; and Cab mtg Sep 21: CAB65/1.
29. Simon diary, Sep 18; Hankey to wife, Sep 19: Hankey papers.
30. WSC to Chamberlain, Sep 10: Churchill, i, 406.
31. Dalton diary, Sep 13.
32. Ibid. He had told Ripka in Jun 1938 one had to be stupid not to know how to handle Italy. Ripka: "Despite this rough language I had the impression Churchill had a soft spot for Italy." Král, 144.
33. WSC to Adml Fraser, Sep 9: cit Gilbert, vi, 18.
34. WSC paper, Oct 18: CAB 66/2.
35. Dugdale diary, Sep 20 and 30; and Weizmann papers.
36. Nicolson diary, Sep 26.
37. Ltr Kennedy to FDR., Sep 30: FDR Library, PSF file Kennedy.

* * *

NAVAL PERSON: Page 190

1. John Colville diary, Sep 28, 1939.
2. R. Cartland, ltr of Sep 26: in B. Cartland, *Ronald Cartland* (London 1945.)
3. The N.Y. Genealogical Society established this: H. Wallace diary, Aug 7, 1942.
4. WSC speech (in absentia) to Univ of N.Y. State, Apr 9, 1954: HST Library.
5. Ltr Kay Halle to Jim Rowe, 1959: Frankfurter papers.
6. C. Murphy memo on dinner, Mar 16, 1946; and ltr W. Graebner to Henry R. Luce, Jan 23, 1947. "You are, of course," WSC told Luce in Apr 1955, "the saviours of the world. . . All of us would have been flattened out by the Muscovites." C.D. Jackson papers, box 32, Churchill: DDE Library.
7. Colville diary, May 13, 1940.
8. Hoare diary, Oct 1, and Simon diary, Oct 7, 1939 (Bodleian Library, Oxford).

9.   Godfrey MS: Naval Historical Branch, Admiralty.
10. Mackenzie-King papers: Public Archives, Ottawa.
11. Ltr Kennedy to F.D.R., Sep 30: PSF file Kennedy, FDR Library.
12. *The Times*, Oct 2.
13. Kennedy MS, 461: in The Hon. James M. Landis papers: Library of Congress.
14. The "1939" file of the Chamberlain—Horace Wilson papers (PREM1/333) and forty-five pages of FO371/22985 spanning Oct 3-4 are closed; as are Hankey's Oct and Nov 1939 files, CAB63/84-5. But see e.g. Bastianini to Ciano, No. 550 of Oct 2, in Ital emb file No. 1054: a talk between Halifax and Ld Brocket on Oct 1 on peace terms — Halifax denied the war was to destroy Germany or even Nazism.
15. Kennedy Tel. No. 1892-3 to State, Oct 2: U.S. emb files and *FRUS* 1939, I, 45. Cf. B.E.T. Gage, FO memo, Sep 20. He added: "I believe that other information in our possession goes to show that Mr Kennedy . . . is not optimistic about our chances." FO371/22827.
16. *Boston Herald*, Apr 7, 1947; Beschloss, 206.
17. ADM199/1928; the declassified FDR/WSC correspondence is on six microfilms of FDR Library. WSC had sent vol.i of *Marlborough* to F.D.R. inscribed: "With earnest wishes for the success of the greatest crusade of modern times. Oct 8, 1933;" vol. iv was published in 1938.
18. Kennedy diary, cit in Landis.
19. Kennedy to FDR, Tel. 1936, Oct 5, four p.m.: FDR film 6/0266.
20. WSC to FDR, Oct 5, 1939.
21. See e.g., Hinsley, i, 141; and for examples, German naval staff war diary, Oct 1-2: PG.32022.
22. "*Aus bestimmter Quelle.*" *Ibid.*, Oct 1. On the attaché's question, Raeder would only say that his source "in neutral Ireland" was very reliable. Tel US naval attaché, Berlin, to OpNav, Washington, Oct 4; and war diary, Oct 3-7, 10: PSF, Box 201, FDR Library.
23. WSC's version of this is in PREM3/467, a Cabinet print of his messages to FDR, Sep 1939 - May 1940; for a British embassy telegram from Washington on the bizarre incident see FO371/23097.
24. See too Ickes diary, Oct 7. F.D.R. had gone to Hyde Park for an early weekend after his Oct 5 Cabinet: Library of Congress.
25. Samples are in RG-84, Series 4: "Records relating to . . . Tyler Gatewood Kent." One item in box 10, file 820.02 I-M, suggests that the British were reading American cypher traffic between Stockholm and Washington. Another item, in box 22, is the interrogation of the German prisoner Laun who worked in Ribbentrop's *Pers-Z* codebreaking section; in 1942 he saw intercepts of American dispatches stamped, "Seen by the Führer." (*Dem Führer vorgelegt.*)
26. Later the Americans paraphrased messages and used secure navy codes. Thus Harriman's ltr from Moscow, Nov 3. 1943 was paraphrased before being forwarded to WSC: U.S. emb secret files, 711-Moscow Conf: box 12, series 2, RG-84.
27. WSC to Halifax, Jan 12, 1940: FO371/24248.
28. Oral History, Rear Adm D.J. Macdonald, Aug 3, 1970: HST Library.
29. See Prof. Warren F. Kimball, "Churchill and Roosevelt: The Personal Equation," in *Prologue*, Washington, Fall 1974.
30. Gilbert, vi, 56.
31. I.M. Maiskii, "Bor'ba za vtoroi front: iz zapisok posla," in *Novii Mir* (Moscow, 1965) Jul (No.7) 185-210, and Aug (No.8) 166-187.
32. Cabinet mtg, Nov 7: CAB65/4; ltr Hoare to Lothian, Nov 11: Templewood, 409f.
33. WSC to DNI, Sep 6: Churchill, i, 655.
34. Godfrey MS, v, 39.
35. Churchill, i, 323: "In the purely naval sphere he [Hitler] had always been building U-boats as fast as possible, irrespective of any agreement." Godfrey (i, 284) comments that this was quite untrue; cf Hinsley, i, 63.
36. WSC to Pound, Apr 24; Roskill, *Admirals*, 310.
37. Godfrey MS, v, 259ff.

38. H. Nicolson diary, Dec 6.
39. Godfrey MS, v, 63. Capt Ralph Edwards (diary, Feb 21) called Winston's sacking of Danckwerts and "all the others in that Divn . . . a great loss & a great mistake." The handwritten diaries of the late Admiral Sir Ralph Edwards (1901-1963), who was Director of the Operations Division (Home) under Churchill are in Churchill College.

* * *

THE JOYBELLS WILL RING: Page 201

1. Ld Camrose, note of Sep 5: Camrose papers: Gilbert, vi, 11.
2. Spears diary. He pencilled in the margin "Best left out."
3. Mtg. Nov 3: ADM116/5458; trip report, ADM1/10250.
4. Prof to WSC, Oct 16: Cherwell papers.
5. Kennedy MS, 469f: Landis papers. After prolonged bargaining with Oliver Stanley, Kennedy managed to increase the Hollywood quota to $20.5m.
6. Kennedy MS, 482.
7. Kennedy to FDR, Nov 3: FDR Library.
8. *Daily Telegraph*, Nov 9, 11.
9. Kennedy MS, 485.
10. Cadogan diary, Nov 2.
11. WSC to Eden, minute M64/1, Jan 20, FO371/26542.
12. Guiseppe Bastianini to Ciano, No.640, Nov 13: Ital emb London file 1054; and ltr of Nov 14, ibid. and *DDI*, (9), ii, Doc.218; and Weizsacker memo, No.916, Nov 20: T-120/234/169846.
13. Reynaud and WSC appointment books.
14. War Cab, Nov 24: CAB65/2; and Gilbert, vi, 87.
15. ADM116/4239 and 205/2; and CAB120/418.
16. WSC to Pound, Oct 16: ADM199/1928.
17. Kennedy MS, 491ff.
18. Kennedy MS, 578.
19. Dugdale diary, Dec 5; Weizmann note, Dec 17: Weizmann archives.
20. Kennedy MS, chap. 38; Beschloss, 200.
21. War Cabinet, Dec 11: CAB65/2.
22. Jukka Nevakivi, *The Appeal that was Never Made: The Allies, Scandinavia and the Finnish Winter War 1939-1940* (Montreal, 1976).
23. Godfrey MS, v, 27 and 302.
24. WSC to Chamberlain: Gilbert, vi, 117.
25. WM 120 (39) 9; Cadogan, minute, Dec 21: Supreme War Council, Dec 19: FO371/23696.
26. MC 10(39) 2, Dec 20: CAB83/1.
27. ADM116/4471; and War Cab., Dec 22: CAB65/4.
28. Diaries of Hoare, Jan 2; Capt Ralph Edwards, Jan 5: Churchill archives: C. King, Jan 13, 17, Feb 2 and 27.
29. Australia's Robert Menzies cabled Chamberlain about this omission. War Cab, Jan 12: CAB65/11.
30. Gort to Halifax, Jan 16: FO800/328.

* * *

NOBODY QUESTIONS THE VICTOR: Page 212

1. War Cab, Feb 2. CAB65/4. A record of the interallied staff talks at Vincennes Jan 31-Feb 1 and other Anglo-French documents fell into German hands at La Charité. T120/115/117116ff and 119964ff; cf FO371/30944B on these documents.
2. Ribbentrop speech, Apr 27: German FO White Book No.4, 1940.
3. Supreme War Council, Feb 5: British text, CAB99/3 and PREM1/437; Ironside diary, Feb 5.
4. Ltr of gunnery officer Fox, Feb 7: Gilbert, vi, 148f.
5. C. King diary, Feb 8; cf ibid.

6.   Spears diary, Feb 10-11. He visited Georges twice at his Paris apartment, the General having left his G.H.Q. specially for the rendezvous. "Every time he was deeply affectionate and his regard for Churchill is boundless."

7.   German naval staff war diary, Jan 30, Feb 9 and 12: *Altmark* was a *Trossschiff*, an auxiliary, neither a "warship" (Gilbert, vi, 151) nor armed (p.154). See the study by the U.S. Naval War College in *International Law Situation and Documents*, 1956, pages 3 et seq.; and Borchard, "Was Norway Delinquent in the *Altmark* Case?" 34 *American Journal of International Law*, 289 (1940).

8.   Edwards diary, Feb 15; Halifax diary, Feb 15-17.

9.   Ibid., Feb 16; WSC to Pound, Feb 16: Churchill, i, 506; Duty Capt's account in Alexander papers, AVAR.5/4, Churchill College, Cambridge.

10. Gen. Geyr von Schweppenburg, ZS-680: IfZ. German accounts of the incident are in naval staff war diary, Feb 20, file PG/33730 and Woermann papers, T-120/40/34183ff.

11. WSC to Pound, Mar 25: Churchill, i, 692.

12. War diary of Gruppe XXI, Feb 21: BA Freiburg, E.180/5.

13. See FO371/24263; *Daily Express*, Oct 13 and Mar 10, 1939.

14. WSC memo, Feb 13; Lothian to WSC, Mar 19 and 30. FO371/24263.

15. *Daily Express*, Oct 22, 1942.

16. Dugdale diary, Feb 7.

17. War Cab, Feb 18; Weizmann to WSC, Feb 23: Weizmann archives.

18. Holma Tels Nos 254-5 to Helsinki Feb 29: Finnish FO archives: Nevakivi, 126.

19. ADM116/4471.

20. Halifax at War Cab, Mar 8; Gripenberg diary, Mar 7; and Halifax-Gripenberg conv, in CAB66/6.

21. Cf *Journal Officiel*, Mar 13, 1940: Daladier omitted the implied threat in reading out the text to the Chamber of Deputies on Mar 12.

22. Cf FO371/26542: 16pp Cabinet summary of principal German peace feelers Sep 1939 - Mar 1941.

23. Kennedy to US emb, Feb 9: FO371/24251.

24. Kennedy MS, 551. He wrote "very extensive notes" on the episode. Ltr Landis to JPK, Jul 2, 1948; and to Welles, Dec 4, 1950: Landis papers: Library of Congress.

25. Kennedy MS, 562.

26. COS Committee, Mar 11: CAB 79/85; and cf. Simon diary, Mar 13, 1939.

27. WSC to Reynaud, Mar 22: Churchill, i, 519. Cf Hankey's file on Royal Marine, CAB63/107.

28. Ulrich Kittel, a senior *Forschungsamt* official, recalled this in ZS-1734: IfZ.

29. Weizsäcker diary, Mar 13; Tanner diary, in Väinö Tanner, *Olin ulkoministerina talvisodan aikana* (Helsinki, 1950), 387; Ribbentrop (see note 2); Tel. R145 from Dr Pakaslahti to Holma, May 14, 1940: Helsinki FO archives, 109/C2e; and interview of Prof Jukka Nevakivi, London, May 1973.

30. Hewel diary Jul 5, 1941: Irving collection: IfZ.

31. Kennedy MS, 567; Welles' reports in box 9, PSF: FDR Library. — On Mar 13 WSC related to the War Cabinet he had told Welles: "Now that we have entered the war, we must, and should fight it to a finish . . . even though this meant putting all to the stake."(CAB65/6).

32. Kennedy MS, chap. 40.

33. C. King diary, Feb 8.

34. Kennedy MS, 578.

35. Kennedy MS, 572.

* * *

TIT FOR TAT: Page 225

1.   And, incidentally, that Mussolini was the greatest man he had ever met. Ickes diary, Apr 6, 1941: Library of Congress.

2.   Berle diary, May 5, 1940: FDR Library.

3.   Mackenzie-King: convs with FDR at Warm Springs, Georgia, Apr 23-4: "When Welles had a talk with him," FDR had continued, quoting Welles almost verbatim,

"he drank a lot of whiskey and made a speech of an hour's length to Welles. At the end of the hour's talking he had become sober." And diary, Apr 29 ; Mackenzie-King's papers, Public Archives of Canada.

4.   Oral History of Brig Gen Garry H Vaughan, 1963: HST Library.

5.   Ltr of Sir Charles Mott-Radclyffe to author, Apr 1978.

6.   Ltr in *Daily Telegraph*, Apr 10, 1981.

7.   Cadogan diary, Jul 14, 1940: Churchill College, Cambridge.

8.   Eleanor Roosevelt diary, Oct 23, 1942: FDR Library.

9.   FDR quoted in Ickes diary, Feb 20, 1943.

10.   Berle diary, Jun 10, 1943.

11.   *Washington Star*, Mar 8, 1958; In Beaverbrook's file C70 are pathetic letters from WSC's secretary Anthony Montague Browne thanking him for keeping stories about Sarah out of the press.

12.   Ltr Agent P.E. Foxworth to J. Edgar Hoover, Jul 27, 1942: FBI archives, Washington DC.

13.   Beaverbrook to Pamela Churchill, Dec 13, 1943: C87. According to a Danish study reviewed by experts of Harvard's Alcohol and Drug Abuse Research Center in *New England Journal of Medicine*, Oct 25, 1979, alcoholism is four times more common in the offspring of alcoholics.

14.   Ltr Sarah to Clementine, Apr 9, 1948 (unpubl.)

15.   Ltr W. Graebner to D. Longwell, Mar 9, 1949: Longwell papers, Columbia Univ., New York.

16.   Cadogan diary, Aug 1941.

17.   Ltr to Lester Pearson, Jan 23, 1952: DDE Library.

18.   Mackenzie-King diary, Aug 16, 1943.

19.   Mackenzie-King diary, May 19, 1944.

20.   FDR Cabinet, May 10: in Ickes diary, May 12, 1940.

21.   "He claims it is good for typhus and deadly on lice which thrive in those parts." Tel. Hopkins to FDR, Jan 24, 1945: Hopkins Papers: FDR Library.

22.   See note 4.

23.   See e.g. ltr from Gabriel Smith, Cdr (retd.) of Royal Norwegian navy, to John Renny, Feb 21, 1940 in Halifax papers: FO800/322. "We have behaved like damned blundering fools, the Germans have been liars and cheaters, but on the other hand not much good can be said for the British action."

24.   War diaries of Gruppe XXI, Mar 12-13 and German naval staff Mar 15.

25.   WSC to Halifax, Mar 14: FO800/328.

26.   C. King diary, Mar 20.

27.   Tel. Kennedy to State, Mar 19; on Mar 16 WSC also voiced concern to Gamelin that Welles might succeed: ADM116/4240.

28.   WSC to Reynaud, Mar 22: Churchill, i, 519.

29.   PREM1/437 shows that Daldier was expected. Spears noted on Apr 4: "Reynaud is completely at Daladier's mercy, and the way Daladier treats him is best shown by the fact that a quarter of an hour before Reynaud started . . . Daladier informed him that he was not going."

30.   Paul Stehlin, *Témoignage pour l'Histoire* (Paris 1964) 215; he saw the map. There was open talk of it in London. Cecil King diary, Feb 29. "Campbell saw Byron last night. . . We are intending to attack the Baku oilfields. The large force we have in the Near East is to be used for that purpose."

31.   Kennedy MS, referring also to evidence that agreement on the July date was reached on Apr 5: Docs 8 and 9 of the German *White Book* No.6.

32.   British text in CAB 99/3. Churchill, i, 519f; Gamelin, *Servir*, (Paris, 1947) 297; Reynaud, in *La France a sauvé l'Europe* 28ff.

33.   Resultats du Conseil Supreme du 28 Mars 1940; and Notes prises par le lieutenant-colonel de Villelume sur des conversations sur les evenements Avril-Mai 1940, in Divers: Reynaud papers: 74AP22, Archive National, Paris.

34.   Edwards diary, Mar 28.

35.   Darlan to Daladier, Apr 12: Daladier papers, Archives Politiques, Paris.

36. Thus his own memo on their conv., Mar 31: in FO800/312 and ADM116/4240; Cadogan diary; cf Captain Edwards diary: "If the French won't play with Oprn. R.M. we don't like R3."
37. See Note 35.
38. Amery diary, Feb 27, 1927.
39. Ltr Chamberlain to sister, Mar 30; Eden diary, Apr 1.
40. Ltr WSC to Chamberlain, Apr 1: Gilbert, vi, 203.
41. Cit Gilbert, vi, 206.
42. War Cab., Apr 5: 11:30 a.m. CAB65/6.
43. Colville diary, Apr 5.
44. See Note 35.
45. Tels Copenhagen to F.O. Apr 6, 00:25 and 14:17: FO371/24815.
46. Ltr Daladier to Chamberlain, Apr 5: Daladier papers, 3 DA 6 Dr 3.
47. WSC to Chamberlain, Apr 6: Chamberlain papers, Birmingham Univ.
48. Admiralty to Forbes, 2:20 p.m. Apr 7: ADM186/798.
49. Pound to Cunningham, Mar 30: MS 52560: British Museum; Roskill, *Churchill and the Admirals* (London, 1977), 296f; Edwards MS; summary in ADM116/4471; Churchill, i, 533.
50. Edwards diary, Apr 7: The author prefers the original diary to the bowdlerized version quoted by Capt S.W. Roskill, and adopted uncritically by Gilbert, vi, 166.

* * *

COMPLETELY OUTWITTED: Page 238

1. Darlan to Daladier, Apr 12: Daladier papers.
2. W. Hewel diary Jul 5, 1941: Irving collection: IfZ, Munich.
3. This was on Mar 28, 1940. Ribbentrops speech, Apr 27: Ausw Amt, White Book No. 4, 1940.
4. German naval staff war diary, Mar 30.
5. Report by D.B. of S.I.S., "The Scandinavian Invasion," Apr 14: PREM1/435. Cf Hankey to Wilson, May 12 about his inquiry into the S.I.S. and MI5, CAB63/91.
6. PREM1/435; and ADM1/9956.
7. Wilson to Chamberlain, Apr 30, PREM1/435.
8. Memo, Dep.C.I.G.S. Lt Gen Hugh Massy to Ironside, Apr 13, WO216/780.
9. German naval staff war diary, Apr 13.
10. Gilbert, vi, 215.
11. Hoare diary, Apr 8; cf Templewood, 427.
12. Summary in ADM116/4471.
13. Halifax, cit Kennedy to State, Tel.887, Apr 9.
14. Capt S.W. Roskill, *War at Sea*, i, 171.
15. Réunion du Conseil Suprême du 9 Avril 1940, in Reynaud papers, 74AP22; British text in CAB 99/3.
16. CAB99/3; and Reynaud papers.
17. WSC to Forbes, Apr 9, 7:14 p.m.: Gilbert, vi, 221f.
18. WO106/1875.
19. ADM199/1929; Edwards MS: Roskill, *Admirals*, 105. Official Historian Roskill found the signals in a guarded "cage" in the Admiralty Record Office; they are now missing, but incomplete typed copies are in ADM199/1929. All WSC/Cork/Mackesy signals are quoted from this file.
20. Roskill, *Admirals*, pp.100f identifies the signal's author as Mr Churchill.
21. ADM116/4471, and Churchill, i, 540f.
22. Eden diary.
23. The author prefers the handwritten original diary; Roskill, *Admirals* 102 quotes this as: "was half-cocked as usual." This bowdlerized text is adopted by Gilbert, vi, 231.
24. Edwards diary, Apr 11.
25. ADM199/1929.
26. WSC to Reynaud and Daladier, Apr 13. FO800/322 and ADM116/4471.
27. Gilbert, vi, 239.

28. Massy to Ironside, Apr 13; Ironside to Stanley Apr 14: WO216/780.
29. Comments by Ironside, CAB101/232.
30. Edwards diary, Apr 15; Bridges memo, Apr 25: PREM1/404.
31. Wilson memo, Apr 25. PREM1/404.
32. WSC to Chamberlain, Apr 16: ADM199/1929.
33. Bridges memo, Apr 25. PREM1/404; cf Ismay to WSC, Apr 16, ADM199/1929.
34. Colville diary, Apr 16; Bridges memo, Apr 25: PREM1/404.
35. Wilson memo, Apr 25, PREM1/404.
36. Edwards diary, May 8, 1940.
37. WSC to Ismay, May 26, 1946: CAB127/50.
38. Note initialled by WSC, Apr 17, 1940, 1:45 a.m.: ADM199/1929; and Churchill, i, 554f.
39. Cork to WSC, Apr 21, 22:29 hrs, rec'd 23:59: ADM199/1929; original in ADM116/4471.
40. ADM199/1929; and cf Churchill, i, 572f.
41. Reynaud papers, 74AP22; English ibid., and CAB99/3.
42. Colville diary, Apr 23: Gilbert, vi, 263.
43. Colville diary, Apr 26.
44. Keyes to WSC, Apr 30: FO800/322. he sent copies to Halifax, Simon, Hoare, Stanley and Chamberlain. PREM1/418.
45. Nicolson diary, Apr 30.
46. Reynaud to Chamberlain, Apr 26, 8:50 p.m.: Doc No.49, captured by Germans at La Charité: German: T-120/115/117196; French: T-120/127/119986; Corbin to Reynaud, Apr 26, 11:00 p.m.: No.50, ibid.
47. See note 41; and Notes prises par le lieutenant-colonel de Villelume: Reynaud papers.
48. Tel. Corbin to Reynaud, Apr 29: see note 46.
49. Ibid., Docs Nos 51, 52.
50. WSC to NC, Apr 30: PREM 1/401.
51. Reynaud conv with Chamberlain, Apr 30, 10:10 p.m.: see ltr SS-Schütze Fritz Lorenz to Himmler, Jan 26, 1943: T-175/124/9424ff; BDC file on Lorenz; *Völkischer Beobachter*, May 7, and Hitler speech, Jul 21, 1940. — A private ltr of Adm A.B. Cunningham shows that Weygand met him at Malta en route to Paris on Mar 28 — "He said [Reynaud] must have heard that he was very old [73] and sent for him to see if it was true." MS 52588, British Museum.

* * *

HENCE PRIME MINISTER: Page 255

1. Dalton diary, May 1.
2. Eden diary, May 1: *The Reckoning,* 96.
3. Hptm Deyhle, Gedanken über die Befehlsführung an erster Stelle, Apr 24: ND: PS-1781.
4. Nicolson diary, May.
5. Reith diary, May 3.
6. Dugdale diary, May 6.
7. Lockhart diary, May 1.
8. John Colville diary, May 1. He entered these thoughts that evening.
9. Ironside diary, May 3.
10. Ld Davies to Beaverbrook, May 3: Beaverbrook papers.
11. A.J.P. Taylor *Beaverbrook*, 408.
12. Churchill, i, 583.
13. Colville diary, May 3, quoting Ld Portal of Laverstoke.
14. This remark, commented one senior F.O. official, was reminiscent of pre-war days and unlikely to inspire foreign confidence; it seemed an easy way of earning dollars. — Macdonald to Halifax, Jan 16: FO800/321; and D Express, Jan 13.
15. Chips Channon diary, May 1.
16. C. King diary, May 3.

17. Alexander, quoted in Dalton diary, May 2.
18. Ironside diary.
19. CAB65/13.
20. *Hansard,* H of C Deb, cols 1086f, May 7.
21. Kennedy to State, Tel.1140, May 8: U.S. emb (London) file.
22. Dalton diary, May 8; *Hansard,* May 7: cols 1075-1198; May 8, cols 1253-1368; ltr Herschel Johnson to Hull, May 10, 1940; Nicolson diary, May 7-8.
23. Colville diary, Dec 12.
24. A.V. Alexander to WSC, May 20: ADM116/4471.
25. CAB79/4.
26. War Diary, Hopkinson Mission (Phantom), May 7: WOP215/1.
27. WO Daily Intelligence Summary, May 8: WO106/1644; the diary, May 7-9, of Lt Gen Brooke (II Corps) shows no hint of coming events.
28. Beaverbrook papers, C88: Churchill; and Kennedy to State, Tel. No.1148, May 9, noon: U.S. emb (London) file.
29. Edwards diary, May 9.
30. Eden diary May 9.
31. Amery, *My Political Life,* iii, 371; cf Spears, *Prelude to Dunkirk,* 131.
32. Ltr Butler to Halifax, May 9: file A4.410.16: Hickleton papers; Dalton diary, May 8-9.
33. Notes: in Taylor, 409.
34. Bruce Lockhart diary, Aug 16, 1946; and slightly different 1963 version by R. Churchill in Gilbert, vi, 305.
35. Eden Diary, May 9.
36. Cadogan diary, May 9; Margesson told Beaverbrook: A.J.P. Taylor, 410.
37. Kennedy to State, Tel. No. 1158, May 10, 2.00 p.m. His source was perhaps Halifax.
38. Eden diary, May 9.
39. Gilbert, vi, 302f.
40. Viscount Templewood, *Nine Troubled Years,* London, 1954.
41. *Hitler's War,* 114: H. Heim, Hitler's Tischgespräch, Oct 17-18, 1941.
42. Cit Gilbert, vi, 306; cf Lockhart diary, Aug 16, 1946.
43. Diary.
44. Kennedy to State, No.1158, May 10, 1940, 2.00 p.m. Kennedy predicted trouble over this. "This may result in another bitter fight while the world is burning." Earlier on May 10 (according to Dalton diary) Sinclair urged Attlee that Chamberlain remain until the crisis was past; he then issued a statement to *The Times:* "Recent events have proved the necessity for a prompt and radical reconstruction of the British Government; but the opening of the first critical battle in the West is not the moment."
45. Dalton diary, May 16: Bracken said it to H. Macmillan.
46. Nicolson, diary, May 10.
47. Diary, May 10.
48. Hankey papers. Under his long-prepared Operation XD, destroyers carried British demolition parties to Ymuiden, Hook of Holland, Flushing, and Antwerp. Each party consisted of 3 officers, 26 naval ratings, plus Royal Engineers: 12 for Amsterdam, 66 for Rotterdam, 24 for Antwerp. Memo by Hankey, May 10, CAB63/132.
49. CAB65/7
50. Greenwood's version, in Bruce Lockhart diary, May 15.
51. CAB65/7. The King (diary, May 10) felt Chamberlain had been treated unfairly and suggested Halifax as the "obvious" successor; Chamberlain explained why the King should send for Churchill.
52. Adm A.B. Cunningham, ltr to Aunt Helen, May 11: MS 52558, British Museum.
53. Kennedy diary.

* * *

ROGUE ELEPHANT: Page 268

1. *Dictionary of National Biography.*
2. Memo of Apr 25, ADM199/1929.
3. Colville diary, May 11.
4. FDR Cabinet of May 10, reported in Ickes diary, May 12. "Apparently Churchill is very unreliable when under the influence of drink," FDR added. "I suppose that he is too old." Library of Congress. When Kennedy (MS) tendered his resignation on Dec 1, FDR spoke of WSC's rudeness.
5. Ltr Hankey to Halifax, May 1, 1941: A4.410.4.5: Hickleton papers.
6. Ltr Hankey to Hoare, May 12, 1940: Beaverbrook papers, C308.
7. Dalton diary, May 16, 1940; and Bruce Lockhart diary, Mar 14, 1946.
8. H. Hopkins diary, *unpub.*, Jan 30, 1941; Mackenzie-King diary, Aug 30, 1941; King to WSC, May 12, 1940: Gilbert, vi, 316. — On Jun 5, Lord Halifax would record after seeing the King: "He was very funny about Winston, and told me he did not find him very easy to talk to. Nor was Winston willing to give him as much time, or information, as he would like. Much surprised and not a little disturbed at being invited to make Brendan Bracken a Privy Councillor."
9. Taylor, 411.
10. Dalton diary, May 14.
11. Ibid., Dec 13.
12. Gilbert, vi, 331.
13. Dalton diary, May 18.
14. Ibid., May 17.
15. Nicolson diary. Halifax (diary) was struck by Churchill's "chilly" reception.
16. Ismay, 116.
17. Reynaud papers, file: Télégrammes; ltr Corbin to WSC, May 14: PREM3/188/1. PREM3 files (Mr Churchill's papers) have been heavily sanitized before their release to the PRO.
18. CAB79/4.
19. Bullitt to State, Paris, May 14: box 26, PSF: FDR Library.
20. PREM3/188/1; Cadogan diary, May 14. Telephone message, timed 8:40 p.m.: Reynaud papers.
21. Bruce Lockhart diary.
22. Colville diary, May 14.
23. Kennedy to State, Tel.1211, May 15, 1940, 2:00 a.m. He concluded that WSC called in Eden, Alexander and Sinclair "and they are very low tonight although they are tough, and mean to fight." Box 26, PSF: FDR Library.
24. Kennedy to State, No.1216, May 15.
25. Bullitt to FDR, noon May 15: box 26, PSF: FDR Library.
26. Reynaud papers, file 74AP22; Seal's memo, PREM 3/188/1.
27. CAB79/4.
28. La Charité files, T-120/115/117019.
29. Beaverbrook replied, "The communications you speak of are a subject I have always fought shy of;" but respected Dowding's right to "hold fixed and firm opinions." C120. — *Sunday Pictorial*, May 31, 1942, article: "Did They Really Die?"; Mackenzie-King diary, Aug 18, 1943.
30. CAB65/7 and /13; cf Dowding to air ministry, May 16: Dowding papers AC71/17/2.
31. WSC to Reynaud, undated üMay 15ö, PREM3/188/1.
32. La Charité files: T-120/115/117018.
33. The author has used the original diary in Brooke papers, 5/2/1: Kings College Library, London.
34. Kennedy to FDR and State, Tel.1237, May 16, 6:00 p.m.: U.S. emb (London) file.
35. This from CAB99/3; the remainder is based on the French minutes by de Margerie (Reynaud papers) and by Daladier (Doc.No. 74 in German White Book No.8: *Dokumente über die Alleinschuld Englands am Bombenkrieg gegen die Zivilbevölkerung*, Berlin 1943.) Cf Reynaud, *La France a sauvé l'Europe*, ii, 98 and 131.

36. Around 10:30 a.m. on May 16 de Margerie briefed the Sous Directeur d'Europe that Reynaud had "chargé [his secretary] Monsieur Leca de centraliser toutes les questions relatives a l'évacuation du ministère." Daladier papers.
37. Dalton diary, May 28.
38. Colville and Cadogan diaries, May 16.
39. *FRUS* 1940, iii, 49-50; PREM3/468.
40. Bullitt to FDR, 6:00 p.m., May 16; FDR Library.
41. Gamelin tel to WSC, May 17, 9:25 a.m.: in La Charité files: T-120/115/117017.
42. Kennedy to State, May 17; WSC to Chamberlain, May 17, PREM3/188/2.
43. Dalton diary, May 18.
44. Historical Record of Signals officer in Chief, BEF, May 10-June 1, WO197/92; and Hankey papers, CAB63/132.
45. Cabinet, May 18, 10:00 a.m.: CAB65/7.
46. Colville memo, May 18, PREM3/188/3.
47. Brian Bond (ed.): Sir Henry Pownall, *Chief of Staff: The Diaries of Lt General Sir Henry Pownall*, vol.i, 1933-40. (London 1972) 328. Cf Ismay, Summary of W. Front, May 28: PREM3/188/6.
48. Eden diary.
49. WSC to FDR, Tel. 12,671, May 20: FDR Library; Map Room papers; also in *FRUS*, 1940, vol.iii, 51; and *Their Finest Hour*, pp.56-7; Colville diary May 19.
50. PREM3/468.
51. CAB65/7; Edwards diary, May 20; and Tel Swayne to WSC and Eden, May 20: PREM3/188/3; ltr Dill to Churchill, May 20: PREM3/188/6.
52. Major General Giffard Martel, history of 50th Div attack of May 21. PREM3/188/6.
53. Ironside and Colville diaries, May 21; Eden: *The Reckoning*.
54. Defence Committee, evening, May 21, CAB69/1; and PREM7/2.
55. PREM3/263/1.
56. Reynaud papers.
57. Reynaud diary, May 22: "10 h Weygand, 11 h Churchill, puis à Vincennes, Churchill et Weygand. Déjeuner, Churchill, puis Mandel arrive après le déjeuner." British text, CAB99/3; the French, in Reynaud Papers, was also among archives captured by the Germans at La Charité and sent to Hitler for his enjoyment.T-120/115/117004. Also, Notes prises par le Lt Col Villelume.
58. Reynaud Papers, 74AP22, file: Télégrammes.
59. See note 44.
60. CAB65/13.
61. Ulrich Liss, Chef der 3.Abt., Fremde Heere West: "Dünkirchen, gesehen mit den Augen des Ic," in *Wehrwissenschaftlicher Rundschau*, 1958, 325ff.
62. Pownall diary, May 23.
63. CAB65/7.
64. Note prise par le Président du Conseil, 23 Mai 1940, 16h50: Reynaud papers; 74AP22: Télégrammes.
65. Bock diary, May 24: he learned "dass an der Somme bei und südostwärts Amiens erhebliche Angriffe . . . im Gange seien und dass Kluge, der Oberbefehlshaber der 4. Armee, drei von der Heeresleitung für die Schlacht im Norden bestimmte Division dorthin, also nach Süden, habe abdrehen müssen." Bundesarchiv, N22/5.
66. King George's diary, May 23.
67. Pownall diary.
68. Ltr Reynaud to Pétain, 25 Apr 1941: FDR Library; and Reynaud papers 74AP23; and FO371/28570 and PREM3/186/A4.
69. Darlan letter, Jul 9: Reynaud papers.
70. John C. Cairns, "Great Britain and the Fall of France," *Journal of Modern History*, Dec 1955: pp.394.
71. Kennedy to State, Tel. 1344, May 24, 1940.

* * *

AN AVOIDABLE DISASTER: Page 287

1. WSC to Ismay, May 18: Churchill, ii, 49; Morton to WSC, May 18: PREM7/2; report by H.V. Johnson: "The Fifth Column in Great Britain," Jul 29: RG-84, US emb file, Box 3; and Cabinet, May 22.

2. RG-84, US emb files, Series 4: Tyler Kent, 1939-42; and Cabinet, May 22, CAB65/13.

3. Mackenzie-King diary, Apr 23-4, 29.

4. Memo, May 25: ibid, MG26, J13. The emissary was Mr Keenlyside.

5. WSC to Reynaud for Weygand, May 24, 5:00 a.m.: Churchill, ii, 61; also in Reynaud papers and captured La Charité documents, T-120/115/117004.

6. Reynaud Papers: Télégrammes.

7. Campbell to WSC, May 24: PREM3/118/6.

8. *Hitler's War*, 125. General Hanz von Salmuth, interrogataed in 1947, was one witness of Hitler's remarks (IfZ, ZS-133).

9. Reynaud to WSC, May 24, 9:00 p.m.: Reynaud papers: Télégrammes; Churchill, ii, 62f. The Germans later broadcast this message.

10. J. Martin private ltr. Jun 2.

11. WSC to Ironside, May 25: PREM3/188/6.

12. Spears diary May 25.

13. Cabinet, May 25: CAB65/7; WSC to Ismay for Nicholson, May 25: Churchill, ii, 73; Edwards diary; Nicholson, Calais diary: WO217/1.

14. Reynaud papers.

15. Churchill, ii, 75; L.F. Ellis, *The War in France and Flanders*, 148f; this is accepted by Hinsley, i, 143. WSC's source was Brooke: ltr, Oct 31, 1946: Gilbert, vi, 397, suggests that G.H.Q. read the documents "that afternoon." Not so.

16. Brooke made no reference to the "document wallet" in his *authentic* (ink) diary. After he visited 4th and 3rd Div., to discuss plans for the attack, "GHQ had another conference at 7:00 p.m. [I] found the atmosphere entirely changed and was at once presented with 5th division to hold Ypres-Comines Canal. They have now realized the danger I warned them about this morning. The penetration scheme [Weygand Plan] is temporarily abandoned." *Later* he pencilled two lines about it under May 25: "Collected German officer's wallet from 3 Div HQ with plan for German attack." In Alanbrooke papers (3/A/iii) is MI14's version, Oct. 1946.

17. CAB69/1.

18. Comité de guerre, May 25, 7:00 p.m.: Daladier papers.

19. Eden to Gort, May 25, seen by WSC May 26: PREM3/188/6.

20. Ltr R. Campbell to WSC, May 25: "The enclosed message to you from Léger has just been brought to me by a friend of his to whom he telephoned it from the country." PREM3/188/6; the message itself has been withdrawn, like much of this file. Horace Wilson would write in Oct 1941, "Léger was violently anti German, equally violently anti Italian, and he must bear much of the responsibility for the failure to take advantage of the opportunities offered from time to time by either Hitler or Mussolini for some kind of rapprochement." CAB127/158. For a similar view on Léger see Feiling, *Life of Neville Chamberlain*, 413.

21. 3pp undated draft, PREM3/174/4.

22. Agende, May 26: Reynaud papers, box 74AP22: Documents.

23. It is in CAB65/13 and PREM3/188/6; cf Ismay summary, ibid; and Cadogan diary, May 26. On May 27 Mackenzie-King noted, "Mentioned [to Malcolm Macdonald] . . . that we might very soon have the King and Queen themselves in Canada."

24. Eden diary.

25. WSC to Spears, May 26: PREM3/188/6.

26. Darlan ltr, Jul 9.

27. Churchill, ii, 73; Ismay, 131.

28. The intercepted order to a panzer division to attack Calais was shown on May 27 by Major General A.E. Percival the Assistant C.I.G.S. to Eden: *The Reckoning*.

29. So King George VI told Hopkins: HLH diary, Jan 30, 1941. "It strikes me," Kennedy reported, "this isn't going to improve the morale of the Dutch much." Tel.1197, May 13.

30.   WSC to Gort, 4:30 a.m., May 27: PREM3/188/6.
31.   Army Gp B, telex to OKH, May 31: Weizsäcker papers, T-120/155/126598ff.
32.   CAB65/13; Halifax diary, May 27, 1940. Major Thomas Ingram, the archivist of Lord Halifax's papers (now at the Borthwick Institute, York) has informed the author (Feb 1987) that Halifax evidently began dictating the intermittent journal for his family in 1940 when his children were dispersed and he himself had moved into the Dorchester Hotel. "These typewritten diary-letters, together with the 'secret' diary, were passed to me by Lord Halifax and are just as I received them." — Halifax appears to have related the Cabinet dispute to Kennedy: see Kennedy to State, No. 1400, May 27, 9:00 p.m.: peace moves were in the air. "Churchill, Attlee and others will want to fight to the death but there will be others who realize that physical destruction of men and property in England will not be a proper offset to loss of pride."
33.   Kennedy to State, No.1415, May 28.
34.   Spears to WSC, May 28: PREM3/188/6; Colville diary.
35.   Tel WSC to Reynaud, May 28, 11:40 p.m., sent by cipher telephone. Ismay papers, CAB127/50.
36.   Bruce memo, May 30: Morton papers, PREM7/2.
37.   Martin private ltr, May 30; Ironside diary, May 28.
38.   Spears diary; WSC to Spears, May 29: FO800/312.
39.   Personal, WSC to Ld Gort, 21:40 May 29: PREM3/175; and PREM3/188/6.
40.   WSC to Reynaud, May 29, 23:45. PREM3/175.
41.   Eden to Gort, 14:07, May 30: PREM3/188/6.
42.   Mackenzie-King to WSC, May 30: Mackenzie-King papers, MG26, Jl, vol.286, and FO800/310. He found the "difficult part" was meeting FDR's wishes "of having the message appear to be from myself rather than from him." (Diary).
43.   WSC to Mackenzie-King, Jun 5. PREM4/43B/1 and FO800/310; Churchill, ii, 128f; and Mackenzie-King diary, Jun 5.
44.   British text, CAB99/3; French text, "Conseil Suprême du 31 Mai 1940. — Discussions rélatives a l'évacuation de l'armee des Flandres." Reynaud papers: 74AP22.
45.   Reynaud MS: Comment Raymond Cartier écrit l'histoire, in 74AP27. "Ainsi, cent dix mille soldats français furent évacuées."

* * *

WE SHALL FIGHT IN THE HILLS: Page 307

1.   Thompson, 82.
2.   Dr Waino W. Suojanen, a psychologist, and professor of management at Georgia State University (ed.): *Management and the Brain*, (1983). As for the curative properties of stress, Dr Neil E. Kay and Dr John E Morley suggested to a Washington symposium that stress increased the body's production of natural opiates.—*International Herald Tribune*, Jul 30, 1983.
3.   Dr Paul A Rosch, president of the American Institute of Stress. Dr Joel Elkes, emeritus professor of psychiatry at the John Hopkins medical school, draws a significant comparison between drug addiction and stress addiction: "Risk-taking and extreme stress produce a pleasurable arousal," he explains, "followed by a feeling of release." cit. ibid.
4.   Diary, Mar 26.
5.   Quoted in Bruce Lockhart diary, May 29.
6.   Diary.
7.   Memoirs, 293.
8.   Spears diary, Jun 1; Darlan ltr, Jul 9: Reynaud papers.
9.   WSC Churchill to Spears for Weygand, Jun 1: Reynaud papers and PREM3/175 (from which many items have been withdrawn); cf Spears diary, Jun 1.
10.   Darlan ltr, Jul 9.
11.   Herschel Johnson to State, Tel.5258, May 17, 1940: US embassy files.
12.   Eden diary; WSC to Lloyd, Seal to WSC, May 23: PREM3/348; Weizmann to WSC, May 29: Weizmann archives.

13. Martin dairy, May 31.
14. Mackenzie-King diary, May 27.
15. Kennedy to State, June 26: "There was a disposition, as much as three weeks ago, even on the part of Churchill, to say, 'Of course we move to Canada and carry on the battle from there.' Everybody, however, since then gives me the same answer which makes me very suspicious. That answer is 'Of course we are not going to move to Canada; we will fight it out here.' "
16. Colville diary, Jun 1. cit Gilbert, vi, 449.
17. There are impressions of Chequers in the diaries of General Hap Arnold, May 30, 1942 and Harry Butcher, Sep 21, 1942.
18. Corbin to Reynaud, Jun 2, 7:30 p.m.: Daladier Papers; also T-120/115/117259.
19. WSC to Reynaud, Jun 3: Reynaud papers, slightly garbled; and PREM 3/175.
20. Dowding (memoirs) and other writers have mistakenly put this episode on May 15, when he also attended the Cabinet. The "graph" figures however only in the Jun 3 Cabinet minutes.
21. PREM3/175.
22. Dalton diary, Jun 3; Bevin also wrote an account of it in his diary, "while the memory was white hot." A. Christiansen to Beaverbrook, Oct 28, 1942: C38.
23. PREM3/175, note of Jun 3. Gallipoli evacuation figures: from Helles, 35,268; from Anzac and Suvla 83,048.
24. Dalton diary, Jul 23.
25. Author's interview of Norman Shelley, Dec 1981.
26. Pownall diary, Feb 9, Mar 12, Apr 10.
27. Ministère de l'Aire, Cabinet Militaire: Note pour le Général Tarnier, Jun 2: Reynaud papers, 74AP22.
28. WSC to Ismay et al., Jun 4: Gilbert, vi, 459f, 472f, 469.
29. Cadogan; and cf Colville diary, Jun 5: "Winston would like to send more than the experts agree."
30. Tel WSC to Reynaud, Jun 5, 4:15 p.m. PREM 3/188/1; Spears recorded on Jun 5: "Winston sent me two very sharp messages to Reynaud and later spoke to me on phone." Reynaud "took my stuffy wires well."
31. Colville diary, Jun 5.
32. The letter is in French files captured by the Germans, T-120/115/117036. Churchill replied to Reynaud on Jun 6: "Fighter aircraft. General Vuillemin's demand was altogether unreasonable and his letter made the worst impression on everyone and greatly increased my difficulties." — Reynaud papers, 74AP22: Correspondence Reynaud/Churchill. Reynaud summoned Spears to his Cabinet: "Very painful and difficult atmosphere," Spears noted in his diary, describing Vuillemin's letter as "incredibly impertinent."
33. Colville diary, Jun 6.
34. Tizard diary, Jun 4: Clark, *Tizard*, 227.
35. Spears to WSC, Jun 6: PREM3/188/3.
36. Ismay to Spears, Jun 7, and Reynaud to WSC, Jun 7: Reynaud papers, PREM3/188/3; 74AP22, file: Angleterre télégrammes . . . Mai-Juin 1940; and PREM3/188/1.
37. PREM 3/188/1; and WSC to Reynaud Jun 8, 7:55 p.m. Reynaud papers.
38. Cadogan diary; and Dalton diary, Jul 16, 1940.
39. For a rough statistical analysis, see Warren F. Kimball: "Churchill and Roosevelt: The Personal Equation," in *Prologue*, Fall 1974.
40. Tel. WSC to Smuts, Jun 9: PREM3/43B/1.
41. WSC to Ld Lothian, Jun 9: FO371/24239.
42. Reynaud papers, 74AP22.
43. Colville diary Jun 10.
44. Kennedy to State, Tel. 1579, Jun 10, 9:00 p.m.
45. Ickes diary, Jun 5.
46. Beaverbrook to Hoare, Jun 11: C308.
47. French text, "Proces-verbal de la séance du Conseil Suprème tenue au Château du Muguet, près de Briare, le 11/6/1940," in Reynaud papers, 74AP22; and Reynaud diary. British minutes in CAB99/3; and see Sir Ronald Campbell's despatch to Halifax,

Jun 27, 1940; transcripts of all these meetings were extracted by the Spanish from the luggage of Reynaud's fleeting staff, and copied for the Nazis.

48. Tel DDE to WSC, Dec 14, 1942, quoting ltr Darlan to WSC Dec 4, 1942.
49. Reynaud papers: 74AP22.
50. Tel. WSC to FDR, No. 1622, Jun 12, 9:00 p.m.
51. Tel Kennedy to State, No. 1603, 2:00 p.m. Jun 12: FDR Library.
52. Colville diary, Jun 12.

* * *

BREAKNECK: Page 323

1. WSC to FDR, in Tel Kennedy to State, No.1628, Jun 13: US emb file. Gilbert wrongly dates this Jun 11 and applies it to Churchill's previous trip.
2. English minutes are in Reynaud papers, file 74AP27; and CAB99/3. Three French participants wrote accounts: Reynaud; Baudouin, first in a memoire titled, "A propros d'un nouveau livre de M. Kammerer" and then in, " *Neuf mois de Gouvernement*"; de Margerie, R's directeau du Cabinet, took an almost verbatim note: in 74AP27. Cf Kennedy to State, Tel. 1650, Jun 14: WSC to Dominion high commissioners, Jun 14, 5:00 a.m. FO800/310; and Beaverbrook memo, Sep 11, 1946: D480.
3. In German captivity Reynaud often recalled those words, *"in her power and her dignity"* e.g. in ltr to Pétain, Apr 23, 1941: in Reynaud papers and PSF Box 34, Biddle: FDR Library. Leahy had sent copies to Washington. Reading them, Churchill ordered them circulated to the Cabinet: "Pray God we never get in such a jam! . . They vindicate us before history. W.S.C. 8.vii." He wanted them published but, to protect Reynaud, the Americans declined. (Churchill however used the "neck wrung like a chicken" quotation in his Ottawa speech.) FO371/28570.
4. Spears, *Assignment to Catastrophe*, ii, 215. Spears is not always reliable. As Reynaud later commented, "Le General Spears . . . est devenu avant d'écrire ses mémoires, l'adversaire de la France, malveillant pour tous les Français, moi compris, du fait du conflit franco-britannique en Orient, auquel il a pris part." Reynaud, MS: in 74AP27.
5. Spears diary, citing M Dejean: Spears papers, 2/18.
6. Deposition by Weygand, proces de Riom. And *Témoignages, l'Armistice*, (Paris, 1944, Edition de Minuit.)
7. Sent at one p.m. Washington time, Jun 13; cf Berle diary, Jun 13. Churchill told the Cabinet, according to Halifax's diary: "If he will consent to have this published, it pretty well commits America to war."
8. CAB65/7. Kennedy takes the credit for this. "The call came through while he was with Churchill and he persuaded Roosevelt to withdraw it [the permission to publish] in Churchill's presence. Said Churchill hated him from then on." — Herbert Hoover, memo dated Apr 19, 1945: Hoover Library. But Berle's diary makes Hull's role plain.
9. PREM3/468.
10. Eden diary, Dec 19.
11. State Tel. No.1643, [Jun 13], 1 p.m. "In no sense was it intended to commit . . . this Government to the slightest military activities."
12. Kennedy to FDR, Tel. 1649, Jun 14: embassy file, and PSF file: Kennedy.
13. Prof to WSC, Jun 13: Cherwell Papers, Nuffield College, Oxford; J Martin ltr, Jun 13.
14. CAB65/13.
15. Bryant, 172-3.
16. Colville diary, Jun 14.
17. FO800/310.
18. Colville diary, Jun 15. The message was despatched at 3:15 a.m., Jun 16. PREM4/43B/1.
19. Mary Soames, *Clementine Churchill* 229; CSC to Prof, Apr 3, 1941; Cherwell papers.
20. Colville diary; and Tel Campbell to F.O. Jun 15, PREM3/468.
21. Colville diary, Jun 15.

22. Notes de Louis Marin: Reynaud papers, Divers, 74AP22; Reynaud diary; Tel. Bullitt to FDR, Jun 16, 1:00 a.m.

23. Diary.

24. CAB65/13.

25. Halifax to Campbell, Jun 16.

26. "Conversations téléphoniques enrégistrées à Bordeaux pendant les journées du 15 au 17 juin 1940 au Palais Gallien." In 74AP22: file Divers. Charles Eade pointed out to Reynaud in May 1953 that in *Le Proces du Marshall Pétain*, (i, 97) he had called these intercepts false.

27. On Jun 16 Lt Col Villelume noted, "Tard dans la soirée, le général de Gaulle revient de Londres. Il revele . . . qu'il est avec Jean Monnet, l'auteur du projet, et que c'est lui qui l'a fait accepter par Churchill."

28. MI5 were shadowing her and reported she exerted "a dominating influence over the Free French delegation" in Britain: RG-84, US emb London, secret files: file 820.02.

29. CAB65/7. Text of the Proclamation from Roosevelt's files: Film 1, 0099f.

30. Hankey to Halifax, Jun 22; reply, Jun 23: FO800/312.

31. Edwards diary, Jun 16. Louis Marin recorded the events of that afternoon: "A 17 h Reynaud annonce que la Note de 12h 30 est retirée. Il lit le nouveau texte anglais apporte par Campbell à 3h 30. Ybar et Pomaret déclarent qu'ils ne veulent pas être sujets anglais. Chautemps: Le texte donne lieu à des observations. Le projet est écarte. Chautemps reparle de l'armistice et de la nécessité de provoquer un choc psychologique sur l'opinion . . . Pour justifier la résistance devant l'opinion, il faut connaî tre les buts de l'Allemagne. . . Un ministre suggère une nouvelle tentative auprès des Anglais pour être rélevés de la parole donnée. Reynaud repond: "C'est un autre qu moi qui fera cette démarche." . . Louis Marin rappelle la parole donnée et le devoir de la respecter. Il demande à Reynaud s'il juge que l'honneur de la France est engagé avec sa parole. Reynaud: Parfaitement — totalement." He resigned, noting in his papers: *"La majorité se prononce par Chautemps sans attacher grande importance a l'offre anglaise. J'annonce mon demission."* Reynaud papers: Louis Marin notes. Ltrs Reynaud to Pétain, April 5 and 23, 1941: Reynaud papers and Campbell despatch.

* * *

THE DIEHARD: Page 334

1. Hewel papers. Some items were retyped on Hitler's special typewriter.

2. In 1946 and 1964. Prytz revealed it in 1965. *Der Spiegel*, Nr.40/1965; *The Times*, Oct 10, 1965; and Prytz's obituary, *D. Telegraph*, Jul 30, 1976.

3. The Italian minister in Stockholm Francesco Fransoni, reported this urgently at 7:30 a.m. to Ciano: "The British representative [Sir Victor Mallet] requested an interview with the Swedish foreign minister and notified him that the British government is inclined to enter into peace negotiations with Germany and Italy. The Secretary General of the foreign ministry here immediately informed me and in reply to my inquiry confirmed specifically that this declaration by the British representative is of official character." — *Documenti Diplomatici Italiani*, 9, v, No.47, Jun 18; cf No.48, Jun 21 (evidently intercepted by German codebreakers: naval staff war diary, Jun 22). Sweden notified her envoy in Berlin, Arvid Richert; and on Jun 22 he related this to von Weizsäcker. — Aufzeichnung Nr.454, June 19: *Akten zur Deutschen Auswärtigen Politik*, Series D IX Dok.487.

4. Swedish foreign minister Christian Gunther showed it to Mallet on Jun 19, and asked — no doubt to satisfy inquiries from Berlin — precisely how it was to be interpreted. Tel. Mallet to FO, No.743, Jun 19: FO800/322. The relevant paras. are blanked out in CAB65/7.

5. WSC to Halifax, Jun 25, and reply, shielding Butler: FO800/322.

6. György Barcza, unpubl. memoirs, MS, in Hoover Library, box 1: chap.xix, "Churchill az uj miniszterelnök," pp. 206f.

7. Dowding to WSC, Jun 17: cit Gilbert, vi, 564; Ld Halifax diary, Feb 8, 1941, and ltr to Simon, Mar 25, 1941: Hickleton papers, A4.410.4.14.

8.   WSC to Campbell Jun 17: Reynaud papers; and A.V. Alexander's memo on WSC's meeting with Pound Jun 17: Alexander papers.

9.   Kennedy to State, Jun 17, 8:00 p.m. US emb London file.

10.   BBC Written Archives. The speech was heard in North America at three p.m. — Harold Nicolson ltr, June 17 (dated "Jun 19" by Gilbert, with consequential misidentification of the broadcast concerned.); and Cecil King diary, Jun 18.

11.   Colville and Dalton diaries, Jun 18.

12.   Norman Shelley, interview, Dec 1979; J Martin ltr, Jun 21.

13.   Colville diary, Jun 18.

14.   Martin MS: Colville diary, Jun 27.

15.   Cadogan diary, Jun 19; C King diary, Jun 21.

16.   Tels Künsberg to Ribbentrop, Jun 24: T-120/127/119648; and Abetz to Ribbentrop, Sep 18: /119890.

17.   To Edwards (diary, Jun 23) this was "a first class blunder. . . This when we're doing our damndest to bring away troops."

18.   Tel Stohrer to Ribbentrop, Jun 27: T-120/127/119655.

19.   WSC to Duke, Sep 6, 1939; in *Sunday Express*, Mar 12, 1967.

20.   *Sunday Express*, Mar 12, 1967. Many Windsor documents in Halifax's file FO800/327 have been closed.

21.   Tel Hoare to WSC, No.437, Madrid Jun 27: closed.

22.   On Jun 28 the Italian chargé d'affaires told Ciano that the Duke had told the Spanish foreign ministry he had "no intention of returning to Great Britain," despite Churchill's pressure on him; he had confidentially asked the Italian government to take good care of his Cap d'Antibes villa. On Jul 3, explaining the couple's move to Lisbon, the same Italian reported: "They intend however to prevaricate and possibly remain on the Continent." (Italian diplomatic archives.)

23.   WSC to Daniel Longwell, Jan 26, 1946: Longwell Collection, Columbia univ.; Lockhart diary, Feb 16, 1946.

24.   It was to the Tories' good fortune that although arrested in April 1945 John Amery would be held outside England until after the July elections contested by Leo and Julian. He had made pro-Nazi and antisemitic broadcasts from Berlin (Bruce Lockhart diary, Nov 21, 1942) and tried to recruit British prisoners for a Legion of St George to fight the Russians. See PREM8/122.

25.   WSC to Mackenzie-King, Jun 24: PREM 4/43/B/1.

26.   WSC to Halifax, Jun 28.

27.   Cit in Gilbert, vi, 584f.

28.   CSC to WSC, Jun 27: in Soames, 291.

29.   Colville diary, Jun 25.

30.   Beaverbrook to A.V. Alexander May 30, 1955, and replies: C2. In general, ADM186/800: *Operations Against the French Fleet at Mers-el-Kébir*; Pound's file, ADM205/4; and Hinsley, i, 150ff.

31.   Ltr Marshall to FDR, Jul 11, 1942: Hopkins papers, FDR Library.

32.   *The Scotsman*, Jul 12, 1923.

33.   E.g., he directed Ismay on Aug 3, 1941, that "an assortment of Boniface" should be flown over to the Atlantic conference in a weighted case in case the plane came down at sea. Beaverbrook papers, D122. Cf too COS tel, Jun 28, 1943 referring to that day's "Boniface" revealing Hitler's intentions in the Mediterranean: tel Marshall to DDE, Jun 30: DDE Library.

34.   See Ismay to WSC, May 13, 1942: PREM4/7/8. At the Washington NA (RG-457) is a Special Research History (SRH-005) evidently of British provenance, "The Use of CX/MSS Ultra by the United States War Department": The text declassified by the National Security Agency blanks-out every reference to the British part of the project. — That Eden was not receiving Ultra: cf WSC to Ismay, Oct 16, 1940: Gilbert, vi, 849.

35. WSC to FDR, Feb 25, 1942: FDR Library, PSF Safe File.
36. An untitled manuscript by Cdr Denniston on breaking diplomatic and other codes is in his papers, DENNI/4, at Churchill College; and see Note 47 to Chapter, "Gangster Methods."
37. SRH-145: U.S. War Dept, Report of Technical Mission to England, Apr 11, 1941: NA., RG-457.
38. Prof to WSC Jun 13 and 17: Cherwell papers; R.V. Jones, interview, May 1978; memoirs, *Most Secret War*, London 1978; A Sci (I) Report No.5, May 23, 1940: Indications of New German Weapons to be Used against England: AIR20/1623.
39. Jebb: Present Conditions in Germany, May 30: PREM3/193/6A.
40. Edwards diary, Jun 18-Jul 2: Forbes returned "a damned rude reply."
41. Kennedy to State, Tels 1715, Jun 18; and 1777, Jun 21.
42. Macdonald briefed Kennedy so that he could inform Roosevelt. Kennedy to State, Tels 1847, Jun 26: and 2001, Jul 5.

* * *

A MISUNDERSTANDING BETWEEN FRIENDS: Page 347

1. C.D. Jackson log: conv with H. Macmillan, Jun 10, 1958: DDE Library.
2. *Sunday Express*, Jul 10, 1966; and see *Yorkshire Post*, Jul 20, 1946.
3. Eden diary.
4. Tel Leahy to FDR, Aug 1, 1941: FDR Library.
5. Spears, 218f. The misunderstanding was widespread. Sir Ronald Campbell reported to Halifax (Jun 27) that WSC had said that "he understood that in her desperate plight" France might be forced to lay down her arms: FDR Library: PSF Box 46. U.S. ambassador Tony Biddle informed FDR (Jul 1) that WSC had told Reynaud that "they would understand France's position."PSF Box 41.
6. On Mers-el-Kébir: Pound's file, ADM205/4; naval staff history, ADM186/800; cf Hinsley, i, 150ff. Signals in PREM3/179/1 and /4; and in Adm. Cunningham papers, British Museum; MS 52566.
7. Hitler's naval conf, Jun 20: PG/32184 and 31762b; author's interview of Konteradmiral Karl-Jesko von Puttkamer, his naval adjutant, 1967.
8. Armistice: German in Handakten Ritter, T-120/733/280529ff; French in *La Délégation Française auprès de la Commission Allemande d'Armistice* (Paris, 1947) i; cf Hermann Böhme, *Entstehung und Grundlagen des Waffenstillstandes von 1940*, Stuttgart 1960; — To his credit, Professor Hinsley, (i, 151) uses "supervision," not "control".
9. Halifax memo, Jun 23: in PREM3/174/1.
10. Cazalet diary, Jul 5:Halifax claimed it was "almost impossible" to get five minutes conversation with WSC. In fact he saw WSC on Jul 3, 5 and 8: the PM's card shows he found time for Cazalet and ghost author Deakin on Jul 2; for Ian Colvin on Jul 5; he lunched with endless peers.
11. A. Bevan, cit in Bruce Lockhart diary, Jul 4.
12. Cordell Hull memoirs.
13. Beaverbrook memo, Sep 11, 1946: D480; and ltr to Alexander, Jun 16, 1955, D325.
14. Bracken, quoted by Chips Channon diary, Jun 25; and John Martin diary, June 24.
15. Ltr Alexander to Beaverbrook, Jun 1955.
16. Beaverbrook to Prof G.S. Graham, Oct 21, 1958: Graham papers: Public Archives of Canada, Ottawa.
17. Beaverbrook memo, Jun 27: Taylor, 439.
18. WSC to Beaverbrook, Jul 1: C88.
19. Marshall memo, Jun 27: Langer & Gleason, 568.
20. WSC to Lothian, Jun 28: Gilbert, vi, 607.
21. WSC to Baruch, Jun 28: Baruch papers.
22. Colville diary, Jun 29.
23. Martin ltr Jun 30.

24.   Maisky, 597; and memo of Jun 10, 1941.
25.   Colville diary, Jul 3.
26.   Cordell Hull memoirs.
27.   Cunningham to aunt, Helen Browne, Jul 18; Sep 9, 1940 ("I never approved of the Oran business & got rather unpopular saying so") and Feb 10, 1941 ("He's a rascal but he's a great leader") MS 52558.
28.   Martin MS and diary; Raymond Lee, diary, Jul 4; Seal to his wife, Jul 5 (Gilbert, vi, 642); Herschel Johnson to Hull, Jul 5; Channon diary, Jul 4.
29.   Duff Cooper told Cecil King in August that Churchill was "quite unaware of his power in the country and strangely afraid of the Tory majority in the House . . . any attempt by the H of C to turn Churchill out would result in the House of Commons being burnt to the ground." Diary, Aug 7.
30.   Dalton diary, Jul 4.
31.   Cttee on French Resistance, Jul 12, Aug 7: PREM7/8. Muselier to WSC, Sep 21; on Oct 4 Morton drafted a reply expressing WSC's sorrow at the killing of the French "comrades in arms" and promising eventual compensation. PREM7/3.
32.   Tel. Alexander Weddell to State, Jul 2: *FRUS 1940* iii, 41; cf Stohrer to Berlin, Jul 2, *ADAP* D X Dok.86: original is in German FO, political archives: Weizsäcker papers, page B002538 of file: Anglo-German relations, Jun-Dec 1940 — the only volume *not* available on the T-120 microcopy!
33.   Tel. Stohrer to Ribbentrop, Jul 9. Once back in Madrid, the latter replied on Jul 11, the Duke should be invited to co-operate against Churchill. B002549ff.
34.   H. Pell to FDR, Jul 17: FDR Library: OF-48, England, 1940-41.
35.   WSC to Ismay, Jul 5: CAB120/464.
36.   PM's card — Pictures of the C.W.R. are in *Illustr. London News*, Nov 10, 1945; Mar 27, 1948; Apr 30, 1949. The author's description is based on a visit of 1964.

* * *

GANGSTER METHODS: Page 360

1.   The diary of U.S. military attaché Raymond Lee observes the London scene.
2.   John Gunther, *Inside Europe* (London, 1940) 321ff.
3.   Mackenzie-King diary, Aug 2, 1943.
4.   CAB120/744. It was a mistranslation, corrected later; Cherwell papers.
5.   Gilbert, vi, 617.
6.   Tom Jones diary, Sep 5, 1926: Gilbert, v, 193.
7.   Milch diary, Aug 19, 1945: author's microfilm DJ-59.
8.   Ismay, cit. Bruce Lockhart, diary, Mar 26, 1946.
9.   Gilbert, vi, 421.
10.   Tom Jones diary, Aug 25, 1926: Gilbert, v, 181.
11.   Dalton diary, Jul 16, 1940.
12.   WSC to Prof, Jun 29: Cherwell papers.
13.   Prof to WSC, Jul 20: ibid.
14.   WSC to Prof, Nov 11, 1942: ibid; on Habbakuk see DEFE2/930 and /1087-90, and PREM3/216.
15.   WSC to Morrison, Jul 7: Gilbert, vi, 655.
16.   Liddell Hart, note, May 23, 1945.
17.   WSC circular, Jul 4, in Spears papers, 1/76b; Beaverbrook papers, D414; etc.
18.   WSC to Jacob, Jul 6: Gilbert, vi, 653.
19.   Seal letter, Jul 6: cit Gilbert, vi, 654.
20.   John Davidson to Baldwin May 6, 1926: Gilbert, v, 160. Hitler likewise visited the *Völkischer Beobachter* after the 1933 Reichstag Fire and demanded a remake of its front page.
21.   WSC to Ismay, Jul 5: PREM3/222 3.
22.   COS(498) 40, Jun 28: CAB120/445.
23.   Gilbert, vi, 622f devotes two pages to this trenchant theme.

24. WSC to Ismay, Jun 9: CAB120/441.
25. Colville diary, Jul 11.
26. WSC at Cabinet, Jul 9: CAB65/14.
27. Ironside diary, Jul 9.
28. WSC to Ismay, Jun 30 and to Morrison, Aug 31: PREM3/88/3; Colville diary.
29. WSC to Ismay, Jul 2, CAB120/453.
30. Dr R.V. Jones (interview, Apr 1984), wakened in London one July 1940 night by a lone plane overhead, assured his wife: "It must be one of ours," but could not tell her why. — Intercepts supplied to Fighter Command are not released: however, Fighter Command's war room log has survived for the period Mar 28 to Jul 15, 1941, and this shows how frequently the Government knew German bombing targets hours in advance from (a) decoding the directives to KG.100, the Pathfinder unit, and (b) the blind-bombing beam activities (AIR16/698); for other summaries pasted into a daybook at MI14 see WO199/911A; and file WO166/3 of G-2 at HQ, Home Forces.
31. Air Staff to WSC, Jul 6: AIR40/2321; and Prof to WSC, Jul 9: Cherwell papers.
32. WSC memo, Jul 19: PREM4/68/9.
33. Prof to WSC and reply, Mar 29-30, 1945: Cherwell papers.
34. Bruce Lockhart diary, Sep 5, 1943.
35. Cadogan diary, Sep 22, 1940.
36. Naval Staff History, *Norway*: ADM186/798.
37. Edwards diary, Jul 15, 17; on Keyes' appointment, see PREM3/330/1 and Pound's ltr to Adm Cunningham, Dec 12: R.K. had "intrigued himself" into the position of D.C.O.; Pound objected on grounds of Keyes' age, "However the PM is as pigheaded as a mule on these things, and his reply was that R.K. was full of the flame of war, etc. etc." Add MS 52561.
38. Pound to Cunningham, Dec 1: ibid.
39. ADM1/19177; North to Admiralty, Jul 4: reply Jul 17: in ADM1/19178; and Alexander to WSC, Jul 17, Alexander papers.
40. Colville diary and PM's card.
41. Colville diary Jul 14.
42. Peter Calvocoressi, in *The Listener*, Feb 3, 1977; ltr W Cdr Oscar Oeser to Jean Howard, Apr 12, 1975.
43. So Cripps told Halifax (who called WSC that day): cf Kennedy to State No.2001, Jul 5. After seeing Ismay, the U.S. military attaché wrote on Jul 3: "There is a lot of wishful thinking that Hitler will go off eastwards."
44. Hewel to Hohenlohe, Jun 30; replies, Jul 18: Jul 24: Hewel papers, on film T-120/776/371052ff. Kelly's report to the FO is Cl3302/89/18.
45. Tel US embassy Moscow to State, Jul 20: *FRUS 1940* i, 608.
46. Lothian to FO, Jul 19: FO C8015/89/18. It reached London at 1:00 a.m. on Jul 20. The Quaker intermediary, Malcolm R. Lovell, was negotiating on the relief of German Jews.
47. German diplomatic ciphers were certainly being read in 1941, as were the Italian: see e.g., Hinsley, i, 345, 363, 368, 410.
48. Thomsen's Tel. No.1488 to Berlin, Jul 19, has vanished from captured files. Churchill denied any but German "feelers" in his memoirs (ii, 229). When Weizsäcker reported Thomsen's message in his memoirs the noted historian Sir Lewis Namier rudely discounted it (*TLS*, Jul 1, 1951.) But see Weizsäcker's diary, Jul 23: "A strange peace feeler turns up, from the British ambassador in Washington. . . Lothian has made advances for which he must have obtained authorization if he were a normal British ambassador."
49. WSC to Halifax, Jul 20: Churchill, ii, 229.
50. Feiling, 426; Cecil King diary, Mar 15, 1944.
51. Cabinet, Nov 14, 1939: cf Nov 6 and 9, Dec 19: CAB65/4.
52. See e.g., WSC ltr to King of Sweden, Aug 3, 1940: Churchill, ii, 231. Replying to Trenchard, on Jan 5, he felt it was still not in Britain's interest "to initiate general and unlimited air war" ADM199/1929.

53. WSC to Beaverbrook, Jul 8: Beaverbrook papers, D414.
54. Ltr Portal to VCAS, Sholto Douglas, Aug 2; AIR14/1930.
55. WSC to Portal, Sinclair, Jul 20; Sinclair to WSC, Jul 23: some documents in PREM3/14/2 are still closed around this episode. Portal checked with Douglas on Jul 20, suggested that the limiting factors were length of night, number of rested crews, and weather. AIR14/1930.
56. See Note 55.
57. Minute D.H.O. (Stevenson) to Newall, Jul 21: last night WSC had asked Portal "what could be done about bombing Berlin at night and gave the date, 1st September." AIR14/1930; Bomber Command's reply, PREM4/3/4.
58. Colville diary, Jul 24; very similar in Halifax diary.
59. Birkenhead, 460.
60. Minute by F. Roberts, Jul 22: FO C7891/89/18.
61. Halifax memo on Lothian's call. C7377; cf Nicolson diary, Jul 22: "Lothian claims that he knows the German peace terms and they they are most satisfactory."
62. Goebbels, Ministerkonferenz, Jul 22. Willi Boelcke, *Kriegspropaganda 1939-41*, (Stuttgart, 1966) 433.
63. COS report, May 19, "British Strategy in a Certain Eventuality; War Cabinet, May 27: CAB65/7 and /13.
64. WSC to Smuts, Jun 27: CAB66/9.
65. Cadogan diary, Jul 11; Atticus, *Sunday Times*, Jul 14.
66. Dalton to Attlee, Jul 2: Dalton papers.
67. Colville and Dalton diaries, Jul 16; the PM's card mentions only Col. Menzies at 6:45 p.m. and Ld Swinton, postponed from 7:45 to 10:30.
68. The identity of MUW is a mystery. On Aug 30, Morton told WSC, "I have . . . invited M.U.W. to consider immediate steps for a bribery and propaganda campaign in North Africa." PREM7/2. To Ismay on Sep 3 Morton mentioned his Committee and "such Departments" as FO, MEW, MUW, and MoI. On Sep 6 he wrote to WSC that his Committee was trying to meet a COS requirement for a coup d'état in Syria and Morocco, "but MUW is unfortunately not in a position to render rapid help, either through bribery, propaganda or other means."PREM7/3.
69. WSC to Eden, Jul 14, 1940: cit Gilbert, vi, 666; Bruce Lockhart diary, Jun 21, 1942.
70. PM's card, and Eden diary, Jul 25, 1940.
71. PM's card, Jul 26; and Gilbert, vi, 686ff.
72. WSC to Ismay, Jul 7: PREM3/361/1.
73. Reith diary, Aug 16. Reith shared Dill's view.
74. Bova Scoppa to Ciano, Jul 22: Ital FO archives.
75. Tels Stohrer to Ribbentrop, Nos. 2474 and 2492, Jul 23-24; both unpublished.
76. Ditto, Jul 25: orig in Weizsäcker papers, B002588; transl. in Beaverbrook papers, D407.
77. Tel Bova Scoppa to Ciano, Jul 25: Ital FO archives.
78. Tel Huene to Berlin, No.749, Jul 26: B002597, *not* publ.; neither was Huene's further message (No.783, Jul 30: B002609) that the Duke's host, a mutual friend, had told the ambassador that his guest assured the Nazis he could fly back via Florida in 24 hours.
79. Michael Bloch, interview of Viscount Eccles, 1983.
80. WSC to Duke, Jul 27: Gilbert, vi, 705.
81. Bova Scoppa to Ciano, Jul 29, who repeated it to Berlin, Aug 3. Ital FO archives.
82. Draft ltr to WSC, Oct 1940: the Duchess tactfully amended the phrase to "dictator methods." — The reference to "assassinated" is in Bova Scoppa's telegram to Ciano, Aug 2 publ. in *Documenti Diplomatici Italiani*, Series ix, vol.v (Rome 1965), 324.
83. Huene to Ribbentrop, Aug 15, 1940: B002655.
84. Attlee to WSC, Aug 25, 1945; and reply, Aug 26: Beaverbrook papers, D407.
85. Winant to Eisenhower, Sep 1945: DDE Library. The royal names were left blank on the carbon copy; but mention of "B002527-3018" leaves no doubt. Weizsäcker's file is now safe in German FO archives.
86. Note by Crozier on a conv with WSC at 5:00 p.m. on Jul 26: Beaverbrook Library.
87. Beaverbrook to WSC, Sep 2: Beaverbrook papers, C87.

* * *

THE EAGLE NEVER LANDED: Page 378

1. Cecil King diary, Feb 19,1941: Boston Univ. Library.
2. Ltr Major I.G. Frhr von Falkenstein to Col von Waldau, Jun 25, in Karl Klee, *Dokumente zum Unternehmen Seelöwe* (Göttingen 1959), 296f, and author's interview of Falkenstein, 1971; Wehrmachtsführungsamt, directive of Jun 28, 1940 signed by LtCol Bernd von Lossberg: T-608/1; cf naval staff war diary Jul 2.
3. Lossberg's plan (Fritz) for the attack on Russia was nearing completion when Hitler arrived in Berlin on Jul 6: Lossberg papers, in my possession. — Wehrmacht adjutant LtCol Rudolf Schmundt notified Luftwaffe adjutant Major Nicolaus von Below at Hitler's Black Forest HQ (interview of Below, 1967.) — General Franz Halder diary, Jul 2; explaining this entry he told British interrogators in Aug 1945: "About this time [von Brauchitsch] asked me to begin operational thinking about Russia." Jodl recalled to gauleiters in Nov 1943 that Hitler told him about the planned attack on Russia "during the western campaign." ND: 172-L.
4. The deception character of Sealion was confirmed by Jodl at Nuremberg, Nov 1945. The OKW's Dr. Wolfgang Cartellieri, in a postwar paper on "Die Amtsgruppe Wehrmacht Propaganda", makes it plain that "special emphasis was placed on deceiving German troops also, up to *high command* levels (hohe Führerstellen.)"
5. OKW operations staff war diary, Aug 8.
6. Maj.Gen.Erich Marcks, draft operation plan, Aug 5: T-84/271/0902ff.
7. German naval staff war diary, Aug 14.
8. ND: NG-2948.
9. Frau Anneliese Schmundt, diary, Aug 27-29.
10. WO199/911a; and Edwards diary, Jul 29.
11. C. King diary, Aug 21.
12. Kennedy to State, Tel. 2486, Jul 31.
13. Kennedy to State, Aug 2.
14. Cadogan diary, Jul 16: Halifax, Butler, and the F.O. continue to debate the "surrender to Japan (insisted on by Winston)."
15. WSC to Chamberlain, Feb 20: PREM1/414.
16. Ltr Weizmann to WSC, May 29: Weizmann archives, Rehovot, Israel; and papers in PREM3/348, from which some items have been removed.
17. Weizmann to WSC, Aug 6.
18. Mtg on Sep 4: Weizmann papers; other participants included Ben-Gurion, Lewis Namier, Morrison, Layton, Boothby.
19. Blanche Dugdale diary, Sep 13.
20. Prof to WSC, Dec 17: Cherwell papers.
21. Pownall diary, May 25, Jul 25, 1941.
22. Cunningham diary, Apr 2, Jul 6, 1944: Add Ms 52577.
23. Cadogan diary, Jun 22, 1940.
24. Morton to WSC, Aug 30, PREM7/2 and PREM7/8.
25. Halifax to WSC, Dec 13: FO800/312.
26. WSC to Ismay, Jun 24: PREM3/119/11.
27. Beaverbrook complimented Morton Jan 3, 1945 on his modesty, suggested "you have been reading a *Life of Warren Hastings.*" D141.
28. The man selected on Lyttelton's recommendation was the Metal Market publicity agent, Richmond Temple. Morton to WSC, Jul 15: PREM7/2. — A.B. Cunningham to Pound, Jun 27: Add MS 52560; Eden diary, Jul 22.
29. Dakar file, PREM3/276.
30. PM's card, Aug 3.
31. Norman Young to S.D. Waley, Jun 6; Hankey to WSC, Jun 7: CAB63/132. Fol.401 summarizes the Gold holdings of France, Belgium, Denmark, Norway and Poland.
32. Cadogan diary, Jun 21; Morton/Vansittart Cttee, Jun 23. PREM7/8.
33. Raymond Lee diary, Jul 30.
34. War Cab, Aug 22: CAB65/14.
35. Ltr Kingsley Wood to FO, Oct 9: FO371/24292. On Oct 13 Halifax submitted to Masaryk a draft agreement for the Czech National Bank's gold to be placed at the British government's disposal: Taborský papers, box 6.

36. Taborský diary (in Czech), and PM's card, Aug 8; Benes message, Aug 15. Taborský papers, box 5: Hoover Library.
37. OKW/WFA, Weisung Nr.17 für die Fuhrung des Luft- und Seekrieges gegen England, Aug 1. Göring's corresponding directive of Aug 2 (Ob.d.L. Füst.Ia Nr. 5881/40) would be in the airforce cipher.
38. Tel. Alfieri to Ciano, Aug 7: *DDI*, 9, v, No.368.
39. R.W. Thompson, *Churchill and Morton* (London 1976.)
40. Eden diary, Jul 29.
41. Colville diary, Aug 9: and PM's card.
42. Cadogan diary, Aug 10.
43. Colville diary, Aug 10.
44. PM's card; Eden diary, Aug 12; passage of armoured reinforcements through Med., Sep-Oct 1940: PREM3/284/1.
45. Eden diary, Aug 13.
46. Harry Hopkins diary Jan 30, 1941; Colville diary, Aug 7, 1940.
47. Taborský diary; and Benes message to Czechoslovakia, Aug 15. "In any case it is vital," Benes warned his agents, "not to do anything against Russia." Taborský papers, box 5: Hoover Library.
48. Pound to Cunningham, Aug 14: ADD Ms 52561.
49. Field Marshal Wilhelm von Leeb diary, Aug 14.
50. Kennedy to State, Tel. 2731, Aug 14. He cast doubts on the R.A.F. claims.
51. Tel. FDR to WSC, 6:00 p.m., Aug 13: PREM3/468.
52. Colville diary, Aug 14.

* * *

IN A SINGLE GULP: Page 393

1.   Morgenthau, memo to FDR, June 18: FDR film 1, 0090; and diary, 0586.
2.   Kennedy to State, Tel. 2001; and Colville diary, Jul 5.
3.   Harold Ickes diary, Jul 5.
4.   WSC to Prof, Jun 21: Cherwell papers.
5.   WSC to Ismay, Jul 17: PREM3/475/1.
6.   Morton to WSC, Jul 21, PREM7/2; Godfrey MS, v, 129f: Naval Historical Branch.
7.   Cadogan to Halifax, Dec 17: quoted in Anthony Cave-Browne, *Wild Bill Donovan, The Last Hero*, (London, 1984) chap.10.
8.   Lee diary, Aug 2, and pocket notes Aug 13; Donovan told Stimson (diary, Aug 6) that he found British morale very high; if invaded they would "probably win," but he stressed the danger of letdown if not (Yale Univ. Library).
9.   Sir Arthur Salter's memo of Aug 17: CAB115/83.
10. Records of Tizard mission, AVIA10/1; Tizard corresp., AVIA9/48.
11. Tizard to A.V. Hill, Jun 25: Clarke, 237.
12. Cecil King diary, Jul 4; cf Jul 7.
13. Dalton diary.
14. King diary, Jul 7.
15. Tizard diary, Aug 1. The PM's appointment card records the archbishop at 5:00 p.m. and Tizard not at all.
16. WSC to FDR Jul 31: PREM3/462/2/3; paraphrase on FDR film 1, 0107.
17. WSC to Ismay, Aug 1, PREM 3/475/1.
18. Ickes diary, Aug 4.
19. Colville diary, Aug 6; Halifax diary, Aug 7 (Hickelton papers, A7.8.5).
20. Morgenthau diary, Aug 14.
21. WSC to FDR, 1:00 a.m., Aug 15: FDR film 1, 0112f.
22. Lothian to FO, Tel. 1789, Aug 23.
23. WSC to FDR, Aug 25: film No.1, pp.0116ff.
24. Kennedy to State, Tel 2948, 7:00 p.m., Aug 29.
25. Kennedy to State, Tel 2948, 7:00 p.m., Aug 29; and Kennedy MS.
26. PREM3/462/2/3.

27.   Adolph A. Berle Jr, diary, Aug 31, 1940. The "foaming" remark is from intercepted ltr, Baron Stackelberg, Washington, to editor, *Financial News*, Nov 9: FO371/24263.

28.   Cecil King lunched with William Sempill of the Admiralty, Lord Hirst of General Electric, and R.B. Bennett, one time prime minister of Canada, and was surprised that they did not even mention the deal. "The press here is unanimously favourable," recorded Cecil King (diary, Sep 4), "which surprises me, as the deal on the face of it is overwhelmingly favourable to the Americans."

29.   Ibid, Aug 21.

* * *

THE ONE SINLESS MAN: Page 401

1.   Leopold Amery diary, Feb 27, 1929.
2.   WO199/911a.
3.   Milch diary and notes.
4.   C. King diary, Feb 19, 1941: lunching with WSC.
5.   Colville diary, Aug 16.
6.   Ismay, 180, and cit: Bruce Lockhart diary, Sep 12, 1946.
7.   Air Min to Bomber Cd., 6:25 p.m., Aug 17: "Operation is postponed indefinitely and will not be undertaken without Air Ministry authorisation." AIR14/775. — And PM's card.
8.   Unpublished, Brooke papers, 3/a/iv, 230f; and Martin diary.
9.   Cadogan diary, Aug 19. Milch diary, Aug 19; Milch docs., vol.65, 7251ff. "Boniface" also reported invitations to a Berlin conference on Aug 19, issued to 7th *Flieger Division*, which had spearheaded Hitler's May attack. On Aug 24 all three Air Fleets were directed to provide air sea rescue launches, "in connection with the Sealion operations."
10.   Colville diary, Aug 20.
11.   In May 1941. Adm. Godfrey, visiting F.D.R. as Director of Naval Intelligence, tactfully said nothing. Eleanor Roosevelt and the others affected not to notice this "rough talk." Godfrey MS.
12.   WSC to Phillips, Oct 14, 1939: Gilbert, vi, 158.
13.   WSC to Lord Lloyd, Jun 16, 1940: ibid, vi, 556n.
14.   Cadogan diary, Oct 13, 1942.
15.   Colville diary, Aug 10.
16.   Spanish amb. in Lisbon, cit: Bova Scoppa to Ciano, Aug 16: Ital FO archives.
17.   Duke of Alba to Madrid, Aug 26: Span.FO archives.
18.   Bomber Command directives file, vol.1, AIR14/775. — As recently as August 24 the German high command (O.K.W.) had issued Most Secret order No.665/40, "regulations for restricting hostilities," forbidding the use of poison gas, attacks on ships not positively identified as hostile, and — air raid on London (*Kriegstagebuch des Oberkommandos der Wehrmacht*, i, 970).
19.   Colville diary; Bottomley minute, Aug 26, AIR14/775.
20.   Martin ltrs, Aug 25, 28, Sep 1.
21.   Cadogan diary, Aug 28; Attlee, cit: Dalton diary, Aug 29; Morton, ibid., Oct 4.
22.   Bottomley minute, Aug 28, 10:30 a.m. AIR14/775.
23.   Col Raymond Lee notebook, Aug 28, ltr Aug 29, diary Oct 3.
24.   Bensuson-Butt to Prof, Dec 21: Cherwell papers.
25.   Portal to Peck, Sep 2: AIR14/3554.
26.   *SAO*, i, 154; Portal's biographer disagrees.
27.   WSC Cab paper, Sep 3: WP(40)352, Churchill, ii, 405: CAB66/11.
28.   COS(40)683, Sep 4: in CAB80/17.
29.   Dalton diary, Sep 3.
30.   *Hansard, Official Report*, H of C., vol.430, Written Answers, cols. 52-7.

* * *

GOOD OLE WINNIE: Page 413

1. Kennedy to State and FDR, Tel.3063, Sep 11, 7:00 p.m.: US emb file.
2. CAB65/9. WSC had written to Air Marshal Peirse on Sep 6 recommending widespread attacks on "the smaller German centres." Portal submitted on Sep 11 a list of twenty larger towns suitable for bombing in reprisal for "each night of indiscriminate bombing." Heavy attack on "a military objective" would by normal spread "inevitably cause a high degree of devastation."AIR14/1925.
3. Cf WSC to Chamberlain, Aug 31; Halifax diary, Aug 29.
4. Colville diary, Aug 28, and Ismay.
5. WSC to Anne Chamberlain, Sep 20: Gilbert, vi, 800.
6. Ismay to WSC, Nov 26, 1946: Gilbert, vi, 775; and memoirs, 183.
7. Ismay, cit Lee diary, Sep 24.
8. Sinclair to WSC, Sep 15: Gilbert, vi, 782.
9. Colville diary, Aug 31. Alexander was refused access to Ultra: Godfrey MS.
10. Air Intelligence assessed on Sep 2, "It may indicate their re-employment on a larger scale in preparation for an invasion. . ." AIR40/2321.
11. MI14 memo, Sep 8: WO199/911a.
12. Jodl, signal to Ausl/Abw, Sep 6: ND, 1809-PS.
13. Note 1.
14. Mallet to Halifax, Sep 5, and to Cadogan, Sep 7, 8, 9: in FO C.9498/89/19; on Sep 8 deputy Führer Rudolf Hess first approached Prof Albrecht Haushofer to discuss peace talks with England: Haushofer papers, T-253/46/9921ff.
15. Cf Cecil King diary, Sep 4: William Sempill of the Admiralty said Churchill was "being very disconcerting to the Foreign Office, as he sends cables affecting foreign policy all over the world without even informing Halifax of what he is at."
16. Cadogan diary, Sep 10; Tel. Halifax to Mallet, Sep 11: FO C.9598/89/18. Halifax told the War Cabinet that day of the rejection.
17. Kennedy said WSC was an "entirely bellicose character." H. Hoover memo, Nov 22, 1940: Hoover papers. — On the Weissauer deal: Stig Jagerskiold of Djursholm, Sweden has unpublished papers on the negotiations between Weissauer and Mallet, and related letters between Professor T. Kivimaki (the Finnish envoy in Berlin) and Ekeberg.
18. Security at Chequers, WO199/303.
19. Knickerbocker, passing through Lisbon, told Bova Scoppa who telegraphed this to Ciano, Oct 2: Ital FO archives.
20. Brooke diary Sep 12, 1940, and notes Mar 4, 1941, 3/a/iv.
21. Milch diary: note on Jeschonnek's conf with Hitler, Sep 14. In view of subsequent developments it is worth quoting the resulting O.K.W. directive: "Air raids are to be continued against London with larger target areas including military targets and targets of vital importance to the city. Terror raids are expressly embargoed as an ultimate sanction."
22. Note 1.
23. Lee diary.
24. Martin diary. Sep 13-14; WSC to Ismay and others, Sep 14. PREM4/69/1.
25. Morton's memo, in PREM 3/276, WSC's file on the Dakar operation.
26. PREM 4/69/1.
27. PREM 3/276.
28. CAB 65/15; Cadogan diary, Sep 17.
29. Pound to A.B. Cunningham, Sep 20: ADD Ms 52561.
30. WSC to Ismay, Sep 19: PREM 3/314/2.
31. Colville diary, Sep 20, 1940.
32. Minute by Gp Capt T.W. Elmhirst, Nov 19, 1940 (AIR16/473) and draft instruction for Duty Air Commodore, Dec 10, 1941 (AIR16/388).
33. Blanche Dugdale diary, Sep 13.
34. Kennedy to State, Tel.3150, Sep 20: we have earlier remarked on J.P. Kennedy's anti-Semitism.

35. Lee diary, Sep 13; C. King diary, Sep 11, 1940; and FO371/26259. Cf Menzies diary, Feb 21, 1941.
36. Godfrey MS, vii, 185.
37. PREM3/276; and diaries of Spears and Halifax.
38. *Hansard,* H of C Deb, vol.365, cols 298-301; Churchill repeated this: ii, 427; Roskill calls the claims "fictitious" in *Churchill and the Admirals*, 161.
39. Admiralty to Bevan, Oct 4; writing to Alexander, Oct 19, WSC claimed Bevan's "serious and disastrous failure in responsibility" had contributed to "a far worse misfortune," meaning Dakar. That day Edwards noted, "I hear W.C. wishes to make Bob Bevan the scapegoat for Dakar."
40. PREM3/71.
41. Pound to North, Jan 3, 1940: North papers.
42. Admiralty to North, Jul 4: Add MS 52575.
43. Tel Menzies to WSC, Sep 29: FO800/310.
44. Knickerbocker memo, Sep 27: Daniel Longwell papers, Columbia Univ.
45. Kennedy to State, Tel. 3247, Sep 27. In US emb. file.

* * *

THE FIXER: Page 430

1. WSC to Beaverbrook, Sep 12, 1939: Beaverbrook papers.
2. Mackenzie-King diary, Aug 21, 1943.
3. Bruce Lockhart diary, Dec 4, 1941; Feb 24, 1942, and Aug 4, 1943.
4. Mackenzie-King diary, Aug 21, 1943; Bruce Lockhart, diary Mar 31, 1942.
5. Author's interview of John Parker, MP, Apr 12, 1978. The Tory MP concerned died in 1945, as did several WAAF's sent over as interpreters from Bletchley, having caught an infection while visiting Buchenwald concentration camp.
6. WSC to Chamberlain, Sep 30; reply, Oct 1: Gilbert, vi, 819.
7. Dalton diary.
8. WSC to Halifax, Sep 29, cit Gilbert, vi, 817f.
9. Seal to WSC, Oct 3: PREM3/22/1.
10. This and what follows from the Hugh Dowding papers, file AC71/17/2: RAF Museum, Hendon.
11. The woman was Irene Ward, MP. PREM4/4/6.
12. The report is in PREM4/3/6; quotations are from Lee diary, Sep 12 and Oct 4.
13. Dalton diary, Oct 3.
14. Cadogan diary, Oct 21.
15. C. King diary, Oct 6.
16. *Daily Express*, Oct 2, 1929.
17. Colville diary, Oct 8.
18. Pile, *Ack-Ack*, 169.
19. Colville diary, Oct 12.
20. Pile, 171.
21. *Manchester Guardian,* Oct 10.
22. WSC to Morrison, Nov 23, 1940: PREM4/40/19; and Jul 19, 1941: Gilbert, vi, 895n.
23. Colville diary, Oct 12; Cecil King diary, Oct 8, 11; Halifax diary Oct 7.
24. Dalton diary, Oct 7: "I hear that on the lower deck they call him Don't-do-it Dudley."
25. Dalton diary, Nov 9.
26. Roskill, *Churchill and the Admirals*, 120.
27. Pound to Cunningham, Sep 20: ADD Ms. 52561.
28. Cecil King diary, Oct 18: Dalton diary, Nov 9.
29. Pound to Alexander, Jun 8, 1942: ADM 205/14.
30. Tovey to A.V. Alexander, Oct 9 (Alexander papers, AVAR 5/4); and to Cunningham, Oct 17, 1940: Cunningham papers, ADD Ms 52569.
31. Colville diary, Oct 21.
32. Brooke papers, 3/A/IV, 241.

33.   WSC to Dill, Oct 19: PREM3/220.
34.   Colville diary, Oct 23.
35.   Alastair Forbes, letter to *The Times* Oct 26, 1978.
36.   Colville diary, Sep 23.
37.   War Cabinet, Mar 24, 1941. CAB65/18.
38.   Colville diary Oct 13, 1940.
39.   WSC to Halifax, Oct 13: CAB120/300.
40.   Colville, The Churchillians, in *Sunday Telegraph*, Dec 7, 1980.
41.   Dalton diary, Oct 16, 1940.
42.   Cadogan diary, Oct 12.
43.   Vice-Admiral Sir John Godfrey MS.
44.   MI14 file, WO199/911A.
45.   Halifax to Hoare, Oct 24, FO800/323.
46.   WSC to Menzies, Oct 2: PREM4/43B/1.
47.   WSC to FDR, Oct 4: PREM3/468.
48.   WSC to FDR, Oct 26.
49.   Johnson to State, Feb. 12, 1941: in 8700.2 Boothby, R.: US embassy file; cf Dalton diary, Oct 31, 1940.
50.   Boothby stresses that he did not run the committee. "It was set up by a very well known Jewish lawyer. They asked me to see them once. I said I would support any Bill which came in to prevent them sending the Gold [out of London]. . . Immediately after the war Speaker Morrison gave a ruling from the Chair of the House of Commons making it clear that the rule of the House regarding the disclosure of financial interests applies only to Votes, and not to Speeches." Interview Feb 2, 1984.
51.   According to his own account. Interview, Feb 2, 1984.
52.   *Hansard,* H of C Deb, Jan 28, 1941, vol.000, cols. 445-461.
53.   Colville diary, Oct 17; WSC to Chamberlain, Oct 20: PREM4/7/8; Deakin to WSC, Oct 18: cit Gilbert, vi, 852.
54.   Nicolson diary, Oct 17.
55.   WSC to Chamberlain, Oct 20, PREM 4/7/8.
56.   WSC to Portal, Oct 20: Portal papers file 1; and PREM3/314/2, Churchill, ii, 604.
57.   *SAO* iv 128-31.
58.   WSC to Portal, Nov 1: Portal papers, Christ Church, file 1, (items 9, 9a, 9b.); and PREM3/25/1.
59.   WSC to Bridges, Oct 22: PREM 4/69/1.
60.   Ltr Douglas Fairbanks to FDR, Nov 19: FDR Library: PSF, Box 53: GB-Kennedy.
61.   Ltr Gerson J. Brown to Stephen J. Early, Jun 6, 1941: FDR Library, file OF.3060.
62.   WSC to FDR, Nov 6, PREM 3/468; and to Ld Lothian, Nov 26, PREM 4/17/1.
63.   Colville diary, Oct 24.

* * *

BRITAIN CAN TAKE IT: Page 448

1.   *Daily Express*, May 2, 1945. On D-Notices, see Min. of Inf. Handbook of Defence [D-] Notices, revised 1941, in file 871 (Press and Postal Censorship): box 11, RG-84, US emb secret files.
2.   *Evening Standard*, Nov 12, 1964.
3.   Dalton diary, May 28.
4.   So this Yugoslav politician told Bova Scoppa on arriving from London on Nov 13. Tel. Lisbon to Ciano, Nov 14: Ital. For. Min. archives. — The other quote is from Churchill, ii, 331.
5.   Tel Bova Scoppa (Lison) to Ciano, Dec 4: Ital. For. Min archives. The "personalita nord americana" is not identified.
6.   Cadogan diary, Nov 4.
7.   Halifax diary, Oct 1.
8.   WSC to Halifax, Sep 29, PREM4/21/1; Halifax diary, Oct 1.

9. Dalton diary, Oct 2.

10. WSC to FDR, Oct 4: PREM 3/468.

11. WSC, note, "Priorities," WP 416(40), Oct 15: CAB120/10.

12. WSC to Hoare, Oct 20, 6:55 a.m., PREM3/186A/2.

13. Churchill, ii, 451-3. Sir Ronald Campbell pleaded that the Prime Minister be persuaded to let someone read the French version for him "since if the truth must be told" his French is not altogether intelligible." FO371/24361.

14. When Rougier first published details in his book, *Les Accords Pétain-Churchill* (Montreal, 1945) he was denounced by the Gaullist press as "valet de Pétain" and "neo-hitlérien" and dismissed as professor of philosophy at Besancon. He defended himself in a paper, in *Ecrits de Paris*, Jul 1948, pp. 95-118: Rougier papers, private possession.

15. King George to Pétain, Oct 25: in PREM3/186A/2: publ. in White Paper, Cmd.6662, Aug 2, 1945.

16. Memo on mtg WSC-Rougier, Halifax, Oct 25: FO371/24361.

17. Rougier, *Mission sécrète*. In his memo for Frankfurter, he said that Churchill wanted "nothing less than to send the British Air Force to bomb the Vichy Government."

18. In file FO371/24361 is one such memorandum headed *Entretien avec Weygand*. Handwritten in Churchill's ink at top, "If General Weygand will raise the standard in North Africa. . ." Cf War Cabinet, Oct 28, and F.O. to Hoare, Nov 1 enclosing a copy: "The French text is Rougier's own, and the passages in English are our additions." Strang also sent a copy to Rex Leeper on Nov 7. "It was seen by the Secretary of State and the Prime Minister and the bits in English are their additions." However several documents at this point have been closed until 2016.

19. Ismay memo, Oct 31: CAB127/14.

20. Published Jul 13, 1945: "Despatch to H.M. Ambassador in Paris regarding relations of the United Kingdom and the Vichy Government in the Autumn of 1940." *The Times*, Jul 17.

21. Paul Baudouin trial, Feb 27, 1947.

22. [Rougier's] memorandum is in Frankfurter papers, box 98: and ltr Frankfurter to FDR, Dec 24, after talking with [Rougier]: Library of Congress.

23. Admiral Moreau would write to Rougier on Feb 28, 1948: "From 1940 to 1942 as naval commander at Marseilles charged with supervising our merchant navy traffic with our colonial empire, I was able to confirm that whether signed or not, it was the agreements you worked on which governed relations between Britain and France and assured our food supplies." On Jan 8, 1941 Mr David Eccles, a ministry of economic warfare expert, would negotiate agreements in Madrid with a Vichy expert, M Marchal, which lifted the blockade: Testimony of Flandin, Flandin trial, pp. 177f; and see Churchill's statement to the House on Apr 9, 1941, welcoming public assurances offered by Pétain, and coupling this with the fact that Britain had eased the blockade; and the pseudonymous letter from an officer of Darlan's staff in *NYT*, Jul 31, 1945. As for the BBC: See Soustelle, *Envers et contre tout (de Londres à Algers)*, 88f: "La BBC refusa desormais de transmettre sur ses ondes aucune attaque contre Pétain, qui demeura pratiquement 'tabou' jusqu'au debarquement de 1941." And Colonel Passy (de Wavrin), *Souvenirs*, 152.

24. Muselier, *De Gaulle contre la gaullisme*, 218.

25. However the F.O. cabled to Lisbon and Tangiers on Oct 30, "Professor Rougier arrived here a few days ago from Unoccupied France with the knowledge and approval of Marshal Pétain to explain to us the situation at Vichy and to take back with him an impression of the situation here and of the attitude of His Majesty's government." FO371/24361.

26. Cadogan (diary, Oct 25) was doubtful about this, noting: "We have already covered that ground and it's no good going on nagging." A summary of the Churchill letter was sent to Weygand by the British consul at Tangiers, Anthony Gascoigne, in a letter dated Oct 31. Since in Jun 1945 Churchill would emphasize to the House that Rougier was acting on Pétain's personal instructions it is clear that the visit to Weygand was a bonus, not the main purpose of the trip.

27.   Colville diary, Nov 1.
28.   Dalton diary, Oct 31.
29.   Prof to WSC, Nov 13: Cherwell papers.
30.   Colville diary, Oct 24.
31.   Defence Committee Oct 31.
32.   Dalton diary, Oct 28.
33.   Colville diary, Oct 31.
34.   Dalton diary, Oct 31; cf Colville diary, Oct 28.
35.   Eden to WSC, Nov 1, PREM3/309/1.
36.   WSC to Portal, Oct 31, Nov 2: CAB120/300.
37.   Colville diary, Nov 3.
38.   WSC to Portal, Nov 2: cit Gilbert, vi, 884.
39.   WSC to Ismay, Nov 9: PREM4/43B/1.
40.   Gilbert, vi, 885f.
41.   Colville diary, Nov 2.
42.   Minute by WSC to Bridges, Nov 22, 1940: CAB 120/744; Gen. Lee diary, Nov 24: "The Information Outline . . . has been cut to the bone;" and Nov 27, Dec 4-6, 17.
43.   Ltr from Jean Howard, Jan 30, 1984.
44.   The intercept is pasted into MI14 report, Nov 6, 5:30 p.m., in WO199/911A. On Oct 27 an intercept had revealed that the invasion forces were merely to "continue training."
45.   *Hansard*, H of C Deb., col. 1246; and Harold Nicolson, diary, Nov 5.
46.   Channon diary, Nov 5; he was not an unbiased observer, reporting inaccurately on Nov 6 that Churchill's "popularity is on the decline."
47.   Dalton diary, Nov 10.
48.   Colville diary, Sep 23.
49.   Memo, Churchill speaking, Apr 14-17, 1955. C.D. Jackson Papers, box 32.
50.   WSC to A.V. Alexander Oct 16: ADM199/1931.
51.   H of C Deb., vol 365, col.108.
52.   R. Tree quoted by Nicolson diary, Nov 22.
53.   Hap Arnold diary, Apr 18-19, 1941; author's interview of Mrs Marietta Tree, New York, 1978.
54.   Colville diary, Nov 11.
55.   In a November 12 minute Wing Cdr C.P. Grant of AI1(w), spelt out to the Director of Home Operations Air Commodore D.F. Stevenson the evidence that Moonlight Sonata must be a massive night attack by moonlight using the beams, KG.100 and both Luftflotten: AIR 2/5238, the main PRO file on the Coventry attack; the related CAS file is AIR 8/352. See too N.E. Evans, "Air Intelligence and the Coventry Raid," in RUSI *Journal*, Sep 1976.
56.   R.V. Jones supplied this Enigma intercept to Miki Clayton who quoted it to Winterbotham, Sep 23, 1980.
57.   Colville diary, Nov 14.
58.   A/Cdre Boyle, D of I, to D.C.A.S., Nov 13, and Air Staff memo of Nov 14. AIR 2/5238: The target possibilities were given as "Central London (not absolutely definite,) Greater London, the area bounded by Farnborough—Maidenhead—Reading and the area bounded by Rochester—Favisham [*Faversham*]—Isle of Sheppey."
59.   Sqdn Ldr S.D. Felkin, AI1(k) to Air Commodore A. Boyle, Director of Intelligence, Nov 12, in AIR 2/5238. Felkin noted, "As this came after S/L Humphrey's visit . . . when he mentioned that a gigantic raid under codename of 'Moonlight Sonata' was in preparation, I thought it well to bring this information to your notice. . . I believe that S/L Humphreys has pretty definite information that the attack is against London and the Home Counties . . . in retaliation for Munich."
60.   Chips Channon diary.
61.   Ltr WSC to Sinclair, Nov 14, 1940: PREM3/466.
62.   Colville diary, Nov 14.
63.   Dalton diary, Nov 14.

64.   Author's conversation with Sir John Martin, Feb 7, 1984.
65.   The diary of 80 Wing (AIR26/580) is silent on this; but the 3:00 p.m. time is confirmed by the report by DDHO (J. Whitworth Jones), "Note on German Operation Moonlight Sonata and Counter Plan Cold Water," Nov 17: in AIR2/5238 and AIR8/352. R.V. Jones, in *Most Secret War*, (5th edition) 536f, challenges this as "tinged with a degree of hindsight and self-interest." He points out that the Duty Group Captain in Home Operations had to send out two telegrams on Nov 14: "Executive Cold Water" when it was sure the raid was on (see Note 70); and the target, when identified. The first was sent at 4:15 p.m., with no mention of Coventry. The draft of the second telegram remains on the file with a blank space where the target was to have been named. However there was a bureaucratic reason for this: the lengthy Operation Orders for Cold Water were issued earlier on Nov 14: four possible target areas were foreseen, but Coventry was not among them. Stevenson commented on this. For security reasons this complicated the issue of the telegram that night, and it was probably communicated verbally. Stevenson minuted later that day "the 1300 hrs signal was made today & acknowledged by HQ Air Fleet 3. CAS decided to go ahead with COLD WATER and *I spoke to Commands* [author's italics] and issued instructions at 16:15 hrs."
66.   The late Miki Clayton, one of the principal WAAF liaison officers between Chichester(?) Sands intercept station and Bletchley Park, as well as F.C. Jones, the senior signals officer at Kingsdown listening post, are certain of this. So Clayton wrote to Winterbotham on Sep 23, 1980; and see her book *The Enemy is Listening* (London, 1980)
67.   Gp Capt F.W. Winterbotham, ltr in *TLS*, Jun 25 1976, and memos of Apr 26, 1979, and May 27, 1980, ltr to author Jan 23, 1984.
68.   Information from the present Lady Tweeddale.
69.   The whole talk of London may have been a decoy. The pencilled diary of General Hoffmann von Waldau, chief of Luftwaffe operations staff (in the author's possession), mentions only Coventry. ". . . to Richthofen's at Trouville for conf with Canaris. Evening: heavy attack planned against Coventry. Weather and visibility conditions good." However London was heavily attacked the next night.
70.   Director of Home Operations, telegrams en claire to Fighter, Bomber and Coastal Commands, and 80 Wing, Nov 14; time of origin 16:15 hrs, time of despatch 16:21: in AIR 2/5238 and AIR8/35.
71.   This is according to Sir John Martin's loyal recollection in a letter to *The Times*, Aug 28, 1976.
72.   Colville diary.
73.   CAB65/10.

* * *

ALL VERY INNOCENT: Page 466

1.   DHO to Bomber, Fighter etc Commands, 10:20 p.m., Nov 15: AIR2/5238. Field Marshal Milch's diary reveals that R.A.F. raids killed 975 Germans from May to November (road accidents had killed 1,845 Germans); fifteen thousand British had died in German raids.
2.   Brooke diary, Nov 16. Re Poincaré: Colville diary, Jan 24, 1941.
3.   Colville diary, Nov 18.
4.   WSC to Naval Staff, Oct 22: ADM 199/1931.
5.   Keyes dates this meeting Nov 19: KEYES 13/5. The PM's card Nov 18 records "9:30: Meeting with 1st Lord etc."
6.   Harold Nicolson diary, Nov 20. From the PM's card it seems his doctor Sir Charles Wilson visited one morning a month.
7.   Eden diary, Nov 20.
8.   Eden diary, Nov 25.
9.   Lee diary, Dec 5.
10.   Alan Brooke diary, Nov 22, 1940: 3/A/IV,246.

11. C. King diary, Nov 26.
12. Beaverbrook to WSC Dec 2, and reply, Beaverbrook Library C/87.
13. Beaverbrook to WSC, Mar 17, 1942: ibid.
14. WSC to Alexander and Pound, Dec 2: First Lord's papers, ADM199/1931.
15. Somerville to Cunningham, Dec 8: BM ADD Ms. 52563.
16. Eden diary, Dec 4.
17. WSC to Dill, Dec 7: PREM3/288/1.
18. Def Cttee, Dec 5: CAB 69/1. — Pound to Cunningham Jan 27, 1941: BM ADD Ms 52578.
19. Duke of Alba to Madrid, Tel 985, Dec 8: despatched Dec 9.
20. *Hitler's War*, 187f. The resulting O.K.W. directive is on film T77 roll 781 p.8325.
21. Lewin, 127.
22. Eden diary, Oct 11, 1940.
23. Eisenhower and Mark Clark dined at Chequers on Aug 25, 1942. Ike's aide Harry Butcher dictated the unflattering description on Aug 25; it was deleted from his unpublished diary by a censor who scrawled "My God" in the margin.
24. Charles Murphy, MS in Jackson Papers: box 32: DDE Library.
25. Michael Eden, op.cit.
26. Chips Channon diary, Dec 9.
27. Eden diary, Dec 12.
28. WSC to Mackenzie-King, Dec 12.
29. Colville diary, Dec 13.
30. Dalton diary, Dec 17.
31. Adml. Godfrey, MS, vii, 236.
32. Michael Eden, ltr, Dec 15: cit Gilbert, vi, 938n.
33. WSC to FDR, Dec 7: WP(40)466: FDR film 1/0161ff; cf Churchill, ii, 544ff; and see his remarks about the ships in ltr of Dec 13: FDR film 1/0183.
34. WSC to Pound, Dec 21: PREM 3/462/1. WSC reported the defects to FDR on Dec 31, but the Washington embassy pleaded with the F.O. not to push their luck: it might seem ungrateful to mention shortcomings in the destroyers to the White House just now.
35. Cabinet, Dec 2.
36. WSC to FDR, No 21: FDR film 6/0331f.
37. Cf PM's card Nov 27, and Colville diary, Nov 30.
38. WSC to FDR, Dec 7: WP(40)466: FDR film 1/0161ff; cf Churchill, ii, 544ff. The file on this ltr is CAB115/14.
39. PM's card, Nov 25, 2:45 p.m.; and WSC to Halifax Nov 27, FO800/362: H/XIV/477.
40. Lisbon Tel. to F.O., Dec 9: Strang raised the question on Dec 15 whether de Gaulle should not be informed of these too. W.B. Mack recommended that distribution be confined to Churchill, Alexander, Pound, Ismay and Morton. FO371/24361.
41. Halifax minute Dec 19: WP(40)486: ibid.
42. A note on this Dec 21 conv is in ADM199/1928. Tel Washington to F.O., Dec 9. Cf Lisbon Tel.903, reporting Baudouin's conversation with the Portuguese chargé at Vichy, Dec 7. FO371/24361.
43. Darlan: D. Dodds-Parker, *Setting Europe Ablaze* (London, 1983.) Huntziger: Leahy diary, Mar 3, 1944.
44. Halifax diary, Nov 25: Hickleton papers, A7.8.3.
45. Dalton diary, Feb 4, 1941.
46. Hewel diary, Feb 14, 1941; and *Hitler's War* 156.
47. Neville Butler to F.O., Dec 15: FO954/29. Lloyd George had met Hitler and held him in high esteem: C. King diary.
48. Colville diary, Dec 20.
49. Halifax diary.
50. Cadogan diary.
51. Eden diary, Jan 20, 1941.

52. Dalton diary, Dec 20.
53. Bruce Lockhart diary, quoting Tedder: May 6, 1944 and Jun 25, 1944.
54. Rawdon-Smith cit in C. King diary Dec 26, 1940.
55. Lee diary, Dec 5.
56. Masaryk to Prague, Mar 15, 1934: Czech state archives.
57. HLH memo, Jan 10, 1941: HLH papers, film 19: FDR Library.
58. ibid.
59. Dalton diary, Jan 9, 1941.
60. Dalton diary, Dec 20, 1940.
61. Harold Nicolson, diary, Dec 23.
62. Cadogan diary, Dec 24-5.
63. James Layton Ralson diary, 1940-41, in Ralston papers, file 41, MG.27.III.B11, Public Archives of Canada.
64. C. King diary, Jan 4, 1941.

* * *

THE UNSORDID ACT: Page 483

1. WSC to Hopkins, Tel., Apr 13, 1945: Hopkins papers: FDR Library.
2. Henry Morgenthau diary, May 15, 1942: FDR Library.
3. Harold Smith (Budget Director) diary: FDR Library.
4. William Mackenzie-King diary, Apr 29, 1940: Public Archives of Canada; and cf Ickes diary, May 10, 1940: Library of Congress.
5. WSC to FDR, Oct 4: PREM3/468.
6. Morgenthau diary, Mar 11, 1942.
7. Henry Wallace diary, Jun 15, 1942. "The President," he added, "says that the nations leading the world are the United States, Australia, New Zealand, China, Russia, the Scandinavian countries, and possibly Holland."
8. Ibid., Dec 16, 1942.
9. Ibid., Dec 18, 1943.
10. Morgenthau diary, Aug 19, 1944.
11. British White Paper, Dec 7, 1945.
12. Alexander Cadogan diary, Aug 7, Dec 24, 1940: Churchill College, Cambridge.
13. Aide memoire, May 27, 1940: Reynaud papers: 74AP22: Archives Nationales, Paris.
14. Harold Ickes diary, Sep 28, 1941. This was in Cabinet on Sep 26. "Russia should turn over to us what Gold she has, which would go to pay for goods here." After that she would get Lend-Lease. FDR also suggested (Morgenthau diary, Mar 10) sending a cruiser to South Africa to pick up the Belgian Gold.
15. John Colville diary, Jan 12. The emissary was Hopkins.
16. Professor Warren F. Kimball in *Political Science Quarterly*, June 1971.
17. Memo on Mtg, Mar 17, 1944 of Stettinius mission. RG-59: State dept files: Office of European Affairs. FDR envisaged the trustees including "one from Latin America perhaps, one from the United States and Canada perhaps, and one other." Wallace diary, Aug 20, 1942.
18. Answers by Harold Smith, hearings on Lend-Lease, Mar 15, 1941; 740.011EW/14061.
19. Ickes diary, Jan 19, 1941.
20. Smith, *op. cit.* In two years up to Oct 1941 Britain would spend £5,668m of a total budget of £7,018m on war services.
21. These were nominal values; market values would be less, particularly in Latin America.
22. Ickes diary, Nov 9, 1940.
23. Tels Phillips to F.O., Dec 10-11. PREM4/17/1.
24. Draft Tel. WSC to FDR, Dec 17: ibid.
25. *PPR*, ix, No.149; *The Times*, Dec 18.
26. Washington to F.O., Dec 23.

27.   Beaverbrook to WSC, Dec 26: ibid; cf A.J.P. Taylor, 439.
28.   Kingsley Wood to WSC, Dec 26.
29.   Phillips to F.O., Dec 27.
30.   WSC to FDR, Dec 28: *draft*, PREM4/17/1, fols. 89-91, and PREM3/469.
31.   Churchill, ii, 507f.
32.   WSC to Wood, Dec 28. *Ibid.*
33.   WSC to FDR, Dec 31 by telephone at 3:45 a.m.: PREM4/17/1, fols 77f. Cf Colville diary, Jan 1. Original in PREM3/469; *FRUS*, 1941, 3:1-2.
34.   Morgenthau lunched with WSC on Aug 10, 1944. He told FDR (diary, Aug 19), "He [Churchill] is going to tell Parliament about their financial condition at the right time after the Armistice, and . . . when he does that he is through." Morgenthau also told this to Sir John Anderson on Aug 11: W.D. Taylor memo on mtg: in H.D. White papers: National Archives; Washington.
35.   Major General Eugene Chaney, report, Mitchell Field, New York, Dec 15, 1940: archives of U.S. Army War College, Carlisle, Pa.
36.   At the signing of the draft Lend-Lease Agreement Phase II. Harry Dexter White, memo, Sep 15, 1944: Morgenthau papers, p.1512: FDR Library.
37.   Memo, Mar 10, 1941: Morgenthau papers, p.0853.
38.   Ickes diary.
39.   FDR to Hull, Jan 11, 1941: FDR film 6, p.0344ff.
40.   Ickes diary, Jan 19. The Secretary of Agriculture also recorded this in his diary. Discussion arose over Britain's available assets. In the "rather warm debate" FDR insisted that only Britain's dollars mattered, not her sterling ("because it might not prove of value after the war") or other worldwide assets. "Railroads or all other property in South America or elsewhere were not wanted by us." Wickard limited himself to the observation "that many people in the country had the idea that the British were holding back part of their resources, their securities." FDR and Morgenthau declared themselves satisfied that these had all been pledged. Claude R. Wickard papers, FDR Library.

* * *

THERE GOES THE EMPIRE: Page 492

1.   Lee diary, Dec 28, 1940.
2.   C. King, and Lee diaries, Jan 11, 1941.
3.   C. King diary, Jan 11.
4.   Ickes diary, quoting Wendell Willkie, Feb 22.
5.   Nicolson diary, Jan 21.
6.   C. King, Jan 31.
7.   C. King diary, Jan 31.
8.   C. King diary, Jan 11.
9.   Dalton diary, Jan 13.
10.   Defence Cttee, Jan 13, 1941: CAB69/2.
11.   Colville diary, Jan 24.
12.   C. King, diary, Jan 17. Ward Price alleged that Censorship found incriminating references to Muselier in Vichy telegrams; and that he was arrested "at a *very* gay party with some young French officers and a few blondes."
13.   Diaries of Cadogan, Jan 3-4, Bruce Lockhart, Jan 15 (and citing Bracken, Jul 18, 1946); and C. King diary, Jan 10.
14.   C. King diary, Jan 10.
15.   Ickes diary, May 7, 1941, quoting the Morgenthau's; and Aug 31, 1942 quoting Anna Roosevelt. On Apr 20, 1937 Hopkins told him he had been wed "at 21 to a Jewess" and had stood this first marriage "as long as he could." On Feb 6, 1938 Ickes talks of the cancer death of the second Mrs Hopkins and of Hopkins' own bad shape through that illness.
16.   Ickes diary, Apr 26, Jun 8, 1941.
17.   Ickes diary, Nov 17, 1940.

18.   Ickes diary, Aug 10, 1940; Sep 28, 1941. Elliot Janeway, source of many tidbits, reported that Stettinius and Odlum also paid Hopkins.
19.   Ickes diary, Feb 8, noting FDR Cabinet of Feb 7.
20.   Ickes diary, Feb 1, 1942.
21.   Harry Butcher diary, conv with H. Hopkins, Jan 20, 1942: DDE Library, page deleted by them opened at this author's request in 1977.
22.   Dalton diary, Jul 24, 1941.
23.   Lee diary, Jan 10.
24.   HLH note, Jan 10.
25.   WSC to FDR, Jan 11, 5:00 p.m.: FDR film 6/0342f. FDR sent instructions to Leahy on Jan 13: 1/0189f.
26.   FDR film 6/0348f.
27.   Colville diary, Jan 20.
28.   Martin ltr, Oct 27.
29.   Colville diary, Jan 11.
30.   Hopkins to FDR, Jan 14: Hopkins papers.
31.   WSC to FDR, Jan 13.
32.   Harold Ickes diary, Feb 8, recording FDR Cabinet of Feb 7, 1941; and cf February 27, 1943: Library of Congress.
33.   HLH memo, Jan 10.
34.   COS(40)27(0) of Nov 25, 1940: CAB80/56.
35.   FDR to WSC, Dec 30: FDR film 6/0334.
36.   WSC to FDR, Jan 3.
37.   HLH memo, Jan 10.
38.   Dalton diary, Jan 13. PREM3/328/7.
39.   Dalton diary, Jan 14.
40.   Charles Peake diary, Jan 15. Birkenhead, *Halifax*, 471.
41.   Ltr Martin, Jan 19.
42.   Hopkins diary, Jan 30; Martin MS, 41; cf Dalton diary, Jan 30.
43.   *Ruth*, 1:16. Johnston related this to Lockhart, diary, on Jul 18, 1944.
44.   Martin MS, 40.
45.   FDR memo, Aug 23: PSF: Atl. Charter.
46.   Hinsley, i, 355.
47.   Defence Cttee, Jan 20: CAB69/2.
48.   Eden diary, Jan 20.
49.   C. King diary, Jan 21. On Jan 17 *Mirror* columnist Bill Greig had told him, "There is a great hoo-ha about Communists" and predicted the *Worker*'s suppression.
50.   Herschel Johnson to State, Tel.246, Jan 22.
51.   Dalton diary, citing Desmond Morton, Feb 2.
52.   Nicolson diary, Jan 22; *Hansard,* H of C Deb., col. 263.
53.   Hopkins, handwritten memo on Chequers notepaper, Jan 25: HLH film 19.
54.   WSC minute Jan 6: cit Gilbert, vi, 979.
55.   Hinsley, i, 353.
56.   Def Cttee Jan 8: CAB 69/2.
57.   HLH memo, Jan 10; Tel. WSC to Wavell, Jan 11.
58.   WSC minute to Cabinet Jan 14: cit Woodward, i, 519f; cf Eden diary.
59.   WSC to FDR, Jan 6: FDR film 6/0340.
60.   WSC to Wavell, Jan 26: PREM3/309/1.
61.   WSC to Inonu, Jan 31: ibid.
62.   WSC to Portal, Feb 6: Portal papers.
63.   Henry Wallace, diary, Aug 7, 1942; Halifax diary, Feb 17, 1941.
64.   Seal, cit Gilbert, vi, 1000.
65.   Hopkins memo.
66.   HLH memo, Dec 19, 1941. The U.S. Naval Hospital found on Dec 8 that the tablets "contain barbital, phenacetin, antipyrine, urotropin and a small amount of material to bind these drugs together. In general it is a sedative-pain reliever type of remedy." HLH papers, film 21.

* * *

AGAINST HIS BETTER JUDGMENT: Page 508

1. Beaverbrook sent Willkie's remarks at the Century Club, New York, to WSC on Jun 6, 1941: D417.
2. J.C.C. Davidson to Lord Irwin (Halifax) Jun 14, 1926: Hickleton Papers.
3. Chamberlain to Irwin, Aug 12, 1928: ibid; the 1903 speech is from Guedalla, *Mr Churchill.*
4. Gp Capt R. Humphreys: "The Use of 'U[ltra]' in the Med. and NW African Theatres of War," Oct 1945. (NA, RG-457, SRH-037)
5. Dalton diary, Feb 3; and cf Cadogan diary.
6. Stimson diary, Apr 15 and 17: Donovan assured him that Wavell alone made the decision. "Donovan had been present [in Cairo] when it was made."
7. Dalton diary, Mar 4; cutlery salesman: Lee diary, Jan 7 and 10.
8. Dalton diary, Feb 4.
9. Def Cttee Feb 10: CAB69/2.
10. Eden diary.
11. Dalton diary, Jan 24.
12. Dalton diary, Jan 29, Feb 1-5; and Portal to Gladwyn Jebb, Feb 1: AHB file 1D3/1588.
13. Dalton diary, Feb 10 and 13.
14. Churchill, iii, 157. Cadogan noted "Jap telephone talks" diary, Feb 5-6; Dalton diary, Feb 7.
15. Stimson diary, Feb 4: "Quite a flurry of exciting news this morning." FDR summoned him with Marshall on "an urgent message respecting the Far Eastern situation" from London. And General Sherman Miles (G-2) showed him a further alarming message, evidently MAGIC.
16. Cadogan diary, Feb 6. Marshall sent Stimson reports from London "that the Japanese were clearing out and getting their Embassy out of Britain." Stimson (diary, Feb 8) adds that these were "discountenanced by later messages."
17. Eden diary, Feb 7.
18. Stimson records (diary, Oct 23, 1940) a heated conference on the release of MAGIC. The U.S. army approved but the navy did not: Admiral Stark finally agreed to exchange MAGIC for British experience on Enigma. See Stimson diary, Oct 24, 1940 and May 15, 16 and 27, 1941.
19. *The "Magic" Background of Pearl Harbor*, US Govt Printing Office, 1979, eight vols. Cited hereafter as *MBPH*. And Japanese German Diplomatic Messages 1940-1, MAGIC intercepts (NA, RG-457, SRDJ series.)
20. WSC to FDR, Feb 15: FDR film 6, 0006ff. Stanley Hornbeck (State Dept. Far East section) commented approvingly on Churchill's suggestion: "The only thing which can effectively prevent further Japanese adventuring is display of physical force and of willingness if necessary to use the said force." NA: Hornbeck papers, box 117.
21. Matsuoka to London, Feb 15: repeated to Washington, Feb 15: MAGIC transl Feb 19: *MBPH* No. 381.
22. Matsuoka to London, repeated to Washington Feb 18: transl Feb 20: *MBPH* No. 382-3. At British ambassador Sir Robert Craigie's request Matsuoka on Feb 16 briefed editors to "exercise restraint."
23. Cadogan diary, Feb 15: "How valuable this form of eavesdropping has been!" On the 23rd he drafted a telegram for Washington summarizing "all the Jap talks that gave their game away."
24. Churchill, iii, 159.
25. Martin MS, 44.
26. Shigemitsu to Tokyo, Feb 24: repeated by Tokyo to Peking etc, Feb 27: *MBPH* No. 384.
27. Quoted in Japanese circular from London: Tokyo to Peking, etc, Feb 27: *MBPH* No. 385-7.
28. Matsuoka to Shigemitsu, Feb 27: repeated to Washington, Feb 28: transl Mar 10: *MBPH* No. 388.
29. Shigemitsu to Tokyo, Mar 10: transl Mar 13: *MBPH* No. 389.

30. WSC to Cadogan, Feb 19: Gilbert, vi, 1012.
31. Eden to WSC, Feb 21.
32. Until his capture and liquidation. S.S. memo, Jun 5, 1943: Himmler files: NA film T175/458.
33. Report from A/D [evidently George Taylor] and D/HY: Certain S.O.(2) Activities in Yugoslavia, Jun 24: Dalton papers, 7/3, 99-116; cf Sweet Escott, *Baker Street Irregular*, 35, 63.
34. Mackenzie-King, diary, Aug 31, 1943. When a Tory MP told WSC years later of his own maiden-speech agony, he replied that he still had butteflies and only recovered when he recognized the sound of his own voice. Ltr from Sir William S. Duthie, Feb 18, 1978.
35. The speeches were those at Ottawa and to the Congress. Dean Acheson to Lester Pearson, Jan 23, 1952: Acheson files: DDE Library.
36. C. Murphy: memo Mar 16, 1946: Jackson papers, box 32: DDE Library.
37. Colville diary, Feb 26.
38. Seal ltr Feb 27: cit Gilbert, vi, 1016.
39. Cazalet diary Feb 27.
40. Menzies diary, Mar 1: National Library of Australia.
41. Henry Scrymgeour-Wedderburn, diary, Sep 21, 1928: Gilbert, v, 302.
42. Menzies diary, Mar 2.
43. Minister of Def. directive, Mar 6: CAB120/10.
44. Dalton diary, Feb 28 and Jun 15, 1940.
45. Churchill, iii, 106.
46. Bruce Lockhart diary, Mar 4.
47. Seal letters Mar 4, 6: cit Gilbert, vi, 1024n.
48. Halifax diary, Jan 15.
49. Tizard diary, Mar 9.
50. Dalton diary, Mar 2.
51. Menzies diary, Mar 2.
52. WSC to Hopkins, Feb 23: FO954/29.
53. Washington *Daily News*, Feb 8. Worried British Purchasing officials urged that Churchill publicize Canada's direct contribution with two divisions on British soil. Canad. Legation in Washington, Tel. to Ottawa, Feb 11: MG 26, J1, vol.302.
54. Colin Cross, *The Decline and Fall of the British Empire*.
55. W.K. Hancock & Margaret Gowing: *British War Economy*, in *History of the Second World War* (HMSO, London, 1949), 234.
56. Presidential press confs, xvi, 393f.
57. Diary, Jan 9.
58. Morgenthau diary, Dec 19 and 23; Mackenzie-King diary, Feb 3, 1941.
59. F.O. to Phillips, Dec 12. No 3496. Beaverbrook file D46. Jn general: R.S. Sayers, *Financial Policy*, 1939-45 (HMSO, London, 1956); Warren F. Kimball, *The Most Unsordid Act: Lend Lease*, 1939-41 (Baltimore, 1969).
60. Beaverbrook to WSC, Feb 19: D414.
61. Stimson diary, Oct 2, 1940 quoting Alfred Loomis.
62. Morgenthau diary, Mar 10.
63. Ickes diary, Aug 9. He called it "skulduggery for the benefit, as usual, of the House of Morgan." Churchill, ii, 506 wrote: "A figure much below its intrinsic worth."
64. King George's diary, and King to Sir Alexander Hardinge, Dec 30, 1940.
65. FDR to WSC, Feb 25, 1941: FDR film 1/0198.
66. Colville diary, Mar 5.
67. WSC to Lds Moyne and Cranborne, Mar 4.
68. Recalled in Bruce Lockhart diary, Jan 28, 1944.
69. King's diary, Apr 25; Dalton diary Jul 24.
70. Colville diary, Mar 5.
71. A.I. analysis, Mar 3: The Move of the German Air Force into the Balkans.
72. Colville diary, Mar 5.
73. WSC to Eden, Mar 6, 2:20 a.m.: CAB69/2.

74. Colville diary, Mar 7.
75. PREM3/224/1.
76. Brooke diary, Mar 9. Cf Martin diary, Mar 10.

* * *

THE MIDAS TOUCH: Page 524

1. Dalton diary, Jan 9, 1942.
2. State dept. conv with Mr Rumbold, Jan 28: State dep file, 841.01B11/190.
3. Agent's report, Feb 6. Ibid., /191.
4. Donovan had again visited No.10 at mid-day on Mar 4, 1941 on a mission for Roosevelt. PM's card; and Brooke, 3/A/IV.
5. Morton to Jacob, Sep 18, cit in Cave Brown, *Donovan*, 166; and Berle to Welles, Sep 27, 1941: FDR Library.
6. William Stevenson, *A Man Called Intrepid* (New York, 1976)
7. Statement by Col H. Montgomery Hyde, a former BSC agent: *Daily Telegraph*, Aug 22, 1979.
8. Berle to Welles, Sep 27, 1941: FDR Library.
9. Berle memo, Apr 17, 1942: FDR Library. There were no such plans.
10. Berle memo on conv with Mr Spruille Braden, U.S. ambassador to Colombia, May 7, 1942: diary.
11. At 64 Baker Street they were handled by Lieut Col James Pearson. Several 1944 samples are in Beaverbrook's file D145, while a memo in D400 begins, significantly, "No.10 have received, through secret channels, the following telegram from Bill Donovan. . ."
12. Memo by Biddle Feb 26: Berle papers box 213.
13. Biddle memo, Feb 26, 1942: FDR Library: Berle diary, box 213.
14. The BSC agent, Paine, fled to Montreal; see Berle memos, Feb 13, 14, 26 and Mar 5 and 10, 1942: FDR Library.
15. Memo by Berle on the conf, Mar 5: ibid.
16. Berle memo, Mar 10, 1942, in State Dept file 841.20211/36.
17. Menzies diary, Mar 10.
18. PM's card, Mar 10-11, 1941.
19. Cadogan diary, Mar 3.
20. Stimson diary, Jun 5: quoting Winant on a brief return to Washington.
21. Cabinet, Mar 17: CAB65/18.
22. Martin diary, Mar 15; on Harriman: James Farley cit by Beaverbrook, May 1943: D.517. Ickes diary, Nov 17, 1940. memo WSC to Bridges, Mar 26: Gilbert, vi, 1034.
23. WSC to Halifax, Mar 15: PREM4/17/2.
24. WSC to Wood, PREM4/17/2.
25. Ltr Cadogan to Halifax, Mar 18, 1941.
26. Cadogan diary, Mar 20.
27. WSC to FDR, Apr 2, 6p.m.: FDR film 1/0293 and 0296.
28. Lt Gen Josef Schmid, speaking in CSDIC(UK) report SRGG.1331, Jul 14, 1945 (NA, RG.407, box 1954.)
29. *The Times*, Mar 19.
30. Führer naval conf., Feb 13, 1942.
31. PM's card.
32. WSC to FDR, Mar 19: FDR film 6/90353f.
33. Ltr Biddle to FDR, Apr 26: PSF Biddle: FDR Library; Colville diary and Seal ltr, Mar 19: Gilbert, vi, 1039.
34. FO371/30253.
35. WSC to Tsvetkovitch Mar 22: Churchill, iii, 141f.
36. German FO files of Task Force Künsberg, Serial 2013H, pp.443373ff: German interrogations of Tsvetkovitch and his secretary.

37. WSC to Campbell, Mar 26: Churchill, iii, 42. In the British Consulate at Skoplje German agents later found remnants of a recent arms and explosives consignment which had arrived as diplomatic luggage from Greece and been forwarded to Belgrade; S.O.E. had used some to sabotage mines at Radusa Tel Burker (O.K.W Abwehr) to German FO, Apr 10. White Book No. 7, Dok.Nr.102.

38. Summary report by A/D, Jun 24: Dalton papers.

39. Heeren to German FO, Belgrade Mar 26: in White Book No. 7, Dokumente zum Konflikt mit Jugoslawien und Griechenland.

40. Dalton diary, Mar 27. The 9:45 p.m. Defence Committee sent its appreciation to him for "the part played by his Organization in bringing about the coup d'état in Yugoslavia." CAB69/2.

41. WSC to Australian acting PM, Mar 30: Gilbert, vi, 1048; and to Eden, Mar 28.

42. Hinsley, i, 371, 451.

43. See the diaries of O.K.W. ops staff, naval staff, Hewel, von Waldau Jan 9, Halder, Jan 16.

44. MI appreciation, Jan 17, 1941: WO190/893.

45. Def Ctte mtg, Oct 31, 1940: CAB69/8. For the opposite Military Intelligence view: WO files 190/891-3; the Air Intelligence view: AIR40/2321. and see the weekly intelligence summaries in WO208/2258.

46. Churchill, iii, 10.

47. MI appreciation, Feb 14: WO190/893.

48. Brooke, notes, 3/A/IV.

49. According to Berle it reached Washington in January. "We had the memorandum for the General Staff," he recalled, "on which the decision to attack was taken, having got it surreptitiously in December [1940]." (Diary, Jul 28, 1944.) With justified misgivings, Sumner Welles passed the gist of it to Soviet ambassador Oumansky on Mar 1; but Moscow took it as an attempt to embroil them with Germany. (*FRUS*, 1941, i, 712, 714.)

50. *FRUS*, 1941, i, 133 and 723; re MAGIC: FO371/26518 and 29482.

51. Washington to F.O. Mar 21 and Jun 17: FO371/26521.

52. Cf Cadogan diary, Mar 28.

53. Colville diary, Mar 29.

54. Churchill, iii, 319f.

55. F.O. memo Mar 31: FO371/29479.

56. On Apr 10, Ribbentrop went further: even if Russia did not attack Japan, he told Matsuoka, "Germany might still start a war against the Soviet Union before the year is out; it depends on how she behaves." Ambassador Oshima's telegrams to Prince Konoye, especially that of Apr 1 reporting Matsuoka's lunch with Hitler, are published in German in *Wehrwissenschaftlicher Rundschau*, 1968, 325ff.

57. WSC to Cripps, Apr 2: PREM 3/252/2. On Apr 12, Hitler was handed a Forschungsamt decrypt of Churchill's message. D. Irving, *Breach of Security*, London 1968, 130.

58. ADM 233/88.

59. Colville diary, Mar 31.

60. WSC to Cripps, Apr 3. PREM3/170/1; Churchill, iii, 323.

61. WSC to Beaverbrook and Eden, Oct 14: Beaverbrook papers.

62. Ltr by Keitel to Africa Korps, Apr 3: Germany navy file PG/33316; text in O.K.W. war diary, i, 1009f.

63. MI appreciation, Apr 2: WO190/893.

64. Hopkins memo, Apr 5, 1941: FDR Library: Hopkins Box 307. Churchill asked F.D.R. urgently (but cryptically) if he had received the message about "his Italian friend" and the president replied, "No." Roosevelt obviously did not understand because on Apr 5 Halifax noted in his diary, "The President told me he had had a telephone call from Winston which he hadn't been able fully to understand, as the connection had been bad, but in which Winston had said something about the Man from Italy. . ." In a telegram to WSC on Apr 2 the president used the phrase "your larger friends" meaning "Your larger warships." A telegram of Apr 11 talked of expectations of making early use of seized Danish and Italian ships.

65.   Hewel diary, Mar 27; Hitler/Sztójay conf, Mar 27.

* * *

MR OPTIMIST FROG: Page 538

1.   Hinsley, i, 320, is coy about *which* night raids were thus revealed, but the Fighter
       Command war room log gives scores of precise instances of the Government's own
       foreknowledge. Mar 29, 1941: "16:00 hrs DAC [Duty Air Commodore] special
       message, 'Target tonight [will be] Avonmouth & Bristol." Apr 1: "20:28 hrs, beams.
       DAC reports, [beam] Cherbourg 345° true on Bristol established, active since 19:00."
       Apr 2: "18:00 hrs DAC reported that Avonmouth will be target tonight." Apr 5:
       "17:44 hrs [DAC reports] KG.100 have no operations for tonight." Apr 10: "17:50 hrs.
       Target tonight. Indications are the East side of Birmingham will be attacked." It was,
       and so the warnings went on — though not of course to the cities affected.
       (AIR16/698).
2.   Winant to FDR, Apr 14: Winant papers, box 1: RG-54, Suitland; notes by Winant,
       ibid; and Harriman's version in Tel. Winant to State, No.1470, Apr 14. And Cdr
       Thompson, MS.
3.   H.H. Arnold diary, Apr 16: Arnold papers, Library of Congress.
4.   CAB120/10.
5.   Cadogan diary, Apr 7.
6.   Colville diary, Apr 7.
7.   Dalton diary, Apr 9.
8.   Nicolson diary, Apr 9.
9.   *FRUS*, ii, 1941, 836f.
10.   Anneliese Schmundt diary, Apr 17 (in this author's possession): her husband was
       Hitler's chief adjutant.
11.   General Lee diary, Apr 22. The war room log (see note 1) shows that the Government
       had precise forewarning. "Special message," the log recorded five minutes before 6:00
       p.m.: "KG.100 [the German Pathfinder unit] are preparing to operate tonight.
       Unlikely to be a western target." Then: "Beam, Cherbourg 30° true through
       London." At 7:42 p.m.: "The attack on London is likely to start at 21:20 hrs. . .
12.   Cadogan diary, Apr 17; Cecil King diary, Apr 16: Boston University.
13.   Arnold diary, Apr 18.
14.   WSC to Longmore, Apr 18: Gilbert, vi, 1065.
15.   King diary, Apr 22; Colville diary, Apr 18.
16.   Note, Apr 18, PREM3/14/3; PM's card.
17.   Benes telegram,Apr 24: "He [Churchill] promised help . . . concerning recognition
       and setting up a provisional government and he will assist us to get American
       recognition." In Taborský papers: box 5: file: "Dr Benes messages . . . to
       Czechoslovakia 1941": Hoover Library.
18.   Beaverbrook papers: House of Lords Record Office.
19.   Hankey papers, Churchill College, Cambridge.
20.   King diary, Feb 19.
21.   Brooke diary, Apr 27; and Hankey diary, May 1.
22.   Quoted in Hugh L'Etang, *Fit to Lead?* (London, 1980), 32.
23.   Cadogan diary, Apr 28; Dalton, Apr 29.
24.   Def Cttee mtg, Apr 28: CAB 69/2; and Churchill, iii, 241.
25.   Lindemann to WSC Apr 28. On May 7, he repeated that Hitler's oil position would
       be permanently secured if he captured Iraq. Cherwell papers, Nuffield College,
       Oxford.
26.   Ivan Maisky memoirs, 637, quoting Swedish minister Byorn Prytz; PM's card, Apr
       30.

* * *

THE "TELEPHONE JOB": Page 550

1. E.g., Oliver Stanley. Dalton diary, Apr 28: confidential annex.
2. General Kennedy, DMO: Lee diary, Apr 15.
3. Lee and Arnold diaries, Apr 21.
4. Lee diary, May 21.
5. Sir C. Wilson (Ld Moran) to Beaverbrook Apr 18, and reply Apr 19: D141. C. King diary, Jul 17.
6. Dalton diary, Jun 11.
7. Ibid., Apr 28.
8. C. King diary Mar 27.
9. Shinwell told Stewart Campbell (*D Mirror*) this: ibid., Feb 19.
10. Ibid.
11. Gilbert, vi, 1090.
12. Ltr Canadian High Commissioner Vincent Massey to Ottawa, Jun 7: MG 26, J1, vol.312: Public Archives, Ottawa.
13. C. King diary, May 1.
14. Cadogan diary, May 5.
15. Colville diary, May 2. Harriman wrote to FDR on May 7 that the PM often took him to the devastated cities. Having an American around was "of value for the morale of the people." He and Winant were at Swansea, Bristol and Cardiff; James Forrestal at Liverpool and Manchester. "This week we go to Dover.": FDR Library.
16. FDR to WSC, May 1: FDR film 1/0228.
17. PREM 3, 469/350.
18. WSC to FDR, May 4: FDR film 1/0306.
19. Winant reported this to Roosevelt, May 6, 9:00 p.m.: FDR Library, PSF Safe file: Winant; and FDR film 6/0371.
20. Colville diary, May 3.
21. Cf Cab mtgs, May 4-5: CAB105/4; Cadogan refers on May 4 to "secret news" that the Germans in Libya were uncomfortable.
22. WSC to Wavell, May 4: Gilbert, vi, 1080.
23. COS mtg Apr 22: CAB79/11.
24. Stimson diary, unpubl., May 15-16: Yale University. Confiding to Stimson on May 27 the progress of talks with the Japanese, Hull again remarked how "bitterly disappointed" he had been to realize that the British could read the intercepts.
25. WSC to Dill, May 13: WO216/5.
26. Hinsley, i, 418: quoting CX/JQ 911, May 6.
27. RG-457, SRH-037: Gp Capt R. Humphreys: "The Use of 'U' in the Mediterranean and Northwest African Theatres of War," Oct 1945.
28. C. King and Colville diaries.
29. WSC to Pound, Portal, Dill, May 10: PREM3/109.
30. FO371/26566.
31. Ltr Karl to Albrecht Haushofer, Sep 3, 1940: ADAP D XI, No.12.
32. Hess/Beaverbrook conversation, Sep 9, 1941: D443.
33. Cf Duff Cooper's account of how MI5 intercepted the Duke's correspondence. Cecil King diary, May 15. The intercepted Hess-Haushofer-Hamilton letters are in file FO371/26565, closed until 2016.
34. Ltr Hamilton to Air Min., Apr 28: Hamilton op cit., 148. The Haushofer papers are on NA film T253, roll 46. Albrecht Haushofer was executed by the Germans, Karl committed suicide in Allied custody.
35. J. Martin diary, May 11: "Arrival of Duke of Hamilton to report on arrival of Rudolf Hess."
36. Hamilton-Hess conv., May 11, Nbg (Nuremberg) doc M116, a certified copy by David Maxwell Fyfe of an original said to be in FO files.
37. Beaverbrook-Hess conv, Sep 9: D443.
38. Berlin Document Centre file 236: Rudolf Hess.
39. C. King diary, May 15.

40. ND: M117.
41. Colville diary, May 13.
42. Unpubl. memos James H. Rowe Jr to FDR and to "Missy" LeHand, May 14: FDR film 1/00242f.
43. FDR to WSC, received May 15: in 800.2 Germany, Hess: London embassy files; and FDR film 1/0241.
44. C. King diary, May 15. FDR wondered on May 20 what was "really behind" the story: Sherwood, 294. For American uneasiness about Hess see Lee diary, May 24.
45. ND: M119.
46. Cadogan diary, Jun 11. The fullest transcripts of Simon's talks (Jun 9) are in his papers at the Bodleian Library, Oxford; and cf IMT, xl, 279-291.
47. Beaverbrook file D443. Cf Dalton diary, Jun 16.
48. Cadogan diary, Jun 16.
49. FO371/26566. Benes learned that the S.I.S. saw the Haushofer approach as "an excellent opportunity" and sent a reply "purporting to come from the Duke." Further letters, Benes learned, had arranged when Hess should fly to the Duke's estate; his actual arrival had created panic in London. Benes, interview with Compton Mackenzie, Dec 13, 1944: Hoover Library: Taborský papers, box 4. A 1941 account of what security sources told Benes is : Prisna duverna zprava z britskeho uredniho prameno [vojenskeho]: ibid., box 6: Haushofer's letter "never reached Hamilton because the Secret Service intercepted it and answered it instead. Several letters were exchanged and in the end Hess actually came to England and he fell into the trap." "Among leading British personages," Benes learned, "a furious argument is raging as to whether Hess set out . . . with the knowledge and consent of Hitler or not. . . He acted as though he was an official negotiator and expected all the prerogatives accruing from this role."
50. Morton to WSC, Jul 28: PREM3/219/2.

* * *

TURNING POINT: Page 563

1.   WSC to Ismay, Dec 11: PREM3/124/2.
2.   Freyberg to New Zealand Govt., May 1: Churchill, iii, 244.
3.   Wavell to WSC, May 15: ibid., 249.
4.   Sonderkommando von Künsberg: Bericht über die Tätigkeit des Britischen Vizekonsuls Pendlebury auf Kreta, Juni 1941: German federal archives: MGFA/DZ III S.29.
5.   Ltr J. Martin to home, May 18.
6.   Churchill, iii, 250.
7.   See note 4; and ltr from Major John Biddulph, a Cambridge contemporary, April 1982.
8.   Gen. Lee diary, quoting Lady Warwick, Oct 11, 1940; Gilbert, vi, 1031n; Spears excised the word louche from the published text of his diary.
9.   Martin MS. Cadogan diary, Nov 5 and 8, 1940.
10. Pétain cit. in Admiral William Leahy diary, Mar 18; and in ltr Leahy to FDR, Mar 19: Library of Congress, Leahy papers.
11. Ibid.
12. Weizmann to WSC, Feb 7; and reply, J. Peck for J. Martin, to Weizmann: Weizmann archives, Rehovot, Israel.
13. Weizmann to Jewish Agency Executive, reporting conv with WSC on Mar 12: Weizmann archives; Harvey diary, Nov 1, 1941.
14. WSC paper: Syrian policy, May 19: CAB120/10.
15. Admiralty to Tovey, May 18: 9:55 a.m., ADM223/78; in general, Ludovic Kennedy, Pursuit (London, 1974.)
16. Admiralty to naval commands, May 21, 6:28 p.m.: ADM223/78.
17. WSC to FDR, May 23: FDR film 1/0323.

18. Admiral Süd-Ost: Kurzer Bericht über Operation Motorseglerstaffel Malemes-Heraklion an SKL v. 23.5.1941: in War Diary of Admiral Süd-Ost, German archives: III M800/2; Karl Gundelach, Der Kampf um Kreta, in *Entscheidungsschlachten des Zweiten Weltkrieges*, 127.

19. Cunningham to Admiralty, May 23: Churchill, iii, 259.

20. Roskill, i, 441; I.S.O. Playfair, ii, 137.

21. Colville diary, May 23.

22. Dalton diary, May 26: quoting Rex Fletcher; Ismay, 219.

23. Capt Ralph Edwards says Churchill insisted on this signal: RUSI *Journal*, Feb 1953: Admiralty to *Rodney*, May 25, 2:48 p.m.

24. ADM 233/88: Colpoys, Admiralty Use of Special Intelligence in Naval Operations, 53-73.

25. Admiralty to Tovey, May 25, 7:00 p.m.; and CX/JQ 993; and ADM 223/78, Ultra signal, 6:12 p.m., May 25.

26. Colville diary, May 24-5.

27. Odyssey, 374f; Admiralty to Cunningham, May 25, 9:32 p.m.: Cunningham papers: British Museum ADD Ms 52567.

28. Cunningham to Admiralty May 26: Churchill, iii, 260.

29. Dalton diary, May 26; and cf Colville diary, May 25.

30. Eden to WSC, May 26: cit in Gilbert, vi, 1095.

31. WSC to Freyberg; and to Wavell, May 27: Churchill, iii, 262.

32. Lee diary, May 26; Winant eventually praised Churchill to FDR, but said that his colleagues were rotten: Stimson diary.

33. It was actually transmitted at 11:37 a.m. on May 27: Kennedy, 225; and Churchill, iii, 282.

34. Kennedy, 225; Roskill, *Admirals*, 125.

35. By noon-thirty Admiral Ghormley had phoned the news from the Admiralty to his embassy.

36. Tovey to Admiralty, May 27, 11:19 a.m.; and WSC's reply, 4:10 p.m. adding ". . .However much we admire a gallant fight."

37. Martin MS: *Hansard*, H of C Deb., May 27: cols 1714-8; Nicolson diary.

* * *

BEAVERBROOK, BATTLEAXE AND BARBAROSSA: Page 576

1. Clementine Churchill to Hopkins, Apr 10, 1942: HLH film 11, FDR Library.

2. Bruce Lockhart diary, Jun 24, 1941: "recently;" PM's card: Jun 19.

3. Colville diary, Jun 5.

4. Bevin, cit in memo A. Christiansen to Beaverbrook, Oct 28, 1942. C38.

5. Brooke diary, May 13 and 27, Jun 19 (orig.): Brooke suggested that 20 percent of AFV output be for spares. "This was not appreciated by the PM, who likes to put the whole of his goods in the shop window."

6. Beaverbrook to WSC, Jun 3: D417.

7. Beaverbrook/Hess conv, Sep 9: D443.

8. Londoner's Diary, *Ev. Standard*, Feb 29, 1940. Beaverbrook's dinner guests were McGovern, James Maxton and Campbell Stephen.

9. *Greenock By-Election Special*, reported McGovern's speech of May 25. According to C. King's diary, Jun 5, Beaverbrook sent *Express* general manager E.J. Robertson personally to kill the rival *Daily Mirror*'s story.

10. Tel. WSC to Beaverbrook, Jun 10. McGovern reminded Beaverbrook of the Mar 5, 1940 dinner in ltr of Jul 2, 1941 (copy to WSC). The sheer number of press communiques, drafts and redrafts on file D446 testifies to an uneasy conscience.

11. Beaverbrook to W.J. Brown, Apr 16, 1942: "I send you my personal good wishes and my hopes and expectations. I cannot oppose the Churchill candidate but I hope the newspapers give you a good show. Mention this telegram to Robertson." State dept file 841.00/1589.

12. Lee diary, May 27.

13. Colville diary, May 29.

14. WSC to Dill, Jun 7; Colville diary, Jun 3.

15. PREM4/68/9. Dowding had taken an airforce mission to North America in November 1940; he quarrelled with Slessor and in Canada he expressed views so obnoxious that Churchill decided in March it was "high time" he came home. "No reason need be assigned." WSC to Beaverbrook, Mar 29 and 31. D29.

16. WSC minutes to Ismay, May 27: cit Gilbert, vi, 1097.

17. Hewel diary, May 31: author's possession.

18. Bletchley intercepts OL 523 and 525.

19. For F.O. scepticism see FO371/29479.

20. COS mtg with JIC on Apr 22, CAB79/11; and file WO190/893.

21. Churchill, iii, 373-7.

22. "Winston," he added proudly, "had said Hitler would attack Russia, and said this some four months before." Mackenzie-King diary, Aug 24: Public Archives, Ottawa.

23. Churchill, iii, 320ff. Cf Eden to WSC, Oct 14: Gilbert, vi, 1051n.

24. CX/JQ/S/11, dated May 31: cit Hinsley, i, 474.

25. Churchill, iii, 326.

26. Churchill, iii, 319.

27. COS to Wavell, May 31: Churchill, iii, 318. Cf Cadogan diary, Jun 2, and Bruce Lockhart diary, Jun 3.

28. Ltr WSC to Randolph, Jun 8: Gilbert, vi, 1107.

29. Conf Justice Robert H. Jackson with First Secretary Donald R. Heath, on Mar 29, 1946: Schacht had told him "on about Jun 6." NA: Jackson papers: Schacht file.

30. Visits by Birger Dahlerus are recorded in Göring diary, Mar 25, 27 and Jun 16; and cf Bernd Martin, *Friedensinitiativen*, 470; Woodward, i, 620f.

31. Sikorski cit in Biddle to FDR, Jun 20: FDR Library: Box 34, PSF, folder: Ambassador A.J. Biddle, Jr, 1937/1941.

32. For typical criticism see Channon diary, Jun 6.

33. Colville diary, Jun 6.

34. C. King diary, Jun 7: quoting the *Sunday Pictorial*'s Stewart Campbell.

35. C. King diary, Jun 12.

36. Cf Bruce Lockhart diary, Feb 27, 1944.

37. Kathleen Harriman cit in Bruce Lockhart diary, Apr 6, 1942.

38. Cadogan diary, Jun 9.

39. Mackenzie-King diary, Apr 16-21.

40. WSC to FDR, May 31: FDR film 1/0337.

41. See e.g. Wickard diary, Jun 8; Stimson diary.

42. WSC to Pound, Alexander, May 28: ADM199/1933.

43. WSC to FDR, Jun 8: FDR film 6/0010.

44. Ltr Johnson to WSC, Jun 12: US embassy file.

45. WSC to Ismay, Jun 14: Gilbert, vi, 1110.

46. Martin and Cadogan diaries, Jun 9; Bruce Lockhart diary, Jun 11.

47. Eden minute, Jun 9: FO371/26521.

48. Cab mtg, Jun 9: CAB65/22.

49. Massey reported this denial to Ottawa on Jun 13. Cripps told him the same on Jun 15: "It is Cripp's view that German motive is not economic, because in his opinion Russia would be prepared to sign any economic agreement which Germany would demand, but that German aim is to remove menace of the Russian Army from her eastern frontiers before it gets too strong." MG 26, J1, vol. 312: Public Archives, Ottawa.

50. Eden cit by Herschel V Johnson, Tel. to State, Jun 11. In his Russian memoirs, 641, Maisky mentions only Cadogan.

51. The telegram was in Oshima's Chef de Mission cipher. Oshima saw Hitler at 7:00 p.m. on Jun 3. Walther Hewel, who made the (now missing) official record, noted in his diary only: "*Andeutungen* [Hints about] *Barbarossa*."

52. Hinsley cites only the (classified) Jun 12 Report JIC (41) 252(O). Sikorski paraphrased this intercept to Biddle on Jun 20: see Note 31.
53. JIC report, Jun 12: cit Churchill, iii, 318.
54. *Izvestia*, Jun 14.
55. P.J. Grigg cit: Nicolson diary, Jun 24.
56. Ltr W/Cdr Oscar Oeser to Jean Howard, Apr 12, 1975.
57. Dalton diary, Jun 16; cf Jun 20 and 21.
58. WSC to FDR, Jun 14: FDR film 1/0355; PREM3/230/1.
59. Brooke diary, Jun 17 (orig.)
60. Colville diary, Jun 18.
61. Bruce Lockhart diary, Jun 18.
62. *News Chronicle*, Jun 18.
63. C. King diary, Jun 20.
64. WSC to FDR, Jun 26: FDR film 1/0358 and reply, Jul 10, 1/0362ff; PREM3/426/3.
65. Colville diary, Jun 19: cit Gilbert, vi, 1112.
66. O. Harvey diary, Jun 25.
67. Colville diary, Jun 20.
68. WSC to Ld Linlithgow, Jun 20: cit Gilbert, vi, 1113; and to FDR, Jun 22: ibid, 1115.
69. Martin MS.
70. WSC to Ismay, Jun 21: CAB120/10.
71. Colville diary, Jun 22.
72. Winant op.cit., 203, says he arrived on Jun 20 at Chequers.
73. Lockhart diary, Jun 20, 1942.
74. Churchill, iii, 371f; only this speech is transcribed in Beaverbrook's files, C87; Lee diary, Jun 22.

* * *

Index

Gupt

$1,500,000

20%	300,000
22.5%	337,500
25%	375,000

UK.

Bob will get $10.00.

$1,800,000

~~20%~~
22.5%

$2.001 ~

20%	400,000
22.5	450,000
25	500,000

restrictions on overflying the frontier before the "general crossing." Cripps took leave from Moscow on the tenth and dined with Churchill two days later. He felt that Russia would hold out under Nazi attack for four weeks at the most.

Whitehall agreed. The War Office gave the Red Army ten days.[55] The Joint Intelligence Committee thought six weeks more realistic. One red-tabbed colonel visiting Bletchley Park gazed at the map of the eastern front smothered in little flags, rubbed his hands and said, "Splendid! Six weeks' breathing space!"[56]

Churchill also anticipated a Soviet collapse. Congratulating Hugh Dalton on S.O.E.'s success in blocking the Danube, Churchill asked him about preventive sabotage operations against Soviet oil installations and he talked of bombing the oilfields at Baku with the Middle East airforce to prevent Hitler getting them. "All this," the minister dictated in his notes, "should be prepared as quickly as possible."[57] That day, June 16, Bletchley appreciated that Hitler might begin Case B in three days' time. On June 21, the airforce Enigma detailed targets for the Fourth Air Corps' opening attacks on Russia.

* * *

Churchill briefed Roosevelt about all this on June 14. He told of the reinforcements he had sent out for Battleaxe, the desert offensive beginning on the morrow. "As it will be the first occasion," he added, "when we hope to have definite superiority in tackle both on the ground and above it, I naturally attach the very greatest importance to this venture."

Then he hinted at the other extraordinary coming event, and inquired Roosevelt's likely attitude:

> From every source at my disposal including some most trustworthy it looks as if a vast German onslaught on the Russian frontier is imminent. Not only are the main German armies deployed from Finland to Roumania but the final arrivals of air and armoured forces are being completed. The pocket battleship *Lützow* which put her nose out of Skaggerak yesterday and was promptly torpedoed by our coastal aircraft was very likely going north to give naval strength on the Arctic flank. Should this new war break out we shall of course give all encouragement and any help we can spare to the Russians, following the principle that Hitler is the foe we have to beat. I do not expect any class political reactions here and trust that a German-Russian conflict will not cause you any embarrassment.[58]

Battleaxe began the next day, Sunday: Wavell confidently hurled 25,000 troops and 180 tanks at Rommel. Rommel was expecting the stroke: on Monday afternoon his own tank forces appeared, twice as numerous and far better equipped than anticipated. On Tuesday mid-day

Churchill called his home commanders-in-chief to what one general called a futile conference, overstuffed with "rather moth-eaten old admirals" and shocked them with the revelation that Battleaxe was a major offensive just like the week-old assault on Syria. Even at this distance from the operational theatre General Alan Brooke suspected that Britain could scarcely attempt offensives on two fronts in the Middle East when she was barely strong enough for one.[59] Outflanked in the desert by Rommel, Wavell's raiding forces had to withdraw, leaving 150 dead and over one hundred tanks on a battlefield dominated by the enemy.

PROBABLY LEARNING OF THIS fresh fiasco from Rommel's own signals before he was officially notified by Cairo, Churchill cancelled his appointments for the evening and retreated to Chartwell for a rare, melancholy visit; the house was shuttered, but he wanted to be alone where he could wander disconsolately about the valley.

By Wednesday this lionhearted man was back at No.10 and already casting about for some new means of launching an offensive.[60] Around 10 a.m. he telephoned Beaverbrook and asked to see him that evening. He talked of holding an inquest on his desert generals.[61]

Against this background, it is not surprising that his war leadership was called into question. His popularity was slipping — down three points to eighty-five; his Government's had slumped to fifty-nine.[62] The Times published a broadside against the Cabinet; when the Sketch echoed this it evoked from yet another editor the observation that even the mice were leaving the ship.[63]

Churchill's interventions became crabby and unhelpful. When he cabled to Roosevelt suggesting an Anglo-American Tank Board the president was able to point out that one already existed.[64] Churchill snappily rebuked Margesson, his half-forgotten Secretary of War, for having foisted the suggestion on him. Private secretaries Colville and Peck were worried by his "inconsiderate treatment" of the service ministries: only the personal loyalty of Sinclair, Alexander and Margesson prevented serious trouble. Colville quietly observed that while Winston supplied "drive and initiative," he was often just meddling, and operations might profit if he would turn instead to Labour and Production.[65] These were serious criticisms. Eden echoed them a few days later to his own private secretary; a separate minister of defence ought to be appointed — no doubt he had himself in mind.[66]

Against these criticisms must be set one compelling fact: that Churchill had greater experience of government, and knew more than any other person: neither Eden, nor Beaverbrook, nor his private secretariat had access to his secret sources. This gave him the right, if not always the ability, to interfere.

* * *

That Friday morning, June 20, he took his train down to Dover, seeking inspiration among the big railway guns and south coast Flak defences. On the return journey he stopped off at Chartwell again. He seemed to be seeking his roots. He dozed all afternoon, then donned purple dressing gown and battered gray felt hat and wandered round the garden with his private secretary, chasing random thoughts out loud — about the marmalade cat and the goldfish pond, and about Tobruk and resuming the offensive.[67] But swimming around the bottom of his mind was a decision to replace the Commander in Chief in Cairo.

No single episode had impelled him to this decision. To Ian Jacob and Pug Ismay he said afterwards, clutching imaginary fishing rods, "I feel that I have got a tired fish on this rod, and a very lively one on the other." The western desert needed a "fresh eye and an unstrained hand." He telegraphed this phrase to the Viceroy of India that day, asking him to take Wavell in exchange for General Claude Auchinleck.[68] That was the lively general who had shown such alacrity over Iraq. Citing "the public interest" for the change, he broke it to Wavell.

Improper though the occasion may have seemed — since Churchill's own Syrian adventure had contributed to the failure of Battleaxe — Wavell's replacement was correct in the long term: after so many reverses no general could command confidence, and that alone mattered on the battlefield. Moreover, Churchill's survival was more important than Wavell's and the General's prestige and experience would be invaluable for an august semi-political command like India.

True, Wavell might sulk, as Colville warned the PM, and write unfavourably of the episode in later years.

Churchill retorted: "I can use my pen too, and I will bet I sell more copies!"

* * *

It was growing oppressively hot. On Wednesday he had gone up to Norfolk to see rockets tested against unmanned target planes, and he had sweltered in the heat — realizing only later that the steam heating had been left on in his train after the endlessly cold spring.[69]

The weekend that now began was even hotter. Those who could, fled to the country. That Saturday, June 21, he himself lunched at No.10 with Lord Louis Mountbatten, and listened distantly to his tales of how

German aircraft had sunk his destroyer off Crete. "Every single one of our plans has failed," he lectured Ismay in a note this day. "The enemy has completely established himself in the Central Mediterranean. We are afraid of his dive-bombers at every point."[70]

He drove down to Chequers alone that afternoon, his mind on the broadcast he proposed to make that night about Russia. Hitler might unleash Barbarossa any day now. Upon reflection, he decided to postpone the broadcast. He conversed with his private secretary, who arrived in time for dinner, about the attack and about whether Hitler was right if he assumed he could enlist rightwing sympathies in Britain and America. After dinner he made his own intention plain: "I will go all out to help Russia."

Colville was surprised. He remarked, as they strolled around the croquet lawn, that for an anti-Bolshevik like Churchill to back Stalin would be to bow down in the House of Rimmon. His life, the PM replied, was simplified by one single purpose: the destruction of Hitler. "If Hitler invaded Hell," he said, "I would at least make a favourable reference to the Devil."[71]

A FEW HOURS LATER his adversary threw three million troops, three thousand tanks, and two thousand planes across the entire Russian line from the Arctic to the Black Sea.

Since Churchill, knowing what he knew, refused to be wakened before eight unless Britain was invaded he was allowed to sleep on. Wakened with the news, the PM grunted that he would broadcast that night.

It occurred to him to send Sawyers to Eden's bedroom with a cigar on a silver salver: Churchill had been proven right, after all. Shortly General Dill arrived from London with the details. The General gave the Red Army six weeks. "I suppose," he commented, "they'll be rounded up in hordes."

Another man than Churchill, dogged by the fiascos that had littered his military career, might have hesitated before supporting Stalin: a shipwrecked seaman seeking rescue by the Titanic? He summoned the foreign secretary and announced that he would broadcast at nine p.m.

The gamble seemed immense: the diversion into Syria had lost him Battleaxe; what great Empire territories might he now forfeit if he furnished its materials and military aid to Stalin instead?*

He telephoned Beaverbrook's successor at the ministry of aircraft production. "Do you not think," the PM challenged him, "we ought to help?" Colonel Moore-Brabazon agreed that they should.

---

*This controversy would arise after the fall of Singapore.

Roosevelt had also sent word by Gil Winant, at that moment returning from Washington. Churchill had the ambassador fetched from the airfield; he arrived at Chequers dishevelled after a transatlantic trip by bomber. The oral reply from Roosevelt was this: if Churchill pledged support for Russia then he would back him to the hilt.[72]

That Hitler had struck, as was his wont, on a weekend, was fortunate: it relieved Winston of the need, if not the obligation, to consult his King, his Cabinet, or his party. He began drafting his broadcast script soon after breakfast, and fetched Cripps and Beaverbrook down from London for advice, still uncertain about how far to go.

Ambassador Cripps counselled circumspection. But Beaverbrook was ebullient. "If you are going to accept Russia as an ally," he said, "you must go all out."[73]

Churchill's script was ready just in time — but too late to show to Eden or the F.O. mandarins.

"Any man or state," he had dictated, "who fights against Nazism will have our aid. Any man or state who marches with Hitler is our foe. . . It follows therefore that we shall give whatever help we can to Russia and the Russian people."[74] After predicting an increasing tonnage of bombs on Germany, "making the German people taste and gulp each month a sharper dose of the miseries they have showered upon mankind," he had dictated a piece of thoughtless rhetoric that sounded well, but boded ill for the peoples of the territories freshly occupied by Stalin's armies.

The Russian people are defending their native soil. The Russian soldiers are standing on the threshhold of their native land.

In truth, *outside* the threshhold: because their boot trod firmly on the freshly expanded crust of the Soviet empire whose frontiers had been sanctified by Stalin's pact with Hitler: they were on Finnish, Lithuanian, Latvian, Estonian, Polish and Romanian soil.

Chequers, nine p.m., June 22, 1941: as he took his seat before the mircrophone installed in his study, this was not the hour for Churchill to dwell upon small print: it was as though a clap of thunder had sounded and lightning had lit up the horizon of his mind; it was one of two Great Events he had been living for since the summer of 1940.

His grand strategy was taking effect. He still waited for that other Great Event, the entry of the United States into the war; after that there could be no doubt as to the outcome of Churchill's War.